The
Successful
Marketing
Plan

The Successful Marketing Plan

How to Create Dynamic, Results-Oriented Marketing

FULLY REVISED AND EXPANDED
FOURTH EDITION

Roman G. Hiebing, Jr., Scott W. Cooper,
and Steven J. Wehrenberg

New York   Chicago   San Francisco   Lisbon   London   Madrid   Mexico City
Milan   New Delhi   San Juan   Seoul   Singapore   Sydney   Toronto

The McGraw·Hill Companies

1 2 3 4 5 6 7 8 9 10   QDB/QDB   1 9 8 7 6 5 4 3 2 1

ISBN   978-0-07-174557-4
MHID   0-07-174557-2

e-ISBN 978-0-07-174897-1
e-MHID 0-07-174897-0

Library of Congress Cataloging-in-Publication Data

Hiebing, Roman G.
  The successful marketing plan : how to create dynamic, results-oriented marketing / by Roman Hiebing, Scott Cooper, and Steve Wehrenberg. — 4th ed.
    p. cm.
  ISBN 978-0-07-174557-4 (alk. paper)
  1. Marketing—Planning.   I. Cooper, Scott W.   II. Wehrenberg, Steve.   III. Title.
  HF5415.13.H523 2012
  658.8'02—dc22

                                                              2011008996

McGraw-Hill books are available at special quantity discounts to use as premiums and sales promotions or for use in corporate training programs. To contact a representative, please e-mail us at bulksales@mcgraw-hill.com.

This book is printed on acid-free paper.

Contents

PART I   BUSINESS REVIEW INSIGHTS

PART II   BRAND PLATFORM AND PLAN OBJECTIVES

PART III   TACTICAL PLANS

PART IV   EVALUATION

Foreword

First of all, I would like to establish some background information so that comments I make later on in this Foreword become clear. During my career I chose to move to companies that were in need of changing their business model. Their performances in generating top line sales growth and bottom line operating profits were not healthy or acceptable in the short or long term.

Over the years, I have been deeply involved in many marketing planning processes while employed by retailing companies such as Famous Footwear, Finish Line, Athlete's Foot, Zales' jewelry corporation, Just for Feet, Lazarus department stores, Oshmans Sporting Goods Stores, and others. These companies were publicly held, privately owned, or foreign owned entities with revenues ranging from billions of dollars to less than $20 million.

I was also involved in the marketing planning process of key wholesale companies, such as Nike, Adidas, Converse, Skechers, Steve Madden, and Nine West, that addressed specific marketing initiatives of the retailers previously mentioned.

Ultimately, the performance of these retailers and wholesalers, and the vendors that supported them, after executing well-thought-out plans and processes was exceptional.

I would like to take credit for these things, but I cannot. But I do credit myself for two things: (1) a strong belief and commitment to great and effective marketing planning that produces results and (2) finding external resources that lead that thinking.

After 20 years at the Hiebing Group, the last 7 as president, Scott joined me and the new leadership at Famous Footwear and Brown Shoe as senior vice president of marketing. We subsequently used the services of the Hiebing Group where I met Roman Hiebing and later also partnered with Campbell Mithun where I met and worked with Steve Wehrenberg, the chief executive officer, when Campbell Mithun became the Famous Footwear agency of record. So I've come to know the three authors' marketing planning process well, from the extensive insight work we did at Famous Footwear to the marketing strategy and tactics that were all shaped by the content that is so clearly laid out in this fourth edition.

Many plans are academic, and most sit on the shelf and aren't used to actually move the business. This one works. It is the best all-around planning tool I've seen. It speaks not only to the needs of the traditionally structured marketing department but also to the entrepreneur, something I think is a critical advantage of the book.

While Famous Footwear was a $1.4 billion business we couldn't afford to run it like a bureaucracy. In the contents of this book, you'll find a disciplined approach that brings the consumer to the table, provides accountability, and demands creativity. Critical to the success of this planning methodology is the fact that the authors don't define marketing as simply communications. They understand the cross-functional nature of the discipline and the fact that the channels you pick, the products you develop, the operational side of the business, and the communications all make the difference in how you actually deliver your brand positioning to your chosen target markets.

So this is a book on marketing that isn't just for the marketing department. It's a book that can change a company, no matter the size, because, in keeping with my own belief in the necessity of doing so, it provides every department with a marketing orientation.

The authors have been helping some of the largest and best consumer, business-to-business, and service businesses in the world with their marketing. But they have also taken the marketing planning process in their book and worked with start-ups, franchise operations, and turnarounds. I believe that, with this book as a guide, any intelligent, persevering person, regardless of experience level, can write an effective marketing plan. The book guides strategy, but it is also filled with tactical direction and ideas. It's a reference guide. It's the one marketing book you want on your shelf. There's a reason that since 1990, when the first edition came out, *The Successful Marketing Plan* has rightfully become the authoritative marketing planning book available today, and the authors have gone and made it even better with the most extensive set of revisions yet.

The marketing planning the authors brought to Famous Footwear and Brown Shoe was superior to any I've been involved with in my career. Together with the management team, we led Famous Footwear and Brown Shoe to record years. A complete turnaround in fortunes that saw most every metric increase—from awareness levels, customer counts, purchase ratios, store-to-store sales, inventory turnover, operating profits (which increased 300 percent), return on invested capital (which moved from under 10 percent to 24 percent)—all working to create the impetus that ultimately raised Brown Shoe stock capitalization from $200 million to $1.4 billion.

There's little more that I could have asked for or expected in following this book's strategies. Take it off the shelf, read it, keep it on your desk, and share it with your partners. It will positively change your business model and its results.

Joe Wood
Retired President
Famous Footwear/Brown Shoe

Preface

REASONS AND GOALS FOR THIS BOOK

While we never could have imagined the success of our first three editions, we continue not to rest on our good fortune, but to continually improve on what we started out to do in the first place: create the best possible marketing planning process with only one target in mind—the practitioners.

This book always was and continues to be for the marketing professionals who have worked many years in the business and know their craft but need a reference from time to time or a proven way of attacking a problem. And it continues to be for the new-to-marketing professionals, those veterans who came from different disciplines or the college graduates who developed a keen academic understanding of marketing but now need a process and understanding of what works in the real world. It's for the practitioners who have picked up other books that provided only to-do lists and who now need a tested process and data-based method to help them systematically gather relevant data and insights and tie them to a proven planning process. It's for marketers in consumer goods, retail, services, and business-to-business companies who need to tailor their plans to their own industry.

And finally, it's an actionable resource for practitioners who need ideas—ways to release the great ideas trapped in their own minds.

What's New?

This is by far our most extensive revision. For starters, you'll notice that there are three names on the front cover instead of two. We are pleased to have added Steve Wehrenberg, chief executive officer of Campbell Mithun. Steve has had a 30-year career working on the who's who of consumer accounts from General Mills to Land O'Lakes to H&R Block. Steve has helped pioneer the Brand Zealotry model and has led many of the innovations around key proprietary marketing processes and tools for the Interpublic Group flagship, Campbell Mithun. His agency is at the forefront of new media, and we felt the opportunity to tap into his desire to partner with us on this fourth edition would be nothing but positive for you who have chosen to read the book. We think you'll agree.

You'll find a new model developed to help combine the necessary elements of strategy and creativity. This is the first time we've revised the original model we used when the book was first published back in 1990.

The fourth edition has a significantly revised business review section (Part I) filled with new ways to find insights.

You'll find a completely new brand platform and plan objectives section (Part II) that updates the thinking and the best ways to answer these critical questions:

- What do you really do for your customers? (Chapter 4, "Scope")
- Whom are you for? (Chapter 5, "Targets")

- How are you really different from your competitors? (Chapter 6, "Positioning")
- What do you need to do? (Chapter 7, "Sales Objectives," Chapter 8, "Marketing Objectives," and Chapter 9, "Communication Objectives")
- What's your story? (Chapter 10, "Message Strategy")
- What's the plan of action? (Chapter 11, "Umbrella Strategy")

You'll notice that there's updated advertising, media, public relations, and interactive media chapters. And you'll quickly notice the addition of social media material. In addition to these major changes, we've added bits and pieces to almost every chapter. An example would be the section "Evaluation Metrics Every Marketer Should Consider" in Chapter 24, "Plan Evaluation."

What's Remained?

What hasn't changed is our belief that while there are a lot of books that provide examples of what others have done, what's really needed, and what we've provided, is a book with a how-to format that helps and directs you in creating effective marketing. We still believe in and practice marketing that links the three disciplines of marketing: research, strategy, and tactical execution around ideas that differentiate. That hasn't changed one bit from the first edition to this, the fourth edition.

To those of you who have an earlier edition, don't worry. The updated planning process itself still quantitatively locks objectives, strategies, and tactics together so that the process can be effectively executed and accurately evaluated, and, most importantly, it can achieve up-front sales objectives. And we feel more than ever that this book provides you with the one definitive source that you can use as a marketing planning guide for a whole plan and with a resource to which you can go back and focus on a specific marketing problem.

While the vast majority of what is presented in this book is based on hard factual data, we've continued to include personal experiences, observations, and opinions. For these we take full responsibility. Likewise, any errors are our own.

ACKNOWLEDGMENTS

From Roman

I have many friends, colleagues, and family members to thank for helping me over the years; they directly or indirectly had a hand in making our previous editions, and now this book, possible.

Thank you to my two mentors. First, my thanks go to Harry Dean Wolfe, who was my major professor in graduate school at the University of Wisconsin, from whom I learned that theory and practice are *both* necessary. Harry was instrumental in my taking a first job out of school with the Leo Burnett advertising agency in Chicago. Second, my thanks go to Rogers W. Zarling, entrepreneur extraordinaire, who from my boyhood to adulthood taught me business by what he called the best school, "the school of hard knocks."

Thank you to the Leo Burnett agency for instilling in me true advertising ideals and the quest for the best.

Thank you to all the McDonald's people I have worked with over the years, and especially Kathy Henry, for what they taught me and for the confidence they placed in me.

Thank you to my brothers, Al and Dick, former partners with me in a group of restaurants, for giving me the opportunity to try new things. In most cases they had to make the new ideas work and pay for them.

Thank you to my parents who were here in mind and spirit to see the completion of the first text. To my father, Roman, thank you for teaching me that I needed to "finish what I started" and that if I were "going to do something," to make sure I did it "right the first time." To my mother, Charlotte, thank you for encouraging me to "go for it" and to take the chance to try something new. I am forever in their debt, and they're in my thoughts always.

Thank you to my wife, Margaret, and my daughter, Laura Rose, for their understanding and constant support and for sacrificing many vacations and weekends because they accepted my need for a continual challenge.

Finally, thank you to Scott, my friend, former partner, and the best coauthor anyone could ever have, whose wife, Liz, encouraged him while he pushed me to do our first text, which was the catalyst for our other texts and this edition. And we did it. Because we know there is a better way.

From Scott

I never underestimate how lucky I've been during my career so far.

Everyone should be lucky enough to have a true mentor, someone whom you work with and who works for you—helping, nurturing, collaborating, pushing, and being a pain in the ass from time to time because he cares. Thank you, Roman Hiebing. We've done it all, from running a marketing and advertising agency together, to playing tackle football in the annual Mud Bowl.

I was lucky to be a member of the band—led by Joe Wood, the president of Famous Footwear, with members Rick Ausick, Doug Koch, Marty Lang, John Mazurk, and Jim Roe, the original Famous Footwear team that turned the fortunes of a company around. Joe created an environment in which we had the permission to disagree but the good sense to put egos aside, do what was right, and stay the course of our convictions. We worked hard, played hard, and won.

Luck had it too that I crossed paths with Steve Wehrenberg. It's the rare person who can both do and teach, and Steve has done both, exceptionally well over his career. Beyond that, you have to be a little positively bent to want to write a book while being the chief executive officer of a large advertising agency. Thanks for taking the time and for bringing another critical dimension to our book.

Finally, I've been lucky in love. To my four boys Seth, Birk, Reed, and Cale: I couldn't be prouder in what you are doing or how you are doing it. And to Liz, this fourth edition, by far the best one yet, is dedicated to you, because you're simply the best.

From Steve

In this book you'll read about how brands can take on archetypal roles in people's lives. But people can also take on archetypal roles in the life of an aspiring author. So, thanks to mine.

Scott Cooper, my **guide**: You coaxed me into the project, showed me the ropes, led me down the path to success, and always made me feel smart, even when I wasn't.

My **sages:** Earl Herzog, a man from whom I've learned so much and the author of our media chapter; Eric Einhorn, perhaps the smartest and gentlest man I've met in advertising; and Adina Dahlin and Lynn Franz, whose great thinking for our clients and contributions to my grad school class quickly found their way into our book.

And finally, my **lover**, partner, best friend, and wife: Sue. You have given me more inspiration than words can describe.

Introduction

The purpose of this book is to provide you with a practical and proven, step-by-step guide for preparing your own marketing plan. This is a text with real-world answers to help you meet specific marketing challenges head on, whatever the level of your marketing expertise or the size and type of your organization. In addition to providing a realistic guide to preparing a marketing plan, this book is a very useful reference and resource that will help you find marketing solutions on an everyday basis.

WHAT THE READER CAN EXPECT

The key to writing a successful marketing plan is disciplined marketing planning. However, before defining *disciplined marketing planning*, it is necessary to first describe each of the components. Let's first define the term *marketing*.

Definition of marketing: Determining the target market for your company, product, or service, determining the target market's needs and wants, and then fulfilling those needs and wants better than the competition does.

Planning then is simply an arranged structure to guide the process of marketing. Finally, *disciplined marketing planning* should be thought of as a comprehensive, sequential, interlocking, step-by-step decision and action process. In using this disciplined approach, you follow a four-step prescribed but logical process that allows you to define issues, answer questions correctly, and make decisions. Each step and the components within, as depicted by a box on the successful marketing planning chart in Exhibit I.1, should be completed before going on to the next.

This approach, although initially more time-consuming, dramatically increases the chances of your product's or service's success because the marketing plan prepared in this manner is just that—totally planned. It is a data-based plan that is all-encompassing, yet feasible to execute.

Why do we say that employing this successful marketing planning methodology increases your chances of success in marketing your product or service? Because this method of marketing planning is the following:

1. *Disciplined:* To truly integrate marketing tools that often overlap, one needs a methodology to sort out and interface them. Integrating can become very complicated and, in some instances, overwhelming. Accordingly, disciplined marketing planning employs a sequential, step-by-step system that asks for consideration of all tools and takes the marketing through a clear incremental building process. The sequential steps put the various planning tasks in a logical order so you do not get ahead of yourself (such as putting together an advertising and publicity campaign before clearly defining the heavy-user target or before considering the interfacing of the promotion and merchandising tools with the advertising and publicity tools).

EXHIBIT I.1
The Successful Marketing Plan

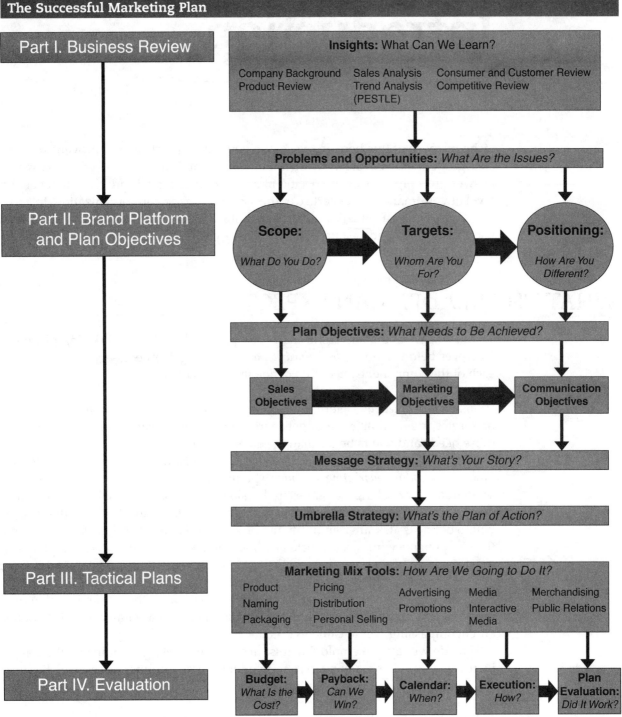

Further, because so much of marketing is not easy to quantify and evaluate, disciplined marketing planning demands that measurable objectives be incorporated throughout your marketing plan. Starting at the top of the marketing plan, there are objectives for sales, marketing, and communications, and there are objectives for every tactical marketing mix tool, such as promotion, advertising, and publicity. Each objective is very specific and quantifiable.

Finally, we end the plan with specific evaluation objectives in order to accurately measure the impact of the marketing program.

2. *Target market driven:* Everything we do to generate sales revolves around the target market. To emphasize this point, the word *marketing* has *market* within it. Of all the things necessary to be successful in selling a product, understanding the target market and target market segments is most important. From start to finish in writing a marketing plan, the target market is the focus—determining its needs and wants and fulfilling those needs and wants better than the competition does.

3. *Interlocking, not just integrated:* Successful marketing planning takes the integrated marketing approach to the next level by providing a sequential, step-by-step methodology that numerically locks the various elements of the marketing plan together. Each element and marketing mix tool is quantifiably integrated to meet the up-front sales objectives of the plan. No longer should the supporting plan elements and communication tools be woefully inadequate to meet the sales objectives. This happens, for example, when the target market is too small to support the sales objectives or when the advertising media weight is half the amount necessary to generate the level of awareness to affect the target's attitude.

   The sequence of steps is important because what comes *after* in the order of the plan is, in effect, making what comes *before* possible. For example, generating advertising awareness for the message is made possible by the amount of media weight put into the marketplace to communicate the message. Likewise, certain elements of the plan are placed directly next to each other because they have a direct quantitative tie to each other. For example, sales objectives rely directly on the size of the target markets and their behaviors as detailed in the subsequent marketing objectives that are tied to behaviors that in turn link back to sales.

4. *Comprehensive:* Successful marketing requires a comprehensive approach. This includes not only the major components of the marketing background and marketing plan but also the actual execution in the marketplace, where the successes and failures take place. Finally, a comprehensive plan includes a thorough evaluation of each component. This step provides the starting place for next year's plan, effectively closing the loop on this continuous, interlocking, and comprehensive planning process.

   Effective marketing cannot take place until every element of the marketing mix is considered and all appropriate elements are incorporated into the marketing plan. Further, because each tactical tool has communication value, each tool must be considered when preparing an integrated communication program. For example, price is not usually considered a marketing communication tool, yet the price charged for a product communicates something about the product image to the potential purchaser. It has been shown that a substantially higher competitive price charged for a product usually connotes an image of higher quality for that product. Accordingly, it takes a comprehensive planning effort to make sure that the communication value of each tactical tool is taken into account and is correctly presented to the target customer.

   In summary, to be comprehensive not only means extra effort but it also means leaving nothing or very little to chance. The net result is that marketing programs developed from comprehensive marketing plans are far more successful when implemented in the marketplace.

THE FOUR STEPS TO SUCCESSFUL MARKETING PLANNING

To bring order and efficiency to the difficult task of marketing planning, we have broken down the process into four steps that we believe need to be addressed when developing a successful marketing plan (see Exhibit I.1). The steps and the components within them combine to make an interlocking and comprehensive process. The following are the four steps of disciplined marketing planning that we employ, and the key components of each step are emphasized.

STEP 1   ## *Business Review*

The business review answers the question, What can we learn? It includes six steps of data gathering and insights and then a summary section titled "Problems and Opportunities." The problems and opportunities step is a summary of the challenges that emerge from the business review. Here the data collected from the business review are distilled into meaningful summary points that form the foundation of the work you do in the marketing plan—solving the problems and taking advantage of the opportunities that have been identified.

The business review helps you discover and then outline all you'll need to know to successfully create a winning marketing plan. Part I, "Business Review Insights," consists of a narrative to help you understand the concepts being discussed, questions to ask yourself to help you structure your business review, and charts (which appear both in Part I and again in Appendix B) that you can tailor to your own situation.

STEP 2   ## *Brand Platform and Plan Objectives*

We view the process of branding as more expansive than most marketing planning developers view it. The brand platform is the strategy section of your plan. It answers the following questions:

- What do you do? (defining your firm's core competencies, markets, and competitive set—that is, the scope of your business)
- Whom are you for? (defining target markets)
- How are you different? (defining your brand positioning—the brand promise you make to your customers that differentiates you in the marketplace)
- What needs to be achieved? (winning by adopting interlocking sales objectives, marketing objectives, and communication objectives)
- What's your story? (creating your message strategy)
- What's the plan of action? (developing your strategies)

STEP 3   ## *Tactical Plans: Marketing Mix Tools*

In this step of marketing planning, you develop tactical plans. The tactical plans incorporate marketing executions that, when implemented, will allow you to meet your marketing objectives and execute the overall brand positioning and marketing strategies you established earlier. Each marketing mix tool should have its own objectives, strategies, and where appropriate, executional specifics.

The following marketing mix tools are included in the tactical planning process:

- *Product:* The product is the tangible object that is marketed to the target market for consumer goods, retail, and business-to-business companies. For service businesses, the product is a future benefit or future promise.
- *Naming:* The naming of the product, service, or company is called *branding*. A brand or name is the label that consumers associate with your product. For this reason, a brand or name should help communicate the product's positioning and its inherent drama for the consumer.
- *Packaging:* For manufacturers, packaging holds and protects the product and assists in communicating the product's attributes and image. For retailers and service firms, packaging is the inside and outside environment that houses and dispenses the products and/or services (stores, offices, and so on), and it helps communicate the company's attributes and image.
- *Pricing:* Price is the monetary value of the product. The monetary value is usually governed by what the target market or buyer will pay for the product and what the seller or company must receive for the product in order to defray costs and generate a profit.
- *Distribution:* We define *distribution* as the transmission of goods and services from the producer or seller to the user. Distribution must ensure that the product is accessible to the target market.
- *Personal selling and service:* Personal selling for retail and service firms, often referred to as *operations*, involves all functions related to selling and service in the store, office, or other environments, such as door-to-door solicitation, in-home selling, and telemarketing. This includes hiring and managing sales personnel, stocking inventory, preparing the product for sale, presenting and maintaining the facility, and providing follow-up service to the customers.

  For business-to-business and consumer packaged-goods firms, personal selling relates to the manufacturer's selling and servicing of its products to the trade and/or intermediate markets (various buyers of the product within the distribution channel from the original producer to the ultimate user).
- *Advertising message:* Communication that informs and persuades through paid media (television, radio, magazine, newspaper, outdoor, Internet, and direct mail) constitutes the advertising message.
- *Promotions and events:* Promotions provide added incentive, encouraging the target market to perform some incremental behavior. The incremental behavior results in increased short-term sales and/or an association with the product (for example, product usage or an event-oriented experience). In addition, the focus of promotions is relatively short term. For the purposes of this book, we will define a *promotion* as an activity that offers added incentive to stimulate incremental purchase or association with the product over the short run, for a reason that goes beyond just the product's inherent attributes and benefits.
- *Advertising media:* Advertising media are paid carriers of advertising, not at the point of purchase. While the advertising message is *what* is being communicated, the advertising medium is *how* it is delivered.
- *Interactive media:* The Internet is an interactive medium with centralized content that is delivered to members of the target market when it is requested. Members of the target market drive their exposures to your organization's

Internet content, while your organization drives exposure to its multimedia content. Chapter 19, "Interactive Media," also covers *social media*, focusing on tactics specifically for social interaction and fostering connections between people. The media found in this space include common networking sites like Facebook, LinkedIn, and Twitter in addition to sites focused on specific interest groups. Also covered are interactive blogs and other forms of two-way communication accessible on the Internet.

- *Merchandising:* Merchandising is the nonmedia communication of the company and/or product to the target market. This is the method used to communicate product and promotional information. Merchandising makes a visual and/or written statement about your company through an environment other than paid media, with or without one-on-one personal communication. Merchandising includes brochures, sell sheets, product displays, video presentations, banners, trade show exhibits, shelf talkers, table tents, or any other nonmedia tools that can be used to communicate product attributes, pricing, or promotion information.

- *Public relations:* Public relations creates goodwill for an organization not just for the short term but also for the long term. *Publicity* is a part of public relations, and it is any nonpaid media communication that helps build target market awareness and positively affects attitudes for your product or firm. Publicity provides your firm or product with a benefit not found in any other marketing mix tool. Since publicity utilizes noncommercial communication, it adds a dimension of legitimacy that can't be found in advertising.

STEP 4   **Budget, Payback, Calendar, Execution, and Evaluation**

- *Budget:* The budget is the cumulative monetary cost of implementing the plan.
- *Payback:* This analysis looks at whether the marketing plan and its specific marketing programs, as well as executions within the plan, will generate the projected revenues in excess of expenses.
- *Calendar:* The calendar is a schedule of the marketing plan's tactical executions.
- *Execution:* This step concerns the implementation of the plan.
- *Evaluation:* In this step, the methodology used to help determine the level of success of the overall marketing plan, and its specific elements, is established. We have also included the research and testing components in this section. While evaluation is the last step in the process, it signals a new beginning to the whole disciplined approach, as evaluation findings become a major part of the marketing background section in the preparation of the next year's marketing plan. Evaluation is one of the most important steps because it is a learning tool that will lead to improved marketing plans and execution of marketing programs in the future.

HOW TO USE THIS BOOK IN YOUR MARKETING PLANNING

Before you begin writing your marketing plan, we recommend that you read through the entire book to understand the complete process and all that goes into preparing a comprehensive marketing plan. Next, as you actually prepare your own marketing plan, go through each chapter again, and very diligently attempt to follow the step-by-step disciplined marketing planning process.

Adapt the Process to Fit Your Business

As you use the disciplined marketing planning process, keep in mind that, while you should understand the basic marketing principles provided throughout this book and follow the recommended methodology, you can adapt the review and planning process to best fit your product or marketing situation. The point to remember is that you want to be open-minded and innovative but also methodical and consistent as you prepare the marketing background section and write the marketing plan.

Strive to Fill Data Voids

While the methodology used in the text is data based, hard data required to write a marketing plan may not always be available. If this is your situation, then first search again and again. If you still cannot obtain the necessary data, consider conducting primary research as discussed in Chapter 1. If there is not enough time and money available to conduct primary research, fill the data voids with estimated data. However, if you are using estimated data, have the information confirmed by more than one person, and note in your business review that the information has been estimated.

Keep Track of Your Ideas

As you go through the whole process, you will come up with all types of ideas for different areas of the marketing plan that might not relate to the specific section of the plan you are currently writing. Don't lose these ideas because they will be very helpful when you prepare the particular section to which they apply. As you prepare the background section and the marketing plan itself, have separate sheets of paper handy with headings of problems, opportunities, and each step of the marketing plan (including a separate sheet of paper for each marketing mix tool) under which you can jot down relevant ideas as they occur to you. Don't evaluate the worth of each idea as you think of it. Evaluate its application as you actually write the section of the marketing plan to which it pertains.

Apply the Material to Your Own Marketing Situation

Also keep in mind that many of the principles, procedures, and examples provided in this book can be applied to your particular marketing situation, even though it has not been written just for your specific product or service. In fact, this book is written for broad application by the marketer of a consumer packaged-goods product, business-to-business product, service, or retail outlet with a private, public, or nonprofit organization. For simplicity and brevity, however, the word *product* is usually used throughout this book in generic planning discussions for whatever is to be marketed. When there is specific reference to consumer or business-to-business products, services, or retail, it will be singled out accordingly.

Use Idea Starters

While this book does not deal directly with execution in terms of preparing a newspaper ad or buying a radio schedule, you will find an "Idea Starters by Marketing Situation" grid in Appendix A at the back of the book. This unique marketing idea grid includes hundreds of idea starters for building businesses, categorized by the most common marketing situations and presented separately for each marketing mix tool—from product, branding, and packaging to advertising, merchandising, and publicity. This grid can be of major assistance to the reader who is beginning to develop the actual marketing plan and its executions.

Allow Sufficient Time to Prepare and Modify Your Plan

Writing a comprehensive marketing plan based on a thorough marketing background is a time-consuming project, particularly if it has not been done before. Therefore, it is wise to begin the disciplined marketing planning process far in advance of when the plan is actually due. It seems to take twice the time originally estimated to prepare a complete marketing plan. To do it right, you can estimate 50 to 100 hours or more to prepare the business review section and half this number of hours to prepare the first draft of the marketing plan section. Although the business review section is usually the most demanding, without this database you have no real objective source from which to make your current and future marketing decisions.

As a side note, you will find that updating the business review data and revising a marketing plan year to year is considerably less time-consuming and easier than gathering the initial background information and writing the first marketing plan. This is particularly true if the initial business review is prepared in a thorough and comprehensive manner. Once you have completed the business review, you will be continually revising the marketing plan as you write the first draft, reworking the elements in the marketing plan so they effectively interface with each other.

Once the plan is written, you must allow adequate time to review the plan, make major changes, and rework the fine points. The time and rewriting are necessary to arrive at a marketing plan that is comprehensive, understandable, supportable, implementable, and in the end, successful.

Good luck from all three of us with your successful marketing planning!

The
Successful
Marketing
Plan

The Successful Marketing Plan

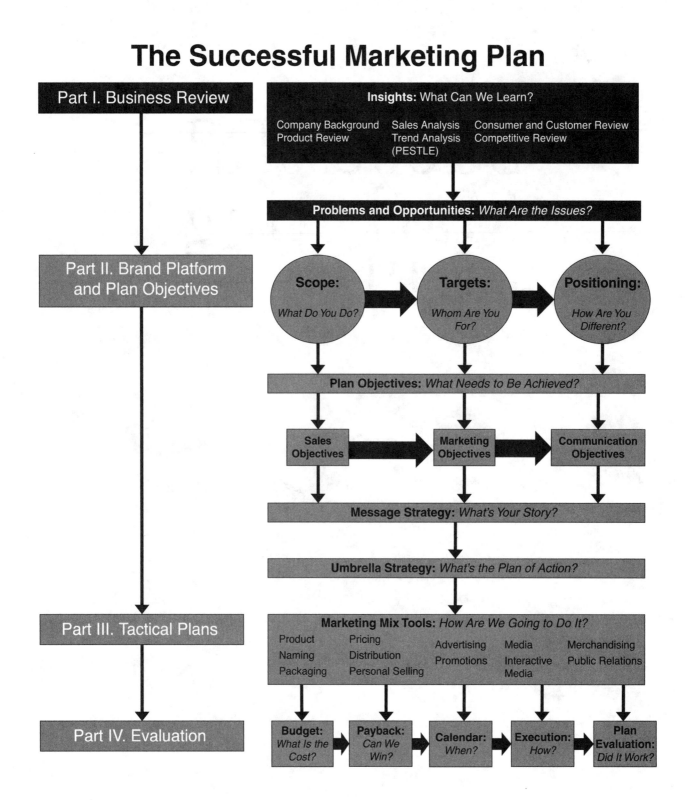

Part I. Business Review

Insights: What Can We Learn?

Company Background   Sales Analysis   Consumer and Customer Review
Product Review   Trend Analysis   Competitive Review
   (PESTLE)

Problems and Opportunities: *What Are the Issues?*

Part II. Brand Platform and Plan Objectives

Scope:

What Do You Do?

Targets:

Whom Are You For?

Positioning:

How Are You Different?

Plan Objectives: *What Needs to Be Achieved?*

Sales Objectives

Marketing Objectives

Communication Objectives

Message Strategy: *What's Your Story?*

Umbrella Strategy: *What's the Plan of Action?*

Part III. Tactical Plans

Marketing Mix Tools: *How Are We Going to Do It?*

Product   Pricing
Naming   Distribution   Advertising   Media   Merchandising
Packaging   Personal Selling   Promotions   Interactive   Public Relations
     Media

Part IV. Evaluation

Budget: *What Is the Cost?*

Payback: *Can We Win?*

Calendar: *When?*

Execution: *How?*

Plan Evaluation: *Did It Work?*

BUSINESS REVIEW INSIGHTS

The following three chapters provide the insights necessary to develop a successful marketing plan.

The Successful Marketing Plan

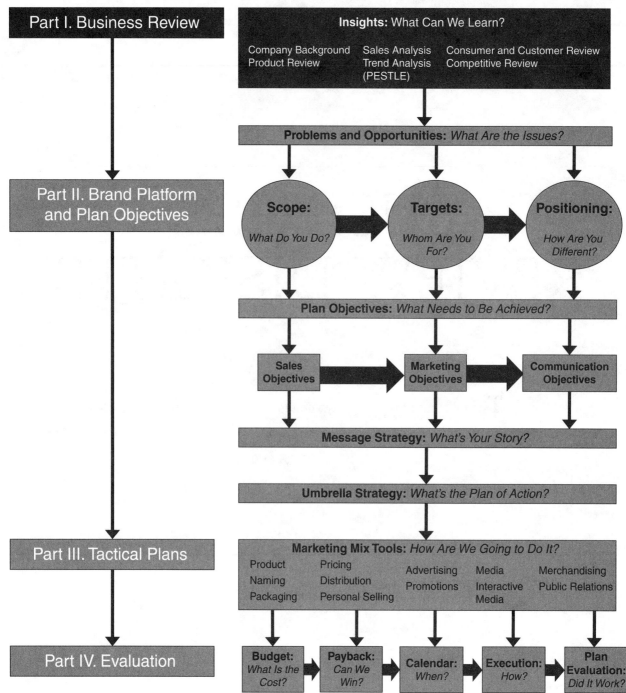

Part I. Business Review

Insights: What Can We Learn?

Company Background   Sales Analysis   Consumer and Customer Review
Product Review   Trend Analysis   Competitive Review
                     (PESTLE)

Problems and Opportunities: *What Are the Issues?*

Part II. Brand Platform and Plan Objectives

Scope: *What Do You Do?*

Targets: *Whom Are You For?*

Positioning: *How Are You Different?*

Plan Objectives: *What Needs to Be Achieved?*

Sales Objectives   **Marketing Objectives**   **Communication Objectives**

Message Strategy: *What's Your Story?*

Umbrella Strategy: *What's the Plan of Action?*

Part III. Tactical Plans

Marketing Mix Tools: *How Are We Going to Do It?*

Product   Pricing   Advertising   Media   Merchandising
Naming   Distribution   Promotions   Interactive   Public Relations
Packaging   Personal Selling   Media

Part IV. Evaluation

Budget: *What Is the Cost?*

Payback: *Can We Win?*

Calendar: *When?*

Execution: *How?*

Plan Evaluation: *Did It Work?*

1

What You'll Need to Know, Part 1

What can we learn? The insights portion of the business review provides an information decision-making base for the subsequent marketing plan and the rationale for all strategic marketing decisions within the plan. Most important, it provides for a consumer and customer orientation to your marketing communications.

FROM THIS CHAPTER YOU WILL LEARN

- Suggestions for preparing a business review

- How to develop an outline to use as a road map for completing your business review

- The steps necessary to complete a business review

- How to utilize primary data (developed through your own company's research and databases) and secondary data (existing data from trade journals, government publications, syndicated research) in the development of your business review

- Where to find the information necessary to complete the charts and answer the questions in each step of the business review

OVERVIEW

This chapter explores why marketing information is not a nice-to-have but a must-have. It also introduces some basic business review terms and the key elements of developing a business review.

WHY MARKET INFORMATION IS IMPORTANT

Today, consumers have more product choices than ever before. They also have more information about the choices. The combination of more competition, from small niche marketers to large dominant category killers, and a bombardment of communication from many competitive alternatives means that marketers have to work much harder to affect target market behavior. Thus, it is more important now than at any time in the history of marketing to really understand your target market and to let this understanding drive not only the marketing decisions but impact the entire decision-making framework of your company.

It is our opinion that many of the business successes of the past 30 years have come about not because of great business management but because of individuals like Sam Walton who have had tremendous consumer insight—insight developed through their deep understanding of the target market, the business environment, and the competition. Walton realized that the rural consumer was underserved from a retail standpoint. He consequently built his business on a unique concept: while the standard doctrine of the day said that there had to be 100,000 people within a 10-mile trading area to support large general merchandise stores such as Walmart, Walton put his stores in small towns such as Viroqua, Wisconsin. He succeeded because consumers in rural areas were willing to drive much greater distances to avail themselves of the deep selection of merchandise and reasonable prices that in the past had been found only in the larger cities.

Many industry leaders such as Best Buy, Famous Footwear, Apple, Starbucks, and Nike have similar stories, stories based on consumer insights that were the foundation for dominating success.

Much of the marketing innovation in today's environment is coming from retailers, service firms, packaged-goods companies, and business-to-business firms that are interacting with their target markets with a new level of urgency. Technological innovations in the retail industry, such as "smart" cash registers and customer databases, have increased the use of customer insights and have provided marketers with a wealth of behavioral information. In addition, firms like Networked Insights and MotiveQuest are mining social networking websites on the Internet to track and interpret the millions and millions of unbiased consumer conversations that are happening daily.

The more successful business-to-business firms are spending less time selling what they have and more time defining their customers' needs in order to sell what their customers really want. And packaged-goods companies, facing product parity issues and a sales promotion environment, are exploring ways to build brand equity and add value to their products. Marketers who are on the front lines, engaging in dialogue with the consumer on a daily basis, are the ones who are often closest to the consumers and target market demands. This "closeness" is bringing about a change in the way many marketing-oriented companies are doing business.

These marketing-oriented companies are now in a position to define specific market segments based on the segment's unique needs or consumption behavior, which in turn allows them to set realistic marketing objectives to affect the segment's behavior. Companies today have the ability to know whether product repurchase rates are different for new versus old customers or for customers of different ages. They have the ability to determine exactly how many customers there are for each unique purchasing segment, and they know what the average expenditure per purchase and the average number of purchases are for the segments. More important, they know what each segment of customers is buying, when and, often times, why. With this type of target and customer information, the marketing-oriented company is able to set objectives that have a more realistic chance of positively affecting consumer behavior. Marketers writing the plan know they have a good chance of achieving the goals because these objectives have been set with the consumers' needs in mind.

For example, an objective to increase the repeat purchase rate might be developed due to a knowledge that the consumers have the desire and the ability to purchase more if the company were to make some basic changes in the way it does business. This might require changing the product to satisfy shortcomings in important attributes in order to stimulate increased repurchase. It might mean changing the packaging to allow for easier storage, adjusting price to encourage multiple purchases, or improving customer service to increase after-sale purchases and repurchases. While all these involve strategic decisions, it is consumer insights that provide the marketer the confidence to set obtainable marketing objectives and to determine the appropriate strategy for achieving them.

Marketing is a broad discipline in which multiple decisions must be made such as which customers should be targeted, through what specific combination of product features, with what price, through what distribution channels, with what type of service, and via what type of communication. Unfortunately very few companies operate in a competition-free environment so these decisions need to be made not only with the consumers and customers in mind but also with the actions of the competitors and the realities of the business operations in mind. A systematic review of all known facts and insights affecting these decisions greatly improves a business's chances for success.

Industry Category Comparisons

To gain insights into marketing planning direction, look not only inward at your own company but also outside it, to the industry in which you are competing. A business review will help you compare trends within your company to those of your industry category and key competitors. The *industry category* is the overall business in which you compete. For example, Sub-Zero makes food freezers, and it is in the kitchen appliance industry.

Consumers versus Customers

Throughout the business review, we use the terms *consumers* and *customers*. In order to analyze *company trends*, we need to investigate the behavior of company *customers*—that is, those people who have purchased a company's product. If we are to compare company trends to industry category and key competitor trends, we also need to look at the purchase behavior of *consumers*—that is, people who have purchased the *industry category product*, a subset of which are company customers.

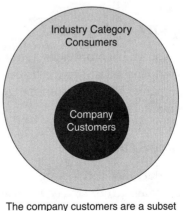

The company customers are a subset
of the industry consumers.

PRIMARY ELEMENTS OF THE BUSINESS REVIEW

A well-developed business review should be utilized as a daily reference source. Your business review should be updated each year to reflect the most recent changes in your industry and company. Therefore, if this is your first business

EXHIBIT 1.1

The Seven Steps of the Business Review

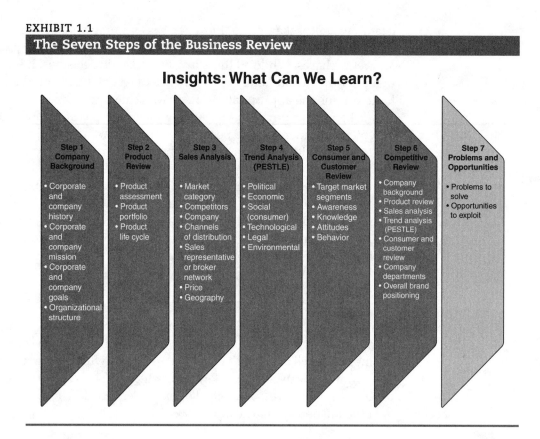

Insights: What Can We Learn?

Step 1 Company Background	Step 2 Product Review	Step 3 Sales Analysis	Step 4 Trend Analysis (PESTLE)	Step 5 Consumer and Customer Review	Step 6 Competitive Review	Step 7 Problems and Opportunities
• Corporate and company history • Corporate and company mission • Corporate and company goals • Organizational structure	• Product assessment • Product portfolio • Product life cycle	• Market category • Competitors • Company • Channels of distribution • Sales representative or broker network • Price • Geography	• Political • Economic • Social (consumer) • Technological • Legal • Environmental	• Target market segments • Awareness • Knowledge • Attitudes • Behavior	• Company background • Product review • Sales analysis • Trend analysis (PESTLE) • Consumer and customer review • Company departments • Overall brand positioning	• Problems to solve • Opportunities to exploit

review, don't be overwhelmed. If you don't have time to complete all sections, work on those that most affect your business. Then, next year, update those sections and further complete some of the others for which you didn't previously have time.

Completing the business review can be more than a one-person job. Request assistance from other people in your company to help compile the information. This step-by-step process is intended to help the marketer to more easily manage the information gathering process.

There are seven sections to a business review, as shown in Exhibit 1.1.

STEP 1 ## Company Background

Where you've been provides a foundation for where you are going. Additionally, if your company goes through a strategic planning process, the strategic direction of the company should be summarized in this section where it can serve as a bridge to the marketing plan.

STEP 2 ## Product Review

Your products and services are your major touch points to your customers. This section provides ways to objectively analyze and assess your products and services portfolio.

STEP 3 ## Sales Analysis

This section provides a first view into both the industry consumer and your customers. This section also establishes a comparison of your company to industry benchmarks. Additionally, sales trends provide you with tremendous insights to your customers' and consumers' evolving likes and dislikes.

STEP 4 ## Trend Analysis (PESTLE)

This section helps bring to the forefront major trends that will affect your marketing decisions. The PESTLE analysis allows you to anticipate the likely major external influences on your business: political, economic, social (consumer)— *social* is defined here as cultural norms, demographics, and shifts in consumption patterns—technological, legal, and environmental.

STEP 5 ## Consumer and Customer Review

This section helps you gain understanding of the various target market segments' awareness, attitudes, and behaviors. This work provides the foundation for defining your primary and secondary target market segments; creating your sales, marketing, and communication objectives; developing your positioning; and finally, deciding on your umbrella strategies in Part II of the plan, "Brand Platform and Plan Objectives."

STEP 6 ## Competitive Review

Know your enemy to know yourself. This section provides a step-by-step question-and-answer methodology to help you understand your company's strengths and weaknesses relative to its key competitive set.

STEP 7 ## Problems and Opportunities

This last section is a summary of the business review. It covers the key problems you need to solve and the key opportunities you will need to take advantage of in your marketing plan.

PREPARING THE BUSINESS REVIEW

Six tasks make up the process of preparing the business review: creating an outline, developing questions, developing data charts, developing reference points for comparisons, conducting data searches, and writing summary statements.

TASK 1 ## Prepare an Outline

It is important to understand that the business review, as presented in this book, is broad and attempts to be all encompassing. You must tailor the business review to your specific needs and situation, in terms of both the information you gather and the format in which you provide it. An auto parts manufacturer might include both business-to-business information and consumer information if its products have both original equipment manufacturer (OEM) market and aftermarket components. A packaged-goods manufacturer may include both a channel and consumer market analysis. Further, the availability and quality of information may dictate the ultimate form of your business review. The outline gives you a framework for gathering the information. Expect the business review to evolve as you go on.

Start your business review by developing a written outline. The outline should be as specific as possible, and it should cover each major area of the business review. The outline helps you stay focused and ensures that you will obtain, in a disciplined and sequential process, the critical data you need for an actionable marketing plan.

In the discussion that follows the outline below, each task section discusses and explains the topical points so that the reader will have a full understanding of how to gather and organize this information for use in the marketing plan.

The following is an example outline for a business review.

Step 1. Company Background
- History and heritage
- Mission
- Corporate and product or service goals
- Organizational structure

Step 2. Product Review
- Assessment of product strengths and weaknesses relative to industry category and key competitors
- Product life cycle
- Product portfolio

Step 3. Sales Analysis (Five-Year Trends)
- Total sales for the company and industry category
- Company's sales by product or service line compared to sales in the industry category
- Market share
- Seasonality for sales by the company versus sales by the industry category
- Channels of distribution
- Sales representative or broker network
- Price influence and price line analysis
- *Geography:* Company's brand development versus brand development in the industry category indexes

Step 4. Trend Analysis (PESTLE)
- Environmental trend analysis: PESTLE
  - Political
  - Economic
  - Social (consumer)
  - Technological
  - Legal
  - Environmental

Step 5. Consumer and Customer Review
- Target market segments
  - Heavy users
  - Decision makers versus influencers
  - New versus repeat buyers
  - Customer tenure
  - Demographics
  - North American Industry Classification System (NAICS) code (business classification)
  - Dollar size
  - Product usage
- Awareness by target market
  - Unaided awareness (first mention and top of mind)
  - Aided awareness

- Knowledge
- Attitudes
  - Emotional
  - Rational
  - Relevancy
  - Esteem
- Behavior
  - Trial
  - Retrial and/or loyalty measures

Step 6. Competitive Review
- Company background
- Sales analysis
- Product review
- Trends
- Media strategy and spending
- Customer service
- Overall brand positioning

Step 7. Problems and Opportunities
- Key problems to be solved in the plan
- Key opportunities to be taken advantage of in the plan

TASK 2 ## Develop Questions

List questions that need to be answered for each section of the business review outline. The questions will provide direction in determining what specific information you need to accumulate.

TASK 3 ## Develop Data Charts

Develop data charts with headings to help structure your search for relevant information. When completed, the charts should enable you to answer the major questions pertaining to each section of the business review outline.

The first part of this task is to organize the headings and columns of the charts in order to determine what information you need to find prior to the data search. This preliminary work forces you to look for data and numbers that will provide meaningful information for your specific situation, and it keeps you from gathering random data and information. Remember, if you look for data before developing your charts, you may tend to construct the charts around what was easy to find, not what should have been found.

TASK 4 ## Develop Reference Points for Comparisons

Always develop charts that have reference points for comparison so that the data are actionable. For example, when you analyze sales growth for your company, compare this against the sales growth for the industry. In this manner, the company's sales growth can be judged against a reference point.

To summarize, a business review, whenever possible, should do the following:

- Provide reference points of comparison within the company (past-year trends).
- Provide reference points of comparison between the company and the industry category.

- Provide reference points of comparison between the company and its key competitors.

The following sections provide some basic reminders that are applicable throughout the business review and pertain to the collection and organization of the data you gather.

Compare Five-Year Trends

It is important to review trends whenever analyzing data that will direct marketing decisions. Five years is a good amount of time—long enough to show trend movement but not so burdensome that it will discourage you from collecting the data. Looking at five-year trends allows the marketer to determine not only increases and decreases from year to year but also shifts in the marketplace over a period of time. For example, while any given product or target market segment may account for the greatest sales volume in one year, a review of five years' worth of data might show that the leader has had flat sales and that another product or target market segment will soon dominate the category if the trends continue. Therefore, it is important to look beyond a static one-year number to get a true feeling for the data trends over a period of time.

Compare Trends within the Company

The marketer must be aware of the trends within the company. For example, what customer market segment accounts for the most volume? Has this same company segment been growing, flattening, or declining in volume over the past five years? Has another company segment been growing faster, and will it be serving the dominant target market segment in the future? If you have a large company, it is also very insightful to compare regions of the company to the overall *company system* data. This regional review is helpful when determining different local target markets or marketing objectives versus company system target markets or marketing objectives.

Compare the Company to the Industry

It is also important to compare the company to its appropriate industry category as a whole. Are the target markets that are responsible for the company's highest product volume the same target markets that are responsible for the industry category's highest product volume? Are your company's sales trends comparable to, above, or below the industry category's sales trends across products with the highest sales volumes, transaction volumes, and profit potentials? What are your company's market share trends (your share of sales or transaction volume relative to the industry) overall and among various target market segments?

Make Competitive Comparisons

Finally, the marketer must also take into consideration the competitive environment and any changes or trends that will make it harder or easier to capture market share against identified target market segments. For example, there might be an increase in the total number of competitors, or a competitor may have developed a product or manufacturing innovation resulting in a price or product attribute advantage.

Use Benchmark Marketing

Although the concept of comparing relative points of data started in the retail industry under the name *deadly parallel*, we apply the principle to all business types—retail, packaged-goods, services, and business-to-business firms. The name *deadly parallel* developed because the technique was often used as a rationale for eliminating the poor performers. We find it far more constructive to use benchmarking to examine comparisons between relative points of data. The true measure of a marketer is his or her ability to use these comparisons to uncover and solve problems and to figure out the best ways to further maximize opportunities.

One of the best ways benchmarking can be successfully utilized today is with businesses that have multiple locations or geographic markets. The concept is to identify departments, product lines, stores, or markets with similar characteristics, such as product mix and sales potential, and then compare results. In order to accomplish this, many firms designate their markets into A, B, and C markets, with each broad market designation demonstrating similar characteristics. Then sales by store, sales by product, customer counts, sales per transaction, purchase ratios, profits, and expenses can be compared across like markets. With these benchmarks established across a marketer's system, strong and weak performances can be identified and management can put focus on both the positive and negative exceptions to improve company performance.

Another way benchmarking can be used is to compare target market segment performance. For the American Automobile Association (AAA), we looked at the performance of customer segments based on age, length of membership, and product use. For example, renewal was considerably lower among members of five years or less than among members of more than five years. And users of specific AAA products had greater cross-sell into the wider range of AAA products.

Remember, benchmarking is most successfully used to identify targets, products, or stores that are the exceptions, either significantly overperforming or underperforming. Then your focus becomes taking further advantage of high performers and eliminating or fixing the problems of underperformers.

A Last Thought

Remember, a single piece of data is really of no use to any marketer. The fact that a company has experienced 10 percent sales growth means very little unless it is compared to some other benchmark, such as sales growth for the industry category. If sales growth for the industry category has increased 15 percent, suddenly the 10 percent sales growth doesn't look as good.

In summary, establishing comparisons within your company and comparing your company to its industry category provides the following benefits:

1. Comparisons allow you to identify customer target market segments, geographic markets, products, and channels and individual stores that are performing below or above the company or industry average, thus providing insight to further exploit strengths or solve weaknesses.
2. Comparisons allow you to identify trends within the target market and the industry.
3. Comparisons allow you to compare or benchmark your firm to its industry, thus providing insight into how you are actually performing versus your competition.

TASK 5   *Conduct Data Searches*

Institute a disciplined data search. Stay focused on what needs to be found by constantly reviewing your outline. This will allow you to feel confident that you have compiled all of the existing data necessary to complete your charts.

TASK 6   **Write Summary Statements**

After the charts have been completed, write brief statements summarizing the major findings and answering the questions you developed in Task 2. Include a summary rationale when needed. Keep the summary objective by strictly reporting the findings; don't provide solutions at this point. The business review is not for developing objectives and strategies; it is for providing facts from which to develop a marketing plan and the supporting rationale. However, as mentioned in the Introduction, you should jot down your thoughts and ideas as you prepare your business review to potentially use later when writing your marketing plan.

ORGANIZING THE BUSINESS REVIEW

The sections of the final written business review should follow the same sequence as the steps developed in your outline. Each section should include summary statements followed by completed, detailed data charts.

We suggest writing the marketing background and plan in the third person, being as objective as possible. Do not interject personal feelings that cannot be documented by fact. Write in a very clear, concise manner so that there can be no misinterpretation of what is presented. And don't assume that everyone who reads the plan will have the same base of information that you, the writer, has. Include all available information pertinent to the issues being discussed so that everyone reading the plan will have the same frame of reference.

CONDUCTING RESEARCH

In preparing your business review, data can be obtained through both primary and secondary research.

Primary Research

Original research compiled to meet your specific data requirements is broken down into two categories: quantitative and qualitative.

Quantitative Research

Data and information are usually obtained through surveys, with results gathered from a representative random sample of a given universe. The samples are large enough to make inferences that are statistically significant. We refer to two types of quantitative research methods most often throughout this book. One is *customer-based research*, which provides information about a company's own customers. The other is *marketwide research*, which is used to provide information about the overall category user or purchaser base.

Qualitative Research

Research methods that do not statistically represent the target market universe provide qualitative data. Qualitative research typically includes talking with small groups of consumers in the format of focus groups, mall intercepts, Internet panels, and one-on-one interviews. Consumers are asked to provide insights into their likes, dislikes, and attitudes regarding a particular company, product, or even activity or why and how they purchase or use one type of product versus another. Qualitative research is particularly good at deep explorations into understanding consumer and customer emotions that drive decisions, shape attitudes, and form the basis for likes and dislikes of a company, product, or service versus alternatives.

Qualitative research is often used in conjunction with quantitative research. For example, quantitative research may determine that a company has a perceived customer service problem relative to the competition. Then, qualitative research can be used to further explain what consumers feel customer service entails in the company's particular industry and what specifically is lacking in the company's customer service as compared to that of other companies. In the reverse example, sometimes qualitative research can be used up front to identify trends or problems with quantitative data used to verify and quantify the findings.

Another form of qualitative research that has gained much acceptance and use is *ethnographics*. This form of research involves watching consumers as they relate to the company's product—in public places such as airports, as they use the product or interact with others who are using it, or in retail stores where the purchase is being made (or not made). A great deal of information can be learned through these observation techniques. JanSport, for example, invests time in this technique to learn how people use backpacks or anything related to backpacks, and it applies these valuable insights in new product development.

Finally, a word of caution. As with any form of research, qualitative research can also be very misleading. It is not statistically based and therefore can be a poor representation of what the marketplace really thinks. However, conducted by researchers experienced in this form of research, the directional findings and insights are consistently very accurate and reliable.

Secondary Research

Secondary research, which may also be quantitative or qualitative, is not specifically compiled for your company. Instead, it is existing information that is available through outside sources. An example of a secondary research source is census information. Just as with primary research, combining this type of secondary research information with your company's data will allow you to develop insights into your customers, your market, and the problems and opportunities facing your company. The only difference is that primary research is conducted to answer specific questions a company might have. To answer these questions with secondary research, you may have to dig a little more and be willing to analyze multiple studies to find your answers. Even then, you may not be able to answer all of your questions, so you will have to rely on judgment. Of course, secondary research is also typically less expensive than primary research. In most cases, a mix of both primary and secondary research is appropriate.

Indexing

Indexing, used extensively in the business review, is a process that presents a number or group of numbers in relation to an average, or base. Indexing is used to show a relationship between two sets of numbers or percentages. Indexing is based on an average value of 100. A number higher than 100 means the index represents a value greater than the average; a number lower than 100 means the index represents a value less than the average.

EXHIBIT 1.2

Indexing Example

Age Category	Homeownership*	Index
18–24	20%	33
25–34	48	80
35–44	60	100
45–54	74	123
55–64	70	117
65–74	50	83
Average, all ages	60	100

*These numbers are used only for illustration. They do not reflect actual homeownership rates.

When indexing, a base number is established, and all other numbers are compared to it. For example, assume that 60 percent of the population owns a home and that homeownership is further broken down by age category as shown in Exhibit 1.2. Since 60 percent is the average percentage of homeownership, it becomes the base number from which to measure any subset of the population. In this example, among 18- to 24-year-olds, only 20 percent own homes; then 20 percent divided by 60 percent equals 0.33. However, for purposes of clarity and easier communications, the decimal result is then multiplied by 100 to give a round number—0.33 times 100 equals an index of 33. (From this point on in the book, we will not explicitly show the multiplication by 100.) Because 33 is substantially below 100, we know that 18- to 24-year-olds own homes at one-third the average across all ages.

In another example, 30 percent of a national company's consumers live in Chicago. With that, you would expect them to consume 30 percent of the company's products (30 divided by 30 equals an index of 100, or average). But if the Chicago consumers consume 60 percent of the company's products, they are consuming at a rate of 60 percent, divided by the base of 30 percent, for an index of 200. Thus, the Chicago market would compare at twice the national average, or 100 points above the expected consumption pattern.

We usually consider an index meaningful if it is plus or minus 10 from 100. In other words, we look for the number 110 and above or number 90 and below. If all age groups index between 95 and 105 in terms of consumption, we determine that our target market is flat across all age groups. However, if the 25-to-34 and 35-to-44 age groups indexed at 115 and 180, respectively, and all other age groups were at or below average (or below 100), then we would determine that those two age groups consumed at significantly higher levels, especially the 35-to-44 age group.

Sources of Information

The following are commonly used sources of information available to most any marketer. These sources will help you obtain the data necessary to complete the business review portion of your marketing plan. Many of the references listed can be found in a public or university library, can be obtained free, or can be purchased at a reasonable cost. The sources are organized here under easy-to-understand category headings:

- *Target market segmentation (consumer, business, and geographic):* Sources here provide consumer, business, and geographic segmentation statistics, which help to define target market segments, product usage, and size of potential markets.

- *Lifestyle segmentation information:* Sources in this section provide attitude, opinion, interest, and lifestyle information to help define target market segments.
- *Media spending and media competitive information:* Sources here provide media planning and buying information along with data on competitive spending.
- *Association and trade show information:* Sources in this section provide trade association listings. Many trade associations provide valuable industry data that are useful for compiling a business review.
- *Media and print production costs and availability:* Sources provide information required by advertisers for buying media and print production.
- *Trending information and analytics tools:* Sources provide information on predicting future data based on patterns in the past. Trends will help provide a direction for marketing efforts.
- *Social media measurement:* Sources provide information on where to find help with monitoring, measuring, and analyzing social media and tapping into the conversations on millions of websites daily.

Target Market Segmentation: Consumer, Business, and Geographic

Experian Simmons
600 Third Avenue
New York, NY 10016
212-471-2850
www.experiansimmons.com

Experian Simmons provides information on the demographics, size, and media habits of the user and purchaser group for a broad range of products, product categories, and brands. Available information from this source includes but is not limited to the following:

- Demographics and size of demographic groups using product
- Heavy user or light user by demographic break
- Brand loyalty
- Media usage by demographic break
- Approximate market share by brand
- Lifestyle psychographics

GfK Mediamark Research & Intelligence, LLC (GfK MRI)
75 Ninth Avenue, 5th Floor
New York, NY 10011
212-884-0200
800-310-3305
www.gfkmri.com

GfK MRI provides data on consumer market segmentation, media usage, demographics, psychographics, and consumer behavior. The Survey of the American Consumer produces a large database of consumer behavior, media usage, and consumer motivations. It also has specialties in supplying the ratings data for nearly all national print; it analyzes magazine readership, performs readership studies, and publishes generational studies (for example, the BoomerView [baby boomers], the American Kids Study, Teenmark, Hispanic Consumers). Available information from this source includes but is not limited to the following:

- Demographics and size of demographic groups using particular products
- Heavy user or light user by demographic break
- Brand loyalty
- Media usage by demographic break
- Approximate market share by brand
- Lifestyle psychographics
- Generational studies

Zipskinny

www.zipskinny.com/

This is a free site that gives you a wealth of demographic information for any zip code in the United States.

Business and Industry Classification Sources

Dialog

2250 Perimeter Park Drive, Suite 300
Morrisville, NC 27560
800-334-2564
919-804-6400
www.dialog.com

Dialog provides the key business target research information including market share and sales figures, competitive intelligence, business directories, and financials on over 14 million U.S. and international companies.

Dun & Bradstreet, Inc.

103 JFK Parkway
Short Hills, NJ 07078
973-921-5500
800-234-3867
www.dnb.com

D&B is a business list company that provides accurate direct-mail lists and information pertaining to the number and size of businesses within specific business category segments and geographic territories. Available information includes the following:

- Number of businesses by NAICS classification by territory
- Dollar size of businesses by NAICS classification by territory
- Employee size of businesses by NAICS classification by territory
- Listing of businesses within specific NAICS classifications, sizes, and territory parameters; trending of sales per employee; and address, phone number, and listing of key personnel

D&B Million Dollar Directory

800-234-3867

The directory provides a listing of information on over 1.6 million U.S. and international businesses. Available information for individual companies includes the NAICS code, total employees, legal status, and annual sales in U.S. dollars or the equivalent.

Hoover's, Inc., a D&B Company
5800 Airport Boulevard
Austin, TX 78752
866-704-3395
512-374-4051
www.hoovers.com

Hoover's database with information on over 65 million companies provides insight and analysis of business targets to marketing professionals. Available information includes the following:

- A company profile complete with employee information, executive biographies, company description and history, industry information, competitors, products, and financial analysis
- A competitive landscape with information on key numbers, profitability, valuation, operations, financial ratios, per-share data, and growth statistics
- An industry report with an industry overview, quarterly industry update, business challenges, trends and opportunities, call preparation questions, financial information, industry forecast, website and media links, and a glossary of acronyms

The List Inc.
1440 Dutch Valley Place NE, Suite 1000
Atlanta, GA 30324
404-350-0600
www.thelistinc.com

The List Online is a database of information on companies and their decision makers that spend significant dollars on marketing services. The database includes contact information, contact locations, news, financial feeds, and more. The search interface allows users to narrow results by brand name, industry, geography, company type, ad spend, media mix, and fiscal close.

U.S. Census Bureau
North American Industry Classification
www.census.gov/eos/www/naics/

NAICS Association
129 Lakeshore Drive
Rockaway, NJ 07866
973-625-5626
www.naics.com/search.htm

The North American Industry Classification System (NAICS) is the standard used by federal government statistical agencies in classifying business establishments for the purpose of collecting, analyzing, and publishing statistical data related to the U.S. business economy. The NAICS provides 10, two-digit industry classifications with further breakdowns of each two-digit classification into six-digit category segments. The classification system can be used to determine the total number of businesses within your category. Additionally, extensive lists that are available for purchase can provide regional segments, prospect data with addresses, and contacts by job title. The NAICS Association provides a searchable database that will enable you to identify the total number of businesses in your specific business category.

Test Market and Geographic Strength

Nielsen DMA Test Market Profiles
The Nielsen Company
770 Broadway
New York, NY 10003
800-864-1224
www.nielsen.com

Nielsen profiles contain demographic, retail sales, and media information for each Designated Market Area (DMA). Available information includes the following:

- Demographics
- Circulation of magazines and newspapers
- Media usage
- Retail purchasing rates and market data
- Households by country
- Forecasting and trends

Sales and Marketing Management

Nielsen Scan Track
770 Broadway
New York, NY 70003

The Nielsen Scan Track measures product transactions on a daily basis in more than 350,000 stores across 30 countries in product categories that range from packaged goods to entertainment to media products. The service tracks product movement, market share, sales by price lines, and sales across a broad array of retail channels.

Marketing Journals
The following two sources provide the marketer with a foundation of journals, articles, books, case studies, webinars, and reports.

Harvard Business Review
www.hbr.org

In addition to receiving the highly respected and user-friendly focusing on business leadership and strategy, membership in the Harvard Business Review provides access to a deep well of content and relationships with thought leaders and practitioners through webinars, roundtable discussions, conferences, articles, blogs, books, and videos. Easily searched topics include content around change management, competition, innovation, leadership, and strategy.

You are provided content about the above topics, which is broken into the following individual skills categories: emotional intelligence, managing yourself, measuring business performance, project management, and strategy execution. You can also obtain information by industry groupings: finance, health care, manufacturing, media and telecommunications, and professional services.

American Marketing Association
www.marketingpower.com

In addition to the association's magazines (*Marketing News* and *Marketing Research*) and its journals (*Journal of Marketing, Journal of Marketing Research, Journal of International Marketing,* and *Journal of Public Policy Marketing*), the association provides:

- An extensive resource library and reference section containing white papers, best practice tips, research, and more
- Events from conferences to webinars and podcasts

Sales & Marketing Management
Lakewood Media Group, LLC
27020 Noble Road
Excelsior, MN 55331
952-401-1283
www.salesandmarketing.com/

Formerly a print publication, Sales & Marketing Management is now a fully searchable online database. Sales & Marketing Management is the leading authority for executives in the sales and marketing field. Its website, regular webcasts, e-newsletters, white papers, broadcasts, and more, all provide its readers easy access to the most relevant trends, strategies, exclusive research, expert voices, and cutting-edge case studies designed to help them sell more, manage better, and market smarter.

Government Publications and Census Data
No one collects more data on business than the government. The Department of Commerce has reference libraries in more than 40 field offices in major cities throughout the United States. The Small Business Administration can also provide information, and it has offices in more than 80 cities throughout the country.

U.S. Census Bureau
www.census.gov

The Census Bureau has numerous sources valuable to researchers:

County and city data book: Provides a variety of statistical information for counties, cities, standard metropolitan statistical areas, incorporated places, and urbanized areas.
County business patterns: Details the number, dollar size, and employment size of businesses by county, state, and country. Breaks information into North American Industry Classification System (NAICS) categories.
Census data: Includes census data on agriculture, housing, general population characteristics, social and economic characteristics, retail trade, manufacturing, and wholesale trade.

Trade and Consumer Publications
Many trade publications with research departments are waiting to help. Standard Rate and Data Service (SRDS) maintains up-to-date listings for business, trade, and consumer publications applicable to your industry.

Lifestyle Segmentation Information

Nielsen Claritas
770 Broadway
New York, NY 10003
800-234-5973
www.nielsen.com

Nielsen PRIZM is a market segmentation system that defines U.S. neighborhoods by 66 lifestyle clusters based on product, media, and lifestyle preferences and survey data. PRIZM can also cluster along industry- and client-specific lines. The clustering information can be used for the following:

- Defining and targeting consumer market segments
- Strategic planning
- Direct mailing
- Site and location analysis
- Media planning
- Product distribution

Nielsen P$ycle segments households into 58 categories based on financial behavior and wealth. The 58 segments fit within 12 life stage groups based on age, family structure, income, and assets.

Nielsen ConneXions tracks consumer communications and new technology adaptation among market segments. The household segmentation system groups consumers into 53 segments based on voice, video, and data consumption, as well as consumer technology adoption. The 53 segments fit within 10 life stage groups based on the combination of technology adoption, age, and family structure.

Scarborough Research
770 Broadway
New York, NY 10003
646-654-8400
www.scarborough.com

Provides in-depth research measuring the lifestyle and shopping patterns, media behavior, and demographics of American consumers locally, regionally, and nationally. Included in Scarborough's suite of products is VALS, which enables marketers to segment their markets using eight distinct groups based on primary motivations and resources. Scarborough measures and reports on lifestyles and shopping patterns across a vast number of categories including automotive, banking and financial, beverage, computer and Internet, drug and grocery, household shopping, restaurant, retail, sports, telecommunications, transportation, travel, and voting.

Strategic Business Insights (SBI) VALS
333 Ravenswood Avenue
Menlo Park, CA 94025
650-859-4600
www.strategicbusinessinsights.com/vals

VALS segments American consumers into eight distinct lifestyle groups for the purpose of predicting consumer behavior. The segments are based on the following:

- Education
- Income
- Self-confidence
- Health
- Eagerness to buy
- Intelligence
- Energy level
- Self-orientation
- Novelty seeking
- Innovation
- Impulsiveness
- Leadership
- Vanity

Media Spending and Media Competitive Information

Arbitron Inc.
575 Fifth Avenue
22nd Floor, Suite 2
New York, NY 10017
212-887-1300
www.arbitron.com

Arbitron's core business measures network and local radio audiences and usage across the United States.

Competitrack, Inc.
36-36 33rd Street
Long Island City, NY 11106
888-604-0260
718-482-4200
www.competitrack.com

Competitrack is a full-service advertising tracking firm. Services include creative tracking, competitive spending analyses, multicultural ad tracking, co-op ad tracking, and ad verification services. Competitrack monitors 18 types of media: network, cable TV, spot TV, syndicated and local cable TV; national, local, and trade magazines; newspaper distributed magazines; national and local newspapers; online; radio; outdoor; viral advertising; cinema; alternative media; and inserts and retail circulars.

Media Representatives

Media representatives serve as valuable sources not only of costs but also of competitive spending information. Contact local print, radio, television, Internet, and outdoor media representatives.

Nielsen Companies
www.nielsen.com

Originally known for its measuring of media usage, the Nielsen Companies have become a multifaceted research organization that operates across a vast number of information categories:

- Nielsen measures media audiences and usage across "three screens": television, Internet, and mobile.
- The company tracks customer market segmentation (see PRIZM/Claritas in previous section).
- It offers a broad array of consulting services such as research, brand management, pricing, and performance tracking.

Nielsen AdRelevance
770 Broadway
New York, NY 10003
888-634-1222
www.nielsen.com

AdRelevance is an award-winning online advertising measurement system that allows you to easily access and customize data. The software reports on nearly 1 million distinct URLs and probes more than 2,000 sites more than 8 million times a week. Features include the following:

- Customized reports
- Enhanced charts and graphs
- House ad tracking
- Extensive industry coverage
- AdAlert e-mail notifications
- AdContact prospecting tools
- Paid sponsored search link reporting
- AdLink checks on sponsored links
- AdCross checks against offline media

Schonfeld & Associates Inc.
www.scibooks.com

SAI provides information specializing in industry advertising, R&D, and financial ratios by industry classification.

SRDS Media Solutions
1700 Higgins Road
Des Plaines, IL 60018
847-375-5000
800-851-7737
www.srds.com

SRDS provides detailed ad rates, publishing dates, and contact information for national and international publications, broadcast media, direct marketing channels, interactive websites, and out-of-home media. It also maintains market-specific data and demographics.

Strategy Software
2722 Colby Avenue, Suite 515
Everett, WA 98201

888-756-4930
425-212-4347 ext. 302

Strategy Software offers a range of information management software (IMS) systems, utilities, and services to help companies easily organize their information about competitors, including sales, marketing, and financials. Detailed custom reports help keep companies in the know on their competitive environment.

TNS Media Intelligence
11 Madison Avenue, 12th Floor
New York, NY 10010
347-748-9551
www.tns-mi.com

TNS provides competitive spending data by medium, including a summary of national advertising expenditures by brand. TNS maintains information on network TV, cable TV, syndication, spot TV, local cable, Hispanic TV, radio, newspapers, magazines, Internet, and outdoor media.

Association and Trade Show Information

Encyclopedia of Associations
Gale Cengage Learning
27500 Drake Road
Farmington Hills, MI 48331
248-699-4253
www.gale.cengage.com

The Encyclopedia of Associations database covers more than 2,500 subjects and details more than 25,000 national associations. It provides contacts to develop leads on how to find difficult information specific to certain industries and customer groups. Available information includes the following:

- 25,000 national organizations
- 29,000 international organizations
- 100,000 regional, state, and local organizations

Management Information Guides
Gale Cengage Learning
27500 Drake Road
Farmington Hills, MI 48331
248-699-4253
www.gale.cengage.com

Each volume includes books, dictionaries, encyclopedias, film strips, government and institutional reports, periodical articles, and recordings on the featured subject. Guides are available from this series in almost every field.

Trade Shows Worldwide
Gale Cengage Learning
27500 Drake Road
Farmington Hills, MI 48331
248-699-4253
www.gale.cengage.com

This directory serves as a guide to conferences, conventions, trade and industrial shows, merchandise marts, and expositions. This list includes more than 10,500 trade show profiles; 6,500 organizers and sponsors; and 5,900 facilities, services, and information sources.

Media and Print Production Costs and Availability

SRDS Media Solutions
1700 Higgins Road
Des Plaines, IL 60018
847-375-5000
800-851-7737
www.srds.com

The following sourcebooks provide information required by advertisers for advertising and media buying:

- *Business Media Advertising Source*
- *Healthcare Journal Research* from Kantar Media
- *Consumer Media Advertising Source*
- *My SRDS Project Manager*
- *Newspaper Advertising Source*
- *Circulation 2010*
- *Print Media Production Source*
- *Radio Advertising Source*
- *TV & Cable Source*
- *SRDS Local Market Audience Analyst*
- *Interactive Advertising Source*
- *Out-of-Home Advertising Source*
- *Direct Marketing List Source*
- *SRDS DirectNet*
- *SRDS Media Property List Rental*
- *SRDS International Media Guides*
- *Canadian Advertising Rates & Data*
- *Hispanic Media & Market Source*
- *Professional Health Solutions* from Kantar Media

Circulation
SRDS Media Solutions
1700 Higgins Road
Des Plaines, IL 60018
847-375-5000
800-851-7737
www.srds.com

This annual issue shows circulation and penetration by county, metro area, and TV viewing area for every daily and Sunday newspaper, all regional sales groups, national newspaper supplements, and leading magazines.

Trending Information and Analytics Tools

American Demographics
www.adage.com

American Demographics Magazine ceased publication in 2004, but it remains a leader in trends analysis through its special sections published in the *Advertising Age Magazine* and its online insights.

eMarketer Inc.

75 Broad Street, 31st Floor
New York, NY 10004
800-405-0844
212-763-6010
www.emarketer.com

Targeted to online marketing, eMarketer provides users with the latest trend information: how it impacts your business and how your business can be better prepared for future challenges and opportunities. Using articles, charts, and analysis, eMarketer provides numerous resources for marketing professionals. Most content is released on a subscription basis; however, eMarketer does make some information available at no cost.

Google Analytics

www.google.com/analytics

Google Analytics is a free Web analytics tool that people can use to track visits and page views on websites. Using the page view and visits data, marketers can analyze the information through charts and customized reports. Available information includes the following:

- Page views and site visits
- Time on each page
- Bounce rates
- Segmentation
- Key words used to find the site
- Clicked links
- Geographic locations of clicks

IconoIQ
Iconoculture, Inc.
244 First Avenue North
Minneapolis, MN 55401
612-642-2222
www.iconoculture.com

IconoIQ is an interactive marketing research database for emerging trends. It provides an integrated view of consumers across categories and demographics. Iconoculture also provides experts on hand to assist in research possibilities. Available information includes the following:

- Values-based observational research
- Unique market facts and media
- IconoCommunities
- Social media analysis

Popcorn Report
Faith Popcorn
One Dag Hammarskjold Plaza, 16th Floor
New York, NY 10017

212-772-7778
www.faithpopcorn.com

Faith Popcorn is a trending expert, well known in the marketing industry. The marketing consulting firm she founded, Faith Popcorn, offers services and information related to long-term corporate planning, strategic positioning, brand strategy, new product development, market segmentation, cultural intelligence products, analysis of trends, and consulting services. Faith Popcorn is also the author of the best-selling trends book *The Popcorn Report.*

Trendwatching.com

A free trend-watching source, Trendwatching.com is a leading trend firm reporting on consumer trends and insights from around the world. Subscribe for free to its monthly trend briefing report.

Yankelovich Futures Company

400 Meadowmont Village Circle, Suite 431
Chapel Hill, NC 27517
919-932-8600
www.yankelovich.com

Yankelovich is an insights company that does research into customer segmentation, consumer attitudes, and trends across a wide range of products.

Social Media Measurement

Forrester Communities

Forrester Research, Inc.
400 Technology Square
Cambridge, MA 02139
866-367-7378

Forrester Research is an independent research company and an industry leader in providing research, consumer insight, consulting, events, and peer-to-peer executive programs. One area of expertise for Forrester is interactive marketing. Their blogs and community forums provide insight, strategy, and case studies on an array of marketing and social media topics. Beside its own team of marketing professionals and staff, Forrester Communities encourages the public to participate and contribute.

MotiveQuest LLC

1578 Sherman Avenue
Evanston, IL 60201
847-905-6100
www.motivequest.com

MotiveQuest monitors online conversations to understand customers' motivations. Using qualitative and quantitative proprietary research software, MotiveQuest tracks marketing-related information in the following areas:

- Consumer motivation
- Market segmentation
- Target market profiles
- Product launches
- Issue tracking and business strategy

Radian6
Radian6 Technologies Inc.
30 Knowledge Park Drive
Fredericton, New Brunswick
Canada E3C 2R2

Radian6 is an Internet-based social media monitoring and engagement platform. The software aggregates conversations into easy-to-use analysis and measurement. The comprehensive tool monitors more than 100 million websites, including blogs and comments, forums, online news publications, photos and videos, and social media sites like Facebook and Twitter. Use Radian6 to listen to your customers, find out what they are saying about your company and products.

Scout Labs
Lithium Technologies
575 Market Street, 12th Floor
San Francisco, CA 94105
888-620-6220
www.scoutlabs.com

Scout Labs is an Internet-based social media monitoring tool designed to function through community management teams. With multiple log-in IDs, teams can coordinate responses and searches simultaneously. Services that the Scout Labs offer include the following:

- Persistent searches
- Rants and raves
- Assignments
- Buzz tracking
- Automated sentiments
- Real-time content
- Conversation digest
- E-mail alerts

SocialSense
Networked Insights, Inc.
33 East Main Street, Suite 251
Madison, WI 53703
608-237-1867
www.networkedinsights.com

By constantly scanning web pages, blogs, forums, and more, SocialSense automatically generates marketing insights. Clustering technology enables SocialSense to group words and phrases into themes, which can help marketers evaluate campaigns and strategies. SocialSense's capabilities include the following:

- Discovery of new words and themes for marketing campaigns
- Engagement measurement
- Influence and sentiment analyses
- Theme- and audience-based data sets
- Relevant verbatims
- Theme tag clouds
- Trending displays

- Buzz across the Internet
- Integrated Quantcast data
- Near-real-time analysis
- Alerts

Additional Sources and Tips

In addition to the foregoing sources, many other references exist that will help you complete a business review consistent with the outline you establish. We suggest the following methodology to help you find supplemental information sources that pertain to your specific industry:

1. Consult applicable SRDS publications, and write down the names of all trade and consumer publications pertaining to your industry.
2. Contact the research department of each trade publication, and ask what information is available. Send them copies of your outline and charts, and ask them for the specific information required for completion of your business review as you have detailed it in your materials. Also ask about other available sources. The research departments of trade publications are often aware of other studies that may help you. One publication told us about a consultant who has made it her life's work to learn about the plumbing and sink business. She saved us many days of searching by referring us to timely studies that helped fulfill required data needs specified in our outline for a national manufacturer of kitchen water flow products.
3. Call the library and ask a reference librarian to do a subject search, pulling all available materials. Utilize your local public library and the nearest college library. Many public universities have special reference services dedicated to compiling secondary research for private industry.
4. Examine companies' annual reports and their 10-K forms (the financial statements companies file with the Securities and Exchange Commission), follow patent and trademark filings through data networks such as CompuServe, monitor news releases through a clipping service, talk to the trade press, talk to consultants, create and make use of a disciplined intelligence gathering system from your sales force, talk with your suppliers, go to trade shows, take plant and company headquarters tours, . . . and finally, see number 5 below.
5. Dig, dig, and dig some more.

DOS AND DON'TS

Do

- Develop an outline and charts before you start digging for information. This will keep you focused on the important issues.
- Consider using both primary research and secondary research.
- Use multiple secondary research sources to find your answers. Many times part of an answer can be found in one source and the other part in another source.
- Most secondary sources listed here have excellent staff resources. You'll find they will take time to help if you are prepared with specific questions.
- Always report data with reference points for comparison—use your company compared to the industry or this year compared to last year.
- Keep your summary statements as objective as possible.

Don't

- Don't give up if you can't find information you need. Call trade journals, the library, media reps, and others. The answers are out there.
- Don't just dig up information. Have a plan on what you want to find and know why this information will be helpful to you.
- Don't limit insights to your customers. Remember, there are often large differences between your customers' awareness, attitudes, and behavior and the total customer (prospects and customers) universe. Learn the difference between what your customers think and how they act and your prospects.

The Successful Marketing Plan

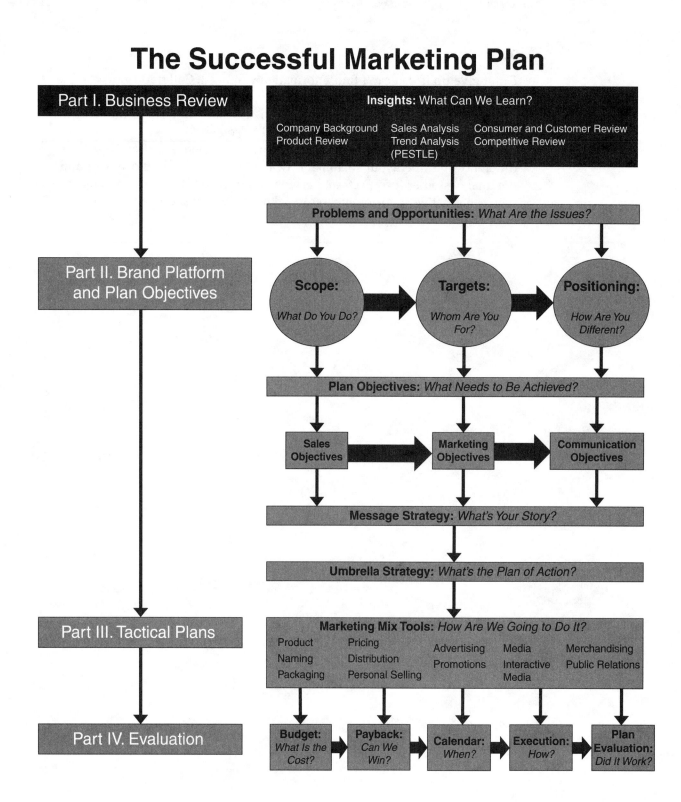

What You'll Need to Know, Part 2

Now *that you have a general understanding of what is involved in developing insights for a business review, you are ready to work through each step of the review process.*

FROM THIS CHAPTER YOU WILL LEARN

- The major steps of a business review and the individual issues you need to understand in each of the business review steps

- The data requirements and the material that needs to be analyzed in each of the business review steps

- How to write succinct summary statements describing the business review findings

OVERVIEW

Each of the business review steps in the remainder of this chapter contains three main components:

1. A general *background discussion* that details each area covered in the step
2. *Marketing questions* that must be answered in order to provide an adequate quantitative database for each section
3. *Charts* to help you organize your information in a disciplined, efficient manner, so you will be able to answer the marketing questions accurately

The charts can be easily adapted to your own situation. Worksheets for each of these charts are provided in Appendix B, which can be found online at www.mhprofessional.com/successfulmarketingplan.

The charts are intended to help you organize your data search. They are not exhaustive, and they cover only the major topical areas. In addition, it is not intended that all the questions at the end of each business review section will have a corresponding chart. Nevertheless, many of the charts provide multiple pieces of information when completed. For example, one of the sales charts seen in Exhibit 2.3 provides sales trending for the industry and for your company, demonstrates differences in industry growth compared to your company's growth, and provides company market share data.

The charts can also be used as support for business review conclusions during presentations. In addition, you may want to consider transferring the information in the charts onto graphs for presentation purposes. Finally, please note that while we have provided charts for all three steps and most of the tasks within each step, there are some topics that warrant charts that are tailored more specifically to your company, and you will need to prepare them on your own.

DEVELOPING INSIGHTS FOR THE FIRST SIX STEPS OF THE BUSINESS REVIEW

The remainder of this chapter will take you through the first six of the seven steps (see Exhibit 1.1 in Chapter 1) necessary in developing specific insights for a business review. Chapter 3 will then conclude Part I, "Business Review Insights," with a discussion of Step 7, "Problems and Opportunities."

STEP 1. COMPANY BACKGROUND

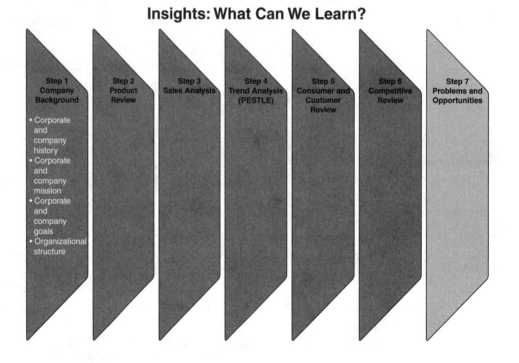

Insights: What Can We Learn?

Through reviewing your company background—its history, its mission, its goals, and its organizational structure—you do two things:

1. You begin to put into place the foundation for telling your company's story later in the marketing plan. Your story is developed from many places. Certainly a big part of it will be your insights into what the customer wants and needs and how you deliver those. But don't forget your company history. Where you've been is oftentimes where you're going—understanding the past helps to shape the future.

2. An understanding of the company's mission, its goals, and its organizational structure will help you ground the marketing plan in reality. In order for the marketing plan to be successful, it has to be part of the organizational whole. Marketing can't be a silo, disconnected from the rest of the organization. To be successful, it needs to be an integral part of the organization, helping to make all the other pieces successful through bringing the customers' voice into the company strategy.

Corporate and Company History

Remember all the stories you were told as a youngster. We bet you remember many of them. A lot of what we learn in any culture has to do not with remembering facts and figures but with remembering ideas as told in a story. George Washington and the cherry tree communicate the positive trait of honesty. Aesop's Fables remain a favorite way to communicate morals to young children (and adults who need reminding). Stories based on reality provide stickiness for ideas that could never be duplicated through charts, facts, and figures. Your company has a compelling story—all companies do. Your first task in completing the business review is to uncover your company's history and tell its story.

Think back to your high school English literature class when you learned that most great stories have four components:

- *Message:* Some idea or learning that is conveyed.
- *Conflict:* All great stories have a conflict—either a villain to combat or some hardship to overcome. Would you have remembered Little Red Riding Hood without the wolf? The conflict doesn't have to be a person. It can be an economic downturn, the outcome of failure, something that's never been done before, a set of circumstances, outdated beliefs, or many other things that get in the way of achieving something quite remarkable.
- *Main character:* Someone you remember and who personifies the story.
- *Main plot:* This is the story—it's how you describe getting from *A* to *B*, from the beginning to the end, so the message can be solidified with your audience. Thus we've come full circle, back to the first point: the telling of the message.

Have you ever heard the L.L. Bean story? Leon Bean (*the main character of the story*) was born in the small town of Greenwood, Maine. His parents unfortunately died when he was 12 within just a couple of days of each other. Leon and his five siblings moved in with relatives in the small town of South Paris, Maine.

From an early age, Leon learned how to take care of himself and survive combining his love of the outdoors and a strong sense of right and wrong with a strong entrepreneurial streak. In young adulthood, Leon worked on farms, peddled traps, and hunted and fished for income. The L.L. Bean lore found on the company's website tells of Leon finally getting fed up with tired, sore, and wet feet. He blamed the generally poor products (*this would be the villain in the story*) made for people like him who spent a great deal of time in the woods. So he took matters into his own hands and designed a lightweight boot with a rubber bottom and leather upper, and then he found a cobbler to make the boot. In 1912, at the age of 40, Leon Bean took out an advertisement to sell the boots to others. Within the ad was the same guarantee that the company has on its website today—one of unconditional customer satisfaction.

That guarantee was put to the immediate test. The first 90 of the 100 pairs of boots that Leon had sold were returned due to cracks in the leather. Leon refunded the purchase price to all of those 90 customers. He then fixed the problem with an even better design, one that would become the hallmark of quality in the industry to this day (*the main plot*).

In 1916 when he opened his store in Freeport, Maine, Leon tacked the following on the wall: "I do not consider a sale complete until the goods are worn out and the customer is still satisfied." Today that guarantee has evolved to say: "100 percent satisfaction in every way. Return anything purchased from us at any time if it proves otherwise."

The history of L.L. Bean and its founder Leon Bean tells a story of the highest-quality merchandise and customer service. It's a legacy (*the message of the story*) to be proud of and one personified in Leon and many subsequent caretakers of the L.L. Bean enterprise.

Go to the L.L. Bean website and scan it for legendary guarantees, and you'll find stories about 20-year-old silk underwear being returned and replaced along with the postage. And stories about old worn-out Maine hiking boots being returned and replaced, no questions asked. These anecdotes, passed on from employee to employee, tell the story of L.L. Bean—what it stands for today and what it will stand for into the future.

Here's another story. It's about a brand losing its way and then finding it again.

❖ naturalizer

In the early 1950s and 1960s, the Naturalizer brand was targeted to women through a very heavy television advertising schedule. Its value promise was a rare combination of both fashion and comfort. This brand promise was summarized through the famous Leo Burnett advertising campaign that included the tagline "A Beautiful Fit." The promise and the campaign made the brand one of the leading women's shoe brands in the country.

In the late 1980s and 1990s, the brand strayed from its roots. The Naturalizer heritage was nearly forgotten and then nearly killed. The brand went younger, it tried to be sexy, it attempted to be at the cutting edge of fashion, and it continually changed whenever the next photographer had another idea about what the shoe should be and how it should be portrayed. See Exhibit 2.1.

With a subsequent change in management, the brand rediscovered its history and who its customers were and who the brand really was to those customers. The brand team went back through the company's history, spending a lot of time talking to customers and noncustomers and researching the brand. The brand team rediscovered what the customers had loved about Naturalizer, and they found that over time, things hadn't really changed. The Naturalizer brand was still about comfortable fashion. It performed best with women who are comfortable in their own skin. The company's customers want to be fashionable, love being fashionable, but aren't a slave to fashion. Simply put, they demand both comfort and style. It was this understanding of the brand's original positioning and essence that led to the brand's reemergence as one of the leading women's shoe brands today. Naturalizer is once again a leading department store brand.

In Summary

Our message to you is this: take the time to really get to know where you've been as a company. Learn about the founders and the important milestones along the way that made your company what it is today. Perhaps you'll find you are in a situation in which it's good to go back and relearn a few keys to success that

EXHIBIT 2.1

| A Brand That Lost Its Way | A Brand That Rediscovered Its Heritage |

Courtesy of Naturalizer. Marthias Vriens, photographer.

Courtesy of Naturalizer. Pamela Hansen, photographer.

were once crucial to the company's success but that have somehow been over-looked or forgotten recently. This knowledge can be used later in the positioning and communications portions of the plan. *Remember, there are no dull companies or products—only dull copywriters and salespeople.*

Where to Find Information about Your Company's History

Search for your company history by going back in time and reviewing old media coverage, PR releases, advertising, and magazine articles. Try interviewing long-term employees, visit the company archives, delve into Internet searches, interview customers—in short, be creative, curious, and think like a historian.

QUESTIONS TO BE ADDRESSED

Note: Answers can pertain to the entire company or individual products and services depending on the orientation of the plan.

- What is the history of your company? Why was it started, who started it, how did it grow, and what are its major milestones in terms of events and people?
- What inspired the founders of the company? What were their visions, their dreams, their passions?
- What did you find surprising in researching your company's history? What were you most proud of? What events do you think are the most relevant to your business success today and into the future?
- What have been the most significant changes to your company and/or the industry in which your company competed over the past 5, 10, or 20 years?

- What are the critical strategies that have driven your company?
- What have been your company's biggest mistakes? What have been its biggest successes?
- Where has your company succeeded or failed? Why? What were the changes it made to succeed? What were the reasons it failed?
- In what years did the company accomplish its greatest successes? (Note that the successes do not have to tie to sales results. A great success can be the hiring of a core group of people that many years later led the company to success, or it can be a product innovation, a change in company policy, a new marketing strategy, or something else.)
- Summarize your company's history in a story:
  - Who were the characters? What did they stand for? What did they accomplish? What was important to them?
  - Was there a villain?
  - What's the message? What's the plot that brings the message to life?

Corporate and Company Mission

What is your company's mission? Quite simply, what is it that you are trying to accomplish? Notice in the examples below that profits aren't mentioned. You won't find the word *profit* in most mission statements. When you work toward accomplishing your mission, the profits will come.

If your company has a strategic plan, the company mission will be located there. If you don't implement a yearly strategic plan, chances are you still have a mission. Include it in this up-front section of your business review. Company missions tell you a lot. The following three examples (Advance Auto Parts, Aflac, and Nike) were found at www.missionstatements.com. The site provides examples of mission statements for a wide variety of entities, from Fortune 500 companies to restaurants, credit unions, technology companies, hospitals, marketing and public relations firms, and many more. Included is the company name, a brief description to make sure you're oriented to what the company does (although you should recognize all three of these examples), and then the company's mission as reported by Missionstatement.com when the edition of this text was printed.

Advance Auto Parts places emphasis on friendly, knowledgeable, professional service with an education and problem-solving orientation. Aflac comes right out and says very clearly that it will be an aggressive marketer and provide value (quality at a good price). And Nike communicates very clearly that it is all about inspiration and innovation. Take particular note as to how you might market each company based on understanding its mission. Think about how you would go about developing new products and services given these missions. How would these mission statements affect where you go in terms of marketing communication? Based on these mission statements, what types of people would you hire for each company?

Advance Auto Parts

Description: Advance Auto Parts is a company that provides customers with automotive products and services that include diagnosing vehicle problems and doing repair work.

Mission: It's the mission of Advance Auto Parts to provide personal vehicle consumers and enthusiasts with the vehicle-related products and knowledge that fulfill their wants and needs at the right price. Our friendly, knowledgeable, and professional staff will help inspire, educate, and problem-solve for our customers.

Aflac

Description: Aflac insurance policies may be able to help you with those expenses not covered by your major medical plan.

Mission: To combine aggressive strategic marketing with quality products and services at competitive prices to provide the best insurance value for consumers.

Nike

Description: Serving the sports and athletic industry, Nike, Inc., is known for manufacturing shoes, gear, and apparel, particularly for athletes in a whole range of sports such as track and field, basketball, and golf.

Mission: To bring inspiration and innovation to every athlete in the world.

QUESTIONS TO BE ADDRESSED
- What is your company's mission statement?
- What things are you doing from a marketing standpoint (product, distribution, pricing, communications) that are consistent with your mission? What things are you doing that are inconsistent? Why?
- If you had to choose one word from the mission statement, which word is the most important? What would be the second most important word and the third most important? Why?

Corporate and Company Goals

The marketer should have an understanding of existing sales goals, profit goals, and marketing expectations prior to the development of a marketing plan. As with the mission statement, many times these goals are found in the organization's strategic plan. The marketer should also review the operating budget to gain an understanding of each product's margins, costs, and potential profit contributions.

In stating corporate objectives and philosophies up front, the marketer will have a base to build on when determining future marketing objectives and strategies. More important, through a thorough review of the market and company in the latter steps of the business review, the marketing manager will be able to judge whether the original overall business goals and philosophies are realistic and consistent with consumers' wants and needs. In this manner, the marketer is making himself or herself responsible for determining the feasibility of achieving the corporate goals given the market conditions and vice versa (achieving the marketing goals given the company conditions).

QUESTIONS TO BE ADDRESSED
- What are the long-term and short-term goals and objectives of the company?
- Are there existing sales goals, profit goals, and marketing expectations?
- What is the operating budget for the company? What are the margins and planned profit contributions of each product?
- Is there a corporate philosophy on how to do business? What are the principles of the business in regard to working with customers, developing and selling product, and managing the company's internal operations?

Organizational Structure

Organizational structure tells a great deal about a company and its chances for successful marketing. Study your company's organizational chart. Analyze whether the marketing department is set up to develop and implement marketing plans efficiently. Identify the people you'll have to work with and the people who will make the final decisions regarding the marketing direction and the marketing policies. Then make sure you have a plan to engage them in the marketing planning process.

Work to understand how the marketing department interfaces with the rest of the organization. Our feeling is that the consumer research plus all areas of the brand platform and the communication portions of the marketing mix tools should be the direct responsibility of the lead marketing individual, who usually has a title of chief marketing officer, senior vice president of marketing, or vice president of marketing. Additionally, this person should report directly to the president of the company, which will mean that this person has a seat at the table that directs company strategy. If this situation does not exist, there is less of a chance for cohesive implementation of the marketing plan. Chances are that there will be a diminished synergistic effect of the marketing tools working together to achieve the companywide sales and marketing objectives established in the marketing plan.

Later, you may want to develop a plan to reorganize your department or to improve communication with other departments in the company so that your department has a more positive impact. If the individual responsible for marketing does not have access to key decision makers in merchandising or operations, create a structure that forces this.

You won't change the way your department communicates and inserts its input into corporate decision making overnight. The purpose of reviewing the organizational structure is to make you aware of your department's ability to provide marketing direction. You must develop a plan to make sure that marketing has the ability not only to formulate marketing plans and get them approved but also to work with the rest of the company to effectively implement them and ensure their success.

QUESTIONS TO BE ADDRESSED
- Do you have a plan to actively engage the individuals who will influence the outcome of your marketing plan—from both a decision-making and implementation standpoint? What is it?
- Is your marketing department sufficiently organized to develop and execute a disciplined marketing plan? Do you have enough resources to plan, implement, and analyze results?
- To what degree is the company committed to marketing? Where does marketing fit in your overall organizational structure? Does the lead marketing individual report directly to the president? Is he or she a part of the company's leadership team?
- Does your marketing department have decision-making authority over the areas of the brand platform and over all the marketing tools and the decisions made regarding communications and consumer touch points? Do these areas include advertising, media, promotion, publicity, Internet, the call center and/or customer service operations, and in-store merchandising functions in addition to having a strong leadership team voice across sales, product, pricing, distribution, and operations?
- Is your marketing department responsible for the consumer research function?
- Does your marketing department have the ability to communicate with and have a positive impact on other departments within the company?

- Is the company driven by operations, finance, merchandise, product, sales, or marketing? In other words, what area of the company is most responsible for the company's success? Will that be true in the future? How does the marketing department fit in? How will this affect your ability to develop and implement effective marketing plans?

See Appendix B, Worksheet 1, to help you capture this information.

STEP 2. PRODUCT REVIEW

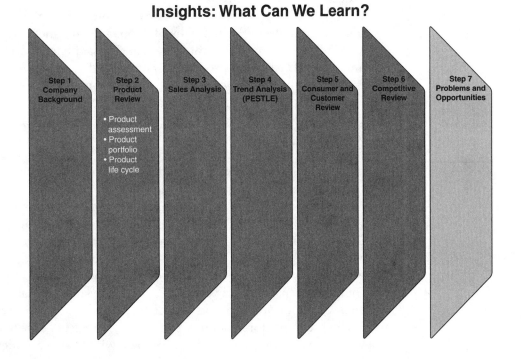

Insights: What Can We Learn?

Your products and services are the face of the company to your customers and consumers within your industry category. This section helps you assess the product strengths in your own business and helps you look outside your business to the industry category in which you compete. It's important to analyze the whole range of competitive product and service offerings to help you determine future product strategy later in your plan.

Product Assessment

Product assessment includes creating a list of your company's products and services, identifying the history of your company's development of those products and services, identifying the strengths and weaknesses of your company's products and services, and assembling information on the trends in the general marketplace for your company's products and services.

Products and Services of Your Company and Those of the Competition
QUESTIONS TO BE ADDRESSED
- What are the products and services sold in the industry categories in which you compete?

- What products and services does your company sell under each industry category in which you compete?

See Appendix B, Worksheet 2, to help you capture this information.

The History, Strengths, and Weaknesses of Your Company's Products
QUESTIONS TO BE ADDRESSED
- Write down the history of your products and services. When did they start? Why were they developed? How have they evolved over time? What are the major milestones in the products' or services' evolution? What are the major milestones in the ways in which consumers have used or purchased your products or services over time?
- How would you describe your company's products and services? What's unique about them? Why are they famous? What benefits do they provide that are similar to the industry category's, and what benefits do they provide that are different? Are your products differentiated?
- What underlying company strengths or combination of company strengths allow you to provide unique and differentiated products and services?
- Does your company provide groupings of products or services that are used together by your customers or their end customers?
- Do the products or services your company manufactures or sells have any manufacturing or service problems? Are specialized parts, labor, or manufacturing processes necessary? Are the products vulnerable to shortages or other consumer, environmental, technological, or economic factors? If so, how?
- What are your company's products' and services' strengths and weaknesses? Develop a chart with your company's name and your key competitors' names along the top. Now list your company's products under your company and the corresponding products that compete with your company's product under your competitors' names. Now develop a list of the strengths and weaknesses associated with your products and services compared to those of your competition.
- Do your competitors offer any product or service benefits to consumers that you don't offer or that you can't compete with? What are they?
- What are your competitors' product and service strengths and weaknesses? (For each of your competitors, develop a chart similar to the one you made for your own company.)
- Based on your knowledge of product sales and demand, which products do you believe will grow, which will remain flat, and which will decline within your company and within the companies of your key competitors?
- Do you have products or services that are critical to initial trial from consumers and lead to the purchase and/or use of other more profitable products and services?

See Appendix B, Worksheet 2, to help you capture this information.

Product Trends
QUESTIONS TO BE ADDRESSED
- How has your product or service category done in terms of growth nationally?
- Which trends over the past five years in terms of product innovations, marketing, distribution, pricing, and merchandising will positively and negatively affect your products and services into the future?
- Which trends in terms of product design, appearance, manufacturing, and technology will affect your products and services into the future?
- Are there product usage or consumer behavior trends that might drive changes in your product or service demand into the future?

See Appendix B, Worksheet 2, to help you capture this information.

Product Portfolio

If you have more than one product or service, you have a product or service portfolio. Products cost you money. They take budget and human resources to adequately grow, maintain, and market. They also either positively or negatively affect your brand positioning in the marketplace. Therefore, each year, you should go through an exercise to evaluate your product portfolio and make decisions in your subsequent marketing plan concerning the following:

- Which products you will feed and grow
- Which ones you will simply maintain
- Which if any, you will get rid of or phase out to make room for future performers

In this way, you will stay current with the ever-changing needs and wants of your target markets.

Later in your plan, there are five major product decisions you can make in your umbrella strategies:

1. Increase penetration or new customers for your product or service within your industry category. This can result in increasing market share, although a company can increase penetration and still have its market share either decrease or stay constant based on what their competitors are doing.
2. Expand use for your product so as to attract new customers. Apple has done this through making its MacBook Pro capable of storing and editing videos, using photographs creatively, being a vehicle for music via iTunes, and being a platform for viewing movies and other video. Note that the iPad is continuing to expand and attract new customers by moving into the book reading area previously dominated by the Amazon Kindle reader and increasing its multimedia capabilities. Another great example is ARM & HAMMER baking soda, which in the 1970s expanded the use of baking soda to being a deodorizer for refrigerators, toothpaste, laundry detergent, and underarm deodorizer.
3. Develop new products in new markets against new customer targets.
4. Maintain certain products while emphasizing others.
5. Divest your company of products that are not generating adequate revenue or are not positively affecting your company's brand positioning in the marketplace.

In the late 1960s, the Boston Consulting Group (BCG) developed a matrix for evaluating a company's products or services portfolio. The matrix is still useful today in providing you with a snapshot of the strength of your products or services portfolio. The matrix looks at two factors critical to helping you evaluate the performance of your products portfolio: market share and the growth rate of the markets. The matrix helps companies put their products and/or services into one of four quadrants:

- *Cash cows:* (a) Products and/or services that have a high market share but are in a low-growth market or industry category, and (b) products and/or services that have a high market share and are in a mature market or industry category
- *Stars:* Products and/or services that have a relatively high market share and are in a high-growth market or industry category
- *Question marks:* Products and/or services that have a relatively low market share but are in a high-growth market or industry category
- *Dogs:* Products and/or services that have a relatively low market share and are in a low-growth market or industry category

The definition of how much market share a product or service has to have to be a market leader is tricky. The "Rule of 123" says a market leader's position is most stable if it has a share lead double the second strongest competitor and triple the third strongest competitor.* So if you were a market leader, you would have a 30 percent market share, the next competitor would have a 15 percent share, the third strongest competitor would have a 10 percent share, and the remaining competitors would all have shares in the single digits. Markets of high growth are typically considered to have growth rates of 10 percent or more per year.

Success for most companies comes from managing a combination of top line sales growth and profitability. The matrix in Exhibit 2.2 shows how a company can examine its products along both important areas. For each product designated by a circle, the size of the circle represents the value of the product's sales relative to the value of the total sales for the company. If you duplicated a chart like this for your company, you'd drop in the total sales volume of the product, the profit dollars, and also the approximate market share.

Cash Cows

In examining the matrix in Exhibit 2.2, we see that the company has one very large product that falls into the cash cow quadrant with a very high market share and a market or industry category with very little growth. Based on the size of its circle, this product also represents a significant amount of the company's total sales. There are a number of ways to look at this cash cow:

- When the Boston Consulting Group Matrix was first developed, the common view was to not invest much at all into this product and to milk profits from it while growing other less sizeable and high-potential products—thus the name "cash cow." This still is a viable strategy for many firms.
- Be aware that there is a counterviewpoint that the worst thing a company can do in a position where the market is not growing and it possesses a clear market

EXHIBIT 2.2

Boston Consulting Group Matrix

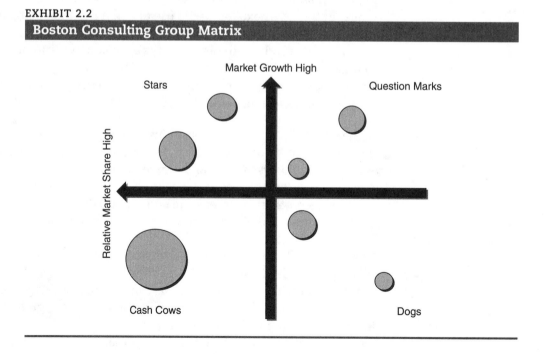

---

*David Mercer, *Marketing*, 2d ed., Blackwell Publishers, Oxford, U.K., and Malden, Mass., 1996.

share leader is to siphon dollars from this product to grow new products in other markets. This happened to Miller High Life when in the 1980s, Miller Light grew while the flagship brand Miller High Life lost share—but the combination of the two could not combat the tremendous growth and the loss of total market share to Budweiser.

Stars

Markets where your company has strong market share and tremendous market growth are typically looked at as generating both high top line sales potential but also requiring cash to support future growth and to sustain or build on the strong market share.

Question Marks

These are the tough choices. The market is growing, but your relative market share is very low. The answer as to how much to invest in these products can be partially answered by how many cash cows and stars you have that also require investment. Additionally, you need to determine if the market growth will continue or if a short-term fad is pushing the growth. A good example of this situation was the introduction of shape-up footwear by MBT. The shoes were priced at $150 and up with many models at $250. Skechers quickly introduced Shape-ups, and Reebok followed with EasyTones. Both were heavily marketed at the end of the decade and into 2011. However, while sales momentum was brisk initially, it appears that what was at first considered a new emerging major category might just end up a fad.

Dogs

These are the products where you have low market share in a market that is stagnant. These markets are very competitive and are often marked by strong price and promotional competition. This is the first place you look to divest effort and put it into something more promising.

See Appendix B, Worksheet 2, to help you capture this information.

QUESTIONS TO BE ADDRESSED
- List your products and services. Which ones fall into the cash cows quadrant of strong relative market share and low or stable market growth? List their sales volume and market share.
- Which products and services fall into the stars quadrant of strong relative market share and strong market growth of 10 percent or more per year? List their sales volume and market share.
- Which products and services fall into the question marks quadrant of strong market growth but small relative market share? List their sales volume and market share.
- Which products and services fall into the dogs quadrant of low relative market share and low market growth? List their sales volume and market share.

Product Life Cycle

Most products go through a product life cycle. Understanding your product's stage in the product life cycle will help predict target markets, competition, pricing, distribution, and advertising strategies. The following is a brief outline of how we view the three product life cycle phases—introduction, growth, and maturity—from five marketing perspectives—target market, competition, pricing, distribution, and advertising.

Introduction Phase

Target market: Usually innovators try new products. The goal is to get people who are opinion leaders to try and use the new product. It is usually more difficult to sell a new product or concept to a mass audience during the introduction period.

Competition: Typically, there are few competitors in the introduction stage, as the technology and start-up costs for a new product or product category are high.

Pricing: Usually the company that first introduces a product has the freedom to set prices as desired. Companies can look to the short terms and "cream the price"—that is, set it high to gain the maximum profit on each unit—or they can set it low in an attempt to obtain as many customers as possible with an eye toward the future. The pricing decision is often a function of the company's ability to produce the product, the product's availability, and the amount of anticipated competition.

Distribution: During the introduction stage, distribution is usually through specialized channels rather than mass distribution channels because a good deal of attention needs to be paid to educating consumers about the product and its use.

Advertising: Advertising of a new product is usually educational and market building in nature, convincing people to try the product and explaining how the product will provide benefits not currently found in the marketplace.

Growth Phase

Target market: The market is still growing, with new customers purchasing the product for the first time. The product is becoming accepted by a wider profile of consumers.

Competition: As product acceptance grows, the number of competitors increases.

Pricing: While competition is focused primarily on product attributes, pricing variations are introduced along with diversification and differentiation of the product. Price cutting occurs, and discounters try to steal market share and broaden the customer base by making the product or service more affordable. Higher-priced, higher-quality products are also introduced and marketed.

Distribution: Distribution expands from specialty stores to more mass distribution channels, such as chains.

Advertising: The communication focus moves away from selling the product category and educating consumers. As a result of product differentiation and increased levels of competition, advertising takes on the role of positioning particular products with specific attributes or benefits against the competition.

Maturity Phase

Target market: The product is now accepted by all or most consumers. When bank automated-teller machines (ATMs) were first introduced, only young innovators used them, with older adults preferring to go into a bank for transactions. Now, with the end of the prolonged introduction period, people of all ages readily use the machines.

Competition: The market is very competitive at this stage.

Pricing: In this stage, pricing becomes very important. Products are often standardized, with fewer product innovations and fewer discernible differences. Thus, the selling emphasis is not as much on product attributes as it is on price and customer service.

Distribution: All channels now have access to the product.

Advertising: By this time, share of mind or consumer awareness is an important component to share of market. The company needs to communicate its brand name and have it included in the "evoke set" of brands that comes to mind when a customer is thinking of purchasing. Thus the communication strategy shifts even more toward keeping and improving brand name awareness with continued effort of differentiating the product from the competition's. However, the effort to differentiate falls more and more to price promotions instead of pure advertising around product attributes and benefits.

QUESTIONS TO BE ADDRESSED

- Where is each of your products in the product life cycle?
- Based on where your products are in the product life cycle, what are the historical ramifications for target market, competition, pricing, distribution, and advertising that you should be aware of for each product when you develop your plan?

STEP 3. SALES ANALYSIS

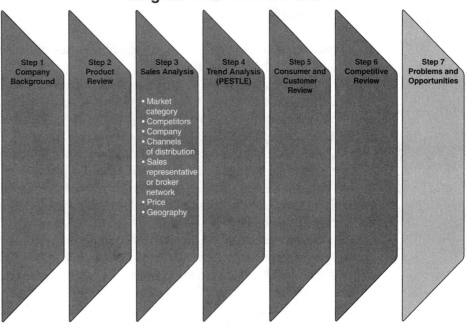

Insights: What Can We Learn?

We start to learn a great deal about consumer behavior through the analysis of sales data. Sales are the broadest indicator of consumer demand, and the industry market category is the broadest indicator of your company's potential sales.

The sales analysis allows the marketer to establish a clear picture of the sales trends for the industry, competitors, the company, and its products. A comparison may find that the industry or broad market category is doing well, yet specific products are doing poorly. Or during your sales analysis, it may be determined that while the individual company is doing quite well, the industry growth is minimal or declining. Each situation would take the marketer in vastly different directions in the development of marketing objectives and strategies.

Market Category, Competitors, and Company

In this part of the analysis, you will be looking at sales across:

- Your industry category
- Your competitors
- Your company
- Your channels of distribution
- Your sales representative or broker networks
- The price of your products
- The geographic distribution of your sales territories

One suggestion whenever you examine sales: if at all possible, analyze sales data over five years. In doing so, you will be able to spot trends that you couldn't see over just one or two years. Trends are often more important than the absolute numbers.

Total Sales
Capture the total sales trends for three areas:

- Your company's overall industry market category
- Your key competitors
- Your company

Analyzing sales over all three of the above will allow you to determine if sales are growing, shrinking, or flattening? In addition, you'll determine if your market share is growing, shrinking, or has remained flat?

Remember in Chapter 1 that we stressed the importance of providing reference points for comparison. The key in this section is to determine if the company picture matches that of the industry or your key competitors.

There's much to be learned in comparing your company's results to that of the overall industry and/or that of individual key competitors. In your plan, you'll have to make many strategy decisions. Insights into how the company is doing relative to the industry in which you compete provide direction for many of these decisions. Here's just one example.

If the industry is gaining sales in a product area significantly more than your company, you'll need to determine why and if you have the competitive strength to compete. Ultimately your plan will need to articulate a change in strategy allowing you to be more competitive. Vice versa, if you are dramatically outpacing the industry sales in a product category, you now have the luxury of examining a different set of options. Should you milk this product category and use the profits to expand into new markets, enhance the current product line with new flanker products that expand the target market to new users, further improve the existing product, or strengthen your position with added-value services? Depending upon the insights you gain from comparing your company sales to the industry category's sales, you have a very different set of strategy options.

Individual Product Sales
Make sure you understand which products offer the greatest potential from a volume standpoint.

Monitor the sales volume trends for your individual products. Break down your sales data to get at both:

- The sales by product
- The number of transactions or actual units sold in total and by product

If you notice a product with a large number of transactions or unit sales, you could use it as a way to further improve traffic and/or interest in your other products or services. In other words, you could use your more popular products or services as a way to cross-sell customers to your other products, perhaps even to your more profitable ones. In working with the consumer products paper company Fort James (Fort Howard when we worked with them), we gave a series of marketing planning seminars that looked at the broad napkin market category. Fort James was a strong player in printed lunch napkins with the Mardi Gras brand. However, the company had little presence in luncheon white or dinner napkins.

In analyzing sales trends, luncheon napkins dominated the napkin category in terms of both units and dollar volume. At the time of our work, within the luncheon category, printed napkins, where Mardi Gras was strong, had increased over 20 percent, and luncheon whites, where Mardi Gras had little presence, had decreased over 20 percent in sales during the past five years. This data matched Fort James's strengths in luncheon napkins. However, dinner napkins, though not the dominant napkin category and not a Mardi Gras strength, had shown double-digit increases in sales over a five-year period.

This type of information by itself should not necessarily drive any one decision. But later, during the planning process, if there are reasons to expand product offerings, such information can be valuable. In our example, the dinner napkins could be a logical area worth investigating for the Mardi Gras brand from a sales volume standpoint.

Profits

Work to understand the gross margin dollars (sales less cost of goods sold) and the operating profit (sales less cost of goods sold and expenses):

- The average profit rate for the industry and key competitors
- The profit rate for your company and each product you sell

Keep in mind that an individual product might have a lower margin, but it might still have very high total margin dollars because of its strong volume.

Market Share

Market share is a measure that quickly tells you how well your company or product is performing from a sales standpoint relative to the competition. Market share is your product's sales as a percent of the total market or category's sales. You might have very strong sales, even sales growth, but if you're losing market share, it's clear that your relative performance is lagging that of your competitors.

There are several ways to examine market share:

- *Total company dollar market share:* Sales as a percent of total market or category dollar sales
- *Total unit market share:* Sales as a percent of total market or category unit sales
- *Individual product market share:* Sales as a percent of individual market product or category sales

The chart in Exhibit 2.3 demonstrates industry performance and percent change in growth relative to your company's performance. The result is a market share figure

EXHIBIT 2.3

Comparison Table for Your Industry Category's Sales, Your Competitors' Sales, and Your Company's Sales

Total Industry Sales

Year	Total Industry Sales, $000	Change, %	Total Company Sales	Change, %	Company Market Share, %
2007	$100,000		$4,500		4.5
2008	$110,000	10.0	$5,500	22.22	5.0
2009	$120,000	9.1	$7,000	27.27	5.8
2010	$130,000	8.0	$8,000	14.29	6.2
2011	$150,000	15.0	$9,000	12.50	6.0

Total Industry Product Sales

Year	Product A, $000	Change, %	Percent of Total Industry Sales	Product B, $000	Etc.
2007	$15,000		15.00%		
2008	$17,000	13.3	15.45		
2009	$22,000	29.4	18.33		
2010	$28,000	27.3	21.54		
2011	$32,000	14.3	21.33		

Total Company Product Sales

Year	Product A, $000	Change, %	Percent of Total Product Sales	Product B, $000	Etc.
2007	$675		4.50%		
2008	$825	22.22	4.85		
2009	$900	9.09	4.09		
2010	$950	5.56	3.39		
2011	$975	2.63	3.05		

Estimated Total Competitive Sales

	Sales 2007	Market Share, %	Sales 2008	Market Share, %	Sales 2009	Market Share, %	Sales 2010	Market Share, %	Sales 2011	Market Share, %
Total										
Competitor A	$6,500	6.5	$7,500	6.8	$9,500	7.9	$11,000	8.5	$12,000	8.0
Product A										
Product B										
Product C										
Product X										
Total										
Competitor B	$3,000	3.0	$4,000	3.6	$7,000	5.8	$8,000	6.2	$9,000	6.0
Product A										
Etc.										

Note: The abbreviation $000 means thousands of dollars.

for your company. Note that the chart could also be utilized for individual products, departments, or product categories. In addition, company profit could be included in the same manner as sales.

See Appendix B, Worksheet 3, to help you capture this information.

QUESTIONS TO BE ADDRESSED
- What are the industry or market category sales over the past five years? Are sales flattening, shrinking, or growing? At what rates? Compare the industry or market category sales to that of your company and that of your top competitors over the same time period.
- What is your company market share in terms of total sales to that of the industry category in which you compete?

- Which products in your *industry* market category have the largest total sales volume? Which products in your *industry* market category are growing the fastest, which are declining, and which are flattening in terms of sales growth? Which products for your *company* and top competitors have the largest total sales volume? Which products for your *company* are growing the fastest, which are declining, and which are flattening in terms of sales growth? Compare your company to the industry category and your key competitors on these questions.
- What are your products' market shares within their respective product categories?
- What products have the greatest profitability for the industry market category, your company, and your key competitors?
- What products have the greatest number of transactions or number of actual units sold over the last five years for the industry market category, your company, and your competitors?

Sales by Seasonality

The sales analysis provides answers to seasonality questions regarding sales performance by time of the year. This type of data is used to help you determine when specific products should receive marketing emphasis, to help you make decisions about whether to support seasonal periods or try to shift some consumption to other periods, and ultimately to help you budget on a monthly basis.

It is important to ascertain the strength of the industry, the company, and each individual brand or department on a monthly basis (and even a weekly and daily basis for retailers). The chart in Exhibit 2.4 tracks seasonality of industry sales as compared to company sales. The chart in Exhibit 2.5 tracks the performance of individual brands or departments within your company on a monthly basis. This chart provides seasonality of sales by month for each brand or department. It is helpful to develop five-year trends of these charts to compare and identify any significant movement or changes in the seasonality from year to year.

See Appendix B, Worksheets 4 and 5, to help you capture this information.

EXHIBIT 2.4

Seasonality of Industry Sales as Compared to Your Company's Sales by Month

Month	Company Percent of Sales	Company Index to Average (8.33)	Industry Percent of Sales	Company Index to Average (8.33)
January	10%*	120*	8%*	96*
February				
March				
April				
May				
June				
July				
August				
September				
October				
November				
December				

*The *percentage* of the company's sales that occur in January is 10 percent. If sales were equal each month, 8.33 percent of the sales would occur in January (10 ÷ 8.33 = 120). January was above average for sales. The industry index of 96 was slightly below average, demonstrating that company sales for the month of January were substantially above the norm when compared to industry sales. Another way to do this would be to take the *total sales* and divide it by 12 to get an average. Use this average as the base, and divide each month's sales by the base to get an index.

EXHIBIT 2.5

Monthly Sales of Individual Brands within Your Company

| | | NOVEMBER | | DECEMBER | | ETC. |
	Base*	Percent of Total Dollars	Index to Total Year	Percent of Total Dollars	Index to Total Year	
Company Brand X	38.2†	41.9%†	110†			
Company Brand Y	18.5	22.8	123			
Company Brand Z	6.2	11.2	181			

*Base equals total figures for the year.

†Brand X accounts for 38.2 percent of the sales volume during the year. During November, Brand X accounts for 41.9 percent (41.9 percent ÷ 38.2 percent = 110). This means that Brand X does better in November than it normally does throughout the year, accounting for 41.9 percent of the company's total business in that month.

QUESTIONS TO BE ADDRESSED

- Does the industry category you compete in have a strong seasonality with sales skewing to certain times of the year?
- Does your company exhibit the same seasonality? Has this always been true, or is this something that has only recently occurred? Is the seasonality of sales for certain times of the year getting stronger or weaker?
- Do you have certain products that have significantly stronger times of the year in terms of sales?

Sales by Store-for-Store Sales by Retailers

Total retail sales for a company often reflect growth resulting from the opening of additional outlets rather than from increases from individual stores. Sales need to be monitored on a store-for-store (or same-store) basis in order to determine the relative health of each unit or outlet as well as the total system of stores. The chart in Exhibit 2.6 shows total sales and per-store averages. Charts would be developed on an annual basis over a five-year period for comparison.

See Appendix B, Worksheet 6, to help you capture this information.

Channels of Distribution

Distribution is the method of delivering the product to the consumer. A review of sales by distribution channel, agent, or broker helps determine which method of distribution your industry, your company, and your competitors use most successfully.

EXHIBIT 2.6

Store-for-Store Sales

Market	Sales Volume, millions	Change from Previous Year	Number of Stores	Per-Store Average, millions	Change from Previous Year	Per-Store Average Indexed to System Average, $840.0 million
Tulsa	$2,202.7	12%	2	$1,356.4	12%	$161†
Minneapolis	6,147.5	24*	8	768.4	15*	91
Milwaukee						
Atlanta						
Tampa						

Note: Make sure your year-to-year analysis of per-store averages includes comparable stores that have been open for the full year.

*The percent change for total sales volume is higher than the per-store average volume due to a decrease in per-store averages and an addition of stores. For example, this would be evident if there were a chart showing seven stores versus eight in the Minneapolis market the previous year.

†Tulsa stores do better on a per-store basis than the system average, which is $840,000. The breakeven per-store average for the total system is $700,000. (Include this figure as another comparison point to be utilized when analyzing market performance.)

Sales by Outlet and/or Channel Type

Determine and review the optimum outlet category or categories for the product or services being sold and the consumer who is purchasing it. Common retail distribution outlet categories include mass merchandise, discount, off-price, department stores, specialty shops, chain stores, direct mail, catalogs, mobile, and interactive Internet channels. Each is a unique distribution method that a retailer can use to sell the product to the consumer.

While the retailers own the selling spaces, the packaged-goods or consumer goods companies sell through retailers. Therefore, the packaged-goods or consumer goods companies must be as aware of the trends affecting the retail locations as the retailers are.

To determine the optimum outlet category, it helps to analyze the current channel trends. The business review may determine that the two fastest-growing methods of distribution for your product category are relatively small, single-line specialty shops and direct mail. If you were not currently using these channels, your marketing plan would need to address the industry's shift in emphasis toward these alternative methods of distribution. This could be done by shifting distribution strategy to these channels or by adapting some of the strengths of specialty store retailing to your channel environment or by experimenting with direct mail. The chart in Exhibit 2.7 details dollar sales and unit sales by outlet type for a retailer. You would customize this chart to fit the outlets that you and your competitors use in your industry category.

See Appendix B, Worksheet 7, to help you capture this information.

Penetration for Retailers

The optimum penetration levels (the number of stores per *market*) should be calculated to determine if more distribution outlets are needed. Note that in the broadest sense, we define markets according to established *Designated Market Areas* (DMAs), also referred to as *television market areas*. But markets can also be defined in terms of the Census Bureau's *standard metropolitan statistical areas* (SMSAs), counties, or city or metropolitan trading areas. Penetration levels are evaluated on three issues:

1. The total number of competing outlets a market can support.
2. The number of your stores a market can support before cannibalization (one of your stores steals customers from another of your stores) occurs.

EXHIBIT 2.7

Distribution: Purchases by Outlet Type

Distribution Outlets*	PERCENT OF TOTAL SALES				POINTS/% CHANGE	
	2007		2011		2007 to 2011	
	Units	Dollars	Units	Dollars	Units	Dollars
Specialty stores	36.2%†	48.4%†	43.1%†	51.2%†	6.9/19%†	2.8/6%†
Department stores						
National chains						
Discount stores						
Direct mail						
Catalogs						
Interactive websites						
Other						

*This chart is set up for retailers, but it could easily be modified for appropriate use by packaged-goods or business-to-business firms by changing distribution outlets to reflect the industry channels. For example, a packaged-goods firm might want to look at sales by chain grocery stores, independent grocery stores, convenience food stores, delis, and specialty grocery stores.

†In 2007, 36.2 percent of the units and 48.4 percent of the dollars were sold through specialty stores, while in 2011, 43.1 percent of the units and 51.2 percent of the dollars were sold through specialty stores. There was a 6.9 point increase in units corresponding to a 19 percent increase and a 2.8 point increase in dollars corresponding to a 6 percent increase between 2007 and 2011.

EXHIBIT 2.8

Store Penetration Analysis Method I

	Number of Stores	Sales Last Year $000	Number of TV HHs $000	Esti- mated Sales per HH	CURRENT ADVERTISING PLANS			FUTURE ADVERTISING PLANS			
					5% of Sales $000	W18–49 GRP Media Weight Level		Average Sales per HH	Number of Stores Needed	5% of Sales $000	W18–49 GRP Media Weight Level
Group 1 Markets (Weaker Markets)											
A	7	$ 3,233.5	1,229.6	$2.63	$161.7	1,587		$4.26	8.22	$ 261.9	2,567
B	9	4,508.9	1,662.1	2.71	225.4	1,896		4.26	11.12	354.0	2,987
C	6	2,292.1	708.9	3.23	114.6	1,983		4.26	4.74	151.0	2,613
D	2	1,597.6	868.2	1.84	79.9	1,535		4.26	5.80	184.9	3,552
E	4	2,079.9	2,518.0	0.83	104.0	512		4.26	16.84	536.3	2,641
F	4	2,122.1	602.7	3.52	106.1	1,901		4.26	4.03	128.4	2.301
Subtotal	32	$15,834.1	7,589.5	$2.09	$791.7	1,358		$4.26	50.75	$1,616.5	2,770
Group 2 Markets (Stronger Markets)											
G	22	$24,400.1	3,016.8	$ 8.09	1,220.0	3,148					
H	15	10,746.9	992.9	10.82	537.3	5,055					
I	5	4,350.4	703.7	6.18	217.5	3,191					
J	3	2,407.8	209.5	11.49	120.4	4,391					
K	5	4,323.6	694.9	6.22	216.2	3,947					
L	14	10,004.4	1,156.6	8.65	500.2	4,023					
Subtotal	64	$56,232.4	6,774.4	$ 6.69	$2,266.0	3,704					
Totals and/or Averages for Groups 1 and 2											
	96	$72,066.5	14,363.9	$ 5.02	$3,603.3	2,461					

Notes: The average per-store sales for Groups 1 and 2: $750,700 (or, $72,066,500 in total sales ÷ 96 total stores). Also, $000 is an abbreviation for thousands of dollars; HH is an abbreviation for household; GRP Media Weight Level is the gross rating points (GRPs).

3. The number of stores that are required in order for mass media such as newspapers, television, and radio to be efficiently leveraged, making the media affordable for your company from a percent-of-market-sales or sales-per-store standpoint.

Two methods, Store Penetration Analysis Methods I and II, for determining the optimum store penetration levels for each market are described below.

See Appendix B, Worksheets 8 and 9, to help you capture this information.

The chart in Exhibit 2.8 shows a method for determining the number of stores needed for Group 1 markets. In this example, Group 1 markets are underpenetrated and thus have not received the type of advertising support as the stores in Group 2. Because of this, Group 2 stores have a stronger sales performance than Group 1 stores.

In essence, this methodology assumes that if Group 1 markets are more fully penetrated with additional stores, the markets will be able to afford more advertising, and the individual store sales figures will increase. Although it would be unrealistic to expect Group 1 stores to equal Group 2 stores in sales in the near future, ideals are established—the average sales per household and per store of the weaker Group 1 markets and the stronger Group 2 markets.

The number of stores needed is calculated by first multiplying the estimated television market households by the average-sales-per-household figure of the weaker Group 1 markets and the stronger Group 2 markets. Then, the end result of this multiplication is divided by the average-per-store sales for the Group 1 and Group 2 markets to produce a realistic penetration figure.

The calculations for Market A in Group 1 are as follows:

New Sales Goal Based on Expected Potential

Estimated TV HHs in Market A 1,229,600	×	Average sales per HH in Groups 1 and 2 $5.02	=	New sales goal for Market A $6,172,600

Optimum Projected Stores for Market A

New sales goal for Market A $6,172,600	÷	Per-store average of Groups 1 and 2 $750,700	=	Ideal number of stores required for optimum penetration 8.22 stores

This method should be applied to all markets, as the chart in Exhibit 2.8 indicates. In addition, Exhibit 2.8 provides an advertising comparison in the form of gross rating points (GRPs) that could be achieved given a 5 percent advertising budget from the new projected sales and store penetration. (Gross rating points are also referred to as *target rating points*, TRPs, when measured against a specific target or group of people. See Chapter 18, "Media," for definitions and more information.) Continuing with the examples, Market A will have a new sales goal of $6,172,600 from eight stores. Five percent of $6,172,600 equals $308,630, which equals a media weight level of 2,567 GRPs.

The chart in Exhibit 2.9 shows yet another way to calculate estimated penetration requirements. As with Exhibit 2.8, this chart takes a group of stores seen as optimum and uses that group's performance as the standard. Through this analysis, it was determined that the best-performing markets from a sales standpoint have approximately one store per 100,000 households. This was accomplished by reviewing sales of those markets meeting sales and profit expectations. Column 7 shows how many stores would be needed in each market to match this goal.

EXHIBIT 2.9

Store Penetration Analysis II

	Number of Stores	Existing Stores per 100,000 HHs	Total Sales Last Year $000	Advertising Budget 5% of Sales $000	Estimated 1-Week Cost	Estimated Number of Advertising Weeks*	Minimum Stores 1/100,000 HHs	Advertising Budget 5% of Sales $000	New Estimated Number of Advertising Weeks*
				EXISTING STORES			PENETRATION OF 1 STORE PER 100,000 HHS		
A	7	0.569	$ 3,233.5	$ 161.7	$24.6	6–7	12.3	$284.1	11–12
B	9	0.541	4,508.9	225.4	13.8	8	16.6	415.8	15
C	6	0.846	2,292.1	114.6	11.4	8	7.1	135.6	10
D	2	0.230	1,597.6	79.9	11.4	7	8.7	347.5	30
E	4	0.159	2,079.9	104.0	48.6	2	25.2	655.2	13
F	4	0.664	2,122.1	106.1	13.8	7–8	6.0	159.2	12
G	22	0.729	13,487.1	674.4	49.6	13–14	30.2	925.7	19
H	15	1.511	10,746.9	537.3	27.0	20	10.0	358.2	13
I	5	0.711	4,350.4	217.5	17.0	12–13	7.0	304.5	18
J	3	1.432	2,407.8	120.4	7.2	16–17	2.1	84.3	12
K	5	0.720	4,323.6	216.2	13.0	16–17	6.9	298.3	23
L	14	1.210	10,004.4	500.2	31.6	15–16	11.6	414.5	13
All stores	146	0.536	$96,445.5	$4,822.3	—	—	272.4	—	—

*Weekly advertising equates to 200 total rating points (TRPs) of 30-second TV spots.

In addition, this chart looks at how many weeks of television the markets could currently sustain, given the advertising goal of 5 percent of sales. This is then compared to the number of advertising weeks that could be afforded, given the optimum penetration level of 1 store per 100,000 households and the subsequent increase (or decrease) in sales this would create in any given market. For example, Market A currently has a per-store average of $461,900 (that is, $3,233,000 ÷ 7). With a projection of 12.3 stores (1 store per 100,000 households), the new market sales figure becomes $5,681,400 (that is, 12.3 × $461,900). A 5 percent advertising budget, given the fully penetrated projected market sales of $5,681,400, is $284,100.

Market Coverage for Packaged Goods and Consumer Goods

As with retailing, you need to determine the number of outlets required to cover a trading area efficiently. However, since the packaged-goods firm doesn't own the outlets, there is less concern with overpenetration. In some cases, the goal is to reach 100 percent market coverage of grocery store outlets in a given market. At the other extreme, some manufacturers offer exclusive distribution to a chain in return for greater sales and merchandising support. In still other situations, the product is distributed on a more limited basis to outlets that are consistent with the image of the product.

In most cases, packaged-goods marketers do not calculate distribution coverage in terms of total stores. *Distribution* is used to mean the percent of total grocery store dollar volume that the stores carrying the marketer's product account for in all grocery commodities, or all commodity volume (ACV). Thus, the term "65 percent ACV" means that the marketer's brand is carried by grocery stores accounting for 65 percent of all commodity grocery store volume.

The ACV unit of measure is used by most packaged-goods and consumer goods companies to establish minimums in terms of considering advertising support, providing co-op programs, or supporting the markets in other ways. It is also used as an important measure in placing more sales emphasis and support against markets falling below levels that the company establishes based on results in other high-performing markets.

The ACV can be roughly determined through talking to retailers in your trading area. However, it is typically purchased through such services as Nielsen's Scan Track. The Scan Track measures daily sales in 350,000 stores across 30 countries in a broad range of product categories ranging from retail packaged goods to entertainment and media products. The Scan Track shows product movement, market share, price lines, and actual sales across stores in a broad array of retail channels.

The chart in Exhibit 2.10 provides information detailing market coverage. The example is for a packaged-goods firm, but it could easily be adapted to business-to-business firms. (A similar chart would be created for each business-to-business segment, such as an NAICS segment category.) From this chart you would determine that your product was represented in eight of the nine major outlets but that those outlets accounted for only 60 percent of the total product category business in the market.

The amount of shelf space a product receives is also critical to how well the product will do from a sales standpoint. Limited shelf space or facings and poor positioning on the shelf are both reasons for concern and need to be corrected. An average shelf space figure for your company could be calculated and included in your market coverage chart, as shown in Exhibit 2.10. Your percent of shelf space can be compared to the shelf space percentages of your major competitors, which can help you establish future shelf space goals.

See Appendix B, Worksheet 10, to help you capture this information.

EXHIBIT 2.10

Market Coverage Chart: Rockford, Illinois

	Coverage for Your Product	Percent of Total Product Business in Market, % ACV	Percent of Shelf Space Given Your Product in Store	PERCENT OF SHELF SPACE FOR MAIN COMPETITORS IN PRODUCT CATEGORY	
				Competitor 1	Competitor 2
Outlet A	X*	10%*	10%*	15%*	10%*
Outlet B	X	20	15	15	10
Outlet C	N/A	40	N/A	20	10
Outlet D	X	5	10	10	10
Outlet E	X	5	15	15	15
Outlet F	X	5	15	20	10
Outlet G	X	5	20	20	10
Outlet H	X	5	10	15	10
Outlet I	X	5	10	15	5

Note: An identical chart would be created for each key market.

*Outlet A sells this company's product. Outlet A accounts for 10 percent of the product category's business in Rockford. The company receives 10 percent of the shelf space given the product category in Outlet A while the major competitors receive 15 and 10 percent, respectively.

EXHIBIT 2.11

Sales Rep Analysis

Sales Rep	Territory	Number of Years a Rep	Total Sales 2010, $000	Total Sales 2011, $000	Percent Increase TY/LY Sales	Sales per Account 2010	Sales per Account 2011	Sales per Account Index to System Average 2011
1	California	5	$400/10 accounts	$450/10 accounts	12.5	$40,000	$45,000	88
2	Wisconsin/ Illinois	9	$350/8 accounts	$380/8 accounts	8.6	$43,750	$47,500	115
3								
4								
Etc.								

Note: While sales rep 1 has more sales, sales rep 2 does better on a sales-per-account basis with an index to all sales reps of 105, which is 5 points over the average. Strategically, barring reasons that can't be solved, sales rep 1 needs to work on increasing sales per account, and sales rep 2 needs to work on increasing the number of accounts.

Sales Representative or Broker Network

Another integral part of analyzing your distribution effectiveness is the personal selling method. Some companies choose to use an in-house sales force, others use independent sales representatives and brokers, and still others use distributors or wholesalers. You need to analyze the sales production of each individual sales rep, broker, or agent. The best way to establish benchmarks of success is to use some version of Exhibit 2.11 to compare the sales for each rep against the total performance of the aggregate rep or sales staff.

See Appendix B, Worksheet 11, to help you capture this information.

Sales by Selling Programs

A final issue that needs to be explored is the selling programs your company has in place to sell the trade. What are they? What's worked best in the past, and why? What innovative things are being done by your competition that you should consider improving upon and incorporating into your program?

QUESTIONS TO BE ADDRESSED

- Where do consumers shop for products in your category? What channel or outlet type do consumers use most when purchasing? Which ones are increasing and decreasing in importance?

- Now compare the above to your company's performance—what channel or outlet type do the customers of your business use most when purchasing? Which have increased in importance, and which have decreased? How is this similar or different from how consumers are shopping the category and your key competitors?
- Are new channels emerging? What trends are noticeable in the stores that dominate the sales for your product category?
- What channels or methods of distribution do your competitors use? If they use different channels than you use, why?
- Do you have adequate penetration of outlets (retail) to maximize sales in any given market?
- If you are a consumer goods company, do you have sufficient all commodity volume (ACV) to allow you to advertise and be competitive? What is the ACV in each of your company's markets? What is the ACV for each of your major competitors in those same markets?
- Is the percent of shelf space your product receives in major outlets greater than, the same as, or lower than your competitors?
- How many potential dealers, wholesalers, distributors, brokers, or retail outlets are there? What are their distribution trading areas geographically?
- Does expansion into new territories make sense? Are there additional areas of the country in which you should be doing business?
- Does your product require mass, selective, or exclusive distribution? Why? Does it require a combination of distribution methods? Who can best provide this type of distribution? Do your competitors' products require mass, selective, or exclusive distribution?
- How do you sell your product to the retail trade or other businesses? Do you use in-house sales staff, independent reps, wholesalers, or distributors? What is the most efficient method of selling to distributors, wholesalers, or the retail trade?
- Do you perform ongoing sales rep analysis? Which reps are the strongest in terms of the number of their accounts, sales per rep, and increases in sales volume year over year? What are the barriers that prevent better performance from those sales reps indexing below the system average? What is it that the best reps are doing that can be duplicated by the others?
- What is the importance of your product to the retail stores and/or distribution channels that sell it? Do you need the channels' services more than they need your product? Who has the channel power? How important is your product to the channel in terms of profit and volume (units and dollars)? Does your product help build or sustain traffic? Is it prestigious? Does it help sell other goods? How do these points differ from your competition?
- How do retailers or other distributors sell or market your product? Does your product receive aggressive sales support, or does your product have to sell itself? Does your product receive a prominent display relative to the competition? Does your product get promoted in the store or to the ultimate purchaser by the distribution channel? Does your product receive the same merchandising and promotion support (more or less) that the competition receives? Does your product receive other promotion, advertising, or merchandising support?
- How established is your product with the trade? How well is it known and accepted by the trade? Is it important to the businesses? Do you receive cooperation from the channels to which you sell? How does your competition rate in these areas?

- What is the minimum order size you require of your customers or channels? Is this standard in your industry? What are the payment terms? How often is restocking needed?
- Do storage, price marking, packaging, or accounting practices help sell the trade or create problems?
- Do quantity discounts, cooperative advertising, promotion allowances, price discounts, trade promotions, or other deals play a large role in the selling of your product category to the trade? How? Does your company have the same programs as your competitors?
- What is the customary markup of your product by the trade? Does this affect your marketing to the trade or the acceptance of your product by the end consumer?
- Are retail sales or sales to the trade subject to taxes or legal restrictions?
- What are the stocking requirements of the trade? How does your company make allocation decisions? Who gets the best fill rates and why? How are out-of-stock situations handled?
- When, how often, and by whom are the orders placed?
- Do interactive media have an impact in your business category? What percentages of your industry category sales and your business sales are made through the Internet?
- For services, what type of office is most consistent with your company's image? Describe the office interiors and exteriors of your competitors. Are they similar to or different from yours? Where, when, and how is your service best sold to the consumer?
- Are there certain sales programs that have worked well in the past? Which ones? Why?

Price

Price is a prominent part of the marketing decision-making process. A price that is too high may discourage purchase of the product and encourage competition in the forms of lower prices and more entries into the product category. Alternatively, a price that is too low may be a deterrent to reaching profit and sales goals.

The business review sales analysis section on pricing is designed to provide pricing data regarding the competition, changes in the marketplace price structure, and strength of consumer demand. This information will provide a reference and help guide your pricing objectives and strategies in the subsequent marketing plan.

The business review should provide you with four major insights on pricing:

1. The prices of your products and/or brands relative to those of the competition
2. The distribution of sales by price point relative to the competition
3. The price elasticity of demand for your product
4. The cost structure of the product category

Prices of Your Products Relative to Those of the Competition

Changes in a competitors' price structure often cause reactive price strategies in the marketplace. Frequent competitive price checks should be made by the marketing department in order to track historical pricing patterns of the competition. To a large degree, competitive pricing information allows you to determine market supply and demand and provides accurate yardsticks from which to make timely pricing decisions of your own.

EXHIBIT 2.12

Price of Your Company's Product Relative to That of the Competition during Key Selling Periods

	Price Nov.–Dec.	Price March–April	Price Aug.–Sept.
Your Company	$15.50	$15.50	$15.50
Competitor A	20.00	22.00	18.00
Competitor B	12.00	13.00	12.00
Competitor C	15.00	15.00	15.00
Competitor D	17.00	19.00	15.00

The chart in Exhibit 2.12 provides your company's prices relative to the competition during key selling periods of the year. It also allows the marketer to determine the pricing policies of the competition. Note that Competitors A and D raise their prices during the spring and lower them in the August–September period. If this happened year after year, it would become evident that it was a planned policy created in response to demand. You may also determine periods when competitors typically lower prices, and you can use this knowledge when developing competitive pricing and promotion strategies.

See Appendix B, Worksheet 12, to help you capture this information.

Sales by Price Point

In figuring the distribution of sales by price range relative to the competition, you determine what percent of the product category purchases are at each price level (low, medium, and high). Then you compare your product's price category to the distribution of category sales by price point. You might be surprised to find that your major price category accounts for a small percentage of category sales or that there has been increased sales growth in your product's price category. This information will allow you to judge the potential impact of your pricing decisions later in the marketing plan.

The chart in Exhibit 2.13 provides details of the percent of sales and percent of items sold by price range for the product category and your company. The chart allows for a trend comparison of sales by price over five years for both the category and the company. It also provides for comparison of pricing between the company and the category as a whole. From Exhibit 2.13, one can easily see the company's sales come from higher-priced items compared to the industry category. This pricing should be consistent with an upscale target market and a positioning based on quality.

See Appendix B, Worksheet 13, to help you capture this information.

Price Elasticity

Consumer purchase behavior responds directly to price changes. The effect and extent of price changes on consumer demand for a product is measurable in terms of price elasticity. Demand for a product is considered to be *price elastic* if sales go down when the price is raised and sales go up when the price is lowered. Demand for a product is considered to be *price inelastic* if demand is not significantly affected by changes in price.

Actual price elasticity can be determined in two ways. One method is through simulation research; the other method is through actual price changes in test markets. However, the way many marketers determine or estimate price elasticity is by monitoring competitive price changes and price changes on their own products and

EXHIBIT 2.13

Distribution of Sales by Price Point

	PRICE RANGE INDUSTRY CATEGORY		PRICE RANGE COMPANY'S PRODUCT	
	Percent of Sales	**Percent of Items**	**Percent of Sales**	**Percent of Items**
2011				
$0–$10	5%	5%	0%	0%
11–20	5	10	5	5
21–30	35	25	5	5
31–40	25	25	15	15
41–50	10	15	15	10
51–60	10	10	25	30
61–70	5	5	25	25
71+	5	5	10	10
2010				
$0–$10				
11–20				
21–30				
31–40				
41–50				
51–60				
61–70				
71+				
2009				
$0–$10				
11–20				
21–30				
31–40				
41–50				
51–60				
61–70				
71+				
2008, etc.				
2007, etc.				

then noting the resulting effects on sales. This can be done by obtaining market share figures through secondary sources; by talking to consumers of your products, sales representatives, buyers, and wholesalers; or by shopping your competitors to determine the results of various price changes.

Cost Structure

The cost structure of your product relative to its selling price should be reviewed. This information will need to be available when you establish your pricing segment later in the plan. The following should be included:

- Gross sales figure
- Cost of goods sold
- Fixed and variable costs associated with the selling of your product
- Gross margin (worked backward from the retail price: the price less the cost of the product sold divided by the price)
- Markup (based on cost: the difference between the cost and the price divided by the cost)
- Margin and profit

QUESTIONS TO BE ADDRESSED
- What is the pricing structure for the product category? Are there price point products, brands, or stores that sell for more or less than yours? Is there a range from premium to discount pricing in your industry?
- What is the pricing structure for your product relative to the competition? Does the relationship of your product's price to that of the competition change during different selling seasons? Has it changed over a period of years?
- In addition to pure price, are discounts, credits, promotional allowances, return policies, restocking charges, shipping policies, and so on important to the ultimate sale of your product?
- What is the distribution of sales by price point for your industry and your company (five-year trend)? Do the majority of sales fall in one price category, or can consumers or businesses be segmented by price points?
- What has been the trend in pricing (five-year trend)? Are there price segments that are growing or shrinking?
- How price elastic is your product category? When you raise and/or lower the price, how does it affect demand? Are consumers price sensitive to your product category?
- Where is your product priced in relation to your major competitors? Why is it priced where it is?
- What is the cost structure of your main products? Which ones do you make the highest margin on? Are they different from the ones you make the most margin dollar profit on?
- Have your margins and/or your margin dollars been eroding, flattening, or growing? Why?

Geography

Finally, sales by geographic markets should be analyzed. This can be done by region of the country, that is, East, West, South, and North; by state; by standard metropolitan statistical area (SMSA); by city; or by any other geographic segmentation appropriate for your industry.

Purchase Rates of the Industry Product Category and Your Company's Product by Geographic Markets

Geographic markets should be analyzed for their importance in sales for the category (Category Development Index, or CDI) and sales for your company's product (Brand Development Index, or BDI).

The Category Development Index determines the *product category's strength* on a market-by-market basis. It provides a quick index of whether the geographical area or any given market's purchases are at, above, or below the average, given the size of its population in relation to the total country's population. The CDI information allows the marketer to determine markets that have strong per capita sales potential. This information can be used in recommending expansion markets, predicting sales, or as rationale for investment spending decisions.

The formula for calculating the CDI is as follows:

Category Development Index (CDI)

$$CDI = \frac{\text{Percentage of product CATEGORY's national dollar volume in a given market}}{\text{Percentage of CATEGORY's U.S. population in a given market}}$$

Exhibit 2.14 presents a chart that can be used to develop this information.

EXHIBIT 2.14

Category Development Index (CDI)

DMA*	Percent of U.S. Population	Percent of Product Dollar Volume	Category Development Index (Volume/ Population)	Population Number, 000	Dollar Volume of Category Product Nationally, 000	Per Capita Consumption
Chicago	3.2%†	4.5%†	141†	8,961‡	$827,548‡	$92.35‡
Madison						
Philadelphia						
Minneapolis						
Atlanta						

*DMA is the Designated Market Area defined by the television viewing audience.

†Of the total U.S. population, 3.2 percent lives in Chicago; 4.5 percent of the category's national sales volume (for example, all shoes sold nationally) is from the Chicago DMA. The Chicago DMA does better in the category business than the average DMA, as is indicated by the CDI of 141 (that is, 4.5 ÷ 3.2 = 1.41, which is converted to the index of 141).

‡Further, 8,961,000 people live in the Chicago DMA. The Chicago population consumes $827,548,000 worth of the product, for a per capita consumption of $92.35.

See Appendix B, Worksheet 14, to help you capture this information.

The Brand Development Index can help you determine whether a geographical market purchases your *company's product* at, above, or below average rates, given its population in relation to your company's national market population. For example, if your company did business only in three cities, those three cities and their surrounding trading area populations would define your company's national market population. The BDI information is used to help formulate geographic spending strategies. Strong company markets can be protected, and weak markets can be targeted for growth.

The formula for calculating the BDI is as follows:

Brand Development Index (BDI)

$$BDI = \frac{\text{Percentage of COMPANY's dollar volume in any given market}}{\text{Percentage of COMPANY's national market population that lives in a given market}}$$

Exhibit 2.15 presents a chart that can be used to develop this information.

See Appendix B, Worksheet 15, to help you capture this information.

The CDI and BDI numbers are often used together. High-CDI markets mean that the potential exists for good sales, as the product category as a whole does well. If these same markets have low company BDI indexes with adequate product distribution and store penetration and/or market coverage, the markets are often targeted for

EXHIBIT 2.15

Brand Development Index (BDI)

DMA	Percent of Company's National Market Population	Percent of Dollar Volume	Brand Development Index (Volume/ Population)	Population Number, 000	Dollar Volume of Company, 000	Per Capita Consumption
Chicago	11.2%*	10.0%*	89*	8,961†	$200,000†	$22.32†
Madison						
Philadelphia						
Minneapolis						
Atlanta						

* Of the company's total market population, 11.2 percent lives in the Chicago DMA; 10 percent of the company's sales are from the Chicago DMA. The BDI for Chicago is 89 (that is, 10 ÷ 11.2 = 0.89, which is converted to the index of 89), which means that the DMA has a below-average BDI as compared to other DMAs in the system.

†Further, 8,961,000 people live in the Chicago DMA. Company sales in Chicago are $200,000,000, or $22.32 per person.

aggressive marketing plans. Thus, strong category sales (high CDI) and low company sales (low BDI) can mean potential for your company's growth. The following analysis will help you determine spending strategies later in your plan.

Situation	Potential Strategy Directions to Consider
Low BDI/High CDI	Strong market category sales and low company sales provide an opportunity market as your company is underperforming in a strong category market. Look at this as an offensive opportunity and investment spend.
Low BDI/Low CDI	Neither the category nor the company does well. Divest or look elsewhere to spend money first.
High BDI/High CDI	Strong category market and strong company market. Protect investment and continue to grow the market.
High BDI/Low CDI	Strong company market but weak category market. Defensive opportunity. Protect what you have but realistically you can only grow the market to a certain point.

QUESTIONS TO BE ADDRESSED
- Where exactly do your customers reside? Where does your high-potential target segments reside? Do they live nationwide, or are they limited to certain regions? Are they living in large cities, suburbs, or rural areas?
- Where are sales for the product category strongest and weakest nationally (CDI)? Where are your company's sales strongest and weakest (BDI)?
- What markets have above- or below-average consumption per household or per person (CDI)?
- What are the markets at, above, or below the average purchase rates on a household or per person basis (BDI)?
- Are national sales increasing at greater or lesser rates than the population growth? Are there specific markets where this is different?

Trading Areas
In addition to the CDI and BDI information, the retail and/or services marketer should determine the trading area for the product. A *trading area* is the geographical territory where consumers and customers live. This is important when making media purchasing decisions (as discussed in Chapter 18, "Media") and also when determining future store locations (as discussed in Chapter 14, "Distribution").

Through a simple in-store customer survey, as shown in Exhibit 2.16, you can determine where your customers come from. Or, if you keep accurate customer mailing lists, the lists can allow you to construct trading areas.

EXHIBIT 2.16

Trading Area Analysis

Zip Codes Surrounding Store	Percent of Customers Over 1-Week Period
53704	20%
53705	30
53703	20
53702	10
53711	10
53708	5
53709	1
Other	4

See Appendix B, Worksheet 16, to help you capture this information.

QUESTIONS TO BE ADDRESSED
- What is the trading area for your product category? How far do consumers in the category typically travel in miles and time to purchase the product?
- How far do customers travel to purchase your company's product?

STEP 4. TREND ANALYSIS (PESTLE)

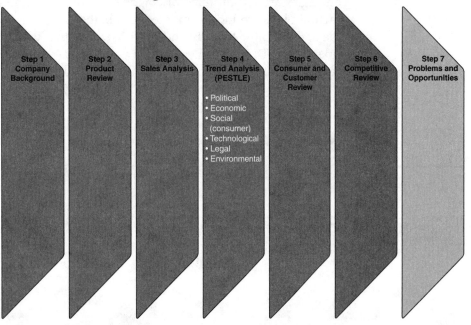

Understanding trends helps you to think long term and to adjust now for change that will happen in the future. We recommend using a rather robust way of looking at and understanding trends by using a technique called the PESTLE analysis.

PESTLE Analysis

PESTLE stands for *political, economic, social (consumer), technological, legal,* and *environmental*. These six categories make up the external audit categories for your trend analysis. The process is a common one in marketing and strategic planning. The earliest known reference to the process, which has gained favor over the past 10 years, was back in 1967 in a book titled *Scanning the Business Environment* by F. J. Agular (New York, Macmillan).

Process for Analyzing Trends
The following provides a process to follow for efficiently analyzing future trends that might affect your business category, your company, and/or your products and services.

1. Assemble a team to collect the information, and assign members to one letter of the PESTLE process.
2. Create an outline of the types of topics you need to cover under each letter.

3. Within each smaller "letter team," identify sources of information on the letter's topic. Then divide and conquer, with each member of the team specializing in using unique sources to find the information.
4. Summarize the information and findings per category under each letter.
5. From the information, identify strategy ramifications or impact going forward, backed by the trend findings for later use in your plan.

The trend analysis chart in Exhibit 2.17 provides a template for you to capture the pertinent trends for your business.

- First, focus on trends that will directly impact your marketing: the targeting of market segments; the development of brand positioning; the development of strategies around product, pricing, communication, and distribution; and the tactical plans around the marketing mix tools.
- Next, think more broadly and capture trends that will affect the total operations of your business. While your focus is on the marketing plan, it is a mistake not to think broadly so you are fully able to incorporate key industry category and company trends into the strategy decisions you make in your plan.

Note that the Questions to Be Addressed for each of the PESTLE sections are included within the chart in Exhibit 2.17.

See Appendix B, Worksheet 17, to help you capture this information.

STEP 5. CONSUMER AND CUSTOMER REVIEW

Insights: What Can We Learn?

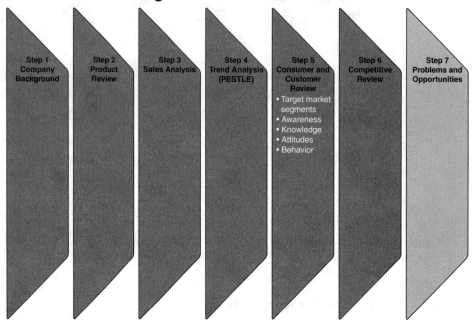

Step 5, "Consumer and Customer Review," focuses on three tasks to complete in terms of developing insights:

- *Task 1, Target Market Segments:* Target market segments for your company and the industry category. It's important to learn about customer segments but also the broader consumer segments (made up of both customers and noncustomers).

EXHIBIT 2.17

Trend Analysis

Trend Category	Questions to Be Addressed	Findings	Impact Potential	Impact Rating	Impact Trend	Strategy Impact
		What are the ramifications of the findings?	How could the factors listed in the Questions column impact your company or your products and services?	Would you rate the impact potential in the previous column: H: High M: Medium L: Low U: Unknown	Would you say the trend identified in the Findings column was: I: Increasing S: Steady D: Decreasing U: Unknown	What are the potential strategy impacts of this finding? How will this trend affect your company into the future? What can be done to either mitigate or accentuate the trend?
Political	Are there any political trends or issues that have surfaced that will affect your company either positively or negatively? Are there any pieces of legislation that if passed will either positively or negatively affect your company? Are there any existing government policies that will either positively or negatively affect your company or its products and services? Are there positive or negative public attitudes that may manifest themselves at the political polls in the future? Other?					
Economic	List the economic factors that are critical to your business (e.g., home sales, disposable income rates, saving rates, or rate of inflation). For each					

Trend Category	Questions to Be Addressed	Findings	Impact Potential	Impact Rating	Impact Trend	Strategy Impact
	factor, are there positive or negative trends that will affect the factor in the near future? What are they?					
	Are there tax trends that will affect your business?					
	Are there historical market trends that will affect your business?					
	Are there specific industry and economic factors that will affect your business?					
	Do there exist company financial factors such as cash flow, capital requirements, cost containment initiatives, or salary requirements for new talent?					
	Other?					
Social	Are there demographic trends such as income, education, place of residence, sex, and age that will affect your business into the future?					
	If you're a business-to-business firm, is there a shift in terms of the types of businesses buying or the influence of various job titles in the purchase of your products? Or is there a different buying behavior that is causing shifts in your business?					

Are there geographic trends that are affecting your business? These might be demographic trends that are stronger in one part of your trading area, the country, or the world than another.

Are shifts in population to some areas of the country and not others going to affect your business?

What are the social trends affecting the purchase of your products (home, activities, purchase trends, time pressures, standards of living, occupations, earning potentials, etc.)?

What are the shifts in attitudes that might affect your business (toward aging, health, diversity, education, fashion, consumerism, youth culture, pop culture, retired people, sports and recreation, etc.)?

Are there changes in the ways businesses purchase from other businesses that will affect the way you do business into the future?

Are there changes in the way people and businesses obtain information or news and communicate with each other?

Has the organization structure changed, or

Trend Analysis (continued)

Trend Category	Questions to Be Addressed	Findings	Impact Potential	Impact Rating	Impact Trend	Strategy Impact
	will there be trends going forward that will impact your business?					
	Are there management trends that will impact your business?					
Technological	Has the ability to capture transaction and customer data affected your business environment?					
	Will a new technology alter the way your industry category or your company conducts its business?					
	Will there continue to be Internet and social media innovations that will impact your business?					
Legal	Are there any legal trends that will affect your business (trademarks, copyrights, patents, organizational structures, etc.)?					
Environmental	Are there staff attitudinal changes that will affect your business?					
	Are there trends that will affect the organizational culture?					
	Are customer values, opinions, lifestyles, and mores changing in ways that will affect your business?					

- *Task 2, Awareness, Knowledge, and Attitudes:* Awareness and knowledge of your company and its products or services. Attitudes and perceptions about your company and its products or services.
- *Task 3, Behavior:* Behavior toward your company and its products or services in the form of initial trials or becoming a customer and making repeat purchases or becoming a loyal customer.

We're going to examine the critical pieces of each.

TASK 1 ## Target Market Segments

The business review provides a format that sorts current and potential customers into segments. Segmenting allows customers to be grouped according to common demographic, product usage, attitudinal, or purchasing characteristics. Segments are groups of people who think, act, and purchase in similar patterns allowing you to focus efforts more efficiently. Segments allow for the determination of which customer group is currently most profitable and which noncustomer group has the most potential for your company. The end result of segmenting is that a company is able to focus its marketing resources against an ultimate target market that has some common characteristics. Instead of trying to be all things to all people, the company can direct its energies (its resources, messages, products, and other marketing mix elements) toward satisfying essentially one person, as characterized by the target market segment or segments. Such directed efforts are considerably more effective and efficient.

The business review provides a format that describes the profile of the current category consumer as compared to the company's current customer. This allows the marketer to determine if the company's customer is different from the general product category consumer. The similarities and differences will be important when determining future marketing strategies. For example, a company may find that its product is consumed by a far older population than the general product category's consumer. This important information can be used in the marketing plan to further target this older age segment or to develop plans to attract more of the younger, mainstream consumers.

Volume and Concentration

Two measures by which target markets can be determined from data are volume and concentration. Experian Simmons and GfK MRI provide these data for most consumer categories. (See Chapter 1, "Sources of Information" section.)

- *Volume:* This is the total number of purchases or the percent of total purchases attributable to any given demographic target market segment. An example would be the total sales in a category equal to $1 million, with 18- to 24-year-olds constituting 15 percent of the total purchases, or $150,000.
- *Concentration:* This is the percentage, within a given demographic target market segment, that purchases the product. An example would be that, of all 18- to 24-year-olds, 80 percent are purchasers of the product.

Volume is the more critical of the two measures from the standpoint that a company must have a large enough target market base and resulting sales base to sustain an ongoing business. At this point in the business review, your job is to analyze the potential target market by determining segments based on similar demographic and purchasing characteristics. However, keep in mind that the segments must be large enough to ensure adequate volume potential. The demand analysis in Chapter 5, "Targets," covers calculating volume potential.

EXHIBIT 2.18

National Demographic Description of Product Category Consumers: Volume Measure

Demographic Descriptor, Age	Percent of Total Population, 210 Million*	Percent of Total Purchases, $900 Million†
Under 18	18%	36%
18–24		
25–34		
35–44		
45–54		
55+		

Note: A similar chart would be developed for all products, product categories, or services your company sells.

*This number provides a total population number. In this example, the total population universe is 210 million. With this total figure you can calculate the total population for each demographic category. For example, the total population for 18- to 24-year-olds would be 18% × 210,000,000 = 37,800,000.

†This number provides the total dollar volume or unit volume of the category depending upon which measure you use for percent of total purchases. In this example, the total dollar purchases for the product category are $900 million. This information allows you to calculate the dollar volume potential for each demographic category. For example, the total purchases for 18- to 24-year-olds would be 36% × $900,000,000 = $324,000,000.

Volume can be measured in terms of purchases (units or dollars) or in terms of actual numbers of consumers (purchasers or users). In the chart shown in Exhibit 2.18, for matters of consistency, we use purchases.

See Appendix B, Worksheet 18, to help you capture this information.

The chart in Exhibit 2.18 demonstrates the demographic profile in terms of age for the product category nationally from a volume standpoint. If more than one brand exists or if there are segments within your business, a chart for each should be developed. If you sell shoes, a chart for total shoe purchases and separate charts for athletic, dress, casual, and children's shoe purchases should be developed.

The easiest way to determine a volume measure is to look at the "percentage of total purchases" column to determine the percent of purchases for which each demographic category is responsible.

Exhibit 2.19 demonstrates the demographic profile of the product category nationally from a concentration standpoint.

See Appendix B, Worksheet 19, to help you capture the information.

Volume numbers are often a function of category size, while concentration numbers are a true measure of the propensity to purchase. There may be more 25- to

EXHIBIT 2.19

National Demographic Description of Product Category Consumers: Concentration Measure

Demographic Descriptor, Age	Percent of Category That Purchases Product, 75%*	Concentration Index: Category/Total
Under 18	40%	53
18–24	50*	66*
25–34	75	100
35–44	90	120
45–54	100	133
55+	50	66

*Nationally, 50 percent of the 18- to 24-year-olds purchase the product; 75 percent of the total population purchase the product. The index of 66 is derived from dividing 50 by 75, and it tells the marketer that 18- to 24-year-olds have a lower propensity to purchase the product category than does the whole population.

34-year-old purchasers of shoes than 18- to 24-year-old purchasers because of the large number of 25- to 34-year-olds in the population. Yet, for particular styles of shoes, while there are fewer total 18- to 24-year-old purchasers, the age category may demonstrate a greater concentration of purchases. For example, 25- to 34-year-olds may constitute 22 percent of total purchases for a particular style of shoe and 18- to 24-year-olds only 15 percent (volume measure), yet the data may show that only 20 percent of the 25- to 34-year-olds purchase that style of shoe, compared to 40 percent of the 18- to 24-year-olds (concentration measure).

Thus, the marketer may find it more profitable to concentrate on the 18- to 24-year-olds when selling specific styles of shoes or whatever the core product being sold. A high concentration of purchasers within a specific demographic category allows for a more efficient and effective marketing effort. The marketer can focus on addressing the similar needs and characteristics of the consumers in the category. There is not much wasted effort since a vast majority of the people in the category demonstrate a propensity to purchase the product.

In summary, both volume and concentration must be taken into consideration when developing a target market database. Volume is a benchmark type of variable. There must be enough people interested in purchasing the product in order to justify any business. Once volume levels are deemed sufficient, concentration numbers can further define demographic target market categories by showing strong propensities to purchase within given demographic categories.

Industry Category versus Company Target Market

It is important to develop target market databases for both the industry product category nationally and your company's purchasers. This will allow you to compare the two profiles to see if your company's target market description matches that of the industry product category. If not, you can spend time determining why and how the differences might help or hurt your situation. One of our retail clients determined that its customer target market skewed younger (18 to 34) than industry category consumers as a whole. However, it wasn't simply a matter of age but a mindset that determined the target. While age was a factor, a greater influence in determining who fit into the target was a mindset innovation, acceptance of new things, and a quest to be the first to adopt new technology. While our client did well against the heavy-user target market representative of the industry category, the data showed that the company could improve relative to the industry through new marketing and product strategies targeting this newly emerging customer market that skewed younger in terms of age and, more important, in terms of attitude. Exhibit 2.20 provides an example chart that indicates the demographic profiles of a company's purchaser as compared to the average purchaser profile nationally.

See Appendix B, Worksheet 20, to help you capture this information.

Review of Consumer Segmentation Methods

The following six segmentation methods are common to many businesses. As just described, you can determine insights for each by looking at profiles that have high volume or concentrations in terms of users and/or purchasers or purchases. Each of the methods should also compare the industry category with the company and product as previously discussed.

Method 1. Customer Tenure Segmentation or New versus Old Customer Segmentation

Many times there are purchasing differences based on how long the customer has been doing business with your company. First-year customers may not buy as

EXHIBIT 2.20

Demographic Description of Company Purchasers Compared to Category Purchasers

Demographic Descriptor, Age	Percent of Purchasers of Product Nationally, $100 Million*	Percent of Purchasers of Company Product, $20 Million*	Index: Company/National Purchasers
Under 18	10%	10%	100
18–24	20†	10†	50†
25–34	40	30	75
35–44	10	20	200
45–54	10	20	200
55+	10	10	100
Total	100	100	

*This provides a total dollar volume figure to help calculate total dollars for each demographic category. For example, the total dollar volume for the category is $100 million. The total dollar volume for the company is $20 million. The company purchases among 18- to 24-year-olds is $2 million (10 percent of $20 million).

†Of all the purchasers of the product nationally, 20 percent are 18 to 24, while 10 percent of your company's purchasers are 18 to 24. This results in an index of 50, meaning that your company sells to 18- to 24-year-olds at half the expected average (the average being an index of 100).

much, purchase as many times, want the same benefits, utilize your entire product mix, or come back next year (retrial) as often as longer-term customers. If so, a natural first segmentation is new versus old customers. In most companies, there are large differences between knowledge and understanding of the company, attitudes, behavior, and loyalty between longer-term customers and new customers. Smart marketers look upon new customers and existing customers as different segments that need and deserve different marketing programs aimed at accomplishing different things based upon the segment's different needs.

Method 2. Demographic Segmentation (Description and Size)

The marketer's traditional method of defining purchaser and user groups and segmenting markets is by utilizing demographic factors such as age, income, education, household size, and type of geographic region (urban, suburban, and rural). There are many examples of segments developed to demographic drivers where a specific demographic is responsible for the majority of the sales. One example would be the use of higher education or colleges. The vast majority of the users of higher education are 18 to 24, with family incomes above $50,000. Another example would be travel. The majority of cruises are taken by older adults. This is a period in people's lives when they are unencumbered by children and have the income, time, and interest to travel.

Demographics can be determined for either individuals or households (the configuration of individuals making up a living unit). The key to determining segments is identifying whether a specific demographic or combination of demographic variables predicts a significant volume or concentration of usage or purchases. For each of the pertinent demographic segments provided in the examples below, you'd want to examine their importance by listing the number of consumers for the category and the number of customers for your product based on the most pertinent descriptors.

Sex: There are often major differences between male and female purchasing and usage habits. For a regional health maintenance organization (HMO), research determined that women were the most influential decision makers in family health care decisions. Marketing, communication, product, and merchandising decisions needed to reflect the particular needs and tastes of this segment.

Age: Target markets can be broken out by age. Age frequently determines consumers' needs and wants for a specific product brand or service. However, age is usually a predictor for a viewpoint, attitude, or belief that is even more important to the target description. Most beer companies recognize the importance of young adults (from legal drinking age to age 34) in the consumption of beer. Studies have shown that males within this age group are above-average and heavy users. The younger beer drinker is more experimental and views beer as a badge that says something about him as a person, and the beverage serves as more of a connector to social good times than it typically will later in life. Most critical to marketers, many beer drinkers form lifelong brand preferences during this time period.

In another example, many banks target groups by product life cycle as determined by age. For instance, 18- to 34-year-olds need access to checking and basic savings accounts, credit cards, and automatic teller machines; 34- to 54-year-olds need mortgages, equity loans, lines of credit, higher-interest checking accounts, and college savings instruments; people in the 55-plus age group need retirement savings instruments such as money market products, CDs, trust fund managers, and brokerage services. By recognizing where a consumer is in his or her life cycle, you can target him or her with products that are most meaningful during that specific life stage and then cross-sell other products over time.

Whenever possible, try to gather demographic information by media age breaks consistent with television and radio (2-plus, 2 to 11, 6 to 11, 12 to 17, 18-plus, 18 to 24, 18 to 34, 18 to 49, 25 to 49, 25 to 54, and 55-plus). This will allow for more accurate media planning and buying. It will also allow for a better direct link from the target market definition to the actual purchasing of media designed to reach the target market. With the advent of nontraditional media, such as the Internet options and social media, this is less important than it was years ago, but it's still a consideration. Unfortunately, media breaks consistent with national rating services such as Nielsen and Arbitron don't always correspond to secondary sources of target market information such as GfK MRI data, but for consistency purposes, try to use media demographic categories whenever possible.

Income: Income can predict in broad terms what a family's lifestyle will be like. There are many product categories, such as cars, appliances, and leisure goods, for which purchases rise with increases in income. Yet purchase rates for other more basic product categories, such as food, remain fairly stable regardless of income growth or decline. Income is often combined with geographic information to further determine the location of specific consumers. Marketers often pinpoint geographic census tracks that have households with approximately the same income range. Identification of these clusters can determine the locations of new outlets for retailers who do well against the identified income range. The clusters can also be used in media selection, such as targeted direct mail, or for the advertising or promotion of income-sensitive product offerings.

Education: In general, the higher the individual's education, the higher the income. Thus, education and income are often analyzed in tandem.

Occupation: Similar to education, income is also a function of occupation. While some of the major differences between white-collar and blue-collar purchasing habits have diminished due to double incomes, there are still major buying patterns affected by occupation. For example, people who are carpenters, craftspeople, and supervisors tend to spend less for clothing and purchase different types of clothing than do service, professional, and clerical workers.

In working with a regional menswear store, it was determined that there were differences in purchasing rates of suits not only between white-collar and blue-collar professionals but also among white-collar professionals. Salespeople, for example, purchased suits at greater rates than did some other types of business professionals. In addition, occupation combined with age further delineated the purchasing segments. Young professionals spent at greater rates than average on suits because they were establishing wardrobes far different from the clothes they wore in college. Conversely, the number of suits purchased dropped slightly as the younger people aged and started a family. Purchases increased again as those individuals got older, reached the top of their profession, and could afford to purchase suits more often.

Family and/or household size: Family size often determines the quantity sold to the household, with larger households purchasing greater amounts. Family size may dictate that greater quantities of a product are used within a given household, but each person within a family may or may not use more of the product than an individual living alone. Thus, per capita rates of purchasing should also be taken into consideration when developing target markets.

Family size is often combined with the age of the family to identify the family's lifestyle as determined by its life cycle. We tend to break the family life cycle into six categories: (1) single under 35, (2) married under 35 with no children, (3) married under 35 with children, (4) married 35 or over with no children, (5) married 35 or over with children, and (6) single 35 or over. Each category has different purchasing patterns and often purchases similar products in different quantities. For example, households with small children purchase products like quick, easy-to-prepare meal packages, appliances, diapers, hot dogs, and household cleaners at greater rates than other family groupings.

Region and/or geography: Many products are not sold evenly across the country due to distribution capabilities of the manufacturing companies or to the differing tastes, lifestyles, and needs of consumers from one region to another. You should determine the geographic location of your potential consumers as well as the varying levels of usage by geographic area. A situation may exist in which a region has very few actual consumers, but those consumers consume at higher-than-normal levels, making that region more important than the small number of customers would indicate. (Actual usage levels by geographic region are determined through the Category Development and Brand Development Indexes discussed in the Step 3, "Sales Analysis," section earlier in this chapter.)

There are many examples of targeting by geography. Small-town women have a much higher incidence of purchasing craft-making materials through the mail. There are a host of weather-related products that have northern geographic targets, such as downhill skis. And there are regional fads and consumption patterns that skew consumption to one area or region of the country. An example would be bratwursts in Wisconsin (due to the German influence), the beignet in New Orleans, and grits in the South.

In preparing a business review for a real estate firm, we discovered that the total population and total home sales outside the city but still within the metro area had experienced twice the growth than that of the city itself. We also found that the firm's share of home sales was high in the city but low outside the city in the metro area, which was the major growth area. Based on this comparative data, the marketing program was developed to target home buyers and sellers in suburban areas throughout the metro area as well as in the city.

The marketing plan called for a targeted advertising strategy that resulted in the advertising theme "East side, west side, all around the county, your home is our profession." In addition, the marketing plan recommended broad metro media coverage and the opening of branch offices on the periphery of the city. The results of this geographic targeting were dramatic increases in the firm's sales and profits, with its market share of home sales going from fourth to first in two years. In another case, the Monona Terrace convention center in Madison, Wisconsin, which was designed by the famed architect Frank Lloyd Wright, had decided to target meeting planners in Chicago because of the city's strong Wright influence. Wright designed many homes and buildings in the Chicago area. However, an analysis of two-year sales showed limited usage of the convention center from businesses in Chicago. Further research confirmed that Chicago meeting planners generally either would stay in the Chicago area, or if they decided to travel, they would most likely go to locations that offered a different climate than another northern Midwest city. A retargeting directed to Wisconsin companies looking for an inspirational meeting location within driving distance proved successful for the convention center.

QUESTIONS TO BE ADDRESSED
- How many total industry category consumers are there in your trading area? How many customers do you have—that is, what is your customer penetration of the total consumer base for the industry category?
- What is the industry category (consumer) demographic profile of the product category nationally? Do the leading target segments differ from your leading customer target segments?
- What is the profile of the individuals who consume or purchase the most from a volume standpoint? Do some demographic categories have a higher concentration of purchasers?
- Do new customers purchase at different rates than older established customers?
- Which industry category target segments and which company customer target segments are growing the fastest in terms of volume?
- How many customers purchase your product? How many potential industry category consumers exist in your product category? Has the number of consumers been growing or shrinking over the past five years?
- Are there geographic areas where the product category is purchased at greater rates? How many industry category consumers and customers are there in each geographic area?

Method 3. Product Usage Segmentation
For some products, demographics aren't as important as the reason the product is purchased or how it is used. Many times purchasers with similar demographics purchase the product for different reasons. This offers the opportunity to segment consumers based on usage of the product. Baking soda is purchased by women who bake from scratch and need the product in the baking process. It is also purchased as a refrigerator deodorizer. Many of the purchasers of baking soda as a deodorizer do not bake on a regular basis, so they do not purchase the product for baking. Thus, usage of this product helps define customer segments, and knowledge of the customers' usage is critical to determining how this product would be marketed to each of the two customer groups.

In another example, some beer drinkers look at beer consumption strictly from a volume standpoint. Others are beer connoisseurs, drinking a little at a time and willing to spend more to do it. How they view or use beer differs, and understanding these different uses or viewpoints of the different segments will be the key to marketing the product.

QUESTIONS TO BE ADDRESSED

- If there are multiple uses of your product, are there consumers who use the product for one type of use or benefit but not another? Are there multiple, independent target segments for the specific uses of your product? How many consumers and customers are there for each of the uses? What's your company's penetration?
- Are there products purchased by a specific target market that might be used as a foundation to cross-sell other company products?

Method 4. Psychographic and/or Lifestyle Segmentation

Marketers use lifestyle factors or psychographics to help them identify target markets effectively. Lifestyle descriptors attempt to define a customer segment in terms of attitudes, interests, and activities of the consumers. This is an attempt to go further than demographic descriptors to really get inside the consumers' mind. A profile of your consumers, taking into consideration some of the following, is helpful in further describing and defining the target market.

- *Personality descriptors:* Do your customers tend to be affectionate, likable, dominating, authoritative, passive, independent, self-assured, sociable, stubborn, followers, leaders, conformists, experimenters, individualists, progressive, conservative, well read or not well read, small town or big city oriented, worldly, or rock 'n' roll or country music oriented?
- *Activities and interests:* Can your customers and prospects be defined by their activities and interests? Do they engage in and are they passionate about outdoor or indoor sports, cultural events, environmental activities, political activities, volunteer projects, social club activities, home entertainment, travel, games, or musical activities?
- *Purchase attitudes:* Are your customers economy minded, impulsive, well organized, price conscious, style conscious, value conscious, quality driven, self-service oriented, status conscious, cash purchasers, or credit purchasers? We just finished work with ProCon, a credit union consulting firm, where we determined that the core member group for a credit union in Florida was a target we described as financial dependents. These were people who regardless of age were more high touch than high tech, wanted and were open to financial advice, and were in fact a bit uncomfortable making financial decisions without guidance. The credit union's primary target market was defined by attitude, not demographics.
- *Opinions:* Segmentation by groups with strong beliefs of one kind or another is also very effective. Some people believe that hunting promotes family values, some people have a strong belief in individualism, some believe it takes a village to raise a child, some have strong associations with faith, and so on. Aligning your company with a specific segment's beliefs and opinions can create a powerful affinity between you and your customers.

Lifestyle segmentation is usually combined with demographics to form a more precise definition of the target market. For example, we worked with a financial advisor firm that specialized in environmentally sound investment options, targeting high-income individuals who were environmentally aware and concerned.

There are two lifestyle systems that are commonly used: the Nielsen PRIZM and the Strategic Business Insights (SBI) VALS systems.

Nielsen PRIZM: PRIZM is an acronym for Potential Rating Index for Zip Markets. Under this system, every neighborhood is assigned to one of 66 clusters, each defined by a combination of demographic and lifestyle characteristics. These clusters have somewhat colorful names describing the type of people that live there. Examples include Young Digerati, Kids & Cul-de-Sacs, and Heartlanders.

(PRIZM is a lifestyle segmentation analysis developed by Claritas, which is now part of the Nielsen Company.)

For example, those living in Young Digerati clusters tend to be the following:

- Tech-savvy singles and couples
- Living in fashionable neighborhoods on the urban fringe
- Affluent
- Highly educated
- Ethnically mixed

In addition, their neighborhoods are filled with trendy apartments and condos, fitness clubs, clothing boutiques, casual restaurants, and all types of bars—from juice to coffee to microbrew.

In contrast, those living in the Heartlanders cluster tend to have the following lifestyle traits:

- They live in small middle-class towns.
- They are older couples.
- They have working-class jobs.
- They have sturdy, unpretentious homes.
- Their communities are made up of small families and empty-nest couples.
- Their tastes are rustic.
- Their leisure activities include hunting and fishing, along with cooking, sewing, camping, and boating.

A Nielsen PRIZM analysis of your customer database might show, for example, a high concentration of people in a Heartlanders cluster. You now have a much better picture of your primary target consumer and are more able to tailor a message or promotion that would tie directly to the lifestyles of these consumers. In addition, efforts to expand the business into other geographic areas can be focused toward those areas that are also Heartlanders clusters since these areas would probably have the highest potential for success.

The PRIZM segmentation system can benefit your marketing in five ways:

1. It provides a better and deeper definition of your primary target consumer.
2. By appending your customer base, it gives you a clear picture of how many customers you have in each target cluster and the penetration of specific trading areas.
3. It helps you find more people just like the primary target consumer.
4. It provides media and messaging insights.
5. It provides product use and channel distribution insights.

Strategic Business Insights (SBI) VALS: Another system that helps define target markets beyond the standard demographic definitions is VALS (Values and Lifestyles, a product of SBI). The VALS system separates the population into eight segments, each defined in terms of attitudes, distinct behaviors, and decision-making patterns. The VALS system is made up of two critical concepts for understanding consumers: primary motivation and resources. The combination of motivations and resources determines how a person will express himself or herself in the marketplace as a consumer.

Primary motivation: As defined by VALS, there are three primary motivations that matter for understanding consumer behavior: ideals, achievement, and self-expression. Consumers who are motivated primarily by ideals are guided by knowledge and principles. Consumers who are motivated primarily by achievement look for products and services that demonstrate success to their peers. Consumers who are motivated primarily by self-expression desire social or physical activity, variety, and risk. These motivations provide the necessary basis for communication with the VALS types and for a variety of strategic applications.

Resources: A person's tendency to consume goods and services extends beyond age, income, and education. Energy, self-confidence, intellectualism, novelty seeking, innovativeness, impulsiveness, leadership, and vanity play a critical role. These psychological traits in conjunction with key demographics determine an individual's resources. Various levels of resources enhance or constrain a person's expression of his or her primary motivation.

The chart below shows a VALS framework for segmentation.

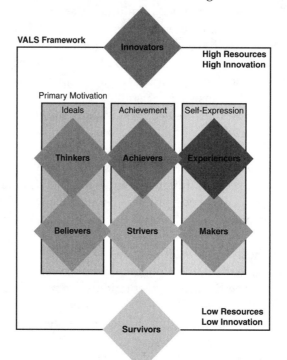

One of the major differences between such systems as the Nielsen PRIZM and VALS is that, whereas the former provides insight into what people do, the latter provides insight into why they do it. Put another way, whereas the Nielsen PRIZM system will help you find the best consumers, the VALS system will help you develop the best message. For that reason, a strong program might be one that makes use of both systems.

Method 5. Attitude Segmentation

Resources like VALS and PRIZM help us develop segments of consumers and customers around attitudes, opinions, and lifestyles. These segments are not defined by age but rather, by specific purchase attitudes or emotions. In our work with Western Publishing, the primary segmentation variable for the game Key to the Kingdom was the desire for adventure in a board game. Boys 8 to 16 bought all types of games, but boys in this age group who liked adventure games purchased Key to the Kingdom. Additionally, males in other age groups who also liked adventure games bought the same game. While the game skewed younger, age alone couldn't define the main purchasing segment.

Whole Foods captures a certain attitudinal target segment around purchasing groceries. The combination of organic options, fresh food, and a more localized, intimate, and connected food purchasing experience appeals across demographics. Go to a Whole Foods store and you'll find young and old, wealthy and students living on a small allowance. The common denominator is the desire for a healthy lifestyle and good health, achieved through taking care of themselves and celebrating what they put into their bodies.

QUESTIONS TO BE ADDRESSED
- Is there a key attitude, activity, lifestyle, or a closely held set of opinions that defines the purchaser segments of your customers and consumers?
- How many industry consumers and company customers are there in each of theses segments? What's your company's penetration?

Method 6. Heavy-User Segmentation
Most product categories have a group of *heavy users*—consumers who purchase or use a product at a far greater rate than that of the average consumers. According to our definition, a category has a meaningful heavy-user segment if approximately one-third or fewer of the consumers account for approximately two-thirds or more of the purchases. A retail example of this can be found in the shoe business, where one-third of the purchasers buy more than 63 percent of the shoes. The demographic description of the heavy-user shoe purchaser is a woman between the ages of 25 and 44 who has children. A heavy-user shoe purchaser is further defined as someone who purchases seven or more pairs of shoes per year. (The average person purchases fewer than three pairs per year.)

Heavy users are important because they offer the potential of marketing to a smaller, more defined group of people who account for the majority of purchases. If you do not have primary research that determines the percent of purchases attributable to heavy users, you can make directional estimates by using information from Experian Simmons, GfK MRI, or other secondary sources. Exhibit 2.21 presents an example of how to calculate a heavy-user segment from either of these resources. Similar methods can be used with other secondary research information. If nothing is available to you, make your best estimate based on your knowledge of the market.

It is also important to determine if there is a heavy-user group in your product category. If so, then develop a demographic profile of the heavy-user group to determine if it is similar to your customer profile.

The chart in Exhibit 2.22 compares the heavy-user demographic profile to the total demographic profile. This is essential information that will help you in making decisions such as whether to focus on a smaller, specialized segment of the market or cater to heavy users. Companies have done well using both approaches, but in either case you need to make sure that there are adequate numbers of potential customers in your defined target market and that you will be able to attract a sufficient number to purchase your product frequently enough to assure profitability. (See the discussion of demand analysis in Chapter 5, "Targets," for further details.)

See Appendix B, Worksheet 21, to help you capture this information.

EXHIBIT 2.21

Example of How to Calculate Heavy-User Segments from Simmons Market Research Bureau (SMRB) Data

Number of Home Plastic Files Purchased per Year*	×	Number of People Purchasing, (000)	=	Total Product Purchased, $ or Units, (000)
1		5,000		5,000
2		4,000		8,000
3		1,000 ⎫		3,000 ⎫
4		1,000 ⎪		4,000 ⎪
5		1,000 ⎬ 4,500		5,000 ⎬ 22,000
6		500 ⎪		3,000 ⎪
7+		1,000 ⎭		7,000 ⎭
Total		13,500		35,000

*Heavy user for home plastic files defined as three-plus purchases per year.

Heavy-User Percentage: To compute, add the number of people purchasing three-plus divided by the total number of people (4,500 ÷ 13,500 = 33%).

Heavy-User Percentage of Purchases: To compute, add the total product purchased by people purchasing three-plus divided by the total product purchased (22,000 ÷ 35,000 = 63%).

Heavy users represent 33 percent of the total population of purchasers and account for 63 percent of the total dollar or unit purchases.

EXHIBIT 2.22

Heavy-User Demographic Descriptors Compared to All User Demographic Descriptors

	Heavy-User Demographic Profile	Total (All Users) Demographic Profile
Age	24–35	18–45
Sex	Female	Female
Household income	$50,000 to $70,000	$25,000 to $70,000
Education	Graduated college+	Graduated high school+
Employment	White collar or professional	White and blue collar
Family size	4+	2+
Geography	Western United States	Midwest and Western United States
Homeownership	Yes	Yes

Note: Lifestyle description of the heavy user compared to the average user: The heavy user is far more socially oriented than the average user. The heavy user is more style conscious and quality driven than the average user. Overall the heavy user is more upscale, with attitudes and purchasing habits shaped by concern over family, neighborhood, and social expectations.

QUESTIONS TO BE ADDRESSED
- Is there a group of heavy purchasers of your product? What percent of the purchasers do they constitute, and for what percent of the purchases are they responsible?
- What is the difference between the demographic and lifestyle and/or attitudinal profiles of the heavy users versus the overall users?
- How many heavy users are there in terms of the industry and in terms of your company's customers?

Review of Business-to-Business Segmentation Methods
Business-to-business firms typically have far fewer existing and potential customers than consumer companies. In addition, each business-to-business customer usually generates larger sales than the typical consumer customer. As with consumer target

markets, it is important to segment so that you can determine which type of business is most profitable and has the most potential for your company and more efficiently market to those customers and prospects.

NAICS Segmentation

One of the best ways to segment businesses is by utilizing the Census Bureau's North American Industry Classification System (NAICS) codes, which were adopted in the late 1990s to replace the old Standard Industrial Classification (SIC) codes. As with the SIC codes, the NAICS classifies businesses into broad categories and then provides subclassifications within each category. The SIC codes included 10 broad categories: Agriculture, Forestry, and Fisheries; Mining; Construction; Manufacturing; Transportation and Communication; Public Utilities; Wholesale Trade; Retail Trade; Finance, Insurance, and Real Estate Services; and Public Administration. Within each two-digit SIC category, there were further breakouts into four-, six-, and eight-digit classifications. For example, within the Retail SIC, category 56 is Apparel and Accessory Stores; and within category 56 there is 5611, Men's and Boys' Clothing.

The NAICS has a total of 20 broad categories with subclassifications within each:

> Agriculture, Forestry, Fishing, and Hunting
> Mining, Quarrying, and Oil and Gas Extraction
> Utilities
> Construction
> Manufacturing
> Wholesale Trade
> Retail Trade
> Transportation and Warehousing
> Information
> Finance and Insurance
> Real Estate and Rental and Leasing
> Professional, Scientific, and Technical Services
> Management of Companies and Enterprises
> Administrative and Support and Waste Management and Remediation
>   Services
> Educational Services
> Health Care and Social Assistance
> Arts, Entertainment, and Recreation
> Accommodation and Food Services
> Other Services (Except Public Administration)
> Public Administration

The subclassifications can be found by going to any number of different websites with drill-down menus. (See Chapter 1, the "Sources of Information" section.) For example, advertising agencies have a six-digit code (541810) within the Professional, Scientific, and Technical Services category, which has a two-digit code (54).

Firms such as Dun's Marketing Services (a Dun & Bradstreet company) and the NAICS Association specialize in providing mailing lists and other market information for businesses according to specific NAICS classifications. We helped generate incremental sales for a statewide CPA firm by determining NAICS categories where its greatest potential was with existing customers and then creating individual campaigns for small businesses within each NAICS code. Differently tailored messages were developed for retailers, service providers, financial institutions, and so on. Each industry received multiple marketing pieces explaining why specialized accounting practices were important for that specific business. The campaign was so successful that for every $1 the CPA firm invested, it had a return of $2—a 100 percent return on investment over a two-year period.

The first step in developing business-to-business target market segments is to break down your customer base by NAICS code. Next, determine how many different business segments you sell to. List the segments in which you have the most customers or clients first, and then continue listing the segments in sequential order from the most customers to the least. Finally, determine the penetration of each segment (percent of the total category that you can classify as a customer). In doing this, you may be surprised to find how fragmented your efforts are against multiple business categories, each one requiring slightly different skills. Further, you may also find that there are some highly profitable segments where you do business with only a small percentage of the total potential, which could represent a large degree of growth potential. This information will help you define target markets and develop marketing strategies later in the plan.

QUESTIONS TO BE ADDRESSED
- To what NAICS segments or other user segments do customers who purchase your product belong?
- What is the demand potential for your product? What is the penetration of your company in each NAICS category? How many businesses that are in NAICS categories that purchase products in your category are not purchasing from you? Why aren't they?
- Which NAICS categories and specific company codes are growing the fastest, are the most profitable for you, and hold the most potential into the future?

Once you have your target market broken into NAICS categories, there are additional criteria you should evaluate to provide for a complete understanding of your target market.

Dollar Size
Determine the total company sales volume for each NAICS code or category in which you do business, and then calculate the average dollar size of each client in the categories. (Divide the total company volume in each NAICS code by the number of clients you have in that NAICS code.)

When combined with the penetration information developed earlier, this can tell you a lot about the current and future potential of the different categories. Exhibit 2.23 provides an overview of clients' revenues within the RETAIL NAICS code. This chart also incorporates additional information by breaking out customers and total

EXHIBIT 2.23
Revenue Distribution of Customers by NAICS Code

NAICS Code	Category	Total Establishments in Total Trading Areas	Enterprises (Headquarters for Multiple-Location Firms)	Total Customers (Enterprise)	Penetration	Total Sales ($000)	Average Dollars per Customer	Index to Average
44–55	Retail	23,000	2,511	1,667	66%	$2,701	$1,620	100
444130	Hardware Stores	10,500	2,257	1,587	70%	$2,381	$1,500	93*
44110	Home Centers	12,500	254	80	31%	$ 320	$4,000	247

*The index of 93 was arrived at by taking the average per customer for hardware stores ($1,500) and dividing it by the average across the retail category ($1,620), or 0.93 × 100 = an index of 93. This is 7 points below the expected 100 index if all were equal to the average of $1,620.

businesses by NAICS codes applicable to this firm's business. If an NAICS code averages substantially above other NAICS codes in terms of average dollar size per client and your company has not fully penetrated that code or category (your company's clients represent a small percentage of the total businesses in the NAICS code), then that classification should be targeted for further expansion. In this example, it's clear that the home centers command further attention due to their lower penetration and their high average-dollars-per-customer index of 247.

See Appendix B, Worksheet 22, to help you capture this information.

Employee Size

Another way to segment businesses is by the number of employees, or employee size, of the firm. Employee size often is an indicator of the company's volume and how it does business. For example, large companies tend to be more centralized and to have formal organizational structures, while small companies tend to be less formal. Pricing, product, and service requirements often differ between large and small companies. Thus, the marketing approach may differ due to a function of the size of the business customer.

Heavy Usage Rates

Are there categories of heavy or light users? Determine the reasons for this. Maybe a category of light users would become heavier users if you modified your product, service, or pricing. Or perhaps you should consider narrowing your firm's focus to concentrate on the heavy-user categories, especially if the earlier analysis determined the potential for growth in these categories.

The chart in Exhibit 2.24 provides the business-to-business firm with an alternative way to look at its business. This chart is for the firm with many types of customers across dealers and distributors. It could also be used to analyze different subcategories within a larger NAICS code. Clearly, from the data presented in the chart, the company would want to look into how it could increase its business in craft stores. The answer may lie in why it does so well in needlecraft stores and discount stores.

See Appendix B, Worksheet 23, to help you capture this information.

Product Application and/or Use

Essentially, this is how the organization uses your product. If you find that there are multiple uses for your product, you can segment target markets by usage type and begin to provide more focused service and expertise to each segment.

EXHIBIT 2.24

Product Category Purchases by Outlet Type

Outlet Type	Where Crafts Are Purchased	Percent of Total Outlets	Company's Business
Business	86%*	21%*	15%
Needlecraft store	67	16	40
Discount store	64	15	30
Mail order	63	15	15
Department store	62	15	—
Craft supply chain store	41	10	—
Art material store	36	9	—
Total	419%*	101%	100%

*86 percent of craft purchasers utilize craft stores to purchase crafts (most craft purchasers utilize more than one outlet, which is why the total equals 419 percent). However, craft stores account for only 21 percent of the total craft outlets and only 15 percent of the company's business.

Organizational Structure

Different companies have different organizational structures. Find out if your company sells better to one type of company than another. You might discover that you get more business from centralized organizations with formal bidding procedures, which would mean that you would want to target these types of businesses within the NAICS category or categories you currently service. You might analyze why you don't do as well with decentralized, entrepreneurial firms and then make changes to increase your success with them. Alternately, you may do well targeting headquarters but perform poorly in generating sales from branches. In summary, you may need to develop independent marketing strategies and executions for different target groups as defined by their organization structure, purchasing habits, and purchasing requirements.

New versus Repeat Buyers

Some companies are good at getting new business and poor at developing long-term relationships. For others, it's just the opposite. Determine the percentage of your business that comes from new buyers versus repeat buyers. Analyze your ability to generate new business or to keep repeat customers. Correct your weaknesses if it becomes evident that you either aren't getting new business or can't develop long-term clients.

This area is a good client satisfaction check and should be analyzed yearly. It also allows you to develop alternative marketing strategies depending on the type of customer (new versus repeat) you are targeting.

Geographic Location

In analyzing sales, you may determine that you are strong in one part of the country but weak in another. It could be the result of your distribution system, it might be caused by a competitive situation, or you may find that demand is higher in some geographical areas than others. In addition, you might discover that you do very well against a particular NAICS category in one region of the country but that you haven't marketed to that NAICS category elsewhere. By analyzing where your current business exists and where you have potential to expand, you can segment your target market by geographic location.

Decision Makers and Influencers

Finally, you need to determine who actually decides to purchase your product and who influences the purchase of your product. Remember, *companies* don't buy products; *people* do. Analyze the purchase decision-making process. Who are the key influencers—the positions and individuals—who shape company decisions? Also decide who makes the ultimate purchasing decision, the purchasing criteria they use, and how they arrive at the purchasing decision. The actual purchaser may in fact be a committee, which means you will need to target many individuals if all have an equal role in the decision process. Typically, the decision makers or purchasers become your primary target market, and those individuals influencing the decision become the secondary target market.

QUESTIONS TO BE ADDRESSED
- How many industry category consumers and company customers are there for each NAICS category or code or other applicable segment you are doing business with currently?
- What is the revenue distribution for the industry category and your company by NAICS code or other applicable segments?

- Based on the preceding two questions, you can now calculate the average dollars of revenue per industry category consumer and company customer. What are they? Which industry category is growing, flattening, or shrinking and why? Will these trends continue?
- What is your company's penetration in each NAICS code or relevant business segment? Do any of the segments with high average dollar sales per customer have low company penetration rates, and do any of the segments hold future potential to capture new customers?
- What size are the companies that purchase from you? Do large companies respond differently than small ones do? If so, why?
- Are there heavy users within your NAICS categories or other relevant target segments? Are some NAICS categories or target segments heavier users than others?
- Do different NAICS category businesses or target segments use your product for different purposes? Why do NAICS category businesses use your product? Is your product used more by some industries, companies, or segments than by others? Is there the potential to expand use to others?
- Are purchasers of your product original equipment manufacturers (OEMs) who utilize your product in the manufacturing of another product? Do they sell to another business or directly to the consumer? How exactly does your product fit into the OEMs' manufacturing structure? Why is your product important? How is it used?
- What is the organizational structure of your customers' companies? Do you have more success with centralized companies than with decentralized? Why? Do purchasing procedures differ among customers? Do you get more business from companies with a single purchasing agent that you do from those with a purchasing committee that requires more formal bidding?
- Are the majority of your customers new or repeat buyers, and why? Do new buyers purchase less or more than repeat buyers, and why? Do they respond differently to your marketing efforts? Why?
- Where are your customers located? Are there areas of the country that have businesses from NAICS categories with which you are successful but that you currently are not covering? Are there potential customers that match your customer profile that you are not reaching? Do some parts of the country provide more business for you than others? If so, why? Is it due to servicing, distribution, sales efforts, or competitive factors? Or do some parts of the country use more product than other parts for other reasons?
- Who are the decision makers and influencers in the purchase of your product? What is the decision makers' function and role in the purchase decision? What is the decision sequence? What are the purchase criteria?

TASK 2 ## Awareness, Knowledge, and Attitudes

We have documented in case after case that an increase in awareness of a quality product leads to increases in purchase rates, or, said another way, *an increase in share of mind leads to an increase in share of market*. Therefore, awareness of your product or service is an important barometer of its future success.

Product Awareness

Awareness is typically measured through primary research on two levels, unaided and aided. *Unaided awareness* is generally considered a more accurate measure because it involves consumers' recalling specific product names without any assistance. *Aided awareness* is the awareness generated by asking individuals which product they are familiar with after reading or reviewing with them a list of competing products.

When analyzing awareness, we typically review the following levels in order of importance.

Unaided Awareness

First mention, top of mind: This is the awareness level that will most closely parallel the market share. It is obtained through telephone research in which the interviewers ask respondents which products or companies come to mind in a specific product category—shoes, propellers, spray-dried ingredients, toothpastes, car repairs, legal services, banking services, and so on. The respondents mention the companies, firms, or products with which they are familiar, the *first* one mentioned being the first mention or top of mind.

Typically, the first mentioned company or product is the first choice or the one most recently purchased—a direct correlation to shopping intent. Try this yourself. Ask a couple of friends to name the pizza takeout restaurant that comes to mind. Since the category is a broad one and people do shop around, they'll probably mention three to four. Now ask them which one they prefer or go to most often. You'll find that the majority of the time, the first mentioned is also the one that they prefer and spend the most money with when purchasing pizza.

Total unaided: All companies or products mentioned without prompting are part of what is known as the *evoked purchase set*—considerations when the respondents purchase. In situations in which several companies or products are mentioned in your unaided survey question mentioned in the first mention section above, it is an indication that the category exhibits less loyalty from its purchasers and that there is more shopping around. This fact should be noted and used strategically later in the marketing plan. For example, in nonloyal categories, special promotions with strong after-purchase retention programs are often heavily used to steal market share and customers.

Aided Awareness

Once respondents have provided unaided responses, the interviewers can ask, "Have you ever heard of _____?" If the respondents say yes, it is considered aided awareness. We feel this is a very weak measure of association or familiarity with a company or product. However, it does serve as a disaster check. If, after prompting, the respondents have not heard of your product or company, there is little chance they will be purchasers or customers of the products or services they have been asked about.

Knowledge

Just being aware of your company or product is often not enough. The final measure of awareness is actual knowledge. We've worked with many companies who say, "Our awareness is very high. We just don't understand why we're not doing better." A large credit union was in this situation. People in a key secondary target market that had little penetration were aware of the credit union, but they had little real knowledge of its products and services or even that they were eligible for membership.

Awareness by Segments

The awareness measures need to be broken out by the target segments developed in the target market section. You may find vastly different degrees of awareness from one segment to the next, signifying a need for different communication strategies and spending levels if in your plan you have more than one target segment.

Some examples of how awareness is used to help formulate subsequent marketing strategies are the following:

- *Low awareness:* Low awareness levels signal the need for a more aggressive or sometimes a more effective advertising and promotional plan that breaks through to the target market. This is especially true if the product has positive attribute ratings (it's liked) from current users and it has a high trial-to-repeat usage ratio (strongly loyal customers).
- *High awareness:* Markets with high levels of awareness often don't need as much media weight to sustain existing sales levels as those markets that have low awareness. It often requires less media weight to generate successful promotions in established markets with high awareness than in newer markets, where a customer base is not yet established and only a minimal number of potential consumers have heard of your product or company. As an example, markets in which a product has low awareness often require larger print ads than those designed for markets with higher awareness levels. Our experience has shown that small newspaper ads are more likely to be seen by current users and that it takes larger ads to attract the attention of noncustomers, infrequent users, or individuals who are not aware of your product.
- *Falling awareness:* Markets with falling awareness levels often indicate isolated, market-specific problems such as increased competitive activity. These problems may require an individual market plan tailored to the specific market situation, along with investment spending over the short term to stabilize and increase awareness levels.

While we would always err on the side of having a professional researcher help you with your insight work, if you cannot afford primary research, you can informally conduct an awareness study for your product. Randomly call individuals in your geographic selling area. Ask them if they have used products and frequented stores in your category in the past year. If they have, ask them to name all the stores in the area where they can purchase the product category or to name all the brands (or companies) they are familiar with in the product category (unaided awareness measure). Try to get between 150 and 200 responses for statistical purposes. Also keep track of first mentions (those products or stores mentioned first by each respondent without assistance), as this is a good prediction of your company's market share relative to the competition.

With this information you can infer what percent of the potential customer base is aware of your product and where it ranks relative to the competition. This will provide a rough approximation of unaided awareness levels for your product and the competition. You can also determine the first mention level, a strong indication of market share, actual use of the product, or propensity to use.

See Appendix B, Worksheet 24, to help you capture this information.

QUESTIONS TO BE ADDRESSED
- What is the unaided and aided awareness of your product among the various target market segments in your industry and among your customers? How do those awareness levels compare to those of your competition? Have awareness levels been increasing or decreasing over the past five years?

- What is the first mention level of awareness (first product mentioned) within each target market segment? Has the first mention awareness level for your company, product, or service been increasing or decreasing over the past five years?

Product Attributes and Attribute Importance by Segment

Product attributes or benefits are derived from consumers' perceptions of the product. It is important to identify which attributes are significant to the purchasing segments and users of your product and then to determine how your company or product compares to the competition on these attributes. There may be attributes that you need to improve for certain segments, or you may find there are certain needs that no one in the marketplace is fulfilling, which will give your company the opportunity to dominate an important niche or purchasing segment.

The repositioning of a menswear chain we worked with was brought about because of insights into the changing attitudes of men toward clothing and styles. Especially important were two factors. First is the fact that most men are not good dressers and not very good shoppers. While most successful businessmen are full of confidence, they lack confidence when it comes to picking out a winning wardrobe. And second is the insight around the changing attitudes toward wearing suits and sports coats and the business casual trends that were affecting the workplaces from Wall Street to the country club to the corporate offices of America. The repositioning of this regional chain tied into the importance of looking good but not stuffy—with it but not disheveled—in a business setting that was rapidly changing. The positioning focused around the idea of "businessmenswear," with emphasis on trend-right quality and business casual fashion expertise for today's businessmen.

Rational Attributes

The first step is to determine which attributes are the most important for each target market segment you are analyzing. For example, with research we did in the highly technical computer diagnostic business, product reliability, service response time, and ease of use were the top required attributes for the research and development target segment, with price, state-of-the-art design, supplier reputation, upgradeability, and application support being more important to the purchasing agents. For a dominant manufacturer of garage doors, reliability was the key attribute, and for a local nonprofit organization, local accountability and program results were the most important attributes.

Emotional Attributes

In addition to ranking the rational attributes, marketers can develop a list of the most important emotional reasons customer segments purchase. For example, the women customers of a large HMO desired partnership. When we explored what that meant, it translated into the willingness to accept the fact that the patient has to do his or her share to stay healthy in today's medical climate. But the doctor has to be willing to listen and should not treat the patient simply as a number or as a disease. In this case, partnership meant two-way communication.

For another client, the American dream was defined by consumers as freedom from debt and financial responsibilities no matter what the individual's income level or potential. This powerful concept became the focus of a very successful and long-standing brand positioning for a regional bank.

For a national auto repair shop we discovered the pride owners of used cars have in getting their car yet another mile and another. "I've got 175,000 miles on my car." "I've got over 200,000 miles on my car!" This led to a brand positioning around the complete auto care capability of getting your used but loved car that extra mile—a sort of used-car dealership where the same care and pride of workmanship is given your used car as the new-car dealer provides for new cars.

Attribute Ranking by Segment

Next, rank your company against the most important attributes of the high-potential target segments relative to the competition. This ranking is typically discovered through survey research. Ready Crisp bacon, for example, was able to say that "fast, no mess cooking" was the number one desired attribute from its most important target segment. In the end, the company judged its product's success on whether it either did or did not perform on these two attributes—fast and no mess. This type of analysis, based on the realities of the marketplace, puts the consumer in the position of guiding the direction the company takes.

Methodologies to Help You Determine Attribute Importance

Note: Chapter 6, "Positioning," has many mapping and matching examples to help you determine both rational and emotional attributes by target segments.

See Appendix B, Worksheet 25, to help you capture this information.

QUESTIONS TO BE ADDRESSED
- How is your product used? What is the product's primary benefit to the industry category consumer segments?
- What does each target segment like and dislike about your product? What are the benefits each target segment likes about your product? How do these compare relative to your competitors' offerings?
- What are the important emotional and rational attributes of your company's industry category against each target segment? How do your company's products or services rank on those attributes versus the competition on a segment-by-segment basis?
- Are there differences between heavy users' likes and dislikes as compared to the other user segments of your product category?
- Are there substitutes that can be used in place of your company's product or the product category?

TASK 3 ## *Behavior*

The third task in Step 5, "Consumer and Customer Review," concerns the behaviors of consumers and customers toward your company and its products and services.

Trial

Trial equates to customers. When consumers have tried your products, they are then considered customers. But within trials, there are several measures that provide additional insights that will be used in your plan: customer penetration, awareness penetration, purchase frequency ratio, and average-dollars-per-customer ratio.

Customer Penetration

Of the total number of potential users (target segment universe), how many are customers, or what is your customer penetration? Target market segments that should be looked to for future penetration and growth are those with strong sales per customer, where the segment is growing in size, and where the target's needs and wants align with your company's capabilities and focus.

Awareness Penetration

Of those that are aware of you, how many are customers? That is, what is your awareness penetration? It's very telling if you have a large awareness but very little penetration. The fact that the percentage of consumers who are aware of your products and services and are also converted to customers is small would signal a potential product or service problem. It could also be a signal that you have chosen to position your brand along benefits that aren't as meaningful as those of your competition.

See Appendix B, Worksheet 26, to help you capture this information.

Purchase Frequency Ratio

How frequently do your customers purchase compared to the industry category average? If you're a retailer, how often do your customers visit, and what percent of those visits turn into purchases?

Average-Dollars-per-Customer Ratio

What are your customers' average dollars per purchase and total dollars spent compared to that of the industry category averages?

See Appendix B, Worksheets 27 and 28, to help you capture some of this information.

QUESTIONS TO BE ADDRESSED
- What percent of the consumer segments have tried the product category?
- What percent of your customer segment has tried your products?
- What is the customer penetration for each important target segment (percent of customers who have tried your product in the past year divided by the total number of potential consumers in each target segment)?
- Of the number of consumers who are aware of your company, products, or services, what percent has tried your product in the past year?
- What is the average dollars per customer for your company's customer segments? Do you have customer segments that perform from an average-dollars-per-customer figure significantly lower than the industry average for those target segments? Have the average dollars per customer been going up or down over the past five years?
- What is the average number of purchases per year, dollar size per purchase, and quantity (number of units if applicable to your business) of each purchase for the industry consumer segments and for your customer segments? What have been the trends for these metrics over the past five years?
- How frequently are purchases made? What is the purchase cycle for your products or services in the industry compared to your company? What is the frequency of purchase for heavy users versus other segments?
- For the retailer, what is the average number of visits per customer per year, and what is the resulting purchase ratio from those visits?
- Do consumers purchase in bulk, stocking up, or do they purchase your products one at a time?
- What is the purchase ratio among industry consumer and customer segments? What percent of consumers and customers purchase when they visit the store or office or receive a sales call? Has it gone up or down over the past five years?
- Is the buying decision spontaneous or planned? What percent of the buying decisions are made at the point of purchase versus at home or over time?
- Is buying by brand name important to consumers in your category? What percent of the consumers in the category are brand loyal most of the time, all of the time, or never?

Retrial

While trials signal conversion of an industry category consumer to an actual company customer, retrials provide insights into brand loyalty. Brand loyalty or retrial provides insights into the following issues:

- How difficult it will be to keep your own customers
- How difficult it will be to steal market share from competitors
- The amount and degree of promotional offers that will be needed to induce trial
- How much media weight will be necessary to increase trial, retrial, and sales
- Whether a true product difference or innovation is needed to compete

If you have extremely high brand loyalty from your customers, your competitors will have to use more media weight, larger promotional offers or inducements, and perhaps even a product innovation in order to steal customers and market share from you. However, if you have low brand loyalty from your customers, it is extremely difficult to keep your own customers. Looked at from a different angle, in industry categories that exhibit low brand loyalty within the category, it is also easier to steal market share through promotional efforts and incentives. Typically strong-brand-loyalty industry categories require more sophisticated brand building efforts as consumers purchase or choose to remain loyal due to nonprice issues related to perceived emotional and product or service benefits.

The following are important brand loyalty measures for you to detail in your business review.

Awareness-to-Trial Ratio

This is a very meaningful measure that examines the percent of customers or prospects in any given target segment that are aware of your company's products or services versus the percentage of those same people who have actually used or tried your company's products or services. If you have a high awareness level but a poor conversion or trial percentage, then you need to examine all the parts of your business—from product to after-sales service and everything else in between—to determine the key problem area.

Trial-to-Retrial Ratio

This is the first of two brand loyalty measures we will discuss. An important area of investigation is trial and retrial by consumer and customer segments. The trial-to-retrial ratio describes the number of people who tried the product to the number of those who also purchased it again at a later date. For example, if 100 people try the product and only 10 purchase it again, the ratio would be 10 percent. This would signal a potential problem.

We did work for a dominant national packaged-goods client that had a specialty line of consumer packaged goods. The products sold were basically the same, but each was packaged for specific uses—packages for the car, the teenager's bedroom, dad's work area, and the woman's purse. The initial thinking was that we would expand usage categories for the products. However, after studying the buying habits of purchasers in the business review, we discovered two things:

1. The overall trial of the family of products was very low.
2. Of those people who tried the products, retrial was very high.

EXHIBIT 2.25

Trial-to-Retrial Ratio

Brand	Percent Ever Used	Percent Used Last 6 Months	Loyalty Measure: Percent Used Last 6 Months/Percent Ever Used
Company X			
A	81%	48%	59%
Competition X			
B	58	22	38
C	43	17	40
D	30	15	50
E	25	17	68

Note: Brand A has a much higher trial (ever used), retrial (used last six months), and thus loyalty rate than any competitor with the exception of Brand E. However, while Brand E has a strong loyalty measure (68), it has a low initial trial figure, a problem that should receive primary attention in the marketing plan.

The challenge in the subsequent marketing plan was not to find more uses for the family of products but to promote trial. Once consumers tried the products, the chances were good they would continue to purchase them. However, if we had found that the retrial rate was in fact very poor, we would have had another set of product-related problems on which to focus and our marketing emphasis would have needed to go in the direction of finding out why customers weren't satisfied with the products. The chart in Exhibit 2.25 provides a summary of trial-to-retrial (consumer acceptance) percentages (found through sources such as Experian Simmons or your own primary research).

See Appendix B, Worksheet 26, to help you capture this information.

Brand Loyalty Ratio

The second brand loyalty measure is a brand loyalty ratio or index that shows the percent of customers who use only your products compared to those who use primarily your products compared to those who don't consider your products either solely or as a primary brand. You can find these data using Experian Simmons or GfK MRI databases, as described in Chapter 1.

There often exists a unique way to measure loyalty by industry. In banking, the *primary financial institution* (PFI) is a critical measure. The determinant of a PFI is sometimes obtained by using survey research and asking which institution is the respondent's primary financial institution. However, the easier way is to simply determine the percent of customers who have a checking account, debit card, or direct deposit with a particular financial institution. A checking account, debit card, or direct deposit will tend to predict whether an individual will have multiple accounts in that bank.

The chart in Exhibit 2.26 provides a measure of the brand loyalty that exists within a hypothetical product category. As mentioned above, this type of information can be obtained for many product categories by using Experian Simmons or GfK MRI

EXHIBIT 2.26

Brand Loyalty Ratio

Brand	All	Sole	Loyalty Index	Sole and Primary	Loyalty Index
Cooper	16.4%	2.7%	16	11.6%	71
Hiebing	12.9	2.6	20	9.5	74
Dorton	11.5	1.2	10	6.9	60
Michaels	9.9	1.9	19	6.0	60

databases (see Chapter 1, "Sources of Information" section). For example, 9.9 percent of all purchasers use the Michaels brand while 1.9 percent use only the Michaels brand. The resulting loyalty index of 19 (1.9/9.9) compares favorably to the other brands in the category. However the category as a whole does not exhibit strong loyalty.

See Appendix B, Worksheet 29, to help you capture this information.

QUESTIONS TO BE ADDRESSED
- Are you converting customers? What is the awareness-to-trial ratio—the percent of your total target (customers and prospects) who are aware of your company or product and also have tried it or become a customer over the past year?
- What is the brand loyalty for your company, product, or service? Do your customers purchase and then remain loyal or do they go elsewhere? What is the trial-to-retrial ratio of industry category consumer segments? How many customers purchase from you and then purchase again once, twice, three times, or more? What is the repurchase ratio for your customer segments (note, you need to determine what repurchase rate is appropriate—1 time per year, 2 times, . . . , 10 times or more, and so on)? Is brand switching common? Are there different target segments that demonstrate different degrees of loyalty? What percent of your customers only purchase from you and no other competitor? How many primarily purchase from you the majority of the time?
- Do heavy users have different loyalty than the overall users?

Putting the Pieces Together: The Hierarchy of Effectors Model

Now, you're ready to use a consumer research model we call the Hierarchy of Effectors. It focuses on helping you organize insights around the relationships between the following:

- Your primary target market segments
- The awareness of your company and its products and services in each segment
- The attitudes toward your company and its products and services in each segment
- The behavior in terms of trial of your company's products and services and the retrial or loyalty of each segment

Once you've either measured through a survey that uses a sample size providing you confidence that the results are an accurate predictor for your total universe of customers and prospects or you have developed best guesstimates for these components, you are in a position to use the information to drive critical insights. These insights will help you position your product and set meaningful marketing and communication objectives later in the plan.

Exhibit 2.27 shows the typical relationships between the components of awareness, attitude, and behavior for a specific target market segment. In almost all cases, the total number for each of the effector components drops. Awareness is lower than target, attitudes are lower than awareness, trial is lower than attitudes, and retrial is lower than trial. Therefore, each successive component of the effectors model is less than the previous.

There Are Exceptions

As just discussed, typically consumers become aware of you, then form an attitude, then decide to purchase, and then decide if they will become loyal and purchase again or make your brand their brand of choice. However, this is not true of all categories. A good example of a product for which this scenario would not play out would be chewing gum. Gum is an impulse item: Customers decide whether or not

EXHIBIT 2.27

Target Market Effectors: What's Needed and How to Use It

Target Market	Awareness	Attitude	Behavior (Trial and Retrial)
Work to Do in the Business Review			
• Describe all major category and company target market segments • Define number of potential consumers and customers in each segment • Determine sales volume and profits accountable to each segment	• Determine target market segment awareness for the company versus competition	• Determine attitude toward company by target market segment through determining company product ranking on attributes most important to those segments • Determine company product ranking relative to competitors by comparing ranking on important attributes for your company to those of your competitors	• Average purchase amount and frequency of purchase for each industry consumer and company segment • Trial and retrial per industry and company segment • Decision-making process for each industry and company segment
Use in the Marketing Plan			
• Defining target market segments	• Communication awareness goals (example: increase in unaided awareness from 26 to 33%) • Communication strategies • Spending strategies	• Communication attitude goals (example: shift in attitude rating from 12 to 17%) • Communication strategies • Spending strategies • Product strategies	• Establish marketing objectives (example: increase in purchase frequency from 1.5 times per year at $38 to 2.0 times per year at $45)

to try a new gum in the grocery store checkout line. In this case, the sequence goes from awareness to trial. Then an attitude is formed, and the decision is made whether or not to retry the product. However, for most other types of products, the hierarchy of effectors describes the sequence of events, which go from awareness to attitude formation to initial trial to retrial.

Hierarchy of Effectors Components
The components of the hierarchy shown in the figure below are discussed in the following section.

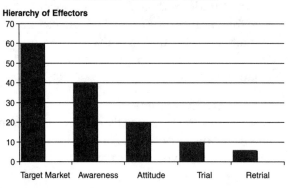

Consumer Behavior Model

Target market segment: The first component of the model is the total universe of the target market segment you are reviewing (the numbers on the left side of the chart could stand for some total number of customers and could be in thousands, millions, tens of millions, or hundreds of millions depending upon your industry category).

Awareness: Some portion of the total consumers in the segment, but not all, will be aware of your company and its products or services.

Attitudes: Of those who are aware, a smaller portion will have strong, positive attitudes toward your company. Attitudes are typically measured around what is most important to the consumers of this segment and also what your company has chosen to stand for within this segment to differentiate. For example, you may be in the financial category of banking. Based on your efforts to be relevant to a large target segment and to differentiate along a dimension that is very important to a large number of both customers and consumers in the segment, you have chosen *ease of banking* as your brand value promise. This might have been determined because of the poverty of time people experience, where today is busier than yesterday. An ability to take a fairly transactional business like banking and make it less time consuming is seen as a great emotional value to people. It gives them a precious commodity, time, to do with whatever they want. To this end, you might have developed an industry-leading Internet banking service, a 24-hour call center, and many other features that provide the benefit of *ease of banking* to your customers. As head of your bank's marketing department, you would be very interested in measuring how you score on *ease of doing business* in total and in comparison to your competitive set. You'd want to know, of those aware of your bank, what percent ranked you number one or very high on attributes that correlated with making banking easy.

Trial and retrial: The next relationship to examine is the total consumers in the segment who have a positive attitude about you. Then you would determine what percent have tried you (or already are customers), and what percent exhibit the behavior of retrial (that is, they are loyal customers). Loyal customers in one industry might be determined by the number of times they repurchase over three-year periods—perhaps loyal customers repurchase every three years. In another industry, loyal customers might be determined by the total number of times they shop at your store or repurchase your products or services over a one-year period. In still another industry, such as the banking example above, loyal customers might be determined by whether they consider your bank as their primary financial institution or whether they have three or more accounts with your bank.

Using the Model Later in the Plan

Let's look at how you will use the information you have gathered in the Hierarchy of Effectors model later in your marketing plan.

Awareness problem: Look at the figure below. What seems to be the problem for this company?

Consumer Behavior Model

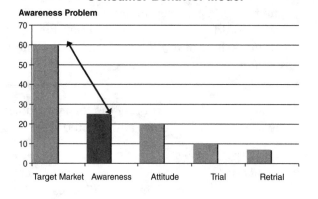

Here there is a big gap between the number of people in the segment and the percent who are aware of your product or company. Yet of those who are aware, most have a positive attitude, and there also is not a big dropoff from trial to retrial. Clearly there is an awareness problem, and this is the area that must be solved before the company can attract new customers.

Attitude and product problem: Next look at the figure below. What needs to be done here?

Consumer Behavior Model

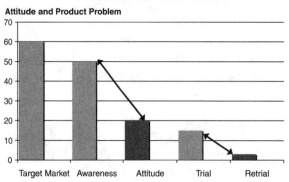

This is a different situation. Here, a very sizable percent of the total target segment universe is aware of the company or product, but very few of those aware have positive attitudes. Of those who do have positive attitudes and have tried the product, very few show loyalty or try the product again. There clearly exists a product, service, or after-sale customer service problem.

If, on the other hand, the relationship between trial and retrial had been strong, and the only gap was between awareness and attitudes, the problem would be isolated as negative perceptions, not product issues. The job then would be to change perceptions.

Summary of How to Use the Hierarchy of Effectors Model

The following figure summarizes the components of the Hierarchy of Effectors model showing where each of the plan objectives of sales, marketing, and communication are determined and the elements of each.

Each step of the hierarchy is used in specific sections of the marketing plan. The target market section helps define the target market and its size later in the plan. The middle two sequences, awareness and attitudes, provide information needed to establish communication objectives and strategies. The behavior sequence is used to develop marketing objectives because marketing objectives affect target market behavior, which quantitatively translates the behavior back to sales.

Insights

Using the Hierarchy of Effectors Model

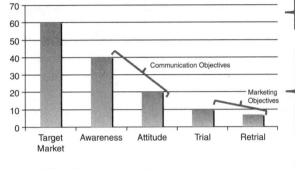

Hierarchy of Effectors and Measuring Plan Objectives

Target Market Metrics

Target market: Total potential customer number by segment, number of customers and penetration by segment, growth of segment

Marketing Objectives

Trial: Increase percent of consumers in the segment that purchases.

Acquisition lapsed customers: Get lapsed customers to purchase again.

Increase purchases from existing customers: Amount and frequency increases.

Retention: Retention and referrals increase.

Communication Objectives

Awareness: Top-of-mind, unaided, and knowledge measures

Attitude: Rational and emotional attributes, relevancy, brand esteem, differentiation measures

Sales Objectives: Sales total the sum of the target market segment's behavior in the marketing objectives.

STEP 6. COMPETITIVE REVIEW

Insights: What Can We Learn?

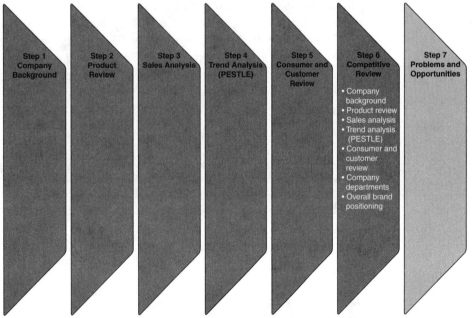

This competitive analysis section is designed to provide you with a summary of how your company is performing in comparison to the competition across key marketing and communication variables. This step forces you to consider strategic and tactical differences and similarities in product marketing between your company and the competition by using the information you have compiled during your business review process. This knowledge will provide insights into potential defensive or offensive strategies that you can include in the marketing plan to capitalize on clear advantages you have or curtail or exploit a major competitor's strength or weakness.

How to Organize and Analyze Competitive Information

The competitive review follows the six steps of your business review, allowing you to consolidate the insights into findings across strengths, weaknesses, opportunities, and threats. In addition, make sure to review the previous two years and, if possible, to project competitive activity into the future. Past years' successes and failures for both your company and your competitors can be great learning tools.

You should also consider the results of your marketing testing and research and development program. Did you introduce any new products, line extensions, services, merchandise, or store concepts in the previous year? Did you test different approaches in your advertising message? Did you test the use of new and/or investment spending? Did you test various promotional offers? What can you learn from past tests that can be translated into future success? If you have been doing the same things year after year, you should explore new uses of your marketing tools to ensure a competitive edge that will help guarantee increased sales and profits year after year.

We encourage you to attend trade shows, shop your competition by purchasing your competitors' products, use clipping services to keep up with key competitors, read the 10-K reports (highly detailed annual reports available when you write for an annual report or request one from the company's website), talk with the trade association journal editors and writers, and be a customer—shop the competition, regularly.

In addition, there is a lot to be learned from media representatives regarding the media expenditures of your competitors. Exhibit 2.28 provides a review of competitive spending as compared hypothetically to your company. The example utilizes banks in a given market and traces share of voice or media spending by dollar amount over a two-year period.

See Appendix B, Worksheet 30, to help you capture this information.

Competitive analyses are not easy to complete because it is often difficult to obtain specific information about competitors. However, you can use secondary sources, some of which are listed in part of this chapter. There are also suggestions for obtaining competitive information at the end of the section detailing where to find sources of information.

EXHIBIT 2.28

Annual Competitive Spending Analysis

Institution	Total Dollar Expenditures	Share of Spending: Total Expenditures, %	Change from Last Year, %
City S&L	$200,000	11%	+10%
First Bank			
State Bank			
Farmer's Bank			
United S&L			

Media	Total Dollar Expenditures	Share of Spending: Total Expenditures, %	Change from Last Year, %
Television	$100,000	20%	+20%
Newspaper	50,000	10	−10
Magazine	10,000	15	—
Radio	30,000	15	+4
Outdoor	10,000	12	−30
Internet media	3,000	5	+25

Note: The above information should also be obtained on a quarterly basis to track seasonality of spending. If available, total dollars for each category should also be obtained.

Competitive Strengths, Weaknesses, Opportunities, and Threats (SWOT) Analysis

Exhibit 2.29 provides an outline for a competitive SWOT analysis. It follows the six steps and reviews of your business review as a guideline for consolidating the

EXHIBIT 2.29

Competitive SWOT Analysis

| | STRENGTHS | | | |
	Your Company	Competitor 1	Competitor 2	Competitor 3
Company Background				
Corporate and company history				
Corporate and company mission				
Corporate and company goals				
Organizational structure				
Product Review				
Product assessment				
Product portfolio				
Product life cycle				
Sales Analysis				
Market category				
Competitors				
Company				
Channels of distribution				
Sales representative or broker network				
Price				
Geography				
Trend Analysis (PESTLE)				
Political				
Economic				
Social (consumer)				
Technological				
Legal				
Environmental				
Consumer and Customer Review				
Target market segments				
Awareness				
Knowledge				
Attitudes				
Behavior				
Company Departments				
Media spending				
Customer service				
Marketing				
Sales function				
Technology				
Other				
Overall Brand Positioning				

Note: Set up and complete the same table for each of the other three components of SWOT: weaknesses, opportunities, and threats.

insights and helping to interpret their meaning. In addition to the six business review steps, there is a section that covers departments that touch the consumer—examples would be the media department allowing for a media strategy and spending review and customer service. Finally, there is an overall category called "brand positioning" that allows you to provide a big-picture review of your company's positioning in the marketplace relative to your competitors.

See Appendix B, Worksheet 31, to help you capture this information.

QUESTIONS TO BE ADDRESSED
Company Background
- What parts of your company's or product's history are different from your competitors' and are most relevant to your customers today? Are there stories from your company's history that contribute to the values and worldview of your company that are also a significant part of your customers' values and worldview? Do you have a unique, authentic company history that provides a competitive advantage?
- What about your company's organizational structure is advantageous to the way you can connect and serve your customers' needs and wants? What is not advantageous or is therefore a weakness? Why?

Product Review
- Compared to your key competitors, what are your product and service strengths and weaknesses? Are there new products that are emerging in the marketplace that will create relative weaknesses or future risks for your products? What will you be doing differently into the future that will add to your product strengths and create opportunities?
- In reviewing the Boston Consulting Group product matrix you constructed (cash cows, stars, question marks, and dogs), are there strengths and weaknesses, risks and opportunities that are evident? Do you have more cash cows or dogs now than you did in the past? Is your company growing emerging stars, or are there more question marks than products that provide you definitive direction? Are there competitive product strengths, weaknesses, or threats that you see? Are there competitive products that present opportunities?

Sales Analysis
- Are there opportunities or risks in the past or future sales trends for your company relative to the market category or your key competitors?
- Do specific individual products show more positive growth and sales momentum for reasons that can be sustained into the future? Are there products that look like they are slowing in terms of sales growth or shrinking significantly compared to competitive offerings?
- Are you gaining market share against key target segments that are growing or are most profitable? Is there a threat to key products and key segments from a specific or new competitive product?
- Does there exist a strong seasonality skew in your industry category? What threat does this pose, and what opportunity? Is the whole industry category affected by the seasonality swings, or are your products affected more severely?
- Are there channels that are growing or poised for growth? Are you competitive in these channels? Will new and emerging channels pose a threat in any way? What would be the opportunities, and why would you be able to take better advantage of them than your competition?
- Does your sales rep or broker network provide you with a strength or weakness? Why? Are there risks or opportunities associated with your selling platform?

- How much does price play in the decision making of your primary target market segments? Is your product price elastic or inelastic? Are the price lines (the range where you price your product) shifting up or down? Are higher-priced or luxury products growing faster than value or lower-priced product categories? What risks or opportunities does this provide you and your company?
- How does the geography of sales affect your future in terms of risks and opportunities? Are there areas where the industry category consumption is very high relative to yours? Why? What weaknesses must you overcome? Conversely, are there areas where you are strong and the category is also strong and growing? Again, why? What strengths exist that lead to this situation?

Trend Analysis (PESTLE)
- What company strengths, weaknesses, risks, and opportunities emerged from the PESTLE analysis relative to your key competitors?

Consumer and Customer Review
- After reviewing the consumer model and links between the various components of the Hierarchy of Effectors, what strengths and weaknesses, risks, and opportunities exist due to the primary target segments where you are strongest or weakest? Are there issues with your ability to penetrate your best segments?
- Are there awareness, attitude, and/or trial and retrial issues for specific target market segments? Are there awareness, attitude, and/or trial or retrial issues relative to your key competitors?

Company Departments
- Is your share of voice comparable, weaker, or stronger than that of your key competitors? What risk or opportunities does this present?
- Do your competitors have significantly different media strategies? What are they doing, and does this make them more effective? Is your ability to partner with media companies a firmwide strength or a weakness? Are there trends emerging in this area that will lead to a competitive strength or weakness?
- Is your customer service, marketing, sales function, technology, or other department a strength or weakness relative to the competition? What's emerging that will create a risk or an opportunity?

Overall Brand Positioning
- Look at your overall brand positioning in the marketplace. Is this a strength or a weakness? Why? Will it lead to opportunities? If so, what are they? Are there weaknesses inherent in the brand positioning that affect your company? If so, what are they?

BUSINESS REVIEW WRITING STYLE

Now that you have answered the questions in each section and completed the charts, it is best to summarize the important findings from each section. This is helpful for two reasons:

1. It is much easier to isolate problems and opportunities (as you'll be doing in Chapter 3) if the business review has been condensed and summarized.
2. The summary statements provide a good management summary and support during presentations.

See Appendix B, Worksheet 32, to help you capture this information.

We have found that there are no real shortcuts in preparing a business review. Marketing is very broad, and marketers need to look at relationships among many numbers in order to come to sound conclusions about the company, the marketplace, the competition, and the consumers' needs and wants.

We recommend developing summary statements for each section of the business review. They should precede each section, where they will serve as summaries for management when the final business review is ready for presentation. Your summary statements should be objective. This is no place for developing strategy. Keep the statements concise and focused on the facts.

Examples summarizing major findings for a canning company would be as follows:

Target market effectors—target market example: Canned-vegetable consumption is dominated by medium and heavy users. Of all canned-goods purchases, 37 percent of all the people who buy groceries account for over 65 percent of the canned-goods vegetables used per month.

Target market effectors—trial-retrial example: Canned vegetables are used by a high percentage (80 percent) of households. Canned vegetables are a relatively high usage category. Fifty-nine percent of homemakers use 4 or more cans per month. Twenty-nine percent use 10 or more cans per month. Thirteen percent use 16 or more cans per month.

Product or market review—sales example: While the canned-tomato category has increased dramatically (140 percent) for the industry over the past five years, Company X has experienced only moderate growth (20 percent). This is far below the industry growth pattern.

DOS AND DON'TS

Do

- Take as much time as possible to compile the business review insights. It will make writing the remainder of the plan much easier and far more effective.
- Make sure each chart you prepare has a descriptive title that explains the purpose of the chart.
- As you work on your business review, keep a notebook nearby in which to jot down ideas for the marketing plan, as detailed in the Introduction. Also keep a list of problems and opportunities that stem from working with the data. Doing this gives you a head start in writing the plan.
- Remember that people buy stories, not just facts and figures. You only have so much time in developing your business review, so make it count. Each piece of information you find should be relevant to the story you're ultimately telling in your marketing plan. You'll be a better storyteller if you take the time up front to prioritize what is most critical to find, then stay focused on finding these insights before you move on to things of lesser importance.

Don't

- Don't just collect information. As you develop your business review insights, start formulating ideas and strategy direction. Based on this direction, make decisions and set priorities against what additional information you need to find that will either strengthen your initial strategy direction or push you in another direction. Simply gathering data for data's sake will get you nowhere. Think like a marketer from the very beginning.

- Don't follow a mission statement based around profit goals. The profits will come if you accomplish something that customers need and want. Your vision and mission should be externally focused not internally focused. The business review's purpose is to provide you with that external viewpoint. In developing a business review, you are bringing the customer to the decision-making table.
- Don't develop a marketing plan without first thoroughly understanding your target market, your product, and your marketing environment.

The Successful Marketing Plan

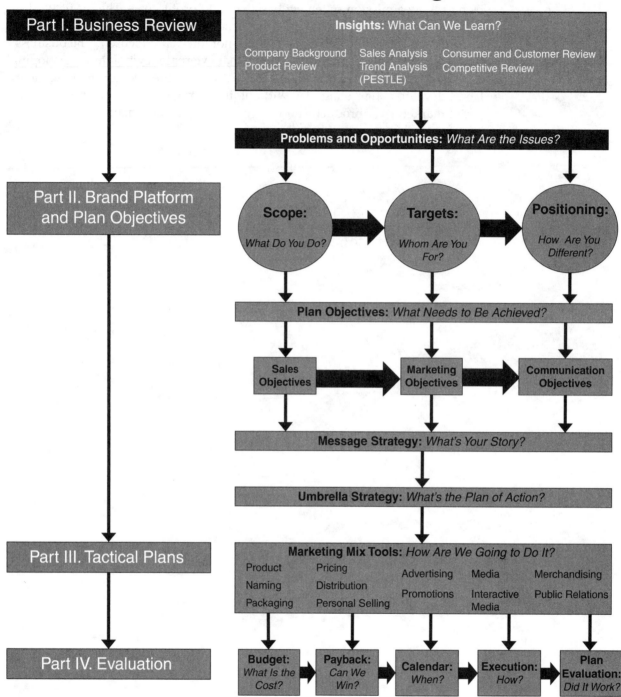

Part I. Business Review

Insights: *What Can We Learn?*

Company Background
Product Review

Sales Analysis
Trend Analysis
(PESTLE)

Consumer and Customer Review
Competitive Review

Problems and Opportunities: *What Are the Issues?*

Part II. Brand Platform and Plan Objectives

Scope:

What Do You Do?

Targets:

Whom Are You For?

Positioning:

How Are You Different?

Plan Objectives: *What Needs to Be Achieved?*

Sales Objectives

Marketing Objectives

Communication Objectives

Message Strategy: *What's Your Story?*

Umbrella Strategy: *What's the Plan of Action?*

Part III. Tactical Plans

Marketing Mix Tools: *How Are We Going to Do It?*

Product
Naming
Packaging

Pricing
Distribution
Personal Selling

Advertising
Promotions

Media
Interactive
Media

Merchandising
Public Relations

Part IV. Evaluation

Budget:
What Is the Cost?

Payback:
Can We Win?

Calendar:
When?

Execution:
How?

Plan Evaluation:
Did It Work?

3

Problems and Opportunities

It is very difficult to develop a marketing plan without first consolidating and summarizing the objective material developed in the business review. The business review is a reference to be utilized throughout the year. It is meant to be exhaustive in the amount of data it presents and analyzes. However, in order to write a marketing plan, the marketer needs to crystallize specific industry, company, and competitive challenges. The major conclusions from the business review should be polarized into problems that need to be solved and into opportunities that can be exploited. Use your problems and opportunities as a simple and effective way to provide focus to the work you do in developing your firm's marketing strategy and marketing plan.

FROM THIS CHAPTER YOU WILL LEARN

- How to identify problems and opportunities from the material you developed in your business review

- How to write succinct, actionable problems and opportunities in a format that allows an organized transition into writing your marketing plan

OVERVIEW

This chapter continues the business review begun in Chapters 1 and 2. "Identifying Problems and Opportunities" is Step 7 in the "Insights: What Can We Learn?" flowchart.

Identifying Problems and Opportunities

When writing your marketing plan, you construct the marketing objectives and strategies directly from the problems and opportunities. Ideally, each problem and opportunity should be addressed in the marketing plan. Therefore, make sure to develop problems and opportunities that are appropriate for each section of the business review.

Insights: What Can We Learn?

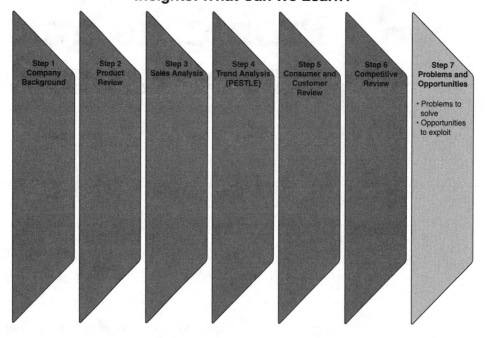

First, make headings that correspond to the steps and sections in your business review. Leave plenty of room to summarize the problems and opportunities under each section heading. Next, review each section of the business review to identify as many meaningful problems and opportunities as possible. Make sure to read each section in the business review at least twice. Ask yourself: Is this information actionable? Is it a current or potential problem that needs to be solved, or is it an opportunity that can be exploited?

See Appendix B, Worksheet 32, to help you capture this information.

Problems

Problems are derived from situations of weakness. As with opportunities, a problem statement can be drawn from a single finding or set of findings that make for a potentially negative situation. Reviewing the target market section in the business review for a consumer apparel manufacturer client, we discovered that there was a heavy-purchaser group in the industry category with 30 percent of the consumers purchasing 65 percent of the product. The heavy-user group concentration was composed of upscale females 35 to 49 with children. They purchased the product for their children with a strong emotional tie to remembering their own childhood. Additionally, they saw their children as extensions of themselves, a reflection of their fashion sensibility. Thus purchasing for and dressing their younger children took on multifaceted meanings and was of significant importance to this target market. As a result, the company faced the following problems:

- While the company manufactured and sold merchandise in line with the heavy-user's attitude around self-expression through their children and a romanticized memory of their own childhood, it was best known for a more casual, durable line that was the signature of the brand.

- The company's purchaser tended to be older mothers with less of a fashion orientation purchasing more out of utility than a fashion statement.

Thus, to target the heavy user, the manufacturer had to focus on building awareness around and focusing more product development against the type of product and brand image that was desired by the industry category heavy-user target.

In summary, problem statements focus on your firm's weaknesses. Problem statements also address market conditions that can result in a disadvantage for your company or the industry as a whole. The common denominator is that problems are defensive in nature; you will be correcting a negative.

Opportunities

Opportunities are developed from strengths or positive circumstances. Often a combination of circumstances makes for a potentially positive situation, creating an opportunity. When we reviewed the competitive situation for a statewide accounting firm, we determined that there were very few accounting firms with aggressive, disciplined marketing programs. Even fewer of these firms actually advertised through mass communication vehicles. Also, we found that within the industry very few of the marketing and communications efforts were targeting small- to medium-sized businesses. An earlier demand analysis had shown that the greatest potential for our client was in providing a full range of accounting services to small- to medium-sized businesses in the retail, service, and financial NAICS categories. This combination of information provided the following opportunities:

- While there was fairly heavy competition in the trading areas of the CPA firm, there was limited advertising of CPA services. Therefore, no single CPA firm dominated either consumer or business awareness of accounting firms.
- No CPA firm was directly communicating to the small- to medium-sized business target market, yet this market represented the majority of potential business in terms of actual numbers of clients.
- Similar to large businesses, research demonstrated that small- to medium-sized firms desired a full range of accounting services recognizing that financial management, not just tax management, was key to a firm's success.

These opportunities meant three things:

1. Because of the limited advertising clutter pertaining to accounting firms, an aggressive, targeted campaign could dominate the accounting advertising and build high awareness levels.
2. If the messages were strategic and meaningful to the target audience, then the increased share of mind or awareness level should be translated into increases in share of business or share of market.
3. The accounting firm could break out of the tax clutter through a more comprehensive positioning around financial management not simply tax management.

In summary, opportunity statements point out strengths of the firm. They also identify areas where your company can exploit a weakness of the competition. They address market conditions that can result in an advantage to your company if positive action is taken. Opportunities are offensive in nature; they will result in an action capitalizing on strengths.

Problem or Opportunity?

Many times, what appears to be a problem can also be an opportunity. An example is the following sales analysis problem:

> While Heartland Men's Apparel sales are strong during the holiday period of November and December, sales are below that of the men's apparel category nationally. This situation occurs because Heartland Apparel stores are not located in malls that generate heavy traffic during these periods.

While this is a problem for the company, it is also an opportunity. If national sales are at a peak during the November and December periods, then the opportunity exists to capture a larger percentage of these sales. However, because of the stores' locations, it is difficult to do as well as the average store nationally during this period. Thus, this statement is both a problem and an opportunity.

As a rule of thumb, try to determine if the statement is more of a problem or an opportunity. In this example, it is very difficult to change locations in retail, so this overriding factor would make the statement a problem. In either case, however, the marketer would probably choose to address the problem or the opportunity by attempting to increase sales in the months of November and December.

HOW TO WRITE ACTIONABLE PROBLEMS AND OPPORTUNITIES

Problems and opportunities should be concise, one-sentence statements that draw conclusions. Following each statement, there should be a rationale using supporting data and findings from the business review as proof to the statement. By using factual data or findings from the business review you will be able to quickly support your problem and opportunity statements during a presentation.

Keeping Your Statements Factual

It is important that your problem and opportunity section stay factual by summarizing findings from the business review. Problems and opportunities do not show what is to be done but, instead, point out areas that need attention. They describe the current market environment. Leave the solutions to the marketing plan.

The following is not an opportunity. It is a marketing strategy:

> Advertise during the strong seasonal times of the year that exist during August, September, December, and April.

It is a strategy because instead of reporting facts, it is demonstrating what should be done. Leave strategies for the marketing plan, when you can review all the problems and opportunities together and then determine what should be done.

An opportunity statement relating to the strategy cited would be the following:

> The industry is extremely seasonal, with strong purchasing months of August, September, December, and April.

Writing Style Examples

The following are examples of problems and opportunities that demonstrate the writing style to use when formulating these statements. These examples cover a wide range of sample problems and opportunities grouped under some respective business review sections. Remember that in your own problems and opportunities section, there will be problems and opportunities for *each section* of the business review.

Example for Step 3, Sales Analysis
Example Problems
The men's suits and sports coats market constitutes a relatively limited market. Total purchases of suits and sports coats by males in a given year are low in the absolute, and the category has lower purchase rates when compared to most other nondurable consumer goods. In addition, while small percentages of males purchase any suit or sports coat in a given year, the majority of those purchasers buy only one suit or sports coat per year.

The Reed Company has experienced a market share decline over the past five years. This loss in market share has primarily been to the market leader, Birk, Inc. which increased share during the last five years. The remainder of the market has remained fairly stable during this time period.

	Market Share	Percentage Change Last 5 Years
Reed Company	10%	−12%
Birk, Inc.	25	+15

Example Opportunity
Sales data show that a small number of distributors accounts for a majority of sales dollars. Forty accounts provide nearly 70 percent of the company sales, yet these forty accounts make up only 12 percent of the distributors who purchase from Seth Cooper & Sons Office Supplies.

Example for Step 5, Consumer and Customer Review, Target Market Segments
Example Problems
There exist four distinct target market segments. Each target market segment clearly has different reasons for purchase and usage patterns, needs, and wants.

The customers for facial tissues skew very old, with a small to nonexistent percentage of users coming from teens and young adults. The brand is developing virtually no new users from which to regenerate the consumer franchise.

Example for Step 5, Consumer and Customer Review, Awareness and Attitudes
Example Problems
Unaided awareness for the Philo Company is fourth. This continues its trend downward relative to the top three competitors over the past three years.

Of the top 10 competitors, the Cale Company ranks fourth in quality of product relative to the competition. Quality is the single most important purchase attribute for the category.

Example Opportunity

Very little clear differentiation of accounting firms exists, except on the basis of size. Service offerings, expertise, and quality of personnel remain relative unknowns among clients, referrals, and prospects.

Example for Step 5, Consumer and Customer Review, Behavior

Example Problems

While the Southwest consumes more of the product on a per capita basis than any other part of the country, the MEG Company has relatively poor sales in this region. This is because it has yet to fully expand distribution to this portion of the country.

The average shopper is extremely brand loyal. Brand choice is developed at a young age, with a majority of consumers continuing purchases for life.

Example Opportunity

Although the total trial of the company's brands is very low, retrial is above the industry category average. Thus, the rate of consumers who become regular users is lower than is normal for the industry category, meaning that product acceptance is very high.

Example for Step 6, Competitive Review

Example Problems

The top three competitors outspend Sunset, Inc., in terms of total media by 20 percent. Furthermore, Sunset, Inc., does not dominate any one medium, and its media spending has declined since last year in television, the medium in which the majority of its media dollars are spent.

The Sunset advertising messages are inconsistent and present no unifying selling theme. In contrast, the top four competitors each communicate one strong, identifiable positioning in all of their advertising.

DOS AND DON'TS

Do

- Draw as many meaningful conclusions as possible from each section of the business review. Read and reread each section.
- Try to look at each set of facts in as many different ways as possible.
- Ask yourself: What are the positive and negative aspects of the data?
- Write concise, factual statements summarizing the business review. Provide a rationale with factual statements from the business review after each problem or opportunity. These provide context and support to your problem or opportunity statement.
- Organize your problems and opportunities so that they reflect each section of the business review.
- If it helps you to better see the big picture, summarize all the problems and opportunities into 5 to 10 key problem areas and 5 to 10 key opportunities, and include them at the end of your problems and opportunities section.

Don't

- Don't try to write objectives and strategies in this section. Keep the statements factual.

- Don't make the statements too long. Keep them short, and focus each one on a single problem or opportunity.
- Don't shortchange the number of problems and opportunities. Compile an inclusive list. Once you have your final list, make sure you go back and eliminate any that are redundant. This will allow you to concentrate on a more focused, manageable list of meaningful problems and opportunities.
- Don't include problems and opportunities that are not based on information included in your business review.

The Successful Marketing Plan

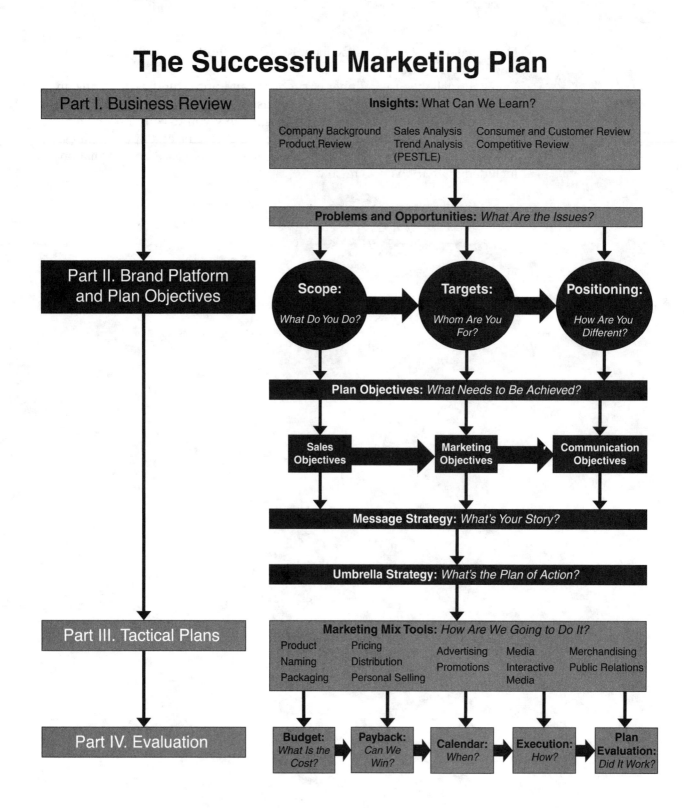

Part I. Business Review

Insights: What Can We Learn?

Company Background | Sales Analysis | Consumer and Customer Review
Product Review | Trend Analysis (PESTLE) | Competitive Review

Problems and Opportunities: *What Are the Issues?*

Part II. Brand Platform and Plan Objectives

Scope: *What Do You Do?*

Targets: *Whom Are You For?*

Positioning: *How Are You Different?*

Plan Objectives: *What Needs to Be Achieved?*

Sales Objectives → Marketing Objectives → Communication Objectives

Message Strategy: *What's Your Story?*

Umbrella Strategy: *What's the Plan of Action?*

Part III. Tactical Plans

Marketing Mix Tools: *How Are We Going to Do It?*

Product | Pricing | Advertising | Media | Merchandising
Naming | Distribution | Promotions | Interactive Media | Public Relations
Packaging | Personal Selling | | Media |

Part IV. Evaluation

Budget: *What Is the Cost?* → **Payback:** *Can We Win?* → **Calendar:** *When?* → **Execution:** *How?* → **Plan Evaluation:** *Did It Work?*

PART

II

BRAND PLATFORM AND PLAN OBJECTIVES

The following eight chapters describe the strategy section of your plan. These chapters establish your business model, your brand positioning, and the message and umbrella strategies that will guide your overall business.

The Successful Marketing Plan

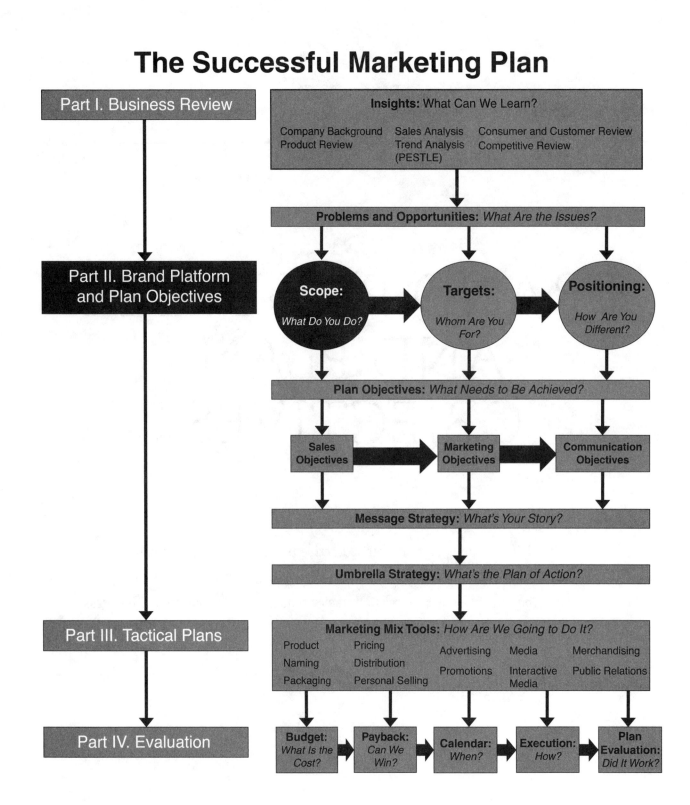

Part I. Business Review

Insights: What Can We Learn?

Company Background
Product Review
Sales Analysis
Trend Analysis
(PESTLE)
Consumer and Customer Review
Competitive Review

Problems and Opportunities: *What Are the Issues?*

Part II. Brand Platform and Plan Objectives

Scope:
What Do You Do?

Targets:
Whom Are You For?

Positioning:
How Are You Different?

Plan Objectives: *What Needs to Be Achieved?*

Sales Objectives

Marketing Objectives

Communication Objectives

Message Strategy: *What's Your Story?*

Umbrella Strategy: *What's the Plan of Action?*

Part III. Tactical Plans

Marketing Mix Tools: *How Are We Going to Do It?*

Product
Naming
Packaging
Pricing
Distribution
Personal Selling
Advertising
Promotions
Media
Interactive
Media
Merchandising
Public Relations

Part IV. Evaluation

Budget:
What Is the Cost?

Payback:
Can We Win?

Calendar:
When?

Execution:
How?

Plan Evaluation:
Did It Work?

4 Scope

The first step in your brand platform work is to answer the question, What is it we really do? That sounds so simple to answer:

- You make dolls if you're American Girl dolls.
- You educate if you're a community college.
- You help people save and provide them money in the form of loans if you're a bank.
- You make drills if you're Black & Decker.
- You make cosmetics if you're Revlon. Right? Right.

But not so fast. Pleasant Rowland, the founder of American Girl, the maker of American Girl dolls, has said that Pleasant Company was in the education business. The company existed to help empower young girls. A community college may really be in the business of being a community engine or a launching pad for getting a job or getting into a four-year college. Maybe your bank is really in the business of making financial transactions easy because consumers don't wake up each morning looking forward to the mundane though necessary task of banking. Or maybe the credit union is really a financial advocate for those of us who aren't very financially sophisticated and could use someone on our side when it comes to money matters.

While Black & Decker makes plenty of drills, it's really in business because it's great at making small 200- to 600-watt motors and has parlayed this competency into solving problems for consumers across three broad markets: the home workshop (drills and power tools), home cleanup (DustBusters), and kitchen appliances (food processors, blenders, and can openers).

And as for Revlon: Charles Haskell Revson, the founder of Revlon, said, "In the factory, we manufacture cosmetics, but in the stores, we sell hope." Yes, Revlon today continues to be in the business of hope. It's what they do. And it shapes how they develop their products, communicate their products, and merchandise their products.

You can't begin to brand your company or product if you don't really understand what it is you do—from the consumer perspective. This chapter is *not a discussion of attributes but, rather, key benefits you deliver to the customers when they buy and use your products. If you don't know what business you're really in, then it's hard to determine who you really compete against, who will be your most valuable customer market segments, and how you will position your brand to win. In summary, if you can't answer the question, What do you do? you won't be able to answer the next two questions in the brand platform: Whom are you for? and, How are you different?*

FROM THIS CHAPTER YOU WILL LEARN

- The definition of *core competencies*—the window to determining what it is you really do
- How to determine your core competency, and how to use this knowledge to discover what it is you really do or what business you're in
- How understanding what it is you really do or what business you're in helps you:
  - Determine the broad markets you will target (users, industry category, channels, and geography)
  - Sharpen your understanding of your competitors set
  - Establish the boundaries of your product portfolio
- Insights on how to let core competencies guide your future actions

OVERVIEW

The most critical part of your scope is determining what it is you really do, that is driven by what key competency you really have, that leads to a differentiated customer benefit. Once determined, this knowledge will help you expand possibilities—of the broad user markets you will target, the industry categories in which you will compete, the geographic priorities with which you will work, the companies you will compete against, and the potential of the range of products you can choose to include in your product portfolio.

We've found over the years that many businesses don't take the time to really answer what it is they really do for their customers and define the scope within which they compete. The result of not doing this is an endless internal focus on things that don't really matter to the customer.

Determining what it is you really do that's of value to the customer allows you to start thinking like your customers (Exhibit 4.1). It provides you with the broad parameters that define your business and allow you to zero in on areas you can differentiate from your competitors as you go through the other components of your brand platform.

Let's figure out what it is you really do for your customers. It's often different and much more interesting than you think.

Core Competency

Definition of core competency. Your core competency is the window to what you really do, and it drives what business you are really in from your customers' perspective.

EXHIBIT 4.1

Scope Components

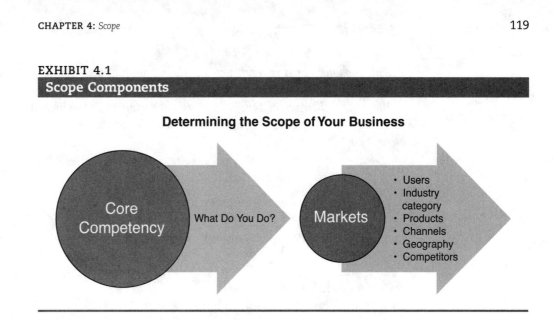

Determining the Scope of Your Business

A core competency describes *why* you can do what it is you really do for your customers. It doesn't outright answer what you do, but in describing why you can do it, you are provided with the insight and connection to determine the scope question: What do you really do for your customers from their viewpoint?

Core competencies represent the consolidation of firmwide technologies and skills into a coherent capability. A core competency is discovered by grouping a number of similar strengths from across the organization together and then working to identify the underlying reason for the strengths. A company's core competency is the trunk of the tree, while its products are the branches. One may not recognize the strength of a competitor by looking only at its end products and failing to examine the strength of its core reason for being. One of the keys to great strategy is your ability to manage your core competency (the trunk of the tree) rather than business units or products (the branches). In the end, it's the core competency that makes a business unique to the target market and thus competitively superior.

Every company has at least one core competency. Very few have multiple core competencies. You've heard it before: "The key to our success is that we . . . ," and then there's a sudden list of four to five different things people tell you their company is great at doing that contribute to its success. You'll also hear this several times in this book: positioning is the art of sacrifice. An ability to focus and sacrifice leads to an ability to expand—markets, products, and customers.

Core Competency Criteria
We believe core competencies must meet the following criteria.

* *Core competencies are usually some combination of company strengths that form a single overriding capability. The capability allows you to have a differential advantage over the competition.* The actual competency is usually a weaving of multiple strengths across processes, assets, specific skills, and organizational culture into one key capability that allows for a competitive advantage. Competitors may have some of the strengths that you possess, but remember, core competencies are a result of a *unique combination of strengths* resulting in a single overriding skill set that drives your company and makes it meaningful to the customer. So while your competitors may have some of the strengths you do, it should be difficult to duplicate the comprehensive combination that makes up the competency.

- *This capability or core competency is the reason that your company has access to and can dominate a specific target audience in that it makes a significant contribution to the perceived customer benefit of using your company's products or services.*
- *The capability or core competency is difficult for other companies or products to imitate or copy.*

In summary, a core competency must do three things:

1. It must be a unique company capability that is made up from a number of underlying strengths.
2. It must make a significant contribution to the perceived customer end benefit to using your company or product.
3. It must be difficult for your competitors to imitate.

A Couple of Examples

Honda and Apple are good examples of companies that have identified and built on their core competencies.

Honda

You hear "Honda" and you think "cars," right? Yet Honda thinks "motors" and "combustion engines." There's a reason the company is called Honda Motors. Honda is the world's largest producer in terms of numbers of internal combustion engines. As a result, while its core competency has helped Honda become the sixth-leading manufacturer of cars, Honda is the world's largest manufacturer of motorcycles. The core competency has also helped Honda successfully enter other markets such as lawn mowers, snow blowers, and trucks. Ask the managers of Honda what business they are in and you'll get the response "internal combustion engines." It's this competency that drives the true benefit their customers receive from doing business with Honda and the underlying reason for the company and its products' positioning around reliable cars that provide tremendous value.

Think about the difference between Honda who has a core competency in motors and Chrysler who essentially assembles components (since the 1990s Chrysler has increasingly outsourced its motors to Mitsubishi and Hyundai). Isn't it interesting that in 2008 the motor company, Honda, passed the car company, Chrysler, in total automobile production?

Core competencies are not built overnight, and it will be interesting to see what happens to Chrysler. Our guess is that Honda will continue to build on its capability with motors and other automobile manufacturers will choose to compete based on their competencies of design, new product innovation, safety, or the dealership network they have established. What will Chrysler build on?

Apple

Apple's core competency is the ability to merge *innovative integrated design and technology*. This competency translates to the suite of industry-leading personal computer and media products from the MacBook family, to iPod and the integration of iTunes to the iPhone, and now the iPad.

Steve Jobs, when interviewed by *Time* magazine said, "Here's what you find in a lot of companies. The designers come up with this really great idea. Then they take it to the engineers, and the engineers go, 'Nah, we can't do that, that's impossible.' And so it gets a lot worse. Then they take it to the manufacturing people, and they go, 'We can't build that,' and so it gets a lot worse." When Jobs came up with the original Macintosh idea, a candy-colored computer that looked cooler and sleeker than any other computer on the market, the engineers wanted to change it. But Jobs hung tough in what business Apple is in: innovative integrated design and technology.* This dogged staying of the course has played itself out again and again throughout the entire product line making Apple one of the most successful consumer companies of the last 20 years.

Let's examine the Apple product portfolio to see how Apple's core competency of *innovative integrated design and technology* has shaped the product line. Think about it, Apple makes its own hardware (MacBooks). It makes its own programs and graphical interfaces that run on the hardware (iMovie, iPhoto, iTunes, Safari Web browser, and so on). Apple then also makes the consumer electronic devices that connect to all those things through (for example, the iPod family) and runs the online services that furnish content to those devices (iTunes Music Store).

There are other music and video players out there but none as cool looking and easy to use as the iPod. And none were developed with an integrated music store. There are many mobile phones on the market but none with integrated Apps, the Internet, instant messaging, video, and photos like the iPhone when it was first introduced. Additionally, there wasn't another phone on the market that had the design pizzazz and was as well designed from its looks to the way it operated by a mere touch of the finger.

Apple doesn't just stop with products but takes its core competency of the *integration of design and technology* straight to the retail and service aspects of its business. When the total company is reviewed, perhaps the most striking success is the ability of Apple to service its customers and users, taking away their fear of computers and making them smart customers and users. Is it the technology that makes Macs easy to use or the service capability? One can argue either side of that question.

There's a reason that the Apple retail experience is like no other. It's because Apple has used its core competency of innovative integrated design and technology to revolutionize the servicing and selling of their product. The first thing you notice when you walk into an Apple store is that it's crowded. It's filled with customers and prospects either sampling the products, taking a class, or being helped in some other fashion. It's rare to see someone simply wandering aimlessly—there's a purpose to every engagement. Then after your initial glance around, you begin to notice a sort of controlled chaos. An Apple employee in blue approaches right away, usually when you are just through the threshold of the store's doorway. You're asked if you have an appointment or what you are looking for. An iPad or iPhone in hand, the staff member either checks you in for the appointment you made at the Apple Internet site or immediately helps you with what you need. Somehow the appointment with the Genius Bar or the class you've come for always starts on time. If you buy something, you'll quickly notice there are not any cash registers—everything is done on a handheld by the individual helping you. When you leave the store, you are still within a keystroke or phone call of help if you need it. Whether it's making another appointment with the Genius Desk through the Apple website, calling AppleCare and getting a real person to walk you through your problem or solution, or interfacing on the Internet with the MobileMe help desk, a well-designed service operation dependent on technology has revolutionized the servicing of the Apple product user. (*Note:* Obviously the three authors are fans.)

---

* Lev Grossman, "How Apple Does It," *Time* magazine, October 16, 2005.

Apple's core competency of the integration of design and technology applies to everything it does—from product to retail. It meets all the criteria of a great core competency. It combines the company's strengths in a single thrust: the core competency provides access to large markets through making a significant contribution to the perceived customer end benefit and it's difficult to copy. It also leads directly to and is the foundation for Apple's brand promise (how they are different) of *effortless*. Apple has learned how to combine the businesses of a fashion design company, a software company like Microsoft, a hardware company like Dell Computer, and a music company like Sony into one company. That's pretty hard to copy!

How to Identify Your Core Competencies: A Case Study

A number of years ago, two of us worked with AAA, the American Automobile Association. The project was to help the national association develop a strategic marketing plan. At the start of the project, we asked them, "What business are you in?" The initial answer was, "We're in the business of providing *peace of mind*." Our quick response was, "Peace of mind in what?" "Peace of mind" could refer to any number of different businesses—banking, insurance, moving companies, travel agencies, estate planners, and so on. Without getting an answer for this basic question, it would be very difficult to gather insights and proceed in the marketing planning process.

After being pressed, the answer changed: "We're in the business of providing peace of mind for insurance, roadside assistance, travel, and financial services." This might seem like a reasonable answer to those of you who are familiar with AAA. They do provide these products and more. That was just the problem. You can't simply just list your products. Products rarely if ever define a core competency or really define what it is your business does. The reverse is true, that business scope or defining what business you're really in, from the eyes of your customers, defines the playing ground where your business will develop products and grow.

So we had a problem that often occurs. We were not developing individual product plans but a strategic marketing plan for the whole organization. We had to find a way to link the entire organization together so that the work we did in insurance would also help the work we did for the travel agency. We had to get to the core of exactly what it was AAA did across its entire product line and business units from the perspective of its customers.

STEPS FOR DEVELOPING THE SCOPE FOR YOUR BUSINESS

The following four steps provide the framework for developing your business scope. We followed the same four steps for AAA. (*Note*: The AAA example does not necessarily reflect the current market environment.)

See Appendix C, Worksheet 33, to help you capture the information described in the steps below.

STEP 1   ### *Provide an Overview of Company Strengths and Weaknesses*

Identify the strengths and weaknesses of your organization across target market needs, products, operations, distribution, pricing, communication programs, personnel, and culture. Use the following definitions of *strength* and *weakness* when developing this section:

Definition of **strength:** Capability or resource that the organization has which could be used to improve its competitive position (share of market or size of market) or improve its financial performance.

Definition of **weakness:** Weakness exists in any capability or resource that may cause your organization to have a less competitive position or poorer financial performance.

QUESTIONS TO BE ADDRESSED

List your organization's strengths and weaknesses across the following categories:

- What are your advantages and/or disadvantages due to target market *needs, wants,* and *consumption trends*? (For example: There is a continuing trend toward short trips taken by car so many of the AAA clubs attract the short trip market through a combination of roadside assistance protection, information, travel packages, and different map products to their advantage.)
- What are your advantages and disadvantages due to the *value* the organization brings the market? What creates these, why do they exist?
- What are your *product* and *technological* advantages and disadvantages relative to target market needs? What creates these? Why do they exist?
- What are the advantages and disadvantages due to *operational efficiencies* that make dealing with the organization a superior experience for the member and/or customer? What creates these? Why do they exist?
- What are the *distribution efficiencies and inefficiencies* or advantages and disadvantages that make the organization unique? Why do these exist?
- What are the *pricing* advantages and disadvantages the organization can offer its customers? Why do these exist?
- What *communication* advantages and disadvantages exist, and why?
- Do you have a real advantage due to *personnel* that is an advantage for your customers? Be very realistic here. Most companies will say yes when in fact, few really do.
- What is there about your organization's *culture* that provides advantages and disadvantages for you customers?

Example Strengths

The following types of statements were a start of the strengths analysis developed for AAA based on the above parameters:

- AAA has a dedicated staff and strong belief in the service concept. Research shows members feel they get excellent service across all the major member touch points. Additionally, the gap between service expectation and actual fulfillment is very narrow.
- The club has the ability to provide a total travel solution at a value. Members can get planning services, reservations, protection from car failure, trip insurance, car insurance, maps and touring advice, special travel discounts, and discounts when they show their card in all types of businesses from automotive services to hotels, restaurants, and entertainment venues.
- AAA has a long heritage in providing safe auto travel as being an early advocate of safe roads, to being a trusted roadside assistance company, to assuring quality from hotels and service stations with the AAA seal of approval.
- AAA has built an extensive network of retail storefronts, auto repair shops, and emergency roadside service contractors that are unmatched in the industry.
- There is a strong loyalty among the membership as demonstrated by the high renewal rate after members have had experience with the club.

Example Weaknesses

Based on this example, the following statements were the start of an analysis of weaknesses facing the organization:

- Membership skews old, with younger members renewing at lower rates than older members.
- Historically, AAA was known for and dominated the emergency roadside assistance category. However, over the past 15 years, due to the advent of competitive emergency roadside assistance programs, auto manufacturer programs, cell phones, and cars and tires that have better service records, the need for emergency roadside service has diminished and has been spread over more options. This perception of diminished need is especially true for younger consumers who have never known frequent flat tires and auto mechanical problems and have had GPS types of devices as a matter of course.
- There exists relatively low membership awareness of the products outside of emergency roadside assistance. Because of this, there is relatively lower use of these services as well.
- While the travel agency side of AAA continues to show great promise, it faces tremendous competitive price pressures and a crowded competitive field. The travel agency continues to be more competitive around shorter automobile-oriented trips than around more exotic travel.

STEP 2 ## Identify the Organization's Core Competency

Combine Your Strengths into a Capability

This step is more art than science. In Step 1 you listed your company's strengths and weaknesses. Go back and review the list of strengths. The challenge is to pull out groups of strengths that together enable your company to be the best at one thing—a competency or capability that provides unique products and access to customer markets.

Think about AAA. It competes across six different industries:

Industry	Competitor Examples
Membership	AARP, USAA
Auto service and collision repair	Local service stations, AutoTowing.com
Travel agency	American Express, Carlson Wagonlit, local travel agencies
Financial services	Large and local banks
Insurance	Leading insurance companies
Lending	Banks

So when asked what AAA does, it's a complex question.

A complete analysis of the AAA strengths helped shed light on the organization's true competency. Known for emergency road service and towing, it was clear that AAA meant a lot more to its customers—that its true value was much greater than simply one product. From the work we did analyzing AAA strengths, it was clear the core competency was connected to the thought, *all things cars*. It also became clear that there was a need to connect cars to *travel and mobility*—travel to work and to social engagements, for pleasure and touring. There are upsides (vacations, going places) and downsides (mechanical failures) to car travel. AAA improves the upside experiences and softens the downside experiences. It can do this because of the unparalleled combination of car-related services it provides, all from one organization. Here's a partial list of the strengths that helped us determine the core competency and ultimately the scope of business of AAA:

- Fifty million members means that AAA can provide buying clout.
- AAA has a historic capability in roadside assistance. It is known for towing and repairs and an emerging capability around "on-the-go" service where the car is fixed on the spot.
- It is partners with 8,000 approved auto repair shops and 30,000 towing facilities—all certified to stringent AAA standards. The repair shops agree to arbitration on the behalf of the consumer if a dispute arises.
- It has a national travel agency capability—from trip planning to reservations.
- It has a strong capability in government advocacy for the motorist.
- It is a large provider of car and trip insurance.
- It provides Visa TravelMoney cards.
- It offers assistance with vehicle financing.
- It offers a complete line of travel maps, TripTiks, travel guides, and GPS applications.
- It is a national organization with a local presence via branches.
- It has a strong recognized brand name.

The chart in Exhibit 4.2 summarizes the synergy effect of the strengths. No other organization can add value to the automobile experience the way AAA can—from assurance of safety, towing and repair services, emergency services, auto travel agency services, insurance, discounts when traveling, and advocacy.

EXHIBIT 4.2

The Synergy Effect of AAA's Strengths

AAA Core Competency

Motor Club:
Keeps You Going

Travel Agency:
Gets You Going

Insurance:
Coverage
Wherever
You Go

Savings:
Membership
Clout Wherever
You Go

Emergency
Road Service

Travel
Discounts

Travel
Planning

Car Insurance

Approved
Auto Mechanics

Secure
Travel
Money

Travel
Packages

Trip Insurance

Show Your
Card and Save

TripTiks Maps and
Guides

Lockout
Services

Providing Added
Value to Car
Ownership:

Taking Out the Worry and
Adding to the Pleasure

Yes, AAA sells property insurance and life insurance. And yes, you can plan an overseas trip that doesn't include driving your car—all are important parts of AAA. But the core competency, the thing that makes AAA great, is a comprehensive competitive advantage around anything auto—insurance, travel, and assurance via emergency road service, and approved auto repair assistance. *AAA is a comprehensive automobile resource; a vast tapestry of services put in place to help the motorist to worry less and enjoy his or her car experience more.*

Ask Your Customers

Another way to get at your core competencies is to ask your customers. It's surprising how clearly they know exactly what it is you really do for them. This can be accomplished any number of different ways—in quantitative surveys or one-on-one interviews. Ask the following types of questions:

- What is the single greatest benefit you receive from _____ or from purchasing _____ or using _____ service?
- If Company X (or Product X or Service X) simply went away, disappeared tomorrow, what would you miss most?

Example: American Red Cross, Badger Chapter, Wisconsin

In another example, the American Red Cross Badger Chapter went through this exercise with key donor targets. The answer was overwhelmingly "the ability to prepare our community for the first response to an emergency." We also heard a lot of responses around the word "hope"—that if the Red Cross simply disappeared, we'd lose the sense of hope that our community would be able to respond in times of crisis. These responses provided a good grounding around the real core competency of the Red Cross—*the ability to train and prepare our community for disasters.*

As is always the case, the core competency led directly to a definition of what the organization really does for the target markets it serves.

> The Red Cross is in the business of:
>
> Providing a unique ability to prepare local communities for the initial response during times of natural disasters or man-made disasters.
>
> This led to the Red Cross Badger Chapter's positioning or value promise of why they are different:
>
> The Red Cross provides the *initial hope* to victims of disasters.

STEP 3
Review the Advantages That the Core Competencies Bring Your Organization

Continuing with the AAA example, take the core competency that you developed and give it the test. Does it pass these five questions?

- *Does the core competency provide a strong point of entry for the consumer?* Yes. Emergency road service has been a strong historical entry point into the AAA organization.

- *Does the core competency provide access to a significant target audience?* Yes. The Department of Transportation reports that there are approximately 245 million cars in the United States with slightly under 210 million drivers.
- *Are there other competitors who have the same core competency?* No. None have exactly the same. For example, AARP provides some of the services provided by AAA, but it does not have AAA's complete 360-degree comprehensive auto travel expertise.
- *Does the core competency apply to cross-functional parts of the organization?* Yes. The AAA core competency affects all major business units of AAA. Everyone on the management team in one way or another is tied to cars and owns a part of the core competency.
- *Will the core competency lead to a continual source of new products and services?* Yes. The unique combination of repair, travel agency, advocacy, insurance, and financial products provides a strong incubator of cross-functional teams all focusing on the same thing—auto travel, safety, and maintenance—all things cars and a better car experience for members.

STEP 4 ### Determine What Business You're Really In

Your core competency should lead you directly to the definition of what business you're in as it holds the key to what you really do for your customers. It allows you to be great at what you do. For AAA, *the core competency of being a 24/7 comprehensive automobile resource focused on reducing worry and providing value to the motoring experience* translated into the following definition of its business:

> AAA is in the business of helping motorists enjoy their cars more and worry less—it's an *Automobile Assurance and Enhancement company*.

This then became the foundation as the organization started to redefine the organization's competitors set, markets, and parameters for the products that would receive emphasis in communications.

This doesn't mean AAA shouldn't offer property insurance, but the combination of auto services is what sets the organization apart. Leveraging, building, and communicating these will continue to provide AAA with a competitive advantage. Looking at this a different way, in the end, if AAA's core reason for being went away—if AAA were no longer relevant to the automobile owner—it would sell a lot less property insurance. It can't compete simply on property insurance or life insurance. It can compete as a membership organization that adds comprehensive value to automobile ownership. Understanding what business you're in and really focusing on it increases the number of core customers, which ultimately increases your ability to sell peripheral products and services. Without the core, this ability would disappear.

HOW TO LET YOUR CORE COMPETENCY GUIDE YOUR FUTURE ACTIONS

1. *Add to your core competency.* Core competencies emerge over time. You can add to your core competency by continuing to develop strengths that complement it. Look for these and cultivate them.

2. *Use your core competency to build on key organizational areas of strengths.* Design your internal organization structure around the functions and activities most critical to the success of the firm's core competency. Honda Federal Credit Union is really in the business of providing easy banking. Yes, it does a lot of other things, but it is in the business of making financial transactions easy and simple. Its members see banking as a necessity, so the best thing Honda Federal Credit Union can do is to make sure the experience is quick, easy, and pleasant. That means that functions and activities that facilitate this are important; those that don't, aren't.

3. *Use your core competency to determine what to start doing and stop doing.* A core competency gives management a barometer to determine what's important and what's not—what to stop doing and what to start doing. Begin this process by making a list of what you need to stop doing—tasks, job responsibilities, projects, things that take your organization's mind share during the day that aren't driven by your core competency or what it is you really do for your customers. Then once you've determined things that you need to stop doing, start the list of things that you need to start doing to take advantage of your core competency and that further add to the benefit your customers see in what it is you do.

4. *Use your core competency to define key markets.* Your core competency provides a direct link to the industry category where you will compete and the broad consuming markets that will drive your organization.

5. *Use your core competency to define your competitors set.* A core competency helps businesses determine their specific competitive set, the products they potentially could market and the broad category target markets against which to focus.

6. *Use your core competency to define your core products and future product direction.* Apply your core competency to help create and focus marketing efforts on products and services consistent with the company's main strengths.

7. *Use your core competency to drive cross-functional work.* Understanding your core competency helps unite and align all business functions in one direction. In many instances, this means more cross-functional work and less work around individual silos.

Defining the Scope of Your Business

Review again Exhibit 4.1.

Determining the Scope of Your Business

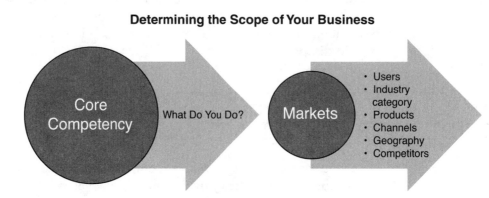

Now that you've defined what it is you really do, use this to help you identify the *market in which you will compete*. A market is a broad body of potential buyers defined by the following:

- *The broad users or purchasers scope*: Broad consumer or business target market
- *The industry category scope*: Industry categories where you will compete
- *Products scope*: The intended product focus of the consumers and within the industry categories
- *Channels scope*: The business channels you sell to and through
- *Geography scope*: Geographic markets where you will compete
- *Competitors scope*: Your competitive set

The work you do here will finish the scope section of your plan. What you are doing is identifying the broad parameters of where you can play and win. After this chapter, the work involves narrowing and getting at smaller segments of these markets to help you form a stronger competitive advantage as you market your company through your plan. We are going to take you through several examples that clearly show how once businesses understand the business they are truly in, they can make the broad interpretations necessary to sketch out the boundaries that make up the firm's scope of business.

Example: Black & Decker

Black & Decker isn't in the business of manufacturing power drills. The company possesses a combination of skills that sets it apart in the manufacturing of electric motors.

Black & Decker Users and Industry Category Products Scope

The company identified three broad user and industry category markets that clearly define both the broad consumer target market and also the industry category. Each of these markets had a need for tools powered by small motors in addition to the specific product varieties that would be sold in those category types:

- *The workshop market* (sanders, drills, and so on for the professional and the home do-it-yourselfer): International focus
- *The home cleaning market* (maintenance and cleaning products like DustBusters for the apartment dweller and homeowner): International focus
- *Kitchen appliances market* (can openers and food processors for use in any kitchen): International focus

Note that each of the three broad markets has a clearly defined *category* (for example, home cleaning) that also points to a broad *user market* (homeowners) and the *products* driving that category (for example, maintenance and cleaning products). Black & Decker's core competency and target market scope are becoming very clear.

Black & Decker Channels Scope

With a little more work, it is possible to also determine the broad *channel markets* that Black & Decker sells through. This can be found through using the North American Industry Classifications System (NAICS). In Chapter 1, you will find details on how to use the NAICS in the "Sources of Information" section.

The Retail Trade Classification is 44-45. But within that classification, there are several subgroups that Black & Decker could list as potential channel target markets or business target markets. We will list a few:

- 444130 hardware stores (There are 25,546 single locations as of the 2009 NAICS statistics.)
- 452910 warehouse clubs
- 443111 household appliance stores
- 444110 home centers
- 454113 mail order houses

Black & Decker Geography Scope
For Black & Decker, the *geographic market scope* of the company is international.

Black & Decker Competitors Scope
For Black & Decker, the competitive set can easily be determined by looking at the companies that compete in the same NAICS categories and market the same products.

Example: Shoe Retailer
In another example, if your core competency led you to determine you were a manufacturer of athletic performance shoes, you would consider targeting the following:

- *Users and industry category scope*: Consumers who use athletic shoes for *fashion* or *performance*. (Fashion athletics and performance athletics are the industry categories.)
- *Products scope*: Athletic shoes
- *Channels scope*: Shoe stores in NAICS category 448210 with further breaks between shoe stores and athletic shoe stores
- *Geography scope*: United States
- *Competitors scope*: Athletic shoe manufacturers

Example: Broadjam Social Media Site for Musicians
Broadjam, www.broadjam.com, is a social media website on which independent bands can post music and to which fans can come to listen and producers can look for new music for videos, advertising, and games. Its core competency is the *access* Broadjam provides independent musicians to getting their music heard and published. What does Broadjam really do? It creates a daily battle of the bands in a virtual performance place that provides music supervisors with an ongoing source of fresh music and musicians with access to getting their music published.

- *Users and industry category and products scope*: Professional services companies who need commercial music from independent artists
- *Channels scope*: Advertising agencies (who would have a need for purchasing music for advertising), NAICS code 54810
- *Geography scope*: Midwest, making it close to the Broadjam home office
- *Channels scope*: Movie production and distribution companies, NAICS code 51211
- *Geography scope*: West Coast, providing a high concentration of targets
- *Competitors scope*: Companies who provide commercial music to advertising agencies and movie production companies

Example: Mercury Marine

Mercury Marine's core competency is its ability to power boats as the world leader in propulsion technology. But powering boats is more than just technology. It's finding ways to keep the power boats running. The company combines its technology with its over 4,300 dealers in the United States and Canada to provide a unique system of getting people on the water and keeping them there.

Mercury Marine, like Black & Decker, would consider a more complex combination of target markets:

- *Users and industry category scope*: Consumers who purchase or have boats—boating category
- *Products scope*: Engines and motors, propellers, rigging, parts and accessories (oil, engine fluids, and so on)
- *Channels scope*: Boat dealers (because they sell the full line of boat motors, props, and accessories) 441222; hardware stores (because they sell boat oil) 444130; wholesale clubs and supercenters (stores like Walmart that sell a high volume of boating oil, lube, and winterizing products); and other, such as direct and Internet sales
- *Geography scope*: International
- *Competitors scope*: All manufacturers of engines and/or motors, propellers, rigging, parts, and accessories

Hints for Determining the Boundaries of Your Scope

Hints for Determining the Boundaries of Your Users and Channels

You can develop an initial sense of the business opportunity by looking at the potential of the users and channels within the scope of your business. You'll go a lot deeper on the targets in the next chapter. The purpose of the scope section of the marketing plan is to define the outer boundaries of what you will consider as you narrow the focus of your plan in subsequent chapters. Exhibit 4.3 continues with the Mercury Marine example. Use the chart in Exhibit 4.3 to compare the potential between different user groups and channels.

Hints for Determining the Boundaries of Your Industry Category and Competitors

Now that you understand what it is you really do based on the work you've done with your core competencies, use this knowledge to more succinctly define your

EXHIBIT 4.3

Comparisons of Types of Buyers

Scope	Potential Size and Number	Yearly Average Boating Sales: Motors, Propellers, Parts, and Accessories
Users scope: Males 25–65 living within a 25-mile radius of water appropriate for recreational boating	Approximately 50 million	To be filled in from business review
Geography scope: Nationally, United States		
Channels scope: Boat dealers	8,905 total dealers (3,400 Mercury dealers) 2009 NAICS	To be filled in from business review
Channels scope: Supercenters and big-box stores (e.g., Walmart)	TBD (to be determined) NAICS or other research	To be filled in from business review
Channels scope: Hardware stores	TBD NAICS or other research	To be filled in from business review
Channels scope: Internet	TBD NAICS or other research	To be filled in from business review

industry category and competitive set. You can use this knowledge to go back and revise portions of your business review in Part I. Then ask yourself the following questions to help add and subtract competitors as you redefine your competitive set:

- Based on the definition of what we do as a company and the true benefit we bring to the broad user markets, what is the scope or the breadth of competitors that we face? What are the different competitive categories? Which category of competitor would be the primary competition, and who would be considered secondary? Now specifically, what are the names of the major competitors in each category?
- Based on the definition of what we do and the true benefit we bring to the broad user markets, industry categories, and channels: Who are the competitors we listed in the business review section that remain very viable? Who diminishes in stature? Who gets added?
- Do the major competitors look like our company in terms of structure and organization?
- What's the biggest competitive challenge we face?

A lot of this will make a good foundation when you do your planning next year. However, now is a good time to at least review if your frame of reference regarding your competitive set has changed at all given the work you've just completed. It can also lead you to go back and redo your competitive analysis in the business review.

Hints for Establishing Boundaries for Your Products Portfolio
Based on your company's core competency and the definition of your business that you developed, along with insights into the broad user markets, industry category, and channels you are considering targeting, make a list of the products you currently have in your portfolio and additional products you don't have that would be consistent with the scope of your business:

- List all current product categories and the products within each category. Then rank them according to their fit within the scope of your business and your company's core competency.
- List products your competitors have that you don't have but that fit your business definition and scope.
- Develop a list of products that you've never considered before but that are consistent with your company's core competency and the scope of your business. This list should include the products and product variations that either are or could be developed and included in your product line based on the scope of your business. Based on your scope, think about products with different features, packaging, alternative uses, supporting products that support other products, and combinations or bundled products.

This exercise provides you with the broad boundaries of the products that you would either use or develop as you go forward with further defining your target markets, positioning, objectives, and strategies.

In summary, the scope section—that is, the definition of what it is you really do—accomplishes the following:

- Defines what business the organization is in and the strategic leverage it will use to compete

- Helps define the markets where you will compete: the key users, the industry category, the channels you will sell, the geographic market you will compete in, and the competitors you will compete against for market share
- Defines the product areas where the organization will grow and concentrate its business efforts
- Sets the stage and foundation for your work completing the brand platform—developing specific target segments, developing a unique brand positioning, objectives, message strategy, and umbrella strategies
- Provides the parameters against which you will direct your marketing background and research efforts into the future

DOS AND DON'TS

Do

- Let your core competency lead into the definition of what it is you really do. Figure out the why before you figure out the what.
- Remember that a core competency is typically a combination of strengths that leads to a comprehensive systemwide capability.
- Make sure your core competency is something that many parts of your business can leverage. A core competency should lead to cross-functional thrusts and focus—a collective effort across company departments in one direction.
- Build on your core competency over time.
- Let your core competency be your guide to stop doing what is not important and start doing what is important.
- Once you have defined what it is you do, use this knowledge to finish defining the scope of your markets (target markets, channels, competitive category, and products).

Don't

- Don't believe that your firm has multiple core competencies. Few do. Find the one that really makes a difference and focus on it.
- Don't just look to your product to define your business. It's the collective benefits your product brings to your customers that provide greater insights into what you really do.
- Don't define what you do from an internal perspective. Think like a customer.
- Don't define your core competency as something that's easy to copy. Make sure it is tied to what creates a customer benefit that is hard to copy. This is why competencies are mostly made up of a number of different strengths that combine to make one core competency.
- Don't expect this to be a five-minute exercise. It's hard work, but as the first step of the brand platform, it lays the foundation to the strategy section of your plan.

The Successful Marketing Plan

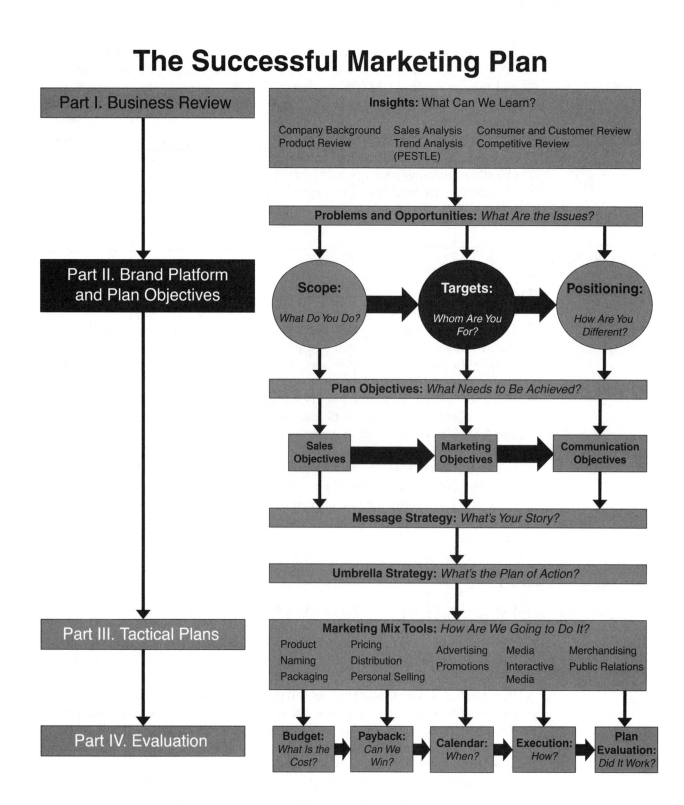

Part I. Business Review

Insights: What Can We Learn?

Company Background   Sales Analysis   Consumer and Customer Review
Product Review   Trend Analysis   Competitive Review
                      (PESTLE)

Problems and Opportunities: What Are the Issues?

Part II. Brand Platform and Plan Objectives

Scope: What Do You Do?

Targets: Whom Are You For?

Positioning: How Are You Different?

Plan Objectives: What Needs to Be Achieved?

Sales Objectives → **Marketing Objectives** → **Communication Objectives**

Message Strategy: What's Your Story?

Umbrella Strategy: What's the Plan of Action?

Part III. Tactical Plans

Marketing Mix Tools: How Are We Going to Do It?

Product   Pricing   Advertising   Media   Merchandising
Naming   Distribution   Promotions   Interactive   Public Relations
Packaging   Personal Selling   Media

Part IV. Evaluation

Budget: What Is the Cost? → **Payback:** Can We Win? → **Calendar:** When? → **Execution:** How? → **Plan Evaluation:** Did It Work?

Targets

"**W**hen you dance with your customers, let them lead."

You have just finished identifying the scope of the marketing plan that establishes what business you are in and helps provide direction to the boundaries of your broad target markets: users, channels, geography, industry categories, and competitive sets. This chapter builds on that work, and it answers specifics around the question, Whom are you for?

The word market in the word marketing reminds us that, as marketers, the most important decision we need to make in developing a marketing plan pertains to focusing on specific customer markets and market segments. Marketing departments exist to understand, listen to, and interpret the needs of the customers. Effective marketing departments bring the voice of the external customers into the daily internal workings of every department in the company.

The most important steps you'll take in developing your marketing plan are to clearly define your customer target market and market segments and then create a bridge of learning and understanding to your target markets so that you can fulfill the definition of marketing.

Let's quickly review the definition of marketing:

- Determining and defining your target customers
- Determining their needs and wants
- Satisfying those needs and wants better than the competition does

FROM THIS CHAPTER YOU WILL LEARN

- The definition of target markets and market segments
- Various ways to segment a target audience
- A methodology for establishing primary and secondary customer target market segments
- How to write descriptors of target market segments

OVERVIEW

In effect, your company exists because of the customers or target markets you choose to serve. In your business review, you analyzed potential targets by looking at many industry categories and then potential company target market segments responsible for product sales volume. One common marketing mistake is to attempt to be all things to all people. It is in this section of the marketing plan that the marketer must decide which target segments will form the core of the business and receive the emphasis of effort and budget.

If you're not something to someone, you're nothing to everyone.

Targets are the key to all that follows in the marketing plan because your target markets and market segments are the reasons for your product's existence and the key to finding marketing answers. Let your customer targets drive your marketing plan.

Segmentation

Definition of **segmentation:** A selection process that divides the broad consuming market into manageable customer or noncustomer groups with common characteristics that determine a meaningful difference in how they purchase, what they purchase, or when they purchase. For example, a broad target market might be moms, but a segment within that market might be new moms, moms of teens, upscale moms, moms of adopted children, and so on.

Segmentation helps you answer the following questions:

1. Who are my customers?
2. How and where can I find more of them?
3. What channels should I use to provide products and services to them?
4. What messages should I use?
5. Which are the best media or how do I best reach and connect with them?

We're assuming you have a limited budget? Segmentation allows you to realize the greatest potential sales at the lowest cost. Segmentation helps you efficiently and effectively allocate your budget in the following ways:

- It focuses your efforts on the customer profiles that you stand the best chance of turning into loyal, long-term customers.
- It directs your efforts more effectively to gain new customers.

Segmentation provides the marketer an opportunity to exploit the common characteristics of the highest-potential target segments through the company's product development, operations, and marketing efforts. Instead of marketing to the "average" consumer, you are able to pinpoint specific clusters of customers and potential customer segments who have unique and unifying characteristics, attitudes, concerns, purchasing habits, and needs and wants.

The most effective marketing communication is essentially the one-on-one sales call, where the skilled salesperson can address the needs of the individual prospect.

Due to the similarities inherent in a given segment, marketers can address groups as if they were communicating with one individual.

There are three main targets to consider when identifying your primary and secondary target segments that determine who you are going to focus on when you market your company or its products and services. Which one or combination you use depends on your type of business. The methodology described in this chapter applies to all three:

1. *Consumers:* Many businesses market directly to consumers. Segmentation allows you to break the mass consumer market into smaller coherent pieces with similar characteristics, similar needs and wants, similar perceptions about the products you're selling, and similar purchasing behaviors. As a result, you are able to more efficiently and effectively spend your marketing dollars in obtaining new customers, retaining existing customers, and creating loyal customers.
2. *Businesses:* Many businesses make their living selling to other businesses. Similar to the consumer segment above, segmentation allows you to break the mass business market into small targets (e.g., the type of business or the titles within a business), each with similarities, allowing for a more efficient and effective marketing effort.
3. *Channels:* Many businesses are involved in marketing both to end user consumers and also specific distribution channels. For example, the manufacturer of consumer products also has to consider the retail channels as targets.

Target Markets and Target Market Segments

There's a difference between a target market and a target segment. We're not going to get too lost in the semantics, but you can think of the differences this way: target markets are large consuming publics and target market segments are subgroups within the larger target markets. In most cases, your business will focus on target segments within a larger target market. Let's look at some examples.

In the preceding chapter on scope, the core competency work you did started the process of identifying broad target markets that define your success. For example, we saw that Black & Decker isn't in the business of manufacturing power drills. In actuality, it possesses a combination of skills that sets them apart in the manufacturing of electric motors. This understanding has helped them to identify three large target markets to focus on:

- The home workshop market (sanders and drills)
- The home cleaning market (maintenance products like DustBusters)
- Kitchen appliances (can openers and food processors)

However, unless Black & Decker has an unlimited budget, unlimited people, and unlimited organizational energy, like any business it needs to focus its efforts. The question now becomes, What are the critical target segments within each broad market defined in the scope section in which the company will compete and win? For example, marketing to all consumers in the home cleaning target market would be a very expensive and inefficient proposition. Compare this with creating a bigger impact against a certain set of consumers defined by demographics, the type of home they have, how they behave, their motivations and emotions toward cleaning (fanatical to laissez-faire), or perhaps something else that takes a subset of the mass market and sets it apart from the others.

EXHIBIT 5.1

Target Markets versus Target Market Segments

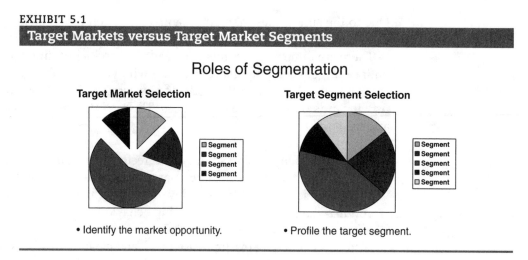

Exhibit 5.1 shows graphically a first choice of a broad target market and the subsequent choice of discrete target audience segments within the first larger target market. In the chart, we've used an example from our experience working with a manufacturer of premium windows and doors. This company took a comprehensive approach to segmenting the market.

In Exhibit 5.1, the graph on the left represents four broad **target markets**:

1. The residential home construction market, which happens to be the largest
2. The residential home remodeling market
3. The commercial building construction market
4. The commercial building remodeling market

During the housing boom years from the late 1990s until the early 2000s, this manufacturer focused a lot of its efforts on the first target market segment, residential home construction.

The graph on the right represents five discrete **target audience segments** of homeowners within the broad target market of residential construction—based on needs, behaviors, attitudes, and sociodemographics:

1. *Price conscious*, who view a window as a commodity, like Sheetrock or insulation
2. *Showcasers*, outer-directed people who view their home as their castle and want the world to see it
3. *Environmentalists*, who care about saving money on energy costs and improving the climate
4. *Family pragmatics*, who place a priority on function over style
5. *Quality conscious*, who want to buy only the best regardless of cost

Based on common wants and needs, this manufacturer chose target segments 2 and 5 against which to place its marketing efforts for its premium line of wood-clad windows within the broad target market of residential home construction.

Then there are also the channels that need consideration. The window manufacturer above had to consider not only the end user target audience segments but also the channels like Home Depot and lumber yards and the influencers of the end users, like home building contractors and architects.

Segmentation Options

The following segmentation categories were reviewed in the business review under the consumer and customer review. Use these to help you think about potential target market segments for your business.

Customers and Noncustomers

There is often a big difference between how your current customers perceive you and even behave in the marketplace compared to how your prospects or noncustomers perceive you. Let's take a typical health care demographic: women 25 to 54 with kids. If you are a health system marketing to this consumer segment, those who are customers may perceive you very differently than do women of the same demographic segment who are not customers but merely prospects. Knowing this, you may need to develop completely different marketing objectives and subsequent strategies for existing customers versus prospects from the same target segment—the difference being the further break or segmentation of customers versus noncustomers.

In Exhibit 5.2 the chart shows the different perceptions of a company that sells computer paper to the office managers of small businesses. Notice the difference between the customer perceptions in all capital letters and the noncustomer perceptions in lowercase. While the company gets consistently high rankings from existing customers, noncustomers score the company significantly worse across all attributes with the largest gap occurring with the attribute that is most important to respondents (highest on the chart), reliable delivery.

Customer Tenure

Existing customers often display different purchasing habits (number of purchases, amount of purchases, different product mixes) based on the number of years they have been a customer with your company. In addition, the retrial or renewal rate is often different by tenure.

We recently found that new members of a national credit union had significantly less knowledge and understanding of the products and services compared to established members. This resulted in less use of things like the call center and Internet banking, services that when used led to greater satisfaction scores and ultimately

EXHIBIT 5.2

Customers versus Noncustomers

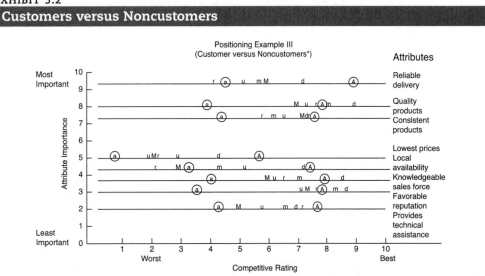

*Uppercase letters represent customers; lowercase letters represent noncustomers.

greater use of the credit union's financial products. The result was a strategy developed to engage new members with the credit union increasing their knowledge of both financial products that were offered and how to access services such as the call center, ATMs, and the website.

Demographics or Description of Businesses

Demographics include descriptors such as age, income, education level, marital status, employment or job classification, race, and homeownership. Demographics are a good first cut at helping to determine common purchasing patterns for many consumer products. Most household durables and consumables, automobiles, bicycles, apparel fashions, vacation destinations, and kids' games are but a few of the many examples of items likely to be purchased by consumers within specific demographic ranges.

For business-to-business marketers, businesses can be segmented by NAICS or other types of classifications that segment businesses by their industry category. For example, an accounting firm could choose to target retailers and then further segment against family-owned retailers for whom the dominant issues are running the business and creating a succession plan to pass it on to another family member or an outsider. The accounting firm could offer its specialized expertise in those particular areas of concern.

Buying Habits and/or Product Uses

Segmentation can be based on how the product is purchased or used, the number of times it is purchased per year, the time of year it is purchased, customers' loyalty to it, or the tenure of its use. For example, baking soda target markets are segmented based on customers' use of the product either for cooking or deodorizing a refrigerator. We selected targets for the Culligan company based on the use of its products for water filtration purposes—water pitchers, sink units, and whole-house systems. Through research, we found that each product type was purchased by a different target market through a different channel of distribution.

Many consumer goods firms target consumers based on buying habits, specifically the consumers' propensity for multiple purchases. We worked with a game company in the puzzle business whose heavy users purchased 8 to 12 puzzles per year. Much of our target market segmentation work and many of the subsequent marketing objectives were developed around this purchasing behavior. We developed objectives to increase the number of our client's puzzles purchased per year and strategies that called for series of puzzles and incentives to generate loyalty to this particular company's puzzles.

In addition, there are many product categories in which the product is used or consumed differently by different target market groups. This is common in the business-to-business area, where spray-dried cheese is used very differently by Frito Lay in the processing of snacks than by Swanson in its TV dinners. Segmentation by different levels of consumption use is also common in consumer packaged-goods marketing. For example, the snack industry segments users by individual, family, and party size, among others, when developing its package sizes.

In Exhibit 5.3, you can see how a financial services firm could choose to target segments based on their behavior category:

1. *Handholders:* Need personalized advice and handholding
2. *Bargain hunters:* Need the best deals, lowest costs, highest rates, and fewest fees
3. *Information seekers:* Need tools and information to make empowered decisions
4. *One-stop shoppers:* Need the convenience of consolidating as many services with one company as possible

EXHIBIT 5.3

Target Market Segmentation Based on Consumer Behavior

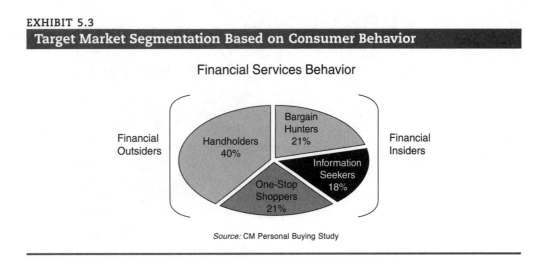

Financial Services Behavior

Source: CM Personal Buying Study

Each segment wants very different things, and given the behavioral preferences, it is very unlikely that any one company is going to be able to satisfy all four segments. Handholding takes a fairly robust organizational structure, higher costs, and a consultative sales force. It would be very difficult if not impossible to construct a business model to deliver personalized advice, handholding, and the lowest costs.

The same becomes true of satisfying the information seekers. The core competencies the business needs to provide tools and information allowing the individual to make empowered financial decisions is very, very different from providing personalized service and handholding. It's hard to envision the same company financially being able to do both. By now you're getting our point, but to finalize the argument, can you imagine a bank that is a full-service, high-touch, one-stop shop that provides the lowest cost across all services? In summary, the businesses in this category need to understand the individual segments that exist in the category and then shape their business to win against one of them.

Lifestyle Characteristics

Psychographics (values, lifestyles, interests, and attitudes) are often used in conjunction with demographics to identify target market descriptors. One example would be a new five-blade propeller that we helped Mercury Marine introduce to the marketplace. We targeted against two lifestyle interests: waterskiing and bass fishing. The five-blade prop provided significantly better "hole shot," or acceleration. Both of these segments had a need for this type of product, and they were predicted to account for a significant percentage of the sales volume for the five-blade propeller. The water-skier target is obvious, but the bass fisherman may not be. Bass fishermen constantly move to find the best spot. They fish one hole, then go to the next. This is especially important during the many contests that the avid fisherman and woman participate in across the country. Both these lifestyle segments were targeted in terms of media, advertising (testimonials from expert water-skiers and bass fishermen), distribution of the product, and point-of-sale merchandising.

Exhibit 5.4 shows a study segmenting the market for women's fashions on the basis of lifestyle.

A brand like Talbots has made a careful and discriminating choice to build its entire retail experience and merchandise selection around the timeless style desires of the modern classic segment. Target, on the other hand, has built its business and brand by providing cheap, chic fashion items for the fun, informed, and influential.

EXHIBIT 5.4

Lifestyle Target Segmentation

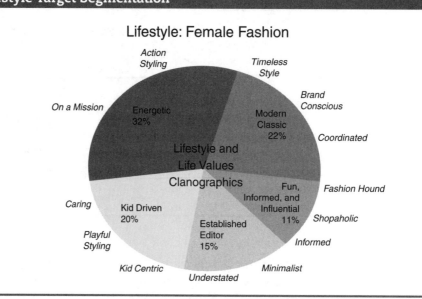

Geography

Purchasing rates often differ according to geography. Segmentation can be based on climate, the consumption habits of certain regions, and other factors that cause differences in volume and usage by geography.

When you developed the company background section of the marketing plan, you determined the regions, markets, and/or areas of markets that have the greatest consumption potential for your product by comparing the overall industry category sales to the sales of your product in comparable geographic areas. (See the discussion of BDI and CDI in Chapter 2.) Based on this analysis, you may want to expand, reduce, or merely refine the geographic focus of your target segment.

Attribute Preferences

Different target audiences purchase different product categories due to product features, attributes, and benefits. Features like sealed gaskets, no-shatter glass, and chrome finish are inherent parts of a product or service. Attributes are a quality or characteristic of your product or service, things such as broad selection, friendly, best price, best quality, best value (the relationship of price and quality together), best service, fashionable, cool, competent, and so on. Finally, benefits are tangible or perceived advantages or feelings the consumer gets from purchasing or using your product or service, things such as safe choice, dependable, feeling attractive, a pause that refreshes, providing a sense of family, and so on.

For a retailer marketing fabric to people who sew, product attributes or benefits became the primary means of defining the target market. As not everyone who sews considers both large selection and low prices of fabrics to be equally important when choosing one fabric store over the other, the retailer made "selection shoppers" its primary target because it could not profitably deliver the price benefit as well as the large selection. Another competitor created an "ideas" store targeting a segment of women for whom sewing was an expression of creativity and not an economic necessity.

Oftentimes with manufacturers of consumer products who sell to retailers who in turn sell directly to consumers, the attribute or benefit target segment determines the channel target as well. For example, the value shopper typically spends time in the off-price, the midtier, or the discount types of retailers. Understanding the channels that match up to the consumer segmentation, in this example the value shopper, is an important consideration when developing target segments.

Emotional Connections

Many times you can segment your target market by emotional connections to your product, company, or service. While harder to define and quantify, emotional segments are often the most powerful because they uncover the real reasons consumers are using and continue to use your products. Beer companies know that their products are badges defining different types of individuals who drink beer—a man's man, a rugged outdoor enthusiast, an intelligent sophisticate. Some soft drinks target the segment of extreme sports junkies who fashion themselves daredevils. For Sonic Foundry's ACID music software, we targeted young adults whose dream it was to be a music rock star through an emotional appeal of "being the star." Even in the business-to-business area, emotional appeals work.

Don't think that emotional segmenting is only for consumer companies. We worked with a large storage systems company and with a large architect/construction company, and both used emotional segmentation to effectively market their companies. One targeted purchasers who feared failure (we're the safe choice when your job is on the line); the other targeted a segment that took great pride in the aesthetic look of their surroundings (we can help you look innovative and modern).

In Exhibit 5.5, we define emotional segments of people who spend less than $30,000 for a new car. Based on our sociodemographic analysis, we've come up with descriptors for these segments that lend themselves to emotional appeals. A brand like Hyundai, for example, might target the segments on the left with its strong value proposition of inexpensive style and luxury. That value proposition would appeal to all three segments: "living *la vida loca*," young urban professionals out on the town; "three-car garage," suburban parents buying the third car for their high school drivers; and "champagne taste on a beer budget," price-conscious consumers who seek the style and luxury of a much more expensive car brand. The two segments on the right, however—"Letterman's mom," representing traditional, older, midwestern Americans, and "born in the USA," traditional, blue-collar, small-town, Main Street Americans—might be more resistant to considering a brand made in Korea.

EXHIBIT 5.5

Target Market Segmentation Based on Customers' Emotional Connections

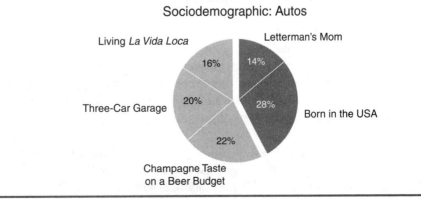

Sociodemographic: Autos

Source: Campbell Mithun Targeting.

Base: 20,000, spent less than $30,000 on car purchases.

Dollar Size or Employee Size

Many times a business-to-business company can segment its customer and potential customer segments on the target companies' dollar sizes or employee sizes. A successful training company for many Fortune 500 companies used this method. Large companies were continually bringing in new managers because of growth and turnover. These companies needed the training company's highly successful and profitable baseline-training program to be implemented year after year. Midsize to smaller companies, however, rarely ran the training company's baseline program in back-to-back years. In fact, it was rare that they would rerun it within even a five-year period. Therefore, in order to retain these midsize and smaller clients (and even get a chance to rerun the baseline program five years down the line), it was imperative that the training company implement a successful follow-up to the baseline program. Marketing the follow-up program to small and midsize businesses versus larger companies required different products, selling effort, and marketing communications in order to be effective.

Organizational Structure

In the business-to-business area, segments are often successfully developed based on the company's organizational structure. There is a very successful advertising agency in Madison, Wisconsin, that has successfully done this: Knupp, Watson and Walman, known as KW2. This agency has developed a highly sophisticated ability to attract government business and also consumer and business-to-business clients. KW2's work with the government requires it to be very adept at writing government requests for proposals (RFPs). It must also adhere to special budgeting, accounting, and other work rules and regulations that are very different from those typically required on the consumer and business-to-business side of the agency. However, the agency successfully bridges the gap between government work and consumer and business-to-business by targeting companies outside of government that have organizational similarities to those in government. For example, the agency does very well with nongovernmental businesses, such as those in the medical field with very complex decision-making structures, service partnerships such as engineering businesses, and associations. Additionally, government work typically involves selling a very emotional idea (reduction of tobacco use, anti–drunk driving, work zone safety). As a result, KW2 also seeks out consumer and business-to-business firms that need ideas and emotional communications to succeed. They call it "disruptive communications for organizations that have a passion." In summary, KW2 doesn't go after everyone, but based on an organizational target market, it is able to successfully grow its agency by obtaining clients across the broad spectrum of government, business-to-business, and consumer firms.

Heavy Users

Analyze the target market data in your business review to determine if there is a heavy user for your product. As a guideline, you have a heavy user in your company or industry product category if one-third of the target purchasers accounts for two-thirds or more of the sales. For example, the last time we worked in the category, 35 percent of canned-vegetable users consumed 65 percent of all canned vegetables.

Define the heavy-user segment based on the descriptive data available to you. For the consumer market, the heavy-user descriptor could include demography, geography, and/or possibly lifestyle and product benefit information, if available. For business-to-business markets, the heavy user might be a specific industry type (NAICS code), a relatively small number of distributors, a specific job function, a specific organizational structure, or a specific customer group identified on the basis of some sort of longevity criteria (new customers, existing customers over five years, and so on).

Short- and Long-Term Target Segments

Remember to develop short-term target segments (those responsible for sales within the next year) and also distinct, long-term target segments (those that you wish to develop over the next two to three years but that will not account for significant sales in the short term). Long-term target segments are either emerging targets that are too small to be a primary focus short term or larger existing industry target segments typically requiring that your company make significant changes in product, distribution, or operational requirements prior to your effectively satisfying the long-term target segments and gaining meaningful market share.

Purchasers or Users?

Many times the purchaser of a product is different from the user. If this is true in your situation, you need to decide who has the major influence over the actual purchase. Does the one who drinks the beer request a special brand, or does the beer drinker drink what the shopper purchases? In many households, the beer drinker is not the beer purchaser. So you have a decision to make. In most cases, the individual who does the purchasing becomes the primary target. However, when the purchaser primarily buys what the user requests, then the user receives primary attention.

Ideally, you'll be deciding whether the primary target group will include segments of purchasers or users. And there will be situations when you target both. However, keep in mind that it is very difficult (not to mention expensive) to effectively market against two primary markets. We would discourage you from targeting both the user and the purchaser if you are not one of the top companies in terms of market share and share of media spend. Consider these three factors in your determination of whether to target segments of the purchaser, the user, or both.

1. The inherent benefits of your product to either the user or the purchaser. Which one will value your product more and why?
2. The strength of your competitors and their focus against either the purchaser or the user. Do your competitors focus their marketing against one or the other leaving you the option to go in a different direction?
3. The size of your budget relative to your competitive set. Do you have the budget to adequately support focus against both the user and the purchaser at the same time?

The following examples will help you see how other companies face this choice and the factors that help them determine whether to target segments of the purchaser, the user, or both? The first three examples are companies that made a choice and picked either the user or the purchaser as their main focus. The last two examples are companies that had the resources to focus on both.

- In the market testing of a hot water faucet for Elkay Manufacturing, one potential target segment was small businesses because the Hot Water Machine eliminated the mess of making office coffee. We knew that business managers and company presidents were the primary decision makers and purchasers in small to midsize businesses. For both of these titles, we could purchase actual names for a direct-mail test. However, every office had a "coffee maker" who was the user and could greatly influence the purchase decision. While we couldn't purchase names for this function, we felt we could effectively use a functional title and each office would know whom we were addressing. We tested different direct-mail lists and found that the "Office Coffee Maker" label on the mailer was by far the most productive.

- In the case of shoe purchasers and users, a mother who buys shoes for her children, herself, and her husband is responsible for 80 percent of family purchases and is the heavy purchaser. With our shoe retail client, two mom segments—fashion value moms and core value moms—became the primary target segments and received the major marketing emphasis.
- Powdered soft drinks are consumed primarily by kids age 2 to 11 but are purchased by their mothers and fathers. Should you market to the kids who are the users or to the moms and dads who are the purchasers? Ideally, if you dominate the category and have adequate marketing dollars, you should target both. But for many companies, that's not economically possible. If you are a low-share competitor and have limited marketing dollars, as was the case for one particular client, you should concentrate on a single target customer segment. In our case, the primary target segment was redefined as kids 2 to 11, with the marketing focus concentrated against the user rather than the purchaser. The result was a revival in sales and a share increase.
- McDonald's is a good example of the exception. It targets both the user and the purchaser. As it is a dominant player in its category, it has substantial marketing dollar leverage. As a result, McDonald's puts major emphasis against its two mass market primary targets: kids because they are users and influencers and they are considered the cornerstone of McDonald's business, and adults because they are also users and, more important, because they are purchasers who bring their kids to McDonald's.
- For Kerry Food Ingredients, our primary focus was on the research and development (R&D) target—the users who first determine whether to incorporate Kerry's spray-dried ingredients into a new or existing food. Our secondary focus, however, was to create different messages for the purchasing agents (purchasers), who often have a major influence on whether Kerry Foods products continue to be purchased after the initial trial generated by the R&D staff. However, it should be noted that we spent significantly more marketing dollars against the primary R&D target market than we did against purchasing agents.

Primary and Secondary Target Market Segments

When you develop and choose the target segments that you will build your marketing plan around, remember that there are varying degrees of importance among the various segment options. We group these segment options into primary and secondary targets. While both are responsible for generating sales, much more is typically expected from the primary target segments. As a result, the primary target segments are allocated a much greater share of the company's marketing budget and are expected to contribute to generating sales and total profits at far greater rates than secondary target segments.

The following will provide you with an overview as to the definitions of primary and secondary target segments and provide practical advice on how to determine whether a target segment is primary or secondary.

Primary Target Market Segments

Your primary target segment will be the one that is most critical to the success of your company. The primary target segment determines where you will place the majority of your focus and commit the majority of your budget as you develop your marketing plan. It's also the target segment that will provide you with the majority of your sales and profits.

A good way to start thinking about your primary customer target market is by using this simple test: Which customer segment, if it suddenly disappeared, would cause you to lose the most sleep at night? Every business has one target segment that if it just disappeared, it would create fundamental problems for the business—probably causing the business to fold. Thinking about your customer segments in this way helps you to realize which is the most important and which should receive the majority of budget for product and service development, marketing communication focus, and even customer research.

The primary target customer segment is often the heavy user (one-third or fewer of the purchasers who account for two-thirds or more of the purchases). While the primary target market isn't always the heavy user, this is an excellent place to start as you are determining your primary target market.

In some situations, there will be a primary target customer segment that is an intermediate channel, such as a distributor, and a primary target that is a consumer or end user. These targets will have different ties to sales (for example, a wholesale price and a retail price, respectively), and both will require separate strategies and programs to fulfill different objectives. Many manufacturers like Mercury Marine find that to be successful, they need to target both the boating retailers and the ultimate consumer of their products.

The following criteria should be fulfilled before you finalize a primary target customer market choice.

- *Focus matters*. Make sure that your primary target can be narrowly defined by one unified profile. The primary target should be a group of individuals or companies with the same basic identifiers, needs, wants, and purchasing behaviors. This will allow your marketing effort to be focused against essentially one type of individual or company.
- *Size matters*. Make sure the customer base is large enough in terms of actual numbers of customers and prospects that match the segment description. Additionally, make sure the total segment does enough business for you to grow into the future. What percent of the product category's volume does your primary target consume? Given your projected market share, is it enough to support your business? And is the target market growing in size and becoming more or less important? (See Task 5, "Analyze Demand for Your Products and Services," at the end of this chapter.)

   A common factor in a plan's failure is a target segment that is too small and limiting. Don't develop neat and tidy primary target segments which are so small that even a huge market share won't ensure that you'll meet your sales goals. Ideally, try to get your primary target profile to be accountable for at least 30 to 50 percent of the industry category's or your competitive set's volume. *Note*: This does not mean you will capture 30 to 50 percent of the category's sales. It does mean, if this is the size of your primary target segment, that a certain percent will be aware of you, a smaller percent will form positive attitudes toward you, a smaller percent will try you, and an even smaller percent will become loyal. Making sure you have a realistically sized target segment universe will help to ensure that you have enough actual customers to meet your sales and profit goals.
- *Sometimes small is beautiful*. The 30 to 50 percent criterion can be lower if you are going to specialize against a narrower purchaser and/or user base as a strong niche player. But remember, successful niche players need to obtain a

larger market share against their target segment than would be possible or typical in a larger market situation with more competitors. In order to accomplish this, you must be certain that your company has some special tie to the narrow niche target segment that will command loyalty resulting in a very high market share against the niche segment. Finally, niche players rarely dominate demographic segments. Instead, they dominate subsegments within the demographic segment like alternative music listeners or alternative sports enthusiasts, within the 18- to 24-year-old target.

- *Profitability matters.* Make sure the target is profitable. Determine that the target's purchases are of sufficient quantity to ensure profitability.
- *The future matters.* Try to estimate the trending of your primary target segment. Is it a growing or shrinking segment? If it is shrinking, will the target be large enough to support your business at its current market share in five years? If not, this should be a danger signal.

In summary, the primary target becomes the company's reason for being. You are in business to determine the primary target's wants and needs and to provide for those wants and needs better than your competition. This pertains to providing the product, service, shopping or sales environment, distribution channel, and price structure that is required by the customer for purchase. The better the definition and description of the consumers in your primary target market, the better you will be able to market to them.

Secondary Target Market Segments

Most plans will identify multiple target segments. The primary target segments receive priority and a majority of the marketing spending because they will most directly influence the short-term financial success of the plan. The secondary targets are also important because they provide additional sales and/or influence on the sales to the company beyond that of the primary targets as well as future sales to the company.

A secondary target customer segment is typically one of the following:

- *Important industry category consumer segment but currently not a strong customer segment:* A secondary target can often be a customer who currently does not purchase heavily from your company but who has high purchasing potential because of the target segment's sheer size and importance to the industry category in which you compete. You can delineate the potential of this customer by estimating your competitors' sales to this customer and determining what additional needs your company is able to fulfill for this customer.
- *A segment that is currently small but is growing rapidly:* In some cases, you may identify segments that have great growth potential but are currently very small in absolute purchasing power. You may want to begin to cultivate and grow this target that is projected to become very important in a few years.
- *A target segment with a low volume but a high concentration index:* Often there is a distinct target segment that accounts for a small percentage of the volume but contains a high concentration of purchasers. For example, 18- to 24-year-olds may account for only 10 percent of the total product category purchases, but 50 percent of the 18- to 24-year-olds may purchase the product. This may be due to the popularity of the product among members of this age group, but this age group may also have fewer total purchase occasions, or they may purchase less expensive product models. In any case, a great percentage of the target market segment uses the product, which provides the opportunity for

efficient use of marketing dollars and little wasted coverage in targeting the segment.

- *A subset of the purchasers or users who make up the primary target segment:* As stated in the previous section, your primary target should ideally be one unified profile of customers accounting for greater than 30 percent of the category volume. This allows for a focusing of resources and message in the marketing effort. However, there are situations in which the volume of any one target segment is not substantial enough to qualify it as a primary target market. In addition, each smaller target market has different demographics, needs, wants, product usage, and purchasing behaviors.

  An example of this is in the target market one of the authors worked on and developed for a regional menswear retailer. The retailer was selling primarily suits and sports coats. There were many purchasing profiles, but no single profile group provided enough volume to allow for targeting against that group. The *primary target* became very broad and encompassed 18- to 54-year-olds for whom more formal suits and sports coats were critical to their jobs. However, the following *secondary targets* were developed, with subsequent marketing emphasis and programs against each:
  - Men in the 18- to 24-year-old age group, college graduates, entering the working world and looking for affordable suits.
  - Men in the 45-plus age group, with higher incomes, at the top of their profession, interested in quality menswear and needing to update their wardrobes.
  - Women in the 18- to 34-year-old age group. Women have great influence over men's purchases of suits and sports coats. Spouses also purchase a substantial number of sports coats as gifts and accompany men in more than 50 percent of their shopping trips, serving as advisors.
  - Blue-collar males who needed an all-occasion suit. Price is a concern for this group.
  - Target markets were also broken out by type of profession, as this helped dictate quantity and style of suit purchases.

- *Influencers:* Influencers can be a primary or secondary target customer segment, though in most situations they are secondary targets. These are individuals who influence the purchase or usage decision of the primary target. A good example of this is the influence children have on their parents in the purchase of many consumer goods, from toys to fast food. Another example is the influence of architects in the use of precast concrete. While the general contractor and the engineer make the actual purchase decision, the architect has tremendous influence both up front in the design of the building and in the final selection of materials.

  Influencers are of particular importance in public sector marketing, where outside forces can affect the success of an organization's marketing program. In a statewide bus transit marketing effort, we concentrated marketing efforts against current and potential riders as our primary target, but for our secondary market, we also targeted opinion leaders, major employers, and education leaders, all of whom would affect the communities' support of the bus system.

- *Manufacturers' intermediate channels as secondary target market segments:* This target might be a fabricator, distributor and/or wholesaler, or retailer that should receive special attention in order to make sure the product is available for the end user to purchase. This is particularly true for consumer goods, because in these markets there is usually minimal retail shelf space available and multiple competitors selling the same type of product. Often, a great deal of time and money are devoted to selling to the end user while the intermediate channel is taken for granted. That's unfortunate because the channel partner has a huge impact in the ultimate selling of your product—from allocating shelf space and the location of that space within the store, to selling support on the floor, to designating co-op dollars for co-marketing programs with your company.

Conversely, many business-to-business manufacturers, because they are selling directly to an intermediate target segment (which is their primary target), *push* these products through the primary distribution channel (often using superior service, a stronger product mix, or low prices and promotions) and put less marketing emphasis on the end user consumer to *pull* the product through the channels. It might be more efficient in the short term to push the product through intermediate markets. However, the end user consumer should not be totally ignored, as this may mean a loss of demand and loyalty for your product or brand over the long term.

TARGET MARKET SEGMENTATION METHODOLOGY

The methodology for determining target market segments involves the following five tasks. Note that the following methodology is designed for a target that consumes a *group of products* within an industry market category as identified in the scope section of the marketing plan (industry market category examples would be shoes, sporting goods, accounting services, construction services, and so on). If you have one product, the same methodology applies, except you eliminate Task 1 and start with Task 2, listing the segments for your one product.

See Appendix C, Worksheet 34, Tasks 1 through 5, to help you develop your target market strategies.

TASK 1 ### Identify Top-Selling and Growth Products

The target process starts with identifying both the **industry category and your company's products** that:

- Constitute the top-selling products.
- Demonstrate the greatest growth potential or are projected to be the greatest growth vehicles.
- Are the main drivers of purchasers to your business and/or have strong profitability. These products may not be the largest sellers or the most profitable, but they are core to your customers' interest in your company.

The top-selling products and services that are growing the fastest are the result of the marketplace's voting on what it likes best. Therefore, top-selling products are of interest to you for a couple of reasons. First, they demonstrate demand and preference from the marketplace, and second, they represent volume to your company. The products highest in profitability aren't a result of the marketplace's vote (they don't choose products based on what makes your company the most money), such as the top-selling and fastest-growing products, but they are of interest internally to your company. Thus in identifying the top-selling, most profitable, and fastest-growing products for both the industry and your company, you accomplish several things:

- You identify whether your company is similar or different to the industry category in which you compete.
- You have started to focus by setting yourself up to examine the profiles of consumers and influencers responsible for purchasing the successful products (Task 2).
- You provide a nod to the future by also identifying those products that demonstrate the greatest growth potential. The target segments that purchase the fastest-growing products may be very different from the target segments that purchase the industry or your company's top-selling products. As a result, in Task 2 you will be able to identify emerging target market segments along with the existing heavy users.

Refer to the business review, and list the products that had the most category and/or company sales, profits, or transactions and are demonstrating the most growth (sales analysis section). Exhibit 5.6 begins a hypothetical example—a manufacturer of cross-country skis—that we will follow throughout this section. The example lists the strongest-selling products for both the cross-country ski industry category and the company we are following. (*Note*: All numbers are purely hypothetical.)

See Appendix C, Worksheet 34, Task 1.

TASK 2 ## Determine Key Industry and Company Target Market Segments

We now move to Task 2 where we identify the segments responsible for the largest share of purchases for each of the products most responsible for driving industry and company sales, now and in the future.

1. Determine the Industry Target Market Segments for Products with the Greatest Industry Category Sales and Growth

Using the work you did in Task 1 that identified the strongest-selling and fastest-growing products, determine the target segments (see the business review and segment descriptions earlier in this chapter) for the top-selling and fastest-growing products within the industry category in which you compete (based on the work you did in your business review and scope section).

2. Determine the Current Company Target Market Segments for the Company Products with the Greatest Sales and Growth

Divide the group of your *current customers* of your company's top-selling and fastest-growing products and/or services into smaller segments with common characteristics (see the segment descriptions earlier in chapter). Determine which customer segments drive the most volume of the company's top-selling and fastest-growing products identified in Task 1. List and describe the first two or three segment descriptions that account for the most purchases, profits, transactions, and/or customers for both the top-selling and the fastest-growing products.

3. Determine If Your Company's Primary (Largest and Most Important) Target Segment Matches That of the Leading Industry Target Segment

Examine the company target segment that accounts for the greatest company sales: Does it match that of the category target segment profile purchaser for the leading products from a sales and growth standpoint? If it doesn't, you are clearly servicing a niche segment, and if you don't know already, you'll need to

EXHIBIT 5.6
Product Sales Volume

List the products in the category that have the largest sales volume, largest profit, and fastest growth. Provide sales trends, profit trends, and the product line's percent of total category sales. Then provide similar information for the products in your company with the highest sales, strongest profitability, and fastest growth. Show the company market share growth for each product and the company's sales growth for key products compared to the growth of those same products within the category. The tables below demonstrate this process for our hypothetical cross-country ski manufacturer.

Cross-Country Ski Example: Category 5-Year Trend

INDUSTRY CATEGORY'S HIGHEST $ VOLUME PRODUCTS	SALES ($ MILLIONS)					PERCENT OF CATEGORY SALES					PROFIT, %					TRANSACTIONS/ PURCHASES (MILLIONS)				
	Yr 1	Yr 2	Yr 3	Yr 4	Yr 5	Yr 1	Yr 2	Yr 3	Yr 4	Yr 5	Yr 1	Yr 2	Yr 3	Yr 4	Yr 5	Yr 1	Yr 2	Yr 3	Yr 4	Yr 5
No-wax touring skis	900	960	1,050	1,020	960	41%	40%	41%	41%	40%	44%	44%	42%	42%	44%	3	3.2	3.5	3.4	3.2
Skate skis	750	800	875	875	900	34	33	34	35	37	44	44	45	45	46	1.5	1.6	1.8	1.8	1.8
Waxable touring skis	400	480	480	400	360	18	20	19	16	15	42	42	43	44	43	1	1.2	1.2	1	0.9
Back–country skis	125	150	175	190	200	6	6	7	8	8	45	46	48	49	49	0.3	0.3	0.4	0.4	0.4
Total category	2,175	2,390	2,580	2,485	2,420	99%	99%	101%	100%	100%										

Cross-Country Ski Example: Company 5-Year Trend

COMPANY'S HIGHEST $ VOLUME PRODUCTS	SALES ($ MILLION)					PERCENT OF COMPANY SALES					PROFIT, %					TRANSACTIONS/ PURCHASES (MILLION)				
	Yr 1	Yr 2	Yr 3	Yr 4	Yr 5	Yr 1	Yr 2	Yr 3	Yr 4	Yr 5	Yr 1	Yr 2	Yr 3	Yr 4	Yr 5	Yr 1	Yr 2	Yr 3	Yr 4	Yr 5
Skate skis*	200	211	243	245	255	63%	61%	62%	64%	66%	45%	46%	47%	47%	47%	0.4	0.4	0.5	0.5	0.45
Waxable touring skis	60	72	72	60	58	19	21	18	16	15	42	42	43	43	43	0.2	0.2	0.2	.0.2	0.15
Back-country skis	35	40	48	50	50	11	11	12	13	13	45	46	48	50	50	0.1	0.1	0.1	0.1	0.1
No-wax touring skis	24	25	27	29	26	8	7	7	8	7	43	43	42	42	42	0.1	0.1	0.1	0.1	0.09
Total company	319	348	390	384	389	101%	100%	99%	101%	101%										

Cross Country Ski Example: Sales Growth Company Compared to Category

COMPANY MARKET SHARE, %					Dollar Volume Products	Sales Percent Change Company (5-Year Trend) Yrs 1–5	Sales Percent Change Category (5-Year Trend) Yrs 1–5	Index Company to Category
Yr 1	Yr 2	Yr 3	Yr 4	Yr 5				
22%	26%	28%	28%	28%	Skate skis	27.50%*	20%	138†
15	15	15	15	16	Waxable touring skis	−3.33%	−10%	33
28	27	27	26	25	Back-country skis	42.86%	60%	71
3	3	3	3	3	No-wax touring skis	8.00%	6.67%	125
15	15	15	15	16	Total company	21.94%	11.26%	195

* $200 in Year 1 to $255 in Year 5 is an increase of 27.5 percent.

†Index = 27.50 percent ÷ 20 percent, or 1.38 × 100 = 138. Expectations would be that the industry category and the company would be the same for an index of 100. The company did 38 points better than expected.

understand who they are and why they purchase your products versus those of your industry category competitors.

The chart in Exhibit 5.7 provides an overview of what you just accomplished. It continues the hypothetical example started in Exhibit 5.6 of a manufacturer of cross-country ski equipment. Note that in Exhibit 5.6, the company's top-selling product differed from that of the industry category. The retailer we're following is significantly stronger in selling to a racing and competitive target market versus a

EXHIBIT 5.7

Defining Segments Based on Sales Potential

Sales and Profits for Top-Selling Products

Top-Selling Industry Products	Highest-Value Consumer Target Segment	Top-Selling Company Products	Highest-Value Consumer Target Segment
No-wax touring skis	Men 35–54, live in 4-season climate range, middle to upper middle income, college educated +, with children 6+ in age, that enjoy winter vacations and other recreational activities year-round. Strong propensity to visit county, state, and national parks.	Competitive skate skis	Men 25–64, live in 4-season climate range, mentally embrace and engage winter, highly educated with college+, upper middle+ income, cross-trains and participates in at least 3 races or other events (running, biking, triathlons, canoe, etc.) per year. High involvement with multiple fitness sports, has subscription to one or more silent sports publications. Skis more than 15 times per year and buys new equipment every 2–3 years.
Competitive skate skis	See description above	Waxable touring skis	See description below
Waxable touring skis	Male and female 24–54. Recreational skier who gets out one time per week or less. Looks upon cross-country skiing similar to a walk in the woods. Very convenience driven and doesn't want the perceived hassle of waxing.	Back-country skis	See description below

Top Growth Products

Top Industry Growth Products	Highest-Value Target Segment	Top Company Growth Products	Highest-Value Target Segment
Back-country skis 8% of category sales, 5-year growth rate: 60%	Men 18–45, with lower (college) income to middle income (occupations that allow for free time), live in areas with access to back-country terrain. Heavy skew toward outdoors, backpacking, cross-country skiing magazines. Participates in backpacking, rock climbing, and other similar activities on a regular basis. Personality profiles of risk takers.	Competitive skate skis 13% of company sales, 5-year growth rate: 43%	See description above

recreational market. This is evidenced in the fact that its strongest product sales come from skate skis used primarily in more competitive skiing. Furthermore, its second-strongest product sales come from waxed touring skis, skis that, again, are used by the more experienced cross-country skier and for racing as well. Clearly the company sells to the real cross-country skiing aficionados.

In reviewing Exhibits 5.6 and 5.7, you can see that while the recreational market is bigger (no-wax touring skis), this manufacturer has a significant market share against a specific target market that is not the industry category's largest target. The exercise would simply help the marketer focus efforts against what is most important to his or her company and to help with future strategy decisions. For example, given complete information in Exhibits 5.6 and 5.7, would the company want to develop a secondary target aimed at the larger recreational market? To answer this question, the marketer would need to review and interpret the following:

• Will the competitive skate market continue to grow, stagnate, or decrease in size over time?

- Has the company's penetration of the target racing skates and wax touring skis reached a saturation point? If it has, does the marketing plan call for significant growth? If penetration share has topped and the market growth has stagnated, the company's growth will need to come from another target segment.
- Would marketing to the recreational target segment hurt the manufacturer's standing with the racing target?

4. Identify the Power Segments, Which Are Those Target Market Segments Responsible for the Greatest Number of Sales across Multiple Products (If Applicable to Your Company)

By listing the top-selling products for your company and the top two or three segments responsible for their sales next to each, you will be able to go back and identify your most important company segments with estimates as to their value in terms of total sales across your product portfolio. For some companies, target segments have mutually exclusive products, but for many companies, a strong customer segment will be the leading segment across multiple company products. Do the same for segments responsible for the industry category sales.

See Appendix C, Worksheet 34, Task 2.

TASK 3 *Define the Primary and Secondary Target Market Segments*

This is the time to make final decisions regarding your primary and secondary target segments.

1. Define Your Primary Target Segment

The first place to look in finalizing your company's choice of primary target segment is to examine the segment that accounts for the majority of your sales. In doing this, you will be examining total sales that the segment is responsible for across multiple products if your company has a multiple product portfolio. In all likelihood, this segment defines your heavy-user group, the one-third of your customers who make up two-thirds or more of your sales and/or profits.

However, you need to also consider the following:

- How relevant and vibrant is this target segment within the industry?
- Is it growing? Are there substantial prospective customers who fall into the segment that you have the potential of obtaining in the future?

The largest customer segment of your company's customers may not be large enough to support your company into the future because it is a market that is shrinking and becoming less relevant. Based on the findings in your business review section, you may want to alter your initial target market profile description to more closely mirror the industry category's largest target market in order to expand your current customer base into the future. We are not saying to automatically do this, but you should at least consider the advantages and disadvantages of this comparison.

The flip side of this strategy is to continue carving out a primary target market that is somewhat unique to your company and that you alone can cultivate and dominate. By developing products, distribution channels, communications, and operations specific to this customer segment's needs, you can intimately connect with the target customers' needs, become part of their lifestyle, and be the preferred brand that is creating loyalty and commanding a premium price in return.

Finally, we're big believers in having **one primary customer segment** and not two. For example, an analysis for a national retail auto repair client experiencing flat traffic per store found that there were two primary target segments: those who go to the dealer after they purchase a new car for up to five years and those whose cars are older than five years who have a behavior pattern of fragmenting the care of the auto between specialists—places like Midas for mufflers, Jiffy Lube for oil changes, and the local service station for repairs. The retailer was splitting its efforts against both targets, but clearly the group consisting of new car purchasers was not going to be large enough due to the pull of the new car dealer in the first five years after the purchase of the new car. The only solution was to focus against the used-car owner with a car older than five years and to capture a greater share of that fragmented marketplace. In doing so, the company could be more effective and be something to someone instead of being just another option to two large primary segments.

2. Define Your Secondary Target Market Segments

Your company's primary segment's respective dollar volume will most likely not add up to meet or exceed your sales goals. The next step, then, in defining your target market is to define your secondary target segments.

Look for one or possibly two of the following scenarios:

- *Identification of a strong influencer target that doesn't make the purchases but influences the purchase decision of your primary target market.*
- *Identification of smaller customer segments that are fairly penetrated:* This would mean that you have a fairly large market share of that segment, you serve it well, and it connects with you, but it doesn't account for large sales volume, and there is not significant room for growth. In summary, you have high concentration or penetration of the target market but low overall volume and growth potential. The target market strategy here is to maintain market share.
- *Identification of a segment with which you are currently very weak in terms of customer market share:* Ideally, this would be a small but growing segment not targeted by the competition. These segments might be connected to products, attitudes, or emotions that your company doesn't perform well against but are becoming more important in the overall industry category. This means that later in the plan you would need to create the necessary products, distribution and communication strategies, and after-sales service capabilities to service this market. Alternatively, these segments might have purchasing needs that are in line with what your company offers; however, the segments have very low awareness or knowledge of your company, making them a potential fit for a secondary target as you work to improve awareness.
- *Identification of segments that are not dominant in terms of size or growth potential but are somehow either a lead-in to the primary target or connected to it in some way:* As an example, one of the authors worked with Allen Edmond Shoes to reach insights on how to motivate a younger male consumer, age 25 to 44, to begin purchasing the very upscale shoes. One of the reasons for this secondary target was to help ensure continuation of purchase into the core 45-to-64 age, higher-income, and upper management target profiles. Work was also done against the female significant other of the core male purchaser, a small target market but with a link to the primary target.

A final word of caution: Before you go on to develop a new market or modify an existing target, make sure you have fully exploited the profit potential of your current customer base. In most cases, your own customers are your most important and potentially most profitable target market because they are responsible for your firm's current existence and are a prime target for future sales. Target your current customers not only to retain their purchase loyalty but also to motivate them to make more and bigger purchases and to refer new customers.

3. Finalize Your Target Market Decisions and Capture the Driver Metrics for the Key Primary and Secondary Segments You've Identified

First, finalize your target market decisions, identifying your primary and secondary target segments. Provide a detailed description of the targets in terms of their demographics, lifestyle, attitudes, opinions, and interests. Then add the critical metrics in terms of size, target segment growth, and purchasing behavior including as much of the following list as you can obtain:

- The total number of customers and noncustomers that fit the primary target segment description or your total penetration of the existing segment
- The average-dollars-per-purchase occasion by your customers and noncustomers that fit the primary target segment description
- The number of purchase occasions or the number of purchases per year for the customers and noncustomers that fit the primary target segment description
- The retention rate and retrial rate for the customers and noncustomers that fit the primary target segment description
- The growth trends in terms of the total number of the primary target segment

See Exhibit 5.8 for an example of a target market description for the cross-country ski example that we've been developing.

See Appendix C, Worksheet 34, Task 3.

TASK 4   ## Refine Your Selections

Now that you have an idea regarding your primary and secondary target segments, there are a number of final considerations that become critically

EXHIBIT 5.8

Primary Target Market Descriptions, Including Customer and Noncustomer Behaviors

Primary Segment Description: Cross-Country Ski Racer
- Male 25 to 64
- Lives in 4-season climate range.
- Mentally loves, embraces, and engages in winter.
- College+, upper middle to upper income.
- Has a competitive mindset. High propensity to compete in off-season races such as marathons or triathlons or participates in multiple fitness sports.
- Very health and nutrition conscious.
- High interest and readership of vertical magazines and websites geared to competitive fitness sports.
- Participates in 3+ races or events per year.
- Skis more than 15 times per year.

	Total Segment	Company Customers
Total customers	2.8 million	780,000
5-year growth rate	20%	28%
Average dollars per purchase	$500	$566
Number of purchase occasions per year	1 every 3.5 years	1 every 3.25 years
Brand retrial rate over 5-year period	55%	70%

important. If your primary and secondary segment selections are not consistent with any of the following, you need to go back and rethink and possibly refine your selections.

1. Your Segments Should Be Consistent with Your Brand Positioning

Your company's primary and secondary target segments must sync with your brand positioning. This is a little like the chicken and the egg because the brand positioning portion of the plan is not complete at this point. Make sure you do the work in developing your brand positioning with your target market in mind. Then once you've finished the brand positioning work in the next chapter, come back and make sure your target segments sync with the emotional and rational components of your brand positioning and company's value promise.

2. Your Segments Should Have Strong Awareness of Your Company and Its Key Products

This is most important for your primary target segment. Refer to the business review to determine if there is average to above-average awareness for your company and/or products among the segment you are considering for your primary target market. If the awareness is not there, keep in mind that you will need to spend considerable dollars to increase it. If you choose your primary target segment for other good reasons and you find that it has very low awareness, consider making this a secondary target segment as you work to increase awareness over time and choosing another segment as primary based on a review of this section. Remember, *share of mind leads to share of market*. Exhibit 5.9 continues with our cross-country ski manufacturer example, examining awareness for the company and its competitors.

EXHIBIT 5.9

Awareness and Attitude Review of Chosen Segments

Male 25 to 64, Avid Cross-Country Ski Racer, Single, Upper Middle to Upper Income of $80,000+

	TARGET SEGMENT AWARENESS RATINGS, %				
	Yr 1	Yr 2	Yr 3	Yr 4	Yr 5
Company	28%	35%	36%	32%	30%
Leading competitor	10	12	15	17	18
Leading competitor	16	15	16	15	16
Leading competitor	15	14	13	12	10

	TARGET SEGMENT ATTRIBUTE RATINGS																			
	COMPANY RANKING					COMPETITOR A RANKING					COMPETITOR B RANKING					COMPETITOR C RANKING				
Top 5 Attributes	Yr 1	Yr 2	Yr 3	Yr 4	Yr 5	Yr 1	Yr 2	Yr 3	Yr 4	Yr 5	Yr 1	Yr 2	Yr 3	Yr 4	Yr 5	Yr 1	Yr 2	Yr 3	Yr 4	Yr 5
1. Overall quality	2	1	1	1	1	1	1	2	2	2	3	3	3	3	3	4	4	4	4	4
2. Lightweight	3	3	2	2	1	1	1	1	1	2	2	2	4	3	4	4	4	3	4	3
3. After-sale service	2	2	2	2	2	4	3	3	3	4	3	4	4	4	3	1	1	1	1	1
4. Price	3	3	2	3	3	2	2	3	2	2	4	4	4	4	4	1	1	1	1	1
5. Innovation	4	4	4	4	4	3	3	3	3	3	1	1	1	2	2	4	4	4	4	4

Notes: 1 = best; 5 = worst.

The data demonstrate that our cross-country ski manufacturer that we've been following throughout this methodology section scores very well on awareness but competitor 3 has been gaining. This is a concern since competitor A competes on the same attributes as our manufacturing company—quality and lightweight skis. While our manufacturing company retains the number one ranking on these two critical attributes (number one and two in importance), the data show that competitor A has historically scored very well on these attributes and has only recently fallen slightly behind on the attribute of lightweight. Competitor C appears to hold the price advantage, a fairly unimportant attribute to this target.

3. Your Segments Should Have Positive Attitudes toward Your Company across Its Most Critical Purchase Considerations

Make sure the attributes and attitudes (rational and emotional) around which you are establishing your positioning and differentiation are those where you already have positive perceptions and where there is reason to believe that you can get even stronger. Exhibit 5.9 looks at the attribute scores for the cross-country ski manufacturer example relative to the competitive set. Note that the attribute examples in Exhibit 5.9 are all rational. They just as easily could have been emotional and attitudinal in nature, such as "wants to feel his equipment is cutting edge," "seeks comfort in a brand that is used by the world's best," "sees cross-country skiing and aerobic exercise as a necessity in life, not an option."

See Appendix C, Worksheet 34, Task 4.

TASK 5   *Analyze Demand for Your Products and Services*

The last step in determining target segments is to attempt to calculate the demand for your product in your chosen customer target segments. The demand analysis is a check to make sure that the target segment is large enough to warrant your effort. The conclusions will be directional and are intended to provide you with a rough estimate of the size of your market and the potential business you might generate. It should give you a first check to make sure the sales goals you set in the plan are realistic and obtainable. The final check will be when you quantify your marketing objectives at the end of this chapter.

The following list outlines the procedures to take in estimating demand for your product.

1. *Target segment:* How many consumers are there in your target? Define the target segment in terms of numbers of potential customers. For example, if your target segment is women 25 to 49, provide the total number of women 25 to 49. Or if you're a financial institution targeting customers who want high touch over high tech, you might be targeting people with a mindset of being financially insecure and unknowledgeable. In that case, you need to provide the total number of people who have this mindset. This is the top-level figure of potential customers. It can be used for calculating future or potential demand.

2. *Geographic territory:* How many consumers are in your defined trading area or geographic market territory? Define your geographic territory, and determine the number of your target segment customers in this area.

3. *Consumption constraints:* What consumption habits exist that limit the potential customer base of your target segment? Determine if there are consumption constraints that will reduce the target for your product. For example, apartment dwellers have no real need for garden tools or lawn mowers. From this review, develop a final estimate of customers in your geographic territory.

4. *Average purchase per year per customer:* Determine the average number of purchases of your product per year. From the business review and the purchase rates and buying habits section, you should have access to the average number of purchases per year for your product category.

5. *Total purchases per year in category:* What is the total number of purchases made by the target segment in your geographic territory per year? Multiply the number of customers in your territory by the average number of purchases per year to get total purchases.

6. *Average price:* Determine the average price of your product. Utilize the pricing section of the business review to obtain this information.

7. *Total dollar purchases:* What are the total dollar purchases of your product category in your geographic target segment? Multiply the total purchases (number 5) by the average price (number 6) to determine total dollar purchase.

8. *Your company's share of purchase:* What is your company's market share? Is it trending up or down? Review market share data and trends from the sales analysis section of your business review, and review the competitive market shares, strengths, and weaknesses from the competitive review section. Also, consider loyalty measures from the target market effectors and the trial and retrial sections (in the consumer and customer review section) of the business review. Multiply your market share by the total dollar purchases (number 7). Adjust this number up or down depending on the increases or decreases of your company's market share versus the competition over the past five years. (For example, if your company has been losing 5 percent market share per year over five years, factor this average loss into your market share projection.)

9. *Additional factors:* What additional factors are there that strongly affect demand for your product? What competitive factors will affect demand? How and why will recent or expected changes in these factors change demand for your product? Additional factors that correlate to the demand for your product—such as a new competitive set, the state of the economy, demographic fluctuations, or changing consumer tastes and lifestyles—should be analyzed for their effect on the demand for your company's product. For example, the influence of rising or falling interest rates on demand should be analyzed if your product is extremely interest rate sensitive and there is good probability that interest rates are going to rise or fall within the next year. Likewise, if your product's sales are teen oriented, determine whether the number of teens is growing or shrinking, and then project the effect this will have on sales. Based on this information, adjust the final share-of-purchases figure you derived (number 8). At this point you should have a fairly reasonable estimate of your company's potential share of total dollars and customers.

Exhibit 5.10 presents an example of how a demand analysis can be calculated for a men's clothing retailer. The chart provides the retailer with a rough projection of

EXHIBIT 5.10

Analysis of Demand Potential

1. Target Market	
DMA population	2,000,000
Target market males 18–65	720,000
2. Geographic Territory	
Target market males 18–65 in trading area of Stores 1 and 3	400,000
3. Consumption Constraints	
None	
4. Average Purchases per Year per Customer	
Average customer purchases 0.40 suits or sports coats per year	0.40 suits per year
5. Total Purchases per Year in Category	
0.40 × 400,000	160,000 suits per year
6. Average Price	
Average price is $150	$150 per suit
7. Total Dollar Purchases	
$150 × 160,000 suits per year	$24,000,000
8. Your Company's Share of Purchases	
Estimated Market Share is 15%	$3,600,000
9. Additional Factors	
None	
Final Demand Expectations for Your Company	$3,600,000

demand for suits in one metro area with two stores. Use a similar procedure for other types of businesses.

Further analysis should be done utilizing information developed in the business review—such as competitive factors, store locations and analysis, competitive advertising expenditures, store loyalty, and the future economic factors affecting the purchase of suits—to provide input for the final adjustment up or down of the demand expectation generated in the calculations.

See Appendix C, Worksheet 34, Task 5.

SUMMARY OF TARGET MARKET SEGMENTATION METHODOLOGY

The process outlined in the preceding Tasks 1 through 5 forces you to develop target market segment plans, not simply product marketing plans. Exhibit 5.11 provides an overview of the target market segmentation methodology.

By examining the top-selling products and then identifying segments responsible for those products, you will naturally be able to identify segments that are common to the purchasing of multiple different products. You will then be able to manage the mix of products in such a way as to maximize cross-selling and minimize cannibalization over time for your primary and secondary target segments. Following this methodology, will lead you to creating target-focused plans versus product-focused plans. Product plans rely on selling only what you have and selling one product or service at a time. A by-product of having product-oriented teams is often that those teams compete for the attention and pocketbook of the same target customers and prospects as other teams within the same company. Our methodology, in contrast, makes sure that the marketer is targeting segments that have the greatest potential to be profitable, which means that the marketing

EXHIBIT 5.11

Overview of the Target Market Segmentation Methodology

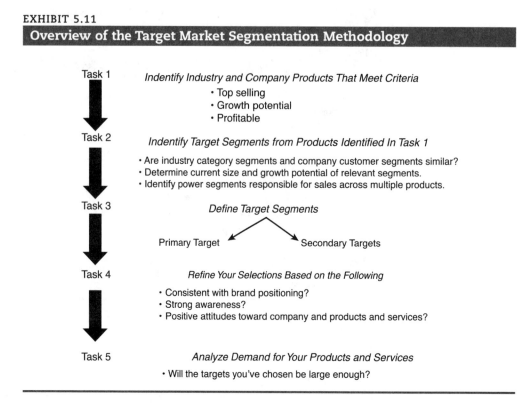

Task 1   *Indentify Industry and Company Products That Meet Criteria*
- Top selling
- Growth potential
- Profitable

Task 2   *Indentify Target Segments from Products Identified In Task 1*
- Are industry category segments and company customer segments similar?
- Determine current size and growth potential of relevant segments.
- Identify power segments responsible for sales across multiple products.

Task 3   *Define Target Segments*

Primary Target   Secondary Targets

Task 4   *Refine Your Selections Based on the Following*
- Consistent with brand positioning?
- Strong awareness?
- Positive attitudes toward company and products and services?

Task 5   *Analyze Demand for Your Products and Services*
- Will the targets you've chosen be large enough?

department can then focus on efficiently and effectively communicating to the targets and building loyalty with one concerted effort against the target segment.

HOW TO WRITE TARGET MARKET DESCRIPTORS

Once you have arrived at your final target market selections, you can use the worksheets provided in Appendix C to list your target markets. You could choose to include a brief rationale under the final target market selection and refer to additional supporting data in the business review. Exhibits 5.12 through 5.15 show alternative examples of how to write target market descriptors for consumer and business-to-business targets. Exhibit 5.15 has been developed in a "persona" format, which is often used to provide insight for web development. You can choose to include data, pictures, quotes, or whatever else may help to more insightfully and deeply describe your choice of target market.

EXHIBIT 5.12

Target Market Descriptor Prepared for a Retail Footwear Chain

Primary Target Market: Fashion Value Moms

Consumers: Women 25–54 with children present in the household. Skews toward household income $40,000–$90,000, suburban or urban residence, and college educated. While demographics are important, the target is defined more by a mindset—the desire for trend-right shoes at a value.

Rationale: The target is the largest shoe purchasing segment within the largest shoe purchasing target market of moms. The fashion value mom currently shops the footwear retailer, but she sees the store primarily for her kids and her husband. If changes were made based on the direction of the marketing plan across product, store environment, and communication, we believe that conservatively, it would be possible to obtain one more pair purchased from this target per year, resulting in a significant increase in total revenues as detailed in the payback section of the plan.

- *Fashion value moms:* 38 percent of the total population, accounting for 48 percent of the shoe sales. Fashion conscious on a budget. However, would rather have today's shoes at a good value than yesterday's shoes at a great price. Takes pride in still being "with it."
- *Major purchaser of shoes in the family:* For kids, herself, and her husband—purchases over 30 percent of her husband's shoes.
- *Values time saving and one-stop shopping:* Her life is busier today than yesterday, and it was busier yesterday than the day before. Experiences time poverty.
- *Wants both comfort and fashion:* Believes she can have both. Believes that shoes make the outfit and is very aware of the fashion trends of today.
- *Tends toward trendy casual shoes, but will still look at and occasionally purchase the pump that turns heads.*
- *Wants her kids to look pulled together:* Sees this as a reflection of herself.

EXHIBIT 5.13

Target Market Descriptor Prepared for a Business-to-Business Research Company

Primary Target Market: Traditional Advertising Agencies

Consumers: Traditional advertising agencies, midsize to large ($50 million-plus in billings). Number would be quantified by using agency Red Book and pulling NAICS industry data.

Rationale: Agencies have significant influence over the types of companies that most use the type of information the research company provides. Additionally, the advertising agencies' job is to provide insights—the company's core competency. Finally, advertising agencies are typically early adopters of new methods of gathering information—a match for the emerging capabilities of mining social media information.

- Agencies with consumer packaged-goods and retail clients who have a history of valuing research and insights
- Additionally, agencies that are experiencing growth, where pitches for new clients are common occurrences and quick turnaround of insight information is valued for competitive and brand messaging input

- User: Creative director
  - There's a tremendous fear of becoming old and not plugged into all that is current and driving today's culture. "I'm afraid of becoming irrelevant, not street level, no longer an integral part of the culture."
  - Every creative fears running dry—not having the next idea. "Ideas are my lifeblood. They are the basis of my craft. And ideas come from insights and knowing the customer and target market."
  - Creatives are distrustful of research. They value listening and observing in a more natural environment. "Traditional research is directed by suits from business schools who never spend time really listening to the consumer. Statistics can prove or disprove anything. I like to get the real sense by talking to and observing my target market customers in their environment, not behind some fake mirror or during a forced 20-minute conversation over the phone."
  - Lives to create something new, to use the newest tool, to be current and with it—in the know. "I read everything, and I stay current with the latest music and art happenings on the macro scale. I do the same around the business categories of my clients on a micro scale. I'm a consumer of culture. I have to be. I'm in the business of communicating that culture."
- Similar descriptions for agency president and agency account planner or research director

Secondary Target Markets

1. The top 30 consumer public relations firms in terms of size
2. New media agencies specializing in electronic, web, and mobile; search engine optimization (SEO) agencies
3. *Consumer demographics:* Adults 25–54 with a median household income of $40,000, high school grads, married with kids; the heaviest users

---

EXHIBIT 5.14

Target Market Descriptor Prepared for a Buffet Restaurant Chain

Primary Target Market: Middle American Pragmatics
Who Are They?

They are people with a practical, matter-of-fact, grounded viewpoint. They are less concerned with lofty higher-order ideals than with the here and now of everyday affairs.

They Put Their Kids First

"I indulge my kids with the little extras."

"I believe that children should be allowed to express themselves."

"I want to provide my kids with things I didn't have."

"I find it difficult to say no to my kids."

They Place a High Value on Faith and Community

"My faith is really important to me."

"It's important to attend religious services."

"I consider myself a spiritual person."

"I am willing to volunteer my time for a good cause."

"We should strive for equality."

"It's important to respect customs and beliefs."

They Are Independent and Self-Reliant

"I would like to set up my own business."

"How I spend my time is more important than money."

"I'm good at fixing things."

They Are Active and Play Well with Others*

Volleyball	136
Soccer	129
Bowling	126
Softball	123
Billiards or pool	122

| Swimming | 120 |
| Camping trips (overnight) | 120 |

They Bond with Family and Friends over Leisure Time*

Visit zoo	143
Play board games	136
Visit state fair	131
Have tailgate parties	127
Play card games	119
Go to the movies	115
Go to the beach	114
Cook for fun	112

*Source: Simmons 2009 Winter. The Simmons database provides demographic and attitudinal data across multiple categories of goods and services. We're showing indexes that represent consumers' responses to statements about their attitudes and behaviors. For example, a 143 index for "Visit zoo" means that these middle American pragmatics are 43 percent more likely than the average person to visit a zoo.

EXHIBIT 5.15

Target Market Descriptor, Using a Persona Format, Prepared for the Syngenta Seeds Company

Primary Target Market: Growers, the Ultimate Purchasers

"I proudly farm about 2,000 acres of corn. This year I planted two different brands. After last year's harvest, I wanted to see if I could do a little better with my yield, but I'm reluctant to 'bet the farm' on a new brand without testing it first for a couple years on just a few of my acres.

"I'm less worried about price than the best value because at the end of the day, yield is what counts. Before purchasing the seed from my dealer, I tried to gather as much of the latest information as I could on product performance in my region, talking to neighbors I trust and reading information from university agronomists and a dealer I like who carries many different brands. (That way I'm not getting biased information the way I would from a seed company.)

"If I see that my neighbor is having great yields, I'm always curious to find out what he's using, and I may look into it for a small portion of my acres next year. Might as well learn from other people's successes, as well as their mistakes. After all, this is about doing my part to feed the world, whether people appreciate it or not."

Derek Ostby
Gender: Male
Age: 55
Location: Boone, Iowa

Source: ©2010 Syngenta Seeds, Inc., Minneapolis, Minn. 55440.
Golden Harvest logo is a trademark of a Syngenta Group Company.

Challenges

- "How do I know I can trust what a company says about seed performance if I don't know them personally?"
- "I have trouble understanding my seed bill and why and where any discounts are coming from."
- "There never seems to be a way to ask questions when I'm gathering information online late at night."

Other Considerations

- "I'm usually looking for a particular brand when researching seed online. Then, I look at product type, followed by available traits."

(Continued)

Target Market Descriptor, Using a Persona Format, Prepared for the Syngenta Seeds Company (*Continued*)

- "Recommendations from people I know personally play a critical role in my decision process, and I tend to build relationships across a broad range of contacts, including dealers, retailers, other farmers in the community, large farmers outside my community, and so on."
- "University research and extension program websites are my primary sources for crop production information."
- "I don't trust a seed company's yield data from their own test plots."

Planting Season Goals

- "Review the latest local weather forecast."
- "Look up current market prices and futures to see what they're selling at the local cash markets and at what price."
- "Get advice on how to market my crop."
- "View product portfolios and compare product yields, ideally from trusted third-party sources."
- "Get tips on how to maximize yield per acre while minimizing production costs."
- "Find a local dealer or sales representative."

Daily Digital Life

- "I access the Internet daily, spending about 5 hours online weekly."
- "My number 1 reason for being on a computer is e-mail, but I also usually visit a couple of websites for ag news, weather, and markets."
- "The information I seek on the Web varies by season."
- "I subscribe to and read a couple online newsletters."
- "I read blogs, but I don't participate myself."
- "I own a basic cell phone and occasionally send text messages."
- "I plan to buy a smart phone this year."

Secondary Target Markets

Farm managers
University extension agents
Crop consultants

DOS AND DON'TS

Do

- Use a step-by-step, disciplined process when reviewing your target customer segments to make sure that you consider all viable targets.
- Make sure you identify the target segments that have the greatest current and future sales potentials.
- To truly understand your primary target market, look to the extremes. The fanatics are found in the heavy-user segment, and they can help describe whom you are really for in terms of a target market and why customers are loyal to you and buy from you.
- Make sure the targets you select are big enough to meet your sales objectives.
- Compare your customer profile to that of the competition and the industry category within which you compete so that you can identify additional target segments and those target segments that you are not fully penetrating to the level you expect.
- Size matters. So do trends. Look to target segments that are responsible for the strongest-selling and fastest-growing products.
- Make sure you define your heavy user as approximating somewhere near the 2:1 ratio of consumption to segment size: one-third of the purchasers purchasing two-thirds of the product; 20 percent of the purchasers purchasing 40 percent of the product; and so on.

- With multiple potential targets and limited marketing funds, focus your efforts against one primary target whenever possible, giving secondary effort to other targets.
- In business-to-business marketing, remember that companies don't buy your products and services. People do. Market to the specific needs of the individual decision makers and influencers.
- Consumer goods manufacturers that have both consumer and trade targets with different sales objectives should consider preparing a separate marketing plan for each target. In this way, the necessary focus will be placed against each critical target, and each plan will more clearly communicate the specific marketing approach.
- Make sure you can deliver the products and services your primary target segment really wants. If there is a disconnect between what your primary target wants and what you can deliver, your marketing plan will fail.
- Bring your customer to life internally through developing a profile, character statement, and mood board that detail not only the description of your target but your target's personality. This will help you educate your internal staff and remind them why you are in business.
- Make sure the target segments you define are uniquely different from other potential segments in behavior, needs, and wants. Then spend time learning how to own the differences that are important to your primary target segment.

Don't

- Don't try to target everyone. A key part of target market strategy is deciding what you will not do and who you will not target.
- Don't expand into markets that have a low target market product usage and a high level of competition.
- Don't just consider your company's targets when you make your target segment decisions. Look instead to the leading consuming segments of the industry category in which you compete as well as the key target segments of your strongest competitors.
- Don't assume that the purchaser of your product is also the user and the only target affecting the purchase.
- Don't pick a primary target that is too shrinking or not large enough to allow you to meet your sales objectives.
- Don't, if you can at all help it, choose more than one primary target customer segment and more than a couple of meaningful secondary target segments.
- Don't expect all your customers and prospective customers to buy your products and services for the same reasons.
- Don't overlook the potential of your emerging current customer segments when considering new targets for growth. Don't just target segments that were important in the past, and don't ignore emerging trends in different targets.
- Don't overlook the influencer targets. Sometimes, there are good reasons to make them the primary target market.
- Don't overlook the potential of the intermediate market (example: grocery store channel for consumer goods companies).
- Don't just go with segments that you have a preconception about. Instead, use the data available to you, and open yourself to looking at things differently.

The Successful Marketing Plan

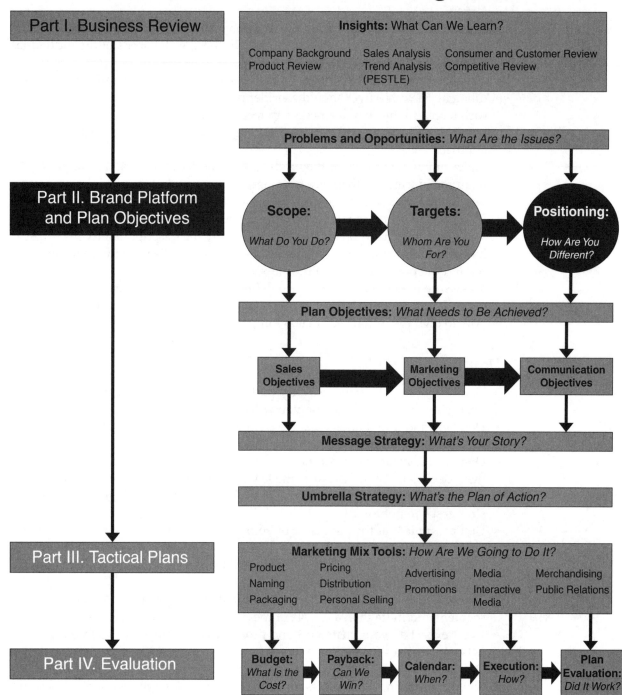

Part I. Business Review

Part II. Brand Platform and Plan Objectives

Part III. Tactical Plans

Part IV. Evaluation

Insights: *What Can We Learn?*

Company Background   Sales Analysis   Consumer and Customer Review
Product Review   Trend Analysis   Competitive Review
                      (PESTLE)

Problems and Opportunities: *What Are the Issues?*

Scope: *What Do You Do?*

Targets: *Whom Are You For?*

Positioning: *How Are You Different?*

Plan Objectives: *What Needs to Be Achieved?*

Sales Objectives

Marketing Objectives

Communication Objectives

Message Strategy: *What's Your Story?*

Umbrella Strategy: *What's the Plan of Action?*

Marketing Mix Tools: *How Are We Going to Do It?*

Product   Pricing   Advertising   Media   Merchandising
Naming   Distribution   Promotions   Interactive   Public Relations
Packaging   Personal Selling   Media

Budget: *What Is the Cost?*

Payback: *Can We Win?*

Calendar: *When?*

Execution: *How?*

Plan Evaluation: *Did It Work?*

6 Positioning

Having completed the first two steps of the brand platform, scope and targets, you are now ready to complete the third step, the one that serves to set the course for how you will differentiate your company or its products in the marketplace. To review:

Chapter 3, "Scope," answers the question,   What do you do?

↓

Chapter 4, "Targets," answers the question,   Whom are you for?

↓

And now . . .
This chapter, "Positioning," answers the question,   How are you different?

Think of the brand positioning discussed in this chapter as the "glue." The brand positioning works to make certain all the strategies and tactics in the marketing mix tools communicate a powerfully differentiated positioning to your staff, customers, and prospects. Your positioning is who you strive to become internally and what you strive to communicate externally. This can also be referred to as your "image," or as we prefer, the "story you tell."

The brand positioning process is both fun and frustrating because it calls for creative thinking on one hand and a sorting out of multiple sets of insights on the other. Be open-minded and visionary; think as a buyer rather than a seller.

FROM THIS CHAPTER YOU WILL LEARN

- What brand positioning is and why it is important
- The five components of a successful brand positioning platform
- How to develop your own brand position

OVERVIEW

Brand positioning is probably one of the most confused concepts in the world of business today. Let's take a look at what a brand position is not before we discuss what it is.

What a Brand Position Is Not

A brand position is not a clever advertising idea, a cool tagline, a slick logo, a graphic standards manual, or a website. While these and other elements combine to contribute to your brand positioning, they are not the foundation.

Okay, now let's look at what a brand position is.

What a Brand Position Is

Brand positioning is the development of your unique promise to the customer. It's the benefit of doing business with your company and purchasing your products and services.

Brand positioning is the thought triggered in the mind of the consumer when he or she hears and/or sees your name. It's how you win the day. It's the tie breaker for consumers:

A brand position is what people tell others afterward. It's the story they tell in the end.

Positioning is the speak of the heart.

Brand positioning is the emotional way customers talk about your brand. Because every product, no matter how boring to you and me, has an emotional connection to some set of consumers. You may have heard the old saying, "There are no dull products, only dull copywriters." We believe this. Products, services, and companies are terribly important to their consumers. There's magic to be mined if you look hard enough and get below the surface.

It's your job to understand the insights into why your customers find your product appealing and then to explode those reasons, build on them, own them, and make them obvious to your target markets. It may be fear of messing up (think about the purchasing agent who doesn't want to make a mistake). It may be that the product saves time for other more important things like spending time with family and friends (retailers that provide convenience). It may be that the product is simply an extension of someone's ego or personality (think what one brand of car says about you versus another—are you a Subaru driver or a Lexus driver?). All these reasons go beyond mere attributes and encompass benefits. Benefits, not attributes, are the emotional hooks to your customers. It's the benefits and the emotional connections that matter and form the foundation to your reason for being or your brand positioning.

Brands Tie Directly to the Values and Beliefs of Your Target Market

Brand positioning is a process of establishing and managing the images, perceptions, and associations that consumers apply to your product based on the values and beliefs they associate with your product. These are managed through application of the brand positioning elements starting with the name and graphic components but encompassing the product itself, your company's service components, personal selling, your channels of distribution, pricing, and your communications. All need to be consistent with the company's brand positioning.

Brand Positions Happen Whether You Actively Choose to Shape Them or Not

No company, product, service, store, charitable organization, or person is unbranded. A brand image evolves whether you are directly involved in shaping the process or not. Think of French people. Think of the redhead, the blonde cheerleader, Irish people, Las Vegas, Nike, IBM, Intel, Starbucks, Ford, Firestone tires, Honda, or simply your favorite brand, store, or service. Words and images immediately come to mind that describe each of these examples. Everything gets branded, whether by a disciplined process or by people's perceptions over time. It's a critical function of the marketing plan to help shape those perceptions not through trickery or slick glossy ads that have little hint of authentic reality, but through a disciplined process that actively solicits consumer insights and a vision of how you want to be differentiated in a way that is meaningful to your target market.

Your Company's Brand Is Just Like Your Personal Reputation

Each of us is known for a few things. Yes, we all like to think of ourselves as very complex and multidimensional, but that's not the way others see us. People have their reputations shaped by a few characteristics, and these few things shape most of what people know about us. "She's a great athlete!" This leads to all sorts of other related personality traits that people would say about this person like "great team leader," "always performs when the game is on the line," or "makes it look so easy." The one or two outstanding personal characteristics shape and form the emotional and rational feelings we have about this person.

The First Lesson of Brand Positioning Is to Practice the Art of Limitation

Brands that try to be all things to all people, fail. Similar to a person's reputation, brands that have strong differentiating characteristics stand out. Furthermore, the authors of this book can attest to hundreds of research studies we've been involved in where companies that are positively known for one thing, raise the perception of other attributes as well. The company known for and dominant around convenience finds that its value, quality, selection, and other attributes important to consumers also improve over time. However, companies that are not seen as having any differentiation have a hard time improving across any measure. They are hopelessly stuck in the middle, a place that leads to what McMillanDoolittle refers to as "the Black Hole."

McMillanDoolittle, the retail consulting firm, has years of research proving that companies that don't dominate one thing eventually die. In the company's book *Winning at Retail*,* the authors discuss what they call the "EST of retail," which is the McMillanDoolittle partners' theory—which has since been validated by research—that a retailer must be best at one proposition that's important to a group of consumers. An example of EST positioning would be a category killer like Amazon.com, which is the biggEST and focuses on selection. McMillanDooltittle points out that every category has one price leader that is the cheapEST, one leader whose fashion is the hottEST, one leader who is known for the bEST quality, or value, and so on.

To accomplish what McMillanDoolittle calls the EST or being the best at something, almost always means targeting one set of consumers to the exclusion of others. McMillanDoolittle has documented the failures of companies that over time had not become the best at what they did but continued to muddle along in the middle. It provides lists of companies that have gone out of business as a result and describe these companies as having gone into the Black Hole, a place where retailers that are no longer relevant to customers go to die. The Black Hole Memorial is filled with names you'd recognize, large retailers who once were dominant but either lost their EST or tried to be all things to all people—Montgomery Ward, Computer City, Circuit City, Linens 'n' Things, CompUSA, Sharper Image, and Mervyn's, along with many more who are significantly downsizing as their position becomes less relevant. One example is Blockbuster who at the time this edition was printed was in the midst of filing for bankruptcy and significantly downsizing as competition from Netflix and Redbox was dramatically changing the distribution landscape.

Brands Are Not Owned by the Marketing Department

As stated earlier, a brand is far more than advertising. It's the identity an entire organization has internally and externally. It represents the values, the personality, and the experience that people associate with the company, product, or service. A brand provides a point of difference—a reason to choose your company, product, or service over the competition. Most important, not only does a strong brand help customers understand your company but it also imparts a sense of mission within the company. A good brand positioning provides guidelines for every action from product development to how to answer the phone. Finally, a good brand positioning provides direction for the rational elements of your company and also the emotional elements, as the chart in Exhibit 6.1 demonstrates.

A brand position is a guideline for the entire company because . . .

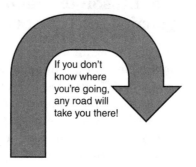

If you don't know where you're going, any road will take you there!

---

* Willard N. Ander and Neil Z. Stern, *Winning at Retail: Developing a Sustained Model for Retail Success,* McMillanDoolittle, Wiley, Hoboken, N.J., 2004.

EXHIBIT 6.1

Brand Elements

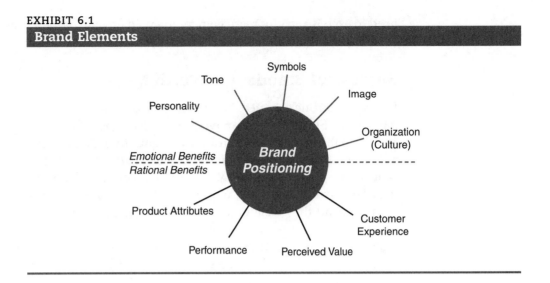

Brand positioning is not something that is owned by the marketing department. Sure, marketing communication plays a big role in the company's brand positioning. But so does any function that touches the customers—product, customer service, sales, merchandising, and the technology interfaces. Brand positioning is strategy, and unless everyone is on the same road, don't expect everyone to be pulling in the same direction. Brands are owned by the full cross-functional management team of any organization. In fact, we'd even go a step further. When we worked with Lionel Train, the model train company, the then new CEO told us a story of receiving multiple letters from customers when his team purchased the company. Many of the letters informed the CEO that he didn't own the company, the customers did. They were that passionate about Lionel. They politely informed and requested that he not blow it for them but to be a good shepherd of "their brand."

Strong Brands Beget Loyal Customers, the Ultimate Benefit of Branding

Developing a brand and building equity in that brand (the value above and beyond the cumulative physical attributes of the product itself) are the broad components of the branding process. In this process, you have one goal for the brand: to generate consistent purchase behavior among a target base (thus providing you with a consistent return on the investment of capital in that asset). In other words, you seek to build and maintain *brand loyalty*. Brand or customer loyalty is the ultimate benefit of building a brand. We believe every company's goal should be to build a strong, loyal base of **fanatics**. The ability to create fanatics is becoming increasingly important in today's parity-product environment.

Our work with McDonald's and Coors showed that both the fast-food retailer and the brewer have strong, loyal consumer bases but that this loyalty is constantly being tested by competitive efforts. The same holds true for the brands developed in the service category with our work for Honda Federal Credit Union, for associations such as the Precast/Prestressed Construction Association, for the nonprofit United Way, for the regional American Red Cross, and for the large diagnostic equipment company PerkinElmer. Our recent work with Firestone Complete Auto Care was focused on the need to increase the lifetime value of their customers. All need to exercise careful management to avoid erosion of their brand equity by their competitors or by their own actions.

Successful Brands Are Worth More

Picture a Starbucks coffee. Now picture a generic cup of coffee. What would you pay for the Starbucks? $2, maybe more? Now how about the generic cup of coffee? Probably somewhere around 80 cents to a dollar. The value of the brand, above and beyond the cumulative physical attributes of the product itself, represents brand equity. Brands help companies command a premium price because of the added value associated with their brands. Brands promise quality; they boost earnings, and they cushion downturns in the economy.

The *brand value* is the absolute financial worth of the brand as it stands today. Accordingly, the brand's value can be compared to the total value of the business, for example, as it would be assessed on the stock exchange. A study by Interbrand and JPMorgan Chase in 2002 and published in *Businessweek* concluded that brands, on average, account for more than one-third of shareholder value. In this study, McDonald's accounted for more than 70 percent. Even more amazing, the brand Coca-Cola accounted for 51 percent of the value of the Coca-Cola company, this despite the fact that the company had a host of other well-known brands such as Sprite, Canada Dry, Tab, Nestea, Fruitopia, and many, many more. Disney accounted for 68 percent of the company's stock market value; Mercedes-Benz, 47 percent; Nokia, 51 percent; and IBM, 31 percent. Studies by academics at Harvard and South Carolina, Interbrand, Millard Brown's BrandZ Portfolio Performance, and others continually point to the fact that great brands outperform the stock market as measured by the S&P 500 or the Dow Jones Average.*

And to think brands are referred to as "intangible assets"!

The top 10 brands valued by Interbrand in 2010 listed in the Interbrand "Best Global Brands 2010," in the "Definitive Guide to the Best Global Brands" on the Interbrand website, are listed below along with their valuation and whether the brand increased or decreased in value from 2009.

The Top 10 Brands as Valued by Interbrand in 2010
1. Coca-Cola: $70,452 million, +2.5 percent
2. IBM: $64,727 million, +7.5 percent
3. Microsoft: $60,895 million, +7.5 percent
4. Google: $43,557 million, +36.2 percent
5. GE: $42,808 million, −10.4 percent
6. McDonald's: $33,578 million, +4.0 percent
7. Intel: $32,015 million, +4.5 percent
8. Nokia: $29,495 million, −15.4 percent
9. Disney: $28,731 million, +1.0 percent
10. Hewlett-Packard: $26,867 million, +11.5 percent

A Short Story

Before proceeding, we want to relate a short story and give you a brief quiz to demonstrate how this thing we call brand positioning really works. The story

---

* T. J. Madden, F. Fehle (University of South Carolina), and S. M. Fournier (Harvard University), "Brands Matter: An Empirical Investigation of Brand-Building Activities and the Creation of Shareholder Value," unpublished paper, May 2, 2002, reported in the Interbrand article "Brand Valuation: The Financial Value of Brands," published on the Brand Channel website.

comes from Lisa Fortini-Campbell and her book *Consumer Insight*.* In a game between the Oakland A's and the Texas Rangers, a promising rookie named Jose Canseco stepped up to the plate. The pitcher, Nolan Ryan, wound up and let his famous fastball go. Canseco swung, connected with a loud crack, and blasted the ball right over the center field wall. As Canseco rounded the bases, one of the bat boys picked up the bat he'd dropped and carried it over to Bert Caulfield, the A's equipment manager. The two of them sat together, heads down, pointing to and talking about a place on the bat.

What were they talking about? The sweet spot. They were talking about one of the things that had made Canseco's hit go so far. They were referring to a special place on the baseball bat, golf club, or tennis racket that drives the ball farther, faster, and with less effort than when it's hit anywhere else.

Consumers also have sweet spots. When your marketing or communications idea hits that sweet spot, your sales will go flying. The sweet spot is the place in the target person's mind where you make the connection between a consumer's insight and the product or brand insight. You might think of it this way:

Consumer insight + product insight = **sweet spot**

What we are saying here is that you must define your customers or potential consumers by the way they think of themselves and how they look at life. You must look at your product not for what you believe it offers but for what they expect and receive from your type of product. Another way you can look at the sweet spot concept is by combining a *rational benefit* via product insight and an *emotional need* via consumer insight—a strong combination for a strong brand positioning.

While the sweet spot concept is one way of describing brand positioning, another way is for you to take the following quiz and answer each question:

1. Who was the first person to fly solo across the North Atlantic Ocean? Who was the second?
2. Who was the first boyfriend or girlfriend you kissed? Who was the second?
3. What is the highest mountain in the world? What is the second highest?
4. Who is first in copiers? Who is second?

If you are like most people, you could answer the "first" question correctly for the first three questions, but you would have a difficult time answering the "second" question for each. And, as for question number 4, most answer "Who is first in copiers?" with Xerox, which is wrong. The correct answer is Canon Copiers, which Gartner's Printer, Copier, and MFP Quarterly Statistics showed in 2009 to be number one again. In fact, Canon has been number one for way over a decade now. However, Xerox is still usually perceived as first in copiers. And that's the point. Securing a meaningful place in the minds of the target market sets the product apart from all the others and causes it to be remembered.

The lesson here is that, like a memory bank, people's minds have slots or positions, with one position or slot for each piece of information they have chosen to keep. You want your product to own that one position. Successful positioning is the art of sacrifice. You can't be all things to all people and create an effective positioning. Positioning is about the one main thing that your company, product, or service stands for. The question is how to develop this positioning equity in the minds of people within your target market.

---

* Lisa Fortini-Campbell, *Consumer Insight*, Copy Workshop, Chicago, 1991.

Positioning Considerations

In order to arrive at a successful long-term brand position, you must take into consideration these factors:

- The inherent drama of the product you are selling
- The needs and wants of the target markets
- The competition

The business review and the problems and opportunities you have completed, along with the scope and target market determinations, are key to arriving at the right positioning. You must understand the strengths and weaknesses of your company or product versus that of the competition. Where is your product comparable to the competition's, and where is it different? Where is it unique? Most important, what do these competitive differences, if any, mean to your company's target market? If the positioning reflects a difference that your product cannot deliver or that is not important to the target group, your positioning will not be successful. Even if your product possesses a meaningful difference, your positioning will not be effective if the target group does not perceive it as meaningfully different. The key point is that, as you develop your product positioning, you must deal with the target group's *perception* of the competing products, even if it is not altogether accurate, because they are the buyers, and consequently, *their perception is truth.*

Further, the odds of arriving at a successful positioning increase dramatically when you have conducted market research on the potential target market. Primary research will help identify key users and/or purchasers and meaningful product attributes. Also, research will show how the primary market perceives these important attributes relative to the competition. Even without primary market research, if you have diligently employed the disciplined marketing plan process, you should have a good start in developing a positioning that communicates effectively to the target market.

Everything in a marketing plan evolves from the target market and how you strategically meet the needs of the target market with your product. Therefore, no matter how you position your product, the target market must be central to the positioning. As you consider various positioning alternatives, let your target market be your guide.

CREATING YOUR BRAND POSITIONING

We use the following five steps to create the brand positioning:

Five Steps to Brand Positioning

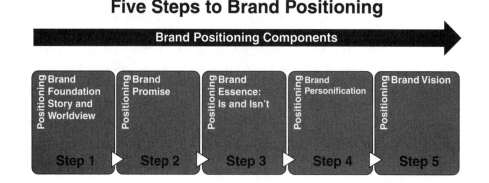

The *foundation story and worldview* provide the context and insights into the compelling reasons as to why the company, product, or service was created or developed. The *brand promise* provides the reason for differentiation, the promise of a unique benefit to the consumer. The *brand essence* provides a concise brand essence—what your brand stands for as opposed to what it does not. The *brand personification* puts into words how your brand feels to consumers. And finally, the *brand vision* takes the organization through the implications of operationalizing the brand promise: What does the future look like? What will remain and what will not when the brand promise becomes fully realized?

STEP 1. CAPTURING YOUR FOUNDATION STORY AND WORLDVIEW

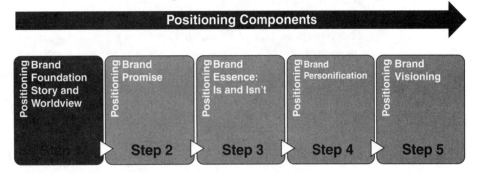

Fritz Gruitzer, a friend of ours and founder and president of Brandgarten, talks a lot about the importance of foundation stories and worldviews. Foundation stories and worldviews provide the marketer with the underlying foundation of who the brand is. Your understanding and connection to a brand begins to come from understanding the heritage, history, and the brand's story. In most cases, capturing your foundation story and worldview is a trip down memory lane into the inherent drama of what you offer your customers, the needs and wants of your customers, and how you're different from your competition. Going through this first step causes many to realize that the very reasons for starting the company or creating your product or service in the first place are at the foundation of why customers still purchase from you. This first step of the brand positioning process helps many to sharpen their focus against the very things that made them great and will make them even greater into the future.

To prepare for writing your foundation story and worldview, go back through the company history section of your business review. As you will recall, we discussed the importance of storytelling and the four main parts of describing your company history:

- The message you want to tell and communicate
- The conflict that occurred
- The characters—villains and heroes
- The plot or how your story progresses to get to your message

The Foundation Story

Your company, products, and services all have rich histories. Get to know those histories. All businesses were started for a reason. If the reason wasn't good enough, the companies failed. The reason your company was started, the story of who started it, and the story of why and how the product was developed or invented tell a lot about the compelling reason your brand is purchased yet today. Found in the foundation story is often just that, a compelling story that helps bring the brand alive. After all, as we've said earlier in this chapter and will repeat again in both this chapter and Chapter 10, "Message Strategy": your brand is your story.

Products are like people. When you meet people at a party, the first question you ask them is usually geared to finding out a little bit about their background, where they came from, where they grew up, how many siblings they have—basically, you're asking about their foundation story. While a foundation story provides a key insight into the brand promise and the brand positioning, it also provides another function. A foundation story provides grounding—a reason to believe that the story you are telling about your brand is true. It helps later in fitting the pieces together in the consumers' minds.

The Steep & Brew Foundation Story

Steep & Brew, a small regional coffee roaster, was started by an individual who had a passion for coffeehouses as a way of providing alternatives to entertainment bars. He was, and is to this day, fanatical about the ability of good, really good coffee to draw people together in what can be the best part of the day. Toward this end, his quest for the perfect coffee bean is never ending. He knows which side of the mountain in the world's best climates for coffee beans is better and why. He has studied the growers, has developed relationships with them, and has developed an acute sense of where to buy and how to roast the perfect cup of coffee. The foundation story was the key to helping Mark position his company as both a coffee shop and a wholesaler to grocery stores, and, ultimately consumers in the Midwest.

The foundation story around Mark the coffee roaster tells a lot about the brand Steep & Brew. It works because it's true. Mark lives this passion, and he still shapes his business around his reasons for starting Steep & Brew in the first place.

The Nike Foundation Story

Nike has a foundation story we all know and can read about in books and articles that have been written. It involves the early lives of two luminaries: Phil Knight and William Bowerman. Phil Knight was on the track team at the University of Oregon where he ran under legendary coach William Bowerman. After graduating from the Stanford Graduate School of Business, he started Blue Ribbon Sports, an importer of athletic shoes under the Tiger brand from Japan, to compete with the then dominant German brands of Adidas and PUMA. Bowerman bought into the fledgling company one year after Knight started Blue Ribbon Sports. He paid the same amount of cash that Knight had originally contributed, $500. Soon after, the company name was changed to Nike. Where Phil Knight was the brains, Bowerman was the heart. Bowerman had been experimenting with developing a new kind of running shoe for the members of his team. Using a waffle iron, he developed the Cortez, the first running shoe with a modified bottom that provided cushioning for serious runners who sometimes trained up to 100 miles per week. From there, the innovations continued with experimentation in different materials like nylon uppers, and the Boston Shoe, the first cushioned midsole shoe.

The company's legendary partnership with athletes started with Steve Prefontaine, and it gave unwavering support to the athletes, who were some of the game's biggest stars and rebels (including Steve Prefontaine, who battled the NCAA establishment; John McEnroe, who battled refs; and Bo Jackson, who had the nerve to think he could compete in two professional sports). From the beginning, Knight thought of Nike as a sports company, and not a running company. He paid attention to the sport of running, the sport of basketball, the people involved, their issues, and what concerned them. It's very telling that when you walk through the Nike headquarters, there are photographs of Wilt Chamberlain and Bill Russell, two of basketball's greatest pioneers who played the game before Nike even had a basketball shoe.

The foundation story for Nike was the foundation for a whole value system that became the company. Nike is a sports company that is all about performance, innovation, and the rebel spirit of sports. These components of the brand came from the foundation story; they were an indomitable part of Nike from the beginning.

The Worldview

A great brand instantly means something, stands for something, and is fundamentally understood by its customers. We believe all great brands have, at their core, a strong belief system that is understood by the company's employees and the company's customers. Belief systems are often polarizing—but so are great brands. We're going to provide you with a couple of belief statements. Our bet is you'll instantly form a galvanizing opinion of them, one way or the other.

Hunting promotes family values. Gander Mountain, L.L. Bean, Bass Pro, Cabela's, and Dick's would be examples of retail organizations that agree with this worldview. Do you? Even if you don't, can you argue the other side? We've given many presentations and seminars where we throw this out. We're always surprised by the passion shown on both sides of the argument. It immediately segments the people in the room with virtually no one neutral on the subject.

Beer enhances our life. Those in favor of this statement would be the American Beverage Institute, the Beer Institute, and those with a German heritage. Those who might vehemently disagree are organizations like Alcoholics Anonymous and Mothers Against Drunk Driving. Many beer companies were started by brewers whose families descended from cultures in which beer was an integral part of the social fabric. The worldview that beer goes with good times is seen in the advertising today and the connection with our favorite pastimes, such as sports and outdoor activities, and in social settings such as holiday gatherings, graduations, weddings, and neighborhood parties.

Two good examples of how worldviews shape brands, with firms that compete in the same space, can be seen in Walmart's and Target's worldviews.*

Walmart's worldview came from its founder, Sam Walton. Walton was a champion of the underserved in our society. Walmart has allowed many people to raise their standard of living by giving them access to low-priced goods. Implicitly there is a worldview that *a hard-working family deserves a decent standard of living*. This worldview is communicated in Walmart's current tagline: "Save money. Live better."

---

* Scott Cooper, Fritz Grutzner, and Birk Cooper, *Tips and Traps for Marketing Your Business*, McGraw-Hill, New York, 2008.

Target and Walmart sell very similar merchandise. Yet Target's and Walmart's worldviews would probably be very different. We imagine at the core of their worldview is the idea that *you don't have to be rich to enjoy fashion.*

These two worldviews create very different companies. Target has followed a strategy of bringing fashion to the masses with designer collaborations using famous, established name designers and artists like Michael Graves and Mossimo Giannulli. Walmart, in contrast, has been centered around taking the cost out of its operations to pass the savings on to consumers. Each retailer is selling value—but in very different ways.

Writing Your Foundation Story and Worldview

Here are some tips for writing your foundation story and worldview. There really are no rights or wrongs in doing this, but the following three tips will keep you on track:

- There is no correct length. These can be as short or as long as you feel appropriate.
- Write from the perspective of what mattered most to those who founded the company and connected to what mattered most to the original (and current) customers. Some things are merely important to the founders and would have no connection to the customers. Examples would be things like how much money the company or founders wanted to make and the ownership structure—really anything that deals with the financial structure. Things that are relevant to the customer are the needs that could be fulfilled, the problems that could be solved, new benefits that could be had, a competitive advantage that could be gained, a way to take pain out of someone's life or to add beauty to it, make something more convenient, improve people's self-esteem, make something easier, make people feel hipper . . . you get the idea.
- Write emotionally. Companies were started on the dreams of a few and loved by many if they survived. Capture those dreams in the language and feelings that they would have used.

Examples of Foundation Stories and Worldviews

You'll see from the following three examples that there is not one way to write a worldview. Yet you'll probably agree that all three provide huge insight into each company's soul.

The following is a foundation story and worldview for Networked Insights, a firm dedicated to discovering insights through mining and analyzing the conversations people have on social network sites.

Networked Insights

Foundation Story

Networked Insights was started with the intent of moving the business to sunny California. But its founder Dan Neely, a serial entrepreneur with successes at three other technology companies, located the business instead in Madison, Wisconsin, a city known for a top-five research university, iconoclastic thinking, and bitterly cold winters. He argued that two of the three were critical to driving a company providing superior technology, analytics, and insights. The company expanded into larger quarters in Madison at the start of 2010.

Networked Insight's collaborative and democratic work environment reflects the dynamics of the Internet and social networks.

Worldview

"The consumer groundswell has already seized control of brand messages. Now customers can do the work fueling insights that drive business strategy and decisions. The answers are out there in the chatter. We've only to listen and interpret correctly."

Work Sharp

The worldview for the Work Sharp brand is very simple. Work Sharp is a sharpening tool that is used to sharpen everything from woodworking tools to lawn mower blades. The brand was built around this worldview: "We believe no one should ever have to throw away a dull tool."

In this day and age of disposables, here is a brand that's all about the do-it-yourselfer, the woodworkers and the professional craftspeople for whom tools are an essential part of work, play, and everyday life. The folks at Work Sharp have built a brand around the recognition of how dull tools can cost their customers money, time, and a job well done.

ELI

The foundation story and worldview for ELI, Inc., a training firm in Atlanta, was critical to developing the firm's brand promise. ELI went from being a firm that helped businesses comply with the laws pertaining to discrimination and sexual harassment to a being a firm that was hired because of its ability to provide a learning platform that helped companies develop higher-performing cultures.

As a lawyer, Steve Paskoff saw the tremendous cost and pain of litigations created by the laws being broken—laws put in place to protect each individual's right to a civil workplace free of discrimination, sexual harassment, unfair wages and hours, and other debilitating employment practices. He began to look at the combination of civil treatment laws as not only the morally right thing for workers but also the right thing for the businesses' bottom line. He came to see that *high-performing companies* all have basic things in common: they create environments of trust, they believe in creating cultures of openness, they embrace diversity, and they create a workplace in which all people are treated civilly and respectfully, irrespective of position. So Paskoff came to believe that he was working at the wrong end of the problem, and out of this realization came ELI, Inc.

ELI's mission has remained the same to this day: to proactively help companies create the types of environments that lead to higher performance, retention of talent, true teamwork, and using each employee's talents fully. ELI does this by helping companies understand how the laws dealing with how we treat each other are about far more than the law. These laws serve as the proven foundation for a better and more productive way for people to work together.

It's always been Paskoff's view that companies who get into legal trouble around any of the civil treatment laws have deeper problems within the company. And those problems if not solved will create far deeper problems than any single lawsuit. The premise today is the same as it was back when Paskoff started the company—that employees and managers want to create a workplace environment that leads to high-performing teams and that there is an innate understanding among most individuals of what the end results of these types of environments look like. The problem is getting there. Communication (both verbal and body language) between individuals and within groups is extremely complex. Most of us are not very good at it when it really comes down to it. Pressure for performance is intense. Words or actions intended to mean one thing are often taken another way. People wanting to do the right thing can do what they think is right, but their actions may in fact have the opposite effect.

Paskoff took his beliefs and created a learning system founded upon the one component common to all high-performing companies: civil treatment. From this idea has sprung a platform of products whose aim is all the same: build respect, trust, and openness with coworkers, suppliers, channel partners, and customers. Each product reinforces the same idea but from a different standpoint, emanating from a different set of laws. But all these laws deal in the end with human's behavior toward other humans. Simple to understand, isn't it? Litigation is expensive, but the legal cost is nothing compared to the crippling effect of a work environment and culture that's damaging to performance and abdicated by management.

In summary, all great companies have one thing in common: their cultures promote civil treatment, which means treating all stakeholders with honesty, caring, and respect. The laws dealing with civil treatment between individuals, and between the firm and all its stakeholders, are the foundation for building a culture that leads to a high-performing company. The highest-performing companies have cultures that are rooted in both understanding and compliance with the most fundamental of each country's laws, the ones that provide inalienable rights, ethical standards, and civil treatment for all in the workplace.

STEP 2. FINDING YOUR BRAND PROMISE

Five Steps to Brand Positioning

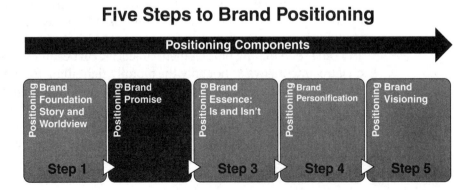

Positioning Components

Positioning Brand Foundation Story and Worldview	Positioning Brand Promise	Positioning Brand Essence: Is and Isn't	Positioning Brand Personification	Positioning Brand Visioning
Step 1		Step 3	Step 4	Step 5

The brand promise is very simply the benefit the consumer receives from purchasing your products or services. It's a pledge from you to your customers. It's the difference between you and your competitors. Fulfilling it becomes what you build your company around.

A brand promise comes from a deep understanding of what the brand provides your target market. This typically falls into one of two areas: emotional and social connections and rational or functional connections.

Emotional and social connections: We connect to brands rationally but also very strongly around emotional feelings. The *Journal of Advertising Research* is filled with articles confirming this. Books like *Passion Branding*, *Emotional Branding*, and *Lovemarks* all provide a strong bias toward branding around emotions. Strongly engaged or loyal customers are almost always emotionally linked to the brand. You know this—simply talk to friends or business associates who would rather not go on living than give up their Starbucks coffee or their Apple computer, iPhone, or iPod. We've viewed focus group tapes where Walmart customers get tears in their eyes talking about how Walmart helps them afford what their families need. Humans are emotional beings, and emotional links last.

The emotional connections people feel toward a company or brand manifest themselves in statements like "The product just makes me feel like I'm in the know and with it," or "In my job as a purchasing agent, I can make a lot of mistakes that really can cost the company a lot of money. I feel I'm making a safe choice when I choose the company I do to do business with." These statements focus on consumer wants and pain points. The consumer in this example wants to feel "with it." And the purchasing agent "wants to make a smart, safe choice."

Brands also provide social promises or assistance in how you want to be seen by others—whether it's others in the business world, within your company, your group of friends, or your family. The product may make you feel like you're making a safe decision, and this in turn helps you to be seen or socially connect to others in your company as a very responsible, careful employee who makes sound decisions.

Rational or functional connections: As important are what we call the *rational attributes*—things like best price, best value (quality price relationship often promoted by saying "Brand X for less"), selection, access, location, and so on. While the feelings of consumers are critically important to your ability to provide a brand promise, so too are the rational factors. Often these are referred to as the *tangible factors*, or the things that provide proof. While the emotional benefits are of the heart, the functional benefits are of the mind. If in the first emotional example above, "you feel like you're in the know" when you use the product, that "feeling" can be substantiated with technological innovations, awards for innovation, or articles that are written about the company and high-profile users that can be seen using the product.

Example of both emotional and rational connections: Dr. Helmut Panke, former chairman of the BMW Board of Management, claimed, "You can destroy a brand if you give into compromises. BMW hasn't, and the brand has created a powerful cachet. BMW has practiced consistency in product and message, and as a result, according to FutureBrand, a consultancy in New York, BMW's brand name is stronger than any other luxury car company, and on par with fashion houses such as Chanel."

For over 30 years, BMW has been consistent in its message around BMW as the ultimate driving machine—a strong *emotional connector* to its target audience. But the *rational connections* are also there. One detail of BMW is the radiator grille, introduced in 1933. With few exceptions, every BMW has been designed with a grille that's split down the middle. Beyond the details, BMW continually puts performance into its engineering another rational connection. Finally, it talks about performance, and it lives performance.

The brand even touts its performance driving school on its website in this manner:

> At BMW, we possess such a profound belief in high-performance driving—and the driver's right to experience every heart-pounding moment of it—that we invested $12 million to create the BMW Performance Center.

Sticking with cars, how do you feel when you drive a Chevrolet truck versus a BMW? Both provide very real emotional and rational feelings but very different feelings. The Chevy truck gives a sense of rugged dependability, "like a rock." And the emotion of driving a "tough" car is backed up by the rational look of the vehicle and the history of dependability. It's certainly no ultimate driving machine. But that's not what its customers are buying it for!

Writing Your Brand Promise

There are three options, discussed below, to choose from when you write and format your brand promise.

Brand Promise Format Option 1

This brand promise format follows the sequence of the work you've already done. You restate your target (whom you're for) and the scope or the industry category you're competing in (what you do), and then in a few words, you state your brand promise followed by an emotional and a rational reason to believe or support it. The reason to believe is the rationale, or why a customer would believe the brand promise. It helps to think along the two distinct ways you connect to your customers discussed in the section above, emotional and rational reasons to believe. The best brand promises have both:

> To_____ [target: whom you're for], brand _____ [your company, product, or service] is a _____ [industry category description] that offers _____ [what you do] and provides _____ [why you're different and why you're famous] because of _____ [reason to believe that's relevant to the target audience].

The following provides an example for ELI, Inc. ELI is a training company using compliance with the law as the basis for teaching organizations a way to avoid litigation but even more importantly a way to build a higher-performing culture and thus company.

> To human resources department heads, ELI, Inc., is a training company that offers a civil treatment learning system providing the ability to translate complex legal compliance concepts into simple-to-understand behavioral norms that are essential to high-performance companies. HR leaders in the most reputable companies in the United States have relied on ELI to help them build cultures based on honesty, respect, trust,

and openness with coworkers, suppliers, channel partners, and clients. Litigation is expensive, but the cost is nothing compared to the crippling effect of a work environment and culture that are damaging to performance and talent retention.

Brand Promise Format Option 2

A second way to write your brand promise is to really focus on the benefit—a benefit that answers the question, "Why are you famous?"

Only brand _____ delivers _____ [unique benefit] to _____ [primary target descriptor].

An example using the Option 2 format is for Firestone Complete Auto Care, the tire, maintenance, and repair retailer. In looking at the Firestone Complete Auto Care communication and examining its repair facilities, the following brand promise is conveyed:

Only Firestone Complete Auto Care will keep your used car running newer, longer.

Note that while not exactly in the format above, the promise includes the brand (Firestone), the unique benefit it delivers (car running longer), and the target or whom it's for (used-car owners).

Brand Promise Format Option 3

A third way to create your brand promise is to use the simple format of adjective, adjective, and noun.

An example of format Option 3 would be Hallmark—"Hallmark, caring shared." It's a simple, powerful promise backed up by the content of their cards and the history of being part of people's most memorable (both happy and sad) life experiences.

"Disney, fun family entertainment." The reason to believe is through its theme parks and endless characters that we identify with from our childhood and the childhood of our own children.

Another would be for Nike: "Nike, genuine athletic performance." The reason to believe would include the host of top athletes who use and endorse the Nike product.

See also Appendix C, Worksheet 35.

Method 1 for Finding Your Brand Promise: Positioning by Emotional Relationship

We are going to take you through three methods to help you find your brand promise:

1. Positioning by emotional relationship
2. Positioning by matching
3. Positioning by mapping

See also Appendix C, Worksheet 35.

All positioning efforts seek to establish a connection between product and target market. But the emphasis can differ dramatically. As a comparison, attribute positioning, which is the basis for the mapping method, focuses on the target's rating of the product relative to the competition; it focuses more on hard attributes like value, quality, convenience, and so on. Emotional relationship positioning emphasizes the *feelings* of the target market customers: their feelings about the product, about themselves or about others, toward the company's personality, and about the meaning of the product in their lives.

This more emotional approach offers a number of advantages:

- Once a relationship is established, it is harder for competitors to attack on the basis of specific product attributes.
- You can maintain the relationship despite radical changes in technology or product features.

There are also some disadvantages to this approach:

- If your product has a unique advantage (for example, a patented process), this approach may not focus enough on the product.
- You must be able to deliver on the emotional promise. If you promise "friendly" or enhanced appeal and deliver "indifferent" or "the same," you will make matters worse.

In many business categories, the marketing battleground has already seen some movement from rational benefits to emotional relationships. The reason? The consumers now face a bewildering array of product choices. Unique product features or technical breakthroughs are quickly duplicated. The result is that the consumers do not have the time or energy to know everything necessary to make the right choice. They need a simple relationship with a company that they can count on over time to be a good choice.

The value of an emotional relationship with the company is even greater in the following circumstances:

- There is high emotional involvement in product selection. Badge products say something about who the wearers are, whom they associate with, where they live, how they live, their values, and their dreams (perfumes, beer, cars).
- The competitive frame is saturated and complex (soft drinks, copiers, fast food, auto insurance).
- The degree of personal, financial, or emotional risk is great (cars, investment firms, lawyers, most jewelry, business apparel, computer or telephone systems for companies).
- Consumers really can't determine competitive differences because of a lack of understanding and knowledge (one doctor versus another, one accountant versus another).
- The business category is perceived as a commodity (sugar).

Having an emotional relationship with a company or product is like having a relationship with another person:

- How does this relationship make me feel about myself? ("If I wear Nike Air Jordans, I feel like a winner.")
- What will other people think of me? (What type of person wears OshKosh B'gosh versus Calvin Klein versus Levi's 501 Originals versus True Religion jeans?)
- What key emotional needs does this relationship meet? (Michelin tires make me feel like I'm protecting my family; Starbucks gives me back a little of my day.)

- What personality characteristics can I count on over time and across product experiences? (Apple versus IBM.)
- What values does this company stand for? (Ben & Jerry's Ice Cream versus Häagen-Dazs.)

Many of these emotional questions are subconscious and irrational. They may even sound silly when stated out loud. You will probably never hear someone say, "I feel like a rich man when people see me in my Cadillac" or "I feel sexy and attractive when I wear Carlos Santana shoes" or "I'll get lucky tonight because I'm wearing Axe body spray" or "I'll perform better than the other point guard because I have Nikes" or "I'm innovative, creative, and more 'with it' because I use an Apple computer." But that is how many people feel. Such feelings can be powerful motivators to buy your product.

Building an emotional relationship starts with the consumer rather than with your company or product. The goal is to build on consumers' feelings, perceptions, and emotional needs. You will have to live in the consumer's hidden emotional world. Get ready to be surprised.

Emotional relationship marketing requires the use of fairly sophisticated qualitative research techniques, the ability to listen "behind" or "below" what consumers are saying and the ability to create a wide range of positioning hypotheses to test. Before you undertake emotional relationship positioning, you may want to seek the assistance of a marketing communications firm, an advertising agency, or a marketing research firm with proven experience in this area.

If you explore how to build relationship positioning, you may find it helpful to look at the following case study from several years ago.

Case Study: A Regional Health Care Clinic

A number of years ago, we did work for a large multispecialty clinic serving 11 counties in southern Wisconsin. The clinic's primary competitor had established a clear brand image based on the quality of its physicians. Focus group research revealed that our client had no clear brand image in the marketplace other than being perceived as "big." Consumers sometimes referred to it as an impersonal "machine." The health care organization wanted to improve its image to keep the patients it had and to attract more patients.

The first step was to identify its highest-opportunity customer. National research available in trade publications revealed that women made 80 percent of all health care decisions for their family, including themselves, their children, their spouse, and their parents. Industry norms and local patient counts showed that the heaviest users of primary care were women with children. Qualitative and quantitative studies confirmed that the choice of clinic was based primarily on the choice of pediatrician. Therefore, the target market was defined as women age 25 to 49 with children. The lowest-opportunity customers were young single men.

By combining national and local demographic information with hospital experience, the following profile of the clinic's heavy user was developed:

"Mary" is a 35-year-old white mother of two young children (preschool and elementary school age). She works part-time. Her husband is the primary

(continued)

breadwinner, and she is the primary caregiver. Their combined annual family income is around $60,000. She has made considerable personal and professional sacrifices to be a mother. She is consumed by the demands of home and family (cooking, cleaning, shopping, chauffeuring, homework, bill-paying, raising children), and she has very little discretionary time. She has traditional midwestern values: her home and family are the most important things in her life. Yet she does not want to be a traditional, 1950s' stay-at-home mom, and she longs for some time for herself. She is responsible for the day-to-day care of the family's health. She takes care of her children when they are sick. She (more than her husband) chooses the pediatrician.

Once the consumer profile had been identified, the health care organization needed to find a key emotional benefit. Based on good logic, the physicians believed that board certification, credentials, knowledge, experience, facilities, technology, and expertise were the most critical attributes in the patient's decision. The doctors believed that a successful interaction was one in which they did a good medical job.

Six focus groups were conducted with the health care organization's patients and nonpatients in which they were asked to identify the difference between a good doctor experience and a bad doctor experience. They were asked to do the following:

1. Describe their best and worst experiences with a doctor.
2. Supply adjectives describing a good doctor and a bad doctor.
3. Describe competing medical systems as if the clinics were people.
4. Rank the competing medical systems based on medical specialties, including pediatrics.
5. Discuss competing medical systems based on a series of photos showing an array of different archetypes. Then choose the archetypal photo that best matched each medical system.

The women in the focus groups said that they really wanted a doctor who would listen to them and treat them like human beings with feelings. Listening, eye contact, personal treatment, and taking the time to explain things were consistently ranked first. Physician experience and knowledge were consistently ranked last because these attributes were taken for granted and were also hard to measure for the average consumer.

Based on this new insight, a positioning opportunity for our client was developed. In the mind of the customer, the health care organization could own "patients" instead of "doctors" and "human feelings" instead of "physician expertise." The positioning became: "the clinic that treats people like human beings with feelings."

A radio, print, and billboard campaign was created to communicate this new positioning. Within the first three quarters of advertising, patient visits increased significantly. In the all-important pediatric category, patient visits increased by double digits. The health care organization was also able to extend the positioning to other medical services and markets, including cardiac care.

Now that you've seen an example of emotional relationship positioning, you can better understand the tasks you will need to undertake for your business.

How to Build an Emotional Relationship

The following six tasks will help you establish an emotional relationship between your company and the customers in your target markets.

TASK 1 ### *Develop an Individual Profile of Your Highest-Opportunity Consumer*

Start by going back to review your Target Market section where you did this work (see Chapter 5, "Targets"). This individual profile, which in many cases will be that of the heavy purchaser, contains information like demographics, lifestyle, values, emotional needs, life experiences, philosophies, hobbies, and interests. This profile is then contrasted with that of the person who is the lowest-opportunity consumer, or in many cases the light purchaser segment. This contrast will often point to the key underlying motivator.

TASK 2 ### **Brainstorm for Motivators**

Brainstorm with your staff or people knowledgeable about the product to develop a wide range of underlying, feeling-generated motivators to test with consumers. It is even valuable to include motivators that you know are wrong in order to get clearer feedback that points you in the right direction. For example, when the regional health care organization in the example extended the positioning to cardiac care, it tested several emotional motivators (fear of dying, joy of living) against several attribute motivators (experience, physician expertise, mortality rates).

TASK 3 ### **Identify the Consumers' Primary Emotional Motivators**

Motivations can differ significantly depending on the purchasing occasion, the stage of one's life, or the role the product plays in your target's life. Through contrasting a good and bad product experience, you gain insight into key motivators or the decision drivers for the positioning concepts you feel consumers liked best in Task 2 above. For the regional health care organization in the example, contrasting their good and bad doctor experiences helped reveal the key motivator—the need to be treated like a human being with feelings.

TASK 4 ### **Use Qualitative Research to Rank the Motivator Choices with Target Consumers**

We recommend showing positionings in the forms of written boards, photo boards, and tape-recorded concept statements. Using audio "theater-of-the-mind" descriptions of the positioning concept is our favorite because they eliminate biases based on colors, how people look, and so on. Use a skilled moderator and/or researcher who can get respondents to talk about their feelings pertaining to each alternative—what they like, dislike, don't trust, trust, believe, don't believe, and why. Through practiced conversation with the respondents, you will be able to determine insights into the strengths and weaknesses of each concept. At the very end of the research, after the discussion, get respondents to force rank each one based on their purchase intent. You should plan to hold a minimum of two to four different focus groups or 12 to 14 one-on-ones against your primary target segment.

TASK 5   ## Validate Qualitative Analysis with Quantitative Survey Results

If at all possible, use quantitative survey research to test several different positionings (both emotional and attribute) to verify the results of the focus groups regarding the appeal of the key motivator relative to the size of the market. This will prevent you from selecting a key motivator that is very strong but that is significant only for a very small group of people.

TASK 6   ## Use the Strongest Motivator for Your Positioning Strategy

This will establish a relationship with your target person and also establish a core brand personality for your company or product.

See also Appendix C, Worksheet 35.

Method 2 for Finding Your Brand Promise: Positioning by Matching

Simply stated, the following five tasks will help you use the positioning method to match your products' inherent and unique benefits or competitive advantages to the characteristics and needs and wants of the target market.

See also Appendix C, Worksheet 35.

TASK 1   ## Analyze Your Products versus the Competition

A good place to start the matching method is with an analysis of your product and your competition's. Based on your business review, list your competition on the top left side of the worksheet (see Exhibit 6.2). The competition could be one major competitor, a number of key competitors, a specific business category, or a number of key business categories. For example, in the positioning of an off-price menswear retailer, it was determined that specific competition varied by geographic market, but the competitive business categories remained the same in all markets—department stores, specialty men's clothing stores, and off-price/discount stores.

TASK 2   ## Identify the Differences between Your Products and Those of the Competition

Next, write down the key positive and negative differences of your product versus those of the competition relative to your primary target market. These differences should be listed as they relate to key elements of the marketing mix that are appropriate to what you are selling.

Sometimes a difference that is seemingly negative can become a positive. A small retailer that has a limited square footage and, therefore, a limited variety of products it can offer can create a positioning of specialty selection and personal attention.

For work one of the authors did with Coors, a meaningful difference was the quality of the beer because it is unpasteurized and made from fresh Rocky Mountain spring water, and the beer is shipped from the brewery refrigerated. For Cheer, it was the one laundry detergent ("All Temperature Cheer") that washes all types of clothes in hot, warm, or cold water. For a retail ski client, being new to a market and offering innovative customer service led to its positioning as the "New age of ski shops." This was a very appropriate positioning because the

EXHIBIT 6.2

Matching Product Differences to the Target Market's Needs and Wants: Retail Fabric Chain Example

Key Competition

1. Specialty chains
2. Mass merchants

Differences from Competition

Product, Store, Service Attributes

Larger selection of fabrics and notions

Slightly better quality

Favorite store of sewers

Always new merchandise

Carries variety of goods for sewing, home decorating, and crafting

Focus and orientation in store toward helping solve sewers' problems—how-to information and new crafting ideas

Store staffed with sewers and crafters

New Products, Improvements

Greater expansion into craft and home decorating merchandise

Packaging, Store Appearance

Best store layout

Larger stores

Does not have promotional appearance

Branding, Name, Reputation

Established reputation

Distribution, Penetration

Greater number of outlets in most markets

Price

Perception of higher prices and less value

Advertising

Has more advertising

Key Target Market

Practical and creative sewers

Women 25–54

Average household income

3+ household size

Characteristics: Needs and Wants

What

Wide selection of merchandise from which to choose

Able to purchase everything at one store

Lowest prices, good values

Quality fabrics

Where

Sews at home

When

After work and weekends (seen as recreation)

Throughout the day (considered part of family responsibilities by practical sewers)

Why (Benefit)

For fun and as a hobby

To express creativity

For herself and children

To save money

For better fit of garments

For feeling of accomplishment

How Purchased, Used

Usually sews alone

Visits a fabric store on average every two weeks

Likes to shop for deals

Shops for enjoyment

Always looking for new creative ideas

How the Target and Its Needs and Wants Are Changing

Less sewing to save money

More sewing for fun and recreation

Not enough time to sew

More sewers working out of the home

Using fabrics not just for sewing garments but for crafting and decorating the home

Buying more fabric-related merchandise for special occasions, holidays

---

skiing target market was young adult, contemporary, and into "change." For a business-to-business firm selling to office supply stores, its established reputation and many office product innovations led to the leadership positioning "Organizing the American office since 1949."

For Elefanten, at the time of our work, Europe's leading manufacturer of upscale kids' shoes, which were purchased by moms, the difference was in moms' experiences or memories of an ideal childhood—of which Elefanten was a big part. The shoes her child wears became an extension of her and of an imaginative, creative, and idyllic childhood that she could readily conjure up in her mind. In other examples, Harley-Davidson promises freedom while Eastpak offers a long-lasting backpack.

Don't stop at one or two differences. Try to list as many as possible. In the last example of the Eastpak backpack, you might start with the overriding difference of longer lasting. But that would lead to the type of material, the care in stitching, the warranty, and so on.

For each area, ask yourself, How is my product different, and how is it better? Is your product different through product superiority, innovation, or size—that is, the number of customers, volume of goods sold, number of outlets?

TASK 3   ## List Your Key Target Market Differences

Insert your key target market on the top right side of the same worksheet (see Exhibit 6.2).

TASK 4   ## List Your Key Target Market Characteristics

Next, list the characteristics of your target market in terms of wants and needs on the right side of the worksheet (Exhibit 6.2). With or without research, ask yourself the following questions, listing brief answers below each question:

- What is the target market really purchasing? Is the product to be used by itself or in conjunction with a number of products? (For example, are women purchasing dress shoes separately or as part of a fashion ensemble? Are moms really buying a doll when they purchase a Pleasant Company doll for their daughter, or are they purchasing an educational experience?) For what purpose is the target using the product? (Is the baking soda for baking a cake, deodorizing the refrigerator, or brushing teeth?)
- Where is the target market purchasing and/or using it—by geography (for example, in sunny, very warm climates) and/or by place (in the home, car, and so on)?
- When is the target market using it—time of the year, month, week, day, during or after work?
- Why are the target market consumers purchasing and/or using the product, or why are they purchasing from one store over another? Is it because of a particular feature? Is it a convenient location or greater selection? Does the product save time or money?
- How is it purchased and/or used? Is it purchased and/or used alone or with other people? Is it a frequent or infrequent purchase? How is it used? (Is the tissue used to wipe one's nose or clean the windows? Is the beer used to relax after work or celebrate and party?)
- How is the target changing? Is the market changing by demographics, lifestyle, size, or industry category? How are purchasing and/or usage habits of the product changing? (Is fashion becoming more important than durability, value more than price, service more than just product quality?)

In Exhibit 6.2, you start to get a picture of an emerging target market consisting of women who sew for recreation and at home, who no longer sew for need and are looking for an outlet for their creativity.

TASK 5   ## Match Your Product's Characteristics to the Target Market's Needs and Wants

Having listed the differences of your product and the key needs and wants of the target market, try to match what is unique about your product to the meaningful needs and wants of the target market.

In Exhibit 6.2, using a retail fabric chain as an example, we have listed the specific competition and retailer's competitive differences on the left and the target market and its characteristics on the right. Now actually draw connections between what the target market wants and how the company is different from the competition. Focus on these connections as the foundation of your positioning.

Based on the listing of the competitive differences, it would appear that this fabric retailer has a competitive advantage by offering an abundance of fabric-related merchandise in larger, better-designed stores. The merchandise selection appears superior not only in the amount but also in the variety of merchandise offered to complete a sewing project, as well as related crafting and home decorating projects. This retailer could be viewed as a leader with an established reputation offering a variety of quality merchandise, though not at the lowest prices or greatest values. The retailer also has a competitive difference in its orientation toward products and services around the growing trend of crafting as a creative expression.

The target market, on the other hand, is a mix of both practically and recreationally motivated sewers who want a large selection of all types of fabric-related merchandise that is very competitively priced and is a real value. This retailer definitely has the desired selection and quality but not necessarily the lower prices and value. The target also wants all of the required merchandise under one roof in order to enjoy a fun and rewarding shopping experience, as well as to fulfill the needs for both practically and recreationally motivated projects.

Further, the matching exercise indicates changes occurring within the target market. It appears that people who sew have less time or need to sew regularly, are creating fewer garments, and are becoming more recreationally oriented, with interest growing in craft and home decorating projects.

After you have prepared your positioning worksheet, draw lines from the major competitive positive differences to the paralleling want or need characteristics of the target market. Ask yourself again what really is important to the target market in terms of how your product is different and better. Based on this, eliminate lines until you have the two or three most meaningful potential positioning connections between product and target market.

In some cases you might combine two product differences or advantages to fill an important want. If you were a retailer, you might combine the attributes of brand name products and very competitive prices to arrive at a *value* positioning, which ties to an important consumer desire.

In some situations you will draw lines between product and target market characteristics and find that a most important consumer need or want is not being fulfilled by your product or the competition. For example, Virginia Slims, a cigarette for women, was created to fill a consumer void or gap. Going to the other extreme, you might find that all of the competing products fulfill the target's needs or wants, but no one competitor, including your product, has claimed it as a reason for being. Or it might be that there are changing needs that are not being met and evolving needs that will provide positioning opportunities.

In the example shown in Exhibit 6.2, there appears to be a number of competitive advantages that are important for meeting the target's needs, including wide variety, quality, fashionability, growing selection, and larger stores. However, it was clear that the store's advantage in having new merchandise, craft-oriented merchandise, and a staff of creative sewers and crafters coupled with the trend away from sewing as a necessity and toward sewing as a recreational and creative outlet provided a strong positioning foundation. These advantages would appear to match the target's growing desire for a fabric store with a large and complete offering of sewing, craft, and home decorating merchandise and ideas on how to more creatively use the merchandise.

Positioning solution: By matching the key differences to the key target market needs and wants, you could arrive at the following positioning statement for this fabric retail chain: "The store that always provides sewers with ideas and solutions." The name of the store was changed from Northwest Fabrics to Northwest Fabrics and Crafts. The tagline for the store became "Northwest Fabrics and Crafts: The More Ideas Store."

Another example of matching, as shown in Exhibit 6.3, is the positioning of a regional accounting firm, Williams Young, selling its services to presidents and financial vice presidents at companies across a wide spectrum of SIC or NAICS codes.

This is an example of positioning around a complex combination of service offerings and the ultimate benefits to the customer that can be delivered better because of the structure of the firm.

The competitors are other regional accounting firms. However, this accounting firm does more than just measure financial strength. It works across a client's business, with

EXHIBIT 6.3

Matching Product Differences to the Target Market's Needs and Wants: Accounting Firm Example

Key Competition

Other regional accounting firms

Differences from Competition
Product, Store, Service Attributes and Benefits

More than measuring financial strength

- Provide added profit to bottom line
- Look at people and processes

Focus on improving operations, not just identifying problems

Recognized experts across departments

Testimonials from clients who have used the integrated approach to solving bottom-line problems

Assurance

Financial audits to performance measurement

Tax assistance

Business tax structuring, mergers and acquisitions, to retirement

Technology

Network design to financial software

Performance

Strategic planning, work flow, to payroll and salaries

New Products, Improvements

Performance

Human resources: Predictive indexes

Packaging, Store Appearance

Traditional office setting

Branding, Name, Reputation

Fragmented, well known in some industry categories and not in others

Price

Competitive

Communication

Direct mail and personal selling

Key Target Markets

1. Presidents and financial vice presidents
2. Closely held businesses in manufacturing, wholesale, distribution, construction, real estate, and professional services

Characteristics: Needs and Wants
What

Assistance in identifying all inefficient business segments

Where

In on-location office visits

Why (Benefit)

Solve problems

Improve bottom line

Someone who can connect problems and provide a unifying solution that translates to profits

Someone versed in today's business solutions

How Purchased, Used

Undivided services

Ongoing relationships

How the Target Market and Its Needs and Wants Are Changing

Looking for integrated solutions, not just help with taxes and auditing

Recognition that the way to improving bottom line is through solving system problems a concentration on how the interrelated parts affect the whole. In order to do this, the firm had to develop centers of excellence throughout a wide number of departments, including personnel, technology, strategic planning, and various areas of financial expertise (ranging from tax to assurance to performance).

Research showed that members of the target market found it difficult to determine the value of one accounting firm over another and thus were looking for a firm with which they could build a long-term relationship over time and that would get to know their business. Accounting clients also wanted more than just reporting; they wanted solutions that would be actionable.

On the left side of Exhibit 6.3, under Differences from Competition, you will see that Williams Young emphasized its integrated approach. The firm had a proven staff of regionally known experts heading up the individual departments. It also had strong testimonials citing proven results from companies that used the firm's approach of attacking the many parts to provide for a better system bottom line. In addition, on the right side of the exhibit, you will notice that businesses were becoming more in tune with the fact that a combination of factors affects profitability. If you fix the accounting system but don't have the right technology or staff, you won't solve the overall problem. The target market also demonstrates repeatedly the desire for one source to bring tangible ways to increase the overall bottom line performance of the company.

Positioning solution: The matching exercise led us to combine the difference of the Williams Young systemic approach with the end benefit of increased profits. The positioning became "Systemic solutions resulting in improved profits." The visual representation of this positioning consisted of inkblots, in the manner of the Rorschach test, with the tagline "Think Black Ink." Related text developed the message that Williams Young might see things differently because the firm looks at the whole and not just the pieces. And in seeing the whole, the company can help clients find ways to improve their bottom line. The firm developed a "Think Black Ink" audit that reviewed the many disparate pieces of any organization that ultimately tie together to determine the bottom line. So, not only did the firm develop products around its positioning but it also translated the positioning into its signage, internal communications, graphic identity, and aggressive advertising program. The accounting firm doubled in size in a little over two years. The new positioning led to many new business wins. Probably just as important, the firm felt the positioning significantly helped its recruiting. The company attracted better, more aggressive candidates who wanted to be part of everything the new positioning communicated versus the traditional, conservative images stereotypical of accounting firms.

A final example of matching is shown in Exhibit 6.4, the company here being a regional microbrewery. The format is the same as in the previous two exhibits.

Based on the listing of the competitive differences, this microbrewer would appear to have several advantages over better-known small breweries and regional brands. Those advantages include the quirky Bavarian brewmaster, Hans Kestler; the heritage of the local brewery in a state known for its beer (Wisconsin); the limited batches of brew that it produces; and its seasonal beers. While these competitive differences are all marketable assets, the matching exercise we performed for the client highlighted the importance for the microbrewer of equating small with quality. Of course, small size is something most every microbrewery could claim. However, as we noted earlier in the chapter, there are many successful examples of companies claiming such a category difference or benefit for themselves and forever owning it.

Positioning solution: When we matched the differences on the left with the needs and wants on the right, we focused on the fact that *little* meant quality. We noted that

EXHIBIT 6.4

Matching Product Differences to the Target Market's Needs and Wants: Regional Microbrewery Example

Key Competition
1. All micro beers
2. Sam Adams
3. Leinenkugel's

Differences from Competition
Product, Store, Service Attributes and Benefits
   Brewed in small, locally owned brewery
   Personally brewed by Bavarian brewmaster

New Products, Improvements
   Introduced seasonal brews and two new
      year-round beers
   Now 10 different varieties

Packaging, Store Appearance
   Fewer facings

Branding, Name, Reputation
   Associated with well-known Chicago restaurant

Distribution, Penetration
   Limited on-premises accounts

Price
   Above Bud and Miller, but below high-end
      micro beers

Advertising (Message, Media)
   Promotion
   Merchandising
   Personal selling and service
   Publicity
   Growth in number of micro beer drinkers
   More variety of flavors

the target believed that small breweries produced a better-quality beer. The target also believed that breweries with a history and heritage produced better beers, and it liked the variety that microbreweries offer. Anything the opposite of mass-brewed meant good beer.

In this example, the matching process showed us that Berghoff could play off the small brewery theme via its brewmaster, location, heritage, and small batches of beer. We positioned the beer as "Small equals quality." The resulting tagline and focus of the communication became "Berghoff, drink a little beer."

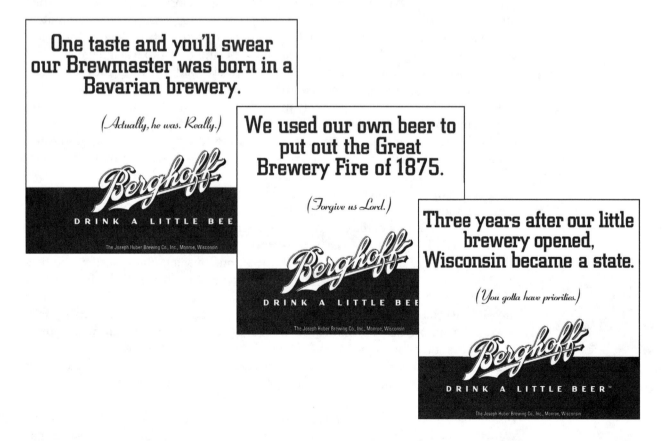

Method 3 for Finding Your Brand Promise: Positioning by Mapping

The following three tasks make up a practical application of the mapping methodology based on multidimensional models. Using this approach, you map out visually what is important to your target market in terms of key product attributes. The competition's products, along with your own, are then ranked on these attributes. This type of mapping is extremely useful in positioning a product and, again, is most effective when based on quantitative research that is representative of your intended target market and the marketplace. Your preconceived notions about what the target market thinks can differ dramatically from what quantifiable research reports.

However, if you do not have market research, it is still helpful to use this method when positioning to sort out what you believe is important to the target market. Further, this positioning approach will help you to more clearly evaluate how your product and your key competition are perceived on each attribute. Because this mapping method is somewhat involved and you will most likely not have research to assist you, read through the three steps before beginning the actual mapping process.

See also Appendix C, Worksheet 35.

TASK 1 **List Product Attributes by Importance**

The first step is to list in order of importance the product category attributes, attitudes, or benefits on the right side of the map, moving top to bottom, from most important to least important. If quantitative research is not available before you begin mapping, it's a good idea to gather a number of people knowledgeable about your product category and have each one of them list the most important attributes. Then as objectively as possible, have them independently assign a number from 1 to 10 (10 being most important and 1 least important) for each attribute. Take an average of these estimates for each ranking. Based on each composite estimate, rank order the attributes.

TASK 2 **Rate Your Product and Competitors' Product for Each Attribute**

Once you have determined the key target market attributes in order of importance in task 1, find out the rating of each attribute, attitude, or benefit for your company and its key competitors.

In your plotting of the competitive market, you might have great disparity between competitors on one attribute and no differences on another. Ideally, you want your product ranked the best versus the competition on all attributes, but particularly on those that are most important to the consumer. The more you see your product's initial on the right, especially on those attributes at the top of the chart, the stronger the position of your product in the marketplace.

A note of caution: Using a knowledgeable group of people to assist in arriving at key attributes and competitive ratings is not very accurate compared to using survey research that will quantify the perceptions of the users and/or purchasers.

TASK 3 **Visualize Desired Position on the Map for Your Product**

Once your positioning map is complete, review how your product ranks on the more important attributes relative to the competition. Next, visualize where you want your product positioned on the map based on what the consumer wants and

EXHIBIT 6.5

Map of Customer versus Noncustomer Rankings

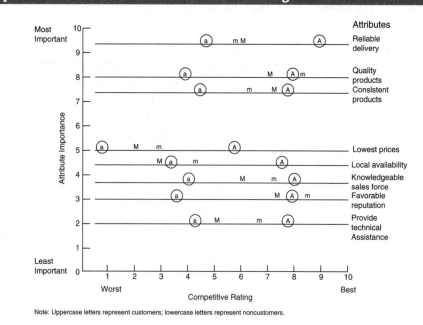

Note: Uppercase letters represent customers; lowercase letters represent noncustomers.

what your product can provide relative to the strengths and weaknesses of the competition. Select the positioning approach that will positively affect the target market's perceptions and attain your visualized positioning.

See also Appendix C, Worksheet 35.

Mapping Customer versus Noncustomer Perceptions

When putting together your maps, another thing to consider is the makeup of your target market. Accordingly, you can put together one map for customers and another for target market noncustomers. Many times, what is important to your current customers might not be as important to noncustomers. Noncustomers will usually rate your product more negatively than will your customers.

To illustrate through a business-to-business case, you can see in Exhibit 6.5 how highly *customers* rated Company A (uppercase) versus its key competitor, Competitor M, and how poorly its *noncustomers* rated the same Company a (lowercase). This firm, which originally emphasized price to attract new customers, changed its positioning to one of "Best performance" in terms of reliable delivery, product, consistency, and quality—all of which the company said it could or did provide. This new positioning was supported with an aggressive advertising and personal selling program built around the new "Best performance" positioning. The result was a substantial increase in new customers.

Look for Positioning Gaps

Using the mapping approach, you can isolate differences for your product versus the competition that will lead to effective positioning. Often, however, there are no meaningful differences but only attribute opportunity areas that no one has taken advantage of.

To find this type of opportunity gap, review your map for an important attribute vacuum that your product can fill. In Exhibit 6.6, for a business-to-business Company B selling its professional services to small and midsize firms, we see no

EXHIBIT 6.6

Positioning by Identifying Gaps

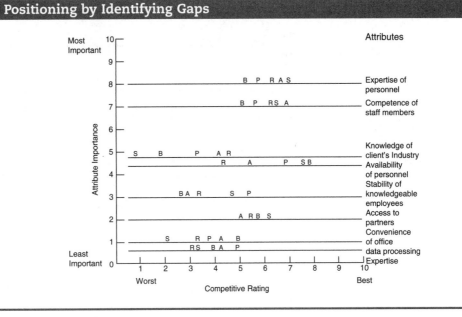

one fully satisfying the target market on the third most important attribute, knowledge of client's industry. Because competitors appeared strong in the two most important attributes, expertise of personnel and competence of staff members, we positioned our client as the accounting firm that understands and tailors its services to the client's specific business. Accordingly, the target market was segmented by SIC or NAICS codes and size. Each industry target segmented by size received tailored-frequency direct-mail advertising. The result was a substantial increase in new clients and a 90 percent return on the marketing investment.

Look for Strengths and/or Groupings

Another mapping example, shown in Exhibit 6.7, demonstrates how you can position by isolating strengths that are meaningful and grouping them under a common umbrella attribute. In Exhibit 6.7 you see a map for analytical equipment manufacturers selling their products to quality control technicians in a wide variety of industries. In this case example, the Manufacturer M was the fourth player in the market by size, selling primarily through attractive pricing against the larger competing companies. In order for Manufacturer M to improve the perceived value of its products and thus increase its share of market and its margins, it grouped together three out of the top four attributes where it was rated most favorably (product reliability, software, and ease of use). All of these attributes were driven by equipment that required state-of-the-art technology. Accordingly, Manufacturer M then made *superior technology* its meaningful difference, avoiding the service attributes, where it was weaker, and making price secondary to technology. Being a fourth-tier competitor in a highly competitive field, Manufacturer M could combine technology strengths to become a major player in a high-tech category against the large competitors who had larger sales and service staffs.

Develop a Visual Space Map

A final form of mapping can be seen in Exhibit 6.8. This map uses a spider web technique. The advantage of this technique is that it allows comparison across multiple attributes with the end result being a visual space that represents each competitor.

EXHIBIT 6.7

Positioning by Isolating Strengths

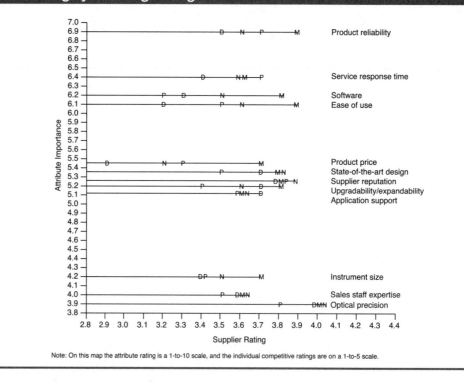

Note: On this map the attribute rating is a 1-to-10 scale, and the individual competitive ratings are on a 1-to-5 scale.

In this example, it is clear how Culver's competes against McDonald's and Applebee's. The chain's appeal comes from its ability to deliver fairly fast food with the perception among adults that they aren't cutting too many corners when they eat there. You still sit down and eat with your kids at a table, the meal is brought to you, and the food is perceived to be fresher and more "homemade." All this contributes to Culver's positioning as "an old-fashioned/modern meal."

EXHIBIT 6.8

Positioning by Making a Spider Web Map

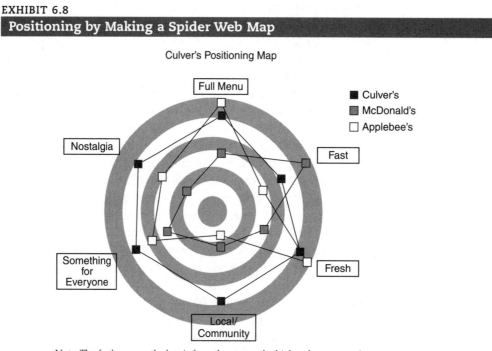

Note: The farther away the box is from the center, the higher the company's score.

STEP 3. EXPRESSING WHAT THE BRAND ESSENCE IS AND ISN'T

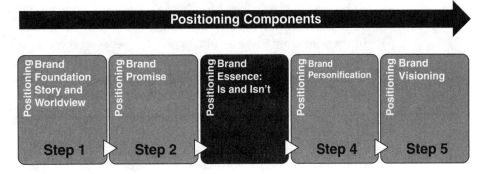

The brand essence is typically three to five words that the brand is and the corresponding word that the brand is not. This is primarily used internally as a continual reminder and boundary for company decisions. We've found that when a company needs more than three to five words to define the parameters of its brand, two things happen. One, no one understands what the brand is because it very quickly becomes "all things to all people." And two, so few people can remember multiple words that the brand essence quickly becomes irrelevant.

Research originally suggested that our working memory (that is, our short-term memory) cutoff point for remembering was seven. However, scientists later revised this idea based on subsequent research. Researchers found that to store seven bits of information, people actually use memory tricks or aids such as grouping (or "chunking") information into smaller units. University of Missouri at Columbia psychologist Nelson Cowan led a study that showed that the number is really closer to four things that people can store in their working memory at one time—that is, the part of memory that allows people to pay attention and still manipulate the information as needed. Whether the number is seven or four, the point is still the same. Keep your list of key brand descriptors or your brand essence to a limited number.

If you are a brand that is all about simplicity and not complex, that says a lot about the customer service systems you'll develop, the product design, and the way you will develop your website. The words that describe what your brand is and is not provide a framework within which everyone in the organization can enhance the brand and develop future strategies and tactics.

Writing What Your Brand Essence Is and Isn't

On first blush, this seems easy. However, we've spent days with clients going through this, and our caution to you would be, don't take this exercise lightly. Words matter.

We suggest you develop your brand essence with a team of cross-functional staff across departments and layers of responsibility within your company. Use your brand foundation and worldview and your brand promise as your guides. The words you develop here should form a sort of border for your brand promise. Picture your brand essence as the house in which your brand promise can live and feel safe.

Start by having everyone bring five to seven words that your brand is and your brand isn't. Make sure the people working on this are versed in your company's consumer research and the brand promise. Often, the best brand essence words come directly from the voices of your customers, for in the end, they know you best.

Start with the "Is" Words

Make a list of the "is" words. Group similar meanings together on a large flip chart. Discuss the differences in meaning of the similar words. Do this across all the different-meaning words until you've discussed the entire list. Use a thesaurus to find new words that are similar in meaning to the ones you've listed. Talk about what it would mean if these words were part of your brand essence. Have people list the tangible actions you would take. This is very important! Make sure you operationalize this exercise. Doing so quickly moves it from theoretical to very tangible. Brand positionings need to be tangible and operational. Now ask if there are other words to describe your brand within the context of the brand promise and the insights provided by your customers. Add those to the list.

Finally have the group go up to the flip charts and pick three of their favorite "is" words that are true to your brand promise and the foundation story and worldview. Review the top three to five words. Discuss, debate, argue, and again, test them by asking, "What would this mean to how we operationalize our business on a daily basis and into the future?" Also, make sure each word is very different from the others and captures a specific area of your brand that is apart from the others. Think about the ramifications of each word to product, marketing, customer service, operations, and even finance.

Now Develop the "Isn't" Words

Once you have agreement on what the brand is, move to what the brand isn't. Take the positive "is" words and have the work group write the opposites. Go through the same basic procedure outlined above. Work hard at really understanding what you would not do and what your brand would not be. How would that understanding affect how you run your business? Again, words matter here.

Example of Brand Essence Is and Isn't: ELI, Inc.

The following is an example of the brand essence for ELI, Inc.: A national business-to-business training firm specializing in using legal compliance issues as the basis of a civil treatment learning platform that minimizes litigation but more importantly, builds higher-performing cultures and companies.

Brand positioning: The brand positioning promise for ELI is: ELI has translated the laws of civil treatment into a foundational learning platform built on universal principles that drive successful workplace and organizational performance.

The brand essence did a great job of putting a box around the brand positioning promise of ELI. The firm brought about real change or transformation with its

ELI, Inc. Brand Essence	
Is	**Isn't**
Transformational	Unchanging
Principled	Dishonest
Simple	Complex
Learning organization	One-time event
Professional	Careless

clients. So much so that the research into customers discovered that the companies ELI served saw the work ELI did as larger and more impactful than even the staff at ELI gave themselves credit for. ELI's clients saw the work that it did for them as far more important than simply compliance to laws, the clients saw it as the foundation for a higher-performing company. The learned traits of civil treatment lead to open, caring, safe environments that breed honest, professional interactions that define successful companies worldwide. Client feedback further highlighted the fact that the ELI training program was simple and straightforward, unlike so many other behavior human resources programs that take years to fully grasp and understand. The work that ELI did led to organizations that continually learned; the classes and workshops of ELI weren't seen as a one-time event but rather as an ongoing series of learnings focusing on the same thing, learned and practiced in different ways.

In this case, as in many, insights from the clients became instrumental in creating the brand essence or the parameters that the company uses to make decisions.

See also Appendix C, Worksheet 35.

STEP 4. DEVELOPING YOUR BRAND PERSONIFICATION

Five Steps to Brand Positioning

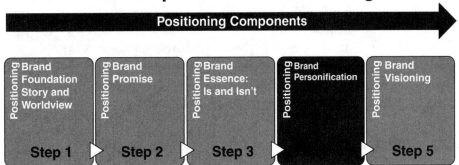

The fourth step in bringing a brand to life is a written brand personification. This is an internal document. It is not intended to be used on your Web page, as part of an advertisement, or in any other form of communication with your customers. It is intended to help communicate and build the brand among the people in your most important target market: the employees and staff of your business.

A good place to start in developing your brand personification is to consider the use of archetypes. Archetypes are the basis for stories that conjure up strong elementary feelings. These stories have been told over time and are embedded in our memories. Think in terms of David and Goliath, the Greek and Roman gods, tales of King Arthur, Rasputin, Johnny Appleseed, Cal Ripkin and Bret Farve, Norm on *Cheers*, the good witch and the bad witch in the *Wizard of Oz*, the bad boys of sports like John McEnroe, the heroes like Michael Jordon, the villains in movies, the innocents like E.T., Merlin the magician, Socrates, the sage, the American Cowboy, bad boy James Dean—archetypes are people we know. They provide a very tangible meaning and context within which we can begin to understand the personification of a brand.

In their groundbreaking book *The Hero and the Outlaw*,* Margaret Mark and Carol Pearson provide example after example of brands whose personifications are embedded through archetypal stories. Here are a few:

- *The Jolly Green Giant:* The personification of fertility—the archetype of the green man, a figure associated with abundance.
- *Ivory soap:* The personification of the innocent. Mothers wash their children with Ivory not only because it will keep them safe from germs but also because Ivory just seems right for our precious, innocent children.
- *Levi's:* The personification of the explorer, the individual who maintains independence.
- *Harley-Davidson:* The personification of the outlaw, the rule breaker.
- *Hallmark:* The personification of the lover.
- *Miller Lite:* The personification of the jester, always having a good time.
- *Nike*: The personification of the hero.

Mark and Pearson go on to discuss 12 signature archetypes in connection to the core desires, goals, and fears of the people who associate with these archetypes. They then discuss which brands typically associate with which archetypes and the characteristics of those brands. The 12 archetypes below are the ones highlighted in *The Hero and the Outlaw*. We'd recommend that you start your exploration of the brand's personification by thinking of your company, product, or service in terms of which archetype it most closely represents. We often use photos of archetypes in qualitative research to have respondents classify the company we're doing research for and its competitive set. The photos people choose associated with each company and the stories they tell surrounding their choice provide great detail and insight into what people think. The list below is just a start; there are many more archetypes that may more closely represent your company. As you start to think of your brand personification, think in terms of the archetypal stories.

Archetype	Helps People
Creator	Craft something new, be creative, and come up with new ideas
Caregiver	Care for others, heal others, solve others' problems
Ruler	Exert control and leadership
Jester	Have a good time and feel at ease
Regular guy or gal	Feel good about their own priorities: being the "salt of the earth," being honest, giving a fair day's work for a fair day's wage, doing what they say they will, being okay just the way they are
Lover	Find and give love
Hero	Act courageously, win the day, be bigger than life
Outlaw	Break the rules, live on the edge, be the "bad boys"

---

* Margaret Mark and Carol S. Pearson, *The Hero and the Outlaw: Building Extraordinary Brands through the Power of Archetypes*, McGraw-Hill, New York, 2001.

Magician	Effect transformations and changes, make things happen
Innocent	Retain or renew faith; be pure, naive, and safe
Explorer	Maintain their independence, search for truth, go their own way, climb mountains just because they are there
Sage	Be wise, understand their world, give advice to others

In thinking about your brand's archetype, it can be helpful to plot out the category on a grid, as shown below. The archetypes work like psychological magnets, pulling consumers toward brands on the axes of "belonging" and "independence" and "stability" and "change."

The best brands understand the power of the archetypes, and they harness them to meet customers' higher-order needs.

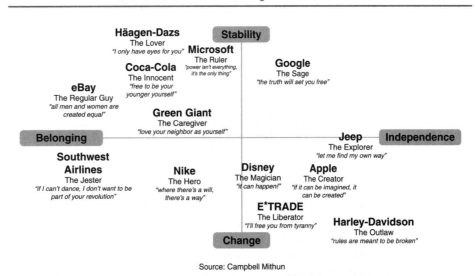

Source: Campbell Mithun

In the following figure, we have used our judgment to plot brands in the casual dining category on an archetypal grid. Notice how brands can tend to crowd the same archetypes in a category.

Casual Dining

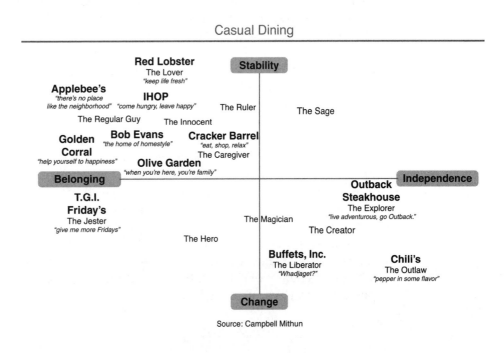

Source: Campbell Mithun

Writing Your Brand Personification

Write in the first person: "I am [your company or product here]." Then go on to describe your company's personality as it relates to your worldview, brand promise, and brand essence words. We think it's a good idea to convert your written brand personification into a video using the tools of sight, sound, and emotion. Do this by bringing the written brand personification to life on a video with photos and music for the background.

Two Brand Personification Examples

- *ELI:* A national business-to-business training firm specializing in using legal compliance issues as the basis of a civil treatment learning platform that minimizes litigation but more importantly, builds higher-performing cultures and companies
- *Networked Insights:* A firm that mines and analyzes consumer insights from social media sites

ELI

I am ELI. I'm a wise and effective *teacher*. Like the earliest teachers, I have a *surprising wisdom* that can be passed on to anyone willing to take the journey. It's a wisdom rooted over time in the most successful civilizations and countries and the best companies of today. The surprise is transformed through the power of individuals to grow and create better, more effective environments, resulting in the higher performance of organizations. This has happened throughout history when organizations have understood and complied with the fundamental laws that deal with respect, trust, fairness, openness—I refer to this as civil treatment. I'm really very *simple compared to the complexity of the law*. Focus on one thing and reinforce it through many—focus on civil treatment and reinforce it through many decision and action areas that matter most in the workplace. I take pride in the fact that over the years, I've become skilled at creating shared visions through talking about the process in very ordinary terms.

I work best with *learning* organizations, ones that are based on continually improving their knowledge and understanding. I detest that "learning" has come to be synonymous with "taking in information." I cringe when I hear, "Yes, I learned all about that in the course yesterday." I believe that taking in information is only distantly related to real learning. As the teacher, I know *practice* leads to real learning and practice can't happen simply by reading a book or taking one class.

I'm interested in *change*. It's my life's work. But change is hard, and meaningful change rarely happens in companies unless the wisdom is transferred to one individual at a time. Organizations learn through individuals who learn. Individual learning does not guarantee organizational learning, but without it, no organizational learning occurs. There is nothing more important to an individual committed to his or her own growth than a *supportive environment*. That's ELI—the teacher that shows companies how to grow supportive and ethical individuals, that when working with like individuals, creates something far more powerful than ever imagined.

Networked Insights

I am Networked Insights. I'm one of the new breed of alchemists who turn today's common material (Internet chatter) into gold (the consumer insights that drive any successful business). I know how to listen, to the thousands and millions of conversations that are occurring right now about your product. But I'm also inquisitive. I don't just eavesdrop and report the gossip. In order to turn common material into gold, you have to be smart, you have to interpret, you have to analyze. We track everything, but we really focus on listening and then understanding the chatter from the individuals and sites that matter most to your business. So unlike the gossipers, we sort out truth from fiction.

We're democratic in our work and work environment because the power of one doesn't transform. It's the power of finding the consistent message and direction of many. We seek the truth no matter where it's hiding or who holds it. The very nature of our process is unabashedly unbiased because it's rooted in listening and not asking.

We're bold innovators. We believe companies need to change the way they look for and interpret insights. Every day, again and again and again your consumers are giving you the answers on how to form a tighter connection in millions of conversations over the Internet. You just need an alchemist to turn those conversations into gold. That's Networked Insights.

See also Appendix C, Worksheet 35.

STEP 5. DEVELOPING YOUR BRAND VISION

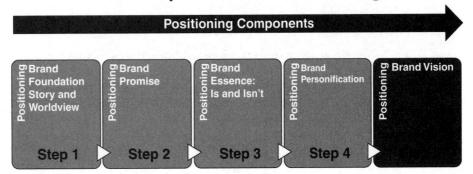

We're sure all four previous steps have been fun, but this is where you really get to soar. This is also where reality starts to hit. The brand visioning allows the key stakeholders in your company or product division to start taking real ownership. Most importantly, the visioning step forces the key internal influencers of the brand to start the process of brand building.

We recommend the following six steps to accomplish your brand visioning.

STEP 1   ## Create Cross-Functional Groups

Include your key cross-functional management team members in one group. Also create a second, and even a third group, composed of individuals who come from all functions in the organization and tend to be forward thinking and idea oriented. These are people who have the ability to leave planet earth but stay in its orbit. Said another way, they are dreamers, but they have a foot in reality at the same time.

Also, it's important to have some 20-year veterans, but within that group of participants, it is equally important to have some people who have been with you only a short time. And rank doesn't matter here either. In fact, you should strive to have people from across all tiers of the company.

We've found over the years that these people exist in every organization, but they aren't necessarily the ones who are on every other committee. Pull people who have had multiple job experiences, who might someday start businesses of their own, who are solutions driven rather than problem driven. Don't put anyone on one of these teams who will say, "We did that before, and it didn't work." Put "yes, and" people, those who take someone's idea and add to it.

STEP 2   ## Send the Participants Your Brand Positioning Work Ahead of Time

Send them your marketing plan's target market analysis, scope, and brand work that you accomplished for Steps 1 to 4 of the brand positioning ahead of time. Send them also the relevant problems and opportunities section of your business review. Ask them to read the complete document twice, one day apart.

STEP 3   ## Start Off the Session with an Overview of the Brand Promise

Start the session with a brief overview of the problems and opportunities and the results of the brand promise development work in Steps 1 through 4. Take time for questions and discussion. Don't set a limit on this. Allow for the fact that the visioning process may take only one session or it may take three. It's important not to rush this process. The participants have to move along together.

STEP 4   ## Have the Participants Work through a Visioning Exercise

Ask the following questions, and take the participants through the following exercises:

- It's the year 20XX, 15 years from now. Write three to four headlines that will appear in the newspaper, on your favorite Internet news site, on your Kindle, or on your Apple Notepad about our company or our products and services based on the brand promise.
- Complete this sentence: By the year 20XX when our brand promise is fully developed, life will be like _____ [mention that this statement is open to interpretation as to whether the response will be focused on financial goals, personal goals, organizational goals, or something else).
- Based on our brand promise, people will describe us as _____.
- If our company, products, and services simply went away, ceased to exist, what would our customers miss the most?
- What are the possibilities for our brand given the brand promise? Where is it now, and where could it evolve to? [Build different collages of the brand as it is now and then as it might be, using scanned material and lots of

photographs—from cars, to people to animals to colors, to buildings. The photographs help people tell stories and are placeholders for ideas and interpretation. This exercise is best done in groups of two.]

- What have we started doing? What have we stopped doing?
- What current things are we doing that distract from the brand promise?
- What current things are we doing that enhance the brand promise? How could we make these even stronger enhancers of our brand?
- Which activities will we stop? Which will we start?

Based on the brand platform you developed, have the groups answer the following types of questions:

- Given your target market description, how will the brand positioning change the participants' expectations?
- How will our product and/or service portfolio change? Will we develop further, add to, or shrink our current product offerings? How?
- What product or service changes will take place? How will we develop our basic set of products and services? Will we have added new ones, eliminated others? Which are more important and less important?
- How will we change the ways in which we interface with our customers?
- How will we communicate differently in terms of what we say, how we say it, and where we say it?
- How will we get our product to our customers differently into the future?
- Will our customer service operations change?
- Internally, what things will evolve due to our brand promise? Will we communicate differently with each other? What will be the structure of the organization? What jobs and positions do we need more of and less of? What types of staff members, in terms of talent and experience, do we need fewer of and less of? How will our physical space look different? How will it change?

STEP 5 ### Summarize the Visioning Sessions

This is simply a base from which to start thinking about how the brand promise could and should change the way you do business. Some of the ideas will be very tangible and actually merit further study as to implementation. Some will serve only to get people thinking about what might be. However, out of this session should come some concrete next steps and areas of exploration for future work.

STEP 6 ### Don't Do This Just Once

This should be a periodic exercise to keep the brand alive and functioning as an integral part of your organization.

See also Appendix C, Worksheet 35.

CASE STUDY OF A COMPANY'S FINDING ITS BRAND PROMISE: FAMOUS FOOTWEAR

To illustrate developing a brand position, we will use the case example of Famous Footwear. This case study covers a 30-year period of working with the retailer in which we worked both separately and together on the account.

EXHIBIT 6.9

Mapping: Famous Footwear Retail Example

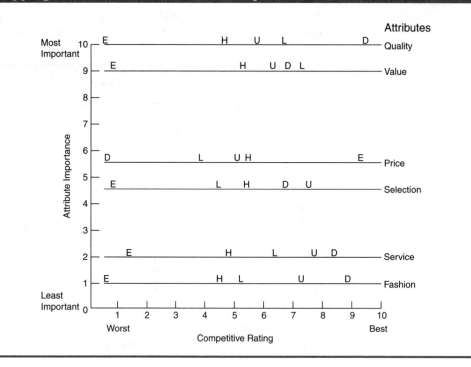

The Early Years

As shown in Exhibit 6.9, Famous Footwear's strongest attribute was price (code letter H), but even though the retailer was very price oriented, it still didn't dominate this attribute. Payless was represented by letter E, and from the chart in Exhibit 6.9, you can clearly see Payless was the leader. Also note that Famous Footwear rated next to last competitively on the two most important attributes to the consumer for this specific retail category: quality and value.

Surprising to Famous Footwear back then was that research indicated that although price was important, quality and value were significantly more important to the target market of middle- to upper-middle-class moms with kids. Based on this set of data, the company changed its position from "A store with low prices" to "The value shoe store"—a store with quality merchandise at competitive prices. Quality shoes at a great price, Nike shoes for $X, you save $X. Translating this goal to the map and visualizing where the retailer would desire to be positioned means it would be the first store on the right for the value attribute. Accordingly, this retailer upgraded its merchandise mix and the appearance of its stores. The advertising was also changed to convey a value image, and the tagline was changed to communicate "Good Prices on Great Shoes!"

The results of this value positioning versus the former low-price/discount-price positioning were dramatic. Comparable store sales for the year increased more than 30 percent. Market research conducted 18 months after the benchmark research study revealed dramatic positive shifts in how consumers perceived this retailer versus the competition on the key attributes. As you can see in Exhibit 6.10, the retailer's competitive rating (H) on *quality* moved from next to last to second. Further, its competitive *value* rating moved from next to last to first, while the *price* rating remained virtually the same. Even the retailer's competitive rating on *selection* showed considerable positive movement from third to second place. This change in positioning resulted in a significant store-for-store sales increase in each

EXHIBIT 6.10

Mapping: Famous Footwear Year-to-Year Tracking Results

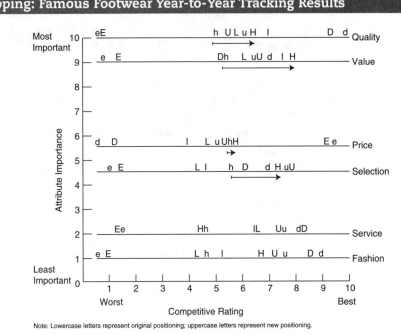

Note: Lowercase letters represent original positioning; uppercase letters represent new positioning.

of the two years following the value positioning. This once-floundering chain expanded nationwide to over 900 stores and thrived into the mid-nineties before hitting a period of five to six years of flat to declining store-for-store sales, customer counts, falling margins, and operating profits.

The Next Evolution

After a long successful growth period, by the middle to late nineties, things changed for Famous Footwear. Positive store-for-store sales and actual store growth started to give way to stagnation in the business metrics. Even more worrisome were the signs that customer connections were dissipating. Customer traffic counts were dropping. Unaided awareness and especially first mention awareness had dropped dramatically between 1995 and 2001. Additionally, the perception of Famous Footwear as a place to get fashionable shoes (a key component of the quality-to-price value relationship) had fallen significantly. One of the two critical target segments saw Famous Footwear as a place to get last year's shoes at a great price, instead of this year's shoes at a good price.

The competitive environment had also changed: the unique concept of brand name shoes for less, the signature of Famous Footwear's value positioning, was merely the price of entry in the midtier (Kohl's, J.C. Penney, and others), and it certainly was not a place to capture a competitively differentiating position. In addition to the old competitive set, new and relatively new midtier players were providing fierce competition (Designer Shoe Warehouse, Shoe Carnival, Shoe Pavilion, Rack Room). Even worse, besides a crowded value tier, the department stores were also hammering brands for less on the upper end, and at the lower end, Payless was starting to merchandise and market brands such as Champion, Airwalk, Dexter, and Shaquille O'Neal shoes at discount prices. And then there was the emergence of the e-commerce competitor Zappos. Famous Footwear was being surrounded on all sides. Everyone it seemed was playing Famous Footwear's value game of brands for less, and the competitive landscape was getting quite crowded.

It was time to reposition again, find the space that no one else could own, Famous Footwear could deliver on, and its customers both needed and wanted. We did the work, going back to both qualitative research, quantitative surveys, and positioning maps to help us develop a clear picture. The following became the cornerstones of our work:

- Identification of two target markets that made up the bulk of Famous Footwear's customer base and also the major drivers in the midtier of value shoppers. The target segments were both demographic and attitudinal.
  - *Core value moms:* 21 percent of the total women purchasing 14 percent of the shoes, in the 25-to-54 age group, middle to upper middle income. This target segment of the mom target market was basically a replacement shoe shopper for herself, purchasing more casual, conservative shoes. The core value mom planned her shopping trips, wasn't a spontaneous shoe shopper, and didn't especially like shoe shopping. Basically she saw it as a chore. The core value target segment would rather have last year's shoes at a great price than current year's shoes at a good value. She shopped Famous Footwear for her husband, her children, and herself.
  - *Fashion value moms:* 33 percent of the total women accounting for 49 percent of the shoes purchased. The fashion value mom had virtually the same demographics as the core value mom. The big difference was her attitude, she **loved** shopping for shoes, felt shoes made the outfit, and had a strong desire to be "with it" and fashionable. She much preferred purchasing today's shoes at a good value than yesterday's shoes at a great price. The fashion value mom was a spontaneous shoe shopper making over 50 percent of her purchases outside of a planned shopping trip. When she saw something she liked, she purchased it. The fashion value mom shopped Famous Footwear for her husband and her kids, but did **not** shop Famous Footwear for herself.
- A focus on getting the fashion value woman, who already shopped Famous Footwear for her family, to purchase more for herself at the store. In order to do this, the brand positioning—what Famous Footwear could promise the customer and create a difference around—would have to evolve, again. However, the trick was to change the positioning to attract the fashion value mom's purchase for herself while keeping the core value mom's patronage. We believed this was very possible and in fact proved that it was.

The New Positioning

We used a combination of ethnographics, focus group interviews, a brand tracking study, and quantitative perceptual mapping using a multidimensional scaling technique to show the competitive landscape and to determine where Famous Footwear was perceived relative to the competition from a merchandise standpoint. See the perceptual map in Exhibit 6.11.

Perceptual maps can have any number of dimensions, but most use the two most important dimensions used by consumers to describe the relationship of one company to another. While the map in Exhibit 6.11 comes from sampling consumers and mathematically plotting the points and the company positions relative to each other, perceptual maps can be developed using the marketer's innate knowledge of the marketplace. These "judgmental maps" are also very effective in providing a common understanding within an organization as to where you are positioned and more importantly, where you want to be in the future.

Given insights from additional research studies we conducted for Famous Footwear, we felt the strongest positioning would be a movement to the open

EXHIBIT 6.11

Famous Footwear Perceptual Map: Polar Quadrants

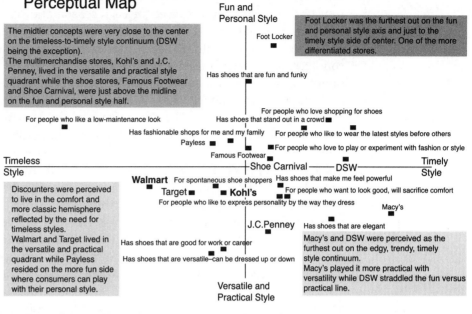

Competitive Market Landscape: Perceptions

2008 Retail Landscape Perceptual Map

The midtier concepts were very close to the center on the timeless-to-timely style continuum (DSW being the exception).
The multimerchandise stores, Kohl's and J.C. Penney, lived in the versatile and practical style quadrant while the shoe stores, Famous Footwear and Shoe Carnival, were just above the midline on the fun and personal style half.

Fun and Personal Style

Foot Locker was the furthest out on the fun and personal style axis and just to the timely style side of center. One of the more differentiated stores.

Discounters were perceived to live in the comfort and more classic hemisphere reflected by the need for timeless styles.
Walmart and Target lived in the versatile and practical quadrant while Payless resided on the more fun side where consumers can play with their personal style.

Macy's and DSW were perceived as the furthest out on the edgy, trendy, timely style continuum.
Macy's played it more practical with versatility while DSW straddled the fun versus practical line.

Versatile and Practical Style

---

space up toward the right quadrant, where Famous Footwear could separate along current, timely styles with a sense of fun and fashion.

See also Appendix C, Worksheet 35.

In addition to the above work, we spent lots of time conducting an extensive ethnographic study to further help us identify customer segments, lifestyles, shopping habits, and feelings about shoes and shoe shopping. We went into women's homes and on shopping trips with them. We heard them talk about their lives, dreams, and aspirations. We talked with them about the place of fashion, clothes, and shoes in their life. We went into their closets and had them pick out their favorite shoes, learned why they bought what they did, and when and for what occasions. This work gave us a tremendous body of understanding, and it was the basis for further survey research around the specifics of what we were learning in the ethnographies.

By combining the insights from the perceptual retail map, the ethnographies, and our other research, we determined that while Famous Footwear could still compete around value, we needed to redefine the meaning of value as it pertained to Famous Footwear. The value Famous Footwear had historically positioned its brand around—value (the combination of price and quality) that resulted in communication about "famous brands for less"—was a tired story that others were doing, sometimes better than Famous Footwear. We worked to redefine the Famous Footwear value along two dimensions:

1. *Value on fashion*: The ability to get today's fashionable, fun shoes she wanted for herself at a good price. This was tricky. Famous Footwear wasn't a department store. It didn't sell shoes over $150. But with a slight change of merchandise mix, especially in the casual and dress shoe areas, it suddenly became a store that sold fun, trend-right shoes that were current to the season's fashion seen in department stores. It also made upgrades in its athletic shoes resulting in an upper end of shoes and fashions that were consistent with those found in the mall athletic stores.

Additionally, we made another big change in how this was brought to life. We stopped being an item/price retailer. We went away from selling individual shoes and price. We listened to our customers, who said time after time that they didn't want to have to hunt for the shoes they were looking for. It took too much time. They wanted to see each current trend in one place. So we found the top four to five merchandise stories for each season and we combined all the shoes across brands that helped tell that story and merchandised them together. Unlike department stores, we didn't sell brands and shoes in separate locations. We consolidated major trends across brands like bows, wedges, Euro look, bohemian, denim, skate, canvas, boots, and certain trendy colors all in one place, in one freestanding insert, in one television spot, and together in our e-commerce site. This helped separate Famous Footwear from both department stores and other midtier shoe stores. It also helped bring the second dimension discussed below to life.

2. *Value on time*: A store that fit her busy lifestyle—there was tremendous value in providing an efficient shopping experience. This included a one-stop shop for the whole family, organizing shoes by trend and fashion stories instead of searching brand by brand for a certain style, home delivery if a customer found a shoe she loved but Famous Footwear didn't have the size, an e-commerce superstore, along with many other time-saving innovations across merchandise, operations, and how the store marketed.

The result: a shoe store full of shoe love for the fashion value mom but one that didn't forget she was a mom who didn't have any time to waste. Famous Footwear solved a paradox for the fashion value mom—trend-right shoes in a store that celebrated the love of shoes without having to waste all day shopping. Famous Footwear was that shoe fix in doses that allowed her to still live her busy life.

Based on these insights and subsequent strategy, the following provides a look at three components of the Famous Footwear brand positioning platform:

1. The Famous Footwear positioning and brand promise
2. The brand essence (is and isn't)
3. The brand personification

Example of Famous Footwear Brand Positioning Platform

Famous ✿ Footwear

Brand Promise
The two value statements discussed above were pulled together by a positioning that combined both: "Positioning Famous Footwear as the ALWAYS IN store for the fashion value mom."

Brand Essence Is and Isn't

Famous Footwear Is	Famous Footwear Is Not
Female	Male
Trend-right fashion	Yesterday
Fun	Expected
Friends	An extension (of my kids and husband)
Fantasy	Everyday standard

The words above were chosen to push Famous Footwear out of its comfort zone. Was the store just for *females*? No, nearly half its sales were athletic with a large percentage of those to men, teenage boys, and male children. There was a very vibrant men's section and no intention of turning the store into a feminine boutique. However, there was the realization of the need to move much closer to the primary female target's ideal or she'd never see it as a store for her. And we knew that the more of "her" we turned into loyal customers, the more of "them" (men and her kids) we would get as customers. Toward this end, the store was redesigned twice during a seven-year period to capture her "love of shoes." And it worked—more of her and more of them.

Additionally the word *friends* became very important. Research showed that she knows she's a mom, and more than anyone, she realizes how hard that work is and, thank you, doesn't need to be reminded of it. In fact, the visuals that tested the worst were photos of her with a smiling face, bags of shoes, and kids hanging on her arm. These images tested just above photos of women models and women athletes in terms of being universally scorned by the Famous Footwear target market. Why women models and athletes? We heard the answers again and again in statements like, "Sure, I could look like that if I didn't have kids, a husband, a job, and a house to take care of."

What did play? Photos of women who looked pulled together and relaxed, and with their friends—basically photographs that captured them when they were just being themselves. While Famous Footwear wasn't a store to go to shop with lots of friends for extended periods of time, the research made it clear: Don't treat me as an extension of someone else. Treat me as me!

Famous Footwear moved toward communicating the *trend-right fashion* even though the store still carried plenty of the timeless basics from yesterday both in the stores and in the advertising. The communication became more *fun*, just like the store environment, and added a touch of *fantasy* instead of the reality of "just getting another pair of shoes." There was a focus on the fun aspect of buying shoes because again and again the customers told us it was important: "Life is short. Buy the shoes first." And even, "Buying shoes is more fun than sex."

The "is" and "isn't" words gave Famous Footwear focus and direction. Like the bumpers in bowling alleys (the authors are from the Midwest), they kept the company going forward in a direction consistent with the brand promise and the basic essence of what the brand was all about.

Brand Personification

I am Famous Footwear. I'm a mom but I'm full of surprises. I'm fashionable, not trendy but with it. I'm casual yet pulled together. I'm current to the season and to the styles that are emerging and here to stay. I'm definitely more female friendly. I'm displays that have curves and aren't just straight lines and boxes. I'm wide aisles, clean and bright with easy site lines, full of shoes and places to sit and see those shoes on your feet. I'm fun, full of unexpected surprises to look at and connect with. But I'm also a shoe authority, a place where you'll see stylish shoes merchandised like stories. I'm that best friend whose fashion shoes you admire, who invites you out to go shopping, who organizes the trip. I'm that shoe fantasy. I'm the high you get just shopping for shoes. I'm that incredible rush you get when you find the right shoe, at the right price, at the right time, with the right experience. That's shoe shopping success. More fun, more fantasy, more female, more friends. I'm Famous Footwear. I'm the joy of shoe shopping success.

The Results

Famous Footwear went to work improving how and what it bought, and it focused on the customer it was buying for. It changed its operations to help the customer

EXHIBIT 6.12

Famous Footwear Store Value Rankings

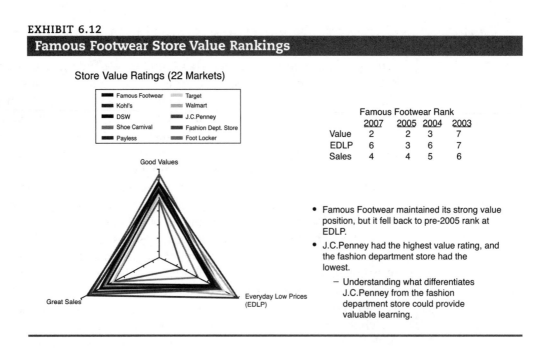

Store Value Ratings (22 Markets)

	Famous Footwear		Target
	Kohl's		Walmart
	DSW		J.C.Penney
	Shoe Carnival		Fashion Dept. Store
	Payless		Foot Locker

Famous Footwear Rank

	2007	2005	2004	2003
Value	2	2	3	7
EDLP	6	3	6	7
Sales	4	4	5	6

- Famous Footwear maintained its strong value position, but it fell back to pre-2005 rank at EDLP.
- J.C.Penney had the highest value rating, and the fashion department store had the lowest.
  - Understanding what differentiates J.C.Penney from the fashion department store could provide valuable learning.

get in and out and find things quickly. It redesigned the store to fit the fashion value mom's love of shoes and to make it look like it was the type of place in which she could find shoes for herself. Famous Footwear found ways to better communicate to her with messages that excited her, hired staff that were fashion value women like herself, and even spent a lot of time rethinking where to place stores and in what geographic locations.

Remember, we stated earlier that the Famous Footwear value position was not expected to come from a price/quality value positioning. The era of "Brand name shoes for less" was over. The positive shift in value would come from the perception of *value fashion* (the ability to get today's fun, fashionable shoes at a good price) and *value on time* (an efficient shopping experience)—the combination to provide the benefit of the double entendre of "Always In."

Exhibit 6.12 shows how Famous Footwear achieved its goal of positively moving the value perception with its repositioning. The retailer moved from seventh to tied for second in the value ranking. And while Payless tied Famous Footwear in value, further exploration of the data showed that consumers were defining Payless value along the lines of everyday low prices (EDLPs), a space where Famous Footwear did not want to compete.

Exhibit 6.13 shows that one of the areas where Famous Footwear was gaining its strong value position was in the consumers' realization that the store did provide *value on time* through the retailer's strong score on *easy to shop*. Further data showed (not pictured in the exhibit) that the perception of *value fashion* increased significantly as the variable *fashionable shoes for me* increased in positive perception.

Finally, note that in Exhibit 6.13 the enjoyable shopping attribute increased to number one since starting the repositioning work—a clear sign that Famous Footwear really was delivering what the fashion value mom wanted: *a little shoe love*.

The maps are graphic representations of statistical ranking data. The further out you are, the better. The key Famous Footwear rankings are summarized in the exhibit.

Over a five-year period, Famous Footwear increased its operating profits in the top quintile of all footwear retailers, increased margins, increased store-for-store sales, and increased customer counts. Furthermore, it saw significant increases in awareness and preference for the brand Famous Footwear.

EXHIBIT 6.13

Famous Footwear Store Shopping Ratings

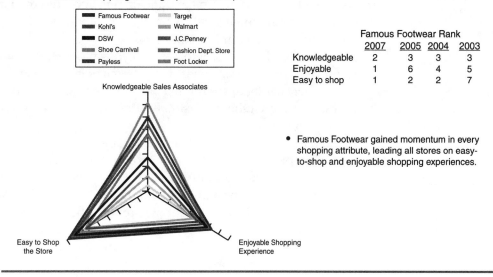

Store Shopping Ratings (22 Markets)

	Famous Footwear Rank			
	2007	2005	2004	2003
Knowledgeable	2	3	3	3
Enjoyable	1	6	4	5
Easy to shop	1	2	2	7

- Famous Footwear gained momentum in every shopping attribute, leading all stores on easy-to-shop and enjoyable shopping experiences.

WRITING YOUR BRAND POSITIONING

Prepare the four components of your brand positioning using the charts in Appendix C, Worksheet 35. Complete each of the following sections:

- Brand foundation story and worldview
- Brand promise
- Brand essence: Is and isn't
- Brand personification
- Brand vision

When developing these, keep in mind that you are writing strategy. You are not writing taglines or advertising copy. You're writing strategy that shapes every consumer touch point—from product development to packaging, customer service, operations, communications, and personal selling.

The key word is *focus* when writing your brand positioning platform, especially when you get to the brand promise and the brand essence. Try to avoid writing a brand promise that reads like a litany. The shorter and to the point, the better the strategy. A succinct brand promise will provide clear and specific direction for the implementation of your message strategy, umbrella strategy, and marketing mix tools.

DOS AND DON'TS

Do

- Position with a meaningful difference.
- Positioning by benefit is more effective than positioning by attribute. Positioning by emotional connection or a consumer group's underlying belief or cause is more effective yet.

- Position from your product's strengths and competitors' weaknesses to fill a target's need. Keep in mind that you could possibly group those strengths that have a common focus to create a stronger positioning of your product.
- Use qualitative research to gain personal insight into the target's mind, particularly on the emotional level. Whenever possible, use quantifiable market research to verify your insights.
- When confused about how to position your product, let your target market and its purchasing and usage behavior in terms of its needs and wants be your guide.
- Remember that there are limited slots in the target's mind and that no two products can own the same slot. Furthermore, the *first* product to own the slot usually wins.
- If you have a parity product, look hard and long for a meaningful need or want that is important to your target market but that has not been taken by a competitor. If you can't find one, take the most meaningful decision factor for consumers and own it through dominating the focus on this factor.
- Look for the sweet spot position where the inherent drama of the product fulfills an important need of the target market.
- Decide up front whether you are positioning your company, individual products, or both your company and products.
- Make sure your product or company's name and positioning are in sync. For example, it would be difficult for Payless Shoes to be an upscale fashion brand.
- Make sure all elements of the marketing mix reinforce your positioning.
- Give your positioning a chance to reap success by supporting it with a substantial investment in time and marketing resources.
- Make your positioning brand promise statement as simple and succinct as possible.
- Ideally, thoroughly search not just for a short-term positioning but for one that can live long into the future.
- Test your new, revised, and/or existing positioning alternatives if there is no clear choice.

Don't

- Don't try to position everything about your products and services to everybody. *To position means to sacrifice.*
- Don't position against a follower if you are a leader.
- Don't position only on price unless you can deliver a lower price profitably and consistently because a price positioning can easily be preempted.
- Don't change your positioning if it has proven successful and there have been no major changes (or you anticipate no major changes) to your product, the competition's product, or the target market. However, attempt to sharpen the focus of your established positioning to present a clearer perception of your product in the minds of the target market.
- Don't position directly against another competitor unless absolutely necessary, and then do so only for a short term.
- Don't position directly against a leader unless you plan to settle for less than first place or you have product superiority and sufficient marketing resources to outlast the leader.
- Don't overdo price promotion or line extensions, as both can destroy a brand's positioning and, in the end, the product itself.
- Don't position your product based on a promise or benefit that it cannot deliver.

- Don't, if at all possible, change your positioning in one large leap if you anticipate losing a substantial portion of the current customer base. Position one step at a time, but still think for the long term.
- Don't take the first positioning that comes to mind. Review a number of alternative positions.
- Don't expect to arrive at your product positioning immediately. Positioning might seem to be a simple concept to understand, but it is extremely difficult to apply. Arriving at the right positioning takes time and concentration. Don't settle for an "almost-on" positioning. If you persevere for the best positioning, the right positioning for your product will come to you almost magically.

The Successful Marketing Plan

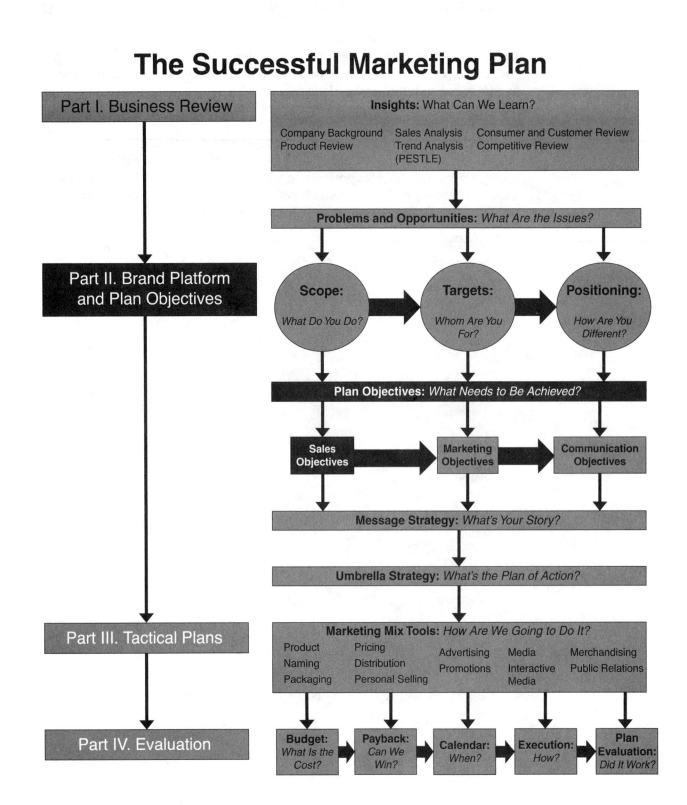

Part I. Business Review

Insights: What Can We Learn?

Company Background   Sales Analysis   Consumer and Customer Review
Product Review   Trend Analysis   Competitive Review
                       (PESTLE)

Problems and Opportunities: What Are the Issues?

Scope: What Do You Do?

Targets: Whom Are You For?

Positioning: How Are You Different?

Part II. Brand Platform and Plan Objectives

Plan Objectives: What Needs to Be Achieved?

Sales Objectives

Marketing Objectives

Communication Objectives

Message Strategy: What's Your Story?

Umbrella Strategy: What's the Plan of Action?

Part III. Tactical Plans

Marketing Mix Tools: How Are We Going to Do It?

Product   Pricing   Advertising   Media   Merchandising
Naming   Distribution   Promotions   Interactive   Public Relations
Packaging   Personal Selling   Media

Part IV. Evaluation

Budget: What Is the Cost?

Payback: Can We Win?

Calendar: When?

Execution: How?

Plan Evaluation: Did It Work?

7 Sales Objectives

Having completed the scope, targets, and positioning portions of the brand platform, you're now ready to set the direction for your marketing plan by completing three objective sections—sales, marketing, and communications. The first of these three, setting your sales and profit objectives, is obviously important, as sales are the ultimate measure of how the company, product, or service is performing.

The next two objective sections tie in to the work you do here in the sales objectives section. Marketing objectives establish the target market behaviors needed to meet your sales goals. Thus there is a direct link between the work you do in the marketing objectives section and the work you do here in setting sales objectives. The final section is the setting of communication objectives. Communication objectives are centered on affecting the influencers of behavior (your marketing objectives)—awareness and attitudes.

The objectives section is one of the unique aspects of this marketing planning process. Understanding the interrelationships between setting sales objectives, marketing objectives, and communication objectives provides you an ability to manage individual pieces. Instead of saying, "We didn't meet sales goals," the conversation should center around which target segment didn't meet its sales objectives, then examining which of its marketing objectives underperformed, and why, based on examining the results of the communication objectives tied to those marketing objectives. In order to get to this point in the next section, marketing objectives, we need to first develop the total sales goal for your company. That's the focus of this chapter.

FROM THIS CHAPTER YOU WILL LEARN

- The definition and importance of sales objectives
- What to keep in mind when setting sales objectives
- The quantitative and qualitative factors that affect the setting of sales objectives
- How to set your own sales objectives using a three-step process

OVERVIEW

Sales objectives are self-defining in that they represent projected levels of goods or services to be sold. Everything that follows in the plan is designed to meet the sales objectives—from establishing realistic marketing objectives, to determining the amount of advertising and promotion dollars to be budgeted, to the actual hiring of marketing and sales personnel, to the number and kinds of distribution channels or stores to be utilized, to the amount of product to be produced or inventoried.

What to Keep in Mind When Setting Sales Objectives

Sales objectives must be challenging and attainable, time specific, and measurable. And they must be established for units sold, not just dollars received.

Sales Objectives Must Be Challenging and Attainable

Because sales objectives have substantial impact on a business, they must be simultaneously challenging and attainable. If not, there could be a negative effect on short-term, bottom-line profits as well as on the long-term success of the business. If sales objectives are dramatically increased, the cost of doing business will also rise significantly to accommodate the projected increase in sales. Accordingly, if your sales objectives are set too high and cannot be attained, your resulting expenses-to-sales ratio will be very high, causing profits to fall below expectations. If you dramatically underestimate your sales objectives and have inadequate production capacity or inventory, you will not be able to sufficiently fulfill demand, meaning that opportunity is lost to the competition. Over the long term, this may translate to the loss of good distributors, loyal customers, and first-time customers.

In summary, a sales objective should be based on as accurate an estimate of the market opportunities and the capacity of the organization as possible in order to put yourself in the best position to fulfill the objectives and realize those opportunities.

Sales Objectives Must Be Time Specific

You must set time-specific sales objectives in order to provide start and end dates for your marketing program. It is also important to set both short- and long-term sales objectives.

Sales Objectives

Short-Term Sales Objectives: 1 Year or Less
Long-Term Sales Objectives: Minimum of 3 Years

Long-term sales objectives are needed to plan the future direction of the company or product in such areas as equipment, real estate, personnel, and capital. Further, what you include in Year 1 of your marketing plan will affect sales objectives set for Years 2 and 3. Testing new products and service programs in Year 1 might be required in order to meet sales objectives in Year 3.

Sales Objectives Must Be Measurable

Setting measurable sales objectives provides the means for determining what must be included in your marketing plan and for evaluating its success. Accordingly, sales objectives are quantified in terms of the following:

- Dollars and units for manufacturing firms
- Dollars and transactions and units for retail firms
- Dollars and number of people served for service firms

Not Only Dollars and Profits but Also the Number of Units Sold, Transactions Processed, and People Served

You must set sales objectives for *both* the dollars and the numbers of units sold, the transactions processed, and the people served. Dollar sales cover your expenses and provide a profit, and they reflect the impact of any increase or decrease in the price of your product. The numbers of units sold, transactions processed, and people served indicate the fundamental health of your business. If you are continually projecting increased dollar sales but decreased unit sales, you will eventually experience a decline in dollar sales because price increases will no longer compensate for the loss of unit sales. Similarly, if sales are going up in a retail environment but traffic is declining, it will become very difficult to grow or even sustain the status quo.

Projected profits, a direct result of sales, should also be included along with sales objectives. Accordingly, as the author of this plan, you must have an understanding of profit expectations in order to effectively prepare and evaluate the marketing plan.

Further, if you are not operating in a pure business environment, keep in mind that sales objectives can be defined in terms other than dollars or units. For a nonprofit organization, the goal might be the funds raised to support its programs. In a government agency such as an employment service, it may be the number of job placements. Or for a political campaign, it may be the percent of votes cast for the candidate. Whatever the organization, there must be sales objectives or a simulation thereof.

Quantitative and Qualitative Factors That Affect Sales Objectives

Both quantitative and qualitative factors must be taken into consideration in the development of sales objectives. Quantitative factors, inputted first, are hard numbers based on objective, historical data. Qualitative factors are more subjective, and because they are driven more by personal interpretation rather than facts, their impact on sales is usually difficult to quantify. Therefore, your interpretation of these additional subjective factors leads to an adjustment of the quantitatively based sales objectives.

Quantitative Factors

Qualitative factors that help you establish your sales objectives include sales trends, the size and purchase rates of your target market, and budget, profit, and pricing considerations.

Sales Trends

When you're preparing sales objectives, the past is a good place to start. The trending of the market and company sales will be major factors to consider when projecting sales.

Industry category sales: Review the trending of the industry category over the past five years in terms of dollars and unit sales. Has the trending of the marketplace been upward, downward, flat, or erratic? Within the total category history of sales and units, what has the trending been of product segments that make up the total market? If you were tracking total industry category shoe sales, you might have found a flat to slowly upward-trending market, but athletic sales as a subset might be trending upward at a percentage rate more than twice that of the total market. Accordingly, if athletic shoe sales constituted a large percentage of the sales in your store, you would take this trend into consideration when setting objectives.

Company versus industry category sales: Next, compare how your company's sales are trending year to year versus the total industry category's sales. In most instances, you can project your sales to equal or surpass the market rate of growth; otherwise, you will be losing share of market.

Market share trends: Another factor to consider is the trending of your market share—for the company or division, for the product line and each product, or for the retail or service category and each major department:

- At what rate has your share of total sales been trending relative to the market?
- Has your share been growing in a growing market?
- Has your share been going up in a market that is shrinking? Or has your share of market been decreasing in a declining market?

If your share of sales has been growing in a growing market, you have more cause to be optimistic about future increases than if your share is flat or trending below that of the market. If you find that your product is losing share in a market that is declining, it would be unrealistic to project sales increases unless your strategy is to reverse this trend through a major product development, service, or marketing communications commitment.

Also keep in mind when setting sales objectives that not only is it difficult to reverse a product's sales decline in a one-year period but it is also extremely difficult to reverse a product's decline within a declining market.

Size and Purchase Rates of Your Target Market

A good double-check of the factors just cited in the determination of accurate sales objective estimates is an independent appraisal of the size and purchase rates of the target market for your product or service (see demand analysis in Chapter 5, "Targets"). Many new business ventures and new products fail because of an overly optimistic estimate of the size and trending of the market. It is very important to review census and industry data, as well as primary research if available, in your business review to determine how big the market really is and how it is trending.

Sales objectives often are set too high year after year because the company's management does not recognize a continual erosion of the target market, an erosion that it could have discovered through searching published industry data, company sales data, and/or primary research. For example, through primary research, our agency was able to document for a fabric chain that the number of women who sew garments had declined approximately 5 percent per year over a 10-year period.

Many times, particularly with new products and the development of entirely new market categories, there is limited market data and no company sales data on which to project sales objectives. In these instances, you can use a simulation approach and track sales growth of categories and/or companies in different, but somewhat related, product and market situations. You can also use the target market approach, as demonstrated at the end of Task 1 later in this chapter, to help you project sales for new products.

Budget, Profit, and Pricing Considerations

In determining realistic sales objectives, it is helpful to have an understanding of your company's historical operating budgets and profit expectations. Ideally, sales cover expenses and provide for profits. The simple fact is that you need a minimum level of dollar sales to stay in business and grow. For this reason, the cost of doing business, or expenses incurred to operate your business, is an important quantitative factor to consider when setting your sales objectives. In setting sales objectives, you should also understand the overall profitability history and expectations of the company and the level of profitability within segments of your product line or retail or service offering.

Along with that input, planned product price increases or decreases must be factored into all sales objectives because they dramatically affect sales volume and profitability. These product price changes, whether they are for the entire year or just portions of it, should be factored in after you have reviewed the historical sales trends but before you apply the qualitative factors, which will be discussed next.

Qualitative Factors

Factors that are not readily quantifiable are important too in establishing your sales objectives. Consider the economy generally, your competition, erratic sales volumes, your product's life cycle, your organization's mission and personality, and the impact of the successful implementation of your marketing plan.

The Economy

One factor affecting sales objectives that is difficult to forecast is the economy. Adjust your sales objectives based on your estimation of the economic factors that will directly affect your business. Are you forecasting sales for a recessionary, inflationary, or relatively stable period? If you are projecting sales for an inflationary period, you will probably be estimating dollar sales to increase at a greater percentage than unit sales.

Interest rates are also an important factor in establishing sales objectives. Businesses that rely heavily on their customers' purchasing on credit, such as auto dealers and real estate firms, usually see their sales slump as interest rates rise.

In addition, you must plan accordingly for any major changes in the tax laws. For example, elimination of an investment tax credit for heavy machinery would affect the sales of companies manufacturing heavy equipment.

Review national economic factors as well as those that might directly affect your product's market on a more local geographic basis. Pockets of unemployment can also seriously affect your sales objectives.

In summary, remember that, although you cannot control economic factors, you can thoroughly evaluate what impact they could have on your business and then adjust your short- and long-term sales objectives. Having just come through the steepest economic downturn since the 1920s, this section is probably all too familiar for those involved in setting sales objectives the past couple of years.

Your Competition

What you identified as a large and growing market can be diluted by strong and growing competition. Before finalizing sales objectives, review the competitive data in the insights section of the business review at the beginning of your plan. Has a major competitor noticeably expanded its sales force, increased the number of trade deals to retailers, added distribution channels or store locations, changed its product mix, or introduced a new product or service? Based on your competitive review of advertising media, is the competition increasing or decreasing its level of spending? Increased competitive advertising spending, particularly in a consumer marketplace dominated by a few major competitors, can negatively affect the chance of your marketing program's meeting its sales objectives.

It is often difficult to determine the direct impact on sales of an increase in competitive advertising. At this point, telephone survey research of your potential market can help you quantify its impact on your sales. Monitoring the increase of mentions of your competitive set on key social networking sites can also provide you insight into increased awareness of specific competitors. These types of insights might identify a significant percentage increase in awareness for your direct competitor. You would then translate this awareness into increased sales for your direct competitor and project an erosion of your market share in the near and long terms. Accordingly, an anti-competitor plan, along with a revision of the short-term sales objectives, would be outcomes of this information.

Emerging Product and Consumer Trends

A critical area is emerging product and consumer trends that might affect demand for your company or product. This area can include a host of factors such as consumption patterns affected by environmental concerns, changes in technology, or socioeconomic factors that have impacted your target market. A retailer that was a client of ours is brilliant at spotting trends and capitalizing on them through its marketing efforts. One example: the retailer successfully spotted the niche skateboard market expanding into everyday teen culture via both apparel and shoes.

Fad Volume

While it is difficult to forecast, many businesses must deal with "fad" or erratic sales volume. You must learn to recognize and deal with it realistically when setting your sales and profit objectives. Fad volume could be occasional, such as a major concert, convention, or sports tournament that brings an incremental number of people to your town and your restaurant.

On a larger scale, international events like the World Cup and the Olympics provide international sales volume opportunities for major sports companies like Nike, Adidas, and other equipment and apparel manufacturers associated with sports. Fad volume could also be much longer lasting, such as that created by a highly publicized health care study indicating that the use of fish oil and/or aspirin prolongs life. Likewise, when there is an event that has negative effects on your short- and/or long-term sales, you must factor in its effects when projecting sales. If your company markets products that are affected by positive or negative fad volume movement, you must estimate the impact of this phenomenon in terms of volume over time. How many consumers will it affect, and for how long?

Your Product's Life Cycle

Another consideration when setting sales objectives is to review where your product is in its life cycle. Do you have a new product with a large untapped target market, minimal competition, and substantial growth potential? If the product was successfully introduced, are the product's sales still growing, have they plateaued, or are they in decline? Your short-term sales objectives should reflect the current life cycle stage of your product, while your long-term objectives should concurrently reflect the stage of the life cycle into which your product is moving.

To ensure a clearer picture of where your product is in its life cycle, it is wise to stand back and review your industry category and the competitive products within it:

- Is your industry category growing? Has the penetration of the product or service your industry category provides reached the overall market penetration you would eventually estimate based on the potential demand of the product? Or is there still a tremendous upside for all the competitors in your industry?
- Are profit margins still very healthy? And for the most part, are you operating in an environment where you are competing on nonprice attributes and nonprice value promises?

In other words, if your industry category is still far away from a commodity environment, you probably are at the front end of your industry's life cycle, and both you and your competitors have the potential of additional positive growth beyond merely incremental gains.

You can also draw comparisons to different products with similar characteristics in other industries. After these companies introduced their products, at what rate did they grow? When did they level off? At what point in their existence did they decline? By determining if specific products they sell are in a growth, plateau, or declining stage, manufacturers and service firms, as well as retailers, can more accurately forecast expected sales growth for their companies.

The Mission and Personality of Your Organization

An important qualitative factor to consider is the mission and personality of your organization. What are your company's expectations? What is its reason for being? What is its philosophy of doing business?

Is your company conservative and careful? Or is it a moderate risk taker? Is it an old-line "don't rock the boat" company, or is it a young and charging "we can do it" company? Also consider the aggressiveness of your organization in terms of growth and innovation—product improvements, new products, and the opening of new distribution channels and new markets. Take all of this into consideration when estimating future sales.

Your Marketing Plan's Impact

Somewhat related to organization personality is another very important qualitative factor: your initial expectation of the overall marketing effort dictated by your marketing plan. You would adjust your sales objectives upward if you intend to change the way you market your product, such as improving your product, investing incremental media dollars, adding promotional dollars, or lowering the price of the product.

Additionally, the employment of a new, well-integrated, disciplined marketing plan will usually generate incremental sales, everything else being equal.

THE PROCESS OF SETTING SALES OBJECTIVES

The methodology of setting sales objectives is both quantitative and qualitative, which means your sales objectives will be a composite of data-based estimates and educated guesses. If you use a disciplined process in setting sales objectives, these goals will be based more on realistic estimates and less on guessing.

EXHIBIT 7.1

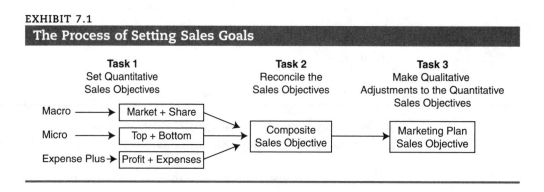

The recommended process to set your sales objectives is based on three tasks:

1. *Set quantitative sales objectives.* Set individual sales objectives for each of three years going forward using three different quantitative methods.
2. *Reconcile the sales objectives.* That is, reconcile the different quantitative goals into composite sales objectives.
3. *Make qualitative adjustments to the quantitative sales objectives.* Adjust the quantitatively based composite sales objectives through the interpolation of the relevant subjective qualitative factors, such as the economy, competition, and the personality of your organization.

A graphic description of the process of setting sales objectives is shown in Exhibit 7.1.

Worksheets for each task and a marketing plan format for writing the sales objectives are provided in Appendix C, Worksheet 36.

TASK 1

Set Quantitative Sales Objectives

We suggest that, if the data are available, you use the following three different quantitative methods:

1. Outside macro approach
2. Inside micro approach
3. Expense-plus approach

Each method will help you develop a sales objective estimate, and each estimate will provide one of three parameters from which to make realistic judgments in arriving at your final sales objectives. Each method can be used exclusively in arriving at a sales objective; however, the final outcome will not be as reliable as when you apply all three approaches. By using the three different approaches, you develop sales objectives derived from three different sets of data—a safeguard against using only one set of data that might not be totally reliable or complete.

Method 1. Outside Macro Approach
In order to execute the outside macro approach, you need two sets of numbers:

- The total market or category sales history
- Your company or product market share history

The basic concept behind this approach is to use projected company market share numbers multiplied by projected industry market category sales numbers to force a projected company sales number. We suggest that you base your projections on at least five years of data, more if possible. If five years of sales data are not available

EXHIBIT 7.2

Method 1. Outside Macro Approach

Market and Share Data

	MARKET SALES VOLUME COMPANY				SHARE PERCENT OF THE MARKET			
Year	$ Millions	Percent Change from Previous Year	Units, Millions	Percent Change from Previous Year	Percent	Percentage Point Change from Previous Year	Units	Percentage Point Change from Previous Year
Previous Five Years								
2007	$ 952.2	13.3%	449.1	5.1%	5.0%	0.1	4.0%	0.2
2008	1,067.0	12.1	484.0	7.8	5.1	0.1	4.7	0.7
2009	1,135.1	6.4	508.2	5.0	6.1	1.0	5.2	0.5
2010	1,202.9	6.0	527.9	3.9	6.5	0.4	5.7	0.5
2011	1,275.0	6.0	544.0	3.0	6.6	0.1	6.1	0.4
Projections Next Three Years								
2012	1,355.7	6.3	567.7	4.4	7.0	0.4	6.6	0.5
2013	1,436.4	5.9	591.4	4.1	7.4	0.4	7.1	0.5
2014	1,517.1	5.6	615.1	4.0	7.8	0.4	7.6	0.5

Three-Year Sales Projections for Company

	DOLLARS				UNITS			
Year	Market Sales Volume, $ Millions	–	Company Share Percent of Market	=	Company Sales, $ Millions	Market Sales Unit Volume, Millions	–	Company Unit Share Percent of Market	=	Company Sales Units, Millions
2012	$1,355.7		7.0%		$ 94.9	567.7		6.6%		37.5
2013	1,436.4		7.4		106.3	591.4		7.1		42.0
2014	1,517.1		7.8		118.3	615.1		7.6		47.0

because you are in a new market situation, use what data you have and provide guesstimate growth rates with available data from benchmark industries that, in the past, were similar to yours in product, price, scope of business, and geography. If you compete in multiple markets or categories, you must include each of them in this calculation. For example, if you are a company like the American Automobile Association (AAA), you compete in the travel agency industry, specific categories of the insurance industry, and the towing business.

Straight-Trend-Line Projection Calculations

The example in Exhibit 7.2 shows how the outside macro approach works with a straight-trend-line projection.

A worksheet that you can use to apply this method is provided in Appendix C, Worksheet 36. Modify this worksheet to include transactions if you are in the retail business; modify it from units to numbers of people or companies served if you are in the services business.

- The market sales volume from 2007 to 2011 increased $322.8 million. This equates to an average of $80.7 million per year.
- Projections for the next three years of market volume use the base of 2011, which is $1,275.0 million. Simply add an additional $80.7 million to get to $1,355.7 million for year 2012. This process is then repeated, adding $80.7 million to the 2012 total of $1,355.7 million to get $1,436.4 in 2013, with the same process resulting in $1,517.1 million in 2014.
- Similarly, the company share history shows that the company's share increased from 5.0 percent in 2006 to 6.6 percent in 2011 for an average of 0.4 percent per year. Taking the 2011 share figure of 6.6 percent and adding 0.4 percent projects a 2012 share figure of 7.0. The same procedure yields a 2013 figure of 7.4 percent and a 2014 number of 7.8 percent.

Other Ways to Project Your Market and Share Numbers

(Content Provided by Hartwig Huemer, Decision Support, Inc.)

The straight-line average provides a good, simple way to calculate growth. However, there are times when it is not appropriate, especially when you anticipate the growth to be at the front end (or back end) of the next three, four, or five years. For example, your company's sales are expected to expand $20 million over the next four years, with $14 million being in the first two years. Reasons for strong front-end growth may be your company's leading position, but the competitors will catch up at some point. Back-end growth may happen due to law changes. A recent example for back-end-loaded sales was the HDTV. Although it was known for several years in advance that HDTVs would become the norm, TV sales didn't really escalate until that mandated switchover came closer. Other reasons for "back-loaded" growth may be the staggered availability of production capacity or the expansion into and development of new geographic markets.

A simple way to go about showing "non-straight" growth is to divide the anticipated total change up into *change units*. In our example from above, we are projecting sales for the next four years, so we get $1 + 2 + 3 + 4 = 10$ change units (a five-year time frame would yield 15 change units). The value of a change unit is computed as the total dollars' change divided by the total number of available change units: $20 million ÷ 10 = $2 million.

Note that the straight-line approach simply uses 1 change unit per year. Thus, for example, four years with 1 change unit per year = 4 change units. The value of a change unit for the straight-line approach is: the total change of $20 million ÷ 4 change units = $5 million per change unit (which is the same as the average yearly change).

To create a "front-loaded" growth projection, you put more change units into the "front" years and the (few) remaining ones into the latter years. Do the reverse for "back-loaded" growth.

The graph below refers to the example, and it shows the difference between the various sales projection approaches. The front-loaded projection uses 4, 3, 2, and 1 units (or $8 million, $6 million, $4 million, and $2 million), and the back-loaded projection uses 1, 2, 3, and 4 units (or $2 million, $4 million, $6 million, and $8 million) for 2011 through 2014.

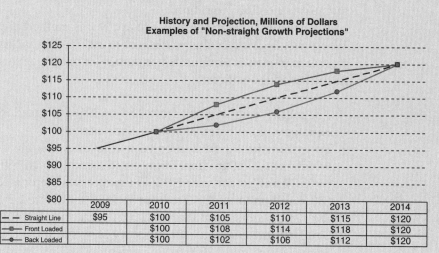

History and Projection, Millions of Dollars
Examples of "Non-straight Growth Projections"

	2009	2010	2011	2012	2013	2014
– – Straight Line	$95	$100	$105	$110	$115	$120
Front Loaded		$100	$108	$114	$118	$120
Back Loaded		$100	$102	$106	$112	$120

Source: Hartwig Huemer, Decision Support, Inc.

The *change-unit forecast approach* can also be used even if the total growth figure is not known. In that case you simply take your average annual growth figure over the last few years. Create 2, 3, or 4 annual change units based on that average dollar figure, and apply that to the next few years—and you will always end up at the same annual dollar figure as if you'd used the straight-line average approach.

For example, your company's recent average annual dollar growth was $6 million, and you need to project the sales for the next five years. But you want to simulate strong sales growth in Year 3 and relatively little growth in Years 1 and 5. You start by splitting the $6 million into more than 1 change unit per year (for example, 2 units at $3 million per unit or 3 units at $2 million per unit). Let's say you use 3 units per year. Since you need to forecast for five years, you now have 15 units (5 years × 3 units per year) at $2 million per unit to be used. Possible projections using 15 growth units are as follows:

	Straight Line	**Option 1**	**Option 2**
Year 1	3	2	1
Year 2	3	3	3
Year 3	3	5	7
Year 4	3	3	3
Year 5	3	2	1
Total units	15	15	15

Source: Hartwig Huemer, Decision Support, Inc.

For Option 1, you would add sales of $4 million to the following year or Year 1, $6 million to Year 2, $10 million to Year 3, $6 million to Year 4, and $4 million to Year 5, for a total of $30 million in added sales over the five years. This is the same total added sales you would calculate if you had used the straight-line approach of $6 million each of the five years for the total of $30 million.

For Option 2, you would add sales of $2 million to the following year or Year 1, $6 million to Year 2, $14 million to Year 3, $6 million to Year 4, and $2 million to Year five for a total of $30 million in added sales over the five years. This is the same total added sales as if you would have had used the straight-line approach of $6 million each of the five years for the total of $30 million.

In summary, the change unit approach allows you to transfer industry projections (which are usually available only in five-year increments) to overall company projections. In particular, it allows you to mold your projections to company specifics, accommodate changes in schedules (such as the moving up or delaying of production capacity), and, last but not least, avoid "hockey stick" projections.

Hartwig Huemer, managing principal of Decision Support, Inc. (DSi): DSi (www.AnalysisSupport.com) is a business consulting group that Huemer founded in 1994. The company designs predictive models, performs data analysis, and builds custom desktop decision tools (such as simulators and optimizers) to assist executives in making the best decisions in their quest to implement their visions. The company has been successfully delivering solutions across diverse industries and sectors, including consumer packaged goods (CPGs), retail, manufacturing, commodities, software insurance, commercial real estate, health care, municipalities, and school boards.

(continued)

Clients are Fortune 500 companies and small and midsized organizations, as well as start-ups.

Hartwig Huemer was born in Austria, where he received his MS and BS in mathematics for engineers from the University of Technology in Graz. He also received an MS in computer science (under a Fulbright Scholarship) and an MBA in finance from the University of Wisconsin–Madison. He can be reached at DSI@AnalysisSupport.com.

Method 2. Inside Micro Approach

This approach projects sales from the trends of your company—reconciling the top-down sales trend with the bottom-up sales trend. After you project sales from both the top and the bottom, you need to reconcile any differences through a subjective touch-and-feel approach.

Top Down

Start at the *top*, with a review of your organization's total sales history. Estimate sales for your company or each product, and project sales into the following three years using the straight-trend-line approach. Or, as demonstrated in the macro approach example, you can use a more accurate and sophisticated method if you have the internal capability. Your output will be sales projections based on your company's past sales history, and your projections will be for your next three years going forward.

Bottom Up

Next, review your sales by dollars and units from the bottom up to arrive at an estimated sales figure. Going from the *bottom up* means estimating sales from where they are generated, such as sales by each channel, store unit, or service office or center. If you are in a manufacturing business, your bottom-up generator becomes the distribution channel (direct accounts, wholesalers, distributors, or retailers). If you are in the retail business, build up to a total sales estimate by estimating by store, by geographical market, and by district or region. Use this same approach if you are in the service business. It is often a good idea to have participation from the sales force or from the retail or service people in the field because they can estimate sales in their area of responsibility.

The actual projections of the bottom-up method are based on using historical data (projecting using a straight-trend-line approach or other method) in combination with a qualitative sense of what's going to happen into the future. The macro approach and the top-down portion of the micro approach are both primarily quantitative and numbers based, but these approaches should include subjective input as well. You have the advantage of personal knowledge that you should use in this sales projection method. Here are a few qualitative insight examples that would cause you to vary from strictly what the numbers are suggesting:

- You've realigned your sales force to take advantage of customer, environment, or competitive shifts.
- You have established a "preferred partnership" with a major distributor or retail outlet.
- You've implemented a new local marketing program or merchandise program that will positively affect certain accounts, stores, or geographic markets.
- There's been a positive change in personnel with a major account that will favor your business.

Based on both historical data trends and your estimated changes in the market-place, project sales for each bottom-up sales generator and add them together to determine each year's projection. Again, you can use the straight-trend-line approach or a more accurate and sophisticated method depending on capability. Keep in mind that if you have very little data or if you are not able to secure pieces of information that you need, you might have to estimate rather than calculate each sales projection. Then, once you've done this, adjust the three years going forward based on the qualitative input you receive from those closest to your markets and your business (internal and external sources).

Combining Top-Down and Bottom-Up Data

Exhibit 7.3 provides an example of how to prepare a top-down and bottom-up sales forecast. To arrive at a final micro sales objective, you must then reconcile the organization's sales estimates derived from the top with those derived from the bottom. Note that the example does not show the buildup of 2006 to 2010 sales in the bottom-up part of this example but only the projections for 2011 or the first year's sales projection going forward. Additionally, to arrive at a final micro sales objective, you must then reconcile this work—something that really is nothing more than the art of negotiation with your internal team.

Worksheets for the micro method top-down and bottom-up sales forecasts are provided in Appendix C, Worksheet 36.

Method 3. Expense-Plus Approach

Once you have the outside macro–based estimates and the inside micro–based estimates, it makes good sense to estimate the sales level needed to cover planned expenses and make a profit. This budget-based sales objective approach is more short term in nature, and it is most useful in helping you arrive at your one-year sales objective. However, you can develop sales objectives for each year of a three-year sales period by employing this approach. A sales objective derived from expense and profit expectations can differ substantially from a sales objective generated from a market or company sales trend projection. This difference in projections may signal the need for a more conservative or aggressive marketing plan. Although very simplistic, it is also very real because it details the sales that have to be generated in order to stay in business and make a profit.

To arrive at a sales objective using this method, you will need budget data. If your company has been doing business for a number of years, it is relatively easy to estimate expenses and expected profits for the next year by reviewing your historical financial data. It is a good learning experience, particularly if you are new in the business, to review the cost of goods, operating margins, expenses, and profits within the industry and for other comparable businesses. Industry guidelines such as these are available from libraries, trade associations, and the Census Bureau's Business and Industry website.

The expense-plus methodology is based on the simple relationships between gross sales, cost of goods sold, and net sales. Keep in mind the following when using this method:

Gross sales − cost of goods sold + returns = net gross margin sales
Net gross margin sales ÷ gross sales = gross margin percent
Net gross margin sales − expenses = net profit before taxes

EXHIBIT 7.3

Method 2. Inside Micro Approach

Projection from Top: Sales Forecast for Manufacturing, Service, or Retail Category*

Year	$ Millions	COMPANY SALES VOLUME Percent Change from Previous Year	Units, Millions	Percent Change from Previous Year
Previous Five Years				
2007	$ 47.7	10.3%	20.2	6.0%
2008	54.1	13.4	22.8	12.8
2009	68.8	27.1	28.8	26.3
2010	78.0	13.3	32.7	13.5
2011	84.2	7.9	34.0	4.0
Next Three Years' Projections				
2012	93.3	10.8	37.5	10.3
2013	102.4	9.8	41.0	9.3
2014	111.5	8.9	44.4	8.3

2011 Projections from Bottom: Sales Forecast by Distribution Channel for Manufacturers*†

	EXISTING			NEW		
	Number	$ Millions	Units, Millions	Number	$ Millions	Units, Millions
Direct accounts	25	$29.2	9.2	6	$5.6	2.4
Wholesalers/brokers	74	62.4	26.5	6	2.1	0.9
Other	—	—	—	—	—	—
Total	99	$91.6	35.7	12	$7.7	3.3

Projections from Bottom: Sales Forecast by Store for Retailers*†

Market	EXISTING STORES $ Thousands	Transactions, Thousands
Green Bay, Store Number		
3	$ 773.7	73.6
4	276.8	25.2
5	449.8	41.8
7	285.6	23.2
8	343.5	30.5
Market total	$2,129.4	194.3
Madison, Store Number		
1	644.1	59.5
2	396.6	35.0
6	534.7	46.0
9 (new, open 9 months)	400.0	36.0
Market total	$1,975.4	176.5

Note: Only two markets represented—total sales rollup to $98 million for 2011. Same process to be used for 2012 and 2013.

*Based on your type of business, include in your sales projections dollars and units or number of transactions or people served, and take into consideration *new* products, distribution channels, stores, or services, and price changes. Service organizations use service offices or centers in place of stores. Manufacturers use net dollar sales to trade or intermediate markets, and retail and service firms use dollar sales to ultimate purchasers.

†For bottom-up projections, develop projections for each year for a three-year period.

Expense-Plus Process

Task 1. Estimate the operating expense dollars for next year. Estimate your operating expense dollar number based on the work you're doing in the marketing and other operational plans for next year.

Task 2. Estimate the gross margin and expense percentage for next year. From historical company or available industry data, review and estimate a target gross margin percentage and the desired (though realistic) profit before tax percentage you plan to achieve at the end of next year.

EXHIBIT 7.4

Method 3. Expense-Plus Approach

Review of Historical Financial Data

			EXPENSES	
Previous 5 Years	**Gross Margin Dollars**	**Profit Percent of Sales**	**Percent of Sales**	**$ Millions**
2006	33.4%	4.5%	29.1%	$13.9
2007	35.1	3.1	32.1	17.1
2008	37.2	3.1	34.1	23.5
2009	35.2	2.0	35.5	27.7
2010	31.3	2.8	30.1	28.0

Estimated budgeted expense dollars for next year's (2011) marketing and operations plans: $28.5 million, planned profit of 3.5 percent.

Expense-Plus Calculations for Next Year, 2011

Planned margin	33.50%
Planned profit	−3.50%
Operating expense	30.00%

Budgeted expense dollars of $28.5 million ÷ operating expense of 30 percent = sales objective of $95.0 million.

Task 3. Subtract your estimated profit before tax percentage from your gross margin percentage. This will force a total expense percentage.

Task 4. Divide the expense percentage into the expense dollars estimated in Task 1 to determine projected sales.

Task 5. Once you have developed your dollar expense-plus sales objectives, you can arrive at a corresponding unit objective by dividing the dollar objective by the average sales unit price.

Exhibit 7.4 presents an example of a review of data and calculations for the expense-plus approach. A worksheet for your computations is provided in Appendix C, Worksheet 36.

Alternative Method for Setting Sales Objectives for New Products or New Product Categories

As mentioned in the discussion of quantitative factors, you can use a target market approach to setting sales objectives when you have limited or no sales history. This approach is particularly useful for new products or product categories, such as the introduction of the first DVD or soft soap. Review the potential target market, and work backward to a sales objective number. An example for a packaged-goods product follows:

Potential target market consumers (defined by demography, geography, usage, etc.)	250 million
Percent expected trial rate	4%
Initial trial units	10 million
Percent making repeat purchases	40%
Repeat purchases	4 million
Number of repeat purchases	5
Repeat units	20 million
Initial trial units	10 million
Units sold nationally	30 million
Cases (12 units per case)	25 million
Gross sales (at $10.40 per case)	$260.0 million

The initial estimates of the target market potential, trial, and repeat projections are obviously critical to these types of sales objectives. Unless based on historical data closely related to your product, sales objectives generated in this manner are highly speculative and thus can be highly inaccurate. It is best to use the target market approach only when data for the other methods of sales forecasting do not exist or in conjunction with one or all of the other quantitative methods previously discussed.

TASK 2 **Reconcile the Sales Objectives**

Now that you have arrived at outside macro sales objectives, inside micro sales objectives, and expense-plus sales objectives, you must reconcile the differences to establish the sales objectives for your marketing plan. After reviewing your sales objective alternatives based on the macro, micro, and expense-plus methods, you may decide to go with a pure average of the three or with a weighted average, placing more emphasis on one result than another. Or you may use the weighted average of two, or simply use one method.

The important aspect of Task 2, reconciling the sales objectives, is that you have reviewed the data from three different quantitative sales objective perspectives. This will help you arrive at a sales objective with your eyes wide open and with an understanding of the dynamics that go into setting a sales objective. For the most meaningful sales projections, attempt to apply all three methods or, at the very minimum, two methods that you can use for comparison. Exhibit 7.5 shows how reconciliation of the three methods' goals into the composite sales objective can be accomplished.

See also Appendix C, Worksheet 36.

TASK 3 **Make Qualitative Adjustments to the Quantitative Sales Objectives**

Now that you have arrived at quantitative sales objectives, you should review the qualitative factors that will have an impact on the future sales. You need to temper the numerically derived sales objectives with the more qualitative forecasting factors. Using the appropriate qualitative factors, you can increase or decrease the composite dollars and the units, transactions, or people served sales objectives through an assignment of positive or negative percentage points, depending on the estimated degree of impact by each qualitative factor.

If the economy is growing and the economic outlook is good, you might increase the composite sales objective by 2 percentage points. Or you may decrease the composite sales objective by 4 percentage points because an aggressive competitor moved into your trading area. If there is more than one major impacting factor, you

EXHIBIT 7.5

Reconciliation of Sales Objectives

Year	MACRO $ Millions	Units, Millions	MICRO $ Millions	Units, Millions	EXPENSE PLUS $ Millions	Units, Millions	COMPOSITE SALES OBJECTIVES $ Millions	Units, Millions
Short Term								
2011	$94.9	37.5	$96.3	38.2	$95.0	37.7	$95.4	37.8
Long Term								
2012	106.3	42.0	103.4	40.1	104.4	40.9	104.7	41.0
2013	118.3	47.0	112.2	45.1	111.0	43.5	113.8	45.2

EXHIBIT 7.6

Qualitative Adjustment of Quantitatively Derived Sales Objectives				
Qualitative Impacting Factors	**+/−Point Change**	**Percentage Adjustment** ×	**Composite Sales Objective, $ Millions** =	**Adjusted Sales Objective, $ Millions**
1. Economy	+2	1.02%	$95.4	$97.3
2. Competition	−4	0.96	95.4	91.6
Total				188.9
Final adjusted average (total of adjusted sales objectives divided by number of calculated factors)				94.5

Notes:

1. List qualitative factors and the extent to which they will impact the previous sales objectives that were numerically derived. Adjust the composite sales objectives accordingly to arrive at your final sales objectives.

2. Use qualitative adjustments for numbers of units, transactions processed, and people served, as well as for the sales dollar objectives for each year's projections. However, the percentage point adjustments may differ from dollars.

can balance their effects through averaging. Exhibit 7.6 illustrates how to calculate these factors.

A worksheet for you to use in adjusting the composite sales objectives by the qualitative impacting factors is provided in Appendix C, Worksheet 36.

FINAL REMINDERS

Be sure to include a rationale with your sales objectives. Also, involve upper management in setting your sales objectives. And plan to revise the sales objectives during the process of writing your marketing plan.

Include a Rationale with Sales Objectives

Once the sales objectives are determined and agreed upon, also include a brief rationale. This rationale should summarize the processes used, assumptions made, and factors considered in finalizing the sales objectives. Although they are not included in the Appendix C worksheets for sales objectives, you can also include specific profit objectives for each year. Any additional pertinent supporting data related to sales and profit objectives should be included in your marketing plan appendix.

Involve Upper Management in Setting Sales Objectives

If you report to upper management, make sure you have an understanding of the company sales and profit expectations and you have reviewed the company business plan, if available. Many times, upper management dictates the sales objectives to the marketing department. When this occurs, it is even more important for you to have systematically arrived at your own sales objectives.

Based on your input, management can adjust its sales objectives (if very different from your sales projections) or, at the very least, gain additional perspective as it reviews the marketing plan designed to meet the dictated sales objectives. To ensure that you have developed a plan that will reach the agreed-upon sales objectives, it is a good idea to involve upper management regarding the sales and profit objectives before you write the remainder of the marketing plan.

Plan to Revise the Sales Objectives

The sales objectives will most likely be revised more than once as you write the marketing plan. You may uncover greater-than-expected sales potential in a particular target market. Or you may determine that your company does not have the necessary capital, that there is greater competition than expected, or that there is not enough consumer demand, all of which could negatively affect the estimated sales objectives.

Once your marketing plan is written (ideally, two or three months before the start of your fiscal year), it is wise to keep your sales objectives current. Review your sales objectives at two months, five months, and eight months into the marketing plan year in order to adjust the sales objectives, if need be, for the second, third, and fourth quarters of your fiscal year. This will help you maximize your sales and control your expenses in a timely and profitable manner. Most companies continue to keep their original *budgeted sales projections* using the revised sale projections to both manage the company and to compare against the original budgeted plan. The original budgeted sales projection is permanent and serves as your benchmark, while your revised forecast sales budgets are flexible and reflect your adjustments to the changing status of your business and the marketplace.

DOS AND DON'TS

Do

- Set sales objectives in a disciplined, step-by-step manner.
- Set short- and long-term sales objectives that are time specific and measurable.
- Make your sales objectives challenging and attainable.
- Review the sales history of the market and your product.
- Consider the size, growth, and decline of your specific target market and its purchase rates as a double-check on those of your projections that are based on sales history or are for new products and new product categories.
- Determine where your product or service or store concept is in its life cycle.
- Get upper management's agreement to sales objectives before finalizing the marketing plan.
- Review industry averages for cost of product or inventory, expenses, and profits.
- Use more than one method in developing your quantitative sales objectives to help guard against a one-sided sales projection.
- Realistically plan for pricing changes.
- Qualitatively adjust your numerically derived sales objectives.
- Once you have arrived at your sales objectives, consider developing a range forecast of high and low to give perspective on upside potential and downside risk. This will provide for contingency options as the year progresses in order to realize unforeseen potential or cut your losses should the business not perform as expected.
- Depending on your type of business, break down your annual sales objectives into smaller segments such as quarters, months, and/or weeks—possibly even days for retail and service firms. This breakdown will be of major assistance when you formulate your annual marketing calendar.
- Revise your sales objectives as needed during plan preparation, and revise your marketing plan budget accordingly.

- Remember the big picture when setting sales objectives. Sales for your product can come from three sources: (1) an all new market in which you have not competed, (2) growth of the market, and/or (3) an increase or a decrease in the competition.

Don't

- Don't guess.
- Don't set dollar sales objectives only.
- Don't accept upper management's sales objectives without independently arriving at your own.
- Don't always believe that your company alone can buck a marketwide decline.
- Don't set sales objectives based on achieving unattainable sales increases.
- Don't overestimate the size of the market.
- Don't feel secure with your long-term sales objectives if your share of market is increasing in a declining market. Increasing share cannot continually supplement a declining market. Look for other avenues that will put your company in a market growth situation.
- Don't consider just the qualitative factors presented in this chapter. Instead, consider other qualitative factors that pertain to your specific industry.
- Don't neglect to get input from upper management and those delegated to generate the sales (i.e., sales force, store managers) before setting sales objectives.
- Don't underestimate the impact of competition when setting sales objectives.
- Don't set sales objectives based on what you or the company wants and needs but on what the market will bear.
- Don't set a sales objective and leave it. Update sales objectives for the fiscal year on an evolving forecast basis, but do not change the sales budget.

The Successful Marketing Plan

Part I. Business Review

Insights: What Can We Learn?

Company Background	Sales Analysis	Consumer and Customer Review
Product Review	Trend Analysis	Competitive Review
	(PESTLE)	

Problems and Opportunities: *What Are the Issues?*

Part II. Brand Platform and Plan Objectives

Scope:

What Do You Do?

Targets:

Whom Are You For?

Positioning:

How Are You Different?

Plan Objectives: *What Needs to Be Achieved?*

Sales Objectives

Marketing Objectives

Communication Objectives

Message Strategy: *What's Your Story?*

Umbrella Strategy: *What's the Plan of Action?*

Part III. Tactical Plans

Marketing Mix Tools: *How Are We Going to Do It?*

Product	Pricing	Advertising	Media	Merchandising
Naming	Distribution	Promotions	Interactive	Public Relations
Packaging	Personal Selling		Media	

Part IV. Evaluation

Budget: *What Is the Cost?*

Payback: *Can We Win?*

Calendar: *When?*

Execution: *How?*

Plan Evaluation: *Did It Work?*

CHAPTER 8

Marketing Objectives

The biggest complaint from other non-marketing departments in most businesses is that marketing is too soft, it's not measurable, it's too squishy, and its practitioners care more about pretty pictures than they do about driving actual business results. Okay, it's easy to throw stones, but if we as marketers are being totally fair, we have to admit that this is the soft underbelly of our craft. Why?

We believe the main problem lies right here, in the development of marketing objectives. This is where many plans suddenly lose focus, ignoring the good work done earlier in the insights section, becoming unmeasurable or worse yet, measuring meaningless things that don't have anything to do with the target market's behavior, the only thing that ties directly back to sales results. Marketing objectives are the rudder that steers the ship. The ship is your company. If the rudder is crooked or off kilter, the ship will simply turn in circles chasing its own tail.

Let's try something we've done in seminars and workshops across the country. Very quickly, list five marketing objectives that you've either created for past marketing plans, that your company is working against right now, or that you feel your company or product plan needs at the current time. If you're like others we've talked to and worked with over the years, you'll have listed marketing objectives similar to the list in Exhibit 8.1.

While all very good goals, we wouldn't consider any of these marketing objectives. None of them will drive your organization directly to sales. They all might be critical in helping you get there, but they wouldn't be the driver. The answer lies in developing marketing objectives that connect target market behavior to sales, the topic of this chapter.

EXHIBIT 8.1

Marketing Objectives or Just Goals?

Would Any of These Be Similar to What You Listed?

Build a new distribution center by a certain date.

Develop a new product to fit a void in the marketplace.

Increase sales to a specific target market segment.

Increase the company's presence and sales from the Internet.

Increase awareness of our company or lead product relative to our competition.

Improve the response rate time in customer service.

Improve the perception of a key target market segment around a particular attribute that is a critical decision factor for the segment.

Become number one!

Use social media more effectively to build connections to new prospects resulting in new initial trial of our product.

After you've gone through the chapter, come back to the list in Exhibit 8.1 and see if you don't agree. Most of these goals might be relevant later in your marketing plan; we're just not ready for them yet.

The first step in deciding your marketing objectives is to analyze what behavior you need from your customers and prospects. What drives the marketing plan are market objectives tied to target market behaviors. The only thing that ties directly to sales that affects sales is an action by the customer, a behavior.

Managing these actions or behaviors becomes the key. None of the examples in Exhibit 8.1 are target market actions that result directly in sales!

FROM THIS CHAPTER YOU WILL LEARN

- The definition of *marketing objectives*
- How target markets and marketing objectives are locked to sales
- How to develop your marketing objectives

OVERVIEW

Think of each of the three components *sales*, *target markets*, and *marketing* in the following manner:

Sales are the reason you are in business.

Target markets—PEOPLE—provide sales. Satisfying the target markets is the way a company stays in business.

Marketing defines the target market behavior required to produce sales—
behavior such as:

○ Retention of current purchasers and users
○ Increased purchases by current purchasers and users
○ Increased trial by new purchasers and users
○ Increased repeat purchases by new purchasers and users

These are all measurable actions that directly tie to a sales result.

Understanding the target market is the key to marketing planning. All too often, however, the target market is not closely linked to each step of the marketing planning process. In our successful marketing planning methodology, target markets are locked to sales through marketing objectives.

Put another way, the marketing objectives quantify the target market behavior needed to deliver the required sales results. The end result is that the marketing objectives under each target market sum to a sales total. Combining the target sales sums of each target market provides you with the aggregate sales objective. Finally, target markets and their corresponding marketing objectives are also locked directly to the communication objectives and finally to the remaining portions of the plan through the strategies developed to accomplish the marketing objectives. Exhibit 8.2 visually demonstrates this link.

In examining Exhibit 8.2, you will notice there are three target segments identified. Each has a different number of marketing objectives, each of which would be specific to one behavior such as retention, new trial, increase customer purchases, or acquisition of lapsed customers. Also notice that each marketing objective or target behavior is quantified to fulfill a specific sales figure and that the sum of the marketing objective dollars results in the sales figure attributed to each target market. Additionally, the sum of the three different target segment dollar amounts equals the total sales figure.

Finally, in examining Exhibit 8.2, note there are umbrella strategies that apply to all the objectives and bring to life the brand positioning across the company or product (these are further explained in Chapter 11). However, below the brand positioning and umbrella strategy bar, you will notice individual tactics or marketing mix tools whose only purpose is to help accomplish the singular objective above it.

A favorite saying of ours in marketing planning is:

You eat the elephant one bite at a time.

The result of this interlocking methodology is that you can now focus on managing the individual pieces, one bite at a time. What you manage are the intended individual behaviors of the target market, which are the marketing objectives. Rarely does a whole plan succeed or fail. For example, you might be successful at retaining customers but not in gaining new trial. Instead of reinventing your marketing plan at the end of the year, you are now able to determine which pieces worked, which didn't, what to keep, and what to revise. This solves one of the fundamental problems in marketing planning—the conclusion that the website isn't working or the brochure is wrong when really, the company needs to start managing the pieces that apply to specific objectives that require vastly different tactics in order to be successful. **With this methodology, you manage the individual objectives and the tactics tied to their performance.**

Exhibit 8.2
How Marketing Objectives Are Interlocked

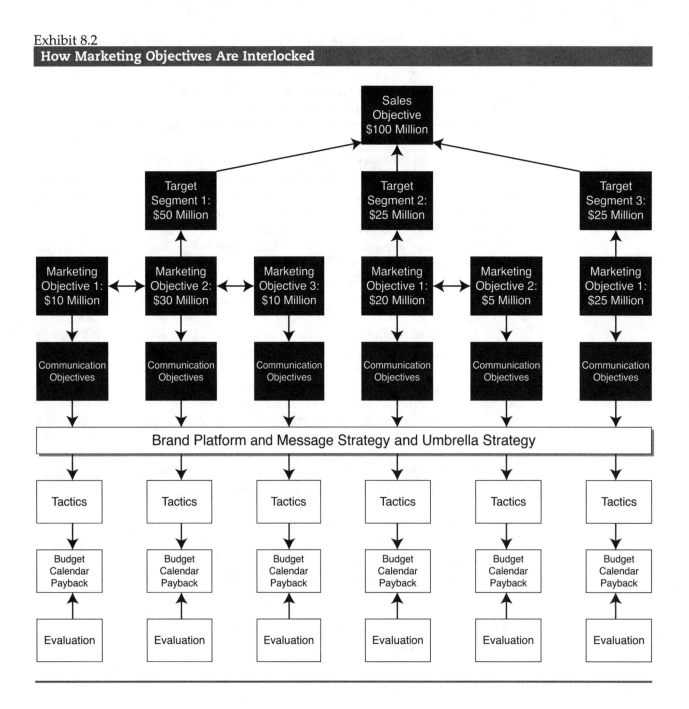

MARKETING OBJECTIVE PARAMETERS

Differentiating between marketing objectives and marketing strategies is not always easy, and it is a source of confusion even for marketing professionals who have been in the business many years. To show the difference between the two, we have detailed those properties that we believe make up a marketing objective. A marketing objective must:

- *Be specific in focus.* Marketing objective should be specific in terms of what needs to be accomplished.

- *Be measurable.* The specific behavior has to be measurable so that you know exactly whether or not you achieved the objective at the end of the period for which you set the objective. There is nothing subjective about marketing objectives!
- *Relate to a specific time period.* This can be one or more years, the next six months, or even specific months of the year.
- *Relate to a specific target.* Marketing objective must relate specifically to a target market segment designated in the target market section of your plan.
- *Focus on affecting target market behavior.* Marketing objectives must affect a specific target market's behavior with that behavior providing a direct link to sales. Such target market behaviors include retaining customers, trials of a product, repeat purchases of a product, larger purchases, and more frequent purchases.

Since marketing objectives are set to direct the business to influence specific target market behavior, they therefore fall into one, two, or all three of the following target market categories:

- Current purchasers and users
- New purchasers and users
- Lapsed purchasers and users

There are several possible objectives to be achieved within each category.

Current Purchasers and Users

Here the objectives might include retention across the entire customer base or a focus on a heavy-user segment.

Retention of Current Purchasers and Users

An important marketing objective is to retain the customer base at its current size from both a number and a dollar standpoint. Most businesses know what a customer is worth in terms of sales per year. So an objective of increasing retention can be directly quantified into sales. Note that this objective is defensive in nature. If your company has been losing customers over the past year or two, it becomes necessary to reverse this trend and maintain your customer base. You need to first direct total focus toward determining why business has been lost and then toward stabilizing the customer base.

Increased Purchases by Current Purchasers and Users

If your customer base is very loyal, the objective can take a more offensive direction, with strategies designed to obtain additional business from existing customers. This can be accomplished in three different ways by getting your customers to purchase:

- More often or more times in a given month or year
- A more expensive product or service
- Greater volume or amounts of product during each purchase

Again, when specifics are added, all these variations on increasing existing customer purchase behavior can be quantified to result in a sales number.

New Purchasers and Users

Marketing objective parameters for this category could include increased trial and increased repeat purchases after trial.

Increased Trial

For retailers, meeting this objective means first getting traffic of a specific target segment into the store. Most retailers have a fairly consistent purchase ratio (percentage of times a consumer purchases versus leaves without purchasing), which means that the retailer can usually rely on a certain percentage of the increased traffic's actually making a purchase. And the retailer typically understands on average what a purchase means in terms of dollars and the average number of purchases a customer makes in a year. So the event of new trial can be directly quantified back to a sales number.

Increased trial for packaged-goods, services, and business-to-business firms equates to actual purchase and/or use of the product from new target segment consumers. However, for both the retailers and the packaged-goods, services, and business-to-business firms, trial relates to obtaining new customers.

Repeat Purchases after Initial Trial

If your company has obtained high degrees of initial trial from new customers, it is important to make sure that you establish continuity of purchase and loyalty with the new users. Similar to increased trial of new customers discussed above, this behavior can be quantified back to a sales number very easily. In some cases, large amounts of initial trial exist, but the repeat purchase ratio is very low. If this is the case, establish an objective to increase repeat purchase and product loyalty and develop a fact-finding program to determine why repeat purchase rates among new customers are low and what can be done to increase them. Even if repeat purchase rates are fairly strong, there is usually some need to make sure they are maintained. Remember, it is far less expensive and more profitable to keep your new customers than it is to prospect, yet again, for new ones.

Lapsed Purchasers and Users

Marketing objective parameters for this category could include increased trial and increased repeat purchases after trial.

Increased Trial

Lapsed customers are a good source of incremental business, especially if you understand why they left and you have made substantiated changes that would give them reason to use you again. Additionally, many businesses operate in environments where loyalty is not as strong and consumers move within a subset of favorite brands or products. If either of these are the case, you should consider establishing a marketing objective to gain trial of these lost customers. Similar to the new trial of new customers above, this behavior can be quantified back into a sales figure depending on the specifics of the objective (percent of lapsed customers that the objective calls for to become activated customers times the average dollars per customer).

Repeat Purchases after Initial Trial

Once you've gained trial from the lapsed customers, make sure to have an objective in place that establishes goals and mechanisms to ensure retention at levels that are at or above what you have historically accomplished. Quantify these objectives in terms of sales the same way you quantified retention of existing customers above.

HOW TO DEVELOP YOUR MARKETING OBJECTIVES

To develop marketing objectives, review the sales objectives and target markets sections of your marketing plan, as well as the pertinent sections of your business review and problems and opportunities summaries. Each provides guidance in developing realistic marketing objectives.

See also Appendix C, Worksheet 37, to help you develop your marketing objectives.

TASK 1 ## *Review Your Sales Objectives*

Sales objectives provide a guideline for determining marketing objectives, as marketing objectives are established specifically to achieve the sales goals. All marketing objectives are quantifiable and measurable. The numerical quantifier used in the marketing objectives must be large enough to ensure success of the sales goals.

The sales goal for an organizational behavior training firm was to increase sales 8.33 percent or $20 million going from $240 million to $260 million.

Let's assume you were working on this. Your first attempt at developing marketing objectives might have been the following:

- Achieve a retention rate of 70 percent with existing customers.
- Increase the number of training modules or purchases from 2 to 2.5 per customer.
- Obtain 125 new customers purchasing 1 training module in the first year.

The question would then become, Would these actions guarantee meeting the sales goal of $260 million?

You'll later see that they did in fact add to the correct number of $260 million, and on the first try! However, in real life, there's a lot of play back and forth to get them to work out. This isn't simply an academic exercise; you can't just force numbers until the objectives give you the correct sales figure. Remember that these numbers need to be directionally accurate because they are the basis for your decisions on where to spend your budget and time resources. Additionally, they will be one of the most important measures against which you evaluate your plan.

In order to develop objectives like the ones above, you would have needed to know a number of things about the total potential industry category customer base, the existing company customer base, and the average dollars per transaction, and the number of purchases and retention rates for the company compared to the industry category or key competitors. This leads us to the next step, a review of the target market.

TASK 2 **Review Your Target Market**

The target market is the generator needed to achieve the sales goals. In this example, the target market in the plan was defined as this:

> Human resources VPs responsible for organizational training in companies with employees over 2,500 where culture is valued as directly leading to a higher-performing organization.

By reviewing the consumer and customer review sections of the business review for this company, we were able to define the following:

- *The potential size of its target segments:* This allowed determination of the number of people in the company's primary and secondary target segments, or the actual potential universe of industry category customers.
- *The size of the current customer base:* This allowed determination of the number of customers versus the number of potential customers across each target market segment.
- *The purchasing rates of the company target segment, including average purchase price, number of purchases per year, and retention rates of the customers:* These data provided the behavior or transactional information needed to quantify the target market's behavior and relate it back to sales numbers.

The business review pointed out that there are approximately 3,700 firms in the United States that had 2,500 or more employees based on census data and NAICS information. It also put us in the ballpark regarding the firm's historic retention rate of 68 percent and the industry category's retention rate of only 55 percent. Additionally, we found the average dollar purchase and the actual or estimated average number of yearly purchases for the main competitive set and the industry category in which they competed.

TASK 3 **Review Your Problems and Opportunities**

The problems and opportunities summaries of the business review provide insight into the content of the marketing objectives. Review each problem and opportunity that relates to the target market's behavior. Solving these problems or exploiting these opportunities will be the basis for your marketing objectives.

For example, one of the opportunities for the training firm was that, although trial of the product was very low, repeat purchase was above average at 68 percent when compared to the industry standard of 55 percent. Research showed that this was due to a strong positive perception that the company's learning system linked individual training sessions into a complex tapestry resulting in a platform of behaviors that enhanced company performance across all levels of the organization.

Another related problem was that awareness of the learning system was very low among the noncustomers in the primary target market. While the lead product and training module had moderately high awareness, the subsequent pieces and their collective connection to a higher-performing company were not understood.

EXHIBIT 8.3

Quantifying Your Marketing Objectives

Sales objective	Increase sales over last year 8.33%, from $240 million to $260 million.
Target market	Human resources VPs responsible for organizational training in companies with employees over 2,500 where culture is valued as directly leading to a higher-performing organization.
Target market size	U.S. companies with over 2,500 employees = 3,700
Company customers	300
Key metrics	
Market share	8.11%
Average dollars per transaction	$400,000
Average number of transactions per year	2 training modules per customer.
Historic retention rate of customers	68%
Marketing objectives	
Current customers	$210 million in sales.
1. Retention objective of 70%	300 customers × 70% = 210 retained.
	210 × 2 modules × $400,000 per module = *$168 million*
2. Increase number of purchases from 2 modules to 2.5 per customer	210 retained customers × 0.5 incremental modules × $400,000 = *$42 million*
New customers	$50 million in sales
Obtain 125 new customers purchasing 1 module in their first year	125 × $400,000 = $50 million
Total sales from marketing objectives	$260 million

TASK 4   ## Quantify the Marketing Objectives in Terms of Your Sales and Target Market Behavior Objectives

The last step is to put the pieces together and quantify the objectives so that you achieve your sales goal using objectives that make sense given your knowledge of your company and the industry.

Exhibit 8.3 illustrates the example that we've just been going through for quantifying your marketing objectives.

LONG- AND SHORT-TERM MARKETING OBJECTIVES

Typically, businesses develop one- to three-year plans while actually operating from the current one-year plan. It is a good practice to develop both long-term (two to three years) and short-term (one year) marketing objectives. Even if you don't have a long-term plan, the exercise of writing long-term marketing objectives forces you to focus on the future and consider the long-term implications of short-term marketing objectives, strategies, and executions. You might conclude that, while your short-term marketing objectives can be realized through increased sales from the *existing* target market segment, long-term marketing objectives will be realized only through the development of a *secondary* target segment. With this knowledge, you can plan for this inevitability sooner rather than later.

In another example, you may determine that you need to increase the number of purchases or the average dollar amount per purchase. With this in mind, a strategy or program can be initiated to study and recommend new add-on or higher-margin products to help you succeed. Then, when the time comes, you will be ready to proceed in an orderly, disciplined fashion.

In summary, most plans have long-term objectives that provide overall direction over the next three years. Short-term objectives and strategies are specific to the current year. However, the long-term objectives are there to focus efforts beyond the near term toward the future.

FACTORS THAT MIGHT INHIBIT THE FULFILLMENT OF YOUR MARKETING OBJECTIVES

The following are a few potential reasons you might not achieve your marketing objectives organized across the three top marketing objective categories. Being aware of these and determining if they apply to your situation will help you set realistic marketing objectives.

Things That Could Prevent Your Retention Objectives from Succeeding
- Product or service quality
- Competitive product innovation; lack of keeping your product or service relevant
- Poor service and customer service
- Competitive pricing
- Poor perception of brand or product across key decision factors (emotional and rational)
- Poor loyalty due to competitive parity within your category

Things That Could Prevent Your Increased Purchase Rate Objectives from Succeeding
- Customer need for wider range of product options than your company provides
- Lack of loyalty due to parity in the marketplace
- Lack of competitive pricing
- Lack of a strong customer relationship management program
- Lack of customer awareness or knowledge of other products and services
- Lack of add-on or bundling (product and pricing) opportunities for the customer
- Poor point-of-sale, in-store marketing
- Lack of a disciplined consultative selling method and effort

Things That Could Prevent Your New Customer Objectives from Succeeding
- Lack of awareness; awareness but misunderstanding or lack of knowledge relevant to the company or product
- Negative perceptions across key decision factors (emotional and rationale)
- Dominant competitor with superior product and/or a stronger link to the consumer
- Product and service that do not match up to the consumer needs and wants

DIFFERENCES BETWEEN RETAIL, PACKAGED-GOODS, AND BUSINESS-TO-BUSINESS MARKETING OBJECTIVES

Marketing objectives reflect the major differences between types of businesses. Marketing objectives for *retailers* affect consumer behavior in a retail environment. This means that there is a concentration on increasing store traffic, transactions, items per transaction, dollar sales per transaction, multiple purchases, and repeat purchases among both current and new users. The following examples of marketing objectives might help a retailer achieve its sales goals:

- Increase purchases per transaction of women 18 to 49 from 1.23 to 1.35 pairs of shoes for the next fiscal year. Concurrently, during the heavy seasonal sales months of back to school in August and the holiday period of November and December, increase purchases per transaction to 1.4 pairs of shoes.
- Increase dollar sales per transaction among the current users by 10 percent from $50 to $55, over the next 12 months.
- Increase traffic of women 18 to 49 by 1 percent from existing levels of 180 people per day over the next 12 months. Maintain the current purchase ratio of 45 percent.
- Generate a two-to-one purchase-to-walk ratio among all customers over the next 12 months.

Packaged-goods and consumer goods marketers also focus on affecting the consumer behavior of existing and new customers, but the emphasis is really on two different target markets, with a separate plan for each: the consumer and the trade. Marketing objectives must be established to achieve sales goals by affecting purchase rates of the trade and the consumer in the store. The following examples of marketing objectives might help a packaged-goods marketer achieve sales goals:

- Trade marketing objectives for next year:
  - Retain 95 percent of current customers at existing spending levels.
  - Maintain current purchase rates of existing trade customers, resulting in three purchase frequencies at an average of $880 per purchase.
  - Obtain increased shelf space for the product line by adding SKUs to 50 percent of the total outlets in the grocery distribution channel.
- Consumer marketing objectives for next year:
  - Retain 80 percent of current customers at existing spending levels.
  - Increase repeat usage of the product from 20 to 25 percent among current users.
  - Increase new trial of the primary market, females 25 to 49, by 5 percent.
  - Increase the total number of purchases per year from 6 to 7—or increase share of wallet from 40 to 45 percent.

Business-to-business marketing objectives are focused on affecting the behavior of other businesses. In business-to-business marketing, remember that there are often multiple target markets as defined by SIC, NAICS, or other user categories. Each one should have specific marketing objectives that, when added together, will meet the sales objectives. The following examples of marketing objectives might help a business-to-business marketer achieve the sales goals for two specific target markets, construction companies and manufacturing businesses:

- *Construction companies (NAICS Construction #23)*: Retain all 10 construction company customers. Maintain current reorder rates of existing customers over the next 12 months—four reorders, at an average of $1,500 per reorder.
- *Manufacturing businesses (NAICS Manufacturing #31-33)*: Develop 10 new accounts over the next 12 months with average sales of $100,000.

See also Appendix C, Worksheet 37, to help you develop your marketing objectives.

In summary, this process allows you to very quickly see where you should allocate your marketing dollars, as certain targets and objectives will result in far more sales dollars than others. Or it will become obvious through the target market and objectives development that a specific sales objective will be more difficult to realize and that a revision of the sales goal might be necessary.

DOS AND DON'TS

Do

- Remember that all objectives must:
  - Be specific in focus.
  - Be measurable.
  - Relate to a specific time period.
  - Relate to a target market.
  - Focus on affecting target market behavior.
- Make sure you have at least one marketing objective per target market outlined in the target market section of your plan. And make sure that cumulatively, the marketing objectives, when quantified for sales, add up to your plan's total sales goal.
- Remember that marketing objectives must be responsible for affecting target market behavior. Make sure that all your marketing objectives result in your target market doing something that leads to a sales result.
- Keep your marketing objectives to one sentence and the rationale to one brief paragraph. The rationale should include support from the work you did in your marketing plan's business review and insights section.
- Take time in developing your marketing objectives. They form the basis of your whole marketing plan. You should give them a considerable amount of thought and review prior to finalizing this portion of the marketing plan.

Don't

- Don't necessarily limit the number of marketing objectives to one. It's fine to have only one marketing objective, but make sure it will meet your sales objective. If not, you may need multiple marketing objectives, each focusing on a more narrow target market or a specific area of consumer behavior.
- Don't write slogans and think they are objectives. "To be the best" and "To provide the best customer service" are slogans. They are not measurable, time specific, or behavior defining. They don't tie directly to sales results that can be measured.

- Don't include communication goals with marketing objectives. Increasing awareness or changing attitudes are communication-based goals, and they should be included in the communication segments of this plan. Concentrate on marketing objectives that change target market behavior. Remember, marketing objectives alter actual behavior while communication objectives alter a thought process.

The Successful Marketing Plan

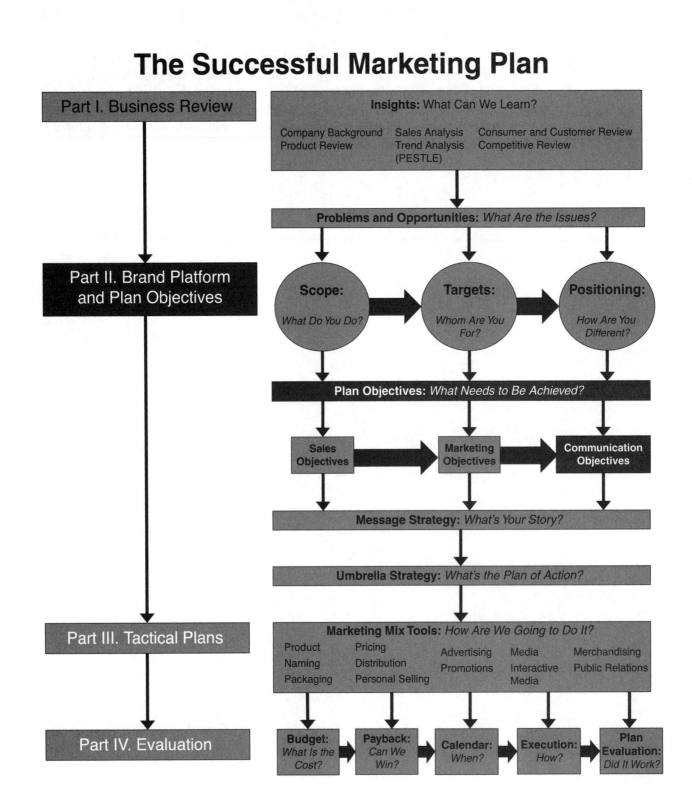

Part I. Business Review

Part II. Brand Platform and Plan Objectives

Part III. Tactical Plans

Part IV. Evaluation

Insights: What Can We Learn?

Company Background   Sales Analysis   Consumer and Customer Review
Product Review   Trend Analysis   Competitive Review
                    (PESTLE)

Problems and Opportunities: What Are the Issues?

Scope: What Do You Do?

Targets: Whom Are You For?

Positioning: How Are You Different?

Plan Objectives: What Needs to Be Achieved?

Sales Objectives

Marketing Objectives

Communication Objectives

Message Strategy: What's Your Story?

Umbrella Strategy: What's the Plan of Action?

Marketing Mix Tools: How Are We Going to Do It?

Product   Pricing   Advertising   Media   Merchandising
Naming   Distribution   Promotions   Interactive   Public Relations
Packaging   Personal Selling   Media

Budget: What Is the Cost?

Payback: Can We Win?

Calendar: When?

Execution: How?

Plan Evaluation: Did It Work?

9 Communication Objectives

The previous chapter demonstrated how to quantitatively lock the marketing objectives to a defined target market that will deliver the sales objectives. Now that you have developed your quantitative marketing objectives, you must build a bridge from your marketing objectives to the remaining portions of your plan—the message strategy, the umbrella strategy, and the marketing mix tools. That bridge consists of the communication objectives within the marketing plan depicted on the page facing this chapter opener.

FROM THIS CHAPTER YOU WILL LEARN

- A review of the Four A's of communication: how the communication objectives of awareness and attitudes affect the marketing objectives of action and action again

- The process of locking sales to the marketing mix tactical tools in your plan

- How to arrive at the overall marketing communication objectives that will help deliver the positioning

- How to allocate the necessary awareness and attitude values for each tactical tool that fulfills the overall communication objectives

- The challenges you will face in arriving at the necessary communication to achieve the intended effect on behavior

OVERVIEW

Setting communication objectives is extremely difficult and can become quite complex. This is because of the many uncontrollable factors found in the marketplace, such as competition and the ever-changing and unpredictable nature of your business's target markets and the media marketplace.

With the advent of social media, some of the new and emerging uncontrollable factors are what we might call "people-driven" versus "brand-driven" communications. People-driven communications can be anything from word of mouth, offline around the kitchen table, to online in a chat room, to independent blogs, on

EXHIBIT 9.1

The Four A's of Communication and Behavior

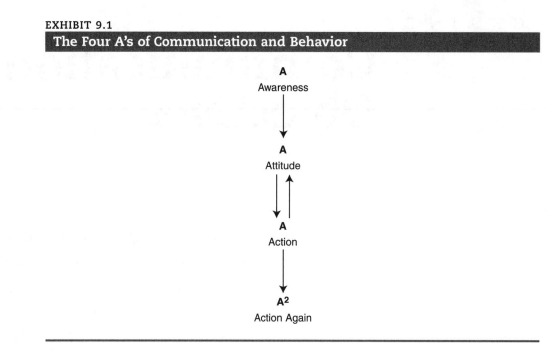

Facebook, a Twitter feed, and other social media sites, or even something said by a store attendant or service representative. We'll discuss this in more depth in Chapter 19, "Interactive Media."

The key point to remember is that everything begins with *fulfilling target market needs and wants* and *not* just with "How do we sell our product?" Therefore, we begin by explaining how the communication objectives of awareness and attitude positively affect the target market behavior that you previously quantified in your marketing objectives.

The Four A's of Communication and Behavior

The "Four A's," representing awareness, attitude, action, and action again (A²) are shown in Exhibit 9.1. This graphic describes the interfacing of target market communication and behavior. In order to have continual target market purchase, it is necessary to have communication down and up the Four A's axis, with attitude affecting behavior and behavior affecting attitude.

Awareness

At the top of the chart is awareness. In nearly all cases, you must first be *aware* of the product in order to form either a superficial or in-depth attitude toward it. As discussed in Part I, "Business Review Insights," there are four different types of awareness. The first three are, from the most to the least effective: top of mind, unaided, and then aided. Once you understand the degree of awareness, you need to understand the knowledge of your company, product, or service.

- *Top of mind* is the first product name given by an individual when asked what product comes to mind in a particular category. When individuals are asked to name the beers that come to mind, they usually rattle off three or four of them. The first one is their top-of-mind choice. The top-of-mind choice usually is the one they go to most. Additionally, it usually has a strong correlation to the one that would lead in share of wallet for those individuals' expenditures.

- *Unaided awareness* includes all the brands in a category one can think of without assistance. In the example above, it would be the other beer choices beyond the one mentioned first.
- *Aided awareness* is an individual's recognition of branded products when their names are given or products are shown to the person. You might say to people, "Now that you've named four beer brands for me, have you heard of Schlitz?" If they say yes, Schlitz has aided awareness. In most instances, there is a huge dropoff in terms of purchase intent from people's unaided awareness mentions and their aided mentions, with their aided mentions rarely coming close to the share of wallet of their unaided mentions.
- *Knowledge* is the last key factor that is a component of awareness measures. While your target market consumers may be aware of you, they in fact may not have much knowledge about you. We recently worked with a credit union for which this was the case with both members and nonmembers. The credit union enjoyed widespread awareness, but the breadth of products and services it provided were not understood, resulting in lower penetration and share-of-wallet figures from members and diminished attitudes from both members and nonmembers.

While the point may seem basic, remember that it is difficult to purchase a product unless you are aware of it and you have some knowledge about it. Many very good new products fail not only because they're not readily available to purchase but also because the target market does not even consider them—it is simply not aware of them.

Attitude
The next step down the chart is attitude.

Perceptions
In most situations, people must have a positive *attitude* toward a product before they can take the initial action. This could involve a long-term attitude development process, such as the case when people are buying a new automobile. In this situation, the consumers' attitude was formed, most likely over time, from a combination of things—advertising, testimonials of friends, test drives, or research they've done via consumer reports. Or it could be a low-attitude-involvement situation formed over a very short period of time, such as the case leading up to consumers' making an impulse purchase of a pack of gum they've never heard of at the checkout register. Even in this case, consumers form an attitude toward the gum, however fleeting, from what is communicated via the brand name, how the gum is packaged and displayed, and perhaps the price.

In both the automobile example and the chewing gum, consumers might have had a positive attitude about the products but after a bad experience with it, the purchasers subsequently formed a negative one. This is why there is a two-way arrow in the Four A's model between attitude and action. In most cases attitude initially affects action, but action also affects attitude. Trying the product or service either reinforces a positive attitude or in turn affects a negative attitude.

Purchase Intent
While most of what makes up attitude are perceptions—positive and negative around the key decision factors and influences of purchasing your product—there is one other component of attitudes that we haven't discussed, and that's purchase intent. If perceptions are extremely positive, a certain percentage of those who have positive perceptions will also have positive purchase intent.

While the two don't correlate 100 percent (you can have positive perceptions but have no intention of purchasing for reasons like the product is too expensive or there is an infrequent purchase cycle), positive perceptions do tend to lead to purchase intent. In almost all cases, a certain percentage of those who have positive perceptions will have positive purchase intent. This measure, like other attitude measures, can be quantified with primary research.

Action

Continuing our move down the chart, a positive attitude typically leads to the next step: action or trial of the product, service, or company. If this initial action is not a purchase, it must be an action that could lead to a potential purchase, such as sampling of the product, asking for additional information, attending a company event, or more important in today's world of consumer participation in marketing, posting a positive comment on a blog or other online advocacy, creating branded content in social media, or engaging in a brand's online channel.

Action Again

The goal of your marketing plan is forming a relationship with your target customers and moving them to loyalty. In most cases, the ultimate goal of this relationship is action by a loyal customer who purchases multiple times or year after year. Thus the bottom of the continuum is action again (A^2).

Action and Action Again: Marketing Objective Definitions

The Four A's process follows a consumer behavior model from initial awareness, to the formation of attitudes (negative, neutral, or positive), to initial action or trial, to action again or retrial. The first two steps, awareness and attitude, are what make up the communication objectives in your plan. The last two steps, action and action again, are what make up marketing objectives.

The Ties between Marketing Objectives and Communication Objectives

Marketing communication objectives involve awareness and attitude formation, and there's a direct link, which the marketer needs to understand, to the marketing objectives of retention, new trial, increased purchase, and reacquisition of lapsed customers established a step earlier in the plan. For example:

Awareness Affecting New Trial
The marketing objective of new trial may not be possible if the target market isn't aware of the product or service.

Awareness Affecting Increased Purchase
Increases in current customer purchase amounts, additional purchases, or additional frequency of purchases won't be possible if the customer is unaware or doesn't have knowledge of the alternative offerings the company provides.

Attitude Affecting Increased Purchase
Increases in current customer purchase amounts probably won't happen if the customer is aware and has knowledge but has a negative attitude. If the targeted

person has not acted on your product in the past year, there still may be attitude issues that have to be dealt with before you can move the person to action. For example, there may be a stronger preference or even a more positive attitude toward a competing brand. While you may find generally positive attitudes toward your product or service, a competitor may own the most important purchasing influence (rational attributes, benefits, or emotional connections). Or in fact, you may have a product problem that needs to be addressed prior to moving the target customer to action or trial of your brand.

Attitude Affecting Retention of Existing Customers or Acquisition of Lapsed Customers
Retention of current customers or acquisition of lapsed customers probably isn't possible if there exists negative perceptions or attitudes.

Therefore, once marketing objectives are established, the marketing planner needs to review exactly which communication objectives need to be met in order to help fulfill each of the marketing objectives.

Communication Objectives

Communication objectives involve increasing awareness and positive attitudes critical to your brand positioning. An awareness communication objective might look like this:

- Increase awareness from 10 to 12 percent over a two-year period against your primary target market.
- Increase top-of-mind, first mention awareness from 5 to 6 percent over the next year.
- Increase the understanding and knowledge through building awareness of the service warranty (or some additional product or service that's an important cross-sell opportunity for your firm) among existing customers from 45 to 55 percent.

An attitudinal communication objective might look like this:

- Improve the value perception for your product from 15 percent of the primary target market to 18 percent.
- Increase the perception that your company's after-sale service is the easiest to deal with in the industry from 22 to 25 percent.
- Improve the perception that your product is the best to help mothers provide the love and care that grandma used to give from 16 to 20 percent over the next year.
- Improve the perception by 5 percent that this fabric and sewing store gives me more ideas, or this motorcycle makes me feel like a rebel, or this shoe is LA cool. All of these would be examples of improving the attitude that is most critical in bringing your positioning alive.

Quantifying Your Communication Objectives of Awareness and Attitude

Just as your sales objectives and marketing objectives can be quantified, so can your communication objectives. However, both sales and marketing objectives tend to be more database based on actual sales figures and behavioral figures, respectively:

- At any given time during the year, internal data will tell a company how its products and services are selling.
- Likewise, most companies have databases tied to their individual customers that can help the marketers determine how many new customers they've gained; if an existing customer has purchased that year, and if so, how many times and the customer's average amount per purchase; and the retention rate of their existing customers from year to year.
- Even mass market retailers can get most of this information for at least that portion of their customer base that is in the customer relationship management (CRM) program or the frequent buyer program.
- Additionally, many mass marketers go deeper and determine fulfillment of marketing objectives across their entire customer base, or they analyze specific segments through primary proprietary market research. This type of research uses sampling techniques to accurately project total prospects for a given target market description, total customers, the percent that have tried or purchased in a given year, and the amount and the frequency of their purchases.

However, communication objectives are not developed from internal databases. Communication objectives are set with the insight using metrics from quantitative tracking studies typically conducted via surveys. You can directionally ballpark this process based on your "feel" for the marketplace, but we would highly recommend spending the money to acquire the research. In one of the awareness examples described above, the 10 percent base in the communication objective of increasing awareness from 10 to 12 percent would have to come from a previous baseline tracking study, and the increase (or failure to do so) after two years would need to come from an additional survey of the target market segments being tracked.

For a final review, Exhibit 9.2 summarizes the various measurements for each component, including the Four A's, of the Hierarchy of Effectors: target market,

EXHIBIT 9.2

Measuring Performance

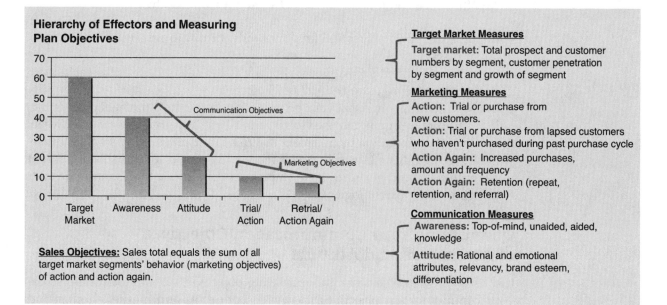

Hierarchy of Effectors and Measuring Plan Objectives

Communication Objectives

Marketing Objectives

Target Market   Awareness   Attitude   Trial/Action   Retrial/Action Again

Sales Objectives: Sales total equals the sum of all target market segments' behavior (marketing objectives) of action and action again.

Target Market Measures
Target market: Total prospect and customer numbers by segment, customer penetration by segment and growth of segment

Marketing Measures
Action: Trial or purchase from new customers.
Action: Trial or purchase from lapsed customers who haven't purchased during past purchase cycle
Action Again: Increased purchases, amount and frequency
Action Again: Retention (repeat, retention, and referral)

Communication Measures
Awareness: Top-of-mind, unaided, aided, knowledge
Attitude: Rational and emotional attributes, relevancy, brand esteem, differentiation

marketing objectives, and communication objectives (see Chapter 1, "What You'll Need to Know, Part 1").

THE PROCESS OF LOCKING SALES TO COMMUNICATION

The task of developing communication objectives is more art than science. While the first two—sales and marketing—of your three plan objectives are hard numbers, the communication objectives are more directional. However, if you have done a good job defining your target market and you have established sales and marketing objectives, you will find that this task does a good job of bridging the brand platform to your tactical tools. The best way to understand this section is to read all the way through the six steps and then go through the comprehensive example in Exhibit 9.8 to pull all the pieces together.

One final note before you start: We suggest you *limit the development of communication objectives to those for your primary target market only*. This target market is the most critical in terms of generating sales. While you can develop communication objectives under each target market and marketing objective, as demonstrated in Exhibit 9.3, we've found that going through the whole process is very time consuming, and given the more directional nature of this step, for smaller target markets, the return on the effort is not as great.

What's Needed to Develop Marketing Communication Objectives?

The six steps that follow will help you develop marketing communication objectives.

Step 1. Describe and Size Your Primary Target Market
List the total number of customers and prospects in your target market's universe (the total number of customers and prospects who could potentially be customers someday). This information was already developed in the business review and target market section of your plan.

Step 2. Quantify Your Awareness
Go back to your business review to find the information needed in this step. From either your primary research or a best guesstimate, identify the percentage of individuals in your primary target market who are aware of your company, products, and services.

Step 3. Quantify Positive Attitudes
In the brand positioning section of your plan, you determined the one or at most two rational or emotional attributes that will answer the question, What are you famous for? Will you win on safety? On reducing the risk of the decision? On providing the widest selection? On performance? Being the coolest? The cheapest? Providing the best care? Offering creative innovation? Prestige, hope, or value? Over time, you need to make sure you increase perceptions around the ownership of the attitude or feeling associated with your unique positioning in the marketplace.

Score your company on the percentage of the target market that has a favorable opinion of your company on the attitude associated with your positioning. The most common way to derive this score would be to assign a top-box or top-two-boxes score—that is, the percentage of the target market that rates your

EXHIBIT 9.3

How Marketing Objectives Are Interlocked

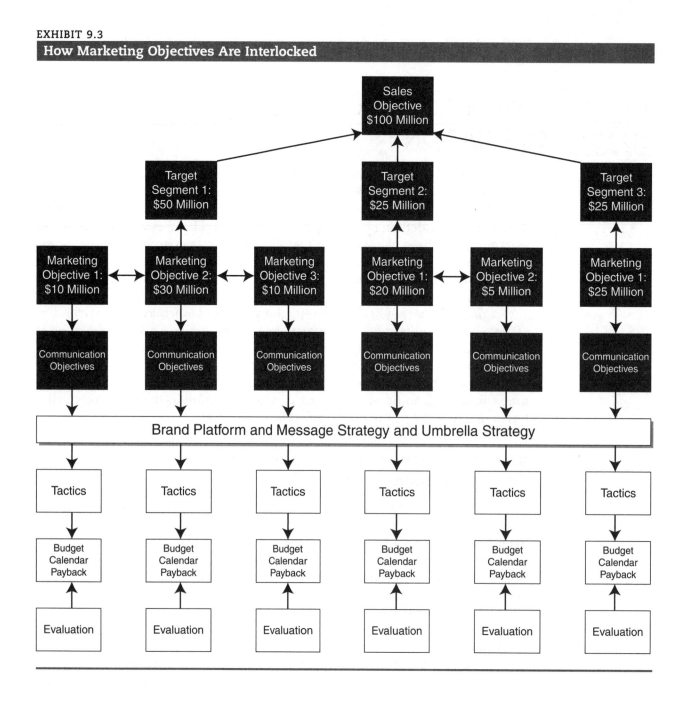

company as either excellent (top box) or excellent and very good (top two boxes) on, for example, a 5-point scale or the top two scores (a 9 and 10) on a 10-point scale. Additionally, this rating could be the percentage that sees your company as either number one or two in the marketplace or the percentage that sees you as dominating the category.

The example in Exhibit 9.4 demonstrates the review process through Step 3 for a business-to-business marketing situation. The target market is sized at 200,000. Company A has top-of-mind awareness equal to other competitors, but also has the best top-box score (or highest rating possible in the survey) for attributes and emotions that are most consistent with Company A's positioning (the attributes along the top of the chart). As you will see, Company A dominates the perception of provides consistent service and the perception of innovative material technology.

EXHIBIT 9.4

Review Process through Step 3 for a Business-to-Business Market Situation

Target Size: 200,000	Top-of-Mind Awareness	Top-Box Provides Consistent Service	Top-Box Innovative Material Technology	Top-Box Rating on Value
Company A	11%	27%	24%	20%
Competitor 1	10	8	12	11
Competitor 2	12	12	5	15
Competitor 3	8	8	10	8

As an outgrowth of dominating these two attributes, the company also ranks number one on value.

Company A is doing a good job of creating positive perceptions around the key attributes that are critical to the company's positioning. However, Company A is not as dominant in awareness, a critical component to building new trial.

Step 4. Quantify Purchase Intent

Many times, your research will indicate what percent of the target market's existing customers and new customers believe they will definitely purchase your product or service in the next year. This number is called *purchase intent*. Score or estimate your purchase intent for customers and noncustomers in your primary target market. If you don't have this metric, again, estimate it for each of your scenarios.

Step 5. Review Your Sales and Marketing Objectives

Review you're sales objectives you set earlier in your plan. Then review your marketing objectives to determine the total number of existing customer purchasers and new customer purchasers you will need to meet the sales goal that corresponds to your primary target market. Review the specific behavior required from the objectives in your marketing plan for your primary target market. What percent of your sales dollars come from retention of existing customers, new trial or obtaining new customers, increased purchase times or amount from customers, or acquisition of lapsed customers?

Examining your objectives and their relationship to awareness and attitude and other tactical considerations is important at this point as you'll use this information when you put all the pieces together later in the methodology. For example, if the marketing objectives were heavily weighted toward new trial from new customers and the company's awareness was very low compared to the competitive set, the marketer for Company A would recognize the importance of increasing awareness over that of increasing attitudes and changing perceptions. Likewise, the plan would also skew toward using tactical tools that would help accomplish the communication objective of increasing awareness.

Conversely, you may have a situation in which the majority of your sales from your marketing objectives fall into the area of *retention*. And you may find you have a lower retention rate than your industry category or key competitors. This may be due to poorer customer service, a weaker-performing product line, or some perception about your company and its products that isn't true (and as we all know, perception is reality).

The above examples are just two of many different possibilities. Reexamine your marketing objectives and then go through the scenarios as to why they might not be fulfilled. There are many possibilities across awareness, attitude, and perceptions toward your company and its products, such as lack of the right product or service mix, customer service, distribution, pricing, or communication.

Step 6. Finalize Your Estimates for Your Communication Objectives

There are two questions to answer at this stage:

1. What percent awareness did you have last year, and what percent do you need this year to meet your marketing objectives and sales goals for your primary target market? An awareness communication objective to address that question follows:
   - Increase awareness from 15 to 16.9 percent across the total primary target market (customers and noncustomer prospects).
2. What percent of the target market had positive attitudes toward your company, products, or services last year, and what percent do you need this year to meet your marketing objectives and sales goals for your primary target market? An attitudinal communication objective to address that question follows:
   - Increase the percent of the target market that considers the company to be in the top box (highest choice) in fashionable trend-right shoes from 10 to 11.3 percent.

THE COMMUNICATION VALUE METHOD: PULLING IT ALL TOGETHER

How to use the 50 percent happening guideline as a starting point: There is a very rough rule of thumb you can follow to help you finalize the link of your awareness and attitude communication objectives to your target market, sales objectives, and marketing objectives. General principles are very difficult to provide when describing the relationship between awareness, attitude, purchase intent, and actual purchase. However, a starting point—and only a starting point—for defining the *total target market goals* (purchaser and nonpurchaser) for the numeric links between target market awareness, attitude, and purchase intent up through purchase or sales is the "50 Percent Happening" premise.

As shown in the following table, this very subjective premise suggests that you begin with the percent of the *total target market* that you project to purchase (including purchasers, past purchasers, and past nonpurchasers) and add 50 percent of each level to the next level of the sequence.

	TARGET MARKET AFFECTED	
	Number*	Percent
Purchase number	10,000	5.0
Purchase intent	15,000	7.5
Positive attitude	22,500	11.3
Awareness	33,750	16.9
Target market size	200,000	100.0

*Note that each row from the purchase number down through awareness increases by 50 percent.

There are more exceptions than rules to this "50 Percent Happening" premise, but it is a beginning sequence to follow if you have no data. Keep in mind that if there is a large number purchasing, if the product is very established, and if there is a great deal of positive trending in the marketplace, you will need to add less than 50 percent for each increment. Likewise, you will need to add more than 50 percent under the opposite circumstances.

Remember, the "50 Percent Happening" approach is a general guide and starting place for the *total primary target market*, which includes both purchaser/customers and nonpurchasers/noncustomers that you project will end up buying and contributing to overall sales.

TASK 1 — ### Link Your Communication Objectives Back to Your Target Market, Sales, and Marketing Objectives

Start the process of developing your final communication objectives by writing in your target market size and corresponding marketing objectives needed to fulfill your sales numbers developed in the sales analysis and marketing objective sections of your plan.

Then based on past knowledge and tracking study research or using a best estimate, fill in the purchase intent and communication objectives against current customers and noncustomer targets.

When you break out the primary target market purchaser/customer and non-purchaser/noncustomer separately, you will find the actual percentages in terms of intent to purchase, attitude, and awareness for *purchaser/customer* to be substantially higher, with a less than 50 Percent Happening for each level, as shown in Exhibit 9.5. On the other hand, there can be a closer to 100 percent difference between the percent purchasing and the percent saying they "will definitely purchase" for *nonpurchaser/noncustomers* and the total target market. Remember, this "50 Percent Happening" is only a starting point, and you will need to modify the percentage levels at each increment based on your review of Task 1.

From this point on, we will build on the example in Exhibit 9.5.

EXHIBIT 9.5

Method for Establishing Marketing Communication Goals to Fulfill the Marketing Objectives: Retail Store Chain Target Market Example

	6,641,000* TOTAL TARGET MARKET	
	Percent Current Purchasers	Percent Nonpurchasers
Marketing Objectives	41.25%	3.1%
Current purchasers: Increase retention to 41.25% and increase purchase frequency to 1.8 times per year		
Nonpurchasers: Capture 3.1% of the noncustomers and obtain purchase frequency of 1.32 times per year		
Purchase Intent		
Believe they will definitely purchase	55.0	7.0
Marketing Communication Goals		
Attitude:		
Rate store as having trend-right shoes	69.0	12.0
Awareness:		
Unaided awareness of footwear chain	95.0	29.0

*4,581,000 noncustomers and 2,060,000 customers

TASK 2 — ### Link Your Communication Objectives to Your Tactical Tools

Review your business data for as many cause-and-effect relationships that you feel confident about. For example, when a manufacturer secures display placements in 25 percent or more of the retail outlets in its service area, there typically is an increase in sales of 5 to 10 percent. Or when a business-to-business manufacturer receives placement of a feature article in a major industry trade publication, it generally sees an increase of 15 to 20 percent in inquiries. With this same manufacturer, over half of the inquiries each year can be tracked back to those trade shows at which there was a booth. Or when a retailer runs a test in which only the execution of one tool was changed (promotion tool changed from couponing to sampling), sales increase 7 to 10 percent in test markets as compared to the control markets where no change was made. (See the discussion of the growth rate of improvement [GRI] in Chapter 24, "Plan Evaluation.")

If you have not been measuring and recording the effectiveness of the various tools or testing their effectiveness, it is something you will want to include in next year's plan. One way to do this is through one of several predictive modeling techniques available that isolate variables and predict their impact on sales, behavior, and communication variables of awareness and perceptions. Another way to measure effectiveness of your marketing mix tactical tools is through educated inferences. While observations like those in the preceding examples measure cause and effect but do not answer the awareness and attitude questions, you can use this basic information to help estimate what percentage of the target market's unaided awareness and attitude caused the behavior. For example, if running twice the number of ads in a given period increased calls by 25 percent, the inference would be that there was some percent increase in awareness created by doubling the number of ads. These types of inferences are far from empirical research, but they do provide some direction.

Predictive Modeling

While many of you will be able to capture only anecdotal evidence around your tests of tactical programs, and thus you will be able to gain only a ballpark idea of the impact of different tactics, there are more powerful quantitative ways to provide marketers certainty in terms of actions and reactions from marketing tactical efforts. The discussion below provides a very brief overview of predictive modeling. Many businesses today are using these methods to accurately predict the cause-and-effect impacts of their tactical tests and programs.

The following content comes from a colleague of ours, Hartwig Huemer, managing principal of Decision Support, Inc.

Predictive modeling is a way of forecasting or predicting business outcomes. Predictive modeling succeeds by combining mathematics, statistics, and databases, and it is able to capture the heart of the business knowledge at hand. That is, it captures the knowledge of "how things work" or "what drives sales in this business." Predictive models are built by analyzing current and historical facts. In the end they are mathematical formulas meant to make predictions about future events. Good predictive models identify the factors that matter (that is, "drivers") and integrate their impact ("dependency") on the overall outcome ("results").

When building predictive models, one looks for trend patterns and data relationship patterns found in historical data. In its simplest form, there are five steps to building a predictive model:

1. Specify the objective of the forecast model.
2. Compile a list of factors that you think affect the forecast.

3. Identify how each factor impacts the forecast.
4. Build and test the model.
5. Apply the model.

Step 1. Specify the Objective of the Forecast Model

The objective is set forth by the business leadership. For example, a marketing group is looking to forecast "promotional sales of Product X." The objective should be kept very focused: "price sensitivity of our midlevel gadget in big-box stores," and not "price sensitivity of our gadget line in the U.S. market."

Since the deliverable of the predictive modeling process will likely be a computer program or spreadsheet enabling you to run simulations, you should seek objectives that you are dealing with on an ongoing basis. Stay away from one-time questions as the goal of a predictive model. These types of questions are answered faster and cheaper via ad hoc studies.

Also, the broader the objective, the more resources (time, people, and money) it will take to build such a model. In addition, the accuracy of a broad model is usually very questionable (at best).

Step 2. Compile a List of Factors That You Think Affect the Forecast

The list of relevant factors is created through brainstorming with the business members. They transfer the business knowledge to the analysts by describing the purpose and characteristics of the factors. For example: marketing dollars (budget for each program); marketing programs (TV, radio, freestanding inserts, in-store advertising, Internet); pricing; distribution and availability; seasonality and timing; competitors; promotions; and demographics.

This is the time when the analysts need to listen to all of the hunches that business personnel have on how these factors tie together.

Step 3. Identify How Each Factor Impacts the Forecast

The goal of this step is to find a mathematical formula whose calculated results mimic the actual performance of the objective. As an example, let's look at the case of attempting to predict promotional sales. When charting your results, you would end up with two lines. Both lines will display "promotional sales": one would represent the actual history, the other the model's projected sales. The goal is to design a formula such that the line showing the projected sales matches the line showing the actual sales history as closely as possible.

What analysts should look for is how changing the value of a factor affects the outcome of the result (objective). Some results are quite obvious (for example, a price discount will spike sales), but others may not be known to analysts (for example, policies for slotting accruals or loyalty programs). Not all factors that were identified by the business team actually make it into the final model. It may turn out that—statistically speaking—a factor is not significant, or it can't be measured, it is too expensive, or it is even impossible to get good data on it.

On the flip side, a factor not identified by the business team won't show up in the model either. In other words, in the very end, the analysts may

(continued)

find that the predictive model can explain only a small percentage of the variation in the objective's outcome, and no one knows what is responsible for the rest of the variation. For example, a model may end up explaining only 40 percent of the variation in an objective's outcome. This means that all the included factors are responsible for 40 percent of the changes that are occurring. The remaining 60 percent cannot be explained by the factors used.

Step 4. Build and Test the Model

Now it's time for the analysts to do their magic. They look for and sieve through lots of historical data to find patterns and relationships between the stated objective and the factors. This is the step where the drivers are found. A *factor* is identified by the business team as having an impact on the real-world objective. A *driver* is a measurable factor that has been identified via statistics and data analysis to predictably alter the outcome of the objective. There are many real-world factors, but very few have a predictable impact on the outcome and can also be measured consistently. For example, weather, traffic, and road construction are all factors that can impact the sales of a restaurant, especially one with outdoor seating. But how can one measure, control, and predict these in a consistent way in order to incorporate them into the model?

Overall, averages are the simplest pattern to find and work with. Averages of ratios are used very often because they are so easy to establish. For example, if a 10-member sales team made sales of $50 million, how much will a team of 15 members sell? The way this question was set up, the answer is $75 million. But is "sales team size" really the only (or main) driver of sales volume? What about the number of customers or the type of company they approach?

Overall there are two things to focus on when searching for and analyzing drivers:

1. *Focus on drivers that the business can control.* Using the above example, you cannot control or predict the weather or traffic. But you can control the location, the price, and the number of seats or tables.
2. *Establish and utilize the marginal rate, not the average rate.* For example, when incorporating "marketing dollars spent," don't use the "average return on the spending." You need to find a formula representing the "return on the next dollar spent."

Step 5. Apply the Model

In its core, a predictive model is a single formula or a set of mathematical formulas. The formulas need input values representing the factors identified earlier in the process. Usually the model is programmed into some commercially available application, or it may be embedded into something as simple as a spreadsheet. The delivery method (for example, desktop software, web-service, or spreadsheet) is an indicator of how many people can use it (for example, its scalability) and whether it can be used for different business objectives (for example, domain). However, the delivery method does not speak to "how good" the model is. In general, a custom model will be a better fit to the business task at hand.

Proper use of the model's formula actually requires a team effort. In order to use a predictive model, the team's members need to cover the following skills. You need someone who:

1. Knows the values to be used
   - Has an understanding of the underlying business challenge
   - Can prevent unreasonable numbers from being used as inputs
2. Knows how and where to (literally) plug numbers into the formula
   - Knows the mechanics and procedures of the spreadsheet and/or software
3. Knows how to interpret the numerical results of the model
   - Can translate the resulting numbers back into the business factors
4. Understands the feasibility of a proposed outcome or required input set
   - Knows when solutions or inputs are "out of bounds"
   - Has the authority to decide on including or excluding suggested business scenarios in recommendations to senior management

Predictive models provide a proven tool set for decision support in fields such as marketing, finance, or operations. They are being successfully used in actuarial science, financial services, insurance, telecommunications, consumer packaged goods, retail, commodities, travel, health care, and pharmaceuticals.

The quality of a model lives and dies by how well its drivers match the underlying factors. To what extent that happens can be judged only on a case-by-case basis. To improve the quality of a model, you need to plan on increasing the number of necessary analysts as well as the development time. Just increasing one but not the other (for example, more analysts but same development time, or same number of analysts but more time) is unlikely to substantially improve the quality of a model.

Hartwig Huemer, managing principal of Decision Support, Inc. (DSi): DSi (www.AnalysisSupport.com) is a business consulting group that Huemer founded in 1994. The company designs predictive models, performs data analysis, and builds custom desktop decision tools (such as simulators and optimizers) to assist executives in making the best decisions in their quest to implement their visions. The company has been successfully delivering solutions across diverse industries and sectors, including consumer packaged goods, retail, manufacturing, commodities, software insurance, commercial real estate, health care, municipalities, and school boards. Clients are Fortune 500 companies and small and midsize organizations, as well as start-ups.

Hartwig Huemer was born in Austria, where he received his MS and BS in mathematics for engineers from the University of Technology in Graz. He also received an MS in computer science (under a Fulbright Scholarship) and an MBA in finance from the University of Wisconsin–Madison. He can be reached at DSI@AnalysisSupport.com.

To help organize, catalog, and summarize this diverse information from many sources as it pertains particularly to the tactical tools, use a structured format like that shown in Exhibit 9.6, and also see Worksheet 38 in Appendix C.

EXHIBIT 9.6

Example of a Communication Value Review

Tactical Tool	Activity	Results	Directional Implications
Product			
Naming			
Packaging			
Pricing			
Distribution			
Personal selling			
Promotions	Trade show sampling of product	Received 180 responses from this trade show handout requesting sales presentations. This is double the rate from same show last year with no sampling.	Sample products at all trade shows.
Advertising			
Media			
Interactive media			
Merchandising			
Public relations	Product feature stories Product news releases	Generated 50 to 150 phone calls per story.	Place greater emphasis on product feature stories even if it means fewer news releases. Generated minimal, if any, phone inquiries.

TASK 3 ## Assigning Values to Tactical Tools

The purpose of this last section is to force you to go through a directional exercise to help you think about the tactical tools and how they will relate to your accomplishing your sales, marketing, and communication objectives.

Rank the available marketing mix tools as important (I), moderately important (MI), or very important (VI) in building awareness and positively shifting attitudes. As shown in the example in Exhibit 9.7, you would rank these values

EXHIBIT 9.7

Example of Tactical Tool Importance Rankings

Tactical Tool	AWARENESS		ATTITUDE	
	Purchaser	Nonpurchaser	Purchaser	Nonpurchaser
Product	VI	MI	I	MI
Naming	I	VI	I	VI
Packaging	I	VI	I	VI
Pricing	I	—	I	—
Distribution	I	VI	I	VI
Personal selling	MI	MI	I	MI
Promotions	MI	MI	VI	VI
Advertising	VI	MI	VI	VI
Media	MI	MI	VI	MI
Interactive media	MI	I	MI	I
Merchandising	MI	VI	VI	MI
Public relations	—	I	—	I

Note: VI = very important, MI = moderately important, and I = important.

by importance as they relate to target purchasers and nonpurchasers. (See also Worksheet 38 in Appendix C.)

Usually, every tool has some importance, but if you believe a particular tool has no importance relative to awareness and attitude, do not give it an importance ranking. For example, you might decide that, while the price tool is very important in affecting attitude, it really has no importance in building the overall awareness for the product.

Summing Up Tasks 1 through 3

Now let's tie it all together. Based on the importance rankings, assign awareness and attitude percentage point values to each tool for purchasers and nonpurchasers so that they total to the awareness and attitude marketing communication goals. An example of this assignment of value point goals is shown in Exhibit 9.8.

Exhibit 9.8 provides an example of how you can *numerically* lock the projected sales from the target market to the marketing objectives to the communication objectives and, in turn, to the tactical tools. The example is for a national retail chain, quantitatively delineating how the ultimate sales objective will be delivered from the target market awareness and attitude communication increments. (See also Worksheet 38 Appendix C.)

In Exhibit 9.8 the total sales objective of $55 million will be generated from the defined total target market quantified at 6,641,000 people. The total market is then segmented into customers (previous purchasers) and noncustomers (nonpurchasers) with each segment receiving its own sales objective. The marketing objectives, which along with the sales objectives would have already been established in your planning process, call for a retention of 41.25 percent of the 2,060,000 *previous purchasers or customers* with a frequency of 1.8 yearly purchases per customer at $32.15 per purchase and new trial by 3.1 percent of the 4,581,000 *nonpurchasers or noncustomers* with an average yearly purchase per customer of 1.32 times $32.15 per purchase.

The estimated average number of annual purchases and average purchase dollars amount (1.8 × $32.15 for previous purchases and 1.32 × $32.15 for new customers) multiplied by the total number of retained existing customers and new customer purchasers equals the $49 million and $6 million segmented target sales respectively, for a total sales figure of $55 million. In order to fulfill these sales objectives, 55 and 7 percent of each respective target market must have a definite intent to purchase.

As you can see, there is falloff from the percent that intends to definitely purchase versus those who are projected to purchase. Using *previous purchasers or customers* as an example, in order to have 55 percent purchase intent, a positive attitude is projected at 69 percent of the target, which falls off from the total unaided awareness projection of 95 percent. In order to deliver the projected 95 percent unaided awareness and 69 percent positive attitude goals, these totals are then allocated among each tactical tool. Each tool is then planned and executed to generate its share of the required marketing plan awareness and attitude communication objectives.

Obviously things are very different for the *nonpurchaser or noncustomer* target market segment. For starters, the unaided awareness is only 29 percent so each of the other components ending with actual purchase projection will be significantly less than the current customer target.

Another point to remember is that if a tactical tool or a group of tactical tools has been given a relatively low goal value (which means minimum expectation for contribution), put a minimum of marketing resources against it when preparing this

EXHIBIT 9.8

Example of How to Lock Sales from the Target Market to Marketing Objectives and Communication Objectives

Target Market Example

TOTAL SALES: $55,000,000
TOTAL TARGET MARKET: 6,641,000

	CUSTOMERS: 2,060,000		NONCUSTOMERS: 4,581,000	
Target Sales Objectives	**$49,000,000**		**$6,000,000**	
Marketing Objectives	**Percent**	**Number**	**Percent**	**Number**
Current purchasers: Increase retention to 41.25% and increase purchase frequency to 1.8 times per year at $32.15 per purchase occasion.	41.25 (retention)	850,000 1.8 times per year $32.15 per purchase occasion	3.1 (new trial)	142,000 1.32 times per year $32.15 per purchase occasion
Nonpurchasers: Capture 3.1% of the 4,600,000 noncustomers or 142,000 new customers. Get them to purchase 1.32 times per year at $32.15 per purchase occasion.				
Purchase Intent				
Believe they will definitely purchase	55.0	1,113,000	7.0	321,000

	UNAIDED AWARENESS PREVIOUS PURCHASERS		POSITIVE ATTITUDE PREVIOUS PURCHASERS		UNAIDED AWARENESS NONPURCHASERS		POSITIVE ATTITUDE NONPURCHASERS	
	Percent	**Number**	**Percent**	**Number**	**Percent**	**Number**	**Percent**	**Number**
Marketing Plan Communication Objectives	95.0	1,957,000	69.0	1,421,000	29.0	1,328,000	12.0	550,000
Tactical Tool Communication Objectives								
Product	10.0		16.0		2.0		3.0	
Naming	5.0		3.0		0.5		0.5	
Packaging	5.0		3.0		0.5		1.0	
Pricing	1.0		5.5		1.0		0.5	
Distribution	7.0		3.0		2.0		0.5	
Personal selling	9.0		5.0		2.1		1.0	
Promotions	12.0		7.0		2.5		0.8	
Advertising	12.0		8.0		3.1		1.6	
Media	17.0		6.0		3.8		0.5	
Interactive media	2.0		1.0		2.0		0.5	
Merchandising	12.0		9.5		8.0		1.6	
Public relations	3.0		2.0		1.5		0.5	

segment of the tactical implementation plan. Unless you can get this tool above the threshold level to make it effective, don't use it. For example, if the advertising communication tools received very low value goals, it might be best to concentrate your resources in personal selling and merchandising (the nonmedia tools), which are concentrated closer to the purchaser and do not have the higher associated costs. Put your major investment or increased investment against the few tools that will drive your plan.

Expect to revise these value goals as you prepare and interface the tactical tool segments of the plan. For example, you might assign more weight to the advertising media tool after determining that effectively communicating a specific promotion will require not only the merchandising tool via store displays but also more media via newspaper ads. Further, as you finalize the marketing budget and reconcile it with the sales objectives and bottom line goals, there most likely will be an adjustment in tactical tool values.

Now You Can Manage the Pieces

In summary, you now have completed the objectives sections of the marketing plan. As a marketer, you can now manage each individual piece. If you don't reach your sales number, you'll be able to dissect the pieces:

• Was it your customer target market segment or new customer (previous nonpurchase target market) or both that resulted in the shortfall?
• If it was your new customer segment that fell short, was it the trial marketing objective, or was it the frequency of purchase that you need to work on next year?
• If it was the trial objective, did you successfully raise awareness enough based on your communication objective to support your marketing objective of new trial? If not, this might be the first area of focus next year.
• If you met your communication objective of awareness but not your marketing objective of trial, do you have attitude problems you will need to address next year?

COMMUNICATION CONTROL CHALLENGES AND INHERENT PROBLEMS REGARDING THE METHOD FOR DEVELOPING COMMUNICATION OBJECTIVES

Now that you have been exposed to the communication goal-setting method, we will review some communication control challenges and inherent problems that make this method only a start to the process of arriving at overall marketing communication goals and allocating awareness and attitude requirements for the specific tactical tools.

Controlled to Somewhat Controlled to Uncontrolled Communication

There is much you can control in the communication of your product and/or service, such as your advertising message, publicity releases, brand name development, packaging, types of promotions and events, company direct service to customers, and point-of-purchase message. However, there is much communication that you cannot control. The sheer noise level in your particular marketplace can exceed your control. This noise level includes the communication of your message and that of your competition, as well as all of the messages your target market is receiving, both within a particular category and on a geographic basis, in their everyday lives. For example, a Google search shows sources saying that the average American is exposed to between 200 and 3,000 ad messages daily! Your advertising messages can easily get lost in this clutter.

There are also many other forms of communication that you cannot control, such as your competitors' sales forces, promotions, and advertising; the retailer's and/or distributor's service level; and independent, third-party communications. For example, a magazine reporter might use your product incorrectly because he did

EXHIBIT 9.9

Brand-Driven versus People-Driven Communication

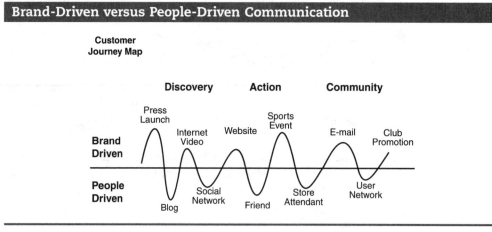

Source: McCann Worldgroup

not read the instructions, he then might have a bad usage experience, after which he writes a negative feature on your product.

Many times you have partial control over what may appear to be uncontrollable communication. In the case of the magazine reporter, perhaps the "facts sheet" sent along with the product and instructions were not clear enough to properly "prep" the reporter. But a phone call highlighting the instructions could have preceded and followed the sending of the material. Further, some believe that the manufacturer has no control over the retailer's displays. However, having a company representative call the retail contact with examples of how to build a retail display, with a corresponding manufacturer's incentive, may provide some control over the retailer's communication of the manufacturer's product. The point is that a well-designed and well-executed marketing plan with detailed follow-through can provide some control over what might originally be considered uncontrollable communication and give your product a better chance to succeed.

And as previously mentioned in this chapter, brands can influence but not control new forms of people-driven communications across the new spectrum of digital and social media. Exhibit 9.9 created by the McCann Worldgroup, outlines this spectrum of brand-driven versus people-driven communication along the customer journey.

Addressing the communication control challenges is critical to determining what overall marketing communication is required to move the target person to action and what is required by each tactical tool to deliver the overall communication for the plan. Yes, there is only so much communication you can control, and yes, because of the control challenge, your communication objectives and values are only directional. However, the key is to be aware of what you truly cannot control, make an effort to control what you can, but not be afraid to invite customers to engage and participate in your brands' marketing activities as well.

Application Shortcomings

In addition to the communication control challenges one faces when relating behavior to communication, you should also be aware of the many shortcomings in the application of the foregoing communication goal-setting approach.

1. *Not all products are alike.* Every product, industry category, and industry is unique, and what applies to one does not apply to all.

2. *Communication is a fluid process.* The effect of communication on building awareness, attitude, and usage is very fluid, with much overlap and no real beginning or ending. Also, you should remember that the communication and behavior relationship can be very time sensitive. The time period needed for the process to take effect could be seconds, such as an impulse purchase, or years, such as a new auto or home purchase.

3. *Subjectiveness is involved in the method application.* While we try to quantify throughout the application of this method, you will still need to apply intuitive judgment. Accordingly, another major problem regarding this method arises from the subjectiveness involved in arriving at the overall marketing communication goals and individual awareness and attitude value goals for each tool.

4. *Marketing activities have a cumulative effect.* Also, there is the problem of attempting to determine what the overall effect will be on target market awareness and attitude when you combine the communication power of the different tools. Is the whole greater than the sum of the parts?

   For example, let's say we give the advertising media tactical tool a value goal of achieving 10 percent awareness among the target market, in conjunction with a 10 percent awareness goal for merchandising and a 5 percent awareness goal for publicity. When you combine advertising media with merchandising and publicity, the awareness contributions of each tool added together are not just the sum of the three media. Rather there is a multiplier effect. What is the multiple progression effect on awareness and attitude from the combination of media advertising, merchandising, and publicity? We believe it is more than just the 25 percent awareness additive sum of the three tools just discussed. No one can really determine the specific multiplier effect. However, our experience tells us that when we do a good job in one medium and then add another communication vehicle, the cumulative effect on sales is almost always positive. We do believe there is a cumulative effect on awareness, attitude, and thus usage.

5. *Communication effects are difficult to measure.* Another problem in the attempt to plan the effects of communication and behavior relates to measurement. How much does a store's display affects awareness and attitude inside the store? How much effect does a personal sales presentation have in the awareness and attitude toward the product? What effect does sampling a product have on attitude? Accordingly, it's difficult to measure the effects of communication and behavior on each other. When it is possible to measure effectiveness, it is difficult to project these findings when planning in different product and market environments.

Keep in mind that, while the interactive communication behavior process is very complex, the proposed planning method is, by design, relatively simple in order to help you cope with the complexities. This approach does not take into consideration all elements of this very involved process. However, no method will ever be totally comprehensive or flawless when you are dealing with human behavior and communication. Nevertheless, this basic approach will give you an opportunity to at least circle the challenges in terms of basic understanding and deal with the very subjective nature of this planning task by providing a man-ageable framework that is a disciplined and step-by-step method. The net result is a process that will literally force you to allocate your marketing resources on a priority basis.

We arrived at this method after reviewing many application cases and primary and secondary research data and after much trial and error. This method has many assumptions and estimates for specific areas where hard data are not available. It is at this point that we have applied our experiences and intuitive judgments to arrive at what we believe is a workable method. Accordingly, we remind you that, while much of this method is directional and represents only a starting point in your communication planning, it does help order the many diverse elements into a meaningful framework, which you can then adapt to your individual product and specific market situation.

DOS AND DON'TS

Do

- Understand that the relationship between communications and behavior is very complex and that, while awareness and attitude affect behavior, behavior also affects attitude and awareness.
- Remember, the Four A's principle is the key not only to introducing and sustaining a product but also to identifying problems such as why awareness or knowledge of your product is not growing or sales is declining.
- Understand the communication control challenges and shortcomings of the goal-setting method to most realistically and effectively apply this method for your product.
- Start now (if you haven't already) to gather cause-and-effect information regarding your product, competition, and industry category.
- Review secondary sources for data on the impact of various communication tools on awareness and attitudes.
- To best apply the communication goal-setting approach, use the findings from survey research whenever possible.
- After detailing the sales objectives and target market segments, go through the exercise of locking marketing objectives numerically to purchase intent, attitude, and awareness to best determine what will be required from each of your tactical tools in order to develop a marketing plan that will fulfill the sales objectives.
- Review the tactical tool value goals before you develop each tactical segment of the marketing plan as described in the following chapters in order to most accurately develop each tactical segment and effectively interface the tactical tools with one another.
- Use your communication objectives at the end of each year to help you piece together where you were successful and where you failed. You can use this information as valuable input for the next year.

Don't

- Don't expect predetermined action without adequate awareness and positive attitude levels among consumers in your target market.
- If you do not follow the steps to arrive at and fulfill the communication objectives, don't expect to effectively lock the marketing objectives and your positioning to the tactical tools.
- Don't expect to fully reap the benefits of the interlocking marketing planning approach unless you first thoroughly immerse yourself in the experiences for

the product, the target market, the direct competition, the industry category, and related categories.
- Don't apply the 50 Percent Happening approach as gospel. It is only a starting point to use if you do not have the directional data from your own product experience to determine the purchase behavior, purchase intent, attitude, and awareness percentage levels for your target market.
- Don't expect your value goals to remain constant once you have set them. Expect to change them as you prepare the tactical tools portion of your marketing plan.

The Successful Marketing Plan

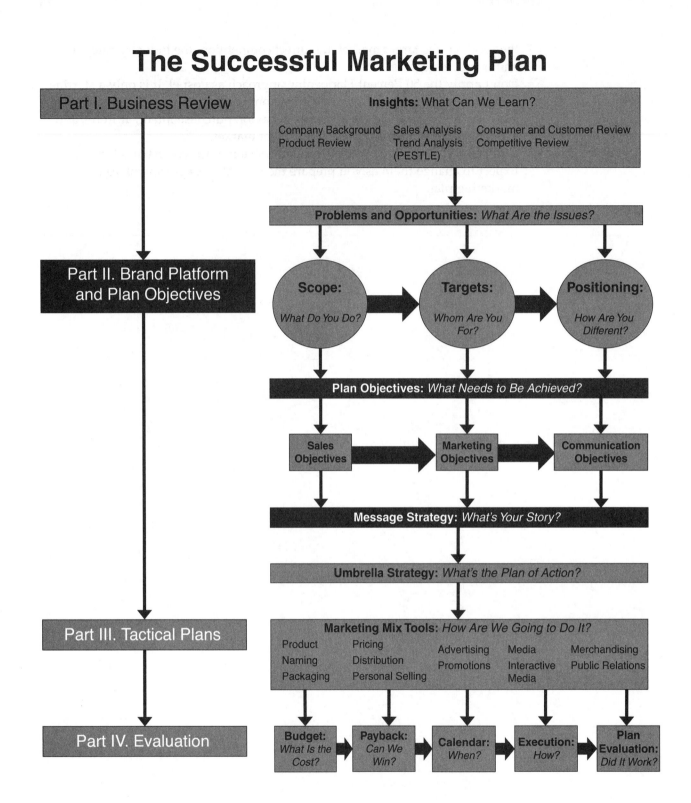

Part I. Business Review

Insights: What Can We Learn?

Company Background   Sales Analysis   Consumer and Customer Review
Product Review   Trend Analysis   Competitive Review
           (PESTLE)

Problems and Opportunities: *What Are the Issues?*

Part II. Brand Platform and Plan Objectives

Scope:

What Do You Do?

Targets:

Whom Are You For?

Positioning:

How Are You Different?

Plan Objectives: *What Needs to Be Achieved?*

Sales Objectives

Marketing Objectives

Communication Objectives

Message Strategy: *What's Your Story?*

Umbrella Strategy: *What's the Plan of Action?*

Part III. Tactical Plans

Marketing Mix Tools: *How Are We Going to Do It?*

Product   Pricing
Naming   Distribution   Advertising   Media   Merchandising
Packaging   Personal Selling   Promotions   Interactive   Public Relations
                                                            Media

Part IV. Evaluation

Budget:
What Is the Cost?

Payback:
Can We Win?

Calendar:
When?

Execution:
How?

Plan Evaluation:
Did It Work?

CHAPTER 10 Message Strategy

The messaging strategy establishes how you will communicate your brand positioning to your targets across all your marketing mix tools. We like to think of this as defining the story that you will tell—because in the end, the best communicators are really the best storytellers. One of the best ways to understand the concept of message strategy is to think about Volvo. What's the one thing that Volvo has been known for over the years? That's right, safety. Remember from Chapter 6, "Positioning": Own one thing and you improve perception across many.

Now stop for a moment and in your mind create three different ways to tell the Volvo safety story. By doing so, you will actually be creating message strategies. In case you've developed writer's block, here are a few we came up with while you were thinking:

1. Demonstrate safety through a story of better materials, better steel, safer air bags, better brakes.
2. Demonstrate safety through testimonials from people who have been in serious accidents and have simply walked away.
3. Demonstrate safety through a story about scientific safety tests.
4. Or maybe, the emotional way is the best way in. Demonstrate safety by connecting with moms and identifying with them in their number one concern: taking care of their family and especially their children.

The first two above used rational message strategies that probably would rely on product or brand news to communicate the positioning of safety. They attempted to connect to the target audience's head, or rational thinking process. The third one used a combination of rational and emotional messaging. The fourth one used an emotional message strategy that attempted to forge a stronger connection to the target audience's heart. As we discussed in Chapter 6, brands evoke both rational and emotional connections. The human being rationalizes with the brain but feels with the heart.

You need to understand the emotional and the rational aspects of your brand and the key communications drivers within the industry category where your brand competes.

For example, clear, simple, and concise communications of brand or product news can often move consumers to switch their purchase behavior in categories like packaged goods. Moms shopping for a new laundry detergent, for example, are making a relatively shallow decision in a short time frame.

In contrast, when the target audience is making a deeper decision over a longer period of time—like buying a car, choosing a college to attend, or planning a vacation trip—some combination of rational and emotional approaches might be more effective. The window manufacturer that we cited in Chapter 6 might tell an emotional story about how its windows enhance the beauty of your family home. But it also might choose to support that story with more specific messages about its craftsmanship and design. We'll talk more about these communications drivers in Chapter 16, "Advertising Content."

However, whenever possible, we will fall into the camp of trying to develop emotional message strategies supported with rational facts. As in all things marketing, there are no hard-and-fast rules, and the cookie-cutter approach doesn't work. But we do know communicating ideas about your company that create a labyrinth of emotional ties to the target will create differentiation that is difficult for competitors to duplicate and market against.

You also need to make decisions about the simplicity or complexity of your go-to-market messaging framework.

You may decide that you have one simple brand message targeted to one easy-to-reach audience segment. You may believe that you have the time, resources, and budget to send out multiple messages to a broad target audience segment. Or, as is more and more often the case with today's atomized customers, you may choose to send out multiple messages to multiple segments, all supporting one central story for your brand.

Exhibit 10.1 outlines these choices.

Getting back to our Volvo example, Volvo could choose to put out one message, let's say the nuts and bolts about why its cars are safer, targeted to a narrow niche target of male-oriented safety geeks. Or it could put out one emotional message targeted broadly to young adult parents. Or with the same target audience, it might put out multiple messages linking its car safety to children and family across multiple phases of the fairly long automobile

EXHIBIT 10.1

Go-to-Market Messaging Options

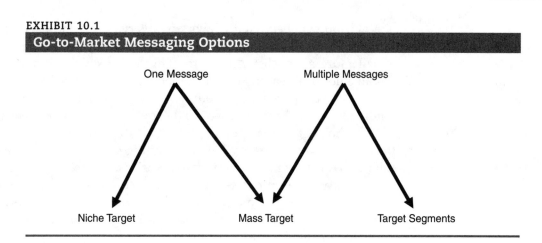

purchase cycle: consideration, comparison shopping, and actual buying. Finally, with its different models and price points, it could choose to craft multiple messages to multiple target audience segments: safety geeks, young adult parents, empty nesters, and so on.

FROM THIS CHAPTER YOU WILL LEARN

- How to determine the key message or messages that tell your brand's story
- Ways to turn your brand messaging strategy into a platform idea
- Why words matter
- Approaches to message testing

OVERVIEW

We all have great admiration for storytellers. Since the beginning of civilized time, stories have been used to communicate. They have been used to keep alive the history of tribes, and they have helped people pass down traditions, cultures, mores, and even the critical learning that ensured survival. Why stories? Because they were the most effective way to make sure people remembered all the information—or more importantly, the main ideas. The point is, people remember ideas. They do not remember excruciating details.

Every strong brand has an interesting story; if it did not, it would be forgotten. That story is wrapped into the real reason the brand is so exciting to consumers. If you turn the message strategy work you do here into a science or math project, or worse, the balancing of your checking account, you'll fail miserably. We talked about how branding is "the speak of the heart." Message strategy is determining for your company exactly *what* to say. Remember, you're not doing this just for you. The message strategy will be used by everyone who is developing communications to your internal or external audiences.

Now you may be saying, "I work in a very boring industry. There's no emotion in what we do." We politely say, "You're not really getting what we're saying." Our e-mail addresses are listed at the front of the book. Give us a try. Whatever you do has an emotional reason your customers are buying. Challenge us.

Let's take the purchasing agent who says, "All my customers want is price. My whole job is to make sure they have the lowest price." We know from working with clients who are targeting purchasing agents that price is critical. They have to be in the ballpark because that's what they get judged on come review and compensation time. However, there are many parts to price and cost. You might have the lowest cost, but your failure rate is high, you don't deliver on time, and you extract an ounce of blood every time someone deals with you. These hidden costs don't go unnoticed. The emotional reason someone might deal with someone else at just a bit higher price could be one of these:

> "The other purchasing agent is far more efficient and saves me time, lots of it. That translates to my being able to see my son's baseball games on a regular basis or getting home at a reasonable hour."
>
> "Another purchasing agent always delivers products on time, on budget, and with a failure rate of 0.0005. That translates to absolutely no time on my part returning products, dealing with complaints, or filling out additional paperwork."

We could go on, but you get the picture. There's an emotional reason for buying decisions and loyalty for what you're marketing. You just have to dig deep enough to understand the consumer emotions involved with the pain if something goes wrong, the gain when things go right, and the ego boost you can provide with your product or service.

TURNING YOUR BRAND MESSAGE STRATEGY INTO A GREAT BRAND PLATFORM IDEA

Bob Greenberg, head of the digital marketing company R/GA, is a terrific iconoclast in our industry. His writings often point out how communications strategies in general tend to flow from the teaching and thinking of storytelling. He pushes his firm, however, to go beyond mere storytelling and to focus on evolving the brand's story into a platform idea, an idea that becomes symbolic, iconic, and visceral. It works in the same way that archetypes work. His examples, Nike and Apple, demonstrate how their brand promises go beyond traditional marketing communications to become platforms for ideas, products, channels, and organizational behavior. That's the power of communications and how they can affect intangible assets.

The way to transform your brand position and message strategy into a platform idea is always a creative exploration. The key is to find the best way to connect to your positioning. That seems obvious, but how do you do this?

Great platform ideas are based on insights. So what's an insight? One of our planners describes it this way: "It's a *new* piece of information about the way an audience interacts with a brand, product, or category." But maybe an insight isn't a new piece of information but a new way of interpreting existing information. The effect is not so much "I never knew that" as "I never thought of it that way before."

General Electric, for example, has developed a platform idea based on an internal insight. Their "story inside" was that people who worked at GE used their imagination to come up with solutions that would profoundly change everything from the quality of health care to the quality of the air. This story became the heart of everything associated with the GE brand, from low-noise jet engines to energy-saving wind turbines to medical technology capable of detecting the onset of Alzheimer's disease. GE's communications strategists and outside agencies created a powerful platform idea for the brand, based on this internal insight: "Imagination at Work."

One of our favorite authors on brand strategy, Allen Adamson of the Landor Associates branding company, describes an insight as "a universally accepted truth hiding in plain sight." He often cites in his books how Johnson & Johnson leveraged a powerful insight around the "sea change" a new mother goes through. J&J's story is that it, better than any other brand, understands that "Having a Baby Changes Everything." (We once delivered this point during our classroom lecture and noticed a brand new mom smiling from ear to ear and nodding along in agreement.)

Insights are obtained mostly from talking, observing, and listening to the intended target market. But they can also come from the product itself, a corporate vision, the category, and often more important, popular culture.

To help you understand the concept of how insights lead to an effective message strategy and platform ideas, we've included a number of different ways to get you thinking from our own client experiences over the years.

Product Insight as a Key Difference Maker That Connected to the Positioning: Hostess

Situation: In the late 1990s, the Hostess brand of Twinkies, Ding Dongs, Snowballs, and other great treats was in great decline after marketing efforts had been abandoned. Moms remembered the brand in a nostalgic way. Kids liked the taste but didn't think the products were cool.

Positioning: The brand and its products were positioned around the attribute of cream filling and the key benefit of *fun.*

Insight: Our research showed that kids would typically break open a Twinkie or cupcake and then use a finger to swipe out some cream filling or lick it out before eating the rest of the cake.

Message strategy: Our Clio, Effie, and Golden Marble award-winning strategy began with an all-consuming cry: "Where's the Cream Filling?" Messaging focused on the products' unique shapes, fun, and ultimately, that delicious cream filling that only Hostess products provided.

Platform idea: "Where's the Cream Filling?"

Cultural Insight That Led to Key Words in the Message: General Mills Whole Grain

Situation: In the mid-2000s, General Mills found itself losing ready-to-eat cereal business as the low-carbohydrate eating craze exploded. Right around that same time, the U.S. Department of Agriculture (USDA) was about to launch a "new and improved" Food Pyramid, and its release would mark a radical change from its decades-old guidelines. One of the biggest changes was a decreased emphasis on protein and an increased emphasis on fruits, vegetables, and whole grains.

Positioning: General Mills cereals are healthier because they are the only line of cereals completely converted to containing *whole grains*. The two key words were *whole grains*.

Insight: Most people have heard about whole grains. Many know that whole grains are good for them. But few realize just how important whole grains are, or where to find them.

Message strategy: "Wake up to the News!" By creatively delivering this important information, we made all of this part of the "morning" news while positioning Big G cereals as the easy solution. The message used information gleaned from studies and health articles to dramatically impact how people think about whole grains. More important, the General Mills Whole Grain icon was used in all advertising and packaging and on websites.

Platform idea: Whole Grain

Source: General Mills Whole Grain® is a registered trademark of General Mills, Inc., and is used with permission.

Target Audience Attitudinal Insight That Connected to the Positioning: Toro

Situation: As technology became better and cheaper, Toro, one of the leading manufacturers of lawn and snow products, sought to create more "brand charisma" in order to help command its premium price points and distribution in key channels, like Home Depot.

Positioning: Toro had long been positioned around dependable performance, adopting the regular guy or gal archetype. The new positioning shifted the brand more toward the creator archetype, centering on a strategy of empowering customers to create their ideal outdoor living space.

Insight: We talked with Toro brand zealots (the heavy users, the ones who know the brand best and are in the best position to provide deep insights around why they love the brand). Through this research, we discovered that although they considered yard maintenance a chore, Toro brand zealots had great passion for transforming their yard into their personal space, especially when given permission to view themselves as designers of their yards.

Message strategy: The key message connected to the soul of this target audience's attitude of yardscaping. It emphasized Toro's role in helping its customers create their ideal outdoor living space: "We make the tools to help you create your ideal yard," and it encouraged them to do what they wanted to do, to love their yard.

Platform idea: "Love the Yard"

Industry Category Insight That Capitalized on a Negative Correlation: Healthy Choice

Situation: In the late 1980s, Con Agra CEO Mike Harper, recuperating from a recent heart attack, couldn't find healthy foods that tasted great. He challenged his company to develop a brand that could deliver on those two seemingly negatively correlated dimensions.

Positioning: Initially we launched and positioned the brand as a caregiver archetype that helped maintain heart health, supported by multidimensional health claims around fat, sodium, cholesterol, and calories. But over time, as the brand grew from zero to nearly $1.8 billion in sales, we evolved the positioning to capitalize more directly on the negative correlation of not having to compromise between good taste and good health. Thus Healthy Choice's archetype shifted more toward that of a liberator, allowing consumers to have their healthy cake and eat it too.

Insight: The bull's-eye market segment consumers for the Healthy Choice brand were not the most health-conscious consumers but those who were trying to find the right balance between taste and nutrition for their families. They wanted to eat healthier, but knew their families didn't want to sacrifice taste.

Message strategy: The brand proudly proclaimed that consumers no longer had to compromise between good taste and good health, culminating with the strong call to action: "Eat What You Like." That overarching promise was supported with clear, simple, and relevant nutritional information like the reduced number of grams of fat and news about exciting new product flavors and ingredients.

Platform idea: "Eat What You Like"

Industry Category Insight That Was Used as an Anti-category Message: National City

Situation: National City, a full-service banking organization headquartered in Cleveland, had built its brand around its retail- and product-oriented communications. The result was no clear, central brand story or idea to create differentiation and preference across multiple target segments and operating units.

Positioning: National City had developed a compelling brand promise: "We're the first bank that actually *cares* about doing what's right for its customers."

Insight: Consumers' negative perceptions about the banking industry had built up. When we talked with consumers, they often cited the "lack of love for the little guy," and they said that banks were "cold, mechanical, and impersonal." But when we spoke with National City brand zealots, we heard testimonials about a different kind of experience, one that wasn't filled with pain. "They have been there for me," we heard. And, "They don't treat me like a number."

Message strategy: Our strategy was to take the brand promise of caring about doing what's right for its customers and tell it through the voice of an advocate archetype. The key message was, "It's Not Just Banking. It's National City." This strategy gave the brand the ability to use "messaging judo," taking category pain points and turning them into proof points about a better banking experience.

Platform idea: "It's Not Just Banking. It's National City."

Competitive Insight That Demonstrated the Positioning: H&R Block

Situation: New competitors and disrupting technology challenged H&R Block's fundamental business model. The brand needed to create one message integrated across its multiple lines of retail and digital tax services that could increase purchase consideration.

Positioning: We created a target descriptor for the brand: the "financial outsider." This was someone of lower to middle income who didn't feel that there were tax and financial institutions "on their side." Their nose was pressed up against the glass, on the outside looking in. H&R Block's fundamental promise was to become the advocate for "middle American financial outsiders," a brand that would put their customers' interests before profit and take action on their behalf.

Insight: The insight was simple and clear. What if every day, normal people, people with very different needs, could say, like wealthier folks, that they had "people" for tax and financial matters? Leveraging "people" allowed H&R Block to showcase its unique, competitive point of difference: more than 100,000 expertly trained tax professionals.

Message strategy: We tied our message strategy back to the core positioning of advocacy: "With H&R Block, you can have an expert on your side, an expert that works for you."

Platform idea: "With H&R Block, You Got People."

WHY WORDS MATTER

When it comes to messaging strategies, and the ultimate creative expression of those strategies, words matter. Think of the power in the two words General Mills chose to leverage and capitalize on a cultural shift toward healthier eating: Whole Grain. During its blitz to announce reformulating its cereal line to contain whole grains, sales shot up 12 percent.

So here's some history to demonstrate the power of words. In 1940, Albert Lasker, an advertising pioneer, described in a recent book as the *Man Who Sold America*, threw his support behind an emerging cause in the United States: birth control. He and his wife contributed energy, time, and money to the Birth Control Federation, which had begun to provide family-planning advice to poor groups across the country. Lasker believed strongly that this "birth control" movement, primarily driven by women, could be something "far beyond the implications of its name." His solution: two new words. "Planned Parenthood." With those words, Lasker redefined or "reframed" the message from that of preventing unwanted pregnancies to a much more optimistic and inclusive cause of family planning.

In his book *Talking Right*, author Geoffrey Nunberg makes a strong case for Republican communicators' messaging skills consistently reframing Democrats' messages during the last two decades and transforming "liberal" into a dirty word. The subtitle of his 2006 book is *How Conservatives Turned Liberalism into a Tax-Raising, Latte-Drinking, Sushi-Eating, Volvo-Driving, New York Times Reading, Body-Piercing, Hollywood-Loving Freak Show*. He suggests that we like to pretend not to be bothered with semantics, but in reality, words work strongly at a subconscious level.

Republicans' communications strategists have mastered reframing through mastering language:

"Death tax" versus "estate tax"
"Weapons of mass destruction" versus "chemical" or "nuclear weapons"
"People of faith" versus the "Christian right"
"Family values" versus "conservative values"
"Personal accounts" (Social Security) versus "private accounts"
"Insurgents" versus "guerillas"

Think about how in everyday life, the precise choice of words can alter associations around the same thing: an "upscale, suburban home":

"Executive home" (status, achievement, social standing)

versus

"McMansion" (keeping up with the Joneses, poor taste)

AVOIDING TRAPS

When developing your message strategy, choose your words carefully. Here are four common traps to avoid:

1. Don't use business-speak in your messages and brand promises. Write and think like your target.
2. Choose your key words carefully. Too many words allow misplaced emphasis.
3. Don't expect the strategy to do everything. Sacrifice.

4. Don't use big-tent words like "quality" and "solutions." They are overused and, therefore, weaker. Go to the next layer and the next when confronted with big-tent words. "Quality" might mean the attention you get from a service representative or the ability of your new running shoe to prevent heel bruising on those long runs.

As you develop your message strategy, think about words that will define your brand. Barack Obama defined his brand in the 2008 presidential election with one simple word: "hope." George W. Bush and his administration convinced the public and Congress to support our war in Iraq with four simple and powerful words: "weapons of mass destruction." Federal Express launched its business and a new category of business services leveraging superlative language: "When it absolutely, positively has to be there overnight." Flat & Scruggs, the duo who popularized "hillbilly" music, described their genre as the happiest of sad songs: "lonesome bluegrass."

TESTING MESSAGES

Sometimes it will be worth your time, energy, and money to test different approaches to messaging. The greater the stakes, risk, and financial investment behind your brand's messages, the more you may want customer input.

We often advocate an iterative approach, using both qualitative focus groups and one-on-one interviews combined with quantitative testing, either online, through mail or in-person mall intercepts. Politicians and large organizations often employ pollsters or consultants, like Dr. Frank Luntz, author of *Words That Work*, to test their messages. Luntz, for example, has tested the differences in voter appeal based on ideological labels like "liberal" versus "progressive" (the latter has more appeal).

When working for a large client that intends to spend a lot of money on a message, we might evaluate several alternatives and put them to the test. One year, for example, we wanted to help H&R Block find the best messaging strategy to communicate a new service we had created: the Double-Check Challenge. We convinced H&R Block to agree to double-check prospective clients' previous years' tax returns for free. If they found a mistake, then the client could pay H&R Block to refile an amended return.

We tested several different ways to describe the benefits of the Double-Check Challenge, which we're paraphrasing:

1. *Fear, uncertainty, and doubt:* "Last year American taxpayers made mistakes that left more than $750 million on the table. Don't be one of them."
2. *The Green Peas Approach:* "Last year when we double-checked returns and found a mistake, it averaged $1,500 in tax savings."
3. *Competitive analogy:* How many times have you done something yourself, like a home repair project or a plumbing project, only to need to hire someone to correct your mistakes later?

Year after year, the Green Peas Approach tested better. (This term was coined by one of our college speech professors, who always hammered home the point that we should turn statistics into "green peas that you can count on your plate." There's also another advantage to the Green Peas Approach: it's personalized. Messages that are optimistic, hopeful, and personalized often test better than messages that are negative and/or filled with fear, uncertainty, and doubt.

Below is an example of a messaging testing approach we took for a large health care provider that wanted to communicate an overall message of "personalization" as a strategy to sign up small businesses.

Quantitative Results

Message		Health Care Decision Makers (n=100)	Health Care Influencers (n=101)	Uniqueness	Believable	Brand Fit
9 - Personal Health Manager	We'll reward your employees to live a healthier lifestyle. Covered individuals can earn up to $125 in gift cards by working toward goals like loosing weight, managing stress, getting in better shape, and eating healthier.	45%	53%	5.87	4.74	5.31
4 - Personal Care Plans	Included within the health care coverage you offer your employees is a specialized plan that caters to an employee's (and covered family members') unique health condition, such as diabetes, asthma, or maternity. This voluntary, custom plan is designed to help your employees manage their condition and incentivize them to maintain their health. The benefit to both you and your employees is better health and reduced cost.	39%	39%	4.97	4.72	4.94
5 - Personal Care Plans	Your employees (and covered family members) can voluntarily enroll in programs like the first-of-its-kind diabetes & pre-diabetes plan. We incentivize subscribers to better manage these conditions and stay healthier. Following the plan can save $500 per year per employee/individual.	37%	28%	5.37	4.62	4.81
2 - Personal Wellness Programs	We work with each of your employees (and covered family members) to create a personal health improvement plan with realistic, actionable goals such as losing weight, smoking cessation, or decreasing blood pressure. Our personalized approach to wellness helps your people stay healthy, and helps you contain costs.	35%	42%	5.07	4.76	5.11
10 - Personalized Health Care	No two employees are alike. And neither are their health decisions. Your employees' decisions impact not only their health, but also your company's costs and productivity. To enable better decisions, our health care company is leading the way with personalized health care solutions designed to help people—and businesses—stay healthy. Better decisions lead to better results.	34%	39%	4.86	4.58	4.89
7 - Personal Cost Estimators	We provide your employees (and covered family members) cost estimates for procedures and treatments based on their coverage and location. With cost estimates in hand they can evaluate their options and choose the right provider at the right cost. Through this personalized approach, we enable better decisions that lead to reduced costs and healthier employees.	34%	23%	5.21	4.44	4.8
1 - Personal Health Assessments	Through tools like our Health Risk Assessment, we find and treat conditions before they become serious. If an employee (or covered family member) shows signs of being pre-diabetic (or other condition), a nurse will contact them and jointly they will come up with a plan to treat the condition before it becomes serious. This personal approach enables better choices that lead to reduced costs and healthier employees.	30%	33%	5.35	4.77	5.11
8 - Personal Health Records	We offer subscribers within your plan access to their health records. This includes an online "health dashboard" featuring medical history, medication records, personal health statistics, and a personal health plan. By giving your employees the tools they need, we enable them to manage their health and make better choices. Better choices lead to reduced costs and healthier employees.	28%	28%	5.26	4.94	4.9
6 - Personal Doctor Selection	We work with your employees (and covered family members) to understand their unique needs and match them with a doctor who can best help them. Getting this relationship right is foundational to enabling your employees to make better choices. Better decisions translate to lower health care costs for you and your employees.	26%	24%	4.82	4.28	4.66
3 - Personal Care Plans	Your employees (and covered family members) can voluntarily participate in programs like the first-of-its-kind diabetes & pre-diabetes plan. For diabetics, we incentivize subscribers to manage their condition through the use of regular blood sugar checks and routine exams. Effective management of diseases such as diabetes lowers health care costs and your employees stay healthier.	25%	23%	4.83	4.8	4.89

Our methodology was to conduct a quantitative messaging test to better understand the target audience's response to personalization.

We tested the messages among the following:

- 100 small business owners
- 100 influencers of small business owners

Respondents were asked to evaluate the individual messages with four criteria in mind:

- *Lead generation:* "Makes me want to learn more."
- *Brand fit:* "Everyone needs to do his or her part to fix the health care system."
- *Uniqueness*
- *Believability*

We exposed 10 personalization messages, which included some that produced reasons to believe, some that made promotional offers, and others that produced higher-level emotional benefits. The results, shown in the figure above, served as guidance in determining which messages we thought could both build brand equity while also driving traffic into Internet and telephone channels. The circled messages were the ones that we thought had the most promise.

Testing doesn't take the place of intuition. But with today's ability to conduct quick, cheap online surveys, you have fewer obstacles to prevent you from involving your target audience in the message development process.

You can test your message strategy many different ways. We've outlined two for you. You would use the first, in Exhibit 10.2, if you wanted to develop a quantitative analysis of different messages from statistically significant sample sizes. This technique uses a tape recording of two different prototype communications in audio form to drive comparisons and insights from each of two different message strategies. We often use audio because it is inexpensive and because, more important, it provides total focus on the concept. Audio allows theater of the mind. People don't judge the messages based on whether they liked the look of the actors or the colors in the ad. The respondents' main focus tends to be on the concepts being communicated.

EXHIBIT 10.2

Example of an Audio Message Strategy Survey

Note that the following is a made-up example for a hospital or health care organization. You can use a similar format and tailor it to your specific company, positioning, and subsequent message strategy.

Survey Objectives

- The objective of the message test is to gain insights into the communication values of two different advertising concepts against a new hospital brand position.
- The message test is not intended to "choose" a creative execution. Its purpose is to provide insight to make the final execution stronger in terms of effective communication and its ability to stand out and be positively noticed among the target audiences.
- Specific questions will be shaped to address the following:
  - Playback of concepts—main points
  - Presence of confusing elements
  - Likability of the communication
  - Positive and/or negative adjective checklist
  - Communication values
  - Effective communication of the hospital's brand
  - Insights into elements that make one execution more effective than the other
  - Recommendation of the hospital to a friend

Survey Execution

1. Two groups of 150. First group responds to Survey 1, which opens with Communication Piece 1. The second group responds to Survey 2, which opens with Communication Piece 2. Each survey is identical with the exception that the audio piece in the second part of the survey is the version not listened to in the opening part of the survey.
   - Women 23 to 54 with children under 18 present in the household: Quantity 100 respondents
   - Women 23 to 35 married with no children: Quantity 50 respondents
2. Eliminate respondents who have health care associations—that is, those who work for a health insurance company, hospital, or medical practice.
3. Geography—the three counties surrounding the hospital.

Statistical Notes

We will be able to, at a 95 percent confidence level, say that broad differences are significant for the total sample and most comparisons in the women-with-children segment. However, in most cases, comparisons in the women-with-no-children segment will only be directional.

Survey 1

1. Please click here to listen to an audio concept for a health care organization—think of it as a form of communication. After listening to the piece, close the viewing window and return to the survey.

   SUBMIT

2. Were you able to hear and understand the piece we just played for you?
   - Yes
   - No
   [*Programmer:* If no, terminate.]

   SUBMIT

3. List the top two or three things you most remember from what you just heard:

_____

SUBMIT

4. Was there anything confusing about this communication? That is, was there anything that was hard to understand or follow?
   ○ Yes
   ○ No
   If yes, please explain:

_____

SUBMIT

5. Of the things you remember, what was most important to you as a consumer of health care?

_____

SUBMIT

6. What do you think was the main point of the communication you heard?

_____

SUBMIT

7. What is the name of the sponsor of this communication?

_____

SUBMIT

8. Each of the following is a feeling you might or might not have received from hearing the concept piece. The exact words in each statement did not have to be present in the ad—but after hearing the communication, did you get a sense of the thought in each statement?

   From the following statements, score each one *in terms of the feeling you got from* listening to the commercial, on a scale of 1 to 5 with 1 being *not communicated* through 5 being *completely communicated*?

Compassionate

1 _____   2 _____   3 _____   4 _____   5 _____

Provides critical care

1 _____   2 _____   3 _____   4 _____   5 _____

Provides extraordinary care, every day

1 _____   2 _____   3 _____   4 _____   5 _____

Excellence in health care

1 _____   2 _____   3 _____   4 _____   5 _____

Helps me stay healthy

1 _____   2 _____   3 _____   4 _____   5 _____

I am personally involved in my health care

1 _____   2 _____   3 _____   4 _____   5 _____

This is a health care partner who is focused on me

1 _____   2 _____   3 _____   4 _____   5 _____

I have options and choices

1 _____   2 _____   3 _____   4 _____   5 _____

(Continued)

Example of an Audio Message Strategy Survey (Continued)

I'll get great care for my family

1 _____   2 _____   3 _____   4 _____   5 _____

The place to go for a lifetime of care

1 _____   2 _____   3 _____   4 _____   5 _____

I'll be treated as a person, not a number.

1 _____   2 _____   3 _____   4 _____   5 _____

SUBMIT

9. Please read through and select the words you feel describe the concept you heard. You may *select as many or as few as you like*. Let this be top of mind: Don't think about these. Simply go through the list quickly and check the ones that you feel apply.

[*Programmer:* Randomly rotate the following choices from top to bottom. Keep the sequence and pattern or the order of the words. Just rotate what comes first through last.]

- Appealing
- Annoying
- Engaging
- Dull
- Thoughtful
- Boring
- Insulting
- Memorable
- Repetitious
- Realistic
- Silly
- Original
- Trite
- Believable
- Commonplace
- Informative
- Unbelievable
- Entertaining
- Unclear
- Credible
- Uninteresting
- Exciting

SUBMIT

10. Overall, how well did you like the advertisement on a scale of 1 to 5 with 1 equaling you didn't like it at all up to 5 equaling you liked it very much.

Disliked very much

1 _____   2 _____   3 _____   4 _____   5 _____

Liked very much

1 _____   2 _____   3 _____   4 _____   5 _____

SUBMIT

11. If a friend came to you looking for a recommendation for health care, how likely would you recommend this hospital on a scale of 1 to 5 with 1 being equal to *very unlikely* up to 5 being equal to *extremely likely*?

Very unlikely

1 _____   2 _____   3 _____   4 _____   5 _____

Extremely likely

1 _____   2 _____   3 _____   4 _____   5 _____

S<small>UBMIT</small>

We're almost done. You have about 3 minutes left.

12. Now click here to listen to one more communication. After listening, please close the window and return to the survey.

S<small>UBMIT</small>

13. Which ad did you like better?
    - Concept 1, the first piece you listened to in question 1
    - Concept 2, the one you just heard

S<small>UBMIT</small>

14. Why did you feel this way?

_____

S<small>UBMIT</small>

15. Which of the communication versions was better at conveying the following thoughts, ideas, or feelings when you heard them?

	Version 1	Version 2	Both the Same	Don't Know
Excellence in health care				
Health care that feels personal				
Preventive and proactive health care				
I'm a partner in my own health care				

S<small>UBMIT</small>

A couple of demographic questions and then we're done. We thank you for your time.

16. Which age category do you fall into?
    - Under 25
    - 25 to 34
    - 35 to 44
    - 44 to 54
    - 55 to 64
    - 64+

S<small>UBMIT</small>

17. Are you single or married or living with a significant other?
    - Single
    - Married or living with significant other

S<small>UBMIT</small>

18. How many children 18 or under are in your household?
    - None
    - One
    - Two
    - Three or four
    - Five or more

S<small>UBMIT</small>

You would use the second method, in Exhibit 10.3, if you wanted to develop a qualitative analysis, doing so by testing your messaging with a focus group. Exhibit 10.3 provides an outline used in the past for Lionel Train, the model railroad company for train enthusiasts of all ages.

EXHIBIT 10.3

Example of a Discussion Guide for a Concept (Message Strategy) Focus

Lionel Train Enthusiasts' Focus Group

Introduction (15 Minutes)

1. Background on focus groups, see-through mirror, videotaping, sessions, and so on.
2. *Respondents' demographic background:* Age, occupation, and number and age of children.
3. *Respondents' railroading background:* Do they collect or run their trains in layouts? How long have they been railroading? What are their railroad interests in terms of products, periods, and/or layouts?
4. *Internet usage:* Do they have a computer and Internet access?

Railroading Benefit and Value Drivers (30 Minutes)

5. How and why did you *first* get into model railroading and/or collecting? [Probe for higher-order benefits and value systems.]
6. Why do you *continue* to collect and/or set up and run your trains? Describe how your train world is different from the rest of your world.
7. *Lionel exercise* [All of the responses from this sensory exercise should be written down on the pads provided before being discussed. Discuss one sensory item at a time.]:
   ○ I want you to think about Lionel. Now close your eyes and inhale deeply through your nose. What does Lionel smell like?
   ○ With your eyes closed again, reach out and touch Lionel. What do you feel?
   ○ Eyes still closed and thinking about Lionel, tell me what you see.
   ○ Last, with eyes closed, smack your lips and tell me what Lionel tastes like.
   ○ *Lionel personality:* If Lionel were a person—could be a celebrity, an athlete, a politician, a person you know, or anyone—who would it be and why? [Have them write responses on a pad before discussing. Give example—for example, Jim Carrey for Pepsi.]
   ○ Describe Lionel as a style of music.
8. Complete these sentences:
   ○ Model railroading and/or collecting makes me feel . . .
   ○ The coolest thing about trains is . . .

Line Reaction (25 Minutes)

9. Another railroad hobbyist used the line "real serious fun." What do you think he meant? What does this line say to you?
10. How important are these concepts or meanings to you?
11. What were your gut reactions when you first heard this line? "When I first heard 'real serious fun,' it made me think of . . . ." Why?
12. Let's dissect this line. [Probe for power and nostalgia connotations.]:
    ○ Let's say you thought this line says it all about training. "This line is great because . . ."
    ○ Let's say you thought this was the most awful line. "This line stinks because . . ."
13. Is Lionel "real serious fun"? [Discuss pros and cons of the line in connection with Lionel.]

Visual Explorations (45 Minutes)

14. [Set up a transition.] Time to stop talking for a minute, and I have some things for you to look at. [Spread out all visuals around the room, and give the participants three to four minutes to look at them with no context provided.]
15. With pads in hand, walk around the room and jot down the numbers of the three pictures you like the most and the three pictures you like the least. I am looking for your initial gut reactions regarding likes and dislikes. [Have them read their selections and write them down on a big pad. Arrange the pictures into piles, and discuss reasons for likes and dislikes.]
16. Write down on your pads the two or three pictures that say "real serious fun" to you and the ones that are furthest from "real serious fun." [Write down on a big pad, and arrange and discuss.]

17. Now let's go around the room one more time and write down on your pads the two or three pictures that say "Lionel" to you and the ones that are the furthest from your image of what Lionel is all about. [Write down on a big pad; arrange and discuss.]

Wrap-up (15 Minutes)

18. If you were to boil down what Lionel stands for in one word, what would it be?

See also Appendix C, Worksheet 39.

DOS AND DON'TS

Do

- Make your message strategy a bridge to your positioning.
- Think about the simplicity or complexity your go-to-market messaging needs: one message to one audience, several messages to one audience, many messages to several audiences.
- Develop your message strategy based on insights into your target's behavior to ensure that your advertising fulfills the emotional as well as the rational needs of the target.
- Seek to create a *platform idea*—that is, an idea that provides the strategic link to your positioning and an idea that becomes symbolic, iconic, and visceral.
- Develop and evaluate alternative message strategies before choosing one. If possible, test the message strategies with the target before choosing a final one.

Don't

- Don't let your message strategy change the meaning of your positioning. It should simply provide a tightly focused way to communicate your positioning.
- Don't ignore the importance of words in conveying your message. Words matter.

The Successful Marketing Plan

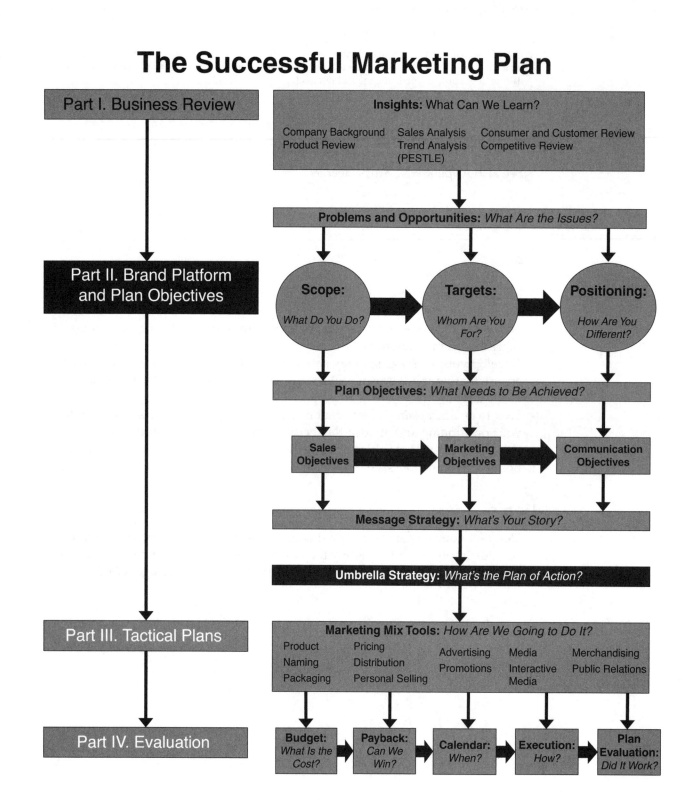

Part I. Business Review

Insights: What Can We Learn?

Company Background   Sales Analysis   Consumer and Customer Review
Product Review   Trend Analysis   Competitive Review
                     (PESTLE)

Problems and Opportunities: What Are the Issues?

Part II. Brand Platform and Plan Objectives

Scope:
What Do You Do?

Targets:
Whom Are You For?

Positioning:
How Are You Different?

Plan Objectives: What Needs to Be Achieved?

Sales Objectives

Marketing Objectives

Communication Objectives

Message Strategy: What's Your Story?

Umbrella Strategy: What's the Plan of Action?

Part III. Tactical Plans

Marketing Mix Tools: How Are We Going to Do It?

Product   Pricing   Advertising   Media   Merchandising
Naming   Distribution   Promotions   Interactive   Public Relations
Packaging Personal Selling   Media

Part IV. Evaluation

Budget:
What Is the Cost?

Payback:
Can We Win?

Calendar:
When?

Execution:
How?

Plan Evaluation:
Did It Work?

11 Umbrella Strategy

One last step and you'll be done with the strategy portion of your plan, the brand platform. In this chapter, you will be developing what we refer to as "umbrella strategies." If someone asks you, "What common things need to be done across target markets, marketing objectives, communication objectives, brand positioning, and message strategies for you to succeed in meeting your sales goals?" this is your answer—the umbrella strategies. They answer the question, What's the plan of action?

The umbrella strategies provide direction for your overall plan, while the marketing mix tools provide tactics that are specific to the individual target market segment and corresponding marketing objectives. The graphic in Exhibit 11.1 is the same one you saw in Chapter 8, "Marketing Objectives." It is also helpful here to demonstrate the concept behind the umbrella strategies. As you will notice, when it comes time to execute your marketing plan, the brand positioning, message strategies, and umbrella strategies are responsible to the whole plan. These elements are in place to help collectively accomplish all the objectives that are individually detailed above them but also give guidance to the individual tactical plans below them.

After you complete this last section of the brand platform, you will move on to the tactical portion of the marketing plan. Unlike the umbrella strategies that provide direction for the whole plan, the individual tactical plans are tailored to accomplishing specific marketing and communication objectives to which they are assigned. (See the marketing mix tools section of the "Successful Marketing Plan" chart found at the beginning of this chapter.)

In summary, the umbrella strategies are also the place in the plan to which you return continually to make sure your organization understands the big picture because, as we always say to clients, "If you don't know where you're going, most roads will take you somewhere else!"

EXHIBIT 11.1

How Marketing Objectives Are Interlocked

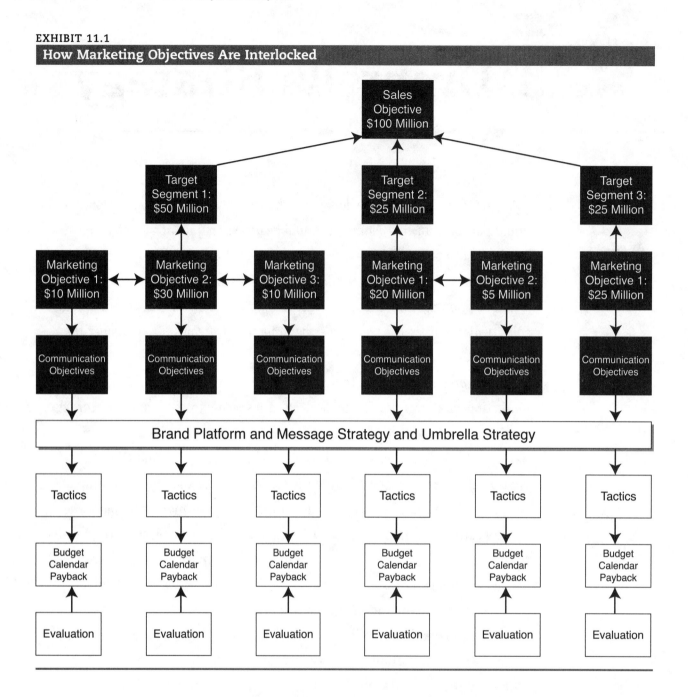

FROM THIS CHAPTER YOU WILL LEARN

- The definition and role of marketing strategies
- Different strategy alternatives to consider in your plan
- How to develop and write your marketing strategies

OVERVIEW

An umbrella marketing strategy is a broad directional statement indicating how you will go about accomplishing your marketing plan. While marketing objectives are specific, quantifiable, and measurable, marketing strategies are *descriptive*.

Within your plan, the umbrella marketing strategies represent top-level decision making. The most commonly addressed strategy issues are discussed in this chapter. Here are two hints for reading this chapter:

1. You should give particular consideration to the first 5 strategy areas that are discussed as decisions in these areas tend to be the most universal to all businesses.
2. In the end, you should address only what is most appropriate for your particular situation. You will most likely end up with somewhere in the range of 8 to 10 key umbrella strategies that will drive common activities in your plan and also lead you to decide which marketing mix tools you will use for specific target segments and subsequent marketing and communication objectives.

Listed below are the 19 different strategy considerations we recommend you consider for inclusion in your umbrella strategies:

1. Target market strategies
2. Pricing strategies: Low cost or differentiation?
3. Building the market or stealing market share?
4. National, regional, and local market strategies
5. Growth and product strategies
6. Naming strategies
7. Packaging strategies
8. Seasonality strategies
9. Spending strategies
10. Competitive strategies
11. Distribution of product and penetration or coverage strategies
12. Personal selling, service, and operations strategies
13. Promotions and events strategies
14. Advertising strategies
15. Media strategies
16. Interactive media strategies
17. Merchandising strategies
18. Public relations strategies
19. Marketing research and testing (R&T) strategies

See also Worksheet 40 in Appendix C.

SPECIFIC UMBRELLA STRATEGIES AND EXAMPLES OF HOW TO APPLY THEM

The following provides a review of umbrella strategy approaches you should consider, as well as marketing strategy examples to get you started.

Target Market Strategies

Your targets section in the brand platform detailed primary and secondary target markets. You must now discuss the emphasis you will place against the various target segments and how you will market to them based on your marketing objectives, which defined the purchase behavior you intend to gain from the targets.

For example, consumer goods or business-to-business firms may decide to target heavy users through the use of a specific product in the product line that has proven appeal to heavy users. A retailer may choose to target a secondary target market only through in-store incentives or point-of-purchase promotional techniques, saving all mass media expenditures for the primary target market. Your company may have recently revised your primary target market to include the heavy users who may have shopped your product only as a second choice in the past. A target market strategy must reflect this change in target market description. This strategy to target primarily the heavy users in all marketing mix decisions affects all subsequent marketing strategies and individual marketing mix tool plans.

Examples of Target Market Strategies

Strategy example: Target women 25 to 54 with children through an emphasis on pediatrics expertise and leadership.

Rationale: Women make 75 to 80 percent of all health care decisions in a family. Mothers tend to align their health care decisions around their choice of a pediatrician. This medical center, associated with a regional HMO, was rated highly on its pediatric care, and it aimed to take advantage of this target.

Additional examples:
- Target only the heavy-purchasing dealers—those that account for over 70 percent of the company's business through highly personalized "top to top" interactions—one-on-one consultative selling and special events tailored to each customer.
- Target the primary target market through the entire spectrum of marketing mix tactical tools. Target the secondary target market only through in-store marketing activities.

Pricing Strategies: Low Cost or Differentiation?

Another important strategic decision comes down to one of four choices. Michael Porter in his classic book *Competitive Advantage* states, "There are two basic types of competitive advantage a firm can possess: low cost or differentiation."* As you can see in Exhibit 11.2, both low cost and differentiation have two options for market focus: broad target and narrow target, or niche focus. Will you depend on service or on the differentiated product benefits for a competitive edge with price being a distant secondary consideration? Or will you depend on the advantage of a low price?

Differentiation

Differentiation is about owning some benefit that is highly valued to the purchasers and influencer targets. In doing so, the company is rewarded by being able to charge a higher price, capture higher margins, and retain loyal customers who

EXHIBIT 11.2

Pricing Strategy: Low Cost or Differentiation?		
	Low Cost	**Differentiation**
Broad Target	Cost leadership	Differentiation
Narrow Target	Cost leadership	Differentiation

Source: Michael E. Porter, *Competitive Advantage: Creating and Sustaining Superior Performance*, Free Press/Simon & Schuster, New York, 1985.

---

* Michael E. Porter, *Competitive Advantage: Creating and Sustaining Superior Performance*, Free Press/Simon & Schuster, New York, 1985.

become champions of the company's brands often because of emotional benefits they perceive through purchasing and connecting with the company and/or brand. This strategy should be consistent with the direction you chose in your positioning and target segment decisions earlier in the brand platform work.

If you will be depending on differentiation, you have two choices to follow. One is broad differentiation of your product or company concept across a large mass market; the other is differentiation through a singular focus on a narrow niche target market. Price always plays some factor, and rare is the company that can charge anything it wants. However, price is not what Microsoft, Apple, Columbia (sportswear), Starbucks, Accenture, Pella Windows, BMW, and a host of other well-known brands are selling to their broad target markets. Additionally, other companies or brands take the differentiation strategy and target small niches and focus on a narrow target market segment within an industry. Examples would be Seven Cycles' focus on the high-end road cyclist who values a quality handmade titanium frame tailored to the cyclists' exact body specs—the ultimate ride. Other examples of a differentiated company and products with a narrow target focus include Prada and Burt's Bees (beauty products positioned as earth friendly). It's not just small and midsize companies that follow a more segmented, narrow target differentiation product strategy. Hewlett-Packard has targeted the smaller home office segment with a machine that copies, prints, faxes, and scans—an all in one machine—while focusing on single-function products for the larger commercial market. In a final example, while the Coca-Cola brand differentiates its product across a large mass market, it has several smaller niche products that depend on a very narrow target focus such as Powerade, which is aimed at young athletes who need hydration, and the very focused Odwalla, a natural health beverage featuring dairy-free shakes and organic juices.

Low Cost

The other option is to follow a low-cost strategy. Implicit in this strategy is that you will be the low-cost producer and provider, resulting in the benefit to your customers of being the day-in and day-out lowest price for a similar or even better product. Low price requires the ability of the company to achieve economies of scale, to have some proprietary technology, to have the necessary raw materials, and/or to have a culture that allows the company to contain costs such that it can charge lower prices while still making the desired profits.

If the low-price strategy emerges from your planning efforts, you again have two choices: broad market or narrow market focus. Remember that history shows there can usually be only one low-price leader. When there is more than one competitor aiming to be the lowest price, the competitive environment becomes very aggressive, and there is a contested battle over every point of market share. Typically over time, only one firm wins this battle. Walmart is a good example of an industry leader that preemptively dominates its category on the price attribute.

Price as a Short-Term Strategy

Price can also be used strategically to spark temporary new trial. Will you consider temporarily allowing for lower margins and lower prices to develop trial? Additionally, will your pricing be consistent nationally? Or will it vary market by market, store by store, or customer by customer?

Examples of Low-Cost Strategies

Strategy example: Follow a differentiated strategy and premium pricing, targeting a narrow segment of boaters who depend on quick acceleration of their boat for the categories of competitive fishing contests and water skiing.

Rationale: The research showed high demand for the new five-blade prop from Mercury Marine among two very targeted segments—fishermen who wanted to quickly get from one hole to the next in fishing tournaments and water skiers who depended on quick acceleration to get out of the water without a tremendous amount of drag.

Strategy example: Maintain slight differentiated premium pricing approach (based on appropriately fitting printing jobs to capabilities) to existing customers, where service and quality are more important than price. Use competitive pricing to gain trial and entry into the new customers' printing "pool."

Rationale: Research indicated that price is an important element of a customer's decision as to whether or not to initially try a printer. Further, the research also revealed that the decision to continue a relationship with a printer was based primarily on print quality and service and only secondarily on price.

Additional example: Utilize a premium-price strategy for the new line extension of black olives. At the same time increase the existing green olive product to premium prices to be more consistent with the overall company premium, differentiated product positioning of olives grown in the European tradition.

Building the Market or Stealing Market Share?

A critical strategic decision facing all marketers writing a plan is whether to build the market or steal share from competitors in order to achieve sales goals. The information regarding product awareness and attributes in your business review, and the product life cycle specifically, will help provide answers to this fundamental question.

A situation with a relatively new product where the current user base is small, the potential user base is quite large, and there is little competition often requires a "build-the-market" strategy. Many times, the company that creates the market maintains the largest market share long into the future, but not indefinitely. An example of this would be Miller Lite, which created demand for low-calorie beer. Miller established the light beer category, and it was the market share leader for decades. However, remember that it is usually easier to steal market share than to build the market, as Miller Lite can attest. Accordingly, as of the writing of this book, Bud Light and Coors have passed Miller Lite in sales by stealing share of the light beer market Miller built.

Because it is a two-step process, building a market takes additional time and money. You have to develop a need for the product and then convince a target market to purchase your particular brand. Many companies intentionally take a "second-to-market" product development strategy. They allow someone else to invest in building the market, and then they introduce their brand.

In a situation in which the product is a mature one with minimal growth (that is, few new customers entering the marketplace), stealing market share from competitors is often called for. In this situation you have to convince product category users that your product is superior to that of your competition. In some cases, the market may be growing, which allows your firm to grow along with it. In this case, the question becomes, "Is the market growing at the same rate I want to grow?" If the answer is no, then you will still need to steal share from your competition. All of these scenarios would be described in the market share strategy.

EXHIBIT 11.3

Building the Market

Market situation	New product, small initial user base, large untapped potential user base
Competitive situation	Limited competition
Target focus	Broad target market
Communication objective	Build awareness
Communication objective	Educate consumers primarily about the benefits of the product category, secondarily about the company and its products
Marketing objective	Induce initial trial

EXHIBIT 11.4

Stealing Market Share

Market situation	Mature product, limited growth potential among users who are new to the category
Competitive situation	Highly competitive, many competitors
Target focus	Move to segments and even niche targets
Communication objective	Maintain awareness
Communication objective	Persuade, provide strong competitive points of differentiation in communication tactics or focus on promotions to steal share
Marketing objectives	Retention of customers critical; increase existing customer business; steal market share from competitors

Exhibits 11.3 and 11.4 provide a snapshot of the market situations and some of the varying marketing and communication objectives you would consider under each scenario—building the market or stealing market share.

The decision of whether to build the market or steal market share must be made up front in your marketing strategy section, as this is a very fundamental strategic decision that will affect all other areas of the marketing plan. A stealing-market-share strategy, such as "steal market share from the leading competitor," requires a very focused target market definition as the highly competitive environment means that companies have sliced up the market and are providing a high degree of specialization against various target segments. Also, the advertising will either communicate specific benefits or an emotional positioning that will allow you to demonstrate a strong point of differentiation in order to retain your existing customers and compete for new ones, or it will move to highly promotional communications in order to induce purchase. This is in sharp contrast to a building-the-market strategy where the goal is to build demand for a new product or category and in doing so, become the market leader. A building-the-market strategy often requires first educating new customers about the benefits of product category usage and then convincing them to use your company's products.

Examples of Building-the-Market and Stealing-Market-Share Strategies

Building-the-market strategy example: Build the market for the new Diaper Genie diaper pail as a gift at baby showers.

Rationale: Research showed that Americans especially were adverse to odors. When introduced, the new product represented a whole new category in diaper disposal. It was felt that the best chance at introduction was to build the market through positioning the product as the new, innovative baby shower gift, giving a reason to buy the gift but also exposing it to a captive audience typically also in the target segment. (Historical context: product was introduced in the 1990s and successfully built the diaper pail category eventually selling to Playtex.)

Stealing-market-share strategy example: Focus on stealing share from other retailers selling off-price branded apparel with a strong appeal to always finding something new because of the rapid inventory turnover and fresh product.

Rationale: The company is not competing on price; instead, it will use the successfully tested appeal of high turnover of inventory, something new every time you stop to look, to induce trial and steal share from other similarly positioned value retailers in the midtier.

National, Regional, and Local Market Strategies

This marketing strategy category should not be—although it often is—overlooked by national and regional marketers. This strategy helps marketers determine whether there will be a core national marketing plan or a combination of national, regional, and local marketing plans. Having a combination of plans requires a lot of work, but it is usually worth the effort. This strategy recognizes the differences between regional, Designated Market Areas (DMAs) or television viewing areas, metropolitan areas, and even local trading areas by allowing for the application of specific territorial marketing programs.

If you are a retailer, for example, you may have a national marketing program as an overlay, with special DMA plans in addition to specific local marketing programs for each store.

If you are a national packaged-goods company, it may be that, to accomplish your marketing objective of increasing new trial by 10 percent, you need to develop a national marketing program. However, to help guarantee your success, you will place special marketing and spending emphasis on specific markets that have demonstrated the potential to grow at far greater rates when given local, tailored types of marketing programs. These local marketing programs often have their own plans with specific marketing objectives and strategies. For instance, the Madison, Wisconsin, and Ann Arbor, Michigan, markets may receive special promotions that are proven sales generators in Midwest college towns, while Chicago may receive extra media spending because of its dense metropolitan size, sales potential, and the amount of advertising clutter in the marketplace. Such an approach allows marketers to tailor the media, message, and spending levels to specific markets. It is important to allocate your marketing resources geographically, particularly when geography is a key variable of purchase rates in your target market. Review the CDI and BDI calculations in the purchase rates and buying habits section of the business review, discussed in Chapter 2.

Examples of National, Regional, and Local Market Strategies

Strategy example (for a printing company located in Wisconsin): Concentrate marketing efforts on customers who purchase directly—versus those that purchase through advertising and/or design agencies—in Wisconsin first, then in the immediate Midwest (Michigan, Minnesota, and Illinois), followed by advertising agencies in the remainder of the United States.

Rationale: All objectives have a local (Wisconsin), regional (Michigan, Minnesota, and Illinois), and national component, and marketing efforts will mirror that.

This "pyramid" essentially allows the marketer—a high-end commercial printer—to focus on direct customers in areas of high potential nearby, where the sales force can most effectively create intimate service relationships to individual companies. This would be followed up with concentrated selling efforts against targeted larger advertising agencies outside of the company's local territory to take advantage of the multiple customer scale opportunities agencies provide.

Additional examples:

- Develop a unified corporate, national in scope, marketing program with all efforts leveraged against one common advertising campaign and dealer sell-in program.
- In addition to the national marketing program, develop a local dealer-marketing program with "turnkey" marketing programs (from "how-tos" to creative material for implementation) designed to meet specific objectives (increase trial, increase retrial, increase dollars per transaction, and so on). This would allow for some local decision making and implementation around those activities seen as most beneficial to each specific market.

Growth and Product Strategies

Products and services are what you sell; they are the tangible worth of the company to your customers. Yet they don't stay static. Products are invented, they evolve, substitutes and alternative products sometimes make existing products irrelevant, and a mature market finds many product line extensions and niche products that appeal to narrower and narrower target segments. You must make strategic decisions regarding development of new products, product line extensions, product improvement, product elimination, and/or whether to build or improve weaker product lines or continue to maximize stronger-selling product lines.

Using Product to Maximize Your Brand Positioning

Think strategically in terms of where your existing products and services portfolio fits with the preceding elements of your brand positioning that you developed earlier in Chapter 6. If your product quality is mediocre and you have a premium positioning, the inconsistencies will kill your positioning strategy if not altered. Your products and services have to sync perfectly with your positioning. If they do not, you need to develop a product strategy that aligns the two areas.

Using Product to Fulfill Marketing Objectives

Stimulate initial purchase through strategy of new product development: The strategy of creating a new product or product line to stimulate demand is common. Not only does new product development fall under this category but so do developing line extensions and product flankers. A line extension adds breadth to your existing product through new flavors, scents, colors, and sizes among multiple other options. Product flankers are complementary products marketed under the existing brand name. An example would be Crest, known for toothpaste but with flanker products such as toothbrushes, whitening strips, and floss.

Stimulate repeat purchase through strategy of improving the existing product: Poor repeat purchase rates are often a result of poor product performance and thus poor customer product perceptions. If repeat purchase rates are low and your company's product ranks poorly across product attributes, you must develop a strategy around how to improve the product in order to meet your marketing objectives.

Stimulate incremental purchase through strategy of expanding alternative product use: Another area to consider is whether to strategically attempt to expand alternate uses of the product. This is a viable strategy when you have a mature product with a static or limited customer base that has been fully penetrated. An example we cited earlier in this book is the expansion of the use of baking soda as a refrigerator deodorizer. Another example would be Apple, which continually expands the use of their computers with music, apps, and book content. These successful marketing strategies were designed to meet the marketing objectives of increasing the purchase and usage rates by current customers and providing a reason for new customers to try the product.

Simulate incremental purchase through strategy of improving weaker brands: Alternatively, building or improving weaker product brands is often the strategy chosen when it is felt that the company's existing product strengths have been fully exploited. This strategic decision requires more initial money, as it is always more difficult to improve a weakness than to build on a strength. However, this approach is worthwhile if it provides a company with additional products that contribute more equally to profits. This also protects a company from major fluctuations resulting from having only one or two strong-selling products.

Stimulate incremental purchase through loss leader or lead product: Many times a specific target market can also be attracted through the use of a loss leader strategy or a specific strong-selling brand in the product mix. You may have a marketing objective of building new trial among heavy shoe purchasers, women 25 to 44 with children. The problems and opportunities section of your marketing plan may point out that women 25 to 44 shop at your shoe store not for themselves but for their children. Therefore, your strategy may be to initiate trial by promoting children's shoes to heavy-user women and then cross-sell to the women's shoe department. Other incentives and merchandising techniques could also be created to encourage the purchase of women's shoes once trial is established. In the razor category, the actual razor is priced very competitively to capture the far more lucrative business of razor blades.

Mitigate demand for competitors' products through strategy of substitution: The development of a substitute product can make existing competitive products less relevant. All bicycles used to be made with steel. Today, only the clunkers are made with steel. The Schwinn brand was one of the preeminent bicycle brands in the 1970s. Schwinn's prominence dwindled as companies such as Seven Cycles used technology developed in the airline business to make top-end titanium road bikes, and other companies such as Trek, Cannondale, and Pinarello learned to use aluminum and carbon fibers to create bikes that were far superior to steel-frame bikes. While Schwinn still exists, the advent of substitute product technology and the slowness of the brand to change have doomed it to a second tier of brands probably never to reestablish itself to past dominance.

Some substitutes such as the disposable diaper changed not only the diaper business but reduced the need for laundry cycles with young mothers. The computer acted as a substitute, eliminating the typewriter but also minimizing the need for the desk calculator, stereo system, CDs, and even photo albums.

Using Product to Improve Efficiency and Cost

Finally, finding more efficient ways to produce the product might also be a viable strategy to help ensure success of a marketing objective if the improved efficiency can permit you to achieve a price advantage. In addition, the improved efficiency might provide greater gross margins, which can help achieve greater profitability or can be invested in stronger marketing programs.

Another way to look at and consider growth and product strategies is to start with a consideration of growth. Do you plan to invest to support growth or to focus on keeping the status quo and milking profits? If your company is on a growth path, there are four ways to think about this. All four have direct links to product decisions:*

- *Horizontal growth:* Horizontal growth happens when a firm expands geographies or the range of its products and services (internally or through acquisition) within the company's core business. Examples would be a newspaper purchasing another newspaper in the neighboring town or starting a neighborhood advertising circular that carried local news and promotional coupons. Another would be a seafood restaurant expanding geographies and opening a second seafood restaurant in a surrounding community or starting a pasta restaurant in the same city as the original seafood restaurant.
- *Vertical growth:* This occurs when a company takes over a function performed by a supplier, distributor, or retailer—either backward or forward of the functions the company currently performs in the supply chain. An example would be a retailer that over time expanded using a vertical growth strategy to control the raw materials, designs, manufacturing, and marketing of its own products.
- *Diversification:* This occurs when the company takes on new growth via companies, products, and services outside of its core business. An example would be the local real estate company opening a restaurant. The only tie would be the knowledge around location, but the operations of running the restaurant would need to be learned.
- *Magnification:* A focus on the existing business and making it better through new strategies, by improving existing products and services, by developing more effective tactics, and by infusing of capital and talent.

Examples of Product Strategies

Strategy example: Link lesser-known training modules or products sequentially to the main lead product to form a learning platform—a sequence of training products linked together through a common foundation.

Rationale: High turnover plagued this national training business due to low awareness of its full product line. Known primarily for its lead training program, the organization determined that the best method to improve retention and increase the value of each customer was to use cross-selling of products bundled to the lead product.

Strategy example: The product portfolio of a social media insights company consisted of one broad software product designed to provide multiple insights across many categories of information. The company's strategy evolved to create smaller killer applications for specific user profiles—that is, limited but powerful applications that were critical to the specific target's needs and unique behaviors.

Rationale: The start-up company using social media sites to develop powerful insight analytics based on consumer conversations was finding it difficult to

---

* Scott W. Cooper, *Marketing Planning Tips for Small Business,* American Family Insurance Business Accelerator Program, http://www.amfambusinessaccelerator.com/go-to-class/Scott-Cooper/index.php.

market a "one-stop-shop" analytical tool because its comprehensiveness created a steep learning curve for its customers. By breaking it down into specific killer applications, it became easier for consumers to understand and for the company to communicate to prospects.

Additional example: Develop new products or modify existing products in order to attract the newly defined target market of adults in the 55-plus age group.

Naming Strategies

If you are going to introduce a new product or line extension, you will want to provide direction for the naming of the product or products. Should the new product stand by itself, or should it be under the umbrella of the family name? Should the name be targeted at current customers exclusively or current and new customers? If you are going to enter a new channel, you might want to modify the name of your product line to appeal to different targets, or you might need a new name for stores carrying your products in discount outlet malls versus regional malls.

Examples of Naming Strategies
Strategy example: Develop a new naming system for the new line of ultralight fast shoes from adidas.

Rationale: Recapture the high school student athlete through a focus on speed, one of the attributes that separates great athletes from average ones.

Additional examples:
- Use research into the characteristics of the target market to predict the most compelling name, taking into consideration the soft drink product's positioning of a fun good-times drink for sociable young adults.
- Provide a new name for the merged health care system that allows for a regional versus local feeling and communicates a strong caring emphasis via the face of health care as seen in such health care providers as physicians, nurses, and technicians.

Packaging Strategies

If you are going to develop a packaging plan later in the marketing plan, establish a general direction for your packaging strategy. Here you will need to consider and address the following issues regarding your product's packaging, referring to your problems and opportunities in your business review:

1. *Function:* Is your product's packaging serving its primary function of holding or protecting the product?
2. *Value added:* Does your packaging add value to the product purchase and enhance its use experience for the consumer?
3. *Communication:* Does your packaging stand out in the retail environment compared to competitors? Does it communicate the inherent drama of the product?

A problem identified earlier in the business review may point out that the company's packaging makes communication or usage difficult. Therefore, a change in packaging strategy might help achieve the marketing objective of increasing repeat usage and consumption among current customers.

Examples of Packaging Strategies

Strategy example: Develop packaging to reflect value positioning, distinct from the current product line offerings, while drawing attention on the dealerships' shelves.

Rationale: A new line of accessories from this manufacturer was positioned differently from its traditional quality-oriented product line. In order to avoid confusion or the possibility of eroding the equity of the original brand, packaging for the new line needed to provide differentiation both from the competition and from the company's original line.

Additional examples:
- Utilize the packaging to more effectively tell the health benefit story at the point of sale.
- Develop packaging consistent with the growing consumer demand for environmentally friendly products.
- Develop packaging that provides a better visualization of the actual product at the point of sale.

Seasonality Strategies

Strategic decisions must be made about when to advertise or promote your product or store. Here, the seasonality portion of the sales section in your business review becomes useful. Several issues are important.

Play to Seasonality Strength

The first issue is whether there are times of the year when your product category as a whole does significantly better than your company does. If so, why? Can you do something to increase sales during that period when customers of your product category are naturally purchasing at increased rates?

Alter the Seasonality

The second issue is whether you are going to advertise and promote all year, during stronger selling periods, or during weaker selling periods. If you have a limited budget, it is recommended that you concentrate only on those times of the year when sales are highest and attempt to capture as many purchases during that period as possible. Often, retail companies utilize in-store promotion strategies, such as bounce-back coupons, during stronger selling periods to entice customers back during down periods, thus using high-volume months to help promote lower-volume months.

Communicate around Seasonality

Third, you need to decide if you are going to advertise and promote prior to, during, or between peak selling periods. In retail, for example, the holiday seasons are heavy purchasing periods. A strategic decision must be made as to whether you are going to advertise earlier than your competitors, throughout the whole selling season, or just during the peak selling weeks. It is often recommended to lead the selling season because there will be less competitive advertising clutter and you can build awareness just prior to the heavy shopping period. An alternative strategy that is also successful is to concentrate advertising during the heaviest weeks of the holiday shopping period. Thus, the advertiser can dominate a critical selling period and be visible when it counts most.

Consider Your Resource Capacity

Finally, you must consider your resource and production capacity. If your current seasonal sales peaks already have you operating near capacity, you're not going to be able to increase sales much in this period. This is true regardless of your product or service. For a restaurant, it may mean space, tables, and waitstaff availability. For a packaged-goods producer, it may be the availability of ingredients. Your marketing expenditures and activities may be used effectively to stimulate demand to accommodate your production or resource limitations.

Examples of Seasonality Strategies

Strategy example: Promote heavily during major back-to-school periods of late summer, as well as winter holidays and spring cold and flu periods.

Rationale: A national paper products packaged-goods company targeted mothers of school-aged children with its travel-sized tissue product, which it positioned as the tissue to keep in your desk at school. The school season influenced the purchase timing.

Additional examples:
- Place the greatest marketing efforts and execute mass media marketing programs during the strongest selling months. Maximize the months with the most opportunity before trying to develop the poorer selling months.
- Build the month of December, a month that performs relatively poorly for the company but is one of the strongest months for the product category nationally.

Spending Strategies

Spending strategies outline how the marketing dollars will be spent. To achieve your marketing objectives, you need to decide on spending strategies regarding issues such as investment spending for a new product; whether to increase sales of weaker-selling brands, stores, or regions of the country; or whether to attract more customers to your stronger brands or stores. In order to make these decisions, you need to determine spending levels by brands, stores, or regions of the country. In most situations you can't increase sales of a weaker-selling brand without making an incremental budget commitment to the brand. We know that one way to increase short-term sales is to place emphasis on a company's strengths. However, there comes a point when strong brands, stores, or markets can't be expected to provide additional growth. Long-term success requires building weaker brands, stores, and sales territories—or creating new ones—and this requires significant investment spending. (Note that this strategy category will affect later media spending decisions.)

Overall spending should also be addressed. Does your company plan to spend at a percent of sales for marketing and advertising consistent with past years? Or because of new aggressive sales projections and marketing objectives, do you need to increase marketing spending from, for example, 5 percent of gross sales to 8 percent? The actual spending detail will be highlighted in the budget section of the marketing plan.

Examples of Spending Strategies

Strategy example: Allocate marketing expenditures between two different tiers geographically. In Tier 1, increase spending by 25 percent; in Tier 2, maintain spending levels comparable to the previous year.

Rationale: This national retailer had allocated spending by markets according to tiers. The tiers were determined by a number of factors including size of market, competitive environment, growth projections, and strength of market management and retail operations. This strategy was developed based on the strength of the Tier 1 markets at that particular time and their growth potential.

Additional examples:
- Increase advertising spending as a percent of sales to be competitive with the market leader.
- Spend at significantly higher levels against the three top-selling products, maximizing their growth potential.
- Increase support of the household products category, which is a strong potential growth market and one planned to be significantly up in sales over the coming fiscal year.

Competitive Strategies

The business review may reveal that a single competitor is almost totally responsible for your company's decline in market share, a new competitor is entering the market, a single company or group of competitors has preempted your unique positioning in the marketplace, or you are grouped in a competitive set with very little differentiation, customer loyalty, and consumer preference of one over the other. If any of these are the case, you will need to develop a competitive marketing strategy in your marketing plan.

Anti-competitive Strategies
Competitive strategies sometimes use an anti-category strategy. This strategy would establish your company as better than all the other competitors in the category. To achieve this, a company often takes a common, consumer-perceived problem in the industry (such as lack of customer service attention in retail or delayed flights in the airline business), establishes the problem as inherent to the industry, and then tries to set itself apart as better than the competition in this area of concern.

Competitor-Specific Strategies
Sometimes competitive strategies focus on one competitor or a group of specific competitors. You may need to reestablish your product attribute dominance relative to a specific competitor, or a competitor may have done a better job of creating a lifestyle image in tune with the heavy-user consumer in your category. In both of these situations, you might consider developing competitive strategies that require comparison advertising or advertising that counters specific competitive claims. You might also consider a competitive media tactic of advertising within the same timeframes and media as your competition. Or you might try to dominate a medium that is lightly used, or perhaps not used at all, by the heavy user of your industry category.

Entry of a New Competitor to Your Industry Category or Market
Another common competitive situation occurs when a strong competitor starts doing business in your trading area or in a market you previously dominated. We developed a competitive strategy for a retail client when an aggressive, nationally known competitor announced it was moving into one of our client's important markets. The competitive strategy centered around taking advantage of the fact that our client was already in business and the new competitor wasn't.

To implement the strategy, our client ran a strong sale for two months prior to the opening of the competitor's stores. This was intended to get customers to purchase prior to the anticipated grand opening of the competing stores. The week of the competitor's grand opening, we mailed a promotional piece to consumers in the five-mile trading area surrounding the competitor's store. We continued the heavy promotion during the competitor's grand opening by having a grand opening of our own to celebrate the opening of the eight-hundredth store in our client's chain of stores. This competitive plan resulted in our client's stores being up 40 percent during the promotional period and gaining market share over the following year.

Countermoves to Your Competitors' Strengths

Finally, competitive strategies also include the development of new or improved product, packaging, selling, or merchandising techniques to counter the competitors' strengths.

Examples of Competitive Strategies

Strategy example: Target the second- through tenth-ranked competitors by aligning with the market leader, and marketing Wyffels Hybrids' seed corn as the second hybrid of choice.

Rationale: This hybrid seed producer recognized the market leader's dominance (40 percent market share) by aiming at the next level of competitors. To do this, Wyffels Hybrids capitalized on the fact that most farmers use two or more brands on their farm. Wyffels positioned itself as the second choice.

Additional examples:

- Create an anti-category strategy by focusing on a category problem germane to all competitors (slow delivery) and making unprecedented changes to set the company apart. Win on something that is a universal problem to the industry category putting all competitors in a box in which the company competes against.
- Minimize Competitor Z's entry into the market by heavily promoting during the three months prior to Z's grand opening—specifically targeting Competitor Z's trading area.

Distribution of Product and Penetration or Coverage Strategies

The strategic decisions that must be made in this area for consumer goods and business-to-business firms differ for retailers and service firms. Consumer goods and business-to-business firms must decide in what areas of the country to target their distribution efforts. They also must decide on the type of channels and/or outlets that will carry their products and on the desired market coverage in the targeted outlet category.

Retailers and service firms, in contrast, must strategically decide if marketing objectives can be achieved through existing outlets, whether new stores need to be added in existing markets without cannibalizing existing stores, or whether new stores need to be added through entering new markets. If sales per store have not been maximized in low-penetrated markets, one way to build sales is to add new stores in existing markets. This allows for greater leverage of store operation and advertising dollars. However, if sales have been maximized in current markets and the markets have been fully penetrated to the point where additional stores or products could cannibalize existing sales, then a realistic strategy is to expand to new markets.

It is helpful to estimate market strengths (BDIs and CDIs as discussed in Chapter 2) by reviewing the channels of distribution section of the business review's sales analysis prior to completing this section.

Examples of Distribution of Product and Penetration or Coverage Strategies

Strategy example: Focus distribution through large retailers nationally.

Rationale: This distributor and publisher of alternative comic books recognized that the vast majority of comics are being sold through the larger comic retailers, who tend to carry alternative comics more than smaller retailers. National distribution was necessary to achieve sales goals.

Strategy example: Focus on the local, family-owned hardware stores in rural areas where the sharpening product would get strong demonstration support.

Rationale: The sharpening tools target market consumers are overwhelmingly rural do-it-yourselfers who often have a personal relationship with their local hardware store staff. Additionally, the local retailer has a much better chance of sampling the product on the floor, something research has pointed out is critical to trial of the product.

Additional examples:

- Do not expand to any new markets until existing markets have been fully penetrated.
- Concentrate on gaining incremental distribution in the Northeast.
- Explore new ways to bypass the intermediary distribution system to deliver the product directly to the consumer.
- Test additional distribution through mobile on-site distribution alternatives (e.g., a Snap-on tools type of channel).

Personal Selling, Service, and Operations Strategies

You need to determine whether you want to address a structured personal selling program through this marketing plan. You may want to address basic elements of that sales program, including whether you will use sales incentives; establish sales goals relative to pure dollar objectives, a particular product, or target market emphasis in terms of calls made, and so on; and define a sales methodology (for example, soft sell or hard sell, consultative sales force or closer to pure order takes, and so on). Your plan might also drive specific sales performance metrics such as total calls, close ratios, percent of new customers, retention rates, cross-selling quotas, and so on. If you are a retailer, note whether your subsequent selling plan should include similar sales metrics specific to retail (e.g., develop sales ratio of purchasers versus walkers based on history and future expectations).

Additionally, you should consider whether you are going to establish service standards such as the number of days it takes to fill backorders or, for a retailer, the percentage of customers who are greeted as they walk in the door.

Finally, if necessary, this section should include a strategy for implementing your marketing department's performance. An example would be to create a marketing liaison between purchasing and marketing to ensure that the proper inventory levels are maintained during peak promotional times that correspond with heavy media and marketing efforts, as well as historically strong seasonal buying periods.

Examples of Personal Selling, Service, and Operations Strategies

Strategy example: Develop detailed target volume objectives with the field sales organization to establish forecasted and performance criteria.

Rationale: This strategy for a national manufacturer of recycled paper products, which holds the market share lead in certain market segments, addresses the lack of quantifiable sales goals for the sales force in spite of aggressive overall company sales objectives.

Additional examples:
- Develop specific sales ratio goals, quantifying the number of specific prospects and those that become customers.
- Provide a strong and innovative incentive program during peak selling periods to improve sales performance.
- Create a stronger consultative sales force with emphasis on providing expertise via problem solving.

Promotions and Events Strategies

Do you plan to use promotions and events? If so, how will you use these tools? Will you use promotions primarily to drive incremental purchases during specific times of the year? Will you use them as countercompetition tools aimed at specific competitors on specific products? Will you use them as a way to engage the target market in learning more about the nonprice aspects of your product or company? Or will you use them as a way to more personally create a connection with the target market?

Promotions should be channeled to meet specific needs, and they must be incorporated into the overall marketing plan in a disciplined fashion. These promotion strategies will establish the areas of emphasis for the specific promotion implemented later in the marketing plan, providing direction for the promotional efforts aimed at addressing specific marketing objectives.

A retailer may have the marketing objective of increasing the number of units per transaction from the target market by 10 percent over the next 12 months. An umbrella strategy to achieve this would be to encourage multiple purchases through promotional incentives. This strategy would then be expanded upon in the promotion section of the marketing plan, but the fact that transaction increases are going to come from multiple-purchase promotional incentives would have been established up front.

Examples of Promotions and Events Strategies

Strategy example: Develop a promotional program to encourage existing advertiser customers to purchase more ad space. (An example tactic later in the plan directed by this strategy could be to introduce a thirteenth issue in the year that would offer special page rates.)

Rationale: The problems and opportunities section for this monthly magazine indicated that the publication was a secondary buy among advertisers, that the advertisers typically purchased more in a special issue, and that the current customer advertiser had a relatively low purchase level. This strategy addressed all of these issues.

Additional examples:
- Increase multiple purchases through in-store promotions.
- Create a smoother seasonality of sales through promotion to encourage purchase during the weaker, seasonal months.
- Create a summer series of multiple events (mass participation, young adult living complex, on-premise bars) to touch the young adult target and involve them with the product.

Advertising Strategies

The marketer needs to provide an overall focus for the advertising and communication. It is important to state up front in your marketing strategy section how you are going to use advertising to fulfill your marketing objectives. Are you going to develop image advertising and build long-term sales? Or will your advertising promote short-term sales through a harder sell, promotional emphasis? Do you plan to vary your advertising message by region? Perhaps you will have both a national advertising program and a localized, market-by-market program. Does your advertising need to take more risk in breaking through the clutter to more effectively build an image? Or will you use advertising primarily as sales support to show the trade that you are supporting them?

Examples of Advertising Strategies

Strategy example: Develop an aggressive and comprehensive consumer advertising program to build awareness for the new product and educate the consumer about its unique features. Include dealer tags to all advertising. Merchandise this advertising campaign to the dealer network to demonstrate support and to help buy-in of the product.

Rationale: The strategy for a new variable-pitch propeller responds to the need to build a market through consumer education and to generate maximum support from the trade to carry and merchandise the product.

Additional examples:
- Dramatically reduce consumer advertising and evolve to primarily trade advertising targeted at the critical distribution channels and their decision makers.
- Develop both a national image campaign and a local, market-by-market advertising campaign that is more promotional in focus.

Media Strategies

The strategies developed in this section should be consistent with the direction established in the product, competitive, and spending marketing strategies. The primary goal in establishing an overall media strategy is to provide direction for the upcoming media plan and to establish geographic and product spending emphasis. You may decide upon a strategy that varies media spending by market or that spends more in markets with greater potential. You may invest in new markets to establish awareness and generate trial. You may consider developing a national media plan or developing both national and local media plans in order to support a dual marketing strategy. You may also address target market reach strategies by identifying how the media will be utilized to reach the primary and/or secondary target market, influencers, and so on.

Examples of Media Strategies

Strategy example: Maintain low-level but consistent advertising throughout the year to maintain awareness among all key targets.

Rationale: Multiple decision makers represent the target for this producer of anesthesia machines—anesthesiologists, biomedical engineers, materials management directors, hospital administrators, and financial managers, among others. Because the purchase of such equipment is not seasonal, awareness must be maintained among these segments on an ongoing basis.

Additional examples:
• Invest media dollars and overspend for a one-year period in new markets to support the grand openings, establish awareness, and generate trial.
• While the target market is teen boys and girls, use aspirational celebrities in the slightly older college age group to communicate the product consistent with the insights gained from the research.

Interactive Media Strategies

Your Internet media strategies can center on the web and e-commerce. The Internet and intranets can be considered as alternative channels of distribution, communication tools, and sales tools. We've found that companies that have a clear direction for the Internet medium for its own purposes will prepare the most effective Internet media strategies.

Beyond the actual tool of the company Internet site, the interactive strategies include other methods for interacting with your target segments in two-way conversation or through permission media on the Internet. New on the scene since our last edition, social media websites have become a driving force that needs to be part of your thought process on two dimensions.

First, social media networks are valuable sources of information, and they have created the opportunity to revolutionize the research or insights industry. Firms like Networked Insights, Radian6, and MotiveQuest all provide marketers with insights gleaned from the millions and billions of consumer conversations that happen every day on the social network sites across the Internet. These conversations provide insights into awareness (conversation volume), attitudes (what's being said by whom), existing consumer behavior, the current language, the sentiment, and future product and behavior trends.

Second, social network websites provide an avenue for communicating with the customer and prospective customers, allowing companies to build favorable sentiments and engage customers with their brands. Marketing campaigns are being augmented and even introduced on well-known sites such as Twitter, Facebook, Myspace, and LinkedIn. Alan Kleinberg in iMedia Connection writes about how Adobe wanted to raise awareness of its discounts to college students. It developed a campaign for Facebook called "Real or Fake"—where the target was engaged and voted whether photos were real or fake. The game got 11,500 plays in the first two weeks, resulting in a 6 percent click to "buy now" for the product promoted.

Examples of Interactive Media Strategies

Strategy example: Utilize the company website to provide ongoing sales engagement tactics to assist the sales force in a challenging selling environment (e.g., a sales workshop, new and existing product content, weekly tips, weekly leads).

Rationale: The product selling cycle is a long one, requiring much detailed information. The web is an ideal vehicle to carry this information and to provide timely advice and communication of best practices.

Strategy example: Become a strong thought leader through creating and disseminating content to sites frequented by the target.

Rationale: The brand currently has a strong engagement component with existing target customers, but new trial has been slow in recent years. In the past, the strongest new customer strategy has been to use existing customers to induce trial. It is felt that the social networking sites will expand the company's ability to help existing customers promote the product to their friends.

Additional examples:
- Use a social networking insight research firm to augment traditional research in areas where real-time information is critical to the knowledge needed to successfully market the company's fad and trend products.
- Join the conversation on the top 10 social networking websites based on research that identifies the most influential websites for the company's target segment.
- Use the Internet to communicate directly to the company end users. Focus on the major customer service inefficiencies that the company's distribution channels continually have problems around (e.g., utilize an intranet to communicate delivery schedules).

Merchandising Strategies

A strategy is needed to set the tone for what will be done from a merchandising standpoint. This applies to all nonmedia communication—for example, in-store signage for retailers, point-of-purchase displays for packaged-goods firms, and personal presentation sales aids such as brochures and sell sheets for business-to-business firms. An opportunity identified under problems and opportunities might tell you that 80 percent of purchase decisions are made in the store. Thus, the marketing strategy in this situation might be to utilize extensive point-of-purchase merchandising to affect in-store decision making.

Examples of Merchandising Strategies
Strategy example: All in-store communication materials should be developed to reinforce the positioning theme line. This may include collateral materials, signage, and continuing-service reference materials for buyers.

Rationale: A theme line based on the brand positioning in the marketing plan had been developed for this large automobile dealership. Considering the fact that car purchase decisions would likely be made at the dealership, point-of-sale materials communicating this theme would be extremely important.

Additional examples:
- Communicate the corporate story through compelling print, web, and visual mediums to be used both in sales calls and internally with new hires.
- Utilize interactive point-of-purchase merchandising to create greater understanding of the product's unique features and benefits.

Public Relations Strategies

At this point in your plan development, you should determine if you are going to make public relations part of your marketing, as you will need to consider PR opportunities when you develop the other specific tactical tool segments of your plan. For example, you might consider supplementing your overall advertising and promotion communication program with publicity. Or you might use media cosponsors of planned promotional events or charity tie-ins to generate publicity. You may decide to develop an extensive public relations program either to take advantage of new product development or ongoing trade show opportunities (e.g., create a speakers bureau) or to become more of a thought leader in your industry category.

Examples of Public Relations Strategies

Strategy example: Create a media tour program to better engage the key dominant media players in the category.

Rationale: This firm needs to build awareness and a reputation as a major player in the high-end segment through targeted publications and other "newslike" formats.

Additional examples:
- Develop a consistent media relations program to obtain articles in the leading trade publications.
- Create a thought leadership program through creating content via a company blog. Another option is to join the conversation on the top five industry social networking sites. Still another option is to publish articles that will form the foundation for a book and speaking tour.

Marketing Research and Testing (R&T) Strategies

Change is often important in generating trial and retrial of a company's product. A disciplined program to initiate this change is critical. In most businesses there is a need to continually expand and/or refine the company's product offerings and marketing in order to continually build sales. This change can be accomplished through a planned and disciplined research and testing program.

Marketing R&T is the lifeblood for the success of your business. It takes time, money, work, planning, and perseverance to research, test, and produce readable results. But it is always worth it!

Research can help define your product's problems and help determine the potential and needs of the target market, optimum pricing, effective advertising messages, and much more. If you plan to conduct primary research, now is the time to establish a research strategy. You may develop a research strategy to solve a specific problem that will help you to build sales and accomplish a marketing objective. You may have a need to incorporate predictive modeling to assist with a companywide test and learn culture. Or you may decide to conduct an ongoing awareness, attitude, and behavior tracking study to assist with next year's plan and to provide a benchmark to evaluate the results of current and future marketing plans.

Testing keeps you ahead of the competition and helps you avoid costly mistakes. It can help you develop a new product or marketing activity, make it better, provide evidence of your program's effectiveness, and eliminate those ideas that aren't going to work before a costly investment has been made. You can test any part of a marketing program, from a product change and price increase to a new promotion, television commercial, or store format.

Once you have committed to some form of marketing R&T, this section should be used to define what you will be researching and testing—new products, services, merchandising programs, store layouts, packaging, media strategies, advertising messages, pricing, promotions, and so on. Incorporate what you will research and test in the appropriate plan segments later in the marketing plan.

Examples of Marketing Research and Testing (R&T) Strategies

Strategy example: Use predictive modeling (discussed in Chapter 9) to test among dealers the pricing elasticity and promotion programs for the variable-pitch propeller.

Rationale: As the variable-pitch propeller is a new product with a premium price, there is little knowledge of how consumers will respond to this price and how dealers would respond to the promotional efforts by the manufacturer. Predictive modeling would help provide answers prior to rolling out the product introduction nationally.

Additional examples:

- Institute a marketing testing program to help effectively provide a continuous cycle of new product alternatives.
- Develop an ongoing research tracking study among the target market consumers to monitor consumer awareness, attitudes, and behavior.

HOW TO DEVELOP YOUR MARKETING STRATEGIES

To develop marketing strategies, review your marketing plan's problems and opportunities, targets, and marketing objectives as well as your positioning strategy. Then use your problems and opportunities as a guide in writing strategies for the marketing strategy considerations.

1. *Review your problems and opportunities.* Read through your problems and opportunities, and make notes regarding ideas you have on how to solve the problems and take advantage of the opportunities. Be creative in this exercise, and identify multiple solutions for each problem or opportunity.
2. *Review your target market and marketing objectives.* Review your target market and marketing objectives. Then reread the problems and opportunities, along with your notes on how to solve the problems and take advantage of the opportunities. Determine which of the ideas will form strategies capable of achieving the marketing objectives.
3. *Review your positioning strategy.* What is the product image you want to instill in the minds of target market customers relative to the competition? It is this meaningful image that must be reinforced individually and cumulatively by your marketing strategies.
4. *Develop your strategies.* Review the 19 strategy considerations in this chapter, and determine which issues you need to address. As stated before, use the strategy approaches that fit your product's or company's particular situation— not all strategies will apply in every situation. Then, based on what you know from the problems and opportunities review, develop clear and concise directional statements about how you intend to address each issue.

In summary, after reviewing the marketing strategies, upper management should have a good understanding as to how you are going to achieve your marketing objectives from a strategic standpoint. However, the details of these strategies will be fully developed in the subsequent tactical marketing mix tool segments of the marketing plan.

How to Write Your Marketing Strategies

Make sure to focus on one single idea at a time when writing your strategies. The strategies should be very descriptive and focus on how you are going to utilize a particular tool, such as promotions or packaging, to achieve the marketing objectives. Following each strategy should be a brief rationale drawing on information in your business review, problems and opportunities, targets, marketing objectives, and positioning sections of your marketing plan.

DOS AND DON'TS

Do

- Make your umbrella strategies descriptive statements of how you will achieve your plan's objectives.
- Look at your strategies as an opportunity for solving the key problems and taking advantage of key opportunities developed after going through your business review.
- Ask yourself: Are my strategies specific enough that anyone in my business will understand directionally how I will accomplish meeting our plan objectives and our overall sales goals?
- Make sure your umbrella strategies qualify as "big ideas"—ideas that excite your organization and are clearly a smart way to go about running your business.
- Take time in developing your umbrella strategies. They form the basis of your whole marketing plan. You should give them a considerable amount of thought and review prior to finalizing this portion of the marketing plan.
- Whenever possible, steal market share. It's easier and less expensive than building the market. Also, it's easier to build on marketing strengths than to improve weaknesses.

Don't

- Don't let the umbrella strategies become too executional. Keep the strategies broad and directional.
- Don't limit the focus to one or two specific marketing areas. Remember that umbrella strategies should include direction across all areas of importance to your marketing plan.
- Don't write long, elaborate strategies. They should be simple, and they should focus on a single idea. These aren't meant to be strategic plans but simply strategic statements to provide direction for the plans developed later.
- Don't create generic, boring strategies. Your umbrella strategy section should be filled with creativity. It should look at your business in new and exciting ways based on solid insights revealed in your business review.

- Don't be stagnant in your strategic thinking and get left behind in the increasingly changing and competitive business environment. Initiate a marketing R&T program so that you are continually developing new and proven marketing programs to replace those programs that aren't working or to help make an existing program even better.
- Don't expect all of your marketing R&T program to be successful. Remember, most new ideas fail. However, only a few successes (and sometimes only one) are needed to keep you ahead of the competition year after year. In fact, one success can often pay for multiple failures in a very short time.

The Successful Marketing Plan

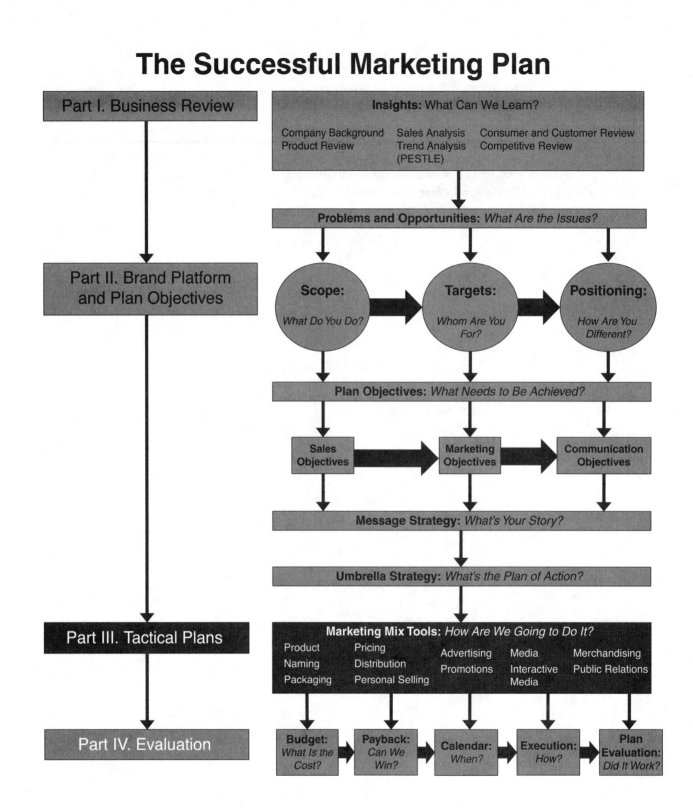

Part I. Business Review

Insights: What Can We Learn?

Company Background Sales Analysis Consumer and Customer Review
Product Review Trend Analysis Competitive Review
(PESTLE)

Problems and Opportunities: *What Are the Issues?*

Part II. Brand Platform and Plan Objectives

Scope: *What Do You Do?*

Targets: *Whom Are You For?*

Positioning: *How Are You Different?*

Plan Objectives: *What Needs to Be Achieved?*

Sales Objectives

Marketing Objectives

Communication Objectives

Message Strategy: *What's Your Story?*

Umbrella Strategy: *What's the Plan of Action?*

Part III. Tactical Plans

Marketing Mix Tools: *How Are We Going to Do It?*

Product Pricing
Naming Distribution Advertising Media Merchandising
Packaging Personal Selling Promotions Interactive Public Relations
  Media

Part IV. Evaluation

Budget: *What Is the Cost?*

Payback: *Can We Win?*

Calendar: *When?*

Execution: *How?*

Plan Evaluation: *Did It Work?*

P A R T

TACTICAL PLANS

The following 10 chapters provide an overview of choices you have to fulfill the individual marketing objectives established in your brand platform. The decision on whether a marketing mix tool is needed or not depends on the individual marketing objective and the insights from the business review that lead to its creation. Remember, few marketing objectives will require the full suite of marketing mix tools. It's better to do a few things well than spread your budget across too many tactics.

The Successful Marketing Plan

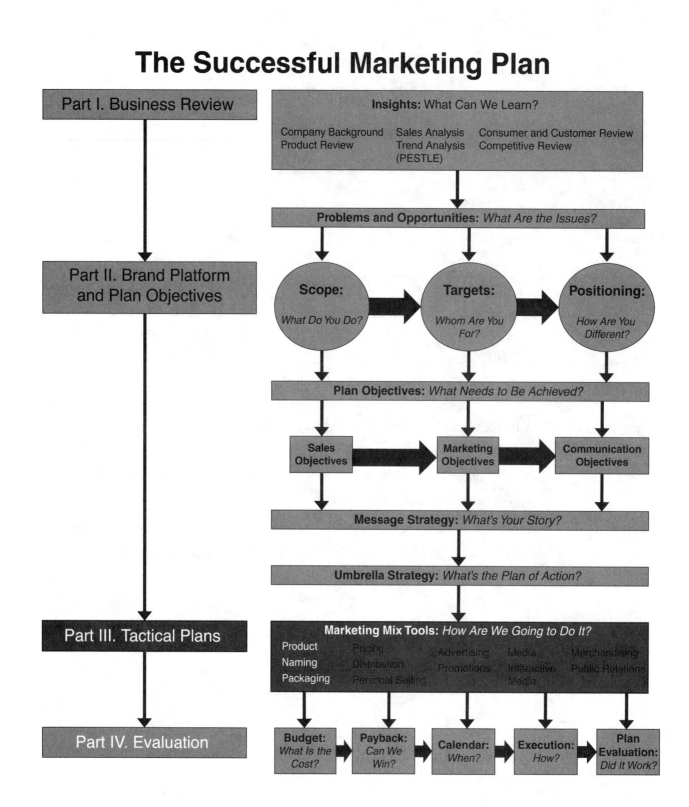

Part I. Business Review

Insights: What Can We Learn?

Company Background   Sales Analysis   Consumer and Customer Review
Product Review   Trend Analysis   Competitive Review
               (PESTLE)

Problems and Opportunities: *What Are the Issues?*

Part II. Brand Platform and Plan Objectives

Scope: *What Do You Do?*

Targets: *Whom Are You For?*

Positioning: *How Are You Different?*

Plan Objectives: *What Needs to Be Achieved?*

Sales Objectives

Marketing Objectives

Communication Objectives

Message Strategy: *What's Your Story?*

Umbrella Strategy: *What's the Plan of Action?*

Part III. Tactical Plans

Marketing Mix Tools: *How Are We Going to Do It?*

Product   Pricing   Advertising   Media   Merchandising
Naming   Distribution   Promotions   Interactive   Public Relations
Packaging   Personal Selling   Media

Part IV. Evaluation

Budget: *What Is the Cost?*

Payback: *Can We Win?*

Calendar: *When?*

Execution: *How?*

Plan Evaluation: *Did It Work?*

CHAPTER 12
Product, Naming, and Packaging

The product, name, and packaging probably have more impact on the success of your brand positioning than any of the other marketing mix tools. They are the most fundamental elements of the entire marketing mix set. While all the marketing mix tools must align with your brand positioning, if these three don't, there is little hope that you will be able to achieve your desired image in the marketplace. Moreover, while the product, name, and package are fundamental in helping you induce trial and repeat purchase, they are also invaluable in helping your company, product, or service achieve the desired awareness levels and in the formation of positive attitudes among both customers and prospective customers.

The product perception is closely linked to the packaging that holds the product and carries the product's name. It is these three elements that make up the reality of the positioning. Effective positioning may induce trial of a product, but beware: nothing will ruin a company faster than selling a poor product or a product that is not consistent with its positioning. Because of all the interrelationships among the product, name, and packaging tools, we have included all three in one chapter.

Before you write the product, naming, and packaging segment of the marketing plan, you must review the direction provided by the problems and opportunities, brand positioning, and the umbrella marketing strategies affecting each of the three areas. If you are not modifying or developing a new product, name, or package, there is no need to address these marketing mix tools in your plan. However, it is recommended that you read through this chapter to help determine your needs for product, naming, or packaging modifications, for their tactical tool value contributions to the plan's awareness and attitude goals, and for additional background in writing the remainder of the marketing plan.

FROM THIS CHAPTER YOU WILL LEARN

Product
- The definition of a product and a service
- The definition and different types of new products
- What type of new product activity is indicated by a business situation
- Issues affecting your new product plan
- How to establish product objectives and strategies

Naming
- Definitions of naming
- The importance of naming
- How to develop a naming plan

Packaging
- Functions of packaging
- Reasons for changing your packaging
- How to develop your packaging plan

OVERVIEW: PRODUCT

In the case of consumer packaged goods, retail, and business-to-business companies, the *product* is a *tangible object* that is marketed to customers. However, for service businesses, the product takes the form of some *intangible offering*, such as a future benefit or future promise. Thus, while all products are offerings to the customer, there is an inherent difference between what is sold by a service firm and what is sold by a retailer or manufacturer.

A new product is one that has not been previously marketed by your firm. We use this definition because, even if a product is not new to the market, if it is new to your firm, it presents new marketing challenges for your company.

New products may come in any one of a number of forms:

- *A new product or brand positioning for an existing product:* This entails changing consumer perceptions of the personality and/or usage of your product.
- *Line extensions:* Line extensions add to the breadth of your product line with the addition of new flavors, scents, colors, or sizes. Line extensions can provide an effective way to reach new customers by leveraging the existing equity in your product's brand name, both at the consumer level and at the trade level, to assist in selling the product at retail.
- *Flankers:* Flankers are complementary products marketed under an existing brand umbrella. As with line extensions, flankers can be an effective way to increase sales by leveraging existing strengths. An example would be Gillette's capitalizing on the strength of its brand in the shaving products market to offer other health and beauty aids products, such as deodorant, under the Gillette name. Similarly, when we worked with Mercury Marine, well known for its motors and engines, the company became very active in marketing a line of inflatable watercraft—small rubber boats that, as we say in the advertising, "get you from here to there." In the biomedical area, an example is Nicolet Biomedical, which expanded from audio testing products to neurological products. In our work in the shoe industry, we see daily the impact of Nike

with its development of flankers in the apparel area. You don't have to work in the industry to notice all the Nike T-shirts, hats, jackets, and other apparel being worn today.

- *Entirely new products:* These are products that did not previously exist. The VCR is a good example. Before the introduction of the VCR, people simply watched what was on TV, generally one show at a time. The VCR was a new product with an entirely new functionality, providing consumers with a new way to use television. Then VCRs gave way to DVD players with significantly improved capabilities. Finally, today we see DVDs giving way to streaming video over the Internet. A stunning example of this it the filing for bankruptcy by Blockbuster and the continuing evolutionary Netflix and other online TV and movie viewing options like Hulu.

Any of these changes to your firm's product constitutes a new product introduction, and the impact and/or opportunities in the other elements of the marketing mix must be reviewed and considered.

Why New Products Are Important

Change is a fact of life for the marketer. It provides the opportunities that allow the firm to grow and prosper, but it also presents the forces that may render the firm's products obsolete and leave the firm without sufficient sales and profits to survive. You must continually review your product's position in the competitive environment and in the context of the constantly changing consumer. This is the best method to ensure that your firm's product offerings remain relevant to the target market and remain competitive.

Issues Affecting the Product

The issues affecting the product are its attributes, segmentation (different product versions for different markets), and innovation (changing the product to fit evolving trends in the marketplace).

Product Attributes

A major focus should be placed on determining if there is a need or an opportunity for product modifications, new products, or extended product lines. In order to accomplish this, it is important to first identify what attributes consumers find most important in the purchase decision for your product category and determine how your product ranks along these attributes compared to your competitors' products. (Refer to your business review—target market effectors awareness and attributes sections, as well as problems and opportunities, brand positioning, and marketing strategies sections.) If there are critical areas where your product is less competitive and/or where there is a product void in the market, then you must develop product objectives and strategies to address the situation.

Product Segmentation

The desirability of segmenting your product to meet specific demographic and lifestyle needs should be addressed. For the manufacturer, one method of segmentation is to develop different product sizes based on product usage. Smaller sizes are often requirements of singles or light users, and larger sizes are often needed by families or heavy users of the product category.

Another way of segmenting products is by utilizing different product features to attract different target markets. Many times new products are developed with a basic appeal to a broad, homogeneous market. As competition increases and the product reaches the growth stage in the product life cycle, differentiation occurs and marketing must more closely target the needs and tasks of specific target markets. Cross-country skis are a good example. Back in 1970, the sport of cross-country skiing was relatively new. There was basically one style: all-purpose, wooden cross-country skis. However, by the next decade, there were touring skis, racing skis (skating and traditional), deep-snow skis, and telemarking skis, not to mention multiple options on bindings, poles, boots, and ski construction. As the sport of cross-country skiing grew, manufacturers targeted specific needs.

Product Innovation

An important area of your business review is the analysis of change and innovation in the product category. Product innovations allow you to map out changes in your company's product. They compel you to determine how your product should evolve to meet customers' needs and the competitive pressures of the future.

There are essentially eight types of new product innovations:

1. *A product with an entirely new function:* Generally, such new products grow out of a technical innovation against an existing consumer need. For example, the first TV was a product with an entirely new functionality (broadcast of picture and sound), but it served an existing consumer need for information and entertainment. Our work with Sonic Foundry involved helping the company introduce and market a new audio software product that allows users to create their own music, starting a whole new category of audio software.
2. *A product that improves performance against an existing function and/or need:* These products perform an existing function in a better way. An example would be the Diaper Genie, an odor-free system for disposing of disposable diapers—a vast improvement over the old diaper pail.
3. *A new application for an existing product:* The classic example of a firm developing a new application for an existing product is Arm & Hammer's positioning of its baking soda product as a refrigerator deodorizer as well as a baking ingredient.
4. *A new product with additional functions or features:* This is essentially an upgrade of an existing product that improves or expands its performance against consumer needs. An example is Mercury Marine's introduction of the High Five Propeller, a new five-blade stainless steel prop that gets skiers out of the water faster than conventional three- or four-blade props.
5. *An existing product aimed at a new target market:* The attributes of the product may be unchanged, but the communications are oriented toward a different target. Marlboro was initially positioned as a cigarette for women. It was later marketed against the male segment, and the rest, as they say, is history.
6. *A product with a new price-and-value mix:* This type of new product entry addresses an existing consumer need with a new price-and-value combination. An example from the retail field would be the repositioning of Famous Footwear (2002–2005) from a store that sells low-priced shoes to a store that sells value with shoes always in stock and always in fashion.
7. *Packaging improvements:* Packaging improvements may essentially constitute a new product when they alter the usage or purchase experience. Procter & Gamble's launch of liquid laundry detergent bottles with a unique no-drip spout designed for neater pouring is an example of this type of product

innovation. In the retail and service areas, packaging improvements include the store or office. We spent more than a year helping Famous Footwear redesign its in-store packaging to be consistent with its new positioning. The research phase included analyzing everything from traffic flow to which color impacted the target market most favorably to the most effective use of point-of-sale materials in the store. We will address this issue again in the packaging section of this chapter.

8. *Changes in appearance or form:* These new products represent incremental changes in the product that result (when successful) in improved performance against consumer needs. A packaged-goods example is the introduction of gel toothpastes.*

How to Develop a New Product Plan

There are two tasks involved in developing a new product plan: establishing objectives for the new product and establishing strategies for developing and marketing the new product.

See also Appendix C, Worksheet 41.

TASK 1 Establish Your Product Objectives

Product objectives will center around one or more of the five following areas:

1. Developing new products
2. Developing line extensions for existing brands
3. Developing new uses for existing products
4. Product improvement
5. Finding more efficient ways to produce the product, in the case of manufacturers, or purchase the product, in the case of retailers

In addition, the product objectives should incorporate specifics on when the product will be available for distribution or inventory.

An example of a product objective for a manufacturer would be the following:

In the upcoming fiscal year, modify the product to reflect the current purchasing habits of consumers interested in low-salt foods.

TASK 2 Establish Your Product Strategies

Your new product strategies should help your firm focus its product development activities against one of five approaches (the first four of which have been previously discussed in this chapter):

1. Developing a new brand positioning for an existing product
2. Developing line extensions
3. Developing flanker products
4. Developing entirely new products
5. Acquiring another firm or the rights to another firm's products that address your company's product strategies

---

* Adapted from C. Merle Crawford and Anthony Di Benedetto, *New Products Management*, Richard D. Irwin, Homewood, Ill., 1983, p. 35.

An example of a product strategy would be the following:

Expand product line offerings to include three new flavors based on product attribute research indicating flavor preferences.

Why So Many New Products Fail

Before we leave the topic of product development, we must briefly address why we believe most new products fail. Various studies have reported new product failure rates up to 90 percent. Why do so many new products fail? Here are some of the key reasons according to George Gruenwald:

- *Poor planning:* Establishing objectives and strategies for your new product and all elements of the marketing mix is crucial to a successful launch. In light of the enormous obstacles facing a new product, it is not surprising that failure to sufficiently plan the introduction is a common cause of new product failures. Part of planning includes determining whether there is sufficient demand potential for a product. Very often, thorough research will show that the current size of the target market, with its current competitive set, is just too small to support another offering that does not have superior attributes.
- *Poor management of the process:* Without proper management attention, the new product development process can produce a final output that does not match the original, promising product concept. Even well-meaning input of many functional groups within your organization, all seeking to maximize the performance of their area, can derail the development process and lead to a less-than-successful product.
- *Poor product concept:* Sometimes the idea is just not good, or it does not provide any benefits or advantages over existing competitive products.
- *Poor execution:* It's true that the genius is in the details. Even the best new product concept, with a thorough and disciplined plan, can fail miserably if the production process, distribution, or any aspect of the marketing plan is not followed through successfully.
- *Poor research:* Good research is key to new product development. Testing should ideally be conducted at the concept stage and the prototype stage, and it should include actual test marketing of the product and the marketing mix supporting its introduction.
- *Poor technology or poor product quality:* If the product does not live up to the target market's expectations, it is destined for failure.

DOS AND DON'TS: PRODUCT

Do

- Review your business review, problems and opportunities, brand positioning, marketing strategies, and sales goals prior to preparing this section of the marketing plan.
- Keep an ongoing surveillance of competitive product innovations in your industry.
- Talk with consumers on an ongoing basis. Find out what they think about your product. Discover which of their needs are not being fulfilled by current products available in the category.

- Be willing to make product changes, especially if market research discovers a product void or shows that your product is not competitive against attributes most important to consumers.
- Research and test product innovations and changes prior to making them standard.
- Expect that the vast majority of new product concepts will fail. However, remember that new product successes are the lifeblood of most successful organizations.

Don't

- Don't copy every competitive product innovation. Use research to determine consumer likes and dislikes regarding your product before modifying an existing product or developing a new one.
- Don't change one aspect of your product without considering what the change will do to the other attributes. Remember that consumers purchase for multiple reasons. A cheaper product from a price standpoint may receive less demand if the quality has also diminished. Consumers may like the lower price but may not be willing to sacrifice quality.
- Don't make changes in your product for purely financial reasons. Consumers purchase your product because of its product attributes, not because the product provides a bigger or smaller margin to your company.
- Don't forget that just as new product development is important to a company, so is the divestment or elimination of historically weak products.
- Don't just concentrate on the short-term bottom line while short-changing product development and long-term growth and profits.
- Don't overestimate the size of the market for your product. Many products fail because the market is not large enough in terms of sheer numbers of consumers.

OVERVIEW: NAMING

Some product categories, such as automobiles, are defined by a relatively high level of differentiation between competing product offerings, while others, such as paperclips, are relative commodities. It is the points of differentiation between your product and the competition, whether real or perceived, extensive or relatively few, and how you, the marketer of your product, communicate those differences that comprise your brand as communicated through your name.

As a marketer, it is your task to develop your brand in terms of the name, graphic identity, and maintenance of marketing mix elements consistent with that identity and your positioning. If successful, the brand will be considerably more valuable to you than the sum of physical attributes that comprise your product.

Definition of Naming

In simplest terms, a *name* is merely the identification of a product's or service's source, whether it is the manufacturer, a wholesaler, or some other entity. In slightly broader terms, the name is composed of the title by which the company, product, or service is commonly known and the graphic forms of identification, including symbols, logotypes or signatures, taglines, and representative characters.

For example, we know through our work with Culligan and the American Automobile Association (AAA) that these are two of the best-known and most respected names in America today. The AAA brand covers a vast number of products and services, from towing to maps to insurance to travel. All these services fall under the well-recognized AAA logo. The Culligan logo in turn stands for water with its myriad softener and filtration products. Likewise, Coca-Cola is one of the best-known names in the world. The name, logo, and packaging rank among the highest in recognition across all categories of products. In a final example, Betty Crocker is identified by its white type treatment in a red spoon symbol or by the picture of the "Betty Crocker" character.

Betty Crocker, which is owned by General Mills, is an example of a *manufacturer's brand*—a name other than the producer's provided specifically for a product or collection of products. Use of a manufacturer's name is typical in consumer packaged goods. However, manufacturer naming does not happen just on the consumer side. Service firms often come up with trademarked names to denote proprietary working processes, and the new forward-thinking business-to-business firms recognize that businesses don't buy products—people do. People relate to names the same way, whether it is a mass-consumed product or a narrow market industrial product sold to a select number of companies. In summary, the name helps position the product, and it is a critical component in establishing your image with that purchase.

In some cases, the manufacturer of the product is not identified either with its own name or with a brand name it owns. Rather, a manufacturer may sell the product to wholesalers or retailers, who provide their own brand names, known as *private labels*. For years, Sears was founded on private-label Kenmore appliances and Craftsman tools. *Generic* products bear no brand at all. Generic products gained popularity among consumers in the late 1970s as a means of saving during an inflationary period.

The Importance of Naming

What's in a name? Shakespeare tells us a rose by any other name would still smell sweet. We don't agree. Would you rather give someone an Orange Passion rose, or a Mud Pie rose; an Orange Passion rose or Old Gym Socks rose? Besides the product, which is the manifestation of the positioning, the name is the most critical link to the positioning itself. A name can add value, add margin, and add positive associations with your company, product, or service.

We had been involved in developing names for the popular teen drink Fruitopia over the past years as the product line repositioned away from a 1960s' counterculture fruit drink to a social fruit drink for young adults who are embracing new experiences and rites of passage. The social drink positioning required new product names for the individual flavors. In all examples, the family brand name Fruitopia stayed the same, as did the flavor and the packaging graphics. One of the first new names we developed was Kiwiberry Ruckus. The product went from last selling to first. The name resulted from a disciplined process that helped us form parameters for the naming (for example, the name needed to have a descriptor of flavor) and insights into names that worked best against the new positioning. *Kiwiberry* combines two of the ingredients into one name, and *ruckus* came out of a "party" bucket that tested very well.

By its very definition, naming products provides a means of identifying your product as distinct from that of your competition, in much the same way branding cattle aids in their identification. Consumers must be able to recognize your company, service, or product in its name, logo, packaging, graphics, and, in some cases, the brand's slogan. Names aid the consumers' ability to make quick, safe product choices. You also want the consumers to make positive associations with your image. What would you expect, for example, from the retailer Shoe Carnival compared with Rack Room? Just the names alone help you conjure up very different places in your mind. Both compete against the same basic target market but with very different approaches as reflected in their names. Names, then, help consumers define whom the product is for, what it does, and how it is different. Names allow consumers to recognize products and determine what the products represent within the purchasing environment. This is particularly important today as the number of available products has increased while consumers' available time to research products and make purchase decisions has decreased.

Developing Your Naming Plan

As we stated earlier, the process of naming is complex and ongoing, involving many elements of the marketing mix. In the naming section of your marketing plan, your efforts center on naming and graphic identity.

See also Appendix C, Worksheet 42.

TASK 1 ### Establish Naming Objectives

The first task in devising a naming plan is to arrive at objectives for your name, graphics, and logo as well as legal protection of these elements. Here, you must be careful to state the objectives in terms of the product strategies defined in the previous section. What are your objectives for how the new name and graphic will be used? Is this a new product, a repositioned product, or an existing product? State your objectives, and include a final decision date for selection of the name, completion of a legal search, and adoption of graphics.

For example, to develop a name by March 1 and logo graphic by June 1, for a new software line:

* Compile a final list of name options by November 1.
* Complete legal name search based on this list by December 1.
* Complete consumer research of names by February 1.
* Make final name selection by March 1.
* Create a logo graphic for the new name by June 1.

TASK 2 ### Establish Naming Strategies

Before proceeding to create a new name and/or graphic, you'll need to formulate appropriate strategies. Working out a naming strategy increases the likelihood that you will arrive at a name that is consistent with the product and its positioning and that takes into consideration the users of the product over both the long and short terms. The naming strategy should highlight those components that will communicate the key perceptions to the key targets.

Your strategy should flow directly from the positioning statement and the product strategies. For example, if you are developing a new product and see long-term potential for line extensions, your naming strategy should address this so that the new name you develop accommodates it. For instance, it is reasonable to imagine the Alpo brand of dog food products extended into cat food products, but Milk-Bone brand cat food products probably wouldn't work. (There really is an Alpo cat food.) Further, the name and graphic treatment should be developed on the basis of the breadth of products to which they will apply. In our earlier example, we saw that the Betty Crocker brand applies to a wide variety of cooking and baking packaged goods. The name is not specific to one product, and the red spoon graphic acts as a unifying element across the product line.

Examples of Naming Strategies

1. Name the new line of marine accessories to reflect the value-oriented positioning—quality products at lower prices relative to the competition.
2. Develop a logo for the marine accessories line that can be used across the wide variety of marine products in the line (with the potential of other products to be added in the future).

TASK 3   ## Establish Naming Property Parameters

The naming strategies should be followed by a list of parameters for the new name and graphic application. These parameters are an extension of the naming strategy and provide specific guideposts for name and graphic development.

Example Name Parameters for Consideration

Reflects positioning of the product, and product attributes or benefits
Provides generic identification and clearly identifies with its functional category
Is preemptive
Contributes to awareness and knowledge of its purpose
Is simple
Is memorable
Elicits a mental image and emotion
Provides potential for growth under its umbrella (new entities, products, and so on)
Possesses a positive connotation in meaning, pronunciation, and visualization
Reflects the personality of the product
Has intrinsic meaning of its own (that is, it is not an acronym or a set of letters that signifies nothing)
Not limited geographically or topically as the organization grows
Lends itself to and allows for creative development both visually and in copy
Must work with current signage and packaging sizes
Is legally acceptable and protectable

Example Graphic Parameters for Consideration

Can be reproduced in large or small form
Can be reproduced in black-and-white and in color
Should incorporate colors that reflect the positioning and are attention getting
Must have visual impact in print and broadcast media
Allows for umbrella look applied to a variety of products and packages

TASK 4   ## Generate and Select Names

Task 3 established naming parameters consistent with the positioning. Remember, the names you develop in this step must meet the parameters established in Task 3.

Keep in mind that a positioning tends to be far broader than a single name. The key word for the Fruitopia beverage positioning, for example, was *social*. While there are many ways to communicate "social," the name you choose has to convey a single thought, or certainly something more narrow than the word *social*. Because of these restrictions, we recommend creating various buckets, each representing a way into the positioning from a potential naming standpoint. Using these buckets, you will generate your list of potential names.

Continuing with the Fruitopia example, the buckets we used to communicate *social* included the following headings:

- Party
- Relationships
- Travel
- Drinking
- Sex
- Sports

With each of these buckets, we developed names that were consistent with the bucket heading. We did this a number of ways. You may want to try a combination of these approaches to help you generate initial names:

- *Target market focus groups:* We typically hold a series of focus groups with members of the target market. Through questions and probes, we encourage them to talk about each of the bucket headings. We don't expect participants to come up with actual names, but we do recognize that these people are closest to the product and the positioning. So we use their responses to generate words associated with each bucket. These words are then turned into actual names by copywriters who develop names for a living.
- *Spider exercise:* This is another group exercise. We start by writing each bucket heading in the center of a large piece of paper that is taped to the wall. The first target market member or participant is asked to write words that come to mind beside the heading. Each subsequent person uses the words that were already developed to come up with more associations. For example, say the heading is *party*. The first participant may write *music* as one of the words he or she associates with *party*. The next person may draw a line off that word and write *jam*, the next might draw a line off *jam* and write *rave*, the next may write *all night*, and so on. Many times you get words that are unique to the target market's culture and that provide insights relative to that particular bucket.
- *Internet:* We surf the Internet and set up chat rooms to find and discuss words associated with the bucket headings.
- *Improv comedy:* Adapting an improvisational comedy technique, we use the bucket headings in a "yes, and" game to generate words and ideas. The game requires each participant to use the bucket to come up with a key word within the framework of a story connected to the bucket heading. The next participant builds on the idea, staying within the context of the story but picking another key word to build on the previous word. This and other improv techniques can be used as rapid-fire fodder for development of names.
- *Development of prefixes, suffixes, and make-believe words:* The goal here is to find partial words or nonwords that sound as if they connect to the bucket. An example is Meriter Hospital. *Meriter* is a made-up name that we thought consumers might associate with quality. When we tested it, we found that it connoted quality strongly among the target market consumers. It became the new name for a hospital that was combining two long-standing hospitals into a new entity.

- *Use of a name generator:* The following chart can serve as an easy reference to help you generate names:

Name Generator	
Combine words	PowerBook; Alka-Seltzer; Microsoft; Netscape
Soundalike	Krispy Kreme; Cingular
Phrase	Gee, Your Hair Smells Terrific; I Can't Believe It's Not Butter; There's Something About Mary
Benefit	Econolodge; 7-Eleven; Pur; Eveready; Gogurt
Visual image	Bell Telephone; Gibraltar Insurance; Apple Computer
Oxymoron	Shell Fire & Ice; Dark Star; Hi-Lo; Stop-N-Go
Alliteration	Big Boy; Stovetop Stuffing; Swiffer Sweeper
Rhyme	Piggly Wiggly; Blue's Clues; Slim Jim
Foreign language	Stolichnaya; eBay; Volkswagen; Evian
Place	Hidden Valley Ranch; Old Orchard; Boston Market
Pun	Frybaby; Slip 'N Slide; Nut & Honey
Gods	Nike; Mercury; Atlas; Sprite; Janus
Animals	The Bulls; Elefanten Shoes; Bobcat; Mustang
Colors	Blue Bunny; Red Bull; Screaming Yellow Zonkers
Person's name	Dr. Scholl's; Smith Barney; Baby Ruth; McDonald's
Acronym	IBM; SHK Foods (Seven Hungry Kids); TCBY; XTC
Borrowed genre	McMuffin; Vegematic; USA Today
Sound effect	Nestle's Crunch; Shout; Ding-Dong; Meow Mix
Verbs	Jolt Cola; Rollerblade; Slice; Surge; Sprint
Personification	Janitor in a Drum; Mr. Softee; Mrs. Butterworth's
Target market	Weight Watchers; Playboy; Hanes for Her
Slang	FUBU; Fuddruckers; Idiot's Guide to Car Repair
Category descriptor	Le Car; Ticketmaster; Master Lock; Juicy Juice

These and other techniques can be used to arrive at initial words for the next step in the naming process. After developing buckets and words that are consistent with each bucket, you need to form a list of potential names based on these suggestions. From there, you can test several of what you think may be the best names under each bucket.

Keep in mind that names related to real words are usually preferable to made-up words. You have a tremendous head start with a name that already means something positively tangible to the consumer in terms of understanding your product and its benefits. In testing the names, you are also essentially testing the buckets. This testing is best done through another series of focus groups. If you don't conduct this research to test your names, we suggest you use the name evaluator guide on the following page. It allows you to rate names across the top of the chart based on some agreed-upon criteria that flow down the vertical column.

TASK 5   ## *Protect Your Name Legally*

The final step is to run the chosen names through a legal trademark search with your corporate law firm. Because names hold value but do not represent assets for the companies that own them, they are subject to extensive legal protection. Walt Disney

Name Evaluator		
Name	**A**	**B**
Short		
Easy to say, conversational		
Easy to remember		
Relevant to category		
Relevant to benefit		
Creates strong feeling		
Likable		
Believable		
Rhyme		
Alliteration		
Oxymoron		
Consistent with brand		
Consistent with name family		
Concrete visual image		
Stands out, unusual, different		
Ownable		
Total		

is extremely sensitive about the use of its characters, and it has been known to file law-suits to protect the value and equity of its brand and the characters that represent it. It is imperative that marketers developing a new name, logo, or graphic identity for their company, product, or service register their final selection. Registration of a trademark takes place with the Patent and Trademark Office (PTO) of the U.S. Department of Commerce. Registration with the PTO lasts 10 years, and it is renewable on the basis of intent to use the trademark and maintain active protection thereof.

This may be your most frustrating naming activity of all, as many product and service categories are heavily penetrated with names that already are trademarked. That's why we always recommend that several names be tested. This practice helps ensure that you will have more than one option.

If you are not in a position to develop names on your own, seek help. Look to your marketing communication agency or a growing number of firms that special-ize in the naming process. Compaq Computers and Verizon are two examples of names that came from companies that specialize in name development.

DOS AND DON'TS: NAMING

Do

- Reflect on the entire naming process, including your overall needs and goals for the brand.
- Review your positioning and product strategies before developing your naming plan. Use these as the basis of your naming objectives and strategies.
- Highlight the key images you wish to communicate to your target market in your naming strategy.
- Outline the qualities, descriptors, and related items that reflect your product and positioning.
- Use a disciplined process when developing a name for your product, firm, or store—from what you want the name to accomplish through a thorough name-generating process.
- If possible, use research to test alternative names, naming buckets, and graphics among the target market.

- Choose the name that best communicates the brand positioning strategy, keeping in mind that the name should be descriptive and have no negatives.
- Consider including your employees in the naming process. Have them generate name alternatives, and communicate to them the reasons for the final selection before it becomes public.
- Make sure you have an established plan to communicate your new name to the audience. Acceptance of a new name is often determined by how well the new name is communicated.
- Have the final list of names go through a legal search to make certain you are not infringing on someone's trademark.
- Once the name is selected, apply for a registered trademark for legal protection.

Don't

- Don't take the first name that comes to you, particularly if you think it's creative, cool, or cute.
- Don't complicate your product name. Keep it simple and memorable.
- If it is a name change, don't expect the new name to be readily accepted. Many people don't like change. However, familiarity breeds acceptability, so build high awareness for the new name quickly.
- Don't go it alone with a name change if your company and agency do not have the time and specific abilities to develop a new name. Consider hiring a consulting firm that specializes in developing new names and brand identity programs.
- Don't necessarily adopt acronyms or the initials of your firm's name as a new name in trade name situations. Don't assume your customers are as familiar with your firm's initials or a short version of your firm's name as you are. Large, well-known companies like IBM or AT&T are the exception, not the norm.

OVERVIEW: PACKAGING

Earlier in this chapter we defined the product as the physical object the consumer purchases and uses, and we defined the *name* as the collection of associations the consumer holds about your particular product.

An important element of every product, which serves as a vehicle for the brand, is the packaging. The package bears the responsibility of holding or maintaining your product and communicating the essence of your brand.

In this section of the chapter we will consider the functions of packaging, why you should consider developing new packaging for your product, and how to develop a packaging plan. If you are a retailer or service firm, the issue of packaging really refers to your store or business environment, and we will address that briefly.

Functions of Packaging

Packaging serves many important purposes: protecting the product, facilitating the product's use, and communicating about the product.

Protection

At their most utilitarian level, packages serve to protect. For the product, packages serve to prevent breakage (eggs), exposure to light (film), exposure to air (wine), exposure to contaminants (drugs), and spoilage (crackers). At the very least, they hold or contain the product for presentation in the store. Today products can safely remain unopened on shelves for months, even years—the result of technology in preservatives and packaging. But the protective function of packaging goes beyond the product. Packaging plays an important role in protecting the consumer as well. For example, special caps minimize the misuse of products, particularly by small children (childproof caps), and packaging has been developed to minimize the potential for product tampering, particularly in pharmaceuticals.

Facilitating Product Use

Packaging serves an important facilitative role in the use of the product. A bottle's shape, the type of pour spout it contains, its ability to be resealed, and other similar packaging attributes all contribute to the consumer's ease in using a product. The package essentially becomes an important component of the product itself. Microwavable food products, for example, would not be nearly as effective if not for the packages that accommodate microwave cooking.

Different package sizes also accommodate differences in the use of a product among various target market segments. Soft drinks are available in cases, 12-packs, and 6-packs of cans and in resealable bottles in two-liter and quart sizes. In fact, the package size can address differences in the benefits sought among segments. Juices can be found in large, family-sized bottles; in individual-sized, 12-ounce cans for adults; or in smaller, lunchbox-sized boxes with straws, for kids.

The package is, in many respects, part of the product. It contributes to the use experience of the product in a way that exceeds a mere supporting role. In many cases it is the package that provides the point of differentiation between one product and another. Your package's ability to aid the consumer in his or her use of a product better than that of the competing brand represents a competitive advantage for your brand. Toothpastes in special squeeze containers, salad dressings with shaker tops, squeezable butter, and resealable luncheon meats are examples of how packaging can contribute to a brand's competitive edge. In fact, a packaging innovation occasionally spawns a new product or line extension for an existing product, as it allows entry into a new target market segment and/or facilitates a different use for a product from the original packaging. Oscar Mayer Lunchables resulted from the technology in packaging that allowed physical separation of component products.

In addition to adding value to a brand through the normal use of the product, a package can add value for the consumer beyond the product's common use or even after the product is consumed. Wines or juices are often sold in decanter-style bottles, which act as premium items for consumers; the bottles obviously serve to hold the wine or juice and accommodate normal pouring, but they can be kept and used by the consumers after the wine or juice is gone.

Communication

Your package represents an important, perhaps the most important, communication tool for you. Labels are used to provide information to consumers to aid both in the product and brand purchase decision and in usage following purchase.

Some of the relatively utilitarian, but nonetheless important, information often conveyed on packaging includes the brand name and product category definition. The box reads, in large type: Kraft (brand) Macaroni and Cheese (product). In extended brand lines, the particular flavor or style is indicated on the package, including grades of oil, flavors of ice cream, applications of shampoo, and so on. The Kraft Macaroni and Cheese example might include a designation indicating regular shapes and special spiral shapes. Finally, the package is utilized to provide warnings, directions, weight or volume measurements, contents and ingredients, date codes, nutritional information, and more.

Packaging also serves an important role in the marketing communications function. This communication effort is provided both explicitly and implicitly. Promotions and offers are often displayed, presented, and explained on packages. Flags, bursts, banners, and other graphic elements on package fronts direct the consumers' attention to specials, premiums, or other promotional offerings from the manufacturer. Cereal boxes are notorious for providing special offers and free gifts. The package can be further used to actually carry the promotional element, rather than simply communicating its existence. Label backs carry coupons or recipes, on-pack or in-pack premiums may be accommodated with the packaging, or contest pieces may be carried in the package, such as letters under soda bottle caps.

The primary way that packaging serves as a marketing communications vehicle is often less obvious than the use of banners and bursts. The package as a whole must communicate the brand's image and positioning. This happens in a variety of ways.

First, the package should appeal to the target market. Industrial products, for example, tend to be much more utilitarian than consumer products distributed through retail channels. Packaging for a brand aiming at the teen market will bear considerably different graphics, language, and size offerings than a brand positioned against mothers with young children.

Second, the package aids in product visibility and awareness, particularly in the retail setting. An important element of branding is product awareness and recognition among consumers. In today's cluttered retail environment, some 30,000 brands fight for the shoppers' attention, retailers are providing less sales assistance, and consumers are making more and more buying decisions at the point of purchase. In this context, your package serves an important role in getting your brand noticed, essentially taking the salesperson's place and encouraging impulse purchases. The package does this through graphics that are attractive or appealing to the consumer, by communicating product attributes and benefits, and by standing out from the crowd.

Finally, the packaging inherently contributes to the brand's image and equity and has a major impact on the target person's attitude toward the product. This role is partially fulfilled through the items mentioned in this section, in the combination of the package's graphics and structure. For example, the fact that a certain brand of paper towels is always packaged using simple graphics on the label, with bursts promoting special low pricing and a coupon for the next purchase, would help communicate the brand's image as a value-based paper towel. By contrast, the higher-quality orange juice is expected to have a better resealable pour spout, perhaps a stronger container, and more attractive graphics. But a package's contribution to a brand's equity is established over time and transcends the functional roles it plays. Eventually, the successful package is clearly identified and associated with the brand. It is, in essence, the physical representation of the brand in the consumer's mind. Coke is the classic example. Coke's bottle shape is as much a part of the brand identity as the name, swoosh graphic, and colors, and it elicits the variety of images and perceptions associated with the Coke brand among consumers.

How the Store or Business Environment Is Like Product Packaging

The retail or service environment serves functions similar to product packaging. It first serves a utilitarian function by housing the products and services you sell. Further, it facilitates the purchase and/or use of the products and services. Grocery stores must provide parking and signage externally to draw customers into the store effectively and efficiently. Internally, shelving is provided to display and hold the products, aisles are maintained for customers to walk along and view the products, signage is available to help them find what they're looking for, and lighting is designed to allow them to clearly see the products and labels. Moreover, the store layout is developed to draw consumers through the store past high-margin items, and displays are used to encourage impulse purchases.

The retail and service environments, both internally and externally, also serve an important communications function. In particular, these settings promote an image to shoppers and reflect the positioning of the firm. Externally, theme decorations, lighting schemes, signage, and landscaping speak volumes to the consumer about the type of establishment he or she is entering. Inside, the interior design, including the color scheme, fixture design, sign style, and even the sound and smell, tell the consumer whether he or she is in Saks or Kmart. All of these elements need to be designed to reflect an image consistent with the positioning for the firm and all of the other communications aimed at the target.

Reasons for Changing Your Packaging

As you get set to begin developing the packaging section of your marketing plan, you need to determine whether or not you need a new package for your product. Clearly, if your plan is for a completely new product, a new package is a must. But if your plan is being developed for an existing product, there are a variety of situations that may indicate it's time to consider new packaging, according to Howard Alport, the principal of Lipson-Alport-Glass & Associates, a design identity firm in Northbrook, Illinois, who writes extensively on packaging and packaging design and whose firm is considered a specialist in the discipline of packaging design. They are as follows:

- *New product or brand positioning:* If you are repositioning your product, you may need to create a new package that reflects the new positioning. As we have stated, the graphics, color, and package shape all must work together in a way that relates and even enhances the positioning of the brand.
- *Poor graphics:* Take a look at your current package. How does it look and feel to you? How does it compare with competitive brands' packages? Refer back to your business review and research—did you get any feedback from the consumers about your package? What do they think about your package? If your package looks cluttered, indistinct, or outdated, it may be time to change.
- *New target market segment for the product:* The target market is the group against which you position the product. If your company is changing target markets, and perhaps the product's positioning as well, you will need to consider changes in your packaging. This is necessary to more closely reflect the new target's needs and to develop packaging (form and function) that more effectively helps persuade the new target market to purchase. Even if the basic positioning does not change against a different segment, the package needs to be reviewed. Its styling and graphics must be relevant to its target audience. Further, a different target group may require different attributes of the package in order to facilitate their particular usage of the product.
- *Line extensions:* In the previous section, we discussed how a brand name and graphic identity need to accommodate future product plans, such as line extensions. Packaging must be adjusted or redesigned to accommodate these changes as they occur. Packages in these situations should reflect an image and general look consistent with the brand, yet communicate the differences between individual product types, whether they are new styles or flavors of the same product or are different products.
- *Wider distribution (new channels):* To gain entry into a particular channel, a package may need to be adjusted in look, style, size, and/or shape to accommodate the display structure and method and the purchase environment. For example,

a videotape sold in packs of six in consumer electronics stores may need to provide single packs in brighter packaging to be carried at checkout displays in grocery stores. The smaller and brighter unit may be more conducive to impulse purchases in an environment that is visually busy and competitive.

Developing a Packaging Plan

As you prepare to develop a plan for your product's packaging, review your positioning, appropriate marketing strategies, and product and branding plans. Your packaging plan should reflect your positioning and flow from the objectives and strategies for the product and brand.

See also Appendix C, Worksheet 43.

TASK 1 **Develop Packaging Objectives**

Establish objectives for your packaging that focus on the following issues:

- Communicating of brand positioning and image to contribute to building equity in your brand
- Generating awareness and drawing attention to the product at the point of purchase
- Encouraging trial
- Providing protection for and enhancement of the product by making usage easier or adding value to the purchase
- Communicating promotional offerings

Provide a time frame for the development and production of your new packaging. The following is an example of a packaging objective:

Have new packaging ready for introduction by March 1 of next year that fulfills the following:
- Communicates the family-oriented positioning and extra servings per container
- Protects the product while displaying the product fully prepared
- Emphasizes the new brand name and graphic scheme
- Addresses the three flavors clearly, yet maintains a consistent look for the brand

TASK 2 **Develop Packaging Strategies**

Your packaging strategies suggest direction for achieving your objectives. They should address specifics about the packaging, such as the following:

- *Physical attributes of the package:* What size is the container going to be, or how many sizes will be provided? What is the type and strength of the package material? What color and design scheme will be utilized? What shape should it be? What copy elements should it contain?
- *Use of an outside packaging firm:* Will an outside packaging firm, design firm, or agency be called upon to assist in your new packaging efforts? If so, when and to what extent will the firm be involved?

Examples of Packaging Strategies
- Develop a uniquely shaped plastic package in a 12- and 16-ounce size that will accommodate extensive home and office use.

- Use bright, bold graphics, and provide product attribute statements to communicate a value orientation.
- Assign an agency to the packaging project by October 1 to assist in design and research.

DOS AND DON'TS: PACKAGING

Do

- Review your problems and opportunities, sales objectives, positioning, marketing strategies, and your product and branding plans prior to developing your packaging plans.
- Since packaging can be used to execute promotional plans, consider the package as a promotion carrier. If your package is to be used in this manner, address this in your packaging plan.
- Make sure the packaging clearly communicates the name and benefits of your product.
- Be as creative as possible with your packaging. Make it unique and make it stand out, but keep it simple and functional.
- Keep it simple. Put less rather than more on the package. Think of your package as a billboard—try to quickly communicate and catch people's attention while portraying the intended image.
- Packaging must provide a message, both explicit and implicit, consistent with the product positioning and brand image. Be sure all packaging conforms to a simple, unified set of graphic standards and guidelines.
- Test packaging options. It is important to know how consumers respond to new packaging or modifications in terms of visual impact, use, and competitive performance.
- If you're a retailer, your packaging includes the total store, from the parking lot and the exterior of the store to the interior of the store. Utilize the store environment in the same ways that manufacturers utilize the package for their products. It should quickly command attention to your product, make a statement about your image, and functionally dispense product or provide convenient shopping for your consumers.
- Compare your current package and new prototype to that of the competition in a real store environment prior to and during package development.
- Make sure your packaging meets legal requirements in terms of communication regarding content.

Don't

- Don't view packaging as just a means of product protection or as a way to dispense the product. Use it as a way to create a product difference and as a communication vehicle to build awareness and to positively affect attitudes.
- Don't change your packaging for change's sake but to increase sales. Like advertising and positioning, familiarity of message can be used to your advantage.
- Don't develop packaging inconsistent with the overall positioning of your firm and your product.
- Don't miss the chance for your packaging to improve your product. The outside of the package usually should enhance the inherent drama of what is inside.
- Don't hesitate to hire outside help for packaging development. Look for firms with knowledge of package manufacturing, design, and research.

The Successful Marketing Plan

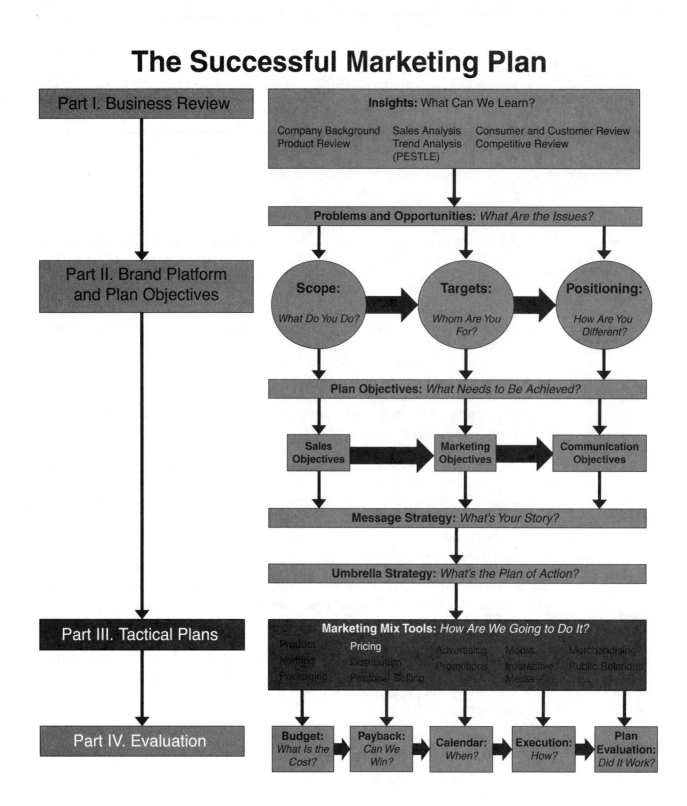

Part I. Business Review

Insights: What Can We Learn?

Company Background   Sales Analysis   Consumer and Customer Review
Product Review   Trend Analysis   Competitive Review
                      (PESTLE)

Problems and Opportunities: *What Are the Issues?*

Part II. Brand Platform and Plan Objectives

Scope: What Do You Do?

Targets: Whom Are You For?

Positioning: How Are You Different?

Plan Objectives: *What Needs to Be Achieved?*

Sales Objectives   **Marketing Objectives**   **Communication Objectives**

Message Strategy: *What's Your Story?*

Umbrella Strategy: *What's the Plan of Action?*

Part III. Tactical Plans

Marketing Mix Tools: *How Are We Going to Do It?*

Product   Pricing   Advertising   Media   Merchandising
Naming   Distribution   Promotions   Interactive   Public Relations
Packaging   Personal Selling   Media

Part IV. Evaluation

Budget: *What Is the Cost?*   **Payback:** *Can We Win?*   **Calendar:** *When?*   **Execution:** *How?*   **Plan Evaluation:** *Did It Work?*

13 Pricing

Pricing represents one of the basic elements of the marketing mix, and it is one of the most difficult elements for which to develop a plan. The importance of pricing is evident in its effect on the target market, as price represents the consumer's primary cost for obtaining your product. Unfortunately, the nature of pricing is very complex, with implications for your firm, your product, the competition, the target market, and the individual consumer. As a result of this complexity, setting prices is as much an art (and perhaps more so) as it is a science.

Our task in this chapter is to present you with an overview of pricing implications and a methodology for developing a pricing plan, utilizing as much hard data as possible. As you begin outlining your pricing plan, review your problems and opportunities, plan strategies, and communication goals for pricing direction. Our recommended methodology will give you a solid framework for your pricing decisions, but it will not guarantee results. You will also need some good, old-fashioned common sense.

FROM THIS CHAPTER YOU WILL LEARN

- The definition of *price*
- Important pricing considerations
- How to develop pricing objectives and strategies
- Additional pricing tactics

OVERVIEW

For the purposes of this book, we will define *price* as the monetary value of your products or services to your target market. For retailers, pricing involves an overall pricing approach for your establishment or chain, as well as setting prices for each individual item. For service firms, there are fees and rates and the application of each in a given transaction. For most business types, there also exist instances of competitive bidding and negotiation, which are components of pricing. We will attempt to touch on all of these elements. Our emphasis, however, will be on arriving at an appropriate pricing approach—lower, higher, or parity pricing relative to the competition.

CONSIDERATIONS IN PRICING

Some issues to consider when pricing products and services are the following:

- Your breakeven points
- The price sensitivity of your target market
- The positioning of your products and services
- The characteristics of the segments within your target market
- Your prices as promotional tools
- The stage of your products in their life cycle
- How your prices differentiate your products within your target market
- The effect of your prices on your competitive bidding situation
- Your overall business goals

Breakeven

Barring the use of loss-leader pricing to drive sales, there is a point below which it would be unreasonable to price your product, known as the *breakeven*. Obviously, the revenue you bring in for a product must be at least equal to what you expend for that product or you are losing money.

Two types of costs must be considered when establishing prices—variable and fixed:

Variable costs: These costs vary with the volume of production or sales—for example, costs associated with incremental payroll and new material purchases.

Fixed costs: These costs do not change with fluctuating sales or production. Fixed costs are usually spread evenly over the company's brands or products, and in this manner they are calculated for each individual product along with the variable costs of selling that product. Examples of fixed costs are rent, insurance, real estate taxes, and depreciation on machinery.

Also there are two pricing scenarios that the marketer should understand when making pricing decisions:

Short-run, excess capacity pricing: If there is excess capacity, management needs to set prices such that the variable costs are covered and there is adequate margin for some contribution to fixed costs or overhead. In the short run, if there is excess capacity, it is far better to take an order with less margin because total year-end company profit will be greater or the total loss will be less than if the order had not been taken and the sale not made.

Long-run pricing: In the long run, prices have to be established so that *all* costs (fixed *and* variable) are covered and there is a profit.

The following formula allows you to determine breakeven points to help ensure that expenditures do not exceed sales. The breakeven analysis allows the marketer to gain insight into the effect of pricing decisions on income and costs and to establish a price that will cover all costs.

$$PX = FC + VC(X)$$

Where:

P = price
VC = variable costs

EXHIBIT 13.1

Breakeven Chart

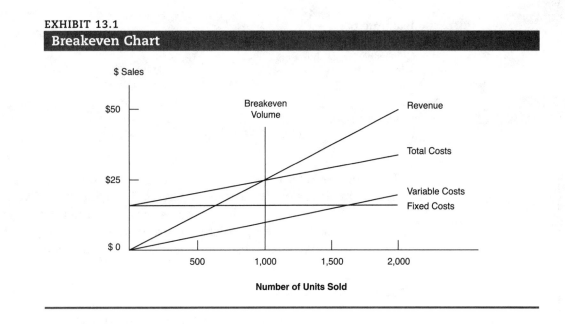

FC = fixed costs

X = volume of units produced at breakeven point (the number of units that must be sold)

Assume you are a shoe retailer, and the average pair of shoes will be sold at $25. Your fixed costs are $10,000 per month, and your variable costs are $15 per pair of shoes:

$$\$25X = \$10,000 + \$15X$$
$$\$10X = \$10,000$$
$$X = 1,000 \text{ pairs of shoes}$$

Based on the breakeven analysis, 1,000 pairs of shoes must be sold at $25 to cover monthly costs.

The breakeven chart is shown graphically in Exhibit 13.1. The marketer can also use the breakeven chart concept to plot fixed costs, variable costs, and revenues. In this manner, the marketer can usually determine the effect of a drop in price and a resulting increase in sales and potential profits.

Let's assume that the shoe company in the previous example was operating at above breakeven, selling 1,500 pairs of shoes per month at $25. As you will recall, fixed costs are $10,000 per month, and variable costs are $15 per pair of shoes.

Example A

Number of pairs of shoes sold	1,500		
Revenue	1,500 × $25	=	$37,500
Costs	$10,000 + ($15 × 1,500)	=	$32,500
Profits per month		=	$5,000

Now let's assume that the marketer, through past experience, can estimate that a drop in average price per shoe to $23 will result in a 30 percent increase in business.

Example B

Number of pairs of shoes sold at 30% increase (1.3 × 1,500)	1,950		
Revenue	1,950 × $23	=	$44,850
Costs	$10,000 + ($15 × 1,950)	=	$39,250
Profits per month		=	$5,600
Profit difference between Examples A and B		=	$600

The shoe marketer would make another $600 by lowering the price $2 with an anticipated increase of business of 30 percent. If the increase in volume were only 10 percent, the marketer would make less profit (try the formula to prove this to yourself). Thus, if you can predict your product's elasticity reasonably accurately, you can use this formula to estimate changes in profitability due to price changes.

Price Sensitivity

The effect of a price on sales volume is the result of change in consumer demand determined by the market's willingness or capacity to pay that price for the product. This concept is known as *price sensitivity*, and it is influenced by two major factors: consumer attitudes and attribute preferences, and the status of alternatives.

The first factor affecting price sensitivity for your product involves the nature of that product offering—its attribute composition—and the attitudes the target has with regard to those attributes. Such consumer attitudes about your product are developed on the basis of their preferences for certain attributes—what they consider important in a product—and their perceptions of the performance of your product offering on those attributes. The better your product performs on important attributes, the more consumers are willing to pay for it. We have discussed this at length in earlier chapters, and your business review should provide information about how your product rates in this regard.

The second factor that influences consumer price sensitivity relates to the alternatives to your product, in the form of your competition or suitable product substitutes. Price sensitivity for your product is affected by the availability, attractiveness, and price of the alternatives. For example, if there are many alternatives available, either in the form of direct competitive offerings or substitutes, if those offerings are "suitable" alternatives with regard to the consumers' attribute preferences, and if the alternatives are "reasonably" priced, then the price sensitivity for your product is likely to be quite high.

The degree to which consumer demand is sensitive to price changes is referred to as *price elasticity*. After reviewing your pricing problems and opportunities from the business review, you may find that demand for your product is elastic—by lowering the price dramatically, you lower your gross margin (selling price less cost of goods sold), but you actually make more profits because of the increased volume. Or you may find that demand for your product is inelastic—higher prices only marginally affect volume, but margins and profits increase substantially. This is useful information in developing your pricing objectives and strategies.

Positioning

The positioning of your product plays an important role in the final price decision. A high, or premium, price suggests product quality. Consumers have come to associate high price with quality. Moreover, higher prices are indeed necessary for premium products to finance the product development and improvements, production technology, and quality components integral to a high-quality final product. By contrast, a product can establish a low-price positioning, generating high sales volume to maintain low unit costs and necessary profit levels.

Appropriate distribution channels are an important component of each positioning and pricing strategy. For example, Rolex watches maintain high prices consistent with their quality image and are distributed through higher-priced jewelry stores, while Timex watches, available through mass merchants, are priced much lower. We see this same conflict where some shoe vendors hesitate to provide Famous Footwear, an off-price shoe retailer, the newest shoe models. They worry that an off-price retailer will dilute the quality and prestige image of their flagship brands, which are positioned around performance, fashion, and style—not price.

As opposed to a strictly low-price positioning, many products, services, or retailers pursue a value positioning, which has many interpretations. Value can mean low price, but it is also evident in a high price. Value is broadly defined as substantial benefits gained relative to the cost incurred from the consumer's perspective, which can translate into a price-to-quality relationship. Consumers are willing to pay more for a product if it is considered a "better value," that is, if they get what they pay for. Famous Footwear began as a budget-priced shoe store chain and then changed to a value positioning. In this particular case, the value results from providing brand name shoes for less.

One of our clients, a business-to-business manufacturer, established a positioning based on product quality, focusing on particular attributes considered important by the target. The firm then adopted a parity pricing approach, based on the facts that the target was very price sensitive and the firm's performance was rated favorably on delivering a low price. In this way, the firm could differentiate itself from the competition in terms of attributes *and* remain competitive in pricing. The firm could not support a low-price strategy, which would have run counter to the positioning of quality, and the market would not bear a high-price strategy.

Target Market

Pricing helps to define your target market. Higher prices, for example, are generally appropriate for higher-income segments. For introductory products, higher prices allow marketers to reach innovators, who tend to be among the least price sensitive segments. Lower prices are appropriate for mass-market distribution.

Marketers can segment the market through the pricing of their product. They can also segment multiple product offerings accordingly. For example, Toyota offers a range of automobiles at various price points for various segments, from the low-priced Matrix to the high-end Avalon. Above that, Toyota's Lexus luxury cars, selling for about $45,000 and up, are available for the higher-income segment. Taking this concept one step further, marketers can also offer the exact same product at various prices for different segments. Movie theaters, for example, charge a lower price for children and senior citizens. This method of pricing is known as *discriminatory pricing*.

Promotions

Price is an important promotional tool for the marketer, and it is used extensively as a customer incentive for a variety of short-term objectives.

Limited price reductions can be used to increase sales quickly in specific markets, to reduce excess capacity or product overstocks, to induce pantry stocking by consumers prior to a competitive introduction, or to increase traffic at the retail level. Occasionally certain products will be priced at or near cost to generate traffic and lead to sales of higher-margin items. Such low-priced products are referred to as *loss leaders*.

Price increases can also be used to address reductions or shortcomings in capacity or to induce trial of a new or other alternative product from the same manufacturer.

Product Life Cycle

The stage of your product in the product life cycle has an important influence on the pricing structure in the industry and presents various implications for your pricing decisions. In each stage, a high- or low-price strategy may be appropriate for different objectives. You determined where your product is in its life cycle when you prepared your business review. The following provides an overview of the ramifications and alternative pricing strategy implications for each stage.

Introductory Stage

Products in the introductory stage see little competition and can be priced relatively freely. Such products sometimes utilize a low price—called a *penetration price*—to build a customer base quickly. Lower prices encourage trial and mass consumption by a broad base of consumers. Thus, lower prices provide an opportunity to quickly establish a trial of your product and a consumer franchise before other competitors enter the marketplace. Also, keep in mind that competitive pricing may serve as a barrier to entry to future competitors. Alternatively, a high price—called a *premium price*—is very often set to generate profits to cover investment costs for the new product and maximize profits while there still is limited competition.

If the product is unique and has little competition, the pricing choice can be one of maximizing profit per unit sold. The strategy involves selling to a narrow group of consumers who are willing to purchase because of unique product attributes. This premium price strategy helps keep the purchaser base smaller than a low-price strategy, thus making allowances for limited production capabilities and/or distribution channels. Premium pricing also allows for maximum margins and potentially quicker payback on the research and development of a new product, as well as heavy levels of introductory advertising.

Growth Stage

In this stage, the market is growing, as a larger number of mass market consumers become users or purchasers. As the market expands, competition increases. Competitive offerings are typically differentiated on the basis of attributes, but price also becomes a competitive tool, establishing low-priced and premium-priced offerings, among others. One option, known as *skimming*, happens when the company sets a high price and thus high margin for the product during introduction and at the start of the growth stage. Skimming is typically a tactic of companies with a product that is unique and has few competitors or has inelastic demand. It allows the company to take advantage of its unique position while at the same time creating a cash cow and building up profits to be used later in the product's life cycle to either defend against competitors or expand the product line. By contrast, a low price can be used to build market share as quickly as possible, essentially buying customers and deterring competitive entries.

Maturity Stage

In this stage, market growth has slowed or stopped. Price becomes important, as well as service, as products become standardized and offer fewer innovations. It is best for a marketer to avoid this stage, or at least minimize its effects, by continually improving the product or service attributes. Pricing alternatives include maintaining high prices to finance new products or using low or promotional pricing to simply compete and maintain market share.

Decline Stage

Once a market begins declining, the remaining competitors should seek simple survival for their product offerings, or leave the market altogether. The appropriate pricing strategy involves recovering variable costs and providing some contribution to overhead.

Product Differentiation

In industries where products are not highly differentiated in terms of attributes, pricing and service become the only real points of differentiation. In some cases, particularly in growth markets, pricing can contribute to maintaining differentiation of a brand. This effort usually requires a higher-price strategy to generate revenues to finance product improvements and R&D, and as discussed earlier, the higher price connotes a quality image consistent with a differentiated product.

Competitive Bidding

For certain industries, a bidding process is common or even required. Construction-related industries rely on this method of determining pricing on a project-by-project basis. For such an approach, prices are calculated on the basis of estimated materials requirements (often at cost plus a standard markup), plus labor hours at appropriate labor rates, and additional services (shipping, for example). Part of the process of setting the price includes determining the appropriate, or best, method of completing the work.

The competitive bidding practice combines a competitive orientation with an internal orientation. The estimator must calculate the firm's costs for a job and apply appropriate rates for specific services to be completed in the process of the project. Further, rates are often based on what the firm wants to earn for each hour of an employee's services. At the same time, rates are also based on going rates, and final project estimates are often adjusted based on the competitive status of the project bidding process, reflecting the involvement of a particular known competitor or an intuition of what the job is likely to "go for."

Business Goals

You should also take into consideration what you need to accomplish in other areas of your business. Such goals, including sales and profitability objectives, can be aided by the appropriate pricing approach or derailed by an inappropriate one. Following are some examples of business goals and the implications of lower, higher, or parity pricing on these goals.

Increase Short-Run Profits

Occasionally, additional profits are needed from a product offering, perhaps to finance a line extension or to offset a particular cost increase. A higher-price strategy overall attracts the less-price-sensitive segment of the market, and thus, a short-term increase will likely not lead to a drastic loss of sales volume. Short-run profits are typically a goal for new products, which cater to the less-price-sensitive early adopters, in an effort to recoup expenditures from the product development process. A mature market product may also maintain a high-price strategy for the sake of short-term profits—an approach known as *harvesting*. In such a case, other costs associated with the product will be cut to increase overall margins on the product, often to finance other investments by the firm. Obviously, an analysis of the price elasticity of demand for your product, along with a breakeven analysis, is important prior to implementing any price strategy to affect short-term profits.

Increase Sales

Often a large spurt of sales activity is needed, particularly with new products attempting to build a market. Typically, this business objective implies a low-price strategy, as the marketer attempts to influence trial to build a base of customers. Such an approach also discourages competitive entry into a market. Finally, a consistent low-price approach can be used to increase sales to a high level; it can then be maintained to create a discount positioning by reducing manufacturing costs due to economies of scale. The Rolex versus Timex example discussed earlier illustrates this situation. By contrast to Rolex, Timex produces and sells a much higher volume of products, allowing for lower overall costs and a lower-price positioning.

Survive

At times the best a product can hope for is sheer survival, as alternative product innovations or consumer preferences and lifestyles make a category obsolete. In such cases, the product should aim to simply recover variable costs and provide a contribution to fixed costs.

DETERMINING YOUR PRICING NEEDS

The last thing you must do prior to deciding the appropriate pricing approach is to review your problems and opportunities, marketing objectives, positioning marketing strategies, and communication goals for overall focus and pricing implications. Then, reflect on the considerations discussed in this section and what they mean for your product. From the problems and opportunities, marketing objectives, and positioning strategies, develop a list that details all of the areas that your pricing approach needs to impact and in what way. Include the implications of all of the issues discussed here, such as the product life cycle stage, the product's cost, and your business's goals.

A worksheet designed to assist you in developing this list is shown in Exhibit 13.2, and it is also available in Appendix C, Worksheet 44. This list, which essentially details what you need from your pricing plan, will direct you toward an appropriate pricing approach.

HOW TO DEVELOP A PRICING PLAN

There are two steps in developing a pricing plan: (1) establish your pricing objectives and (2) establish your pricing strategies.

See also Appendix C, Worksheet 45.

TASK 1 ### Establish Your Pricing Objectives

The first major step in the development of a pricing plan is to establish your pricing objective—whether you intend to implement a lower, higher, or parity pricing

EXHIBIT 13.2

Pricing Considerations

Consideration	Specific Situation	Pricing Implication	Potential Price Approach
Problems and opportunities	The company's "standard" line is continually underpriced by the competition.	This line is losing share and losing distribution.	Match price of top three competitors.
Marketing objectives	Increase new customer trial by 15% over previous year.	Price is an important attribute sought by first-time customers.	Provide price incentives around new customer promotions.
Positioning	Position as the most affordable competitive option.	Looking to position based on a price relative to competition.	Maintain price just below top three competitors.
Marketing strategies	Build sales volume in off-season months of May and September.	Price incentives could be used to pump sales during the off-season.	Use price promotions to tie off-season sales to seasonal purchases.
Price communication goals			
Breakeven			
Price elasticity			
Product life cycle stage			
Product differentiation			
Business goals			
Competition pricing			
Other			

approach relative to the competition. All other objectives, such as increased sales or higher margins, are overall goals of your business or marketing plan to which pricing contributes.

Parity, Lower, or Higher Pricing

How you price your product or service has a significant impact on many aspects of your overall marketing efforts. Used in conjunction with the other elements of your plan, a given price approach supports your product's positioning, while contributing directly to consumer demand (thus sales volume) for your product and providing income to cover costs and contribute to the profitability of your firm. The following is an overview of each of the three approaches to pricing.

Parity Pricing

Often referred to as a *going-rate strategy*, this approach maintains pricing levels at or near those of the competition. This is appropriate where other means of differentiation are common or are considered more important by the target. These other forms of differentiation often include specific product features and attributes as well as nonproduct advantages such as service, guarantees, location for retailers, or additional distribution channels. Interestingly, it is also utilized when product differentiation is low and price is the basis of competition.

In mature categories with few competitors and little differentiation, such as the airline industry, parity pricing is the norm. If one carrier were to raise prices, demand would shift to the competition with lower prices. If one airline lowers prices, the others would be forced to lower theirs in response, which would lower profits for all in the industry and create a *price war*. Often, in such industries, one major player, typically the market leader, is considered the *price leader*. Others in the industry watch this leader for price activity.

Lower Pricing

This objective involves maintaining a price lower than the competition. One specific execution of this approach includes discount pricing, a direct result of a low-price positioning. This approach aims for a high volume of sales to offset typically low margins to achieve desired profit levels (low margin dollars but high volume). It also requires appropriate capacity and distribution channels to support the volume requirements. The reasons for a low-price objective are usually these:

- To expand the market, allowing new consumers who couldn't purchase at higher prices to become purchasers.
- To increase trial and/or sales due to price incentives.
- To take advantage of a strong price elastic product for which a low price generates increased demand. The result is lower margins but increased profits because of the increased volume.
- To preempt competitive strategies, helping to steal market share. This is often necessary in a mature market.
- To remain competitive with your competition. If a majority of the competitors have reduced their prices, oftentimes you will need to do so, especially if you are in a price-sensitive product category. If a strong competitor is also offering an attribute such as service with which you cannot compete, you may need to lower your price to counter the service offering.
- To keep competitors from entering the marketplace by having a price that is difficult for a new company with high initial investment costs to match. This policy of expanded market pricing allows a company to develop a large, loyal consumer base while keeping competition to a minimum.

Higher Pricing

As we have discussed many times, a premium price—a higher price relative to the competition—supports a quality positioning and provides high margins to support higher product and promotional expenditures. The reasons for a high-price objective are usually these:

- A need for a fast recovery of the firm's investment.
- A need for faster accumulation of profits to cover research and development costs. The profits can then be used to improve the product and to sustain competitive marketing tactics once competitors enter the market.
- To substantiate a quality image positioning.

- The product is price inelastic—the demand or sales decrease only marginally with higher pricing.
- The product or service is in the introductory phase of its product life cycle and represents a substantial innovation within the product category. Also, the company may wish to skim profits while there are no substitute products that are forcing competitive pricing.
- The company is stressing profits rather than sales; thus, margins must remain high.
- The product has a short life span. An example would be fad products which last for a relatively short time. This necessitates a high price policy which will help recover the firm's research and development costs in a short time period.
- The product is difficult to copy and reproduce or has patent protection.

Determining Your Pricing Approach

Based on your list of pricing considerations, you should be able to establish a price objective that is either one of parity, lower, or higher pricing for your product or company. Your product, its positioning and other marketing communication goals, the target market's perceptions and behavior, the competition, and the industry will all suggest the most appropriate course of action. Once you have determined which approach you wish to take, it becomes the basis of your pricing objectives.

Addressing Geography and Timing Issues

Many times a company's or industry's pricing structure is not consistent across the entire country. One market may have greater competition, greater price sensitivity, or higher distribution costs, for example, than others. Thus, your objectives should state any differences that exist from market to market.

Finally, timing should be addressed in your price objectives. Are the sales increases to be addressed by a particular price approach needed constantly or just up to a certain point in time? Will price changes for promotional purposes take place during certain seasonal periods or for another, very specific, period? While timing relates to the changing of your price on a seasonal basis, it also relates to the changing of prices in a timely fashion to address competitive price changes, cost changes, market changes, and so on.

Writing the Price Objectives

The following examples present the appropriate style for writing price objectives that include your price approach, geography, and timing:

- Utilize higher pricing relative to the direct competition (minimum +10 percent) within the first year of the plan in all markets, consistent with a quality positioning.
- Increase prices during the strong tourist months of May to September, then lower prices during the off-season, while maintaining a relative parity price approach.

TASK 2 ## Establish Your Pricing Strategies

Pricing strategies state how you will achieve your pricing objectives. They provide the specifics you need to finalize your pricing plan. In developing your pricing strategies, you should take the following steps:

- *Review your pricing objectives.* As the strategies are intended to provide direction for achieving price objectives, it is important to truly understand what price approach you need to achieve and when and where you need to achieve it.

- *Review your marketing strategies.* Again, relate your pricing decisions not only to the direction provided in the pricing portion of your marketing strategies but also to the effect your pricing will have on the implementation of other strategies.
- *Review the product category and the competition.* What is the competitive price structure of the industry? At what stage is the category in terms of the product life cycle, and what is the competitive structure? What are the costs and pricing strategies of your competition?
- *Review your product.* Determine whether your firm has the capacity and/or capability to maintain a low-price strategy. Determine if your product has unique and defensible product attributes that could support a high-price objective. What are your costs associated with the product, and what is the breakeven at various price points? Calculate at what price you are most likely to break even.
- *Review the marketplace.* Consider the target market makeup and segmentation, and determine the price sensitivity among the segments. What attitudes does the target hold with regard to the product category and the importance of price?

Finally, develop strategies that address how price levels, geography, and timing objectives will be accomplished. Using the information acquired in the foregoing tasks, detail specifics as to your pricing strategy. Consider the following two sample marketing strategies:

> *Marketing seasonality strategy:* Increase sales among current customers during the off-season.
> *Marketing pricing strategy:* Maintain a 45 percent margin for the year.

The *pricing objective* might be to utilize a parity pricing structure relative to the competition during the strong selling season nationally and a low price relative to the competition during the off-season nationally. Price then would be one of the tools used to execute the seasonality marketing strategy along with promotion and advertising. And pricing certainly would be used to execute the pricing marketing strategy.
The subsequent pricing strategies might be these:

> Utilize a price consistent with the top three market leaders in the northern markets and the top market leader in the southern markets during the strong selling months of August through December.
> Utilize a price at 5 percent below the top three market leaders in the northern markets and 7 percent below the market leader in the southern markets during the off-season of January through July.

DOS AND DON'TS

Do

- Review your problems and opportunities, your marketing strategies, and communications goals related to pricing before developing your pricing plan.
- Closely monitor the competition and keep consistent records of your competition's pricing.
- Be flexible. Be prepared to adjust to competitive pressures and the marketing environment. Be willing to change your price and use it as a tool for achieving marketing strategies.

- Review the product category life cycle and pricing structure as you develop your pricing strategies.
- Use the pricing tool to help communicate the positioning of your product.
- Consider the logistic implications of your pricing decisions for your firm in terms of capacity and resources. You must be able to support whatever price strategy you implement.
- Test your price often. Test higher and lower prices, and monitor the response in test markets. Apply what you learn to your total system. Make sure you test your pricing strategies for a long enough period to obtain realistic results.
- Determine your pricing approach on the basis of the target market, not just on your firm's costs and needs. Calculate the market's price sensitivity. Analyze the importance of price relative to other attributes and how your firm or product is currently perceived by the target on these issues prior to initiating a price strategy or change.
- Remember, the more intangible (service firms) or unique your product, the more flexibility you will have in setting higher prices.
- Price your product to provide ultimate value to consumers. Remember, you can still give real value through high price (for example, the product is higher priced than the competition, but the customer receives a special or better service).
- Be aware of both the obvious and the hidden costs when determining your selling price (for example, shrinkage through employee theft).
- Make sure your pricing policy follows the legal guidelines.

Don't

- Don't look at pricing as static. Your cost of doing business and the competitive activity in your marketplace are not fixed, so your pricing shouldn't be either.
- Don't set pricing without first determining how it will affect sales, margins, and the ability of the company to cover variable and fixed costs.
- Don't be afraid to use price to achieve other marketing goals, such as trial. Successful companies often plan for a period of lower prices in an effort to increase trial and build the customer base. Though profitability is reduced temporarily, it is often offset by a sustained period of repeat purchase at full price by the expanded customer base. However, it is a good idea to test this premise to make sure you are receiving adequate repurchase from the new customers to justify a rollout of the program.
- While being flexible, make sure you don't confuse potential purchasers by constantly changing prices.
- Don't overreact to the competition. Before you change your long-run pricing strategy, wait to see if the competitive price changes are temporary or permanent. At the same time, learn to anticipate and react to short-run competitive price changes.
- If you are attempting to build a value image, don't lower an already competitive price. Instead, put greater emphasis on the quality of your product.
- Don't forget that your competitors are probably watching you as much as you are watching them. Consider their reactions to your pricing strategies prior to implementation.

The Successful Marketing Plan

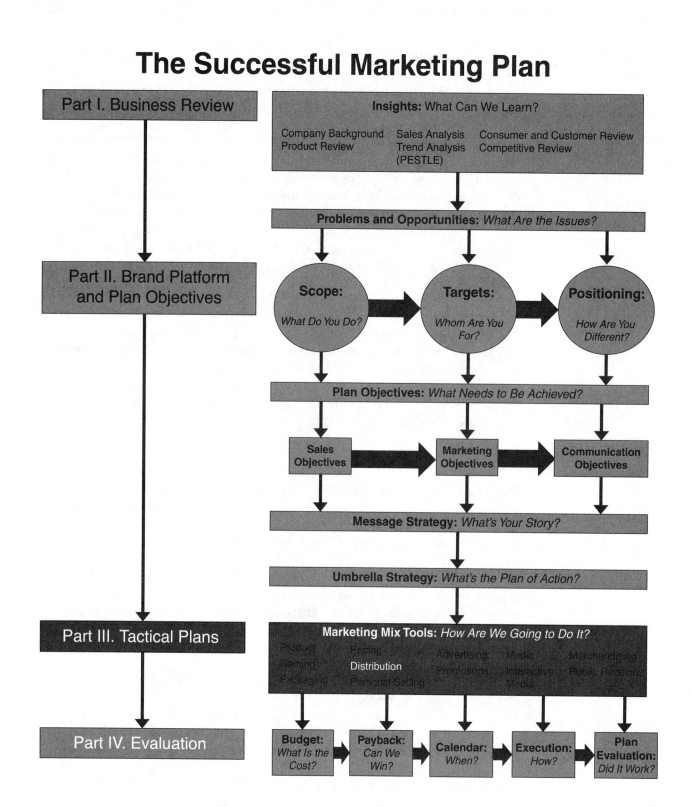

Part I. Business Review

Insights: What Can We Learn?

Company Background   Sales Analysis   Consumer and Customer Review
Product Review   Trend Analysis   Competitive Review
                       (PESTLE)

Problems and Opportunities: What Are the Issues?

Scope: What Do You Do?

Targets: Whom Are You For?

Positioning: How Are You Different?

Part II. Brand Platform and Plan Objectives

Plan Objectives: What Needs to Be Achieved?

Sales Objectives   **Marketing Objectives**   **Communication Objectives**

Message Strategy: What's Your Story?

Umbrella Strategy: What's the Plan of Action?

Part III. Tactical Plans

Marketing Mix Tools: How Are We Going to Do It?

Product   Pricing   Advertising   Media   Merchandising
Naming   Distribution   Promotions   Interactive   Public Relations
Packaging   Personal Selling   Media

Part IV. Evaluation

Budget: What Is the Cost?

Payback: Can We Win?

Calendar: When?

Execution: How?

Plan Evaluation: Did It Work?

CHAPTER 14 Distribution

You now need to consider the marketing mix tool of distribution. Up to this point, your efforts have been focused on developing plans to persuade the target market customer to purchase your product. Distribution focuses on making sure there is accessible product for the target market to purchase once you have initiated demand.

Begin this chapter by reviewing the distribution issues summarized through your problems and opportunities, the overall distribution direction provided in your marketing strategies, and the communication goals for the distribution tactical tool. Then utilize the specific information provided in this chapter to develop a comprehensive plan that will allow for effective distribution of your product.

FROM THIS CHAPTER YOU WILL LEARN

- The definition of *distribution*
- The issues affecting your distribution plan
- How to develop your distribution objectives and strategies

OVERVIEW

We define *distribution* as the transmission of goods and services from the producer or seller to the user. By this definition we mean the method through which the target market user receives the product from the producer. It could be direct or through one or more intermediaries or channels that make available the right product at the right place and at the optimum price, time, and quantity.

ISSUES AFFECTING DISTRIBUTION

In developing your distribution plan, you need to address five main areas:

1. Market penetration (retailers and service firms) or market coverage (consumer goods and business-to-business firms)
2. Types of outlets or channels
3. Competition

4. Geography
5. Timing

Market Penetration (Retailers or Service Firms) or Market Coverage (Consumer Goods and Business-to-Business Firms)

Penetration or market coverage relates to the number of stores or locations your company has in a given market or how well you are doing at gaining distribution of your product in the outlets that carry your products.

Market Penetration Levels for Retailers and Service Firms

Charts completed in the business review will reveal whether your firm has enough penetration to maximize sales, fully utilize the media, and pay out the marketing investment in any given market.

If you do not have enough stores or office locations to take advantage of the market's sales potential, this market is *underpenetrated*. In this situation, you probably cannot afford broad-scale advertising in the market because the expense is too burdensome for just a few stores and offices to carry. It is important to realize that each store has a natural trading area that can usually be defined in terms of geographical size and number of people. Thus, each market, depending on its population and the competition, can support a certain number of stores. If you are underpenetrated, say, with one store in a market of 300,000 households, and the business review determines that there should be one store for every 100,000 households:

* *You will not maximize your sales in the given market.* There are major areas in the market where customers will not be exposed to the store and will not drive out of their way to purchase items that they can purchase at closer alternative outlets offering similar merchandise.
* *You will not be able to maximize your marketing investment.* Instead of leveraging, for example, media and operation costs across three stores, all expenses are shouldered by the one store. Expenses will run above average because personnel and shipping costs cannot be amortized over the total sales of a multiple number of stores. Further, in order to keep advertising expenses within budget, the store will have limited media support, given the size of the market and the cost of the media. When mass media advertising is purchased, there will be much waste because the communication will be received by consumers outside the store's trading area. Given this scenario, effective, broad, marketable media such as television probably cannot be utilized.

Being *overpenetrated*, with too many stores or offices in a trading area, also has negatives associated with it. Too many outlets result in inefficiency, with duplication of coverage. Often the effect is cannibalization of one store's customers by another store. Accordingly, consideration should be given not just to opening new outlets but also to the need to eliminate one or more outlet locations within a market or to dramatically increase sales from the current locations in order to deliver the required profits.

Market Coverage for Consumer Goods and Business-to-Business Firms

The coverage calculation for consumer goods firms includes three pieces of information:

* The number of potential outlets or distribution centers that carry your product
* The all commodity volume (ACV) of the stores that carry your product
* The amount of shelf space allocated to your product

The most important distribution measure for manufacturers is not necessarily the number of stores carrying the product but the ACV of those stores. The ACV is the percent of the total category volume in the market controlled by the stores carrying a specific manufacturer's product. This is the critical measure of a manufacturer's distribution.

Refer to distribution in the product and market review section of your business review to determine how many outlets there are in each market in which you do business and the percentage of total business in your product category for which the outlets that carry your product account. If you are in only 3 out of 10 grocery stores in a given market but those 3 account for 80 percent of the category's sales (ACV), then you don't have to spend a great deal of time trying to expand your market distribution. But if the 3 grocery stores have an ACV of only 30 percent of the business, an objective should be to increase market coverage.

In addition, review the distribution data in your business review to determine the percent of shelf space your product has relative to the competition. If it is substantially less than the competition, either nationally, in specific markets, or in specific grocery chains, then a distribution objective should address this problem.

Further, with an increasing number of consumer products available and with limited amount of shelf space, more retailers are requiring up-front slotting fees from the manufacturer to carry a product. You must either devise a means to avoid these allowances (sell-in your product to departments of the store that do not require slotting allowances—often the produce and meat departments) or build them into your cost of distribution.

For business-to-business firms the same process should be undertaken, except the focus of consideration should be intermediate channel targets. And instead of shelf space, the business-to-business marketer should consider the percent of his or her product purchased by each company, distributor, wholesaler, broker, or outlet within a particular channel. In this situation, you might want to consider the development of an intranet to maintain continuous communication with your intermediate channel targets.

Types of Outlets or Channels

Under distribution in the business review, you should have developed a chart that traces sales by distribution outlet for your product category. Analyze the data for any trends your firm should take advantage of during the next year. We did a business review for a manufacturer of sinks and disposals that had built its business through traditional plumbing channels via wholesalers. However, data showed that, due to the advent of the do-it-yourself movement, more sinks and disposals were being sold to do-it-yourselfers through lumberyards and home building centers than to contractors through traditional channels. Thus, the company developed a dual-channel strategy, using both the wholesale plumbing channels and the consumer home building center channels.

In addition, as with price, the type of product and the product life cycle greatly affect the channel decision. If your product is new and is still being tested, production levels will most likely be relatively small, requiring very specific and limited distribution. Also, the product may require more in-depth, personal selling to the target market because of its complexity and newness. If this situation applies to your firm, determine what type of outlet can provide this level of service before establishing distribution objectives.

If your product is already established, production levels will be higher and the product may be more standardized. This would require less demand for a specialized selling effort. Or it may be appropriate to sell your product in a self-service, self-help type of environment.

There are many different types of distribution vehicles or outlets. Study the Internet or the distribution data in your business review to determine the different distribution channels for your product category. Note which channels have the most volume and which are a growing influence in your industry. Then, list the different attributes of each distribution choice in terms of customer target market segmentation, customer service provided, and price orientation (discount, full price, and so on) to help you make the correct choice for your product.

A whole new distribution force that has emerged in the last 15 years is e-commerce: doing business on the Internet. In its purest form, the product or service is communicated, sold, and delivered over the Internet. Banking and long-distance learning are both examples of applications of this type of e-commerce, with all business and communication able to be completed via the Internet.

E-commerce isn't limited to sites that offer shopping carts and online purchasing. The ability to generate sales leads, provide customer service, and gather target market insights also falls within the parameters of e-commerce.

We've participated in studies that showed over three-fourths of the most successful retail Internet sites are online channels of established brick-and-mortar companies. In these instances, e-commerce is integrated as part of a multichannel marketing strategy that enables target markets to purchase items either online or through retail locations. Properly implemented e-commerce cooperates, rather than competes, with existing channels. It expands the target market by providing advantages that may be unavailable at retail locations.

Competition

Review competitive distribution patterns when making decisions regarding market penetration or market coverage, type of outlet, geography, and timing. Consult your business review to determine competitive distribution patterns. This knowledge is helpful when deciding what markets to further penetrate. If there are two equal markets in terms of potential, the obvious choice for further penetration would be the one with the weaker competitive situation. In another example, if a competitor has shown dramatic sales increases utilizing a new channel of distribution that you do not use, this might provide the rationale to at least test the alternative channel structure for your products.

Finally, what channels does the competition dominate? Are these channels or outlets so important to the way that the target market makes purchases in the category that you cannot afford to not be in these channels? Or can you seek distribution in alternate channels in which your product could have a dominant position?

Geography

The marketer should also consider the Brand Development Index (BDI) and Category Development Index (CDI) data developed in the business review. A BDI demonstrates the sales-to-population ratio relative to other markets in the company's system. Distribution plans often take BDIs into consideration after they have completed the penetration or coverage analysis detailed earlier. A low BDI in any given market coupled with a penetration or coverage analysis that shows that a firm is underpenetrated points toward a potential geographic expansion in those markets.

Also, geographic expansion should be considered for those markets that are underpenetrated and have high CDIs. A high CDI means that consumers in a given market purchase a product at higher rates than the country on a whole. Of course, the competitive situation would also have to be taken into consideration, but the CDI provides a good benchmark for the success rate potential for different expansion markets. The following is a simplified BDI and CDI matrix that you might want to review before you establish your distribution objectives:

	High CDI	**Low CDI**
High BDI	—Strong market with good market potential and product sales worthy of continual development —May require strong support to limit competitive entry	—Cash cow; don't spend marketing dollars to level of sales; use these dollars to fund development of other markets —Will need to look to other markets for growth
Low BDI	—May be a market right for development or a competitor's stronghold to be avoided	—Not promising; generally a market to be avoided unless your firm can develop a dominant (and profitable) share

In summary, distribution objectives should detail penetration and/or coverage goals and/or the use of specific types of outlets and channels on a national, regional, or local basis, depending on the potential of the market and the situation of your product.

Timing

Finally, timing must be addressed in the distribution objectives. State whether the objectives are to be completed in a matter of months or years. Because distribution involves a commitment to actual construction or long-term leases in the case of retailers and requires the development of working relationships between the wholesalers, brokers, and the retail trade and the manufacturers, the distribution timing is often longer term than some of the other tactical tools of the marketing plan. A retail store expansion program is usually a multiyear, ongoing development. What started this year may not be finished until next year and beyond.

HOW TO DEVELOP A DISTRIBUTION PLAN

There are two steps in developing a distribution plan: (1) establish your distribution objectives and (2) establish your distribution strategies.

See also Appendix C, Worksheet 46.

TASK 1 **Establish Your Distribution Objectives**

Establish quantifiable distribution objectives for the following five categories:

1. Market penetration (retailers and service firms) or market coverage (consumer goods and business-to-business firms)
2. Competition
3. Types of outlets or channels
4. Geography
5. Timing

Distribution objectives for a retail firm could be as follows:

- Fully penetrate the firm's two largest BDI markets (Chicago and Detroit, which account for 25 percent of the firm's business) to attain the ratio of 1 store for every 100,000 households within the next two years (8 stores in this plan year and 10 stores the following year).
- Continue to utilize strip centers in existing markets, testing outlet centers in new markets.

TASK 2 ## Establish Your Distribution Strategies

Your distribution strategies should describe how you will accomplish your distribution objectives. The following points should be considered by each business category.

Retailers and Service Firms
- Describe the criteria or methodology for penetrating markets or adding new locations. Where will you locate new stores? What demographic, location, cost per square foot, competition, or other criteria will you use to make these decisions?
- If you are expanding geographic penetration, detail whether this will occur on a systematic, market-by-market basis or whether it will occur wherever the opportunity develops within the total system.
- If a change is warranted, describe how you will make the change from one type of outlet to another.
- Describe your purchase or lease strategies.

Consumer Goods and Business-to-Business Firms
- Describe how you will attain market coverage goals and/or shelf space goals. Some of your strategies to achieve these goals will be incorporated into your promotional plan. If your business review details that your product does not differ from your competition's, your product is not established with the trade, and your product does not make a large impact on the trade in terms of profits, then you will have to rely more heavily on promotions and trade deals to meet aggressive market coverage and shelf space goals.
- If your objective is to increase market coverage, describe how you will choose the types of channels to target for increased coverage and detail specifically what stores you plan to target.
- Outline whether you are going to use a push or pull strategy. A *push strategy* focuses on marketing to the intermediate targets, such as the distributors and the outlets, to obtain distribution and shelf space. A *pull strategy* involves marketing to the ultimate purchaser or directly to consumers to build demand, forcing the outlets to stock the product.
- Describe how you will enter new distribution channels if this is an objective. One of our clients had developed an all-new power tool. Because the product was not established with the retail trade, the company used an informational TV commercial (*infomercial*) communication strategy and delivered the product directly to the customers. While the company was selling its product direct via the infomercials, it was also building awareness for the product that then helped open distribution with the retail trade. Will you try to place your entire line or one top-selling product in the stores? What kind of merchandising and advertising support will you provide? Will you offer return privileges or lower your minimum-order requirements? If storage, display, dispensing, price marking, or accounting specifics are important to the new channel, describe how you will make allowances to gain distribution trial. Will you provide special introductory pricing?

Assume that a distribution objective for a packaged-goods firm is to increase ACV market coverage 20 points among grocery stores in all top 100 markets over the next year. The strategies to achieve this objective might be the following:

- Place additional sales emphasis against large independents with multiple store outlets.
- Concentrate on first establishing the top-selling line of frozen foods before attempting to gain distribution of the entire line of frozen and canned foods.
- Utilize special promotions developed in the promotion plan to help sell-in product, such as special display allowances designed to encourage initial trial and special introductory pricing incentives.

DOS AND DON'TS

Do

- Review your problems and opportunities and your marketing strategies as guidelines for developing distribution objectives and strategies, and consider the effect of distribution strategies on awareness and attitudes in contributing to the marketing communication goals. The number of stores in a market and their exposure alone has a major impact on the level of unaided store awareness by the target market.
- Study your competitors' distribution patterns. Learn from their mistakes and their successes. Look for opportunities to exploit channels that the competition is not in and/or channels that you can dominate.
- Make sure your distribution structure is consistent with your positioning and your target market's purchasing patterns.
- Be willing to change or add distribution channels if the marketing environment changes.
- Remember that the location of the store and its proximity to the consumer must still be considered king in retail.
- Continually test new methods of distribution.

Don't

- Don't make quick decisions. Distribution of your product requires the development of long-term relationships and usually requires a fixed investment of capital. Don't change retail distribution patterns without thoroughly testing alternatives first. If you are going to expand distribution, do it on a market-by-market basis or on a regional basis in a disciplined, rolled-out fashion.
- Don't remain static in your distribution patterns. Customers change their behavior and so must you.
- Don't just use intuition in making distribution decisions. Use hard data and the BDI and CDI method.
- Don't be inflexible with your distribution policy. There may be regional differences that you should consider.
- Don't expand distribution if you can't fully penetrate markets or consistently deliver product. Retail and consumer goods firms need minimum distribution levels within any given market to leverage advertising and other marketing resources.
- Don't expand your distribution at a rate that you cannot effectively support (adequate levels of product, quality service, media weight and support, and so on).

The Successful Marketing Plan

Part I. Business Review

Insights: What Can We Learn?

Company Background   Sales Analysis   Consumer and Customer Review
Product Review   Trend Analysis   Competitive Review
                          (PESTLE)

Problems and Opportunities: *What Are the Issues?*

Part II. Brand Platform and Plan Objectives

Scope:

What Do You Do?

Targets:

Whom Are You For?

Positioning:

How Are You Different?

Plan Objectives: *What Needs to Be Achieved?*

Sales Objectives   **Marketing Objectives**   **Communication Objectives**

Message Strategy: *What's Your Story?*

Umbrella Strategy: *What's the Plan of Action?*

Part III. Tactical Plans

Marketing Mix Tools: *How Are We Going to Do It?*

Product   Pricing   Advertising   Media   Merchandising
Naming   Distribution   Promotions   Interactive   Public Relations
Packaging   Personal Selling   Media

Part IV. Evaluation

Budget: *What Is the Cost?*

Payback: *Can We Win?*

Calendar: *When?*

Execution: *How?*

Plan Evaluation: *Did It Work?*

15 Personal Selling

Personal selling and service involve the personal, one-on-one contact your company has with the specific target customer and the day-to-day administration of the selling program, the retail outlet, or the office. Whether it's business-to-business or consumer marketing, personal selling is a very important tool that incorporates the critical human factor into the marketing mix. It is the **one** personal and direct link between the target market and your company. Further, the degree of personal contact with the target customer will affect the level of impact the personal selling and service functions will have on the awareness and attitude toward your product.

FROM THIS CHAPTER YOU WILL LEARN

- The definition of *personal selling and service*
- The issues affecting your personal selling plan
- How to develop a personal selling plan

OVERVIEW

In this book, *personal selling for retail and service firms*, which is often referred to as *operations*, involves all functions related to selling, operations, and service in the store, office, or other environments, such as door-to-door solicitation, in-home selling, and telemarketing. This includes hiring and managing sales personnel, stocking inventory, and preparing the product for sale, as well as the presentation and maintenance of the facility. For business-to-business and consumer goods firms, *personal selling* relates to the manufacturer's selling and servicing of its products to the trade and/or intermediate markets (various buyers of the product within the distribution channel from the original producer to the ultimate user).

Maintaining constant communication with salespeople, whether it be at the retail, service, distributor, or manufacturing level, is critical. Accordingly, many organizations are employing intranet technology to enhance sales force communication.

ISSUES AFFECTING PERSONAL SELLING AND SERVICE

The issues that affect retailers and service firms are slightly different from those that affect manufacturers (that is, consumer goods and business-to-business firms).

Retailers and Service Firms

The overriding issue facing retailers and service organizations is to determine a realistic and achievable sales ratio. You must determine a goal for the percentage of individuals walking into the retail outlet who will be persuaded to purchase versus those who will leave without purchasing. Or, if you are a service organization, you must develop a goal regarding the number of prospects versus the number of converted clients when making sales calls. If you have primary research, you will be able to track your sales ratio and that of your competitors from year to year. This should provide direction when establishing your sales ratio in the marketing plan. If you do not have primary research, we suggest that you initiate an information survey among your prospects and customers similar to the one discussed under buying habits in the target market effectors section of the business review to help guide you.

Whether you have primary research or not, you should analyze the amount of traffic (retailers) or number of sales calls made (service) in daily and weekly increments. Next, estimate your current sales ratio, and project what an increase of even 1 to 3 percentage points would do for your sales. Finally, ask yourself if it is realistic to expect a 1- to 3-point increase. In some businesses where there is a lot of competition and consumers shop two or three stores before purchasing, the answer may be no. But in other businesses it may be very realistic to expect a higher sales ratio given the proper selling focus.

In addition, retailers and service organizations must address other *customer behavior goals* when developing personal selling and service plans. If you determine that customers are more likely to purchase if they have been given a demonstration or they have tried the merchandise, develop plans that encourage this type of behavior.

When developing a personal selling and operations plan, retailers must also consider the in-store selling presentation, and service firms must consider their basic selling environment. The retailer must determine to what degree the store is going to employ a self-service or full-service selling environment. Are you going to employ minimal sales pressure, or utilize a harder and/or commission-based selling structure? In deciding the type of selling environment, you must analyze the needs of the target customer, the merchandise being sold, the competition, and the positioning of your firm.

Providing service during and after the sale is critical for many products. Many retailers believe in the philosophy that *to service is to sell*. For example, in a shoe store environment, whenever a salesperson can provide the service of personally fitting the shoes for the customer, the chances of selling that customer can increase up to 50 percent. Likewise, in most retail environments, good service after the sale can dramatically increase the chance of a repeat sale. A good example of this is how superior service by auto dealers dramatically impacts the chance of getting continued new car purchases from the same customer.

If the product is extremely technical and/or requires a major dollar outlay, the customer will probably require a great deal of information and a more professional selling technique. If the product is a standardized, utilitarian type of product, there probably is less need for an informational and/or hard-sell approach. For example, many self-help or self-service store environments carry less technical and less expensive products with which the consumer has had previous experience. This type of selling environment addresses consumers' familiarity with the products. The customers can shop and make decisions independently and comfortably without the services of a salesperson.

Consideration of the consumer's need for information and the technicality of the product is only one part of this decision-making process. After you have considered these factors, also review the capabilities of your sales staff. It takes a great deal of product knowledge and selling skill to effectively sell potential buyers and not turn them off. If you decide on an aggressive selling philosophy, your company must make the commitment to sales training and ongoing refresher courses.

Finally, the cost of selling is another key factor you must consider. A sales or in-store staff may be very necessary, but it is very expensive to maintain. You must determine the optimum number of salespeople and the dollar investment required to support the selling effort. The cost of selling as a percent of sales will vary depending upon your company, what you are selling, and the needs of the target market. You might want to review industry sources to help you determine what your company's selling and payroll cost should be.

Manufacturers

When addressing personal selling issues, packaged-goods manufacturers consider brokers, wholesalers, and outlets while many other business-to-business companies think in terms of intermediate markets. As with retailers and service organizations, a key selling issue for manufacturers is a ratio of selling effectiveness. A sales ratio for manufacturers is determined by the number of prospects contacted versus the number that actually become customers. In order to arrive at a sales ratio objective, other quantifiable objectives need to be established, such as the number of sales calls and demonstrations made and the number of products sold to wholesalers, outlets, and intermediate markets. Many times the key to meeting a sales ratio objective is not only selling effectiveness but also arriving at a specific and qualified prospect list. These types of parameters provide direction to the sales force and also serve as a measurement tool when analyzing sales personnel results at the end of the year.

Manufacturers must decide how to sell the product to the outlets, distributors, and other businesses. Manufacturers use three basic methods to sell their product:

- *Direct:* To purchasers through an in-house sales force
- *Indirect:* To purchasers through agents (independent sales reps and/or brokers) or wholesalers and/or distributors
- *Mixed:* A combined selling system that uses both direct and indirect methods

The decision of which of the three selling methods to use is made after consideration of the following factors.

Vertical or Horizontal Market?

A *vertical market* is one that is made up of only one or two industries. It is very specialized. For example, craft manufacturers sell to craft wholesalers or directly to craft retail outlets. The number of wholesalers and retailers in the total industry is very small. Direct distribution is often used because selling is very personal and individual relationships become very important. However, if the market is *horizontal*, with the product being sold to buyers in many industries (for example, plastics manufacturers sell to multiple industry types), then the opportunity to reach large numbers of potential purchasers might be better with an indirect sales approach.

Quality of the Product

With a direct sales staff you can control the selling effort because the sales force is made up of your company's employees. For this reason, businesses with rigid product quality standards often use a direct sales force to ensure the integrity of the quality associated with the product.

Market Potential

Many times a company's only choice is to go through indirect channels. If the firm has only one product with limited sales potential, it is very difficult to generate enough demand to justify the cost of an individual sales force.

Geographic Concentration

If the market is geographically concentrated, it is easier to go direct. If clients are dispersed, indirect channels tend to be more favorable, as it becomes very costly to make time-consuming sales visits.

Technical Aspects of the Product

The more technical the product, the more a direct sales force is favored. The firm needs to supervise the training of the sales force and have a high degree of control over the selling and servicing process.

Standardized or Specialized Product?

If the product is standardized, you can move the product through many different types of channels and selling methods. If it is specialized and requires a high degree of maintenance, specialized care, or instruction, then a direct sales force is often required.

Financial Strength of the Company

The manufacturer must consider the cost of each selling method and weigh this against specific market conditions and options for selling the product. A direct sales force is far more expensive than utilizing independent representatives. However, there are certain advantages of a direct sales force, as previously outlined, that may justify the extra cost.

HOW TO DEVELOP A PERSONAL SELLING AND SERVICE PLAN

There are two steps in developing a distribution plan: (1) establish your selling and service objectives and (2) establish your selling and service strategies.

See also Appendix C, Worksheet 47.

TASK 1   ## *Establish Your Personal Selling and Service Objectives*

Your sales, operations, and/or service objectives should be as specific as possible and should include the following types of goals.

For Retailers and Service Firms

- Customer contact, that is, the percent of store visitors who have contact, and the number of contacts they have, with store staff during their visit
- Customer behavior goals such as percentage of customers who are persuaded to try a product or experience a demonstration of merchandise
- The specific sales ratio

Examples of personal selling objectives for a retailer would be the following:

- Establish a minimum of one contact with 90 percent of store visitors and a minimum of two contacts with 60 percent of visitors.
- Achieve a 50 percent trial ratio of customers—customers who actually try the merchandise during a hands-on demonstration in the store.
- Achieve a 40 percent sales ratio (40 percent of the people who visit the store make a purchase) over the next year during the holiday selling season and a 30 percent sales ratio during the remainder of the year.

For Manufacturers

- The number and type of companies that must be contacted by the sales force
- The number of sales calls that must be made to each prospect and/or current customer by company type (industry, dollar volume, and so on)
- The sales ratio (number of contacts versus the number of sales)
- The average sales dollar volume and the number of orders per salesperson per year
- The number of actual product presentations and/or demonstrations or percentage of product sampling or trial that must be achieved during sales presentations
- Additional customer behavior goals, such as the percentage of customers who are persuaded to sign up for future sales and/or product information

Examples of personal selling objectives for a manufacturer would be the following:

- Contact each current customer twice, and make a sales presentation to the top 50 percent of prospect companies in the newly developed construction and manufacturing SIC or NAICS target markets.
- Make full product demonstrations to 75 percent of the prospects.
- Obtain a sales ratio of 85 percent among existing customers and 30 percent among new prospects.
- Obtain an average dollar sale of $2,500, and generate an average of 200 sales per salesperson per year.

TASK 2   ## Establish Your Personal Selling and Service Strategies

It will be helpful first to review the questions pertaining to selling under distribution channels in the business review. Answering these questions will help you to form specific selling strategies for your company. In addition, addressing the areas listed below when you establish your specific selling, service, and operations strategies will also help you meet your selling and service objectives.

- *Type of selling environment and selling method.* A retailer must decide whether the selling environment will be self-service or full-service. If there is a full-service sales staff, a decision must be made regarding the selling orientation—hard sell or soft sell. A manufacturer must determine whether to use a direct, indirect, or mixed sales staff.
- *Administration parameters of the sales force.* The selling strategies should outline hiring qualifications, training, and evaluation procedures.
- *Seasonal and geographic requirements.* If staffing is a function of seasonal sales or if there are different staffing requirements by store or by market, there should be a selling strategy developed to address these issues.
- *Demonstration requirements.* This personal selling and service strategy section should also direct service and/or demonstration techniques. For retailers, is there a certain technique that should be followed to increase the chance of closing a sale? A shoe retailer may require that its sales force initiate as many trial fittings as possible. This might result from data that show fitting customers and allowing them to try walking in the shoes lead to a sales ratio that is 50 percent higher. Similar selling technique decisions should be considered for manufacturers.
- *Timing and priority of sales presentations.* Manufacturers and brokers and distributors must determine when and in what priority accounts will be given sales presentations. For example, if you were a manufacturer selling to retailers, you might make sales presentations to some retailers before others because you want some retailers to have your product before others.
- *Selection of sales staff to make presentations.* Depending on the customer or potential customer, the manufacturer or broker or distributor must determine who should make the sales presentations. Should it be the salesperson alone, or should a sales management person, technical person, or corporate executive also be involved?
- *Sales force compensation.* Other things being equal, people will tend to perform in ways that will get them the maximum compensation. In a highly measurable area such as sales (number of contacts, individual sales ratios, and the like are generally easily tracked), employees will tend to act in ways in which they are motivated to behave. Therefore, it is critical that the sales compensation approach be in sync with the desired type of selling environment. For example, a retailer that wishes to position itself as a low-pressure, self-service-oriented store would be unwise to structure a large sales commission component into its sales force compensation, as this tends to encourage aggressive closing efforts.
- *Special sales incentives.* If they are going to be used, special sales incentive programs should be developed in this section of the plan. When special incentives are provided for a special event or promotion, for example, make sure the sales staff is made totally aware of the specifics of the special incentive program that apply before, during, and after the event.

- *Store operation guidelines.* Selling and operation strategies should cover the following:
  - Retail staffing requirements in terms of when, where, and what
  - Stocking and merchandising procedures
  - Store maintenance considerations
  - Organization and appearance of the store, office, and shelf display for retailers, service companies, and manufacturers, respectively
  - In-store product presentations (visual diagrams—that is, *planograms*), office presentations, and displays of product for retailers, service companies, and manufacturers, respectively

Examples of Retail Selling Strategies

The following are examples of selling strategies for a ski retailer whose selling objectives were to increase the sales ratio from 30 to 45 percent during the next year and to obtain a 35 percent ski equipment demonstration ratio among customers in the store.

- Develop an aggressive selling environment designed to sell customers during an in-store, one-on-one sales presentation.
- Develop a program that ensures that all customers are greeted upon entry to the store. Utilize the training hill outside the store as a means to get customers to actually try the equipment, and achieve the demonstration goals established in the selling objectives.
- Utilize 2 percent commission plus salary to encourage salespeople to sell. Establish a bonus system to reward the top producers for each week and each month of the year.
- Utilize mystery shoppers to rate service and selling effectiveness. Rate each salesperson at least once every six months.
- Utilize annual and semiannual reviews of the sales staff to improve performance. Send each salesperson to one selling seminar per year.
- Develop quarterly seminars to keep salespeople aware of the latest technology and products in the industry.

Examples of Manufacturers' Selling Strategies

The following are examples of selling strategies for a manufacturer of a new plastic patented toy boomerang that has a distribution objective of 50 percent ACV of toy stores and 30 percent ACV of college stores in Year 1. The selling objectives for this manufacturer are 90+ percent contact rates for both targets, sales ratio of 60 percent toy stores and 40 percent college stores, and an annual average dollar volume of $500 for toy stores and $200 for college stores. The strategies are the following:

- Employ sales representatives and brokers to call on toy stores.
- Employ a national rep organization that calls on college bookstores. Compensate reps and brokers with 10 percent commission on initial orders and 7 percent on all follow-up orders.
- Make Toys"R"Us the number one priority, and follow up with sales calls immediately thereafter to the top tier of toy stores.
- Train sales representative groups with a demonstration video, CD-ROM, and/or DVD.

DOS AND DON'TS

Do

- Review your problems and opportunities, marketing strategies, and personal selling communication value goals before developing your selling, operations, and service plan.
- Review your customers' shopping habits and product information requirements before deciding on a selling method.
- If you are a retailer, make sure you plan to train your sales staff properly before you decide to utilize a hard-sell approach.
- If you are a manufacturer, review the seven considerations outlined in this chapter before deciding whether to use a direct, indirect, or mixed selling method.
- Make sure your sales force compensation plan matches your desired selling approach.
- Have your sales staff reinforce the positioning of your product and your advertising and promotion efforts. Your individual marketing mix tools are far more effective if each one complements and reinforces the other.
- Support your sales staff. They will be more effective salespeople if they have been given the support of brochures, samples, and special offers for when they are interacting with the customers.
- Manufacturers, make sure you are selling to the real decision makers when calling on new prospects.
- Make sure there is diligent, detailed monitoring of each selling program in terms of personal sales calls made and follow-up of sales leads received.

Don't

- Don't expect your company to change selling methods overnight. It takes a lot of training and the right type of personnel to perfect different selling styles.
- Don't overlook the importance of making sure you have a sound operations system in place to execute your sales plans. This is particularly true in the service industries in which there has not been a strong selling orientation, such as health care and legal professions. Operations is also important in retail, where you have many variables to control, including people, product preparation and inventory, presentation, and maintenance of the facility. It is our experience that many marketing plans fail not because they are strategically wrong but primarily because of poor execution in the field.
- Don't forget that the selling function needs ongoing attention from management in order to be effective and to show improvement. The development and use of intranet technology could be helpful in the monitoring and management of the selling effort.
- Don't forget that although money motivates, a formalized program to recognize an individual's accomplishment also increases selling effectiveness.
- Don't expect to sell everyone at one time. Set priorities in terms of when prospects should be sold based on short- and long-term potential.
- Retailers, don't expect your salespeople to sell from an empty wagon. You can't sell the product if it is not available for the shopper to purchase. The operations

plan must ensure that there is adequate communication between marketing and the merchandisers so that adequate inventory is stocked in the stores prior to heavy, seasonal selling periods and promotions.

- Don't just provide service. Use service as a method to *sell* your customers and generate repeat sales!
- Don't let your sales force forget that, while selling new customers is important, the reason for your company's existence is to service and satisfy existing customers.

The Successful Marketing Plan

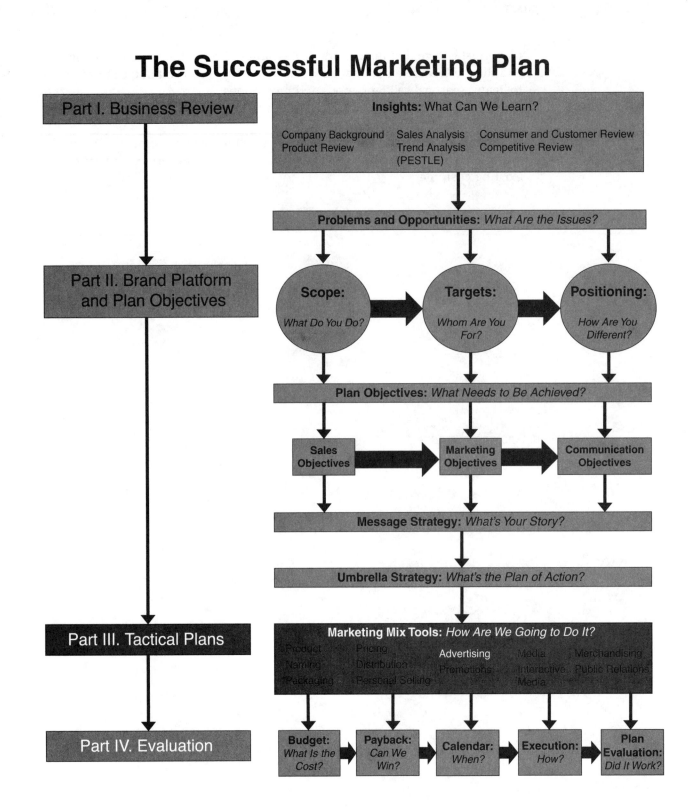

Part I. Business Review

Insights: What Can We Learn?

Company Background   Sales Analysis   Consumer and Customer Review
Product Review   Trend Analysis   Competitive Review
          (PESTLE)

Problems and Opportunities: *What Are the Issues?*

Part II. Brand Platform and Plan Objectives

Scope: What Do You Do?

Targets: Whom Are You For?

Positioning: How Are You Different?

Plan Objectives: *What Needs to Be Achieved?*

Sales Objectives

Marketing Objectives

Communication Objectives

Message Strategy: *What's Your Story?*

Umbrella Strategy: *What's the Plan of Action?*

Part III. Tactical Plans

Marketing Mix Tools: *How Are We Going to Do It?*

Product   Pricing   Advertising   Media   Merchandising
Naming   Distribution   Promotions   Interactive   Public Relations
Packaging   Personal Selling   Media

Part IV. Evaluation

Budget: *What Is the Cost?*

Payback: *Can We Win?*

Calendar: *When?*

Execution: *How?*

Plan Evaluation: *Did It Work?*

16 Advertising Content

Now that you have decided on an overarching messaging strategy for your brand, complete with a positioning and platform idea, you are ready to turn to one of the most fun and challenging tasks: creating compelling advertising content. Advertising content can often be your most visible communication to your external and internal targets. While developing the messaging strategy and platform idea portions of your plan requires strategic and innovative thinking, the most fun will come when you and/or your agency actually get into developing the advertising executions.

Because this is a how-to for marketing plan preparation, this chapter will not review how to develop the advertising executions. Instead, this chapter will discuss how to provide the direction for advertising content, which has changed dramatically over the years and continues to evolve as this edition goes to press. Here, advertising will refer to the creative content. Later, in Chapter 18, "Advertising Media," it will refer to the message delivery method and the context surrounding the content.

With the advent of Web 2.0, user participation and social media have created opportunities to do more than just interrupt audiences using traditional advertising within paid media. Now, with the right idea and content, a brand can engage audiences through earned and social media and create audiences through its owned media platforms.

FROM THIS CHAPTER YOU WILL LEARN

- Communications drivers and advertising models
- How to develop an integrated blueprint for creative content
- How to distinguish strategy, creative idea, and execution
- New rules for creative content

- Approaches to testing advertising content
- How to hire an outside agency

OVERVIEW

Before analyzing how the communication elements are factored into a marketing plan, it is necessary to understand the differences between these communication elements. It is a common error to bunch advertising, public relations or publicity, promotion, and merchandising together as one and the same. In fact, all of these forms of communication are very different from each other in terms of what they are capable of doing and what role they each play in the marketing plan.

But what is advertising these days? The lines between traditional paid advertising, earned media through publicity and social media, brand-sponsored owned content like websites, mobile applications, and programming are blurring. For this marketing plan discussion, we will define *advertising* as that which informs and persuades through *paid* media (television, radio, magazine, newspaper, Internet, outdoor, and direct mail).

The Expectations for Your Advertising

Before you begin developing the advertising section of your marketing plan, you must decide what your advertising can realistically accomplish. We know that advertising can build awareness and positively affect attitude. For your product, advertising can build recognition, help create a positive image, and differentiate it from the competition. Advertising can also build store traffic, assist in introducing new products and line extensions, feature product improvements, and announce promotions. Specifically in the business-to-business category, advertising can also generate customer leads ("please send me more information") and open doors for the sales force. You must make sure you know what you expect advertising to accomplish for your product.

In addition to building brand awareness and positively affecting attitude, advertising can sometimes move the target to action and to buy your product through a direct response channel. Direct mail is a good example of this.

The Concept of Communications Drivers

About 10 years ago, our friend and mentor, Eric Einhorn, global director of strategic planning for the McCann Worldgroup, introduced us to his concept of the seven irrefutable "communications drivers." These are what your messaging and communications programs can affect. These are the things that you put money behind to help drive brand and business performance. They can work as a verbal shorthand to articulate the purpose of your messaging. They help define how your target audience should behave, the answer to the "what you want them to think, feel, and do" questions. We will go into these in more depth in Chapter 18, "Advertising Media."

So think of your paid media and the advertising creative content you develop as an investment in affecting these drivers. Usually paid advertising content has the most effect on five of the marketing drivers: brand awareness, emotional bond, product news, activation, and, with the right content and idea, even buzz.

Brand awareness	Keeping the brand name at the top of mind
Emotional bond	Forging a connection with the heart of consumers
Product news	Creating new relevance through news and innovation
Activation	Encouraging immediate purchase or use
Loyalty	Developing customer relationships and retention, beyond the product experience itself
Experience	Enabling prospects to get to know or use a product
Buzz	Creating advocacy through a third-party source

And more important, you can choose to develop certain models of advertising, which we'll discuss next, that can affect these communications drivers.

HOW ADVERTISING STRATEGY CAN LEAD TO VARIOUS COMMUNICATION MODELS

Our combined advertising experience approaches over 100 years. But the one thing about advertising is that no matter how deep your experiences, just when you think you've figured out how it works, somebody comes up with a new idea.

Activation

For example, ads in the 1920s were black-and-white press ads inviting mail order responses. Color printing hadn't been invented. Most people didn't have phones, so you couldn't ask them to call 1-800 numbers. So even back then, technology shaped content. The majority of the ads were about products and their features and attributes. Most of those features and attributes were unique. And brands hadn't yet really been invented. This is what you might call an *activation model*.

Auto manufacturers and brands with dealer organizations often call this model "Tier 3 advertising." It's the hard-hitting stuff you see and hear every day on TV, in Internet banners, newspaper ads, and radio ads with a strong call to action, price points, promotional offers, and incentives to ACT NOW. In this model, the creative concept usually revolves around the reason to act now.

Product News

In post–World War II America, Procter & Gamble invented the Unique Selling Proposition (USP) and used it to promote brands in a new medium, television. Ivory soap promised dishwashing soap that made your hands as soft as your face. There were mass, passive audiences to be persuaded. Things were efficient. And effective. Products solved problems. And the role of paid advertising content was to show and tell. This is what we would call the *product news model* of advertising. The approach is to own the mind share among the target audience consumers of one salient benefit and drive it home as the reason to buy. In this case, you need, what the research firm Hall & Partners, describes as "a difference that makes a difference."

The award-winning creative content that we developed for the Hostess brand and cited in Chapter 10, "Message Strategy," is an excellent example of the product news model. The Campbell Mithun platform idea—"Where's the Cream Filling?"—made that unique product attribute relevant in a new way both to parents and kids. The advertising creative drove home the "product difference that makes a difference"—cream filling leading to a more fun product experience. So in the product news model, the creative concept needs to spring from the product's attribute or benefit.

Brand Awareness

As media choices became even more efficient, and as brands proliferated across many categories, another model evolved: *brand awareness*. In this type of model, the objective is to deliver and register the brand name as efficiently and effectively as possible. This model is often used by market leaders or new brands that need to stand out in a crowded category where their distribution channels can more effectively communicate salient, and often complex, product benefits.

One of the best contemporary examples of the brand awareness model of advertising creative is what Aflac did historically with its duck icon. If you ask the question "What insurance companies come to mind?" chances are that Aflac will be one of them. But if you ask the question "What's different or better about Aflac?" you might get a blank stare. For nearly a decade, Aflac chose to affect the marketing driver of brand awareness, using the duck and the mnemonic device of the Aflac quack to register its brand name. With a brand awareness model, the most successful creative content will leverage some kind of visual, verbal device—or both—that has "stickiness" and quickly and clearly associates itself with the brand's name. The platform idea itself becomes the iconic device.

Emotional Bond

Then in the early 1960s, somebody came up with a new idea. Bill Bernbach, creator of the famous "Think Small" campaign for VW, said "Telling Isn't Selling." Bernbach pioneered what many would call the *emotional bond model* of advertising. The approach is to connect a brand to the heart of a customer and to make the brand a positive reflection of that customer's values and identity.

One of the classic examples of this model, and one of the longer-running contemporary advertising campaigns, is MasterCard's "Priceless." For the most part, credit cards are thin blades of plastic, with little differentiation. With Visa owning mind share around the benefit of ubiquity, and American Express positioning itself as the business card, MasterCard leveraged a platform idea around being the "One Card for the Things That Matter Most in Your Life." It connected to the heart of its middle-American, family-oriented target audience with its poetic copy around priceless family values: "For Everything Else, There's MasterCard." So with the emotional model of advertising, the creative concept needs to capture with truth not what the brand does but what it really *means* to its target audience.

Buzz

As the fourth generation of consumers came of age in the middle 2000s, advertising craftspeople begin to develop another new approach to lift brands above their myriad, high-quality competitors and engage and involve target customers to become advocates for the brands themselves. We call it the *buzz model*. In some ways, it's advertising masquerading as a publicity stunt attempting to engage brand zealots to engage and involve more and more potential customers. In this model, the brand's advertising itself creates the impression that the brand has something going for it because the advertising gets talked about by the target audience.

Old Spice recently rejuvenated its brand using this buzz model of advertising. Their platform idea, "The Man Your Man Could Smell Like," became a talked-about campaign by its youth-oriented target. The brand accelerated its buzz, or third-party endorsements and engagement, by leveraging social media, like Twitter and YouTube, to gain zealots or advocates. The brand advocates talked about the advertising and participated in Twitter feed question-and-answer sessions, through which they became ambassadors for the brand themselves. So with the buzz model of advertising, the creative concept needs to have a concept that creates talk value.

All of these models are used effectively today. And they are not necessarily mutually exclusive.

Our experience has been that the more precisely you can define the problem that you want your advertising to solve—in other words, which marketing driver you want to affect—the more likely that your advertising creative will be effective. Think about prioritizing marketing drivers and focusing on one of these models. That can become your working hypothesis for effective creative content.

If your brand has enough money, time, and energy, you might choose multiple models. We'll discuss next how we helped H&R Block use different models to affect different communications drivers against different target audience segments.

DEVELOPING AN INTEGRATED CREATIVE BLUEPRINT

In order to help manage all of this complexity, we use a tool you can easily use to build a common framework in order to integrate your brand's advertising content. It takes the form of a creative blueprint. It combines a corporate communications message linkage technique with your brand positioning to create a foundational document for your creative teams. If you have multiple creative agencies—separate agencies for traditional advertising, direct mail, promotions, digital advertising, and/or point of sale communications—you can use this document to brief them all.

So this is where you have to make tough choices about what to say and what not to say, about whom to talk to and whom not to talk to, about where and when in the purchase process to spend time, money, and energy on messaging and where and when to sacrifice. This is where you place bets on strategies to tell your brand's story, to affect key marketing drivers, to motivate your target segments to take the desired action, to change perceptions, to address barriers.

Exhibit 16.1 shows the fundamental outline of a strategic messaging architecture. We like to make it look like a bit of a blueprint, but any format works as long as the thinking and content is right. The key is to address the issues in our eight-question test. Two of the answers should be clear, based on your brand positioning: your brand promise and brand persona.

Question 1. What's Your Brand Promise or Brand Idea?
This should be a simple, brief, and clear articulation of your brand positioning as you developed it in Chapter 6, "Positioning." Or if you've articulated your positioning with a platform idea in Chapter 10, "Message Strategy," you can use it here. Think about how great platform ideas, like "Having a Baby Changes Everything" (Johnson & Johnson) or "Imagination at Work" (GE) or "Just Do It" (Nike), could influence the execution of your creative content.

EXHIBIT 16.1
Integrated Creative Content Blueprint

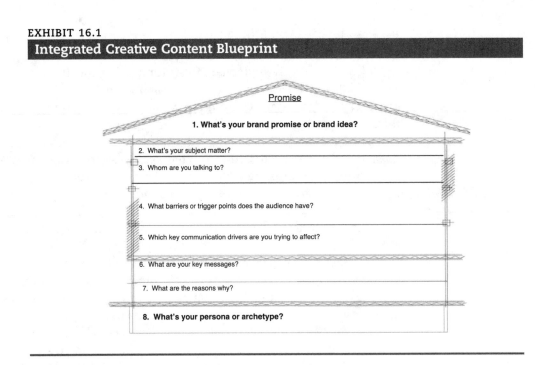

Question 2. What's Your Subject Matter?

In Chapter 4, "Scope," you determined the scope of your brand. Now you need to determine what, of What Do You Do?, you should leverage. Making this choice is critical, and it is, perhaps, the most challenging strategic one to make. What's the best way to tell your story and achieve your desired marketing objectives? Depending on your organization, you can either figure this out from the top down or the bottom up. But this is where you need to make choices about putting messages behind different brand proof points, products, lines of business, and emotional elements of your brand's story.

And this is where you can begin to marry messaging strategy with overarching communications and channel strategies. For example, as we discussed with our window manufacturing client, do you need different messages at different points in the purchases process? Or perhaps your brand is developed differently in different geographic markets. Thus, you might choose to have different messages dealing with different barriers and marketing drivers in different markets.

Question 3. Whom Are You Talking To?

This is Whom Are You For? as determined in Chapter 5, "Targets." You might decide, as we discussed at the beginning of this chapter, to have multiple messages to the same target audience, or multiple messages to multiple audiences. Or you might decide it's important to integrate your marketing communications messages with your corporate communications messages to employees and shareholders. The key is to decide the most important audiences and to make smart choices about your time, money, and energy when it comes to telling your brand's story. Try to paint a picture of your audience.

Question 4. What Barriers or Trigger Points Does the Audience Have?

We've found that over the years our messaging becomes much more effective when we analyze the barriers our target audience might have toward accepting our brand's story. These barriers might be related to awareness, a competitor brand's offer, a lack of knowledge, or a cultural mindset or predisposition. The advertising content needs to overcome these barriers or release the appropriate triggers.

Question 5. Which Key Communications Drivers Are You Trying to Affect?

This choice should be to direct your advertising model: activation, brand awareness, emotional bond, product news, or buzz. It tells the creative teams what kind of advertising content they should think about developing.

Question 6. What Are Your Key Messages?

These connect your brand's story to the positioning, as you developed in Chapter 10, "Message Strategy." And they should serve as proof points to your overarching brand promise or idea.

Question 7. What Are the Reasons Why?

Why should I believe you? These should be the proof points, whether rational or emotional, that help overcome your target audience's barriers. The key point is to be real and *authentic*. Some companies call this the "reason to believe." For example, Johnson & Johnson's Bedtime Bath was one of the most successful baby products launched in decades. Emotionally, it helped consumers feel like good parents because it soothed babies before bedtime. The reason parents could believe it would calm their babies at bedtime was because the product contained a soothing fragrance of lavender and chamomile—and it was from a trusted brand: Johnson & Johnson, a brand whose platform idea is based on the insight that "Having a Baby Changes Everything."

Question 8. What's Your Persona or Archetype?

This is your chosen brand archetype, the social identity or persona that your brand takes on. This was part of your brand's positioning, as developed in Chapter 6. The advertising content needs to reflect that archetype. For example, the Marlboro cigarettes brand takes on the explorer archetype in the form of the American western imagery. When the brand develops creative content, it always answers the question, "Would a cowboy do that?"

The key in developing a great integrated blueprint for your creative content is to make sure that your foundation is solid and that it supports your overarching brand promise, platform idea, and story. And as we discussed in Chapter 10, "Message Strategy," words matter. Your creative blueprint should be crafted with clarity, simplicity, and brevity.

See also Appendix C, Worksheet 48.

Exhibit 16.2 is an example of a prototype integrated creative content blueprint that we developed internally for a former client. See how we've answered each question and how the messages support the brand promise and the persona, and how it all works together to reinforce H&R Block's platform idea, "You Got People."

H&R Block, with a marketing communications budget of about $100 million, over a four-month period actually used three to four advertising models to speak to different target audience segments, all with one voice and one brand persona, all of which supported one platform idea: "You Got People."

HOW TO DISTINGUISH BETWEEN THE PLATFORM, CREATIVE, AND EXECUTIONAL IDEAS

For a client like H&R Block, we might create more than 300 pieces of communications as part of an integrated creative campaign. So how do you evaluate each of these individual pieces?

EXHIBIT 16.2

Integrated Creative Content Blueprint for H&R Block

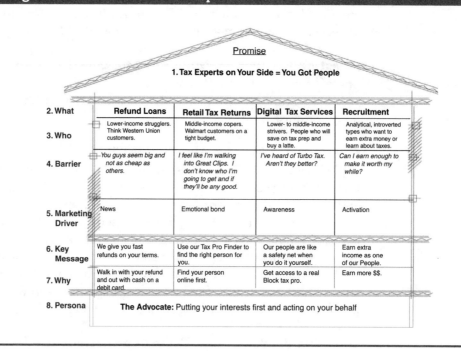

	Refund Loans	Retail Tax Returns	Digital Tax Services	Recruitment
2. What				
3. Who	Lower-income strugglers. Think Western Union customers.	Middle-income copers. Walmart customers on a tight budget.	Lower- to middle-income strivers. People who will save on tax prep and buy a latte.	Analytical, introverted types who want to earn extra money or learn about taxes.
4. Barrier	*You guys seem big and not as cheap as others.*	*I feel like I'm walking into Great Clips. I don't know who I'm going to get and if they'll be any good.*	*I've heard of Turbo Tax. Aren't they better?*	*Can I earn enough to make it worth my while?*
5. Marketing Driver	News	Emotional bond	Awareness	Activation
6. Key Message	We give you fast refunds on your terms.	Use our Tax Pro Finder to find the right person for you.	Our people are like a safety net when you do it yourself.	Earn extra income as one of our People.
7. Why	Walk in with your refund and out with cash on a debit card.	Find your person online first.	Get access to a real Block tax pro.	Earn more $$.
8. Persona	**The Advocate:** Putting your interests first and acting on your behalf			

Over the years, we've seen countless clients react to advertising viscerally, emotionally, analytically, and, occasionally, strategically. In their defense, one of the harder things to do when evaluating creative content is to clearly distinguish between the strategic *platform idea*, the *creative idea* shaping the advertising campaign, and the individual *executional idea* within an ad or the creative content.

Without this clear distinction, researchers can often measure the wrong things in the wrong way. Creative people can misunderstand client feedback. And marketers and brands can lose powerful larger ideas because they react negatively to a small executional element or idea.

The lesson in the following examples is to distinguish between these three different types of ideas, all of which will be reflected in creative content, and to judge the creative work based on the strength of each idea.

You Got People

Go back and look in Chapter 10, "Message Strategy," at what we affectionately referred to as the "ice cream cone" ad for H&R Block. Now let's dissect the three different ideas in it:

1. *The platform idea is obvious:* When you have H&R Block, you have experts on your side. "You Got People."
2. *The creative idea*: A real-looking person with character in common, everyday situations giving an honest, heartfelt testimonial about having people.
3. *The executional idea:* A young guy with an ice cream cone being accompanied by his dog.

The platform idea, that you, the common everyday person, now have people, forces the strategic direction and focus of the creative idea. If you thought that the executional idea was weak, you could have changed it. In fact, we created lots of executions with other types of people in other kinds of situations. And if you thought that the creative idea was weak—not breakthrough enough, for example—you could have changed it to something more focused on the benefits of having people, visuals of things that were purchases from the money H&R Block tax pros saved their customers. (In fact, we did a campaign with that creative idea.) Changing the executional idea doesn't have to change the creative idea. And changing the creative idea doesn't have to ruin a great, broad platform idea.

The Unconvention

Here's another example.

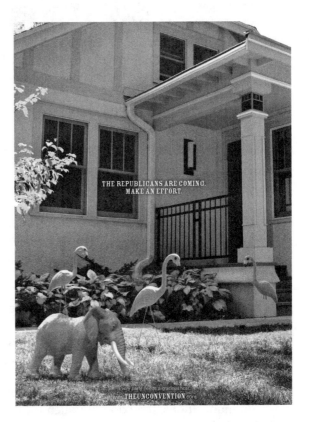

We developed the pro bono effort to welcome Republican delegates to Minnesota for the 2007 national convention. Since Minnesota has been one of the few states to vote consistently for Democratic presidential candidates, we leveraged that irony along with the fact that Minnesotans play nice.

1. *Platform idea:* Make an effort to be a gracious host.
2. *Creative idea:* Lightly humorous static scenes showing the ironic lengths that the nice, Democratic-leaning people of Minnesota have gone to in order to make Republicans feel welcome.
3. *Executional idea:* A pink elephant lawn ornament surrounded by the traditional pink flamingos.

RULES FOR CREATIVE CONTENT

Some of the greatest ads work effectively to achieve objectives without breaking the rules. In fact, sometimes what really works is a new way to be cliché. When you and your creative agency or partners develop creative content against your brief, here are some things to remember.

1. Be authentic.
2. The consumer is the audience—not other creatives, marketing people, or even your spouse.
3. Reward the viewers and give them something for their time.
4. Make the ad the logo.
5. Be honest to a fault.
6. Try not to look and sound like an ad.
7. Be careful with sex. Not everyone is Victoria's Secret.
8. Use celebrities to play roles, not to be props.
9. Showing is better than saying.
10. If an ad doesn't work in the short run, it rarely works in the long run. (MasterCard's "Priceless" campaign may be the exception to this rule, as it didn't initially test well in a copy test best suited to evaluate the product news model of advertising.)
11. You need to be both equally interesting and relevant. Think about dating and mating. People still find babies and puppies interesting.
12. The most effective ads are funny ads. But you have to get it right for the target. Men and women can laugh at the same things, but they often think that different things are funny.

TIPS FOR TESTING ADVERTISING CONTENT

The key when testing creative advertising content, we believe, is to line up the right testing methodology with your chosen advertising model.

Some basic philosophy:

- Advertising content that is efficiently remembered, like Aflac's duck, is not necessarily the best content. For advertising to be effective, it needs to be *engaging*—either through the enjoyment it creates or the news that it shares.
- While traditional measures of recall and persuasion signal efficiency of communications, they do not vouch for the quality of communications.
- "Likability" may seem to be only a diagnostic measurement, but studies are beginning to show a consistent correlation between it and marketplace performance.

Exhibit 16.3 captures a checklist for the product news, emotional bond, and buzz models of advertising.

HOW TO SELECT A CREATIVE AGENCY

Once you have completed your marketing plan, you might find you need additional expertise to help in the execution of the advertising and other elements of the marketing plan. If this is the case, here are some things to keep in mind when selecting an advertising agency:

1. Do not select an advertising agency before comparing a few different agencies.
2. There are a number of ways for you to arrive at a list of different agencies to evaluate:

EXHIBIT 16.3

Advertising Testing Checklist

Model or Framework	Philosophy behind the Model	Examples	How Does It Work? (Deciding on a Model)	How Do You Measure It?	What Is the Downside?
Product news	Seeks to convince people of a Unique Selling Proposition (USP) by giving them a functional reason as to why your brand works better. This approach argues that your product works better than your competitor's.	Packaged goods	Questions to ask: Does your brand actually work better than other brands? Do they care?	Ad recall, main message, brand registration, and persuasion data are obtained.	Highly rational. Model, product, or service must have a benefit consumers want.
Emotional bond	Develops and reinforces the relationship with the user of the brand. Seeks to involve the targets with your ad values so they identify more closely with your brand values. Seeks a moment of understanding.	MasterCard Beverages	Questions to ask: Does the brand say something about the person who uses it? Does the brand have nonproduct values you can easily build on? Does the brand mean a lot to people, and what makes this so? Does brand value make more of a difference than product value right now?	Involvement during exposure: the extent to which the ad is considered important or interesting because it ties in with the recipients' values, concerns, or interests. Likability is important.	Works best with established brands with parity products. Less emphasis on short-term consumer behavior.
Buzz	Seeks to stand out as different—forcing your consumers to reappraise their brand relationship. Model aims to create advocacy for the brand.	Old Spice	Are your products bought on impulse? Is there little product differentiation in industry category?	The extent to which the communication succeeds in distinguishing itself from the customs in the category—"The sort of advertising you'd talk about." Recall and advertising awareness are criteria.	Aims for a short-term effect. Attitude change isn't critical; awareness is. Of least importance is communicating a message.

- Solicit agency referrals from fellow business associates.
- Review advertising in various media, and ask the management of the particular media vehicle (magazine, newspaper, station, and so on) for the name of the agency that placed the specific advertisements that impressed you. Also, ask the media management for their agency recommendations.
- Check out the *Standard Directory of Advertising Agencies* (referred to as the *Red Book*). It is probably available in your local library, and it lists agencies by geographic areas, along with each agency's clients, size, and key personnel.
- Check out the agencies' websites.

3. Once you have arrived at a number of agencies to evaluate, interview them. Or if you have a large list of agencies (five or more) to evaluate, have each agency complete a questionnaire. An advertising agency questionnaire is shown in Exhibit 16.4. After reviewing the completed questionnaires, select three or four agencies for personal presentations. Involve others in your company when reviewing the agencies to provide both more perspective and consensus.

4. The agency you ultimately select should:
    ○ Be genuinely honest and not promise miracles.
    ○ Sincerely care about you and your business and work with you as a partner, not just a vendor.
    ○ Provide the optimum in personal attention, experience, and expertise.
    ○ Have real credentials.
    ○ Be a leader and not a follower. You should not have to tell the agency what to do with your advertising; it should provide sound recommendations.
    ○ Not consistently have turnover of staff and clients.
    ○ Be looking for a long-term relationship, not quick fixes.
    ○ Develop good advertising but also thoroughly understand good marketing.
    ○ Provide a real value (good advertising at competitive rates) and be able to document it.
    ○ Have financial strength, accurate accounting systems, and a billing program to fit your needs.
    ○ Have full-service capability. The agency should be able to provide expert assistance in meeting your creative (including campaign development) and media needs, along with some of your marketing, promotion, merchandising, public relations, and perhaps even research needs.
    ○ Have the right ingredients and staff personalities to match your organization's needs in terms of the agency's size, consumer and business-to-business experience, and level of expertise. Is your advertising account or budget too small or too big for the agency? There must be a match between agency ingredients and client needs in order for both to find the right chemistry for a mutually rewarding relationship.

5. Before making a selection decision, it is also a good idea to give the agency finalists a real product problem to solve in order to assess their strategic thinking and execution abilities.

6. Before making the final decision on an agency, actually visit their offices and check with a few of their current and past clients.

EXHIBIT 16.4

Advertising Agency Questionnaire

Your Business Strategy
1. What objectives are your agency, as a business enterprise, pursuing?
2. What business strategy has your agency adopted for achieving these objectives?
3. What do you consider to be the principal product sold by your agency? What is the main competitive advantage it has over that of other agencies?
4. What method do you have for controlling the quality of your agency's service (specifically in the areas of marketing counsel and creative development and execution)?

Your Marketing and Advertising Philosophy and Practice
1. What is good marketing?
2. Do you prepare marketing plans, and, if so, what is your approach?
3. What makes advertising effective? Include three examples of your most effective advertising.

Advertising Agency Questionnaire (*continued*)

4. How do you measure the effectiveness of advertising?
5. What is the method you use for developing effective advertising?
6. What are your attitudes and/or opinions on the role of research in advertising?
7. To what extent do you feel an advertising agency should or could act as a marketing support function?
8. To what consumer and/or business-to-business marketing successes has your agency recently contributed in a major way? When were they completed? On what basis do you judge them successful? Please limit your examples to no more than three.

Factual Information about Your Agency and Its Services

1. What was the total billing of your agency office (and of the entire agency if applicable) for each of the previous five fiscal years?
2. Which 12 months make up your fiscal year?
3. What percent of your billing is in each of the major media?
4. What is the amount of your largest account billing? Your smallest? Please submit a list of your current clients.
5. Describe the stability and/or longevity of your relationships with your clients in some way that will be more meaningful than a single average figure that covers the number of years they have been with you.
6. What accounts have you added, and what accounts have you lost in the past three years? Why? What is or was their approximate annual billing? (This can be a total figure if confidentiality is required.)
7. What experience does your agency have with consumer goods, retail, service, and/or business-to-business accounts, and which of these accounts do you believe would be of distinct value to our business?
8. Who are the senior general managers and department management executives in your office? *Briefly*, what is the background of each one, including his or her length of service and experience with your agency and other agencies or client organizations?
9. To what extent, if any, would these key executives participate in work on our business?
10. Does your agency have a good history of profitability? Are you currently financially sound?
11. Briefly describe your standard billing policies. What services would be covered by commissions earned? What would be billed net (and at what rate)? What would be marked up?
12. If you prefer a fee, how do you compute the fee?
13. Are you willing to negotiate a compensation plan?
14. Describe your agency's research capabilities and how they have contributed to the success of one or more of your clients.
15. Describe the interaction of the research department with the account service, creative, and media departments.
16. Describe your agency's media capabilities, including information on the following: planning, execution, and postanalysis for national and local broadcast and print media; marketing and media measurement and/or planning sources; and media planning and experience.
17. Briefly discuss how the agency's media expertise has contributed to the successful marketing of one or more of your clients' products.
18. Include a brief discussion of your media department's organization and/or operational structure.
19. If available, describe your promotion, merchandising, and publicity capabilities and experience.

New Product/Concept Development

1. What role do you think your agency could play in the development of new product ideas?
2. Do you have a specific system for product idea generation? If so, please describe it.
3. What are some of the major contributions you have made to the development of new products for your clients? Have these new products been successful?

It's amazing what you will learn. How many talented and experienced people does the agency really have? Do clients receive the agency's account supervisor's personal involvement? Does the agency come up with big ideas that can be affordably implemented? Does the agency pay attention to details?

DOS AND DON'TS

Do

- Measure your advertising objectives of awareness and attitude through quantitative research whenever possible. If you use research, make sure to measure the three awareness levels—first mention and top of mind, unaided awareness, and aided awareness.
- Remember that unaided awareness is the most accurate measure of how you are doing with the target relative to your competition. Use it to determine your real impact with the customer and noncustomer segments.
- Make your message strategy a bridge to your positioning.
- Use the disciplined message strategy approach in developing creative communications.
- Develop your message strategy based on insights into your target's behavior to ensure that your advertising fulfills the emotional as well as the rational needs of the target.
- Develop and evaluate alternative message strategies before choosing one. If possible, test the message strategies with the target before choosing a final one.
- Remember that you are developing campaigns and not just ads. Your message strategy should drive multiple pieces of communication across not just advertising but many of the other marketing mix tools as well.
- Make sure that your advertising is based on your strategy and that it communicates first, and then make sure it's creative—meaning that it commands attention and has an emotional impact on the target.
- Keep in mind that there are no dull products, only dull copywriters! However, compelling message strategies are the single most important determinant of great copy. Your job in the marketing plan is to lay the groundwork for great creative tactics.
- Before producing the final advertising, ask others not directly involved with the executions what the advertising says to them and what feeling they get from it. This last "red flag test" can save you the expense of producing the worst of mistakes: an ad that no one understands.
- If you plan to use an advertising agency, conduct a thorough agency search and screening.

Don't

- Don't confuse advertising with other communication tools.
- Don't expect advertising to make the sale by itself. Make sure you have taken a marketing orientation to your product, distribution channel, pricing,

and all the other marketing mix tools before you turn the blame to advertising.

- Don't advertise if you can't deliver the product as advertised.
- Don't expect to sell anything if you haven't first made sure you've spent enough money to make the target aware of your message. A great advertising campaign won't work if there aren't enough impressions against the intended target.
- Don't begin creating any advertising until you have agreed to a written objective and message strategy.
- Don't accept any creative approach (whether it's your idea or the agency's) unless it's keyed to your strategy.
- Don't create advertising that you cannot afford to produce.
- Don't create advertising that is so expensive to develop that you can't afford adequate media to deliver the message.
- Don't make your advertising different just to be different but to better sell your product.
- Don't drop a campaign because you and your agency become tired of it. Drop it only if it doesn't communicate and motivate. Most likely, your target market has not tired of the advertising.
- Don't create advertising that pleases a boss or a committee. Create advertising that pleases and resonates with your target market. "When you dance with your customers, let them lead!"
- Don't begin creating an advertisement until all the executional details are clearly spelled out.

The Successful Marketing Plan

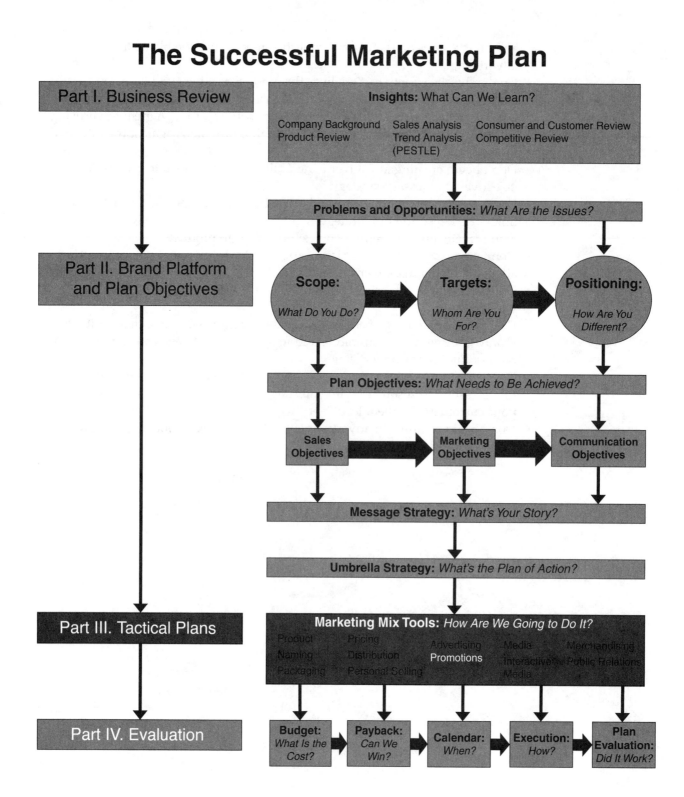

Part I. Business Review

Part II. Brand Platform and Plan Objectives

Part III. Tactical Plans

Part IV. Evaluation

Insights: What Can We Learn?

Company Background | Sales Analysis | Consumer and Customer Review
Product Review | Trend Analysis | Competitive Review
| (PESTLE) |

Problems and Opportunities: *What Are the Issues?*

Scope: *What Do You Do?*

Targets: *Whom Are You For?*

Positioning: *How Are You Different?*

Plan Objectives: *What Needs to Be Achieved?*

Sales Objectives

Marketing Objectives

Communication Objectives

Message Strategy: *What's Your Story?*

Umbrella Strategy: *What's the Plan of Action?*

Marketing Mix Tools: *How Are We Going to Do It?*

Product | Pricing | Advertising | Media | Merchandising
Naming | Distribution | Promotions | Interactive | Public Relations
Packaging | Personal Selling | | Media |

Budget: *What Is the Cost?*

Payback: *Can We Win?*

Calendar: *When?*

Execution: *How?*

Plan Evaluation: *Did It Work?*

17 Promotions

*Promotion is a powerful short-term marketing tool. Developing a promotional plan requires strategic thinking and creativity. In many instances, marketers begin at the execution stage and randomly consider idea after idea without any thought as to the ends they are trying to achieve. The result is usually costly, with time and effort spent on developing promotion ideas that are inappropriate to the target market and the competitive situation and, consequently, do not pay out. The key is to establish promotion objectives and strategies first and then develop innovative, yet **targeted**, executions. Also, keep in mind as you write this promotion segment of the marketing plan that, once executed, it must help fulfill the awareness and attitude communication value goals.*

FROM THIS CHAPTER YOU WILL LEARN

- The definition of *promotion*; promotion differences by industry, incentives, and categories; and the five keys to successful promotions

- How to develop promotion objectives

- How to develop promotion strategies

- How to develop alternative promotion executions utilizing a promotion format

- How to determine the costs of promotions and analyze promotion payback

- How to select the most appropriate promotion execution alternatives and integrate different executions into a total promotion plan

- What event marketing is and how to select and plan an event

- The available promotion tools and how they can be delivered

OVERVIEW

Promotion provides added incentive, encouraging the target market to perform some incremental behavior. The incremental behavior results in increased short-term sales and/or an association with the product (for example, product usage or an event-oriented experience). For the purposes of this book, we will define *promotion* as an activity offering incentive above and beyond the product's inherent attributes and benefits to stimulate incremental purchase or association with the product over the short run. While this promotion segment of the planning process focuses primarily on direct product movement, we do address how to approach event marketing from a planning perspective in terms of product association or experience in the latter portion of this chapter.

Consumer and Trade (Business-to-Business) Promotions

There are two broad categories of promotion—consumer and business-to-business, or trade. The goal of *consumer promotion* is to influence the end consumers or the ultimate purchasers and users to *pull* the product through the channels or, for example, off the shelf. *Trade,* or *business-to-business, promotion* influences the trade or intermediate markets that purchase and resell the product to *push* the product through the channels or onto the shelf. In most cases, some combination of push and pull will be most effective. This chapter discusses both types of promotions.

One major difference between consumer and trade promotions, other than different target markets, is delivery. With consumer promotions, the incentives are delivered either by mass media, online, or in-store devices such as on-pack/in-pack offers. However, because of the relatively narrow customer base for trade promotion, mass communication media are usually not cost efficient—there is too much wasted coverage. Therefore, with trade promotion, added incentives are usually delivered through such targeted media vehicles as direct mail or trade publications or through the sales force.

Promotion Incentives

Promotion incentives fall into one of four major areas:

1. *Price incentives:* Offering some form of savings off the original price of the product.
2. *Product:* Providing a sample of the product.
3. *Merchandise or gifts:* Giving customers the opportunity to obtain merchandise or premiums with the purchase of the product.
4. *An experience:* Giving individuals or groups of individuals the chance to participate in such special events as contests, sweepstakes, parties, or some unique experience. Participants are rewarded with the chance to win a prize, such as money or a trip, or with the pure enjoyment of the event.

Types of Promotions

There are many different types of promotions. Each has unique advantages and disadvantages that are listed in the appendix to this chapter. Following are the 10 promotion categories most commonly used by marketers to communicate or deliver incentives in both consumer and trade (business-to-business) situations:

1. Price reductions
2. Coupons
3. Samples
4. Bonus packs or multipacks
5. Refunds
6. Premiums
7. Contests, games, and sweepstakes
8. Repeat-purchase offers

9. Trade (business-to-business) promotions and allowances
10. Events

Timing of the Incentive Payback to the Target Market

The target market receives the incentive to make a purchase over the course of one three time periods:

- *Immediate:* The consumer receives the incentive instantly with or without the purchase of, or association with, the product.
- *Delayed:* The consumer receives the incentive at the next purchase or within a specified period after the purchase of, or association with, the product.
- *Chance:* The consumer has the chance of receiving the incentive within a specified period of time (immediate or delayed) after the purchase of, or association with, the product.

In summary, promotions are a short-term, behavior-oriented, multifaceted marketing tool that provides flexibility to the marketer in terms of the incentive offered, the promotional vehicle used, and the time period in which the incentive is awarded.

FIVE KEYS TO DEVELOPING SUCCESSFUL PROMOTIONS

As you proceed with this chapter in the preparation of the promotion segment of your marketing plan, keep in mind the five keys to successful promotion development:

1. *Promote what the target market wants.* Don't promote what you can't sell or what is out of fashion. Develop promotions around what will be most appealing to the largest segment of your target market.
2. *Provide the necessary incentive to stimulate behavior.* If you want to get maximum promotion participation, make sure your incentive has the pulling power to get the target market to act. For example, we have found in many retail promotions that "10 percent off" does not move the consumer. It must now be 20 percent or more!
3. *Build the necessary awareness for the offer.* Many marketers do well in promoting what the target market wants with a meaningful incentive, but then they do not make enough of the target market aware of the promotion to garner the participation required to make the promotion successful. Staging a promotion means very little if you don't tell enough people about it.
4. *Limit barriers to promotion participation.* To reduce the liability or cost of promotions, many promotions are overly constrained. Review what barriers or requirements you put in front of the target person in terms of amount of purchase, time made available to participate in the promotion, and incremental behavior required to participate in the promotion. For example, is it too much of a hassle for your target person to participate in your promotion? You can remove many barriers by looking at the promotion from the target person's viewpoint rather than a company viewpoint.
5. *Develop optimum value perception at minimum investment.* Finally, keep in mind that there are two parts to the promotion equation: company cost and target market participation. Accordingly, a promotion should attempt to provide the perception of optimum value to the target market at the minimum of investment by, and/or maximum payout to, the marketer.

THE IMPORTANCE OF ESTABLISHING SHORT-TERM PROMOTION SALES OBJECTIVES

Prior to developing promotion objectives, strategies, and executions, you need to set short-term promotion sales objectives for the promotion time period. In our development of a marketing plan, *promotion is the only marketing mix tool for which we develop specific sales objectives*, and we do so because promotion is both exclusively short term in nature and it affects customer behavior. Customer behavior is affected through tangible incentives, resulting in incremental sales generation and/or an incremental association with the product. With promotion, the marketer will incur short-term expenses in the form of incentives and communication of the incentives in order to achieve the desired short-term consumer response.

The marketer needs to establish promotion sales goals for two reasons. One reason is to enable the promotion to be evaluated against projected payback both prior to and after execution. This will help the marketer determine if the expected incremental sales from the promotion will be greater than the incremental costs (incentives and marketing costs associated with communicating the incentives). The second reason is to set a definite sales goal that the promotion must fulfill.

In Chapter 7, you were urged to develop both annual and short-term, monthly sales goals. In most cases, your promotion sales goal will be a portion of the corresponding month's or week's sales goal. This is because promotions are executed to reverse a downward sales trend or provide necessary incremental sales in any given short-term period.

HOW TO DEVELOP YOUR PROMOTION OBJECTIVES PARAMETERS

Promotion objectives and marketing objectives are very similar in that both are designed to affect consumer behavior. The difference is that promotion objectives should be designed to affect *specific incremental* behavior over a *short period of time*. Therefore, promotion objectives must:

- *Induce incremental consumer behavior over what was anticipated with no promotion.*
- *Be specific.* The objective should focus on one goal only.
- *Be measurable.* The results must be quantifiable.
- *Relate to a specific time period.* However, because promotion objectives are short term in nature, the time period can be from one day to several months.
- *Provide direction as to the geographical focus of the promotion.*
- *Include budget constraints or profit parameters.* Remember, promotion is a marketing mix tool with its own sales objectives.
- *Focus on affecting target market behavior to retain current users, increase purchases from the target market, increase trial from new users, obtain repeat usage after initial trial, and affect attitudes through association with an event.*

Promotions should be viewed as one method to help execute marketing strategies. In order to develop promotion objectives, you must first review the marketing objectives and strategy section of your marketing plan and then restate your marketing strategies in quantifiable promotion objectives.

TASK 1 **Review Your Marketing Strategies**

Review your marketing strategies, paying particular attention to those listed under the promotion category and those for which the implementation tool of promotion might be appropriate. A marketing seasonality strategy such as "increase sales during the weaker selling months of May through August" could be implemented through promotion. Obviously, a marketing promotion strategy such as "develop in-store promotions during peak selling seasons to encourage purchases of weaker-selling product categories" should be addressed in the promotional plan. Thus, the first task requires isolating those marketing strategies that you feel promotions can help implement.

TASK 2 **Review Your Selected Marketing Strategies and Corresponding Marketing Objectives**

This task involves reviewing each marketing strategy selected in Task 1 to be implemented through promotions and its corresponding marketing objective. In order to form promotion objectives, you review the marketing objective to determine *what* needs to be accomplished and *who* is being targeted. Then, you rely on your marketing strategy to guide you on *how* to develop a promotion objective. By linking your promotion objective to your marketing objective and strategies, you ensure greater probability of developing promotions that will accomplish your marketing strategies and fulfill the marketing objectives established earlier in the plan.

Assume the following situation:

Marketing objective: Increase the number of total users and trials among the current target market customers by 10 percent.
Seasonality marketing strategy: Increase the purchasing level during the off-season while maintaining purchasing rates during the peak selling seasons.

Note that there would typically be other marketing strategies to achieve the marketing objective. However, assume that only the seasonality strategy is being implemented through promotion and that the other marketing strategies will be accomplished using other marketing mix executional tools.

In the following example, the marketing objective specifies what the promotion objective should be and to whom the promotion should be targeted:

Increase number of users [marketing goal, *what*] from the current target market [target market goal, *who*].

Continuing, the market strategy will help determine how the promotion objective is developed:

Increase purchasing during the off-season [method of achievement, *how*].

TASK 3 **Create Quantifiable Promotion Objectives**

In combining what, who, and how, the marketing objective and strategy can be restated into a quantifiable promotion objective as follows:

Increase the number of users from the current target market by 25 percent during the off-season of May and June in all markets, with a positive contribution to overhead.

Note that geography and timing considerations and a measurable target market behavior are incorporated into the objective statement to make it as specific as possible. Geography and timing in the promotion objective would be consistent with the geography and timing constraints developed in the marketing strategy section of the plan.

Also, note that a budget constraint is mentioned. In this case, the objective has to be achieved in a manner that contributes positively to fixed overhead. In a different situation, the objective of new trial might outweigh any short-term profit requirement because the company would be investing in new customers or trial for future profits. However, there would be a budget constraint at the end of the promotion objective to limit the amount of the investment in new trial. The promotion objective might be "increase the number of new users 25 percent during the off-season with a promotion budget not to exceed $500,000."

The measurable amount in the promotion objective (in this example, 25 percent) must be realistic. Past experience provides the best assistance in deciding just how much you will affect target market behavior through promotions. Remember that promotion is just one of the marketing tools you will be using to achieve your marketing objectives. If promotions were the only tool, then the measurable goal in the promotion objective would have to equal the measurable goal in the marketing objective. In this example, the goal would have to be to add enough incremental new users during May and June to increase the total new user base for the year 10 percent above last year's results. This is highly unrealistic and points out why there are usually multiple marketing strategies for any given marketing objective. In addition, promotion is most often only partially responsible for the implementation of any given marketing strategy. Other marketing tools, such as advertising, distribution, pricing, and merchandising, might be used in conjunction with promotion to implement a specific marketing strategy.

In going through the process, you may develop several promotion objectives, as there may be several marketing strategies that can be implemented and accomplished through the use of promotions. Each promotion objective will require one or more promotional strategies.

PROMOTION STRATEGY AND EXECUTION CONSIDERATIONS

Once the promotion objectives are established, promotion strategies must be formulated demonstrating how to accomplish the objectives. Promotion strategies should include the following:

- The type of promotion device
- The promotion incentive
- Whether to implement a closed or open promotion
- The delivery method

The Type of Promotion Device

The marketer has to determine which promotional device (samples, premiums, or something else) will best meet the promotion objective. The 10 most common promotion categories were listed earlier in this chapter. Further details and the advantages and disadvantages of each of these promotion vehicles are presented in the appendix to this chapter.

The Promotion Incentive

The promotion incentive must include a basic reward for the consumer. Since promotions are responsible for affecting target market behavior, the incentive needs to stimulate demand. The promotion incentive must be strong enough to move the market to participate in the promotion or event and/or purchase the product.

Keeping in mind profitability goals, the promotion incentive should be broad in scope in most instances. This means that the incentive must appeal to a broad category of consumers. Avoid spending substantial promotion dollars on promotion incentives that affect only small segments of the target market and thus have limited payback potential. A footwear retailer found that it was much more effective to promote a 20 percent discount on all athletic shoes than to promote price reductions on five individual running shoes. The broader nature of the 20 percent discount on all athletic shoes (court, running, fitness, walking) message appealed to a much larger cross-section of consumers. The result was more interest in and trial of the store, greater sales of athletic shoes, and ultimately, more sales in nonathletic departments because of the increased traffic.

One exception is when an individual product or a narrow group of products is promoted with substantial incentives. The larger the individual incentive, the greater the impact of the promotion. The strongly promoted individual product often acts as a loss leader. A *loss leader* is a product intended to build trial for the product or traffic for a store. Another exception to the principle of developing broadly targeted promotion incentives is when the marketer is aiming at a narrow target market. In this situation, an incentive that appeals to a select group of consumers might be very appropriate. Accordingly, you should expect a more limited response.

Finally, as a counter to the broad-scope incentive parameter, the cost of the incentive must also be considered in conjunction with the promotion budget parameter. A half-price sale or a free premium would certainly be broad and appeal to a large cross-section of consumers, but the cost in terms of reduced margins must also be considered and weighed against the anticipated increase in sales generated from the promotion. The key is to develop promotion rewards that are perceived to have high value by the consumer but provide adequate margins, given the anticipated volume of sales, to ensure profitability.

The promotion incentive must achieve the promotion objective. If the promotion objective is to increase purchases among existing customers nationally by 20 percent over the first quarter with a positive contribution to profits, then the promotion can't just generate additional purchases; it must do so profitably. The incentive must be enough to generate additional purchases, yet it cannot be too costly or the promotion will not be profitable. However, if the promotion objective is to increase new trial nationally by 20 percent among the target market customers with a budget of $500,000, then the strategy doesn't need to address a profit constraint, only a budget parameter. This promotion objective might be used by a company concerned with generating new trial as an investment for future profits. In this example, the budget constraint makes certain that a realistic investment is made and that the promotion is developed in a fiscally responsible manner.

Whether to Implement a Closed or Open Promotion

A promotion can be open or closed. There are also degrees between these two extremes. An *open promotion* is one for which the company offers an added incentive to purchase, with no specific behavior required to take advantage of the offer. A good example of this would be a retail-level sale of 20 percent off. In order to take advantage of this incentive or offer, consumers merely have to shop at the store. Anyone can participate with no restrictions.

Open promotions have the ability to generate maximum participation. Our experience has shown us that any restriction will reduce the consumers' interest and propensity to respond and, ultimately, the effectiveness of the promotion. In retail, the sales results between an open sale (one where 20 percent off is advertised with no restrictions) and a closed sale (one where consumers are required to bring a coupon to receive 20 percent off) is substantial. However, because of the increased potential participation, open promotions are more costly because consumers who were going to purchase at regular price will also receive the discount. But remember, greater promotional cost doesn't necessarily mean less profit. Greater sales volume can make up for a loss in margin. We ran a promotion for a client that reduced overall margin by 6 percentage points but added $500,000 to the bottom line. An open promotion also means greater trial and potentially more repeat purchases in the future.

With a *closed promotion*, an added incentive to purchase is offered to consumers, but they are required to do something in order to take advantage of the offer. An example would be a coupon that must be redeemed at purchase or a refund that requires 10 proof-of-purchase validations.

There are varying degrees of a promotion's being open or closed. Consider the example of instant coupons. In this case, the requirement of the individual consumer, beyond simply shopping, is very minimal. The customer has to tear a coupon off the package and present it at the checkout counter. However, a promotion such as a refund requiring multiple proofs of purchase may prove to be very restrictive. This type of promotion requires a great deal of purchase commitment on the part of the consumer before the incentive is received.

Closed promotions are used when the marketer wants to target a specific target market group or limit the cost of the promotion. When Chalet Ski & Patio entered the Twin Cities market, it staged a grand-opening promotion in which it offered a free pair of ski goggles to shoppers who redeemed a coupon at either one of the company's two new stores. The ski shop wanted to limit the cost of the promotion, and it wanted to make sure that the people who visited the shops and received the goggles were skiers and potential future customers. The promotion was delivered via a direct-mail coupon to a targeted list of skiers in the Twin Cities area. The closed promotion allowed Chalet Ski & Patio to achieve its objective of developing trial of the two new ski shops among existing skiers.

The Delivery Method

Promotions can be delivered by four basic methods or a combination thereof:

1. *Media:* There are multiple forms of media-delivered promotions. Direct mail, magazines, newspapers, and the Internet are the most common media delivery methods for packaged goods and business-to-business firms, while television, newspapers, direct mail, and radio are the most common media delivery methods for retail firms.
2. *On, in, or near the package:* For manufacturers, promotions can be delivered on the package itself, in the package, or near the package via a point-of-purchase display. For retailers, the promotions can be delivered in the store through signage and point-of-purchase displays.
3. *Salespeople:* Many companies, especially manufacturers such as packaged goods or business-to-business firms that sell to intermediate markets, use salespeople to deliver a promotional offer. If the target market is not a major consumer

group but a more limited purchasing group, direct personal communication of an offer can be efficient and very effective.

4. *Mobile phones:* Increasingly, promotions are being delivered to consumers' mobile phones via Twitter alerts, text alerts, phone apps, and e-mail. Gift cards and coupons can easily be redeemed from the phone at checkout. In addition, the future will see smartphones increasingly helping consumers locate the best promotions and then find coupons online that can be instantly redeemed at checkout. Manufacturers and retailers will link consumer purchases with up-selling and cross-selling opportunities. The app world is where the Internet was 15 years ago. It's going to explode, and the impact on promotion will be immense. In the coming years, retailers and manufacturers are going to be less concerned about what's in consumers' wallets than what's on their phones.

The fastest-growing delivery methods, according to Nielsen, between 2009 and 2010 are listed below. These provide an indication of where consumers are increasingly looking for promotion information.

Top Five Redemption Growth Methods

Internet	+263%
Direct mail	+ 69%
Magazine	+ 51%
Instant redemption	+ 48%
Direct-mail co-op	+ 45%

HOW TO DEVELOP PROMOTION STRATEGIES AND PROGRAMS

Now comes the fun part. The process of actually establishing promotion strategies is fairly simple and allows for a great deal of creative flexibility.

TASK 1 ## *Review Your Promotion Objectives*

Review your promotion objectives to make certain you are focused on what you are trying to accomplish. Be particularly cognizant of whom you are targeting and the measurable result that you expect.

TASK 2 ## *Review Your Problems and Opportunities*

Review the listing of your problems and opportunities, as these are your knowledge base and will provide insights and ideas on what direction you should pursue in developing your promotion strategies.

As you are reviewing your problems and opportunities, refer to your idea page (discussed in the Introduction of this book), and write down any ideas you may have. Refer to this later when you are actually formulating your strategies.

Two purchase rate/buying habit problems might be the following:

The average shopper is extremely brand loyal.
The Southwest consumes the product category at below-average rates on a per capita basis, and the company has poor sales in this region of the country.

These two problems will affect your promotional strategies in the area of what incentive to offer. Knowing that the category is extremely brand loyal means that it will be very difficult to induce trial, so the incentive will have to be greater. And if you are going to target the Southwest, the challenge will be even greater because it is a low-consumption area where your company has poor sales.

These are examples of how your problems and opportunities will provide direction and insights concerning development of your promotion strategies. Study your problems and opportunities very carefully. They will help you in developing intelligent, data-based promotion strategies.

TASK 3   **Finalize Your Promotion Strategies**

A promotion strategy must incorporate each of the issues outlined in the section on strategy parameters:

- The type of promotion device
- The promotion incentive
- Whether to implement a closed or open promotion
- The delivery method

Assume the following situation:

Marketing objective: Increase usage rates among the target market customers nationally over the next year by 20 percent.

Marketing strategy: Expand alternative uses of the product from being considered exclusively a hot drink to include being also considered a cold drink.

Promotion objective: Obtain initial trial of 100,000 new customers nationally for the product as a cold beverage during the months of April and May. Achieve initial trial with a budget of $2 million.

Note that with this situation there would probably be an alternative promotion objective aimed at stimulating trial from among the existing customers. This objective would have separate promotion strategies and executions.

The following promotion strategies could be utilized to accomplish the promotion objective. Each of four strategy parameters will be addressed. The cost parameter is addressed only indirectly through the choice of an incentive amount. It will be covered in more detail in Task 5.

See also Appendix C, Worksheet 49.

Utilize in-store sampling of the product to soft drink purchasers.

Provide potential customers with in-store coupons worth 50 cents off the purchase price the day of the sampling.

Incorporate a trade program offering price incentives as a way to induce shelf space and merchandising support.

TASK 4   **Develop Alternative Promotion Program Executions**

The first part of this task is to develop alternative executions for each promotion strategy. The second part is to choose the most appropriate execution for inclusion in your program. Multiple executions can be developed for each promotion strategy. Be creative and think of as many as you can. One alternative promotion execution is presented in Exhibit 17.1 This alternative was developed to meet two of the strategies: (1) Utilize sampling of the product in the store, and (2) provide 50-cent coupons to potential customers in the store.

EXHIBIT 17.1

Example Promotion Execution

Program Theme

"Have one on us."

Sales Objective

Develop sales of $20 million over a two-month period.

Promotion Objective

Obtain initial trial of 100,000 new customers nationally for the product as a cold beverage during the months of April and May. Achieve the initial trial with a budget of $2 million.

Promotion Strategies

1. Utilize in-store sampling of the product to soft drink purchasers.
2. Provide coupons to potential in-store customers worth 50 cents off the purchase price wherever the product is sampled.

Description

Display a giant self-serve beverage bottle with the product being served hot from one side and cold from the other in grocery stores carrying the product.

Offer free samples in paper cups to all shoppers during four weeks in April and May, effectively leading the summer selling period.

Provide a 50-cent instant coupon to all consumers who sample the product.

Support

In-store signage and display.

Rationale

The promotion will build trial and exposure for the new cold drink. Serving the cold drink with the established hot drink will show customers alternative uses for the product and link the new brand to an established and accepted product. April and May were chosen as the time to sample because the time period effectively bridges cold and warm weather months.

The instant coupon will encourage immediate purchase after trial. The 50-cent coupon incentive will be strong inducement and, along with the sampling, will lower the risk of trying an unknown product.

Note: Other possible executions would be developed for the same objectives and strategies. You could then choose the execution that most effectively and efficiently met the objectives.

Worksheet 50 in Appendix C will help you channel your thinking and stay consistent from one execution to another.

Note that there is a sales objective included. Since promotions are a short-term marketing tool affecting customer behavior, there will be short-term sales results generated by the promotion. Thus, it is a good idea to establish a sales goal along with the promotion objectives, strategies, and executions. When you analyze your promotion results, you will then have two results against which to gauge your success—the sales goal and the quantitative promotion objective.

TASK 5 ## Calculate the Cost and Payback Potential of Your Promotions

Expenses must be projected for each promotion in your promotional plan. All costs associated with communicating and delivering the promotion to the target market should be included. This includes the media costs associated with delivering the promotion. (This does *not* include the media costs associated with your normal nonpromotion and/or image advertising.) In addition, you must also estimate the cost of the offer or incentive. If you use 50-cent coupons, you must estimate the redemption number and multiply it by 50 cents plus the handling cost of each coupon to calculate a dollar cost of the coupon incentive. (Coupon handling costs will be discussed in detail later in this chapter.)

EXHIBIT 17.2

Average Redemption Range		

	AVERAGE REDEMPTION RANGE	
Promotion Technique	**Low**	**High**
Instant coupon	15.0%	55.0%
In the product	6.0	17.5
On the product	6.0	15.0
Electronically dispensed in the store	4.0	21.0
On-shelf distribution	4.0	16.0
Internet	4.0	10.0
Crossruff or cross-packs	2.0	6.0
Direct mail	1.0	9.5
Freestanding inserts	0.7	3.0
Magazine on page	0.5	4.5
Refunds	0.5	4.5
Newspaper (ROPs)	0.5	2.5
Newspaper co-op	0.4	1.7
Self-liquidating point-of-purchase (POP) premium	0.3	1.0

Cost Calculation for Closed Promotions

In order to calculate the cost and potential payback of closed promotions, you need to accurately project redemption rates for your offer.

The participation estimates shown in Exhibit 17.2 are based on a combination of our client experience and redemption averages published by industry sources. These are ballpark estimates for participation or redemption rates using different closed promotion vehicles. Actual participation rates should be individually adjusted as they are a function of the following:

- *The offer:* Greater incentive and fewer restrictions equal greater participation.
- *The delivery method:* The closer the delivery method is to the product itself, the greater the redemption. For example, on-pack/in-pack promotions will have high redemption rates.
- *The timing:* Immediate incentives such as instant coupons will have relatively high rates of redemption. Also, promotions that are run when the target category customers are purchasing (bicycles in the spring) will have greater participation than those that are run when category purchasing is at a low level.
- *The product category:* Health and beauty aids, for example, have average redemption rates lower than those of household products or beverages.
- *The price of the product:* The higher the purchase price of the product, the lower the participation. However, a higher promotion incentive can have some positive effect on participation if the high price of the product is not out of the economic reach of the majority of your target market customers.

Exhibit 17.3 demonstrates how to calculate the cost of a promotion. We used a coupon promotion as an example because it has applications to retail, packaged-goods, and business-to-business firms. Three different redemption rates were used in order to provide the marketer with a range of expected responses. The cost of this promotion would be somewhere between $110,000 and $101,250, with a medium estimate of $105,000. This cost will be used, along with incremental sales and profits, when calculating potential payback for a closed promotion.

See also Worksheet 51 in Appendix C.

In addition, if you are a consumer goods firm with coupon redemption in grocery and other stores, there are handling charges to be included. If you are utilizing a clearinghouse, you must pay a charge for each coupon handled. Also, the retailer

EXHIBIT 17.3

Calculation Example for the Cost of a Coupon Promotion

	High	Medium	Low
Redemption Costs			
Value of coupon	$ 500	$ 500	$ 500
Number of coupons distributed	500,000	500,000	500,000
Estimated redemption rate	4.0%	2.0%	0.5%
Number redeemed	20,000	10,000	2,500
Dollar value of offer			
(number redeemed × value of coupon)	$ 10,000	$ 5,000	$ 1,250
Advertising and Media Costs			
Printing of coupons (500,000 × $0.01)	$ 5,000	$ 5,000	$ 5,000
Postage and envelopes (500,000 × $0.19)	95,000	95,000	95,000
Total cost of promotion	$110,000	$105,000	$101,250

charges for each coupon handled. At the time this book went to press, the average total cost was approximately 20 to 35 cents per coupon redeemed.

Additional promotion administrative costs to consider are the following:

- *Costs of employing fulfillment house:* There is an incremental cost for fulfillment regarding refunds, samples, premiums, and sweepstakes and/or games. Most companies aren't equipped to adequately fulfill promotion programs.
- *Cost of production:* For example, production lines are often slowed to accommodate on-pack/in-pack incentives.
- *Packaging costs:* For example, with bonus packs there will be a cost to reconfigure the package.

Finally, the cost of the promotion must be compared to the incremental sales the promotion is expected to generate. This can be determined through a payback analysis.

Payback Analysis

Before you execute any planned promotion, you should make sure to review the numbers to determine if the promotion makes sense from a payback analysis standpoint. We recommend calculating the contribution to fixed costs,* as this method isolates the promotion and takes into account any incremental variable cost associated with the promotion. In this method, incremental costs of the promotion (communication of the promotion and incentive costs) are subtracted from incremental sales generated from the promotion.

Exhibit 17.4 presents an example of a sporting goods retailer considering a 20-percent-off sale as an open promotion. The retailer had experience with similar sales in the past, and it had a rough estimate on the incremental sales that could be generated by the promotional offer. This method looks at incremental sales and costs to calculate what the promotion will generate in terms of a contribution to fixed overhead. The incremental margin sales are sales above and beyond what would normally be expected for the time period. In this case, the retailer had a good idea of what to expect. If you haven't run the promotion before, make a high, medium, and low estimate based on similar company promotions run in the past and promotion experiences for the product category. This provides best- and worst-case estimates.

See also Worksheet 52 in Appendix C.

---

* This method is commonly used by retailers, service firms, and manufacturers. However, manufacturers also utilize a method that compares the gross margin to the net sales, and this method is detailed in Chapter 22.

EXHIBIT 17.4

Payback Calculation Example for an Open Promotion

Situation

Promotion: 20% off women's department merchandise
Estimated storewide margin decrease from 50 to 45% during promotion
   time period: First two weeks of March
Geography: All three stores in Madison, Wisconsin

Sales

Estimated sales for period without promotion	$300,000
Estimated gross margin dollars for period without promotion ($300,000 × 0.50)	150,000
Estimated sales with promotion	360,000
Estimated gross margin dollars with promotion ($360,000 × 0.45)	162,000
Estimated net margin dollar increase with promotion ($162,000 × $150,000)	12,000

Media and Advertising Cost

Estimated ongoing advertising and media costs with or without promotion*	15,000
Total advertising and media costs with promotion	20,000
Incremental advertising and media costs due to promotion	5,000

Payout

Incremental margin sales	12,000
Incremental advertising and media expenditures	5,000
Contribution to fixed overhead	7,000

*What would have been spent in regular, mainline advertising and media.

Note that the cost of the promotion (reduction in gross margin dollars) was calculated directly into the projected incremental sales figure. In some cases you may want to break this step out to show what the promotion costs were, particularly if you are a packaged-goods marketer and you wish to show redemption projections.

Remember, the promotion must stand on its own. The only way to determine its potential success or failure is to weigh the projected incremental sales against the expected incremental expenses of the promotion. If the promotion contributes a meaningful positive dollar figure to fixed overhead (expenses that occur no matter what happens—for example, rent) and meets the promotion sales goals, then the promotion should be executed. If the payback analysis shows that there is a negative contribution to fixed overhead, then you should consider another promotion, or rework the promotion with less incentive or a different product mix. The exception to this is the case in which there is no payback parameter specifying that the promotion must contribute to profits. If the firm is simply trying to gain trial, which it feels will translate into future profits, then the major constraints will be the budget parameter and the amount of desired trial.

TASK 6   ## Select the Most Appropriate Promotion Executions

You have developed promotion objectives and strategies, created promotion execution alternatives, and analyzed costs and paybacks for each execution. Now it is time to select those executions that will best achieve the promotion objectives within the established budget constraints.

When choosing your promotion executions, try to make sure the executions complement each other and work together through the year. Two consecutive premium offers would probably be ineffective as compared to other combinations of promotions. The best method to determine if your promotions properly interface with each other is to list the promotions in calendar form according to when they will be executed. This will allow you to make judgments on whether you have selected promotions that complement each other. It will also be useful when you are transferring your marketing tool executions to one master calendar, as is detailed in Chapter 22, "Budget, Payback, and Calendar."

HOW TO APPROACH EVENT MARKETING

While we have discussed in detail most of the promotion categories, one important category into which we have not delved is events. Event marketing, sometimes known as "event sponsorship" or "lifestyle marketing," is a rapidly growing area. Event marketing expenditures by U.S. companies are in the billions annually, and they are showing double-digit growth each year. The largest portion of these expenditures is devoted specifically to sports sponsorships, although event marketing as a whole certainly encompasses much more than just sports marketing.

The growing popularity of event marketing can be attributed to its ability to cut through the advertising clutter and reach consumers (as well as other important audiences) in impactful ways. Well-planned and well-orchestrated events also integrate two or more communications objectives for maximum effectiveness. For example, an event that is promotional in nature may also achieve media publicity and/or build relationships with dealers or distributors.

TASK 1 ## *Establish the Goal*

Although events can be "leveraged" so that they accomplish several communications objectives, it is best to begin your planning with one central goal. This will keep your planning and execution focused, helping you choose from among the myriad options that are open to you in event marketing.

Events can make a strong element in the marketing mix when any of the following is your goal:

- Launching a new product
- Introducing your product to a new market or target audience
- Increasing product trial
- Positioning your product or company
- Building personal relationships with the product and people associated with it
- Differentiating your product or company from the competition
- Building brand loyalty
- Establishing your company as a good corporate citizen
- Educating and informing the target audience
- Strengthening relationships with distributors, retailers, or other partners
- Recruiting, training, or motivating employees

The event you select, and the features you give it, should grow naturally out of your primary goal. As an example, if increasing product trial is a key objective, you should choose an event that reaches the maximum number of people in your target audience and gives them an incentive to try the product via on-site trial or couponing. Also, remember to make every effort to quantify your specific event objectives such as providing a specific number of people you want to attract to try the product on site.

TASK 2   ### Select an Event

Event selection and design is the most critical component in ensuring an event that will meet your marketing objectives. Successful events share the following characteristics:

1. *There is a clear and meaningful connection between your product or company and the event itself.* A shoe retailer, for example, can reinforce its area of business and convey corporate citizenship by giving away discontinued shoe styles to low-income children in the area. An event for the same retailer that is focused on building brand identity might tie an important product line, such as running shoes, with sponsorship of a marathon.

   At the same time, the presence of your product or company message should not be so intrusive that it interferes with people's enjoyment of the event itself. The sincerity of your company's commitment to the event or cause must be apparent, or the target audience may feel that they are being manipulated into buying a product.

2. *Your company or product identity comes through clearly.* This is particularly critical in sponsorship situations, where your company may "own" an event exclusively or "share" the event with other sponsors, media partners, or charities. You need to be sure that your identity is not lost on the target audience.

3. *There is a compelling appeal to the target audience.* Events are costly and time consuming to stage, and nothing is worse than discovering that your event has attracted low participation. You must select an event with clear appeal to those you are trying to reach and integrate features that will ensure maximum interest from your target audience. This includes everything from pre-event promotion and advertising to selecting a high-traffic location for an event designed around public participation.

4. *The event has news value.* Virtually every event can be enhanced with the addition of media coverage. Your event may have an element of "hard news" (that is, a happening that merits coverage), or it may offer publicity opportunities in the form of human interest features or photo opportunities. When designing your event, you should give consideration to including features that will make the event more newsworthy, such as unusual contests or record-breaking events.

   There will be occasions when media publicity is not vital to your objective. For example, you might hold a seminar to educate a narrow group of prospects about a new technology that only they are in a position to use. While media coverage in a technology-oriented trade journal could be a helpful enhancement, the event would be a success without media coverage as long as it attracts a good number of attendees and generates their interest in the technology.

5. *You can incorporate related communications elements that support the event and further your marketing objectives.* What are the opportunities for tie-ins with sales promotions, direct mail, advertising, point-of-purchase displays, and/or dealer programs? These elements can be used to bring additional attention to the event and, in some cases, to extend the reach of the event to members of the target audience who may not experience it personally.

One of our clients designed a promotion to donate $1 to charity for every purchase. The same charity was benefiting from the sponsor's criterium bicycle race, which took place at the conclusion of the promotional period. As a result of this promotion, communicated primarily through outdoor advertising and point-of-purchase displays, even those consumers who were not spectators at the bicycle race became aware of the race and our client's sponsorship of it.

TASK 3 ## Ask These Questions When You Are Planning an Event

- *Do you have the resources (time, money, staff, connections, and so on) to create your own event?* Or are you better off "piggybacking" onto an existing and already established event?
- *Can you establish a tie-in with a timed event?* Examples would be an anniversary, sporting event, or designated week or month (for example, "June is Dairy Month").
- *Are there opportunities to localize the event?* Any event that relates to the community in an integral way will be more meaningful to the target audience. If you are creating a new event, you can survey the community to determine issues and concerns that are important to people's lives.
- *Are there opportunities to affiliate with a suitable charity or cause?* If you and a non-profit organization share a common interest, you can form a mutually beneficial relationship. The charity receives exposure and the implied endorsement of your company, while you receive the legitimacy and additional media coverage that come from being associated with that particular charity and charitable works in general.
- *Can you ally with a media partner who becomes a cosponsor?* For many years, we helped plan and execute young adult events for Coors Beer, with contemporary radio stations' cosponsoring the event. With a media cosponsor, you can negotiate a regular schedule of media coverage prior to, during, and after the event. This is a commonly used technique for charitable events, fairs, telethons, and sports sponsorships. Bear in mind, however, that news coverage from competing media is far less likely when one or more media outlets are linked to your event as sponsors.
- *Can you ally with other business partners who can provide resources and add an extra dimension to your event without overshadowing your involvement?* For example, a local food manufacturer could be invited to serve free samples of its food at your event. This stretches your budget and enables the food company to reach consumers. Regardless of how you choose your cosponsors, make sure both parties benefit.
- *Is there a theme or creative concept?* A "big idea" that gets attention and appeals to the target audience makes it easier to leverage your event with promotions, direct mail, point-of-purchase coupons or discounts, and more. In our work with Coors, the big idea was the Summer Series, which included a number of high-impact events such as the Coors Downtown Beach Party.
- *Is a celebrity or expert spokesperson a possible draw?* Celebrities with recognizable names (whether they are local or national in stature) can help attract attendance at your event and generate additional media coverage. If your event is a seminar or convention, the most appealing speaker may be someone with strong credentials in the field, even if the person is not a recognizable name outside of that field.
- *How can your company or product identity be reinforced?* Signage, banners, giveaways, displays, clothing, and equipment are just some of the ways you can add your identity to the event. If you expect media coverage from television stations and/or newspapers, make sure your identity is positioned where it will be picked up by the camera.
- *What is the timetable?* Building a realistic and detailed timetable is a critical step in any successful event marketing program. Extremely long lead times are often required to plan, promote, and implement a successful event. Remember, detailed planning is the key to successful events.
- *What is the budget?* Budget is another factor that should be planned for in advance. A realistic budget can help you evaluate, while still in the planning phase, whether the event you are designing is likely to be worth the investment. Naturally, careful budgeting also helps ensure that you have the

resources to execute the event of your choice. Usually, it is best to use the task method in budgeting and then pare back accordingly on a priority basis.

- *How will the success of your event be evaluated?* Consider evaluation methods during the up-front planning, so that you can build in any appropriate success measures from the start. Evaluation methods can range from simple counts of attendance, product sold, coupons distributed, and the like. Or evaluation can incorporate primary market research for measurement of pre- and post-event target market awareness, perceptions, attitudes, and behavior.

TYPES OF EVENTS

A wide variety of events are available as marketing communications tools. This list will serve as an idea starter:

Announcement of a new entity or product
News conference
Celebrity appearance
Spokesperson tour
Contest or competition
Professional sporting event
Amateur sporting event
Walkathon or bikeathon
Grand opening or open house
Product couponing or sampling event
Remote broadcast
Dedication or groundbreaking
Commemorative ceremony
Award presentation
Carnival
Parade
Street festival
Vehicle appearance or rides
Community cleanup
Cultural fair
Science fair
Concert
Book release
Telethon
Lecture, demonstration, or exhibit
Information display
Seminar
Meeting or convention
Research presentation

DOS AND DON'TS

Do

- Utilize promotions to encourage incremental target market behavior.
- Make sure promotions are measurable.

- Utilize specific promotions for short-term durations.
- Remember that while promotions are effective in increasing sales in the short term, they also can have long-term attitudinal and behavioral consequences.
- Try to utilize promotions that are consistent with and will enhance your positioning.
- Use the Internet as appropriate. Although somewhat limited in penetration of some target markets, the Internet is becoming more popular for promotion implementation because it is targeted and relatively efficient in promotion delivery.
- Plan your promotions so that they complement the use of the other marketing mix tools. (An example of this would be national image advertising complemented with co-op in ad features of the product and point-of-sale displays in the stores. All advertising would also incorporate the same basic selling theme and tone.)
- Make sure you determine the cost and the potential payback of your promotions before implementing them.
- Evaluate the success or failure of each promotion to help in developing stronger promotions in the future.
- Plan and evaluate carefully. Promotion can be a powerful, but expensive, marketing tool.
- Be aware of an ever-growing promotion problem: promotion fraud. Specifically, learn about coupon fraud among consumers and retailers, as well as refund and/or premium fraud among consumers where promotion offers require proofs of purchase.
- Whenever possible, test new promotions before making a major investment and using them on a broader scale.
- Use incentives that are appealing to your target market and that are realistic for the vast majority of your target market customers to obtain.
- Remember, successful promotions have an optimum value perception among target market customers with a minimum monetary investment by the marketer.
- To have a successful promotion, remember that you need broad target market appeal for the product, a strong promotion incentive, high promotion awareness, and minimum restrictions for participation.
- Remember, over 90 percent of an event's success is in the preplanning of the event itself.

Don't

- Don't expect promotions to solve long-term sales declines or create a loyal consumer franchise among those who purchase the product for its inherent benefits—leave those goals to such other marketing tools as packaging, product improvements, and image advertising.
- Don't rely on only a few promotional devices. Consider all the promotional tools available to you, but use only those that are appropriate to your product.
- Don't overuse or develop a dependence on promotions. Too many promotions can cause an erosion of value and image.
- Don't schedule promotions without reviewing the entire marketing calendar and the specific promotion schedule. Consecutive use of similar promotions will diminish the success of the second promotion.
- Don't run promotions just because you ran them last year. Think strategically about what you are trying to accomplish.
- Don't give deals unless you can document that it builds the business.
- Don't use promotions simply to replace other tools of the marketing mix. Use this marketing tool for its inherent strengths.

APPENDIX OF PROMOTION VEHICLES

Definitions of Promotion Vehicles

Couponing	A type of promotion involving the distribution of a coupon that has a value upon redemption.
Newspaper run-of-press (ROP) ad	A method for delivering promotion incentives that involves the printing of an incentive in the newspaper, usually in an ad, on regular newsprint, with no special paper or inserts.
Magazine and supplement	A method for delivering promotion incentives, commonly coupons, printed on the page as part of an ad. Two variations are the pop-up coupon, printed on separate card stock and inserted into the magazine's binding, and tip-in coupons, which are glued to supplement inserts.
Crossruff coupon	An execution method for couponing that involves taking the consumer from one product, store, or department to a different product, store, or department for which the coupon is redeemable.
Sampling	A type of promotion that involves the free trial of a product.
Premium	A type of promotion involving a product (gift) of perceived value that is given away, or made available, with the purchase of the product.
Self-liquidating premium	An execution method for premiums by which the customer is required to cover the cost of the premium via payment.
Proof of purchase	An execution method for premiums by which the premium is sent to the customer in return for proof of one or more purchases.
Sale-price reduction or cents-off label	A method for executing the price reduction promotion; it can be in the form of advertised sales prices, prepriced goods, labels on the product that flag the price reduction, or price packs, which are specially priced makeups of different size than the regular package.
Free-standing insert (FSI)	An insert with coupons or other promotional offers that is loosely inserted in a carrier such as the newspaper. Co-op FSIs carry multiple coupons for different product categories.
Instant coupons	A method of coupon delivery where the coupon is attached to the outside of the package. The consumer can pull it off in the store and utilize it during purchase.
Bonus packs	A method for executing the price reduction promotion. It involves providing bonus product for the price or close to the price of the original product.
Refunds	A type of promotion offering money back after the purchase and usually requiring some proof of purchase.
On pack/in pack	A method of promotion delivery where the offer is either flagged on the package or included in the package.
Stamps	Stamps may be redeemed for some item of value once specific levels have been accumulated.
Contests and sweepstakes	Games and events in which customers participate for the chance of winning a prize. Many of these games and contests are being delivered via the Internet.

Evaluation of Promotion Vehicles

Promotion	Objectives	Execution/Delivery Methods	Advantages	Disadvantages
Couponing	Stimulate trial	Sales force	1. Allows pinpoint targeting of customers	1. Very high delivery costs per coupon
	Increase frequency of purchase		2. Creates a value-added sales call	2. Distribution of coupons limited
	Increase multiple purchases	Direct mail	1. Higher redemption rates	1. High delivery costs per coupon
			2. Permits selective customer targeting	
		Newspaper ROP ads	1. Low delivery cost per coupon	1. Lower redemption rates
			2. Permits limited geographic distribution	2. Clutter and competitive advertising

Promotion	Objectives	Execution/Delivery Methods	Advantages	Disadvantages
			3. Offers flexibility in timing, size, and layout of coupon ad	3. High potential for misredemptions
		Magazines and supplements	1. Low delivery cost per coupon 2. Permits mass distribution to segmented audience 3. Allows some geographical selectivity through regional editions of national magazines 4. Allows high-quality reproductions for creative appeal	1. Loss of flexibility in timing due to long lead times for insertion 2. Lower redemption rates relative to other vehicles
		Freestanding inserts (FSIs)	1. Higher redemption rates than ROP coupons 2. Lower delivery cost per coupon than direct mail 3. Permits limited geographic mass distribution 4. Permits more creativity than does ROP	1. High potential for misredemptions 2. Needs longer lead time to print and insert than with ROP
		In-package/on-package coupons	1. Draws attention to package at point of purchase 2. Higher redemption rates 3. Lower delivery cost per coupon 4. Effective stimulant of repeat purchase	1. Limited stimulus for trial by new category users 2. Customer may seek simultaneous redemption of coupon on package and previously distributed coupon 3. Distribution limited to users of the product category
		Cross-ruff coupons	1. The product the coupon is promoting receives implied endorsement from brand carrying the coupon 2. Package with coupon is perceived as having added value 3. Can obtain trial of promoted brand by new users with demographics similar to carrier brand 4. Strong-selling brand can cross-sell for weaker-selling brand 5. High redemption rate if promoted brand has natural relationship to carrier brand 6. Low delivery cost of coupon	1. Effectiveness of coupon is a function of the effectiveness of carrier product 2. Limited distribution and target market reach

(Continued)

Evaluation of Promotion Vehicles (*Continued*)

Promotion	Objectives	Execution/Delivery Methods	Advantages	Disadvantages
		Instant coupon	1. Very high redemption rate 2. Very low distribution cost per coupon	1. More likely to appeal to current users than to attract new trial 2. High gross redemption rates
		On-shelf instant coupon machine	1. Simple to use 2. High redemption rates	1. Limited distribution of in-store machines 2. Costs per redemption high due to the technology investment
		Coupons generated electronically at checkout lane	1. Based on consumer profile generated by purchases 2. High redemption rates	1. Shopper must hold on to coupon until the next visit to retailer 2. Coupon is restricted to the retailer that issued it
Sampling	Develop initial trial of new products	In pack or on pack	1. Low distribution costs 2. Sample receives implied endorsement of carrier brand 3. Pack with sample increases trial of carrier brand 4. Selective distribution of pack with sample permits testing of sample's promotional effectiveness	1. Distribution is limited to buyers of carrier brand 2. Trade may reject package if unusual size creates special handling requirements 3. Expensive because of cost of the sample and delivery of product 4. High cost of sample
		Direct mail	1. The ability to aim at specific target segments permits a variety of creative product presentations 2. Delivery may be timed to tie in with other promotions and advertising 3. May create consumer interest forcing the trade to carry the product 4. Permits mass distribution	1. Some products' size, weight, or fragility prevents mailing 2. High delivery costs per sample 3. Any wasted coverage due to inaccuracies in mailing list is very expensive
Premiums	Provide added value to the purchase of your product, thus increasing trial Create impulse trial Develop continuity of purchases and multiple purchases	Self-liquidating premiums	1. Potential value added to product at minimum cost to the marketer 2. Premiums of value often get trade display 3. Image of brand may be enhanced through association with quality premium or premium consistent with brand's positioning	1. Typically, unused premiums cannot be returned, forcing testing of consumer rates; even then, an unpopular premium may result in an inventory of costly and unwanted premiums 2. Stimulates less sales than free premiums because consumer must make cash outlay

Promotion	Objectives	Execution/Delivery Methods	Advantages	Disadvantages
			4. Repeat purchases can be increased by requiring multiple purchases for premium eligibility 5. Permits geographic and creative flexibility	
		In pack or on pack	1. May force increased shelf space and merchandising support from the trade 2. Provides added value to the consumer 3. Premiums can be targeted to specific consumer segments 4. Promotes trial and repeat purchase 5. Permits geographic selectivity	1. Premium should be tested to accurately predict consumer response 2. Physical size of premium may cause trade to refuse to handle product due to space limitations 3. Poor quality or inappropriate premium may detract from brand's image
		Bonus pack	1. Increases perceived value at point of purchase 2. Stocking up takes customers out of market for competitors' products and habituates them to using your product	1. Potential trade resistance to larger pack without profit incentives 2. Customers may feel cheated when package returns to original size
		Proof of purchase	1. Encourages multiple purchases and continuity of purchases 2. Low redemption rate permits use of higher-value premium 3. Consumer can be encouraged to trade up to larger size or more expensive item	1. Lack of immediate reinforcement reduces consumer interest 2. Impulse sales are weaker than with instant premiums 3. Supporting advertising often needed to promote longer-term purchasing commitment
Price reductions	Stimulate incremental purchase/trial Influence purchase decision/increase purchase ratio at point of purchase Increase purchases per transaction Increase dollar amount per transaction	Sale price reduction	1. Greater profits may result if expected increase in sales exceeds effects from margin decrease 2. Can counter competitors' activities by encouraging repeat purchases by current users	1. Continued price reductions can erode brand image over time 2. Potential for price wars 3. Too-frequent price reductions make reduced price the expected norm, so consumers won't purchase at full price

(Continued)

Evaluation of Promotion Vehicles (Continued)

Promotion	Objectives	Execution/Delivery Methods	Advantages	Disadvantages
		Cents-off label	1. Increased attention from flagging of package can influence purchase decisions at point of purchase 2. Increased trade support results from anticipated increase in product demand 3. Sales force provided with opportunity to increase sales to the trade	1. Some stores will not accept flagged or prepriced packaging
Refunds	Develop trial and continuity of purchase Encourage multiple purchases (where multiple proofs of purchase are required)	Same methods as for couponing	1. High perceived value by consumers 2. Relatively low-cost promotion because of large percentage of nonredemption 3. Can extend buying period of seasonal products with multiple-purchase requirement 4. Flagging package with refund offer increases point-of-purchase and impulse sales	1. Lack of immediate gratification reduces incentive to buy 2. Tends to reward current users rather than creating new trial
Repeat-purchase offers	Develop repeat and continuity of purchases Increase purchases per transaction Encourage seasonal purchases Reduce competitive purchases	Refund program On-pack or in-pack premium program Stamps	1. Continuity programs help to create brand loyalty and establish consumer purchasing habits 2. Repeat-purchase requirement often creates multiple purchases, temporarily taking the consumer out of the market for the product class and reducing chances of success for competitors' programs	1. Requires consumers to make a long-term commitment to the product 2. Thrust of repeat-purchase program is to maintain current users, not to develop new trial
Contests, games, and sweepstakes*	Develop multiple purchases Enhance brand image and develop attention through excitement of contest	Product in store, point of purchase media	1. Contest can be built around inherent drama of the product and communicate specific product attributes 2. Contest can be directed to specific target audiences 3. Contest's excitement can help generate trade support and point-of-purchase displays	1. Impact is limited, since there is no guarantee of reward; participation is less than that of price incentives, bonus packs, and other instant-gratification promotions 2. Contest targets current users more than developing new trial 3. There are many legal issues that must be considered before execution

Promotion	Objectives	Execution/Delivery Methods	Advantages	Disadvantages
Trade promotions and allowances	Increase trial by new customers	Price reductions or incentives	1. Promotions to the trade help ensure the product's availability for consumers and result in favorable merchandising	1. Trade can come to expect deals
	Create multiple purchases	Refunds		2. Can take away funds from consumer advertising and promotions so that even if the trade stocks the product, the ability to generate consumer demand is diminished
	Increase distribution	Contest aimed at the trade	2. Limited target market for promotion makes it easier to implement	
	Increase shelf space	Point-of-purchase displays	3. Promotion easily tailored to meet specific needs	
	Obtain point-of-purchase merchandising support		4. Can limit competition's in-store efforts	
	Introduce new or improved products to the trade			

* The law in many states makes purchase an illegal requirement for participation in sweepstakes or games, but association with the product is often necessary. While customers are not forced to purchase to receive a game card, they must visit the establishment or write the company to participate. In the case of mass participation events (a brand-sponsored concert), association usually equates to attending the event.

The Successful Marketing Plan

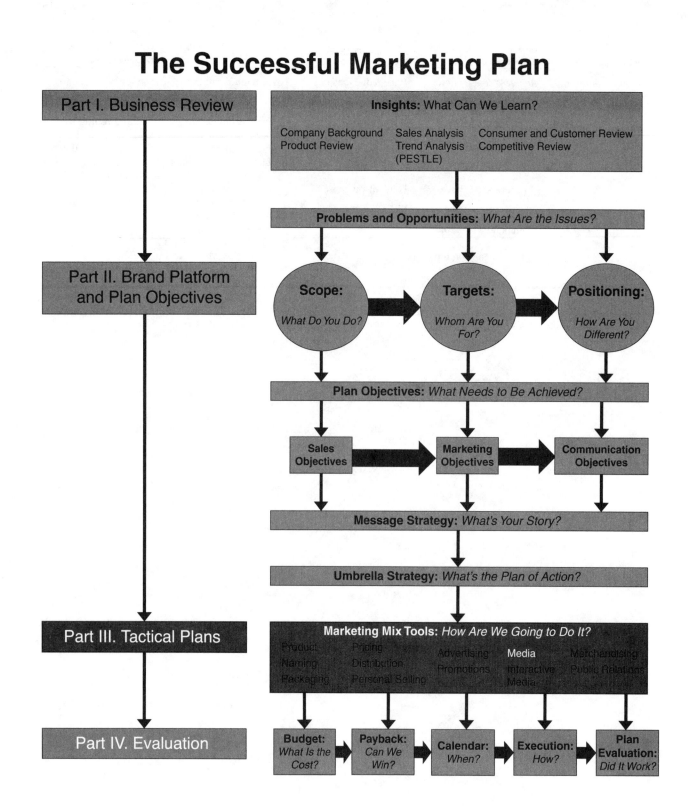

CHAPTER 18 Advertising Media

Developing an advertising media plan is first and foremost an exercise of establishing priorities and allocating investments against those priorities. It is most often an iterative process and best done in concert with message development.

The media environment has changed dramatically and grown more complex over the last decade: increasing media fragmentation, tremendous growth in digital and social media consumption, hyperinflation in television pricing, ever more multitasking and time shifting consumer behavior. This has led to hundreds of more choices and greater complexity in the media planning process. But with the complexity has come the opportunity to better address marketing, communications, and advertising objectives.

And despite this growing complexity, when we stay focused on five critical media strategies, the process is manageable and leads to tactical plans and ideas that will accomplish our objectives. The critical issues around which to frame our objectives are these:

1. What behavior, understanding, and change in perception are we trying to accomplish?
2. Who is our target?
3. When will our message be best received or have the greatest impact?
4. What geographical region will give us the greatest rate of return?
5. How much media pressure is required to create the necessary impact?

The goal is to deliver the right message, at the right moment, in the right medium. The process of media planning is setting objectives and then developing and evaluating alternatives within given budget parameters.

It is important to point out that the media process has two components: planning the media strategy and executing that strategy. This chapter focuses on planning the media strategy. Media execution involves negotiating, and then purchasing once the plan is developed. The execution process also includes

417

schedule stewardship and postbuy analysis that ensures that the appropriate value was received. Depending on your organizational structure and the size of your budget, you may have an outside agency assist you in media planning and execution.

FROM THIS CHAPTER YOU WILL LEARN

- The marketing and media background information required to prepare a plan
- How to think about budget development and allocation
- How to develop media strategies based on marketing and communication goals
- How to evaluate and select specific media and media vehicles
- How to cost and schedule a media plan

OVERVIEW

Too often the media planning process begins with or becomes overly focused on media consumption data and media audiences and the corresponding costs associated with them. Those priorities overlook the most critical part of the process, which is defining the role of each discipline or media form in addressing the marketing and communication strategies. In Chapter 16, you were introduced to *communications drivers*:

Driver	Definition
Brand awareness	Keeping the brand name at the top of mind
Emotional bond	Forging a connection with the heart of the consumer
Product news	Creating new relevance through news and information
Activation	Encouraging immediate purchase or use
Loyalty	Developing customer relationships and retention
Experience	Enabling prospects to get to know or use the product
Buzz	Creating advocacy through third-party endorsement

Each category and brand has different drivers. The airline industry invests heavily in developing loyalty through their frequent-flyer miles programs. New packaged-good products rely on sampling programs to generate product experience. The highly competitive auto insurance category invests nearly $2 billion in television to keep their brands top of mind.

The various communication disciplines and media forms perform differently against the drivers. In using these drivers, we both define the role of communications disciplines and media forms and decide the investment allocation against the discipline and media form.

If brand awareness and emotional bond are the drivers, you will rely heavily on television and mass media mixes.

If activation is the driver, then direct marketing programs, search, direct response television (DRTV), or newspapers for sale pricing and Sunday freestanding inserts (FSIs) for coupon delivery become critical.

If loyalty is the driver, then CRM programs including e-mail and direct mail are most important.

If experience is the driver, then event marketing and sample distribution play the bigger role.

If buzz is the driver, the role of public relations and social media become much more important.

These drivers or the objectives they represent—not necessarily how the various target markets consume a medium—are the most critical influences in the communication and media planning process.

DISCIPLINED APPROACH TO MEDIA PLANNING

There are five steps involved in media planning: (1) gathering the information, (2) developing the budget, (3) developing the media strategies, (4) selecting the media and the media mix, and (5) costing the final plan and developing the final flowchart. See also Appendix C, Worksheet 53.

TASK 1 ### *Gather the Necessary Data and Information*

Developing a media plan is a data-driven process. Much of the data has already been developed in either the business review or the marketing plan. Other data will come from syndicated data and other outside sources. Because gathering the data is time consuming and sometimes the data we need are not available, the planning process usually begins without all the data, and refinements are made as the data become available.

The data usually cover five areas:

1. *Overall size and scope of sales including share of category:* These are likely part of the growth goals in market share and sales volume that the marketing plan is being developed for.
2. *Historical sales information:* Since timing and geography are critical to the plan, data should be broken down by month or week or even day of week in some categories as well as by geography.
3. *Past marketing efforts and corresponding results:* This should include spending by discipline and medium as well as any consumer or target metric available. If brand awareness, attitude, and intent to purchase tracking analyses have been done, comparing these analyses to investments is critical in establishing new objectives. If the plan is heavily based on direct marketing, then response and conversion rates by medium are critical data points.
4. *Competitive background:* If available, this should include sales data as well as marketing and communication programs. In the media area, weight and investment levels by medium can help establish weight levels and aid in budget development. Kantar Media and Nielsen Monitor Plus provide competitive advertising data for all major media. Nielsen Net Ratings and comScore provide the data for Internet display.
5. *Audience and pricing for the media likely to be used:* Exhibit 18.1 gives you a potential list of sources for this information.

EXHIBIT 18.1

Audience and Pricing for the Media Likely to Be Used

Medium	Audience Data	Cost Data*
Television	Nielsen Company (NTI, NAD, NSI-Spot)	Sales representatives
		Spot quotations and data (SQAD) in network, cable, spot
Radio	Radar, Network	Sales representatives
	Arbitron, Spot	Spot quotations and data (SQAD)
Magazines		
Consumer	Audit Bureau of Circulation	SRDS: Consumer magazines
	Experian Simmons	Sales representatives
	GfK MRI	
	Sales representatives	
Business	BPA Worldwide	SRDS: Business magazines
	Sales representatives	Sales representatives
Newspapers	Audit Bureau of Circulation	SRDS: Newspapers
	Scarborough Media Audit	Sales representatives
	Sales representatives	
Digital	comScore, Ad Metrics	SpyFu—Search terms
	Nielsen Net Ratings	Sales representatives
	Google Ad Planners (free)	
Out of home	TAB, EyesOn	SRDS: Outdoor
	Sales representatives	Sales representatives
Direct mail	SRDS: Direct mail	SRDS: Direct mail

Notes:

1. For digital media, Google has numerous information and planning tools.

2. A handy and portable reference to current media rates, data, and demographics for most consumer media, updated quarterly, is *Adweek's* "Marketer's Guide to Media."

*Today, all media are highly negotiable. The data sources are broad estimates for planning purposes.

TASK 2   ## Develop the Budget

This is usually the most challenging part of the process, but it has the most impact on the setting of objectives and the final plan. In most cases there is not one but four methods that are considered, and the final approach is usually a combination of a few of them.

1. *An analysis of the historical investments and allocations:* This is usually a starting process, involving the review of past investments and past performance. If positive results are occurring and we want to continue, we will increase budgets modestly and hold close to current allocations.
2. *An analysis of marketing or advertising expenditures as a percentage of sales:* These vary dramatically by category, and the data can be difficult to develop, but they are often used as a rough starting point.
3. *An analysis of the competitors' investment levels:* Share-of-voice and spending analyses compared to the brand's sales and industry category share are helpful in building budget ranges.
4. *An analysis of the costs of the tasks being considered:* What does it cost to accomplish goals? What does it cost to buy a certain level of reach and frequency on a national basis throughout the year, versus what does it cost to buy a higher level of reach and frequency during key seasonality in 30 percent of the country? The task-based method generally works best for companies that are relying on *activation* and direct marketing efforts, where response and conversion rates are more predictable.

No matter which method is used, two things are critical: (1) If aggressive objectives are established, a corresponding investment is required, and that needs to be weighed against the financial risks and rewards. (2) If less budget is available, the objectives need to be pared down to be realistic.

In the end, budget allocation is usually somewhat subjective although the approaches above usually work to help focus the process. The prioritization of the communications drivers laid out earlier is also a good way to think about budget.

Today there are companies that use sophisticated return-on-investment (ROI) analytics and modeling to help establish budget allocations by discipline and medium. This approach can be expensive, and it requires historical sales and media delivery data broken down by week for specific geographic regions or markets.

Another approach is to test investment levels and media mix approaches. Historically, incorporating a test budget was a standard practice in most plans. Today with inflated media costs and more challenging business pressures, this approach is used less often.

The final budget allocation will likely be a work in progress while all the elements of the marketing plan are developed and new ideas and alternatives are explored.

One last word on budgets and financial commitments: Media investments (especially in television) need to be made months in advance. Often plans need to be built to ensure sufficient flexibility during a fiscal year. This frequently impacts timing and media selection.

TASK 3   ## *Develop the Media Strategies*

There is often debate about what is a media objective or strategy and what is a media tactic. Since we use media to accomplish the marketing and communication strategies developed in Chapters 8 and 9, we will focus on and identify them as media strategies.

It is important that your media strategies are clear and provide definitive direction in the following critical areas:

Target audiences: To whom will the advertising be directed?
Timing and seasonality: When will the advertising be most effective?
Geography: Where will the advertising be most effective?
Media weight levels and schedule duration: How much media pressure is necessary to accomplish the advertising objectives?
Media selection: Which media are the best environments in which to accomplish the advertising objectives?

Also, if the marketing plan calls for testing, it should be stated as a separate strategy since budgets need to be allocated. When developing a test plan, it is best to finalize the base plan first. Then build the test options at different spending levels or with a different media mix.

The process of finalizing strategies is iterative. It requires developing and costing alternative approaches in each of the areas and then making sacrifices to manage within budget. The most critical element in setting strategies is making sure they can be realistically delivered within the budgets allowed.

Target Audiences

You developed your target audience strategies in Chapter 5.

No matter your approach, when it comes to defining your media target, prioritization is critical. The selected behavior or segments must be in alignment with marketing and communication strategies. They also need to be described so that you can analyze and measure media for the target. For most media this is done using demographics.

Some media targeting strategy examples follow.

For packaged goods, presweetened cereals:
  Primary: Kids 8 to 12 (influencers)
  Secondary: Mothers 18 to 49 (purchasers)

For financial service products sold via financial advisors:
  Primary: Financial advisors (influencers)
  Secondary: Adults 35 to 64, with investment portfolios of $250,000 or more

For lawn mowers:
  Men 35 and older, living in single-family dwellings in suburban or rural areas

For shampoo:
  Employed women 18 to 34

In certain media forms we can target on a more granular basis. For instance, in Internet display advertising, we can target based on Internet behavior. For instance, we can target people who used online banking in the previous month, or people who shopped online by any category. Since the opportunities are nearly endless, a subtargeting strategy is built into the online plan.

It is somewhat similar in direct mail where the databases allow more focused targeting including life stage, which is critical in many categories.

Before we leave targeting, it is important that we point out that in most cases the media form is not necessarily selected based on the selected targets' media consumption. The advertising objective and marketing drivers, as well as the absolute budget, usually drive the decision as to which medium we use. Where targeting and media evaluation come together is the selection of specific media vehicles within a medium—which magazines, which television dayparts and programs, which radio stations and formats, or which websites or outdoor locations.

Geography

Once you have determined your media target audience, you must decide where and with what emphasis you want to place your media. Geographic media weighting depends on the marketing strategies, as well as sales potential and profitability differences on a market-by-market basis or within a market. It is also a different thought process depending on the brand's footprint: national, regional, or highly local.

It is important to clarify the marketing area descriptions being used. Here are some market descriptions:

DMA: Designated Market Area (Although developed for television, it is a
  marketing standard since all counties in the United States are included.)
SMSA: Standard metropolitan statistical area
Sub-DMA: Highly local areas usually developed on the basis of zip codes to
  reflect trading areas

Geographic weighting of media levels by market is based on many factors. A few to be taken into consideration when developing geographic media objectives are the following:

Size and growth trends

Distribution levels or number of outlets or stores

Media efficiency

Competitive set and corresponding media activity

Brand sales per population (Brand Development Index, BDI)

Category sales per population (Category Development Index, CDI)

For national or large regional brands, BDI and CDI analyses are developed and grow out of marketing strategies that reflect an offensive or defensive approach:

High BDI and high CDI: Higher media spending to protect share—defensive

High BDI and low CDI: Maintenance-level spending to protect share—defensive

Low BDI and high CDI: Higher media spending to steal share—offensive

Low BDI and low CDI: Limited, if any, support

The above analysis is always modified based on potential competitive activity and a realistic assessment in low-BDI markets of the brand's distribution or footprint in that market.

Media efficiency can also drive market selection. Television, radio, and newspaper efficiencies vary dramatically by market and thus are usually factored into most market weighting objectives.

National advertisers or those with a large regional footprint also have to consider the efficiency of national media versus local media. Depending on the media form and absolute budget, it may not make sense to sacrifice national media efficiencies to concentrate in a specific geographical region. This is especially the case if television is being used. (See Exhibit 18.2.)

EXHIBIT 18.2

TV Breakeven

Daypart	Percent U.S. HHs*
Early morning	85%
Daytime	80%
Prime time	60%
Cable	35%

*Percentage of U.S. households where spot (local) TV equals network TV.

Some industry categories are impacted by weather, and that needs to be factored into geographic strategies. Categories like allergy relief (pollen levels), agricultural chemicals (rainfall), or snow blowers (snowfall) take into account these weather conditions.

Some examples of geographic strategies follow.

For a national packaged-goods company:

Provide national media support.

Deliver incremental media weight in the five high-BDI markets below representing one-third of sales:

DMA	Percent HHs	Percent Sales	BDI
New York	7.1	10.2	144
Los Angeles	5.9	9.3	157
Chicago	3.3	4.7	142
Philadelphia`	2.6	3.6	139
Dallas	2.4	3.8	158
Total	21.3	31.6	148

For a regional business-to-business company:

Primary: Provide introductory support in central regions where new products are being introduced.

Secondary: Provide broad-based media support behind existing lines across all distribution areas.

For a local retailer:

Primary: Provide marketwide media coverage.

Secondary: For underperforming stores, deliver incremental support within a two-mile trading area.

Seasonality and Timing

As important as it is to advertise to the right person, in the right geography, messaging to them at the right time can often be the more impactful strategy. Although seasonality and sales by month are usually the first considerations, it is also important to think about the day of the week and even the time of day. (A message for a new flavor of soup delivered at 10 a.m. on a cold Saturday in January to a person on the fringe of the target will likely drive trial better than a message to the bull's-eye target in July.)

Today only a few large advertisers can afford reasonable levels of mass media on a year-round basis. Many brands (especially packaged goods and retailers) have significant sales skews on a seasonal or monthly basis. Generally you will schedule heavier levels of support during highest sales months. With limited budgets, the questions usually are: Which months do we choose not to support? and/or How much support should we deliver prior to the peak sales months?

For brands that have limited skews but also have limited resources to cover the year, you might want to capitalize on the quarterly differences in television efficiencies created by marketplace demand:

Time of Year	Efficiency Index
First quarter	80
Second quarter	120
Third quarter	85
Fourth quarter	115

Moment of receptivity: It is also important to think about those days of the week or times of day that consumers are most receptive to messages. For example, 60 percent of evening weekday meals are not planned by 4 p.m. This is an ideal time to message for prepackaged dinners. Consumer durable goods purchases are heavily weighted to weekends so Thursday through Saturday is a most opportune time to schedule messages.

For many categories impacted by climate factors, combining geographic and timing strategies together best capitalizes on that moment of receptivity. Some examples are the following:

Cold and flu remedies: These sicknesses hit different regions of the country at different times over the course of the winter.

Lawn mowers: Those first weekends of "green up" and the corresponding first cutting occur much earlier in the Northwest and Southeast than they do in the Midwest.

Property casualty insurance: Catastrophic storms in specific areas need to be quickly capitalized on to get information to current customers.

Allergy medication: Pollen counts vary dramatically by week and month in the different markets and regions.

For Toro snowthrowers, markets are selected and weighted on the basis of historical snowfall, Brand Development Index, and Category Development Index to optimize the budget. To capitalize on the moment of receptivity, morning and evening drive time radio advertisements are placed in advance and triggered when a market receives significant snowfall in a single- or two-day period.

Some examples of seasonality and timing strategies follow:

For a local retail apparel store:
Primary: Deliver significant media weight to support promotion and sales pricing during the July and August back-to-school period and the November and December holiday period.
Secondary: Provide media coverage throughout the year.

For a packaged-goods, frozen entrées, company:
Concentrate media weight during highest sales months: October through March.
Overweight the 4 to 6 p.m. time period to capitalize on the meal planning period.

For an agricultural chemical company:
Provide a base level of media support throughout the decision-making and purchasing process—September through March.
Overlay the base plan with heavier support in the most critical October through January periods.
Maintain budget flexibility to add tactical support in specific regions in March capitalizing on changing early season conditions.

Media Weight Levels and Schedule Duration

Most often the most challenging part of the media planning process is to determine how much advertising to run. It includes how much media coverage is required in a specific time frame and how many weeks of the year it should be scheduled. This is most challenging because of the number of factors to be considered and the limitations of advertising budgets. Here are just a few of these factors:

The marketing communications goals and objectives—communication drivers
How fast the goals need to be accomplished
The level of consumer involvement in the category
The effectiveness of the advertising
The media spending and weight levels of competitors
The effectiveness of the medium used to accomplish the communication driver

Today building and maintaining high levels of top-of-mind brand awareness and emotional bond throughout the year costs hundreds of millions of dollars so it is important to be realistic when developing media weight level and duration strategies.

For decision-making purposes, we establish numerical values for impressions, reach and frequency, and number of weeks of advertising, with the idea of developing and benchmarking alternative strategies and plans. It is important to start with some basic definitions before we go into the process of setting benchmarks.

Important Definitions

Target impressions: The number of target audience impressions or exposures a media vehicle or schedule delivers.

Target rating point (TRP): One percent of the target universe. So if you are targeting men 18 to 34 years old in a specific geography and there are 20,000 of them, 1 target rating point would deliver 1 percent, or 200 men age 18 to 34. A television show that has 1 TRP for men age 18 to 34 would deliver 200 men age 18 to 34. It is important to think about this not as just the demographic universe but also the geographic universe.

Reach: The number of different people a media schedule delivers at least once. It is expressed as a percentage.

Average frequency: The average number of times those reached have been exposed to a message.

Target rating points (TRPs): The sum of rating points a media schedule delivers. For example, 120 women age 25 to 54 national TRPs is equivalent to 120 percent of the *universe* of women age 25 to 54. The target rating points measure is a function of reach and frequency. The reach times the total frequency equals the TRPs. A target rating point schedule of 300 that is reach oriented could deliver a 75 percent reach with an average frequency of 4.0. An equivalent 300-TRP schedule that is frequency oriented could deliver a 25 percent reach with an average frequency of 12.0 (25 percent of the defined target sees the ad 12 times: $25 \times 12 = 300$ target rating points).

Effective frequency: The number of exposures deemed necessary for a media schedule to be effective. The number is expressed as a percentage of the target delivered at that frequency goal (that is, 60 percent reached four or more times). The frequency goal is usually subjective, often based on creative message, awareness objectives, and competitors' spending.

Different Approaches to Media Weight Levels and Schedule Duration

There are two different approaches to setting media weight level and duration strategies:

Effective frequency planning
Recency planning

Effective frequency planning is based on the premise of generating a frequency of message exposure to establish brand awareness, persuasion, and behavior. This is the standard for most categories that are highly competitive, that are highly considered purchases, or that have long purchase cycles. Measurement is based on reach, average frequency, and effective frequency, and it is generally based on either a four-week or a promotional period. Effective frequency planning applies more often to longer and more considered purchases. Categories like automotive, other consumer durables, and financial investments most often use this approach.

Recency planning is based on the premise that an exposure closer to category purchase is more impactful than frequent or multiple exposures. This approach grew out of highly refined research in the packaged-goods categories where purchases could be tracked to the timing and frequency of exposure. It has become the standard for most packaged-goods advertisers and retailers as well as other categories that have short purchase cycles. Measurement is focused on weekly reach and number or weeks of advertising. Recency planning usually calls for a *continuity* or *blinking* (on for a week, off for a week) scheduling approach.

EXHIBIT 18.3

Media Weight Guidelines: Target Rating Points (TRPs)		
	Weekly Range **Low–High**	**Annual Range** **Low–High**
Auto insurance	100–500	3,000–20,000
Financial advisors and funds	25–150	500– 6,000
Quick service restaurants	150–300	4,500–15,000
Packaged goods	75–150	1,500– 5,000
Retail	100–400	2,000–20,000

Setting benchmarks is usually done with either a combination or one of the following approaches:

The brand's historical weight levels: If communication goals remain the same, then you would likely approximate previous years' schedules. If the goal is to make significant improvement on consumer metrics like brand awareness or persuasion, then the media weight levels need to be increased.

Competitive benchmarking: This is usually the most common approach to setting media weight levels. Weekly TRP levels can vary dramatically by category. See Exhibit 18.3. When setting benchmarks, your brand's category share should be taken into account. This weight level comparison is easiest in television where the data are available. In other media forms, we generally look at spending levels and share of spending and translate them to a weight level estimate.

Situations that require higher reach and frequency goals include the following:

- New products or campaign introductions
- Seasonal products that have been out of advertising for an extended period
- Products with highly complex messaging
- Highly competitive categories
- Goals that include increased brand or category penetration
- Promotional or sales periods that require a high volume of *activation* and sales

When establishing effective frequency goals in the above areas, it is important to set the level much higher. If the norm is somewhat close to a 3 or 4-plus frequency in the above situations, it is best to set them at a level of 7 to 10-plus.

Most often the TRPs and the reach and frequency goals are established for broadcast media. For magazines, consider monthly TRPs or the number of insertions. For newspaper benchmarks, consider the TRPs or the number of insertions. For digital, goals are usually established based on impressions.

Duration and scheduling strategies are a part of establishing media weight levels. How many weeks of coverage and how they are scheduled are as important as reach and frequency. The trade-offs and decisions to be made are challenging when dealing with budget issues.

The following are some scheduling strategies that will be helpful in the process.

Continuity: Consider schedules that run at relatively fixed weekly TRP levels for most of the year or seasonal sales periods. For our client General Mills Cinnamon Toast Crunch, we use a continuity strategy to compete in the continuously competitive cereal category.

Blinking: This schedule strategy is similar to continuity, but it involves a scheduling pattern of a week on and a week off to stretch coverage through the year or during seasonal sales periods. This approach is used by many packaged-goods brands where budgets do not allow continuous weekly support.

Flights: This scheduling strategy concentrates the media weights in three- to six-week periods. For Airborne, we use flights during the cold and flu season to ensure effective frequency levels and to cover the entire season.

Heavy-up schedules: With this strategy, the flighting approach is used to increase weight around key sales periods or high promotion periods. SUPERVALU supports other *activation* media for its retail brands, like Albertsons, Jewell, and Cub, with heavy-up television schedules during key promotional support periods in the grocery retail business.

Front loading: This strategy uses the heavy-up approach to introduce new products and new campaigns or to kick off the sales season. Our client Toro uses this approach to kick off the seasonal activity for lawn and snow products.

The continuity and blinking approaches are usually used when planning on a recency basis. Flight approaches are used when planning on an effective frequency basis.

Budget limitations dictate that seasonal and geographic strategies need to be incorporated in the weight level and duration decisions. You will often need to sacrifice annual or seasonal coverage to reach meaningful weight levels within budgets. You may have to sacrifice geographic coverage to reach weight level goals. It is critical to be realistic when developing geographic, seasonal, and media weight level goals.

Here are some examples of weight level strategies:

For a packaged-goods, cereals, company:
To introduce the new campaign, schedule a four-week flight delivery with 80 percent reach and an average frequency of 4.5 (150 TRPs per week).
On a sustained basis, deliver a 50 percent weekly reach (75 TRPs per week) with a minimum of 26 weeks on air.

For an auto insurance company:
Match the category average weekly TRP levels of 200 delivering an effective frequency of five or more times to 55 percent of the target.
Schedule a minimum of five 4-week flights.

TASK 4   ## Media Selection and Media Mix

Media selection strategies are driven by the following:

- Communication objectives (with a focus in this section on communications drivers)
- The realities of messaging requirements and the associated production timing and costs
- Qualitative values of a medium's impact and the environment in which messages are received
- Quantitative audience delivery, cost efficiency, and the medium's ability to build reach
- The pragmatics of absolute budgets and the cost of a meaningful presence in a medium

Communications drivers help select and define the role of each medium. Although there are no absolutes, the following generalizations are a helpful starting point:

Brand awareness: Television, out-of-home magazines, digital display
Emotional bond: Television, digital video, magazines
Product news: Television, magazines, newspapers
Activation: Newspapers, direct mail, search, direct response television
Loyalty: Direct mail, e-mail, social media
Experience: Product sampling via newspaper and radio
Buzz: Social media

Messaging realities often dictate the media forms used. If messages need to be changed frequently or quickly, media forms like newspaper, radio, or digital become more important because of low production costs and speed to market.

Eric Einhorn, global director of strategic planning for the McCann Worldgroup, (mentioned also in Chapter 16) has developed a concept to think about balancing the relative influence and power of each marketing discipline and medium against the marketing drivers. It combines the qualitative judgments of a vehicle's messaging impact with the quantitative audience delivery versus cost.

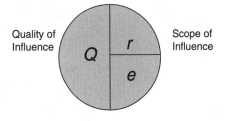

The *Q* is the power of the message and medium to break through and deliver on the marketing driver. This has to be balanced against the number of target prospects reached (*r*) and the relative efficiency (*e*) with which the prospects are delivered.*

Some examples to help think about this:

- A 60-second unit on the Super Bowl, which has high attention value and relatively high one-time reach but is very expensive, versus a schedule of 15-second units scattered on various cable channels, which can deliver greater reach and frequency and is significantly more efficient at delivering the target.
- A polywrapped sample of a new cereal in a Sunday newspaper versus a coupon in the insert section. Due to costs, the polywrapped sample is delivered in a limited geography, which limits reach, while the more efficient insert coupon covers most Sunday newspapers in the country.
- A highly visible digital message in Times Square versus outdoor bulletins placed in markets across the country generating greater reach and target delivery.

The media strategies developed have to take both the qualitative and quantitative deliveries into account. The strategies must include alternatives within the budget and decisions as to which media mix and media vehicles best deliver on your marketing drivers.

Quantitative measures are best used to select vehicles within a media form (networks, programs, magazines, websites). Each medium is measured with different methodologies, making inter-media comparisons irrelevant.

---

*Source: Eric Einhorn.

The most critical measures are these:

Reach: The number of different people a media schedule delivers at least once. It is expressed as a percentage.

Cost per thousand (CPM): Determines the relative efficiency of a media vehicle's target audience delivery. It is developed by dividing the vehicle's cost by the target audience delivered (in thousands):

$$\frac{\text{Media cost}}{\text{Target delivery (000s)}} = \text{CPM}$$

$$\frac{\text{Network daytime unit cost}}{\text{Women 25 to 54 (000s)}} = \text{CPM}$$

$$\frac{\$10,000}{754} = \$13.26$$

Cost per target rating point (CPP): Provides the same efficiency measure but also aids in costing out alternatives:

$$\frac{\text{Media cost}}{\text{Target rating points}} = \text{CPP}$$

$$\frac{\text{Network daytime unit cost}}{\text{Average women 25 to 54 rating}} = \text{CPM}$$

$$\frac{\$10,000}{1.2 \text{ average rating}} = \$8.33$$

The optimal reach for the media strategy is best accomplished through schedule diversification. All consumers have their favorite media—broadcast programs, Internet portals, periodicals, driving patterns, and so on. Schedules focused in fewer of these components will tend to build frequency. If the goal is to expand reach, then within a particular medium, marketers need to broaden the use of the individual vehicles used:

Broadcast (television and radio): Multiple dayparts, program genres, stations, and days of the week

Digital displays: Multiple portals, websites, and ad networks

Magazines: Multiple categories and titles

Out-of-home displays: Multiple venues and locations

The best and quickest way to increase reach is to mix media. Start with the medium that best accomplishes the marketing driver to serve as the primary. Then select a secondary medium to increase reach. The challenge in adding a second or third medium is to ensure that the primary medium is used sufficiently to deliver meaningful impact.

The realities of the budgeted versus the absolute cost not only influence the media mix strategy but also the medium selected. For example, $5 million for a national brand targeting adults 25 to 54 using an efficient cable schedule will generate only 400 to 500 target rating points. Unless the brand is seasonally focused, it is difficult to generate much impact: $3 million will deliver only a modest 25 outdoor showing for one month in the top 25 DMAs. For a national advertiser, it can cost approximately $1.5 million to run a single half-page black-and-white ad in the top 25 DMAs.

EXHIBIT 18.4

Adults 25 to 54 Television Reach

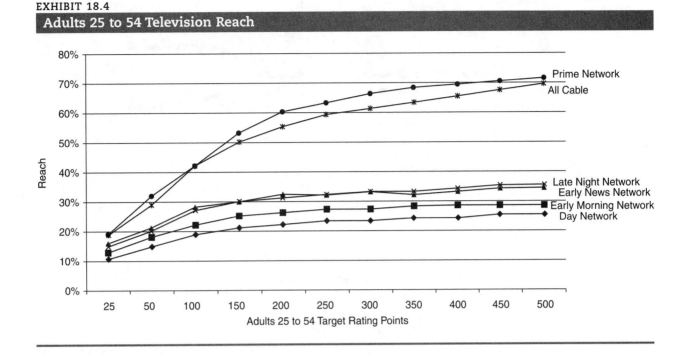

The following section will give a brief explanation of some of the considerations that need to be dealt with in selecting a media platform and the tactics utilized.

Television

Despite the headlines, television remains a dynamic advertising medium. Total television viewing continues to increase, with the average adult now viewing over 35 hours per week. Reported advertising expenditures in the United States are nearing $50 billion annually, more than double any other media form.

Television's intrusiveness, generated by sight, sound, and motion, makes it the best medium to drive brand awareness. Its ability to deliver messages that engage and entertain audiences offers the best opportunity to drive emotional bond. Its immediacy and ability to quickly build reach and frequency are the reasons many retailers look to it to drive product news and activation.

Since television is the most mass of the media, the challenge is to deliver efficient reach and frequency against selective targets. As Exhibit 18.4 indicates, prime network can quickly develop significant levels of reach, but it is challenged by the high cost per target delivery. National cable (which now represents 60 percent of television viewing) can also build reasonable reach if the schedules are spread over multiple networks and times of day. Other dayparts are limited in their ability to develop reach. Most often reach is built by combining more efficient dayparts.

For clients like Land O'Lakes spreads or Freschetta pizza targeting women, we include daytime, early morning, and cable to build reach.

Exhibit 18.5 provides cost per thousands (CPMs) against broad male and female targets. Media efficiencies are a result of target viewing levels and advertising demand. Generally targets that are female or older or less affluent are most efficient. Targets that are male or younger or more affluent are most expensive. Delivering older women in daytime is highly efficient—high levels of viewing and less advertising demand. On the other hand, delivering affluent professional males in golf is relatively inefficient—low levels of viewing and high demand.

EXHIBIT 18.5

Television Cost per Thousands

| | | COST PER THOUSANDS | | | |
| | | WOMEN 25–54 | | MEN 25–54 | |
Daypart	Time Period*	National	Spot†	National	Spot†
Early morning	5–9 a.m.	$25	$30	$45	$50
Daytime	9–3 p.m.	15	25	N/A	N/A
Early fringe	4–8 p.m.	N/A	35	N/A	55
Early news	5–7:30 p.m.	35	40	40	50
Prime time	8–11 p.m.	55	75	70	110
Late news	10–11 p.m.	N/A	45	N/A	65
Cable	All day	20	50	25	65

*Eastern Time Zone.
†Top 50 markets.

Looking at Exhibit 18.5, you can see that the national prime time CPM for women 25 to 54 is $55 compared to the $70 CPM for men 25 to 54.

In selecting dayparts, efficiencies are often qualified by subjective factors. Prime-time viewing tends to be more attentive than other times of the day when more multitasking is taking place. In addition, prime time network television has less commercial clutter with fewer commercial minutes per hour.

Television is planned and purchased either on a *national* basis (using the traditional and cable networks and syndicated programming) or on a *spot* basis (using local affiliates, cable interconnects, or individual cable systems). Spot TV is also referred to as *local television*; the terms are used interchangeably. As Exhibit 18.6 indicates, spot is less efficient than national, but it offers a broader array of dayparts and programming in the early morning, afternoon, and late nighttime periods.

Cable is significantly less efficient on a spot basis. (Looking at Exhibit 18.6, the national CPM for women age 25 to 54 is $20 versus the spot CPM of $50.) For local advertisers with aggressive reach goals, local cable is still important because 60 percent of the viewership is on the cable networks. Also, local cable bought at the system level has allowed advertisers with a sub-DMA footprint to gain access to the medium at a realistic absolute budget.

For advertisers with a national or near national footprint, we look at breakevens to determine when it makes the most sense to capitalize on national efficiencies. (See Exhibit 18.2.)

The 30-second unit is the standard, although the use of 15s is significant and continues to grow. As Exhibit 18.6 indicates, 15-second units cost 50 percent of a 30-second unit. On a spot basis they are often only 25 percent more efficient than the 30-second unit. Many advertisers will test the 15s versus 30s on a persuasion basis. If performance exceeds the cost trade-off, they will use 15s exclusively or in a rotation with 30s. Many packaged-goods brands with simpler messages rely

EXHIBIT 18.6

Television Unit Length Cost Index

Unit Lengths in Seconds	Network	Spot
:30	100	100
:15	50	75
:10	Limited	50
:60	200	200

heavily on 15s while categories that have more complex messaging like retailers, telecoms, and banks are weighted 30s. Many pharmaceutical brands use 60s because of contraindication requirements.

The major challenge with television is the absolute cost to make a meaningful impact for advertisers with limited budgets (less than $10 million nationally). To make a meaningful impact on *brand awareness* metrics, one generally needs to look at TRP levels in the 1,200 to 1,500 range. Also because advertising demand is high, commitments need to be made well in advance of scheduled airings. For national television, commitments are made either on an annual (upfront) or quarterly ((scatter) basis with limited cancellation flexibility.

The other challenge is both the timing and cost of production. Generally television production requires long lead times and can be expensive. It does not offer the production efficiency or timing flexibility to quickly rotate multiple messages.

Radio

Radio listening continues to decline, as it continues to be most impacted by MP3 players and iPods. Listener decline is also being impacted by the role-out of *personal people meters* (PPMs), which are reporting more accurate but lower audience numbers. Advertising revenue has declined as a result of shifts to digital media and the latest recessionary period. It is primarily a local medium. Network radio represents only about 5 percent of the total revenue, and local advertisers represent nearly 75 percent of the total spending in the medium.

Radio offers great flexibility and localization, making it a highly tactical advertising tool. Short production timetables and low production costs are a significant advantage for both low-budget advertisers and advertisers with multiple messaging requirements. Localization includes local personality endorsements, on-site remote broadcasts, product and ticket contests, sponsorships, and promotional tie-ins with local sports teams: profession, college, and high schools.

For national and larger budgeted advertisers, radio is often a secondary medium complementing television to drive *brand awareness*. Low-budgeted local advertisers capitalize on the low absolute cost to drive brand awareness and product news. Retailers use the medium for changing price and item messaging, delivering on activation.

For SUPERVALU's brands we capitalize on radio's production flexibility to change price item copy on a weekly basis. Personality endorsement and local event and sports sponsorships deliver on buzz.

Local radio is planned by daypart, weighting target efficiencies and mixing dayparts and stations to build reach. The numerous stations and various formats offer great targeting opportunities. News, talk, and sports formats tend to skew more male and older. Various music formats deliver along an age spectrum varying from teens to adults 50 and older.

EXHIBIT 18.7

Radio Cost per Thousands*

	Women 25–54	Men 25–54
Morning drive	$33.00	$26.00
Midday	25.00	20.00
Afternoon drive	30.00	24.00
Evening	15.00	12.00
Weekend	15.00	12.00
Network radio (:30)	8.00	8.00

*Top 50 markets.

EXHIBIT 18.8

Radio Unit Length Cost Index	
	Cost Index
:60	100
:30	75
:15	60
:10	50

Hispanic and urban-gospel formats are dominant stations in many markets. The low costs of production allows for targeted messaging building high levels of reach against the Hispanic and African American communities.

Network radio is highly efficient and often serves as a secondary national medium to television, interactive media, or magazines. It is generally used at modest weight levels (50 to 100 TRPs). Reach can be limited, and ratings often skew to smaller markets.

Radio is highly tactical so weekly weight levels vary dramatically, but the following generalizations may be helpful:

For lower-budgeted B2B advertisers, 50 to 100 weekly TRPs with schedules focused on a few stations can build frequency.

When used as a secondary medium to television, 50 to 110 weekly TRPs will add incremental reach.

For retailers using it to drive traffic, 200 to 300 weekly TRPs are often employed.

The standard unit length for local radio is 60 seconds and for network 30 seconds. Costs are highly negotiable, but Exhibit 18.8 provides a relative benchmark.

The medium's local orientation and the struggle to find new revenues provide advertisers the opportunity to capitalize on value-added programs. Program sponsorships and promotional mentions, product and ticket contests, and links to stations' websites and Facebook pages can often be negotiated into a schedule. When negotiated upfront, these programs can often increase the media value by 10 to 15 percent. For Great Clips, we have developed a program called "Great Seats from Great Clips." Station-developed promotions and contests providing listeners tickets to events are sponsored by Great Clips, increasing exposure and visibility.

Clutter levels and the background nature of radio consumption are the biggest challenge in using the medium. More frequency is usually required to break through. Most radio listening is consumed while other activity is taking place. Over 50 percent of the listening occurs while driving to work or being at work. Nearly 90 percent is consumed between 6 a.m. and 6 p.m. Although multitasking occurs and distracts from every media form, it is most acute for radio.

Interactive Media

Chapter 19 will give you a more thorough understanding of the role of interactive media, but it is important to discuss it in the context of the media selection process as well.

No other media form requires greater integration between messaging strategy and media planning and execution. The tremendous oversupply of inventory, combined with the efficiency of production and rapidly changing technologies, presents new opportunities daily. It requires a higher level of collaboration between strategists, planners, and the creative messaging team than other media forms.

The rapid adoption rate of the medium by consumers far surpasses the development of any other medium. Today time spent online is surpassed only by television viewing. Interactive media advertising investments are higher than all other media but television. Traditionally revenue has been driven by search. Today it still represents 40-plus percent of interactive media revenue. Display advertising, which includes banners, rich media and video, continues to outpace other media. The rapid adoption of social networking is changing the landscape and presenting new opportunities, but it has not negatively impacted search or display performance.

As an organizing principle, we have divided interactive media programs as follows:

Display advertising
Search
E-mail marketing
Social networking

The following will be focused primarily on display with search and e-mail marketing, as referenced in the "One-to-One and Direct Media" section at the end of this task (Task 4).

Display advertising most often delivers on the communication drivers of brand awareness, activation, and product news.

Plan goals related to display are generally stated in terms of impressions and/or clicks and/or actions. These could include an engagement at the website or leads or transactions. Options and alternative programs are then evaluated against CPM impressions, *cost per click* (CPC), or *cost per action* (CPA). One of the advantages of the digital medium is the near constant feedback of performance data, allowing for constant optimization. One of the challenges with this much data, however, is making sure you focus on the right data and metrics to optimize against it.

With thousands of formats and messaging options, it is critical that media, creative, and productions teams stay linked both in the planning and executional phases. The standard messaging opportunities include banners, rich media, and video:

• Over 60 percent of display impressions are generated by banners in one of three standard sizes, as shown in the figure below:

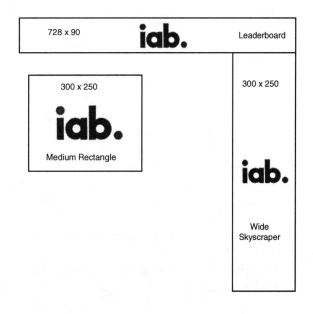

EXHIBIT 18.9

Display Adult Cost per Thousands

	Banners (Range)	Video
Ad networks	$0.05–2.50	$15.00
Social media	$0.25–0.00	N/A
Portals	$2.00–15.00	$20.00
Data targeted networks	$3.00–8.00	N/A
News and information	$4.00–8.00	$25.00
Local news	$7.00–12.50	$35.00
Women's lifestyle	$12.50–20.00	$30.00
Auto	$10.00–50.00	$50.00
B2B	$35.00–100.00	$300.00

- *Rich media* are banners with enhanced functionality that increase attention, engagement, or interactivity. Today this represents nearly half of display advertising.
- Video—generally a 15- or 30-second preroll—has been growing at the rate of nearly 50 percent annually for the past few years. (Preroll is the commercial message that runs prior to the news or entertainment contents.)

Today plans and schedules are built working with individual websites, portals, and ad networks. Schedules for sites tend to be target or content based. Many of these schedules are a result of multiple media buys with traditional broadcast, newspaper, and magazine publishers. Sponsorships are often developed to "own" or dominate specific content on the site. This approach tends to be less efficient and is declining in terms of share of display revenue. See Exhibit 18.9.

Portals dominated by Yahoo!, MSN, and AOL provide huge numbers with targeting capabilities across their array of content. They garner a significant share of ad revenue and are more efficient than individual websites.

The growth of ad networks is rapidly changing the display landscape, and they offer much greater targeting capabilities. There are hundreds of networks, but Google Display Network and Ad.com dominate with nearly 50 percent share. Estimates vary, but ad networks represent over 50 percent of the display revenue. The ad networks' opportunities exist because a significant amount of inventory goes unsold, and they have streamlined the negotiating and scheduling process. Ad networks offer both significantly lower CPMs as well as more advanced targeting capabilities.

The advanced targeting capabilities include these:

Contextual targeted: Display media placed on many websites with relevant or related content. Some examples would be financial content for financial services advertisers, recipe content for ingredient products, and fitness content for nutritional products.

Behavioral targeted: Display media served to consumers based on their online behavior. Some examples would be personal investors, home entertainers, book enthusiasts, and health enthusiasts.

Data targeted: The ad networks are practicing the same data mining techniques that direct and e-mail marketers use: pairing household data against website registrations and modeling offline behavior to online.

Exhibit 18.9 indicates the dramatic differences in the cost per thousands of various programs. Ad networks can often deliver CPM impressions below $1.00, but a highly targeted B2B site can be a $100 CPM. Ad serving charges ranging from $0.04 to $0.10 need to be added to the above cost per thousands. The companies serving ads also provide the data to verify impressions, clicks, and action levels, which allow for ongoing ad optimization. The ad serving companies are Dart Communications, Atlas Solutions, PointRoll, and EyeWonder.

In Chapter 19 opportunities to create advocacy via social media are discussed. In addition to these strategies, most paid display programs now include some display on social networking websites. This is a result of such tremendous growth in social networking sites and the time spent on them. Today over 20 percent of the available display inventory is on Facebook alone.

Magazines

After years of oversized circulations, the magazine industry has been challenged in recent years by the loss of advertising revenue to digital media. With the exception of the celebrity category, general-interest magazines have lost significant revenue, and most have had corresponding circulation cuts. Despite these challenges, publishers of well-run magazines that are tightly targeted to specific industry categories garnering endemic advertising are doing well.

Product news and emotional bond are the communications drivers that lifestyle or special-interest magazines are most often used for. General-interest magazines are used in support of other mass marketing vehicles to drive brand awareness.

Magazines deliver relatively efficient national audiences. As you can see in Exhibit 18.10, celebrity and women's service magazines are highly efficient against women 25 to 54, and these magazines have CPMs of $15 and $10, respectively. There are limited choices at the local level, but each market generally has one or two strong city magazines.

Many magazines offer the advantage of endemic targeting. Marketers can align products or services with a magazine's editorial focus. With hundreds of magazines, the opportunities are endless:

Automotive to arthritis
Fashion to fishing
Food to financial investing
Travel to television
Weight watching to wine
Yachting to yoga

These special-interest magazines tend to be less efficient against broader targets, but the relevant editorial attracts a highly engaged audience in the category, and these people are often category influencers. Broader lifestyle magazines can be included to increase reach. In these cases try to develop editorial adjacencies or advertorials.

EXHIBIT 18.10

Magazine Cost per Thousands

Category	Women 25–54	Men 25–54
Celebrity	$15.00	$35.00
Newsweeklies	35.00	25.00
Women's service	10.00	N/A
Men's lifestyle	N/A	25.00
Business	N/A	50.00
Epicurean	25.00	100.00

For our client Land O'Lakes Butter with an ingredient and recipe strategy focused on baking enthusiasts, we use a combination approach:

Epicurean magazines to deliver the most engaged
Food editorial adjacencies in women's service magazines
Women's lifestyle magazines to extend reach

Magazines lack the immediacy of most other media forms. Long lead times to publication and slower audience accumulation are a challenge to the industry. To counter this, magazines with strong brand recognition have built strong and viable websites that are sold in combination with the traditional magazine space.

Four-color pages are the standard unit, and they offer the most scheduling flexibility. Inside and back cover positions are usually sold at premium or to higher budgeted advertisers. Smaller units—halves, quarters, or thirds—are more efficient, but they usually are scheduled further back in the magazine or in continuing editorial.

Cross-Platform Opportunities

With the changing landscape, publishers have realized that they need to capitalize on their content's full potential. Consequently they are distributing content beyond the printed medium. This presents engagement opportunities for advertisers to leverage content in full-surround platforms, including print, digital, video, place-based, and event platforms. This presents a unique opportunity for lower-budgeted clients who have either a very focused target or a narrow promotional timing window.

For our client Chex Party Mix, *Reader's Digest* offered significant audience scale and targeted content platforms to leverage the traditional holiday aperture. Allrecipes.com, *Everyday with Rachael Ray*, and *Taste of Home* were leveraged in book, online, and in-store content and through events using a recipe contest to unify across all contact points.

Profession and Trade Publications

Thousands of trade magazines cover every industry and nearly all job functions. For B2B marketers, they have been primary advertising tools. As media behavior has moved to the Internet, they have developed corresponding websites to complement the magazine titles.

Product news is the communication driver trade magazines most often deliver on.

There is limited third-party readership data, so the primary tool used to select magazines are detailed circulation audits. Most trade magazines have controlled (free) circulation, and the magazines are delivered in exchange for information on industry, job title, function, and company size. Magazines are generally broken into two categories:

Horizontal magazines serve the entire category covering the broader business issues.
Vertical magazines serve sectors or specific job functions.

Automotive News would be an example of a horizontal magazine, and *Automotive Manufacturing and Production* and *Successful Dealer* would be examples of vertical magazines.

Generally horizontal magazines are used when the target includes C-level executives or financial decision makers. They tend to cover all titles and job functions in the broader industry. Vertical magazines are used to focus on decision makers of expertise, or job functions making recommendations. Since there are so many magazine choices in each category, it is best to select one or two of the strongest publications in each category and build frequency in those publications.

Because of the movement to digital and an assumed decline in trade magazine readership, consider developing digital programs with the publisher in combination with the magazines.

Newspapers

The newspaper industry has been hit with dynamic challenges because of the growth of the Internet. Free news and information updated by the minute have caused many consumers, mostly younger, to forsake newspaper subscriptions and readership. More devastating was the loss of classified advertising revenue to the Internet. In 2000 classified advertising revenue was estimated to represent about 40 percent of major newspapers' advertising revenue, and it has dropped nearly 30 percent since then. There were numerous leveraged buyouts in the late nineties. These factors have forced many newspapers into bankruptcy. Yet despite this, it is still America's retail medium. The immediacy and daily reach of newspapers are ideal for activation and delivering product news.

Over 40 percent of adults claim to have read a newspaper yesterday, and over 50 percent have read the Sunday newspaper, delivering a high single-day reach. Readers tend to be older but also more affluent.

Newspapers are utilized in two ways: (1) *run-of-press* (ROP) *advertisements* inserted in the editorial content of the newspaper, and (2) distribution of *preprints* or *freestanding inserts* (the terms are interchangeable).

Run-of-Press (ROP) Newspaper Ads (or Simply, Newspaper Advertising)

Space units can vary from double-page spreads to column-inch ads. The most common units are pages, halves, and quarters. Large ad spaces deliver both a strong presence on the page and provide room for more copy for more complex messaging, which can include multiple product and price offers, store or dealer locations, or disclaimers for pharmaceuticals. The addition of color delivers more breakthrough and impact. In terms of placement, main news is considered the best read.

Estimating costs for planning is difficult. Traditionally rates were based on volume and category—national versus local; retail; financial services; telecoms; and so on. Today rates are highly negotiable. For national advertisers, there is a significant amount of remnant space being placed. To capitalize on these rates, a little flexibility is required on section and day-of-week scheduling.

Preprints and Freestanding Inserts (FSIs)

This continues to be a major portion of the newspapers' revenue. Preprints are primarily used by large retailers for mass market coverage in most markets, but they do offer smaller or targeted advertisers the advantage of distribution by neighborhood or zip code. Exhibit 18.11 provides rough planning costs.

For national and regional advertisers, co-op FSIs offer mass coverage. Dominated by packaged-goods advertisers, they are used primarily for coupon distribution. News America and Valassis are the major vendors in this category.

More impactful opportunities include poly wraps (with or without a sample) and Post-it Notes on the front page.

In most markets the local newspaper is also the largest news and information website in the market. Programs packaging both the website and the traditional newspaper are common.

EXHIBIT 18.11

Cost per Thousand of Estimated Circulation

	Space	Printing*
Preprints		
Single sheet	$40.00	$20.25
8 pages	60.00	60.70
12 pages	80.00	90.00–100.00
Poly bags	60.00–80.00	N/A
Post-it Notes	60.00	N/A
Co-op FSI	12.00–15.00	N/A

* Influenced by volume.

Ethnic, Lifestyle, and Suburban Newspapers

Most of the focus and data on newspapers is for the major metropolitan dailies. Although major metropolitan newspapers have struggled, ethnic, lifestyle, and suburban newspapers have held their own and are growing. For more focused and targeted programs and for more localized retailers, they offer great advantages.

Out of Home

Out-of-home (OOH) and *place-based media* opportunities continue to expand. The growth of digital technology has increased opportunities not just in traditional out-door settings with digital boards being built along major traffic routes but also in other settings that can be set up with video equipment, from movie theaters to gas pumps to elevators.

It is most often utilized to drive *brand awareness*. However, dynamic locations combined with dynamic messaging are also being used to drive buzz.

The medium is frequently used to create highly targeted or tactical programs. These can include elements like these:

Airports for business travelers
Supermarket showings around grocery stores
Bulletins near corporate campuses or around convention centers to reach B2B decision makers
Mobile units with street teams around stadiums to sample products
Dynamic wallscapes around fashion centers or entertainment venues
Train station dominations with one brand owning all the visual space
Stadium signage, including both inside units and traditional units outside

Each of these programs will have varying deliveries and associated costs based on the dynamics of ad units and the uniqueness of the event or target. Most often the evaluation is based less on media efficiencies than on other softer metrics. These programs tend to be expensive so they are generally planned on a market-specific basis to control absolute budgets.

For The Hartford investment products company, to support its sponsorship of the NCAA, at the basketball tournament site, we used building wraps, video mobile, and high-impact boards around the tournament venue and hotels to create visibility and buzz to their partners and guests.

A plan for general market coverage will usually include a mix of posters and bulletins, and depending on the market, it will often include transit. Schedules are planned and purchased on a monthly basis. Because of high production and posting costs, the bulletins are usually in place for three months to a year. A market coverage

EXHIBIT 18.12

Out-of-Home Cost per Thousands		
Category	Women 25–54	Men 25–54
Bulletins	$10	$13
Posters	7	8
Digital	12	15
Shelters	17	20
Buses	12	14
Airports	25	25

plan is developed on a *showing* or *daily gross-rating-point (GRP) basis*. A 25 showing would deliver a number of impressions equivalent to 25 percent of the target universe each day. If *brand awareness* metrics are aggressive, the 25 showing would be a minimum level.

Digital boards are changing the landscape. The rotation of messaging every 8 to 10 seconds allows for multiple advertisers to share the same locations. In most cases advertisers buy the full network of highly visible boards generating more reach and less frequency. Digital production efficiencies provide opportunities to change messages by day of week and even time of day. Although pricing per exposure is higher, the orientation to more reach and less frequency is generally a cost-effective trade-off.

Pricing can vary dramatically by market and by element. Exhibit 18.12 provides a rough estimate of cost per thousands for various units. Before developing a plan, it is best to get pricing from the OOH companies for the appropriate market.

Before building OOH into a media plan, it is necessary to ensure that messages can be communicated quickly. The medium suffers from cluttered environments and exposure opportunities of only a few seconds each. Industry experts state that messages of six to eight words are most effective.

The other challenge of OOH is the absolute costs to cover significant geography. Covering the top 25 markets for one month at a 25 showing can cost up to $2.5 million. National advertisers need to have significant budgets (Verizon, GEICO, and McDonald's are reportedly the leading OOH spenders) or be highly selective in the markets they target for OOH.

Video-placed media is growing dramatically. Nielsen has begun to measure audiences, and indications are that the medium is attracting younger audiences that are difficult to reach with television. Each venue will have different target deliveries, but if your target is difficult to reach, you should consider this platform.

The following are the most common platforms:

Movie theaters, delivering young audiences
Bars and restaurants, delivering younger on-the-go consumers
Hotels, delivering business travelers
Elevators and office lobbies, delivering B2B prospects
Gas pumps, delivering broader audiences but growing rapidly

One-to-One and Direct Media

One-to-one and direct media continue to grow in importance as marketers look for better metrics and ROI in acquiring new customers and building stronger and deeper relationships with current customers. This growth has also occurred with the new tools and technology that have grown with the Internet. Data mining and modeling have also increased the performance of one-to-one and direct marketing, increasing its share of the marketing communications budget.

In other media forms, the first metrics are audience impression levels and reach and frequency. In contrast, direct plans are based on the performance metrics of the cost per response or acquisition and/or the frequency of purchase. In many categories we look at customer lifetime values to determine a cost allowable for acquisition. Historical performance is used to set benchmarks, and programs are designed for continuous testing of new approaches and vehicles to increase performance.

The following pages will provide a brief description of these tools:

Direct-mail and e-mail marketing
Search
Direct response television
Yellow pages

Direct-Mail and E-mail Marketing

These approaches are focused on the communications drivers of activation and loyalty. Direct-mail activation programs can range from low-cost bill stuffers and shared mail to three-dimensional high-impact units. Data mining and modeling allow for highly sophisticated targeting based on household behavior and life stages. For categories like financial services and retail, life stage targeting is often a critical part of their direct-mail and e-mail programs. Life stages frequently include these:

Graduations
Marriage
New children
New home or recent moves
Changes in employment

For H&R Block, we developed a life stage program targeted at recent marriage, first child, and first home to capitalize on life stage events that impact taxes.

With better targeting, more costly higher-impact units or offers are delivered to fewer households as a way of controlling costs while delivering higher response rates.

Direct-mail and e-mail approaches are the main drivers of customer relationship marketing (CRM). Data on rewards programs and the timing and value of offers are modeled to maximize loyalty and lifetime customer value.

Because of more limited communications opportunities, direct-mail and e-mail play a more important role in B2B communications. This is even more important when small businesses are the target.

Search

This medium is primarily used as an activation driver. Chapter 19 will discuss it in more depth, but it is divided into two approaches:

- *Organic search:* Search terms that include the company and brand terms. Organic search is driven by on-site search engine optimization and offline media.
- *Paid search:* An auction bid system based on specific words. SpyFu is a low-cost tool that can provide a starting point on the cost of specific-word searches.

Direct Response Television (DRTV)

This approach is focused solely on activation, generally using longer-form commercials:

:60s
:120s
Infomercials

The television time is purchased on a remnant basis without regard to audience. Commercial airings are paired to responses on a 24-hour basis, and schedules and clearance are adjusted based on cost per call or acquisition.

Yellow Pages
This medium is also focused primarily on activation. Although considered a dated medium, recent data suggest well over half of the phone searches are still made via the telephone book. Programs should include the interactive yellow pages. This tool can be critical for small local businesses with limited brand awareness. For national or advertisers with local dealer, franchise, or agent relationships, co-op programs are available with the national advertising picking up the cost of a trademark and listing purchased by the dealers, franchisees, or agents.

TASK 5   ## Obtain the Final Costs and Develop the Final Plan and Flowchart

It is critical that alternatives with associated costs and budgets be developed across all media forms and against each of the targeting, timing, and geographic strategies. Equally important is developing alternatives within each medium selected and the associated audience deliveries (impressions, TRPs, reach and frequency, and number of weeks advertised). Weighing the pros and cons within each medium and across strategies will lead to the best recommended media plan.

Alternatives are generally priced on the following basis (Exhibit 18.1 provides data sources for gathering costs):

For broadcast: Cost per target rating point
For Internet display: Cost per impression or click
For print: Cost per insertion
For out of home: Cost per daily GRP or showing (for tactical programs the absolute cost)

As the final plan is developed, it is important to tighten down all costs and audience deliveries. A calendar flowchart is usually developed that provides a full synopsis of the plan. The flowchart should include the following:

Description of each medium and vehicle used (TV and/or radio dayparts, magazine categories, Internet display approaches, and so on)
Media deliveries by medium (TRPs, impressions, number of insertions, and circulation for preprints or direct mail)
Appropriate geographic groupings
Scheduling patterns and timing

Exhibit 18.13 is a sample calendar flowchart.

Budgets summaries usually include breakouts by medium, geography, and month. It is also important to prepare a budget summary based on commit dates to ensure sufficient financial flexibility.

See also Appendix C, Worksheets 54 and 55.

EXHIBIT 18.13

Sample Calendar Flowchart

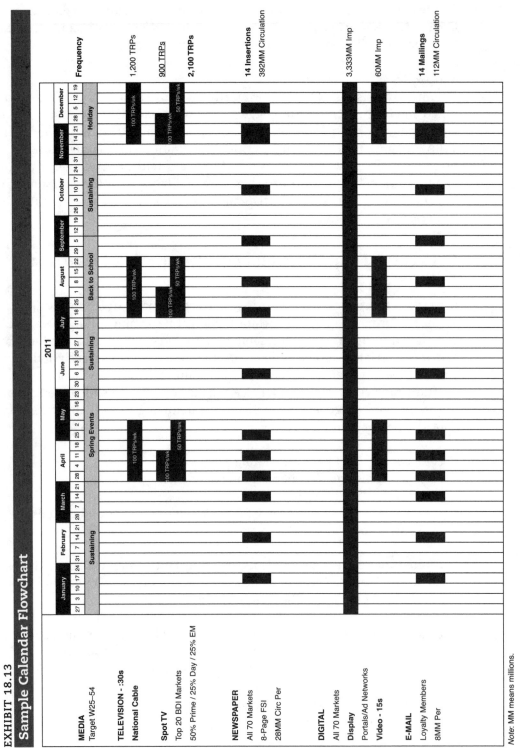

Note: MM means millions.

Note: MM means millions

DOS AND DON'TS

Do

- Be sure targeting, timing, geographic, and weight level strategies are addressed, and prioritize them.
- Be realistic about budgets relative to marketing and communication objectives.
- Make sure your target audience is defined demographically so that media can be evaluated on an objective delivery basis.
- Be sure that the role of each medium is defined for specific communication objectives or drivers.
- Be sure to use both objective data and qualitative judgments on a medium's impact when making media selection decisions.
- Be sure to develop alternatives across strategies and within media before making a final recommendation or decision on a plan.
- Be sure that the selected media forms work in concert with and optimize messaging.
- Ensure that adequate weight levels are delivered in the primary and secondary media before adding additional media.
- Be willing to sacrifice schedule duration or geography to ensure adequate weekly weight levels.
- Budget for continuous testing and learning, if direct and one-to-one programs are part of the plan.
- Recognize the realities of messaging requirements and the appropriate costs and timing before selecting a medium.
- Remember inter-media comparisons are based on different survey methodology and generally not the reason to select a medium.
- Remember that media planning is an iterative process when establishing both media strategies and marketing and communications objectives. As objectives and budgets are adjusted, media strategy priorities need to be adjusted as well.
- Remember that the best media plans require a high level of collaboration with the creative team developing the messaging.
- Remember that the media plan can be adjusted throughout the year as new inputs come in.

Don't

- Don't be unrealistic in establishing communications objectives relative to the budget.
- Don't spread dollars too thinly across the geography or the calendar.
- Don't waste media investments by using too many media forms.
- Don't finalize a plan without developing alternative options both across media strategies and within selected media.
- Don't force fit messaging into a medium just because of audience delivery. Either change the messaging or the medium.
- Don't make media decisions based solely on the audience delivery.
- Never buy a deal from the media without relating it to strategic priorities or creating other alternative within the same costs and evaluating pros and cons of the deal versus the alternatives.

The Successful Marketing Plan

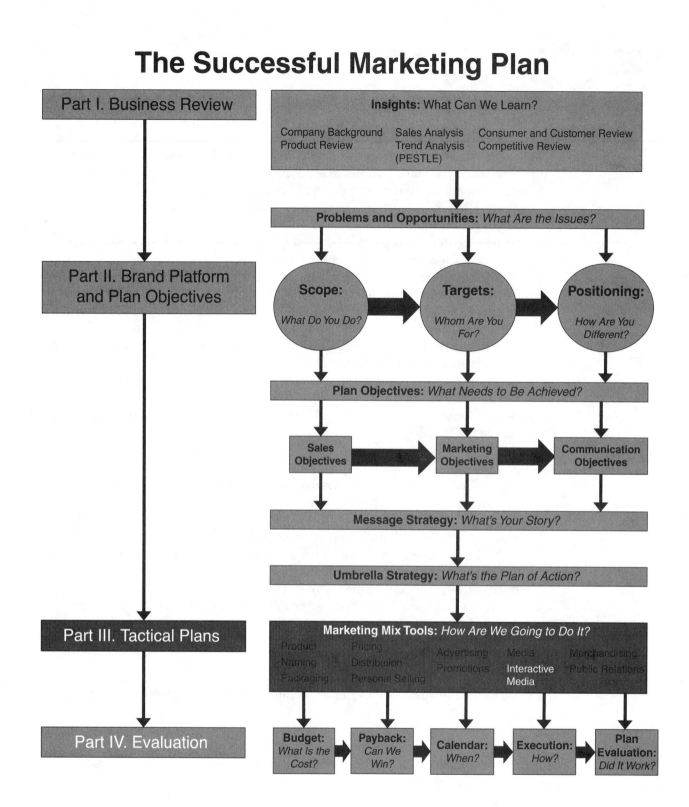

Part I. Business Review

Insights: What Can We Learn?

Company Background   Sales Analysis   Consumer and Customer Review
Product Review   Trend Analysis   Competitive Review
                      (PESTLE)

Problems and Opportunities: *What Are the Issues?*

Part II. Brand Platform and Plan Objectives

Scope:
What Do You Do?

Targets:
Whom Are You For?

Positioning:
How Are You Different?

Plan Objectives: *What Needs to Be Achieved?*

Sales Objectives   **Marketing Objectives**   **Communication Objectives**

Message Strategy: *What's Your Story?*

Umbrella Strategy: *What's the Plan of Action?*

Part III. Tactical Plans

Marketing Mix Tools: *How Are We Going to Do It?*

Product   Pricing   Advertising   Media   Merchandising
Naming   Distribution   Promotions   Interactive   Public Relations
Packaging Personal Selling   Media

Part IV. Evaluation

Budget: *What Is the Cost?*

Payback: *Can We Win?*

Calendar: *When?*

Execution: *How?*

Plan Evaluation: *Did It Work?*

19 Interactive Communications

*I*nteractive marketing and communications have become the nexus where creativity meets technology meets connectivity. The result is a dramatic increase in two new important measures: utility and community. This powerful combination is profoundly affecting marketing and communications, and it is opening up new doors and possibilities for brands to play a more meaningful role in their customers' lives.

With interactive communications, the end customer is no longer always passive but instead is often an active participant in the brand's marketing and communications.

With the advent of social media channels, mavens can now influence the masses.

With the consumers or end users having more control, how brands behave has become even more important than what they say. Truth matters.

And with interactive communications, everything's measurable.

FROM THIS CHAPTER YOU WILL LEARN

- How to relate interactive marketing channels back to the communications drivers
- How to create a strategic interactive "connections" blueprint
- Website strategies and tips
- Principles of creating advocacy through social marketing
- Approaches to interactive media measurement

OVERVIEW

What we hear a lot from our interactive media and digital specialists is that interactive media communication requires a *different mindset*. One of our digital media experts has described it as "lean-in communication" versus "lean-back communication." And if you think about the media discussion in Chapter 18, traditional advertising forms and vehicles like television, magazines, and radio allow the target prospects to lean back and absorb a message passively. In contrast, interactive marketing communications require those target audiences to "lean in" and *participate, engage,* and, quite often, even *create brand content.* In many examples of digital communications, it's difficult to separate classic editorial content and marketing communications content.

Thus, the mindset for interactive communications must incorporate new parameters:

- An iterative, versus linear, process
- Communication without interruption
- Marketing and communications with functionality and utility
- Personalization and customization

INTERACTIVE MARKETING CHANNELS AND KEY COMMUNICATIONS DRIVERS

When it comes to interactive marketing and communications, there are myriad tools, channels, and opportunities. By the time this new edition goes to press, there, no doubt, will be even more, as new technology leads us to new advances in things like augmented reality, enhanced search, browserless Internet use, and supercharged crowdsourcing. But for now, let's review some of the basic channels or tools and apply them to the concept of key communications drivers, which we introduced in Chapter 16: brand awareness, emotional bond, product news, activation, loyalty, experience, and buzz.

Websites

Websites are one channel that can be designed to affect nearly all of the communications drivers. We see websites falling into the following three big buckets.

1. Brand-Focused Websites

In these types of sites, the focus is often put on deeper communications of the brand's key message, or, in other words, the focus is on telling the brand's story within a richer, deeper context. Often the key communications driver affected is the *emotional bond.* Our Burger King client, for example, shifted its site strategy a few years back to leverage fun and its king icon rather than food product news, in an attempt to deepen its emotional connection to its core target audience of young male heavy users. With that shift in communications drivers, it also shifted the site development assignment from its digital marketing agency to its brand agency. And the new agency subsequently shifted some of the content from food to fun.

2. Transaction-Focused Websites

Amazon.com is a great example of a website that has been highly successful with billions of dollars in annual revenue. It's all about product-product-product, and there is very little branding for Amazon.com itself. However, the brand delivers a great user experience for people who are looking to buy, and Amazon.com makes it very easy to find products and purchase from every page. This site has been designed to affect *product news* and *activation.* The design itself is extremely simple, clear, and utilitarian. There is a prominent "Add to Cart" button next to every product—it is not just on a product detail page the way the shopping cart button appears on most sites—right from a search results page. A transaction-focused site such as Amazon.com is obviously great for *activation*, but Amazon.com also does a nice job of incorporating detailed descriptions, user ratings, and reviews including "likes," customer rewards, hot deals, contests and sweepstakes, online customer service—all of which engage consumers and affect product news. Amazon.com discovered that 20 percent of the people using their website were influenced by user reviews in making their ultimate purchase decisions. When they added the "Was this review helpful?" feature to bubble up the best reviews to the top, it turned out to be a $2.4 billion decision for them.

The content you create even within a transaction-oriented site, assuming it provides value to your target consumers, can be geared to creating relevance to users through such features as product news, video product demonstrations that provide virtual product experience, programs to retain customers, and third-party reviews and likes that generate buzz.

3. Mixed-Focus (Hybrid) Websites

Some of the more forward-thinking retailers who want to use their websites to build the brand relationship (emotional bond) *and* sell product (activation) have found ways to do both. A great example is REI, which is an easy-to-use, e-commerce site that also incorporates "travel, learn, and share" into the experience of being an REI customer and website user. On the company's website, you'll find how-tos and handy checklists that contain many of the products that REI also sells. Nike has also had much success in combining both lifestyle and transactions into their online experience.

We encourage you to ask yourself this fundamental question: What key communications drivers are top priority for your brand's website?

E-mail

E-mail is often the stepchild of interactive marketing because it's been around for a while, but it's still a highly efficient way to affect several key communications drivers. A periodic e-mail message can keep you at the top of mind for existing customers and has proven to help with *loyalty*. For example, we created an electronic newsletter e-mailed to "retention" target audiences for H&R Block with the goal of deepening the brand's relationship and ensuring loyalty.

A quick e-mail blast is a great way to get the latest updates out to your customer base to create renewed relevance for your product (that is, product news). A sale or promotional announcement with a time-sensitive offer can generate an immediate purchase (activation), especially when you include a downloadable coupon. LivingSocial and Groupon are great examples of companies who have succeeded with this model.

And an e-mail continues to be one of the easiest ways to forward detailed information to friends, albeit usually to a smaller audience than your entire social graph on Facebook.

On the other hand, e-mail is a very poor awareness driver because, unless you're sending it to a list of people who have already opted in to receive communications, you're just spamming them.

Our experience has been that e-mail marketing campaigns can be extremely cost-efficient ways to communicate to "win-back" and "retention" audiences but much more challenging with "acquisition" targets.

EXHIBIT 19.1

Search Ads on Google

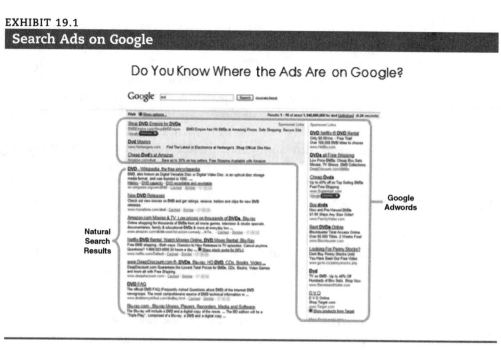

Do You Know Where the Ads Are on Google?

Search

Search is the mortar of an integrated campaign. You use other mass market vehicles to drive awareness, and then once consumers hear about you, their next step is often to go online and conduct a search before they buy. So search can be a critical activation tactic.

Search engine marketing (SEM) is not just about paid search. By now, most people know which ads are the paid ads and which are the natural or organic search results that are the payoff from your *search engine optimization* (SEO) efforts.

Exhibit 19.1 shows the results of an eye-tracking study by Google to map where users' eyes focused on the page. Google found that the darker the color, the more views that portion of the page received. This phenomenon has been consistent over the years, but more users are now scanning farther down the page than in the past to form the F-shaped pattern. Therefore, having strong paid *and* natural search results provides optimal performance for your SEM efforts—between 30 and 60 percent more traffic than just natural search alone.

Search Terms

To improve your search effectiveness and efficiency, you need to understand how to optimize your search spending by volume and topic because search has a *long-tail effect*. Think of the most common search words in a given category as the "head," and the long list of thousands of other related words in a given category as the "tail."

Let's discuss one of our clients, Airborne, a popular homeopathic cold remedy, as an example.

High-volume terms (or head terms): These search terms are typically broadly applicable and not specific to your brand or situation. Key words can be expensive to buy because there's a lot of competition—for example, in Airborne's case, "allergies," "sick," "cold," "stress," and "flu."

EXHIBIT 19.2

Search's Long Tail

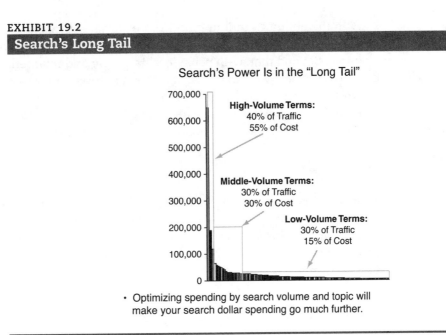

Search's Power Is in the "Long Tail"

High-Volume Terms:
40% of Traffic
55% of Cost

Middle-Volume Terms:
30% of Traffic
30% of Cost

Low-Volume Terms:
30% of Traffic
15% of Cost

- Optimizing spending by search volume and topic will make your search dollar spending go much further.

Middle-volume terms: These terms are slightly more specific and can be applicable to multiple brands, such as "cold remedy" or "immunity support supplements," but there's still a lot of competition to drive the price up.

Low-volume terms: These are very specific and often apply only to your brand; in Airborne's case, the term would probably be "Airborne effervescent formula." Often "Airborne" won't appear in the natural results of very specific terms. Note that having both a paid and a natural result has been shown to boost overall traffic 35 to 65 percent on branded terms. These terms are often very cheap because buying them would be less efficient for your competition than for your own brand, so costs are lower. (See Exhibit 19.2.)

Since there is no pricing available that is based on the number of impressions (that is, the number of times a website advertisement is delivered to site visitors) to buying very specific words, the aggregation of thousands of words getting less than 10 clicks often drives as much traffic as the most popular word at a fraction of the cost. Unless your budget is unlimited, it is nearly always wise to focus your spending on the long-tail terms.

Banners and Rich Media

Contrary to what people were saying a year or two ago, display advertising is not dead. In fact, spending on website advertising is on the rise, and often it's the simple Adobe Flash banner ads, which are relatively cheap to produce and place, that can still get the job done. The content of the ads can be tailored to what you're trying to accomplish, and the ads can be suitable for awareness, product news, or activation.

With the ability to deliver interactive functionality, *rich media, display ads with interactive content that build, move, contain calculators, or even video,* provide a larger palette for the marketer. Brands can create highly engaging experiences with rich functionality, such as product demonstrations, and an expandable unit can serve as a mini-website that does not require users to ever leave the context of the website they're currently on.

With the ability to pull in data from external sources, an ad unit can be highly customized to an individual's location and even the local weather conditions, for example. Beyond that, with behavioral targeting and retargeting, subsequent offers can be dynamically customized based on a number of user-driven factors.

Streaming video is another area of display advertising that has seen dramatic growth. It's an effective vehicle for increasing awareness, creating emotional bond, generating product news, or enabling product experience.

Gaming

There is actually about a 50/50 percent split between men and women gamers, and with the mid-2000s' introduction of Nintendo's Wii and Sony's PlayStation Move, couples and entire families are into gaming. With the ability to leverage product placement within a game or develop a branded game, many drivers can be applied to this channel.

Social Media

Back in 1992, James Carville made the now-famous comment, "It's the economy, stupid." And many believe this simple phrase was a major driver behind Bill Clinton's becoming our forty-second president. A lot has changed since 1992. Back then, the Internet was not even considered mainstream. But now, and hopefully this isn't a news flash for anyone, the Internet has revolutionized almost every facet of our business and personal lives.

What is news, however, is that we are in the early stages of yet another far-reaching revolution, driven by people and enabled by social networking media. That's why in 2009, Erik Qualman, author of *Socialnomics*, took some liberty with Carville's statement and said, "It's a *people-driven* economy, stupid."

Social media is best known for its ability to generate word-of-mouth buzz. Later in this chapter, we will discuss in detail strategies for creating buzz or advocacy through social marketing.

We're also in the early phases of a new customer service model where social media has empowered consumers. Furthermore, it has become a critical tool for many brands in understanding their customers, as well as building deeper relationships via two-way conversations with them. In other words, it is now a critical loyalty tool.

Mobile Applications

Mobile is no longer the next wave. It's here NOW, and its capabilities will continue to grow, whether through mobile-friendly Internet content or smartphone applications. With mobile, access to content travels wherever you do, and its location-aware features compound its power. The possibilities are endless. The simplicity and immediacy of most mobile applications seem best suited for driving awareness, activation, and buzz.

CREATING AN INTERACTIVE CONNECTIONS BLUEPRINT

Interactive media, digital media, social marketing, and mobile media are so multi-faceted, so fast, and so cutting-edge that, to quote the old saying, "If you don't know where you're going, any road will do." We've worked with countless clients who feel pressured to "just do something" rather than take the time to think about

EXHIBIT 19.3

Interactive Connections Blueprint for Famous Footwear

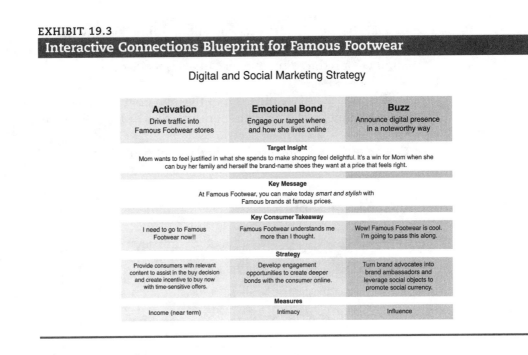

Digital and Social Marketing Strategy

Activation	Emotional Bond	Buzz
Drive traffic into Famous Footwear stores	Engage our target where and how she lives online	Announce digital presence in a noteworthy way

Target Insight

Mom wants to feel justified in what she spends to make shopping feel delightful. It's a win for Mom when she can buy her family and herself the brand-name shoes they want at a price that feels right.

Key Message

At Famous Footwear, you can make today *smart and stylish* with Famous brands at famous prices.

Key Consumer Takeaway

I need to go to Famous Footwear now!!	Famous Footwear understands me more than I thought.	Wow! Famous Footwear is cool. I'm going to pass this along.

Strategy

Provide consumers with relevant content to assist in the buy decision and create incentive to buy now with time-sensitive offers.	Develop engagement opportunities to create deeper bonds with the consumer online.	Turn brand advocates into brand ambassadors and leverage social objects to promote social currency.

Measures

Income (near term)	Intimacy	Influence

their desired outcomes. So the best place to start with interactive communications is what we like to call a Connections Blueprint. It marries marketing drivers, target insights, messages and takeaways to interactive media content and contextual strategies, along with the appropriate measures.

Exhibit 19.3 shows how we developed an interactive Connections Blueprint to help our client Famous Footwear approach its experimenting with digital and social marketing.

Based on this strategic blueprint, our client was able to evaluate, prioritize, and focus on three core interactive programs:

1. A promotion to drive Internal channel sales
2. A social marketing idea with a philanthropic cause marketing component and Facebook application
3. A new mobile app with tremendous "talk" value

Notice how we also begin to set measurement strategy for our programs: income for the activation program, which is more of a financial metric; and intimacy and influence for the other programs, which are more related to brand metrics. We'll discuss these in more detail at the end of the chapter.

WEBSITE STRATEGY

Many people make the mistake of thinking that user experience design is just about one thing like good functionality or the look and feel of the visual design. In reality, a good user experience is *all* of these things:

Useful	Customers can accomplish their goals.
Usable	Customers can easily perform tasks.
Desirable	Customers enjoy their experience.

Useful: The website delivers content and functionality that is relevant to the customers' needs. Ideally, your design strategy creates a personalized experience with minimal or reduced prominence of extraneous content.

Usable: Website navigation is intuitive and obvious. Content is in the right place at the right time, and it's easy to perform tasks or locate content of interest.

Desirable: The website establishes an emotional connection with the brand. This is where the importance of the visual design and tonality come in.

You Need a Plan

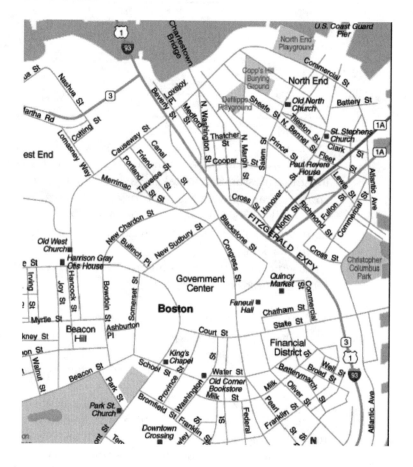

But in order to do this right, you must have a plan. During Colonial times in Boston, one person built a house, then another person built a house, and then they built a path between the two. Then another person built a house with another path, and so on. As a result, Boston's layout was accidental, and if you've ever driven the streets of Boston, you know that it can be quite frustrating.

Similarly, if you create a website without a plan, the results will be accidental and will leave your users frustrated.

Worksheets 56–61 in Appendix C contain some useful tools for organizing your website development.

Competitive Website Analysis

In developing a site strategy, we find it helpful to apply some of the fundamental principles of competitive analysis that we discussed in Chapter 1 in the business

EXHIBIT 19.4

Competitive Website Analysis

Leading Dog Food.com

Content	◑	• Product and offer information is featured prominently on home page— perhaps catering to visitors' primary goals. • Content is fresh and updated frequently with new offers and promotions.
User Experience	◑	• Site has clean, fresh design. • Navigating the site is fairly easy with top navigation. • Interactive Flash navigation areas supplement the top navigation with a more visually engaging experience.
Customer Utility	◯	• E-newsletter, dog age calculator, and dog breed profiles, Puppy Newsletter, Dog Calculator, 131 dog care articles, online donation, food finder, offers, coupons. • Puppy Program.
Campaigns and Promotions	◑	• Million Dog Mosaic promotion (2008) deemed successful. • Adoption Drive integrated with Super Bowl ad (February 2009) has donated *xx* million meals to dogs.
Community (On Site or Off Site)	◯	• Content area caters to an active community who feel passionately about helping sheltered and/or abused dogs. • Active in social networks with two Facebook fan pages.
Other Items of Interest	◯	• iPhone application for converting your dog's bark into your ringtone. • Behind-the-scenes content of the biggest dog show in the world.

● Has and Is Best in Class	◯ Has and Is Above Average	◑ Has and Is Below Average	● Nonexistent

review sections. Exhibit 19.4 is an example of an analysis we prepared for a client in the pet food category. We focus on six aspects of a good website, but you may have more or less, depending on your objective and which marketing drivers you are trying to affect.

ESTABLISHING WEBSITE OBJECTIVES

For those within the target market who visit your site, you should identify objectives based on other communication, marketing, and sales objectives. These may include the following measures:

• The number and/or percentage of target market site visitors who subscribe to receive ongoing information from your company via e-mail
• The number and/or percentage of target market site visitors who request additional information about your organization's products or services
• The number of customers who successfully resolve customer service needs online
• The number of products and services sold online, or transactions originating from the website visits
• The number of new monthly visitors and repeat monthly visitors to your site

EXHIBIT 19.5

Website Statistics

Site visits by hour

Top trails followed: Most common routes from page to page used by visitors to the web server

Top exit pages: Visits typically ended at these pages

Content use by directory

File types (extensions)

Top proxy sites

Top web browsers (also known as "user agents")

Top referring URLs: External pages that link to this site

Top search key words: Key words used to reach your site via search engines such as AltaVista and InfoSeek

Top search key words by server: Search key words used to reach this site, indexed by search server of origin

Top visitor domains

Referring URLs by "document not found": External pages that link to pages that do not exist on this site, sorted by document referred to

Site visits by day

Top entry pages: Visits typically begin at these pages

Example visits: Documents accessed by a sample of individual visitors to the website

Most popular pages

Authorized users

Top proxy domains

Top operating systems used by visitors

Top referring sites: External sites that link to this site

Top search servers: Search servers used to reach your site such as AltaVista and InfoSeek

Top visitor sites

Referring URLs by document: External pages that link to this site, sorted by document referred to

---

Setting quantifiable objectives for your website that relate to your overall marketing and communication goals is essential. Equally important is the ability to accurately measure whether the objectives are met.

See Worksheet 56 in Appendix C for creating your website objectives.

Each time an individual visits your organization's website, information about the visit can be saved. This information can be used to generate website statistics that characterize your site's overall use. The statistics that are available may vary based on the server that hosts your website. Exhibit 19.5 provides a list of commonly available website statistics.

Website statistics are a helpful tool for measuring site use. For example, based on website statistics, you can calculate the following marketing-relevant indicators:

$$\text{Penetration} = \frac{\text{unique visitors to home page}}{\text{unique visitors who go beyond the home page}}$$

Penetration is the percentage of site visitors who go beyond your organization's home page. It's not uncommon for a website to lose 50 percent or more of its visitors before the home page finishes loading. A home page that has 5,000 visitors a month with a penetration of less than 50 percent may be less effective than a site that has 4,000 visitors with higher penetration.

$$\text{Conversion} = \frac{\text{unique visitors taking desired action}}{\text{unique visitors}}$$

Conversion is the percentage of site visitors who take a desired action. You can measure the conversion for several actions simultaneously—for example, the percentage of site visitors who purchase online, and the percentage of site visitors who subscribe to your organization's electronic newsletter.

$$\text{Connection} = \frac{\text{desired content views}}{\text{referral click-throughs}}$$

Connection refers to the number of visitors to your site from another location, such as a website or a website's banner advertisement, who view your desired content. A high connection rate is an indicator of the effectiveness of an online promotion.

$$\text{Migration} = \frac{\text{site exits from a specific content area}}{\text{visits to that content area}}$$

Migration refers to the number of visitors who leave your site from a specific content area. Content areas with the highest migration are typically less effective than areas with lower migration.

$$\text{Clicks to action (CTA)} = \text{average number of clicks to get from the home page to the desired action}$$

The *clicks to action* (CTA) is the number of clicks it takes a visitor to get from your home page to the desired outcome. Your goal is always to limit this number. For example, reducing the CTA to complete an order should result in a measurable increase of customer conversion for online orders.

$$\text{Intro skip factor} = \frac{\text{number of visitors to intro page}}{\text{number of visitors who bypass intro}}$$

This indicator is the number of visitors who view your site's introduction page, if applicable. If a large percentage of site visitors bypass the introduction page, it can indicate an ineffective introduction or a high percentage of return visitors.

Since standard website statistics are not collected with specific marketing, communication, or sales objectives in mind, other methods of measuring objectives are also required. Data for measuring the success of website objectives can be incorporated in the processes used to track the success of communication goals, marketing objectives, and sales objectives overall. For example, customer surveys should include questions related specifically to the unaided awareness, attitude, trial, and retrial levels of the organization's website.

If you establish objectives prior to using interactive media, it may also be possible to integrate objective-specific reporting features. In the same way that site visits yield information for website statistics, information can be collected for evaluating whether objectives have been met.

Technology and Infrastructure

Potentially effective Internet strategies often are delayed or quickly become cost prohibitive because the organization lacks the technology and infrastructure required to implement the strategy. For instance, it may be desirable for a company to sell its products or services online, but doing so requires the ability to update product information and process incoming orders.

Also, once implemented, Internet strategies may require ongoing support or third-party maintenance.

Technology Integration

Internet media can present a world of possibilities. For each Internet objective and strategy, you will find a wide array of vendors offering "off-the-shelf" technology solutions, turnkey Internet services, and prepackaged content. It's important for your company and the vendors you select to carefully evaluate existing products and services and how they can be integrated with your Internet media project. This allows your organization to consider the costs and benefits associated with buying preexisting products and services versus buying custom solutions.

Maintenance Costs

The cost of your organization's website involves more than the development cost. Your organization must consider the total cost of owning and maintaining the site. Be prepared to ask related questions: How often will the site be updated? Who will update the site? What is the anticipated return on investment?

It's a good idea to prepare a maintenance plan that identifies ongoing tasks associated with the website, who will complete the tasks, and the anticipated costs. If your site is developed by a vendor, it may be appropriate to require a maintenance plan within the scope of the project.

A maintenance plan ensures that your site is maintained on a regular basis. It does so by meeting five objectives:

1. *Defining site-related tasks:* The maintenance plan identifies daily, weekly, monthly, quarterly, and annual tasks associated with maintaining and protecting website-related content.
2. *Specifying responsibilities associated with each task:* Every site that is developed has associated maintenance responsibilities. The maintenance plan specifies maintenance tasks and appropriate levels of responsibility for the client and its vendors.
3. *Identifying ongoing procedures:* The maintenance plan identifies ongoing procedures for updating and revising site content and reviewing site visitor information.
4. *Scheduling planned additions and enhancements:* The maintenance plan provides a tentative schedule and plan for any site enhancements and additions to be implemented within the next 12 to 18 months.
5. *Detailing maintenance costs:* The maintenance costs associated with a website are based on the scope of the site. The maintenance plan identifies all ongoing and anticipated costs related to maintaining the website and integrated applications. Maintenance costs include hosting fees, domain registration fees, and the cost of adding and revising content.

User Experience

We've been talking mostly about good user experience design for destination sites. However, it's important to think more broadly about designing experiences in a world where online and offline continue to blur and one in which the online experience is taking place across a wide array of sites, social networks, blogs, games, mobile apps, and so on, on a wide array of devices: computers, phones, game consoles, e-readers, and TVs. So a great user experience on a destination website is one that is consistent with all other channels and rewards the users for their visits by providing continuity and delivering upon their expectations for an even deeper, richer experience with the brand.

CREATING ADVOCACY THROUGH SOCIAL MARKETING

Social marketing is not new.

For example, more than two decades ago we had the pleasure to work with the Brown-Forman company during the early stages of their development of the

Gentleman Jack super premium whiskey. The model for that brand's introduction was the same as the social marketing model for its parent brand, Jack Daniel's, when it expanded its penetration in the 1950s.

A fairly well-kept secret, whispered to us in the back rooms of focus groups around the country, was the lore behind the Jack Daniel's company's marketing campaign in the 1950s. The campaign created an "illusion of discovery." What the Jack Daniel's company did was place its new whiskey in select bars around the country, where bartenders could "influence" the right kinds of patrons—cool, hip, "influentials"—to try the spirits. Those "influentials" spread or "broadcast" the word throughout their own social circles. And to jumpstart the brand's "earned media," it placed Jack Daniel's whiskey in trendy Las Vegas bars where Rat Pack members Frank Sinatra, Dean Martin, Sammy Davis, Jr., Joey Bishop, and Peter Lawford frequented. As the coolest guys around, they, in turn, influenced the cool people descending on the United States' new adult playground.

Or so the story goes.

But this all took a while because there was no social technology, other than the telephone, or social media networks. Sammy Davis couldn't Tweet that he had knocked back a few Jack's and found the taste to be smooth and mellow.

Now social marketing can quickly, efficiently, and effectively build a brand's equity and business.

What Is Social Marketing?

Let's define some terms because *social marketing* has become a buzzword itself:

Social marketing: Using social networking technology and media to stimulate action.

Social media: Activities that integrate technology.

Social networks: Communities and/or places where people are connecting. Facebook is an example of a mass social media network.

Social technology: Tools that enable social actions.

Social actions: Act of social interaction, such as sharing of content, opinions, insights, experiences, and media (video, audio, and photos).

An Alternative Communications Construct: BIER

In Chapter 9, we discussed the Four A's construct of how communications work: awareness, attitude, action, and action again (A^2).

David Rabjohns, head of the innovative online anthropology firm MotiveQuest, believes that social technology and media networks have permanently shifted marketing and communications to a new model he calls BIER: buzz, influence, engagement, and repeat. Exhibit 19.6 compares and contrasts the old model to his new construct.

If we go back to the example of Jack Daniel's marketing campaign in the late 1950s, we can see a modified use of the BIER model. The missing piece is using "online masses" to influence media, offline influencers, and offline masses.

Rabjohns is doing exciting new research, at the time this edition is going to press, which he believes shows a strong correlation between increasing online mavens' online brand buzz or advocacy and increasing sales.

EXHIBIT 19.6

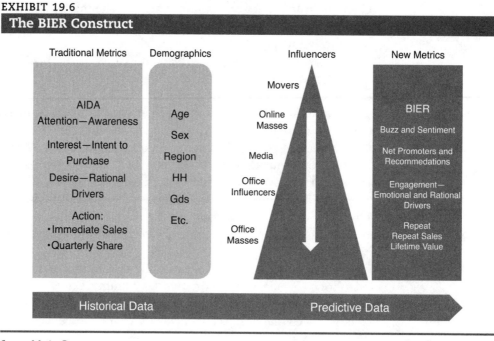

Source: MotiveQuest.

Conventional research has shown that certain industry categories lend themselves more to social marketing than others. High-interest categories such as cars, movies, vacation destinations, and entertainment technology have much higher levels of both social conversations and peer influence on recent purchases than do lower-interest categories like packaged foods, insurance services, and everyday clothing.

But the advent of new social technology and social media networks can create greater opportunities across all categories.

How to Think about Your Advocates

One key task in social marketing is profiling and determining your brand's best advocates—those people who are likely to recommend your brand to a friend. It is probably even more important to identify which of those advocates are most likely to become mass influencers—those people most likely to create online content:

Publish a blog
Upload a video
Upload an audio
Write articles or stories
Post positive ratings or reviews
Comment on another's blog
Contribute to articles on a wiki

Forrester Research has conducted extensive studies on the use of social technology. About 30 percent of adults 18 and older use it. And they tend to be a bit younger. Chances are that adoption will continue to increase as new technologies become simpler and ubiquitous. So, for example, someone who is a Facebook fan may be a joiner but not necessarily an advocate who creates social content for a brand.

A good exercise for any brand is to develop a social advocate profile:

1. Who they are
2. Characteristics
3. What they talk about
4. Whom they talk to
5. How to contact them

This can be done through qualitative research, online quantitative research, by hiring word-of-mouth (WOM) specialty firms like BzzAgent, or by leveraging emerging online tools that help identify influencers based on their Twitter presence.

Finding Insights from Online Anthropology

One way to leverage social marketing is to gain insights into what your potential advocates and/or mass influencers care about and talk about. A great way to do that is often called *online anthropology*. Online anthropology mines conversations from thousands and even millions of customers within a category and about a brand.

For example, a few years back we were asked to consult with the now-defunct Northwest Airlines brand regarding its positioning and communications strategy. The brand was looking for a platform idea and an efficient way to communicate to its myriad, different target audience segments. By harvesting and analyzing more than 1.5 million online conversations about air travel, MotiveQuest helped us uncover an insight that little of the dialog involved the in-flight experience. As you can see from Exhibit 19.7, people talked most about the prices, reservations, technology, and elements of the loyalty programs, and they talked least about the planes, amenities, and meals.

EXHIBIT 19.7

Online Anthropology Conversation Harvesting

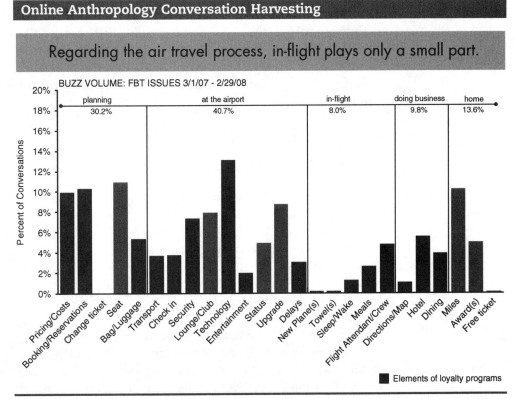

Regarding the air travel process, in-flight plays only a small part.

Source: MotiveQuest.

EXHIBIT 19.8

Motivations from Online Anthropology

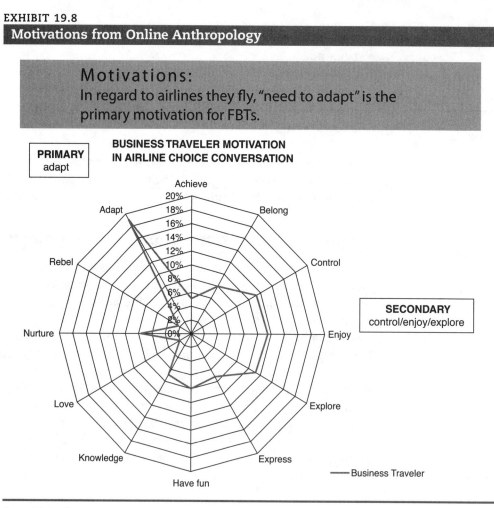

Motivations:
In regard to airlines they fly, "need to adapt" is the primary motivation for FBTs.

Source: MotiveQuest.

Deeper analysis, demonstrated in Exhibit 19.8, showed that the primary motivation of the frequent business traveler was not enjoying the ride but adapting to the journey of getting to and from the flight. Online anthropology told us what potential advocates—frequent business travelers (FBTs) who both influence their peers and their employees—talked about most.

Engagement Strategies

There are five strategies available to you for engaging an online audience:

- *Lassoing a topic:* The key to igniting a social marketing program is often to find out what your advocates and/or mass influencers care about and talk about and then, in the words of David Rabjohns, to "lasso that topic." For example, the Suave brand once sparked a social conversation around motherhood and letting appearances go. A bank might create conversations around financial literacy.
- *Going where the mass influencers hang out:* Forrester Research has shown that those likely to influence the masses are three times more likely to use Twitter than the average adult. So use Twitter and other emerging social networks to spread, recruit, inform, and coordinate advocates.
- *Asking for people's opinions:* Asking for feedback, ideas, and advice is one of the simplest and quickest forms of engagement.
- *Offering authentic experiences:* One way to create buzz and ultimately leverage it through social marketing can be to offer up a great product or brand experience.

EXHIBIT 19.9

Nature Valley's "Where's Yours?" Community

Source: Nature Valley® is a registered trademark of General Mills and is used with permission.

Think about the Jack Daniel's example cited at the beginning of the chapter. Starbucks tried this recently for the launch of its Pike Place Roast coffee, and it gave out its new coffee free to 100 Twitterers that it had identified through the social influencer tool Klout.

- *Creating communities:* Digital technology and social networks make it easy to create and unite communities around common interests. Before the days of Facebook popularity, our Nature Valley client launched its "Where's Yours?" campaign that involved users' sharing their favorite places by writing stories, uploading videos and photos, and connecting with other travelers and nature enthusiasts. (See Exhibit 19.9.)

Social Marketing Going Forward

Social media is more than just Facebook. It's broad and growing.

It is really "people driven versus brand driven," as we discussed in Chapter 9. What's not new is targeting advocates who can influence the masses. What is new are the ever-changing, evolving, and complex social technologies, social networks, and social media choices.

INTERACTIVE MEDIA PROGRAM MEASUREMENT

Establishing the right objectives is key to true measurement. Below are some broad examples, which we cited earlier in the chapter in the context of the Connections Blueprint, that have been identified by the Forrester Research organization, a leader in thinking about both social and digital research and measurement. Forrester's construct applies to overall media engagement, which, of course, is what's unique about interactive media channels. The firm's point of view is that marketers should link together a host of metrics that capture how target audiences participate with interactive advertising content.

The Five I's can help you create a framework for measuring how interactive programs return both brand and financial equity. You will need to customize the measure to fit your program objectives.

We've added the last one: income, or revenue or sales or however your brand would want to measure the financial part of an interactive media program.

Involvement

Presence of a person at brand touch points, like a website, Facebook page, Twitter feed, subscription to an e-newsletter, or mobile application.

Key Metrics
    Website and page visits
    Application use
    Subscriptions

Tracking Options
    Nielsen
    comScore

Interaction

What they do while they're engaged with your interactive content—visiting your websites, Facebook pages, blog posts, and so on.

Key Metrics
    Videos played
    Community contributions: Ratings, reviews, votes, photos uploaded

Intimacy

Sentiment toward a brand.

Key Metrics
    Word analysis in blog posts, chat lines, call center feedback

Tracking Options
    MotiveQuest
    Radian6

Influence

Likely to share

Key Metrics
    Forwarded content
    Tagged content
    Friends and fans
    Net Promoter Scores

Tracking Options
    Social tracking sites: Digg, Delicious

Income

What really matters in terms of revenue per activity, especially related to transactional sites, search, activation-oriented display, and e-mail.

Key Metrics
    Cost per click
    Cost per sale or transaction
    Cost per fan

DOS AND DON'TS

Do

- Include your website address with the name and logo of your organization whenever feasible.
- Encourage word-of-mouth promotion of the website among employees and customer service representatives.
- Include unique metatags on individual website pages.
- Use a search engine registration service. If possible, find a service that periodically resubmits the site to the same search engines.
- Include a search engine that is integrated in the header of each page. This allows site visitors quick access to information on the site.
- Solicit input and feedback from organization leaders when developing Internet media. Obtain buy-in and support from sales, technical, and customer service departments.
- Use simple, intuitive navigation.
- Update your website content as regularly as possible.
- Have a maintenance plan.
- Make an effort to accommodate people with disabilities whenever possible.
- Consider using a database to manage website content.
- Use a scalable web page design that looks good on both small and large computer screens.
- Optimize graphics to achieve the smallest file size possible without degrading the quality of online viewing.
- Provide a means for site visitors to submit feedback using a web page instead of their e-mail application.

Don't

- Don't include a Flash intro to your site. Avoid pages that create layers between site visitors and your home page.
- Don't post a site map of the final website. Site maps are not a remedy for bad organization or a poor navigation system.
- Don't encourage or require site visitors to use a specific web browser for viewing your site.
- Don't use animated images that continuously repeat.
- Don't use browser framesets if it can be avoided.
- Don't allow your IT department to develop nontechnical aspects of your site such as its "look and feel" or visual identity.
- Don't add features to the site that you cannot sustain. For example, avoid adding discussion boards if they are unlikely to be used.
- Don't use Java Applets.
- Don't use image-based text. Download time is greater, and it is not compatible with search engine technology or screen readers used by some site visitors with disabilities.
- Don't require horizontal scrolling.
- Don't use pop-up windows for advertising.
- Don't change the mouse pointer.
- Don't create "under construction" or "coming soon" pages. If the content isn't ready, don't provide a link to it.

The Successful Marketing Plan

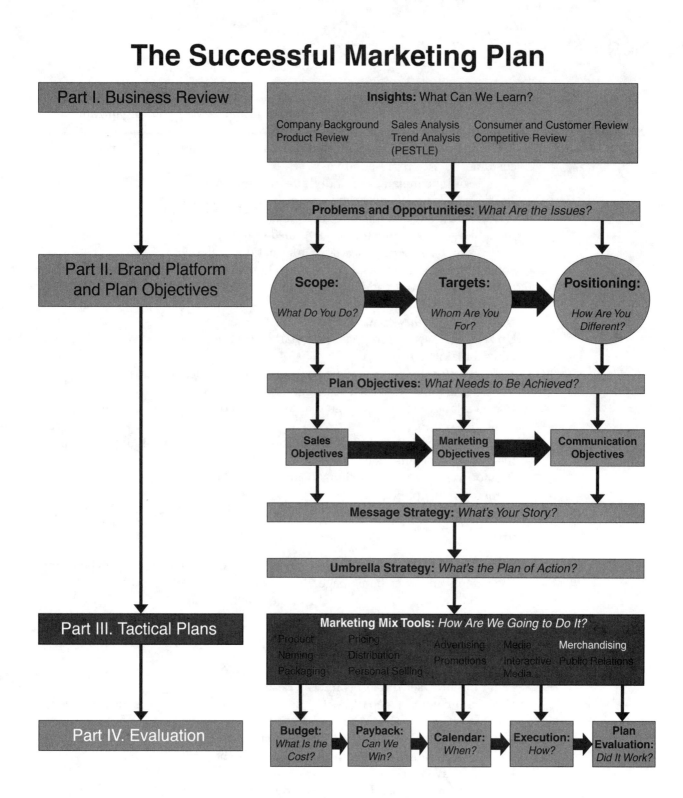

Part I. Business Review

Part II. Brand Platform and Plan Objectives

Part III. Tactical Plans

Part IV. Evaluation

Insights: What Can We Learn?

Company Background   Sales Analysis   Consumer and Customer Review
Product Review   Trend Analysis   Competitive Review
                      (PESTLE)

Problems and Opportunities: *What Are the Issues?*

Scope: *What Do You Do?*

Targets: *Whom Are You For?*

Positioning: *How Are You Different?*

Plan Objectives: *What Needs to Be Achieved?*

Sales Objectives   **Marketing Objectives**   **Communication Objectives**

Message Strategy: *What's Your Story?*

Umbrella Strategy: *What's the Plan of Action?*

Marketing Mix Tools: *How Are We Going to Do It?*

Product   Pricing   Advertising   Media   Merchandising
Naming   Distribution   Promotions   Interactive   Public Relations
Packaging   Personal Selling   Media

Budget: *What Is the Cost?*

Payback: *Can We Win?*

Calendar: *When?*

Execution: *How?*

Plan Evaluation: *Did It Work?*

20 Merchandising

Now that you have developed advertising, promotion, and media and interactive media plans, it is time to focus on how nonmedia communication can enhance the effectiveness of your overall marketing program. Don't overlook the sales generation potential of this very basic, but effective, marketing tool.

Start by reviewing the marketing strategies that apply to merchandising and the related problems and opportunities. Then, when you are developing your merchandising objectives and strategies, remember that your merchandising program can effectively support and complement your broader marketing and communication efforts. Further, remember to develop a merchandising program that will deliver the awareness and attitude levels required to fulfill the merchandising communication value goals, which were discussed in Chapter 9.

Merchandising is a tangible communication link between your product and the consumer. Therefore, you need to make sure that this marketing tool is used in a manner consistent with the product's or service's positioning and that it will complement the other tactical tools.

FROM THIS CHAPTER YOU WILL LEARN

- The definition of *merchandising*
- The issues affecting your merchandising plan
- How to develop your merchandising objectives and strategies

OVERVIEW

We define *merchandising* as the method used to communicate product information, promotions, and special events and to reinforce advertising messages through *nonmedia communication vehicles*. Merchandising is a way to make a visual or written statement about your company through a medium other than paid media with or without one-on-one personal communication. Merchandising includes brochures, sell sheets, product displays, video presentations, banners, posters, shelf talkers, table tents, and any other nonmedia vehicles that can be used to communicate product attributes, positioning, pricing, or promotion information. More and more marketers are using interactive technology, such as interactive kiosks, in their merchandising programs.

ISSUES AFFECTING MERCHANDISING

Issues that need to be addressed when creating merchandising plans are the delivery methods to be used, the geographical reach, the timing of the delivery program, and perhaps most important, the purpose of the merchandising program.

Delivery Methods

Merchandising communication can be delivered through the following methods: personal sales presentations, point-of-purchase (POP) materials, and events.

Personal Sales Presentations

Brochures, sell sheets, catalogs, PowerPoint visual presentations, and other forms of merchandising are often used to enhance a personal sales visit. The material can guide the sales visit, provide visual and factual support for the sales presentation, and serve as a reference that can be left behind for the customer or prospect.

Point-of-Purchase Materials

In many product categories, over two-thirds of the purchase decisions are actually made at the point of purchase. For this reason, merchandising is a useful tool at the point of purchase to help affect purchase decisions that are made in the store. Among other options for point-of-purchase merchandising materials are shelf talkers, table tents in restaurants, product displays, interactive kiosks, and banners. Merchandising at the point of purchase allows the marketer to make an impact on the purchaser above and beyond what can be expected from a product's packaging. Point-of-purchase communication may be in the form of permanent product displays that enhance the presentation of your product or that provide additional information. Point-of-purchase materials may also be of a more temporary nature. Temporary POP display materials can support a special promotion, a new product launch, or a specially discounted sale price.

Merchandising, especially POP, often requires another channel member (most often a retailer) to devote some resources in order for implementation of the program to be a success. These resources may include shelf or floor space and/or labor to set up and stock a display. The question is, How do you sell the merchandising to the channel? Accordingly, it is often necessary to include trade incentives to help ensure successful implementation of the program. These incentives may be in the forms of, for example, special pricing or discounts during the program period, special advertising support, or participation in a sweepstakes.

Events

Merchandising is utilized through special events or company functions where contact with the target market occurs through sales meetings, conventions, mass participation events, concerts, and so on. Banners, product displays, or flyers are commonly used at mass participation events to communicate brand name and product benefits to the target market.

Geography

Your merchandising plan should address where your merchandising programs will be executed. Will they be national, regional, local, or even in selected stores within a market?

Timing

The timing of your merchandising programs is also important. Therefore, the timing of the merchandising execution in relation to the other marketing mix elements must be decided. For example, your plan may require a brochure to be delivered prior to sales visits or after the advertising campaign kickoff. Or you may want a retail store's featured inventory displayed for the duration of an advertising media blitz.

Purpose of the Merchandising Program

Also address what the merchandising is being used to accomplish. You need to describe what marketing tool the merchandising will be assisting. Will you be merchandising product attributes, a new or lower price, a promotion, an advertising message, a personal sell-in presentation, or something else? In summary, you must decide on the communication focus of the merchandising prior to writing this merchandising segment of the marketing plan.

HOW TO DEVELOP A MERCHANDISING PLAN

There are two primary tasks in developing a merchandising plan: establish your objectives, and devise your strategies.

TASK 1 ### Establish Your Merchandising Objectives

Your merchandising objectives should include the following:

- The number of merchandising pieces delivered or displayed at specific target locations
- The geography
- The timing
- The merchandising's purpose: the communication focus of the merchandising program

Examples of merchandising objectives include the following:

Achieve placement of the new product display, which communicates the product's benefits, in 40 percent of the grocery stores carrying the product line nationwide in the month of September.

Obtain placement of price promotional tents from June through August in 50 percent of the current accounts in the top 10 markets.

Display four product banners at each event during the concert series in all markets.

TASK 2   ## Establish Your Merchandising Strategies

Your merchandising strategies should detail how to achieve your objectives in the following areas:

- The delivery and display method that should be used
- The placement of the merchandising elements and the nature of the necessary trade incentives
- The creative parameters for the development of the merchandising materials

Examples of merchandising strategies include the following:

Use the personal sales force to deliver the new product brochure during sales presentations.

Test the effectiveness of coupon use and contest participation via an interactive store kiosk.

Obtain placement of the shelf talkers by offering a competitive discount on each case in return for participation in the shelf talker program.

Incorporate visible brand identification on the shelf talkers, and highlight the rules of the sweepstakes. An entry pad should be included.

Obtain placement of the brand identification banners by the sales force. Employ a weekly monitoring system to ensure that the banners remain in place for the four-week period.

See Appendix C, Worksheet 62, to help you develop your merchandising objectives and strategies.

DOS AND DON'TS

Do

- Review your marketing strategies and your problems and opportunities prior to developing your merchandising plan.
- Think of more than one way to use merchandising. There are multiple uses, and there should be multiple merchandising executions in your plan.
- Tie in existing creative content from advertising, promotion, and publicity to your merchandising. An overall look projects a unified communication effort and allows one marketing mix tool to reinforce the other.
- Find out from the sales force what merchandising is needed to help them increase their selling effectiveness. Then make sure they use it.
- Make sure the merchandising materials sent to the field are properly utilized. All too often, there is a great deal of time and effort put into producing merchandising materials only to have them receive limited attention or not be used at all.
- Make sure the merchandising materials that you develop are designed to fit into the retailers' store and shelf formats.
- Make sure to provide your distributors and retailers with adequate incentive to participate in and effectively execute the merchandising program.

Don't

- Don't ignore the importance of execution and persistence to a successful merchandising program.
- Don't think of merchandising at the last minute. Strategically incorporate this powerful tool into your mix.
- Merchandising materials are expensive. Don't be wasteful; make sure they get used.
- Don't expect your merchandising materials to be readily accepted by the trade. Develop a well-thought-out program that will ensure acceptance.
- Don't overlook the many new ways to communicate via merchandising using interactive media and advanced point-of-sale techniques.

The Successful Marketing Plan

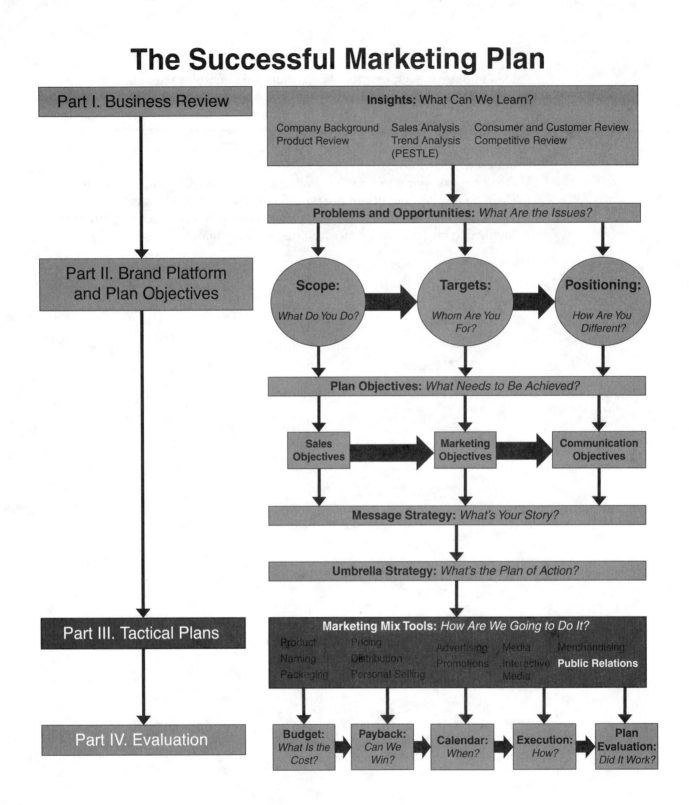

Part I. Business Review

Insights: What Can We Learn?

Company Background   Sales Analysis   Consumer and Customer Review
Product Review   Trend Analysis   Competitive Review
                      (PESTLE)

Problems and Opportunities: *What Are the Issues?*

Part II. Brand Platform and Plan Objectives

Scope: What Do You Do?

Targets: Whom Are You For?

Positioning: How Are You Different?

Plan Objectives: *What Needs to Be Achieved?*

Sales Objectives

Marketing Objectives

Communication Objectives

Message Strategy: *What's Your Story?*

Umbrella Strategy: *What's the Plan of Action?*

Part III. Tactical Plans

Marketing Mix Tools: *How Are We Going to Do It?*

Product   Pricing   Advertising   Media   Merchandising
Naming   Distribution   Promotions   Interactive   **Public Relations**
Packaging   Personal Selling   Media

Part IV. Evaluation

Budget: *What Is the Cost?*

Payback: *Can We Win?*

Calendar: *When?*

Execution: *How?*

Plan Evaluation: *Did It Work?*

21 Public Relations

Public relations is one of the most rapidly growing marketing disciplines. This is due, in large part, to audience fragmentation because of the influx of new media and message delivery options. This growth also is fueled by increasingly better informed consumers who drive an educated, or knowledge-based, sell. Even with this broad expansion of the public relations field, media relations, undertaken with the goal of gaining publicity or unpaid media communications, remains among the most important avenues of communication within public relations. This chapter gives you an overview of the public relations discipline and shows you how to develop a media relations plan as a segment of your overall marketing plan.

FROM THIS CHAPTER YOU WILL LEARN

- The definition of *public relations*
- When using public relations is right for your business
- The advantages and disadvantages of using public relations
- How to develop a media relations program

OVERVIEW

By the standard definition, *public relations* is the process of evaluating public opinion and identifying your organization's policies and practices with the interests of your audiences in mind. Then that analysis is followed by the development and execution of plans that earn public awareness, understanding, acceptance, support, and action.

Often, the practice of public relations is thought of as getting "free" publicity. However, in reality, the key functions of PR are quite in-depth.

- *Anticipating:* Looking ahead and discovering issues that might either positively or negatively affect your company so you can either increase your association with the positive or negate the negative.
- *Counseling:* Reviewing and taking into account the ramifications of company policy and actions on your many publics and audiences.

- *Planning and implementing:* Planning and implementing programs to change and solidify the public opinion of your company across its many audiences (internal, customers, influencers, political, and the general public).
- *Research and evaluation:* Continually researching and evaluating the outcomes of your company's actions to gain insights into your various audiences' opinions and perceptions.

As can be seen from the list above, in practice, public relations is a multistrategy, multitactical means of reaching various external and internal target audiences, called *publics* by practitioners. Public relations enables you to deliver messages that inform, educate, and create or change opinions, attitudes, and actions that have an impact on your objectives. In today's information age, the kind of detailed information delivered through public relations is often required by consumers before they make a decision to purchase. In a Harris Poll National Quorum survey on buying influences conducted by Wirthlin Worldwide (part of Harris Interactive since 2004), 87 percent of respondents agreed with the statement "Before I make a major purchase, I spend a lot of time finding out as much information as I can about which brand is best."

As evidence of just how multifaceted the public relations discipline has become, a list of commonly used tools would include everything from websites, video news releases (VNRs), product and service case studies, newsletters, and institutional ads to speaking engagements and hosting of industry symposia or social events.

For our work on Orkin, public relations was selected as an effective and cost-efficient strategy for building awareness of a new program and reinforcing advanced technology positioning. The company sought to introduce and build credibility for its new Acurid commercial pest control service across five horizontal markets: food service, food retail, food processing, health care, and hospitality. Advertising and direct mail played more limited roles in the marketing mix.

Quantifiable public relations objectives included securing specific numbers of speaking engagements at industry forums and placements in leading trade publications. The image of the commercial pest control industry suffered in these markets, in large part because the market environments imposed inherent obstacles to effective pest control. An even greater challenge was posed by new Acurid technology and practices that the company had not offered in the past, many of which required Orkin to educate the market in order to reach the levels of customer confidence required before prospects would make the decision to contract for the new service. We also needed to educate many targets in these markets, including the media, about the health and sanitation risks of pest infestation.

Orkin allied with leading entomologists, who provided information crucial to the Acurid program and added credibility to the company's endeavors and messages. As part of an industry relations effort, Orkin entomologists and technical staff, armed with electronic presentations customized for individual markets, addressed attendees of major industry trade shows, conferences, and workshops.

A comprehensive pest control reference guide was developed for the media, as were extensive press kits. These tools were combined with an aggressive media relations campaign, which included ongoing media contact, regular mailings, and editor briefings with Orkin entomologists and entomologists affiliated with leading universities. The campaign enabled the agency to exceed all objectives.

Public relations also encompasses internal communications, informing and motivating employees and other internal audiences—the people at the front lines of your organization. Other areas of public relations include investor relations, issues management, crisis communications, and gatekeeper, shareholder, and legislative relations. A broad range of communications tools and channels may be used to reach the many audiences targeted in these areas of practice.

WHEN YOU SHOULD USE PUBLIC RELATIONS

Consider adding public relations to your marketing mix if any of the following situations applies to your business:

- You want to improve all aspects of your brand's reputation and credibility—from building awareness and understanding to changing opinions and increasing loyalty.
- You need to communicate with a variety of internal and/or external audiences.
- Your customers are barraged with selling messages from many communications fronts.
- Your customers, like most today, are becoming better educated, more skeptical about advertising, and more demanding of information to make an informed decision to purchase.
- Your product or service is complex, technical, new, or unique. Under these circumstances, consumers must be educated so they understand your benefits and points of differentiation from your competitors.
- You want to add value to your existing product or service—through information.
- You face current or potential damaging issues or crises that must be managed in order to protect your brand.
- It is important for you to influence the resolution of legislative policy or issues that have an impact on your business.
- You are going to introduce a new product or service.
- You need to educate or motivate internal audiences and other stakeholders.

ADVANTAGES OF USING PUBLIC RELATIONS

Public relations is a vital link between your company and the many audiences who can affect your organization. In that role, public relations often performs the following functions:

- Public relations enables you to access the rapidly increasing number of media channel options, which can be prohibitively costly if you must purchase the media space or time.
- Areas of public relations such as media relations and gatekeeper relations—the establishment of relationships with people whose approval can open the "gate" for your entry into an industry—can significantly boost your brand's awareness and credibility.
- Publicity and involvement with influential trade organizations and industry efforts give you the advantages of implied endorsement by these groups.
- Public relations can advocate for both your company and your audiences. In doing so, it facilitates proactive, ongoing communications, promoting better understanding and cooperation among all parties.
- Public relations tools and communication channels enable you to deliver messages of greater depth and breadth than other marketing media.

- Public relations practitioners can serve as the social conscience of your company and the industries you serve, first identifying social concerns and needs, and then providing the impetus for positive corporate social response.

DISADVANTAGES OF USING PUBLIC RELATIONS

- It takes longer to influence opinion among multiple audiences than to create a single actionable response, or transaction, within a limited target audience.
- Publicity always carries a certain risk because it is not a controlled form of message delivery. No matter how perfectly your publicity message is crafted, ultimately it may be subject to reinterpretation by the media.
- You also can't control when, where, and how often your publicity message will be published or broadcast. In fact, there's no guarantee it will be used.

PUBLIC RELATIONS AS PART OF YOUR MARKETING MIX

In much of our work, we usually provide public relations services in concert with other marketing disciplines. Remember that your advertising should focus on a single target with a single message. Public relations reaches out to all your audiences, often with individually targeted messages of greater length. Combined, these activities give you an integrated communications force that truly is greater than the sum of its parts.

Public Relations Audiences

Because public relations is extremely cost effective compared with many other marketing methods and provides a wide range of communication tools, it is an efficient means of communicating with all of the audiences who purchase or who may purchase your products or services, your brand's stakeholders, and those who influence your customers' decision to purchase. Typically, audiences are identified as *internal* and *external*.

Internal Audiences

Your organization's staff, its field or independent sales representatives, and its investors and shareholders are all part of your internal audience.

Staff

Too often, staff members are overlooked in marketing planning. Since they are the foot soldiers on the front lines of your organization, it's critical that they understand and communicate specific information:

- The basic tenets of your organization, including your mission, objectives, positioning, marketing communications strategies, and message strategies
- Product specifications and benefits
- Company practices and policies
- Your company's culture

In addition to providing messages that staff convey outside your company, public relations tools can help motivate and educate this key audience. When identifying internal audiences, pay particular attention to sales, customer service, marketing, and management personnel.

Field or Independent Sales Representatives

As with your staff, field and independent sales representatives have significant face time with your customers and people who influence them. Reps should possess the same information about your brand, marketing, and products as your staff. Additionally, public relations is a means for communicating company and industry news as well as motivational messages to reps who often can't benefit from your on-site information pipeline.

Investors and Shareholders

Investors and shareholders are designated as internal audiences because since strategies and messages for communicating with this group more closely resemble those developed for internal audiences than those meant for external publics.

External Audiences

Customers and potential customers, members of the media, and influencers and gatekeepers are all part of your external audience.

Customers

It's more cost effective to keep and grow existing business than it is to acquire new customers. Customer communications can help you sell more products, reinforce your expertise and benefits, add value to your products or services, and solidify customer relationships.

Potential Customers

Public relations can help you relate selling messages as well as messages that address your broader marketing communications objectives, including building awareness, understanding, and credibility and changing attitudes that have a direct impact on desired behavior.

Media

Although publicity is a communications channel for reaching consumers and industry influencers, the requirements of media are so specific and specialized that we designate the media as an external audience.

Influencers or Gatekeepers

Influencers or gatekeepers are highly visible people in a specific industry who influence the attitudes or behavior of others. Industry association leaders, academics, and trade publication editors all may be gatekeepers to your industry.

SPECIALIZED AREAS OF PUBLIC RELATIONS

Public relations opportunities can arise in the context of events and promotions, value-adding programs, charitable and educational causes, and issues management and crisis control situations. In addition, opportunities can arise with gatekeepers, organizations within your industry, investors, your organization's surrounding community, not-for-profit organizations, and local, state, and federal government entities.

Event Marketing

A successful event—be it a social event for customers and prospects or a technical symposium, road show, or seminar—builds awareness and leaves a lasting impression of your company. Events are marketing tools to help you meet your marketing objectives, and they reflect your company's positioning and culture.

Gatekeeper Relations

As previously stated, gatekeepers are people who influence your customers or whose approval, or lack of disapproval, is requisite in your industry. Win them over, and they can contribute significantly to your success. For example, members of the small community of university entomologists who work in the livestock field maintain active roles with dairy and beef producers through personal relationships and extension programs. Their influence in the industry is substantial.

As part of the gatekeeper relations program for Orkin Agribusiness, we established personal contact with these entomologists, seeking information from them and often incorporating their suggestions in our program. Each year, we attended the group's annual conference, where we presented our technical data and held meetings with researchers whose work was relevant to Orkin's services. Recognizing that funding and incentives for students to pursue studies in the field were dwindling, we developed the Orkin Livestock Entomology Award for outstanding student research, presenting it at the conference each year. Over time, many of these gatekeepers attended editor briefings with Orkin, and in their writing and presentations, they included information supportive of methods used by Orkin.

Industry Relations

An industry relations program can help you demonstrate expertise, boost credibility, and establish a leadership position in your field and with many people who have an impact on your business—from trade association members, to governing and rule-making bodies, to industry influencers and media. Common industry relations tactics include speaking engagements, serving on boards and committees, and hosting roundtables and other high-visibility events.

Investor Relations

At one time, the primary role of investor relations was to produce annual reports and other basic or required materials. Today investor relations efforts resemble fully developed public relations programs that build visibility and credibility with the many publics that influence investor relations, including shareholders, venture capitalists, and financial analysts.

Community Relations

Too many organizations overlook the importance of maintaining good relationships with the communities in which they have operations and the advantages of good corporate citizenship. Yet it's likely that much of your employee recruitment takes place right in your own community. Furthermore, you'll need the approval of local government, which is highly influenced by public opinion, if you plan expansion or new construction. A thoughtful community relations program will enable you to build important relationships where you live and work.

Government Relations

Few businesses are not affected by public policy. Many organizations have a governmental relations program to favorably influence new policy or policy changes.

Value-Adding Programs

In today's information age, product differentiation can be achieved by adding value in the form of educational support. For instance, in working with Culligan, we developed water quality literature that educated Culligan customers on the risks associated with poor water quality and steps they could take to minimize exposure.

Not-for-Profit Organizations

In many situations, tying in with the right not-for-profit can help promote your product or event and add an emotional connection from the target market to your company, product, or service. Two of the authors successfully helped Coors beer become part of the urban young adult experience through staging a summer series of large mass participation events. One of the cornerstones to these successful promotions was the charity tie-in. The events provided the charities with a significant fund-raising opportunity, which added to the draw of the events. In turn, the charities provided a labor force to help implement the events. Other examples of successful charity brand tie-ins that benefit both the for-profit company and not-for-profit charities include:

- *Famous Footwear and March of Dimes:* Famous Footwear's key target is moms with kids, a natural tie to March of Dimes. The shoe retailer supports in-store programs and the retailer stocks a one-of-a-kind March of Dimes walking shoe that gets big play in the hundreds of walks sponsored each spring by March of Dimes.
- *American Airlines teams up with UNICEF in a coins-for-kids program:* The airline passes a hat at the end of many of its international flights collecting spare coins from travelers who have yet to convert their currencies.

Cause-Related Marketing

A 1999 *Cone/Roper Marketing Trends Report* found that a company's support of a social issue could affect consumers' purchase decisions and that two-thirds of consumers would be likely to switch brands or retailers to one associated with a good cause when price and quality were equal. In a report cited by Sales & Marketing Management (SMM), 83 percent of consumers said they had a more positive image of a company that supported a cause they cared about.

Companies such as General Motors and Levi Strauss have discovered that linking their brands to a cause people care about improves image and sells products. When the Hiebing Group established the Orkin Livestock Entomology Award for outstanding research by a student, gatekeepers bonded with the company in a way that other methods could not achieve.

Issues Management and Crisis Control

Issues management is the practice of preparing your communications response to accidents, emergencies, and other situations that threaten your brand's reputation before an actual incident or potentially damaging media interview occurs. This preparation reduces the risk of someone's issuing a damaging, unprepared response to an emergency and gives you far greater control over the way your message is given—and received.

We've worked with Kalahari Resorts, a large water park and convention center. Because the potential for accidents is great in this kind of facility, we created a plan that anticipates and addresses emergencies at the park, including dedicating spokespeople, suggesting responses to various emergencies, identifying all the audiences who must be addressed, and preparing for responding to media inquiries.

DEVELOPING YOUR MEDIA RELATIONS PROGRAM

Media relations encompass all the activities that contribute to building positive relationships with media, with the goal of generating favorable publicity about your brand. *Publicity* frequently is defined as "nonpaid media communications." Media relations includes media contact—phone calls, editor briefings, informational meetings with editorial boards, media interviews, and written communications via regular mail or e-mail.

In a Wirthlin Worldwide survey on buying influences, 8 out of 10 Americans agreed with the statement "News articles are more believable than advertising." To get positive news articles published about your company, you'll need to establish a strategic media relations program.

Your media relations program should resemble a mini–communications plan, whether it's designed to be a stand-alone program or to be a part of the larger context of your marketing plan. Because public relations addresses many more audiences than may be identified in the target audience section of your overall marketing plan, and because it offers many more message delivery methods, the media relations portion of your marketing plan may very well have its own objectives, strategies, and target audiences, in addition to those outlined in the target market section of your marketing plan.

See Appendix C, Worksheet 63, to help you develop your public relations objectives and strategies.

TASK 1   ## Identify Your Target Audiences

Identify all internal and external audiences you wish to reach via publicity. Review the target section in your overall marketing plan and your list of internal and external audiences to determine your targets. Remember to put media on your public relations target list; they're gatekeepers, and you must meet their needs in order to reach your audience. After listing prospects, customers, and media, think about adding industry influencers, policy makers, and your field staff or sales representatives to the roster. Consider all the people who may be reached via your targeted media who are likely to form a favorable impression of your business by reading or hearing about it in the media.

TASK 2   ## Establish Your Media Relations Objectives

One of your media relations objectives—what you want to achieve—may be to build awareness for a product or technical capability. You may also want to boost your brand's credibility or change a negative perception. Your media relations objectives may be the same as your overall marketing communications objectives, or they may be an addition to your primary plan objectives because of the distinct capabilities of media relations. If these objectives differ, they must be compatible with your other marketing objectives.

Measurable media relations objectives may include gaining a specific number of media placements or speaking engagements at desirable industry forums. Without including quantifiable objectives and other methods of evaluating your public relations program, you'll have only a vague, subjective impression of your effectiveness.

For instance, when the Marcus Corporation sought approval of its bid to build a hotel adjacent to the Frank Lloyd Wright–designed Monona Terrace Community and Convention Center, the objectives were these:

- Narrow the field of five proposals, becoming one of two finalists for the project.
- Gain approval of the bid.
- Gain five favorable placements overall in Madison's three newspapers and two positive television interviews.

TASK 3 ## Develop Your Media Relations Strategies

Like your public relations objectives, your public relations strategies—how you're going to achieve your objectives—may be different, but they must be synergistic with your overall marketing communications objectives. These strategies may be specific to objectives achievable through the use of public relations tactics—the tools you'll use to achieve your objectives. Examples of public relations strategies are the following:

- Establish a leadership position in the industry via an industry relations program.
- Use media relations to build visibility in secondary and tertiary markets.
- Provide instructional materials to educate consumers about complex new technology.

TASK 4 ## Craft Your Key Messages

Unlike the highly refined message you composed for your advertising, in public relations you have the opportunity to deliver several key messages. When the Conseco Finance Corporation needed assistance helping the company rebuild market confidence, we developed the following key messages:

- Conseco Finance is one of America's largest consumer finance companies, with managed finance receivables of nearly $46 billion.
- In just four years, Conseco Finance has gained ranking as the country's fifth issuer of private-label credit cards.
- The company holds leading market positions in retail home equity mortgages, home improvement mortgages, and consumer and floor plan loans for manufactured housing.
- Conseco Finance's mission is to grow market share for its partners through innovative credit marketing programs and to become an integral resource for all customers' financing needs.
- Conseco Finance has a number of key private retail credit card business partners who are leaders in their industries.
- Conseco Finance has Retail Credit Cards, Manufactured Housing, Mortgage Services, and Commercial Lending product groups.

TASK 5   ## *Determine Your Media Relations Tactics*

A wide range of tactics can be used in media relations, and such tactics include the message delivery vehicles you'll use. Following is an overview of options that may be effective in your media relations campaign.

News Releases

Your most basic tool for relaying information to the media, a news release, tells a story that's of interest to audiences of the media outlets you're targeting. A news release may be about a range of topics, including a new product or service, company or industry news, and personnel changes. A cardinal rule of media relations: If your information is not newsworthy, don't waste journalists' time by sending a lightweight release.

A standard format is used for news releases, and most public relations practitioners follow guidelines published in *The Associated Press Stylebook and Libel Manual*. Your adherence to this format will make it easier for the media to use your information, and it will indicate the professionalism of the news release. A sample is shown in Exhibit 21.1.

EXHIBIT 21.1
The Standard News Release

THE **HIEBING** GROUP

FOR RELEASE: Immediately
SOURCE: Renaissance Learning, Inc.
CONTACT: Carolyn Bishop
The Hiebing Group (608) 256-6357

**James Earl Jones to Address Renaissance Learning
School Improvement Conference**

WISCONSIN RAPIDS, Wis.—Celebrated actor, author, and education advocate James Earl Jones will address more than 6,000 educators at the second annual National School Renaissance™ Conference on Wednesday, March 28, in Las Vegas. The three-day event will draw educators from across North America, many of whom are using Renaissance™ methods and technology to achieve comprehensive school improvement.

Known for his rich baritone voice, Jones was mostly mute until the age of 15 because of a stuttering problem. To help control his stutter, he took acting lessons and later studied theater at the University of Michigan. He details his triumph over adversity in his memoir, *James Earl Jones: Voices and Silences*. Jones is a multiple Tony- and Emmy-award winner for his stage and theatrical work. He has appeared in more than 60 films and is

[- More -]

315 WISCONSIN AVENUE. MADISON. WI 53703 **PH. 608. 256. 6357 FX. 608. 256.0693** WWW.HIEBING.COM

MARKETING **ADVERTISING** PUBLIC RELATIONS

[Renaissance Learning, J. E. Jones
Page Two of Two]

the familiar voice of CNN. In addition, he has supported the importance of reading and education with speaking appearances throughout the nation.

The Renaissance Schoolwide comprehensive school improvement process aligns with state and federal funding initiatives such as Title I, the Reading Excellence Act (REA), and 21st Century Community Learning Centers Program. The comprehensive package is designed to accelerate learning and student achievement in reading, math and writing. More than 20 districts across the country have adopted the Renaissance Schoolwide process.

Renaissance Learning, Inc., is a leading provider of comprehensive school improvement, through research-based software products, teacher training, and consulting. The company's software products, called learning information systems, give students and teachers continuous constructive feedback.

This feedback helps motivate students, dramatically accelerate learning, and improve test scores, and it helps students master all standards, while reducing teacher paperwork. Adopted by more than 55,000 schools, these software products are among the most popular in schools nationwide, including Accelerated Reader®, Accelerated Math®, STAR Reading®, STAR Math®, PerfectCopy,™ and others.

Approximately 300,000 pre-K–12 educators have received Renaissance training. The company also provides electronic assessment products and services to educational publishers, and sells enterprise software for training and knowledge management. The company has six U.S. locations and subsidiaries in Australia, Canada, India, and the United Kingdom.

For more information about the National School Renaissance Conference, contact Carolyn Bishop, The Hiebing Group, (608) 256-6357 and cbishop@hiebing.com.

Stick to the facts when writing your news release. The title and *lead*—the first sentence or paragraph—should state clearly and concisely the main message you want to relate. If possible, cover the most important elements of your message in the first paragraph or two. Rushed or inexperienced editors tend to lift a couple of paragraphs and the contact information without using the entire release.

News releases are not the venue for verbose or overtly self-serving copy. Follow the accepted rules of journalism; answer the Five W's: who, what, when, where, and why—and how. Provide detailed and accurate contact information.

Remember too that you're writing a news story, not advertising copy. Minimize the use of superlatives, and avoid blatant commercialism. Use your word processing software's spelling check program, and have another person proofread your news release and review it for accuracy.

News Advisories or Alerts

News advisories normally are used to alert media about breaking news and to announce news conferences and other media events. Although they should, if possible, answer who, what, when, where, and why, detailed information is normally not given. Instead, media are directed to an event and to a contact person for more information.

Case Studies

Case studies are the success stories of your business or product. Because these stories are told about and by your customers, they are often effective as endorsements.

In most instances, comments coming from your customers can be more effusive than any you could tell without sounding as if you're chest pounding. Case studies may be used in a number of ways, including as printed personal selling tools, press kit content, handouts at trade shows and at the points of sale, and placements in print or broadcast media.

If you are providing a written case study to a newspaper or magazine, it should closely match the style of the targeted publication. Let the customer tell as much of the story as possible, preferably through direct quotes. The "plot" normally is written in a problem-solution-results format. Visuals, particularly quality photos that illustrate the story, will enhance the case study and increase the likelihood that the story will be published.

White Papers

White papers and related scholarly papers clearly state a person's—or a company's—stance on a specific topic or issue.

Advertorials

As the name implies, advertorials are hybrids of paid advertising and editorial content. The appearance and copy of an advertorial should closely resemble editorial content of the publication in which it is placed. Like print news releases, advertorials are provided ready for publication. An infomercial is the broadcast version of an advertorial—airtime for infomercials is purchased, and the content more closely resembles a news report. Advertorials are particularly effective when your message is time sensitive and of significant interest as news.

One client of the Hiebing Group, the Wisconsin Health and Hospital Association (WHA), faced a major risk to the reputations of member hospitals when, in 1998, the Department of Justice (DOJ) began sweeping investigations of hospitals across the United States. The DOJ alleged that the institutions had filed fraudulent Medicare claims. Doubtless, there were errors in some instances—hospitals must comply with 17,000 pages of Medicare rules and regulations when filing claims. These rules are so numerous and confusing that Medicare's own enforcement agency interprets them in widely varying ways. One of the most disturbing side effects of this case, though, was the potential damage to the hospitals' credibility in the communities they serve.

Upon learning that investigations would be conducted on several hospitals in the state, the WHA decided to assume a proactive stance, educating the public about the complexities of Medicare rules and the allegations. This education process began with WHA members: the organization provided informational literature and conducted meetings to explain the problem and gain a consensus on how Wisconsin's hospitals would respond. For external publics, we also developed advertorials that hospitals could personalize and place in their local newspapers and a presentation that hospital administrators would make before civic groups. Exhibit 21.2 reproduces one of the advertorials.

By providing communities all the facts of the charges and the details of Medicare's controversial system, the WHA was able to gain control of the issue. As a result, the organization was successful in minimizing negative public exposure and maintaining the good reputations of hospitals across the state.

Broadcast Vehicles

Audio clips or "sound bites" usually will suffice for radio, although contemporary technology has significantly improved the quality of telephone interviews, and these normally are easy to arrange. *B-rolls*—unedited video recordings—are cost

EXHIBIT 21.2

Issue Advertorial

Source: Wisconsin Health & Hospital Association, 1998.

effective and preferred by most television producers. As with your print materials, broadcast communications must be newsworthy, and they will not be used by the media if they're too commercial or self-serving.

Video News Releases

A *video news release* (VNR) is a complete, fully produced videotape. Unlike an infomercial, a VNR is submitted to the broadcast media for consideration, and the airtime is not purchased.

News Conferences

The news conference is the pinnacle of media contact. A news conference is appropriate only if you have information that's timely and of highly compelling news interest.

For instance, it's likely that the Monona Terrace Community and Convention Center in Madison, Wisconsin, will be the last Frank Lloyd Wright building to be constructed. The legendary architect fought, unsuccessfully, for most of his adult life to have Monona Terrace erected near his birthplace and Taliesin. The project had long been highly contentious in Wisconsin and on the larger world stage, commanding international interest.

The Hiebing Group handled communications for the pre- and postconstruction periods and for the grand opening of Monona Terrace. Reporters clamored for exclusive interviews and tours prior to the building's opening. To manage the media and give representatives equal access to interviews and the building site, we held several combined news conferences and hard-hat tours during late stages of construction. City officials addressed the media and guests; hard-hat tours were given by the Taliesin architect supervising the job and an articulate construction executive. During the grand-opening weekend, we staffed a pressroom on site.

The news conferences were well attended and covered widely in the national news. We gave members of the media exhaustive press kits containing the information they would need to write about all aspects of the building, Frank Lloyd Wright's involvement, and the grand-opening festivities. By the end of the grand opening, we'd gained significant coverage in media outlets such as the *New York Times*, the *Wall Street Journal*, *Time* and *Architecture* magazines, CNN, all the major U.S. television networks and news wires, and National Public Radio.

News conferences require meticulous planning. You must consider myriad details, physical as well as interpersonal.

The Location for Your News Conference

Select a site that is relevant to your topic, provides good photographic or video opportunities, and has space as needed to accommodate reporters, camera operators, and other attendees.

Photo Opportunities and Other Visuals

One reason representatives of the media attend news conferences is for photographic and video recording opportunities. Your speakers and site should provide visual appeal for newscasters. Mounted charts, logos, and other relevant graphics may also be used if the site or speakers do not provide good visuals.

Story Support Materials

At your news conference provide written support materials. You don't always need to distribute a complete press kit, but you should give enough information to accurately cover the story—with correct names, titles, dates, and locations.

News Conference Timing and Other Caveats

- You'll not find a time that is equitable to all media organizations, so select a time that will enable reporters from your priority media to file stories for their next edition or news show.
- Holding a news conference? Pray for a slow news day. Breaking news of significant interest can kill even a solid news story.
- As with any news story, if one reporter "scoops" the story—publishes or airs the story before any other media venues—you'll lose most, if not all, additional coverage. Make this clear with everyone involved when arranging your news conference.

Webcasting

News conferences no longer require the attendance of all parties in one location. Technology now enables us to conduct interactive news conferences, "roundtables," and briefings via webcasting.

Take a Leadership Position

Comment regularly by posting to blogs and online publications. Contact the local radio talk show with content and show ideas that could involve you or your business. Send press releases to the media. Write letters to the editor. Think before you send something—is it relevant to a specific audience or am I simply self-promoting? Thought leadership is different from self-promotion—experts get business.

Post Your Event

Use www.meetup.com or traditional "upcoming events" sections in your local newspaper to post your company's events or to look for events in your area that you might want to participate in to gain exposure.

Use Twitter as a Newsroom

Using Twitter is a great way to release information. Utilize www.tweetdeck.com as a way to interface your tweets with Facebook, LinkedIn, and the addresses in your phone address book immediately. However, don't just promote, give back—comment, ask questions, and provide answers.

Meetings with Editorial Boards

If you have a strong position on a major issue in the community, consider scheduling a meeting with the editorial board—the group that determines editorial policy and endorsements—of each of your target publications. Prepare meticulously and provide compelling support for your position. Press kits are appropriate and good—and white papers are even better. And the added participation of a third-party expert who supports your position will add credibility to your visit.

Editor Briefings

Editor briefings are more informal than meetings with editorial boards. Typically, these briefings are attended by one or two editors, and they are conducted in their offices or in meeting rooms you secure at trade shows or conferences. You should have specific goals in mind for briefings: to build awareness for a new product, to present findings from recent research you have conducted or funded, or to gain media placements on topics of importance to your business.

Be certain that the information you plan to share is of interest and value to the media and their audiences; otherwise, don't waste editors' time. Prepare thoroughly, and provide product samples, white papers, research findings, press kits, or other relevant support materials. It is particularly effective to include staff or independent researchers, scientists, or experts in your briefings.

Interviews

Media interviews are an opportunity—and a challenge. Reduce the risk associated with tough media interviews by thoroughly preparing and rehearsing. When possible, disseminate information in advance—or at least provide it at the time of the interview for follow-up coverage. Most public relations practitioners can help you get media training that will enable you to successfully navigate the interview process. There are several fundamental rules to follow if you're interviewed:

- Before the session, consider all questions that could possibly be asked, positive and negative, and prepare and rehearse your response.
- Always tell the truth.
- If you don't know an answer, don't try to bluff or guess the correct response. Explain that you don't know the answer but will get back to the reporter as soon as possible with the information. And do just that.
- Don't overexplain, particularly when responding to tough questions.

Website Media Sections

Create a media section on your website to which the press can refer when writing a piece. Include all the information from your media kit. Consider too providing information that would be of particular use to consumer or business editors, such as industry glossaries, descriptions of technologies and capabilities, and down-loadable visuals.

Dimensional Mailings

Dimensional mailings (nonflat mailings of size, scale, and unusual shapes) may be used to circumvent the mountain of competing news releases received by the media and to gain attention for your press kit or other materials. A dimensional mailing is an excellent creative opportunity; however, its concept and content should never-theless be consistent with your message strategy and appeal to your audience with-out being overly gimmicky. Remember that your primary audience, in this instance, is the media—the link you must win over to gain access to the ultimate target.

Gardetto's is a manufacturer of snack products with national distribution in the retail grocery, food service, convenience store, vending, and mass merchandiser mar-kets. This client sought media coverage, for the company and for three new line exten-sions, in the primary-market trade journals and major-market newspapers. Because the news value of this information was limited, we recommended use of a dimen-sional, one-of-a-kind media mailer, "A Food Writer's Survival Kit," that spoke "to one editor from another," poking gentle, sympathetic fun at the editors' daily dilemmas.

This mailing was exceptionally effective, and we gained placements in nearly all targeted media venues, including offers to develop four feature articles. Editor John Lawn of *Foodservice Distributor* summed up the media response to the mailing: "I've been in this business for a long time, and I've never seen such an entertaining way to introduce a new product. Whoever put this together really knows our business. We will be publishing your information and visuals this fall."

Press Kits

The press kit is your primary tool for providing in-depth information to the media. It typically will contain your news, in the form of a news release, and the support-ing materials a journalist will need to write a more detailed piece about your news or business. Think of the editor working on deadline, often at night when sources are not accessible. In this common scenario, the most comprehensive press kit is likely to command the most focus in the journalist's piece. Press kit contents may include the following elements. These pieces also may be effective when used alone, or with a press release covering a specific news topic.

Contents of Effective Press Kits

Corporate overviews: This document provides a detailed history of your company and the milestones you've reached in the years since the business was founded. Corporate overviews frequently are presented in a chronological format.

Fact sheets: Fact sheets can cover a news topic, product, or company. They serve as easy-to-use and comprehensive sources of details for the media. Fact sheets nor-mally are not written in paragraph form but instead are concise listings of facts from which the journalist may select.

Background pieces: Background pieces provide support for your story. For instance, the Hiebing Group held a news conference to announce a sizable gift of land that a real estate developer, the Blettner Group, was donating to the city of Madison to be used for a light rail corridor. We assembled a press kit for attending media, and we sent the same press kit, via courier, to the media not in attendance. The press kit contained a news release about the gift, a corporate overview on the Blettner Group, slides of the property, and a detailed background piece about the revival of light rail in response to urban land use concerns, pollution, and changes in the way workforces function. Together, these pieces provided the bulk of information required to write a detailed and accurate story on the donation and the potential it held for the community.

Feature-article leads or story starters: Feature-article leads or story starters are one to three brief paragraphs that pique media interest by suggesting strong story concepts and offering assistance in their development. Normally you should provide several feature-article leads in one document, each with a different news angle. Article leads and story starters are effective as part of a media kit and invaluable in editor briefings. It's not unusual for an editor to "select" several story concepts to be used at various times throughout the year, particularly if you've developed them to fulfill information that was covered in the specific editorial or special sections calendar, as discussed later in the chapter.

Interview pieces, especially in Q&A formats: Interview pieces, typically provided in a question-and-answer format, may be used by the media for insight on your company's news, related issues, or plans from senior management when there's no opportunity for an actual interview. Your company president or an industry pundit typically is the subject of the document. Journalists often will use several quotes from the interview piece for their stories.

Visuals: It's easier for the media to get stories than to get visuals to illustrate their pieces. Providing visuals will greatly enhance your ability to land placements and may increase the size of the placements. In most instances, newspapers prefer black-and-white photos, slides, or transparencies; magazines prefer color transparencies. Don't send visuals that have been screened for printing; they can't be used. *USA Today* was a pioneer in making wide use of *infographics*—graphics that illustrate a concept or topic. *Hoard's Dairyman*, the bible of the dairy industry, published a two-part article bylined by the general manager of Orkin Agribusiness. Both issues used infographics and photos we had provided.

Example of an Effective Press Kit

Just weeks before the National Restaurant Association's large annual trade show, we were hired by Baker & Baker, a newly formed processor of baked goods for the food service industry. Baker & Baker's story was complex: the company represented the purchase and partial merging of two well-established brands. The original companies had some overlapping product lines and market segments. They also had other well-established and lucrative product lines that did not compete. The difficult story, and the advantages the merger represented to customers and prospects, had never been clearly explained to the industry; this was our challenge for the restaurant show.

The press kit we prepared helped us meet that challenge:

- A detailed news release explained how Baker & Baker was established and the status of all product lines, distribution processes, plants, and sales staff under the merger.
- Baker & Baker was introducing four new products at this important show, so news releases were provided for each product.
- A fact sheet gave an overview of company management changes, plant capacity, production capabilities, product packaging sizes, distribution, and other details of interest to a trade editor writing a feature article.

- A pocket-size brochure provided a complete listing of Baker & Baker products, with product numbers and carton sizes.
- The Q&A interview piece with new president Paul Baron reassured loyal customers, explained the merger, and detailed the new company's vision, mission, and plans for the future.
- Feature-article leads provided strong ideas for in-depth coverage of the company as well as for articles on topics such as food service trends, product applications, and how to use baked goods to boost business.
- Attached to the releases were color slides of the new products along with cutlines, or captions, on a back sheet. A photo of Paul Baron, with a cutline, was attached to the Q&A piece.
- The press kit was housed in a pocket folder, newly printed to conform to Baker & Baker's new brand identity. Inside the folder the graphics of the letterhead, product brochure, and business cards also sported the new brand identity.

EXECUTING YOUR MEDIA RELATIONS PLAN

There are several aspects to executing your media relations plan successfully: selecting media targets, selecting media databases, identifying publicity opportunities, contracting media mailings, scheduling media relations efforts, following up, and budgeting.

Selecting Media Targets

When selecting media for your media relations campaign, you should first review your targeted audiences. Then you will need to determine which media options will best reach those audiences. If yours is a business-to-business product or service, your efforts in most cases should be directed to trade publications rather than consumer media. If you're marketing packaged goods, you may use trade media to reach the retailers and use consumer media to communicate with the end users of your products. A sample media profile sheet is shown in Exhibit 21.3.

As with paid media readership and viewership, audience profiles will help you determine which media you should target. Consider too the style and caliber of the media outlets and their suitability for your positioning and messages. Don't overlook other means of disseminating your messages such as through websites and industry newsletters.

Selecting Media Databases

Publicity services such as Cision and BurrellesLuce provide electronic media databases that are updated regularly via the Internet. Although not inexpensive, these services are reliable and efficient unless the list of media you wish to target is limited. If that's the case, you can manage your own database.

Identifying Publicity Opportunities

Most publications provide annual editorial calendars of content planned for the coming year or schedules of special sections that cover specific topics. They are

EXHIBIT 21.3

Media Profile Sheet

Detailed Publication Profile

Publication:

Contact information:

Circulation:

Reader demographics:

Frequency of publication:

One-time page rate:

Lead times and/or deadlines:

Written by [staff editors only, contributing editors or freelancers, consultants or vendors]:

How editors prefer to receive information and the mechanical requirements for submissions:

Visuals preferred:

Editors' personal favorite topics:

Sections (description of materials published by section):

Web page or e-zine:

Editorial calendar opportunities:

Additional comments:

Recommendations:

Sample articles:

---

available free of charge from the publications' advertising or editorial staffs. As noted earlier, both are good sources of opportunities for media placements.

There's no substitute for knowing your media targets firsthand and no excuse for communicating with media unless you have reasonable knowledge about their format and content and the type of information they publish or broadcast.

Contracting Media Mailings

In many instances, you'll probably choose to mail your own press materials. If your mailing is large, however, you may want to contract with a media distribution service. Common service providers are PR Newswire, Business Wire, and Video Monitoring Services of America. Each offers distribution to different media and industry segments and a range of distribution methods, including fax and e-mail. State newspaper associations are another inexpensive option if the mailing is within your state.

Scheduling Media Relations Efforts

Timing can make or break your media relations efforts. You'll need to schedule opportunities you've identified in your review of editorial calendars and special sections, compile additional opportunities you'll want to pursue, and determine when you need to pitch them in order to meet deadlines. Don't forget to identify and schedule guides to new products and annual directories; requests for content to be used in these guides almost always come at the last minute, if at all. Take the following variables into consideration when scheduling the release of information or planning press conferences or other media events.

- *Lead times*: Certain publications, newspaper sections, and television and radio shows taped for broadcast at a later date have widely varying lead times. Consumer magazines and trade publications, for instance, have a minimum two-month lead time.
- *Dates*: When planning news conferences or other media events, check city and events calendars for affairs that may conflict with, and overshadow, your efforts.
- *Days of the week*: Weekdays, particularly earlier in the week when news viewership is highest, are the best days to release information or hold a news conference when you want good attendance and coverage. If you're disseminating information about a negative issue that you must address but don't want to receive much coverage, release it on a Friday so the coverage will run over the weekend, when news viewership and readership are lowest before picking up again Sunday evenings. Or release your information at a time when major news is breaking—a technique often used by politicians.
- *Time of day*: It's inevitable that morning and afternoon newspapers will have conflicting deadlines. So too will different broadcast news programs. Consider which print and broadcast outlets are most crucial to reach your target audience, and schedule your release of information at times that enable reporters to complete their stories to meet closing deadlines for their top edition or news show.

Following Up

Public relations practitioners often disagree about following up with the media after providing all the information and assistance needed to complete a story. Many believe follow-up communications about specific placement times and dates are unnecessarily intrusive and fear they may alienate busy editors and reporters. At the Hiebing Group, we gauge all media contact individually and observe the following ground rules:

- Don't call an editor or reporter who is on deadline.
- Avoid unnecessary calls to check the status of a placement.
- Observe the cues you get from the media. If an editor seems harried or annoyed, back off immediately.

Budgeting

Few companies have the luxury of unlimited marketing funds. To focus your planning more realistically, you'll want to start the process with a budget range in mind. That given, you'll not want to entirely stifle the creativity and possibilities that always should be part of planning. After you've determined your tactics, you can develop a firm budget.

MEASURING AND EVALUATING MEDIA RELATIONS

Evaluating your media relations efforts is one way of keeping score on your performance. It tells you where you had wins—and where you just placed. And it shows how you can improve in the future. Nevertheless, accurate, quantified measurement of publicity placements has been called the Holy Grail of public relations. Without precampaign benchmarking and postcampaign research, it's difficult to accurately quantify changes in awareness and attitude.

There are, however, useful practices for evaluating your media relations efforts without primary research. Most practitioners evaluate both *output*, such as articles placed, number of public appearances, or quantities of literature disseminated, and *outcome*, such as changes in awareness, understanding, attitude, and behavior.

Publicity Placements

You'll want to monitor targeted media for placements of your materials. If your media distribution list is limited or your publicity effort is of very short duration, you'll be able to monitor placements yourself. On most other occasions, you'll need to use print and electronic clipping services that specialize in this service. Two of the most common are Cision Information and Burrelles*Luce* Information Services. The form shown in Exhibit 21.4 is useful for tracking your efforts.

Advertising Equivalencies

In advertising, *equivalency* is the value of paid advertising for the same amount of space or broadcast airtime in which an article or interview has been placed via unpaid media relations efforts.

Many practitioners in the industry calculate the value of publicity as three to six times greater than the value of commensurate paid advertising space or time. Although this type of quantification is controversial, research does show that media placements have far greater credibility than do ads because of the media's implied endorsement of a news story or article. As a result, multipliers are widely used when reporting advertising equivalencies and generally are an accepted means of evaluating media relations campaigns.

For example, monitoring of placements after our first 10 months working with Spacesaver, a leading manufacturer of stationary and mobile storage systems, revealed considerable media coverage—more than 40 placements in 26 trade journals and 7 regional newspapers. The advertising equivalency for this coverage was $194,000. If you were to use a multiplier of 3.3, the value of the coverage would be $640,200.

Lead Tracking

Common methods of tracking the number of leads from media placements are a boost in inquiries after an article has been published or an interview has been broadcast and lead inquiries from "bingo" cards following publication in a magazine.

EXHIBIT 21.4

Media Relations Opportunities Checklist

Client: _____ Job no.: _____ Due: _____

Today's Date: _____ Assigned to: _____ Completed: _____

Publication: _____

Contact name: _____

Phone: _____ Fax: _____

E-mail: _____

□ **Image of** _____

Format: □ Slide □ Print □ B&W □ Color □ Digital

Digital specifications: _____

Cutline: _____

_____

Sent by: _____ Via: _____ On: _____

□ **Interview re:** _____

Person to be interviewed: _____

Interview questions requested on: _____ Received on: _____

Forwarded questions to interviewee on: _____

Interview scheduled for: _____

Confirmed with interviewee on: _____

□ **Article or case study re:** _____

Topic: _____

Issue date: _____ Word count: _____

Format: _____ Sent on: _____

Notes and results: _____

_____

Percentage of Coverage Owned

Monitor the number of articles or amount of print space of editorial coverage on topics of relevance to your company. Then compare the percentage of coverage you "own"—because you were interviewed, you placed an article, or your products or technologies are featured—with coverage owned by your competitors.

The Clipping Report

Most public relations practitioners prepare quarterly or biannual clipping reports containing copies or "clips" of articles, a review of what media provided the coverage, when the story ran, the topic of the article or story, media circulation or viewership, and advertising equivalencies.

DOS AND DON'TS

Do

- Be patient about developing relationships with industry editors. It takes time, but the rewards can be great.
- Be available and accessible—on the editor's schedule. Editors almost always work on tight deadlines. If they have trouble reaching you, they may not call you in the future. Become an accommodating and expert resource to the media, and you'll be called more regularly.
- When sending news releases or other information to the media, make sure they are of real news value and not overly commercial.
- Provide thorough and accurate background materials. Today most print and broadcast media operations are run with shoestring staffs and resources. Often the company that provides the best background materials will get the most coverage and subsequent media inquiries.
- Be consistent with your media contact. Establish a continuity schedule of news releases each year, and promptly send out communications regarding every item of real news value, such as notices about company news, installation fact sheets, personnel announcements, and new product releases.
- Tune in to what editors want—and when they want it. Read their publications. Send notes in response to articles you like—or articles on which you have a different point of view.
- Select and prepare primary and backup spokespeople. Determine which people are to address specific topics.
- Assign responsibility for developing and fulfilling a schedule of annual product guide and vendor guide requirements and deadlines.
- Develop a case study form for you and your frontline team that will provide the basic information needed to pitch a case study to an editor.
- Assign responsibility and establish a system for tracking company news and disseminating press materials to the media.

Don't

- Don't pester editors about when your placement is going to run. If an editor is on deadline, back off. Most editors are specific about how and when they want to be contacted. Their wishes should be respected.
- Don't attempt to leverage advertising buys to gain editorial or news coverage.
- Don't attempt to reward the media with gifts or favors. It may work in some instances, but most media organizations find such attempts unethical and offensive.

The Successful Marketing Plan

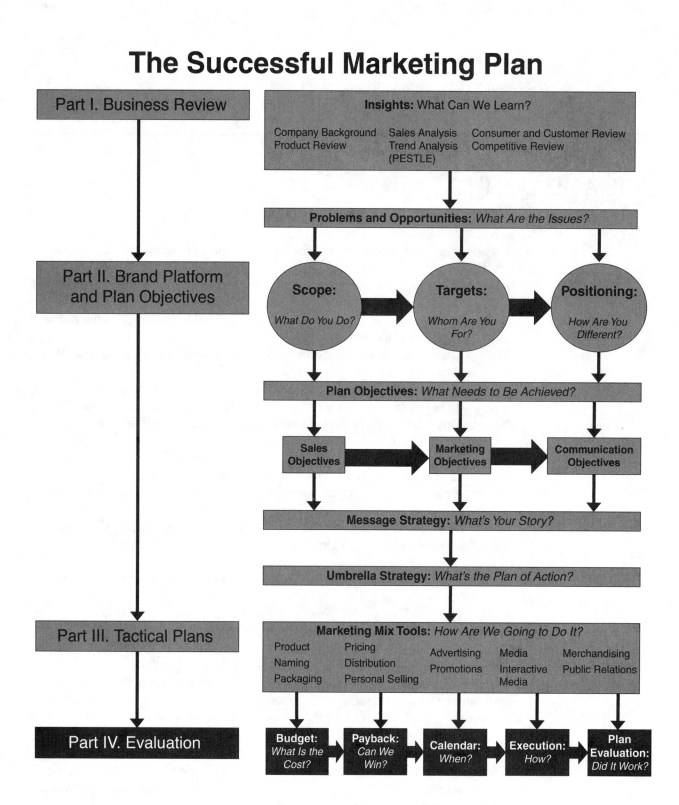

Part I. Business Review

Insights: What Can We Learn?

Company Background   Sales Analysis   Consumer and Customer Review
Product Review   Trend Analysis   Competitive Review
                      (PESTLE)

Problems and Opportunities: *What Are the Issues?*

Part II. Brand Platform and Plan Objectives

Scope: *What Do You Do?*

Targets: *Whom Are You For?*

Positioning: *How Are You Different?*

Plan Objectives: *What Needs to Be Achieved?*

Sales Objectives

Marketing Objectives

Communication Objectives

Message Strategy: *What's Your Story?*

Umbrella Strategy: *What's the Plan of Action?*

Part III. Tactical Plans

Marketing Mix Tools: *How Are We Going to Do It?*

Product   Pricing
Naming   Distribution   Advertising   Media   Merchandising
Packaging   Personal Selling   Promotions   Interactive   Public Relations
                                              Media

Part IV. Evaluation

Budget: *What Is the Cost?*

Payback: *Can We Win?*

Calendar: *When?*

Execution: *How?*

Plan Evaluation: *Did It Work?*

PART

IV

EVALUATION

The following three chapters conclude your work in developing a successful marketing plan. They tie the pieces together financially, provide timing direction, and help you evaluate your plan.

The Successful Marketing Plan

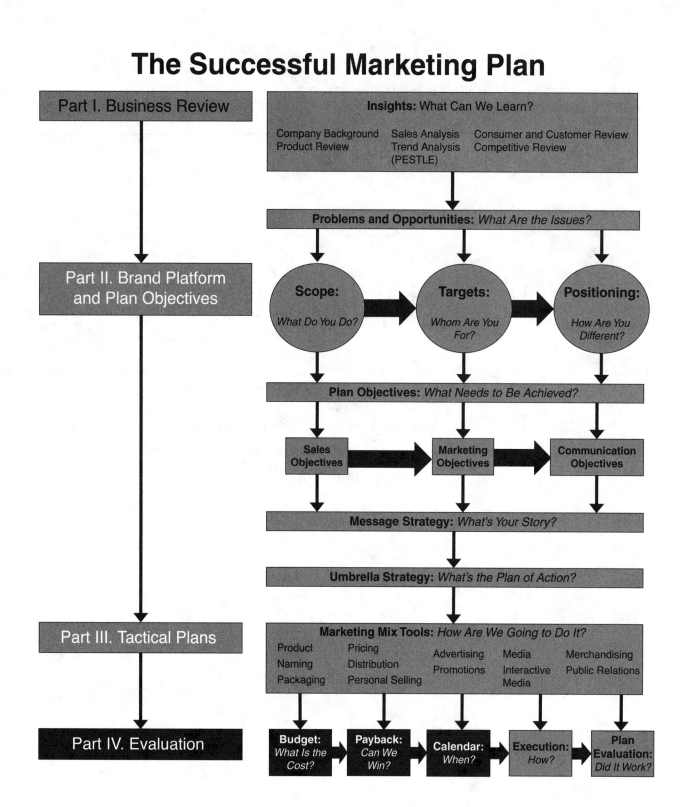

Part I. Business Review

Part II. Brand Platform and Plan Objectives

Part III. Tactical Plans

Part IV. Evaluation

Insights: What Can We Learn?

Company Background   Sales Analysis   Consumer and Customer Review
Product Review   Trend Analysis   Competitive Review
                     (PESTLE)

Problems and Opportunities: *What Are the Issues?*

Scope: What Do You Do?

Targets: Whom Are You For?

Positioning: How Are You Different?

Plan Objectives: *What Needs to Be Achieved?*

Sales Objectives → Marketing Objectives → Communication Objectives

Message Strategy: *What's Your Story?*

Umbrella Strategy: *What's the Plan of Action?*

Marketing Mix Tools: *How Are We Going to Do It?*

Product   Pricing
Naming   Distribution   Advertising   Media   Merchandising
Packaging   Personal Selling   Promotions   Interactive   Public Relations
                                                Media

Budget: *What Is the Cost?* → **Payback:** *Can We Win?* → **Calendar:** *When?* → **Execution:** *How?* → **Plan Evaluation:** *Did It Work?*

22 Budget, Payback, and Calendar

Now that you have completed the objectives and strategies for each tool of your marketing plan, you need to prepare a budget, project a payback from the results of your marketing efforts, and develop a marketing calendar. This process involves three separate steps:

1. Develop a **budget** to provide estimated costs associated with each marketing tool used in the marketing plan.

2. Utilize a **payback analysis** to determine if the results of your marketing plan will generate the required revenues to meet sales and profit goals. If the payback indicates that your plan will not allow you to meet sales and profit goals, you may need to revise your budget and/or your marketing plan objectives, strategies, and executions.

3. Once you have reconciled your budget and payback analysis, you should develop a **marketing calendar** to provide a summary of all marketing activities in one visual presentation.

FROM THIS CHAPTER YOU WILL LEARN

- How to utilize three basic budgeting methods: task, percent of sales, and competitive
- How to develop a payback analysis
- How to develop an integrated marketing calendar for your marketing plan

OVERVIEW

The budget is the cumulative monetary cost of implementing your marketing plan. The payback analysis tells you whether the marketing plan and its specific marketing programs, as well as executions within the plan, will generate the projected revenues in excess of expenses. And the marketing calendar will give you a schedule for the plan's tactical executions.

HOW TO DEVELOP YOUR BUDGET

Based on our experience, it seems there are never enough marketing dollars regardless of which budgeting approach is employed. For this reason, you need to determine priorities for the plan, along with corresponding executional costs for the various marketing activities.

Then, based on the priorities and associated costs, pare back the activities to meet the predetermined budget level, striking a balance between what needs to be accomplished and what you can realistically afford. Ideally, you will be able to develop a budget that is realistic from a total spending standpoint and yet will provide the necessary resources to support a successful marketing plan.

TASK 1 ## Start with the Task Method

We recommend that you begin your budgeting process using the task method as the first step because with this method you set a budget (without bias) based not on what the industry category or key competition is spending but on what needs to be accomplished for your product. This method attempts to develop a budget that will adequately support the marketing mix activity in your plan to achieve the sales and marketing objectives.

To arrive at the total dollars budget, you must estimate the costs for each marketing tool execution involved in the plan. The assumption is that, through a disciplined planning process, challenging yet realistic sales objectives were established, along with a marketing plan to meet those objectives. Thus, the budget will allow the objectives to be met in an efficient manner.

An aggressive marketing plan will result in a more aggressive budget utilizing this method. However, there is no *real* test of affordability or profitability, which is why a *payback analysis* is presented in a later section of this chapter.

TASK 2 ## Then Apply the Percent-of-Sales Method

The second step in developing a budget for your marketing plan is to benchmark your marketing budget total as a percent of total sales. You can review the amount spent on advertising and media, promotions, and total marketing by other firms in your industry as a percent of sales. Usually, an industry standard exists that will provide the average percent of sales that will account for the advertising and media budget, the promotions budget, and sometimes even the total marketing budget.

The major disadvantage with this method is that it creates a situation in which sales determine marketing expenditures. However, the whole idea behind a disciplined campaign development is the belief that marketing affects sales. When sales decline and there are problems to be solved, there is less money available to solve them with the percent-of-sales method.

The percent-of-sales method makes most sense if used as a way to determine whether your task method budget is realistic. Additionally, if your firm has no real history with the effects of marketing and specific tactical tools, then the percent-of-sales method will act as a way to allocate expenditures that should be fairly consistent with industry standards.

You can find the industry advertising-to-sales ratios for the North American Industry Classification System (NAICS) codes and the Standard Industrial

Classification (SIC) codes from reports published by Schonfeld & Associates. *Advertising Age Magazine* also publishes the advertising-to-sales ratios of the top 100 advertisers each year. Additionally, a corporation's or company's annual reports, including the Form 10-K reports that it files with the Securities and Exchange Commission (SEC), are also excellent sources for this information.

TASK 3 ## *Finally, Apply the Competitive Method*

The final method is to estimate the sales and marketing budgets of the leading competitive firms and compare those estimates to your sales and marketing budgets. This method might allow your firm to match or beat specific competitive expenditures, helping to ensure that you remain competitive in the marketplace.

The advantage of this method is that it provides the potential for an immediate response to competitive actions. The disadvantages are that it is difficult to estimate competitors' budgets, and it does not take into consideration the inherent potential of your firm based on data developed from the business review. Utilizing this method alone, you may be restricting the actual potential of your firm based on your competitors' lack of both insight and marketing ability. However, as with the percent-of-sales method, you can use the budget derived from this method as a means of comparison to the task method to arrive at your final budget.

Using a Combination of the Three Methods to Finalize Your Budget

If the data are available, we recommend using a combination of all three steps in finalizing your marketing budget. First, use the task method. This will provide you with a budget that will be your best chance to achieve the stated objectives in your own marketing plan.

As the task method budget is based solely on what is required to provide for the success of your individual marketing plan, the task method is not as biased or as limiting as other methods. Product history and industry averages play lesser roles in the budgeting process. However, if the task method budget varies substantially from the percent-of-sales method budget, you need to review the reasons why your plan requires either substantially more or less spending than the industry average. If, for example, you are introducing a new product, you may be required to spend at greater levels than the industry average to obtain initial trial of the new product and still maintain sales of your existing lines.

Second, use the percent-of-sales method to provide a guideline or rough, ballpark budget figure based on the historical spending of your product and of the marketplace. Used properly, the percent-of-sales budget will help provide insight into whether your task-generated budget is too low or too high based on the experiences of other similar companies in your industry.

Finally, consider using the competitive budgeting method as a device to help you respond to competitive pressures in the marketplace. If your company is consistently spending less than a major competitor and is losing market share while this competitor is gaining market share, then you might want to develop a budget that allows you to be more competitive from a spending standpoint. There is not much any marketer can do, no matter how sophisticated, if continually and dramatically outspent by the competition.

HOW TO DEVELOP YOUR BUDGET FORMAT

When preparing your budget, you should begin with a rationale that outlines what the budget is designed to accomplish. The rationale covers the following:

- Restatement of the sales objectives
- Marketing objectives
- Geography parameters
- Plan time frame

Following the rationale is a breakout of planned expenses by line item under each expense category. The budget line item categories include all applicable marketing mix tools and any other miscellaneous marketing expense items, such as research. The example shown in Exhibit 22.1 can serve as a prototype for your budgeting process. The only difference between this budget and one you may develop is that your budget may have more line item expense categories.

See also Worksheet 64 in Appendix C.

If you are going to be developing new products, there will be a new product development expense category. If you include publicity in your plan, this marketing

EXHIBIT 22.1

Heartland Men's Apparel 2012 Marketing Plan Budget

Rationale

The budget for the fiscal year is designed to accomplish the following:

1. Provide support necessary to meet the aggressive sales goal of increasing store-for-store sales 15 percent over the previous year.
2. Provide support necessary to meet the following systemwide marketing objectives:
   - Increase existing customer purchasing rates from 1.2 to 2 purchases per year.
   - Initiate new trial, increasing the customer base 20 percent above current levels of 5,000 active customers per store.

Marketing Mix Tool (November 5, 2011)	$ Thousands	Percent of Total Budget
Media		
Television (6 markets)	$350.0	31.8%
900 TRPs :30s		
900 TRPs :10s		
Newspaper (12 markets)	202.0	18.3
30 half-page insertions		
Direct mail (12 markets, 24 stores)	120.0	10.9
10,000 per store per drop		
Postage (4 drops per year)		
Media total	$672.0	61.0%
Production		
Television	$100.0	9.1
One :30 and one :10 spots		
Newspaper		
Type, photography, and/or illustration for 30 ads	18.0	1.6
Direct mail	100.0	9.1
4 direct-mail drops, 240,000 pieces per drop		
Photography, type, printing		
Production total	$218.0	19.8%

Promotion

Redemption cost:	$120.0	10.9
Redemption cost of $5 off coupon in 2 of the 4 mailings.		
Estimated response of 5%:		
5% × 480,000 mailings = 24,000		
24,000 × $5 = $120,000		
Media		
Media costs calculated in media section		
Production		
Product costs calculated in production section		
Promotion total	$120.0	10.9%
Internet media	$5.0	0.5
Update website		

Merchandising

Store signage	$25.0	2.2
20 signs per store per month to support planned media promotions and in-store promotions		
Point-of-purchase displays	10.0	0.9
2 POP displays per store to support the April and December promotions		
Merchandising total	$40.0	3.6%

Selling Costs

Sales incentive programs	$20.0	1.8
Sales total	$20.0	1.8%

Research Costs

Market research	$32.0	2.9
Marketwide	$20.0	
In-store	$12.0	
Research total	$32.0	2.9%
Total budget estimate	$1,102.0	100.0%
Total sales estimate	$24,000.0	
Marketing budget as a percent of sales		4.6%

tool will also have a budget line item. Exhibit 22.2 shows how you can compare your budget to that of the previous year, industry average, and the competition. See also Worksheet 65 in Appendix C.

HOW TO ANALYZE YOUR PAYBACK

An important part of any budget is the payback analysis. The payback analysis provides the marketer with a projection of whether the marketing plan or specific marketing programs in the plan will generate revenues in excess of expenses. The payback analysis should review both short-term and long-term projected sales and associated costs to estimate the initial program payback in the first year and the projected payback in the second and third years.

Reconciling Your Budget and Payback Analysis

If the payback analysis determines that the marketing plan dollar investment cannot be justified, it may be necessary to rethink and adjusting the sales objectives

EXHIBIT 22.2

Heartland Men's Apparel Marketing Plan Budget Comparison

Marketing Mix Tool	$ Thousands	Percent of Sales
Total Budget Compared to Industry Average and Previous Year		
Marketing as a percent of sales per plan	$1,102	4.6%
Marketing as a percent of sales per industry average		4.0
Index: Company budget percentage to industry average	115*	
Index: Company budget to previous year ($1,102,000/$1,000,000):	110	
Total Planned Budget Compared to Competition[†]		
Total planned budget for company	1,102	4.6
Total estimated budget Competitor A	2,000	4.5
Total estimated budget Competitor B	1,000	5.5

*In this example, the planned budget would be 15 points above the industry average for marketing as a percent of sales and 10 points above the previous year's plan.

[†]If the data exist, we recommend that this analysis be accomplished on an individual market basis and a national basis. This will help demonstrate localized geographic spending policies of competitors.

and marketing plan objectives, strategies, use of the marketing mix tools, and budget expenditures. After this is accomplished, another payback analysis is needed to determine if the new plan will meet payback expectations.

Developing Your Payback Analysis

We recommend using one of two payback methodologies: the contribution to fixed costs or the gross margin to net sales.

Contribution-to-Fixed-Costs Payback Analysis

Retailers, service organizations, and sometimes manufacturers use a contribution-to-fixed-costs payback analysis method. It focuses on two sets of figures:

1. Sales and revenues
2. All direct marketing costs associated with the sale of the product to the customer

The contribution-to-fixed-costs payback results are determined by first calculating the estimated gross sales and then subtracting the cost of goods sold to derive a gross-profit-on-sales figure. Next, all variable selling expenses directly associated with the sales of the product (selling costs, advertising and media expenditures, and so on) are subtracted from the gross profit figure to provide a contribution-to-fixed-costs figure. This method can be used to analyze an individual marketing program or a whole year's plan.

The contribution-to-fixed-costs method is utilized because it accurately demonstrates the results of the marketing executions. Only the revenues and expenses directly attributed to each marketing effort are used in the analysis. By doing this, the marketer can judge each marketing program on its own merits and on the basis of whether it will contribute to covering the company's fixed costs.

The short-term objective is to make sure that the marketing programs generate enough sales to adequately cover the direct marketing costs necessary to generate the sales. The longer-term objective is to develop programs that cover both direct marketing costs and fixed overhead, resulting in a profit to the firm.

EXHIBIT 22.3

Contribution-to-Fixed-Costs Payback Analysis for a Direct Response Marketing Program

Projected Mailing to 10,000 Customers	ESTIMATED RESPONSE		
	Low 1%	Medium 2.5%	High 5%
Responses	100	250	500
Gross sales ($26 per order)	$ 2,600	$6,500	$13,000
Less refunds (5% of sales)	130	325	650
Less cancellations (2% of sales)	52	130	260
Net sales	2,418	6,045	12,090
Less cost of goods sold (40%)	967	2,418	4,836
Gross profit	1,451	3,627	7,254
Less selling expenses:			
Catalog production mailing (at 20 cents per piece)	2,000	2,000	2,000
List rental	N/A	N/A	N/A
Photography	N/A	N/A	N/A
Type	N/A	N/A	N/A
Boxes, forms, supplies (2% of gross)	52	130	260
Order processing ($3.20 per order)	320	800	1,600
Return postage	N/A	N/A	N/A
Telephone	10	10	10
Credit card (30% credit card sales with 3% charge from store's bank)	23	59	117
Total expenses	$ 2,405	$2,999	$ 3,987
Contribution to fixed costs	$ (954)	$ 628	$ 3,267

Exhibit 22.3 provides a contribution-to-fixed-costs payback example for a start-up, direct mail/direct response program for an existing firm.

See also Worksheet 66 in Appendix C.

There are few limitations to this methodology for most companies. However, the question of capacity needs to be addressed. If, for example, you brew beer and you are at full capacity, you would need to make sure that the revenues from *all of the marketing programs* together cover both the total variable marketing expenses and the total fixed overhead. Unless there is the issue of full capacity, *individual marketing programs* should be judged only on their ability to cover variable expenses and contribute to fixed overhead. The overhead will be there whether the program is executed or not. Thus, *if there is excess capacity*, it is always better to execute an additional program that covers the variable costs associated with the program and contributes some additional revenue toward covering some of the fixed costs.

The payback analysis shown in Exhibit 22.4 is for a retail chain considering the implementation of its yearly marketing plan. The analysis determines whether projected sales will cover marketing expenditures and allow for a contribution to fixed costs and overhead.

See also Worksheet 66 in Appendix C.

Gross-Margin-to-Net-Sales Payback Analysis

For packaged-goods marketers, payback calculations are sometimes analyzed slightly differently than for retailers. The *gross margin* is often defined as covering advertising, promotions, and profit, and it is referred to as the *gross margin to net*

EXHIBIT 22.4

Contribution-to-Fixed-Costs Payback Analysis for a Retail Marketing Plan

Assumption

The plan will result in a 10 percent store-for-store increase in sales over last year. Cost of goods sold will average 50 percent throughout the year.

9 Stores	$ Thousands	$ Thousands
Sales	$7,920.0	
Less cost of goods sold	3,960.0	
Gross profit		$3,960.0
Less variable costs		
Media	$ 316.8	
Production costs	31.7	
Promotion costs	50.0	
Internet media	10.0	
Merchandising	20.0	
Selling	25.0	
Research	20.0	
Public relations and miscellaneous	5.0	
Total marketing mix tools		478.5
Contribution to fixed costs		$3,481.5
Fixed costs		3,081.5
Profit before taxes		$ 400.0

sales figure or, sometimes, as the *advertising, promotion, and profit* (AP&P) *figure*. For example, if there is a 40 percent gross margin, 40 percent of all sales would cover advertising and promotion costs (consumer and trade) and provide the profit. Furthermore, 60 percent of the sales would cover all allocated fixed costs (plant, equipment, and so on), as well as the variable selling costs (selling costs, salaries, raw material needed to produce the product, and so on).

The example shown in Exhibit 22.5 utilizes the gross-margin-to-net-sales payback methodology. We are assuming a 40 percent margin on a new product. The payback analysis is projected for three years in order to determine both the short-term and

EXHIBIT 22.5

Gross-Margin-to-Net-Sales Payback Analysis for a New Packaged-Goods Product

Assumptions

1. $100 million product category, with growth rate of 10 percent per year
2. Three competing brands in the category and miscellaneous private labels
3. Introduction of new product at an expected margin of 40 percent

	Year 1 Projections	Year 2 Projections	Year 3 Projections
Net sales	$10.0 million	$12.0 million	$13.0 million
Gross margin (40%)	4.0	4.8	5.2
Less promotion	3.0	2.5	1.5
Less advertising	2.0	1.5	1.5
Profit or (loss)	(1.0)	0.8	2.2

the longer-term profitability for the new product. In this example the product is projected to pay back sometime early in Year 3.

See also Worksheet 67 in Appendix C.

Using Your Finance Department for Help

If you are using the contribution method, you should review your financial operating statements to determine the amount needed to cover fixed costs. Or your finance department can provide you with further details specific to your company, which will allow you to arrive at the sales needed to cover fixed costs and provide a profit for your company.

Furthermore, if you are using the gross-margin-to-net-sales method, your finance department should be able to again provide you with an accurate margin figure as defined in this chapter.

HOW TO DEVELOP YOUR MARKETING CALENDAR

After the marketing plan budget and payback have been completed, it is time to summarize the plan on a single page. (See Exhibit 22.6.) This summary should be in the form of a marketing calendar. When completed, the marketing calendar will serve as a visual summary of the marketing plan for the specific designated period or, more likely, for the coming year.

A marketing calendar should contain the following elements:

- Headings, including product, service, and store name; time period; date prepared; and a geographic reference (national, regional, group of markets, or tier) or individual market name
- A visual summary of the marketing program week by week, outlining all marketing tool executions and including all other marketing-related activities such as research
- A visual summary of media weight levels by week
- A separate marketing calendar for markets with substantial geographic differences and for test markets

Exhibit 22.6 provides a prototype for you to follow when developing your own marketing calendar. A retail chain plan is used for the example.

A blank calendar is provided in Worksheet 68 in Appendix C.

DOS AND DON'TS

Do

- Develop marketing budgets utilizing the task, percent-of-sales, and competitive budgeting methods.
- Be prepared to change your budgets and/or your marketing plan after the payback analysis is completed if you are over your predetermined budget or if you determine that your plan is not paying back at the expected rate.
- Visually show your entire year's marketing plan activities on a single page in calendar form. Always note the date when the marketing calendar was prepared.

EXHIBIT 22.6

2012 National Marketing Calendar

(December 1, 2011)

Media	January 29 5 12 19 26	February 2 9 16 23	March 1 8 15 22 29	April 5 12 19	May 3 10 17 24	June 31 7 14 21 28	July 5 12 19 26	August 2 9 16 23	September 30 6 13 20	October 27 4 11 18 25	November 1 8 15 22	December 29 6 13 20
MARKETING PROGRAMS												
Ongoing price/item												
Major promotions	Clearance Sale		Half-Price Sale				Clearance Sale			Anniversary Sale	Thanksgiving	Holiday
MEDIA SUPPORT												
Television (50% :10s/50% :30s) 12 weeks of 200 GRPs												
Newspapers—half-page ads 18 insertions												
Newspapers—half-page ads 18 insertions												
Direct mail—4 mailings 10,000 per store per mailing												
NONMEDIA ACTIVITIES												
Point-of-purchase displays												
In-store signage												
In-store seminars												
In-store-only price promotions												
In-store volume discounts												
OTHER												
Research (market and in-store)			Market						In-Store			

Monday (Bdcst) Dates

Source: Copyright (c) 2002 by Telmar Information Services.

508

Don't

- Don't substantially reduce your budget without rethinking your sales objectives and marketing activities.
- Don't prepare a payback analysis such that it gives you the results for which you were looking. If your plan will not generate sufficient sales to cover expenses, change your plan.
- Don't forget to continually update your marketing budget and calendar whenever you make changes in your marketing plan.

The Successful Marketing Plan

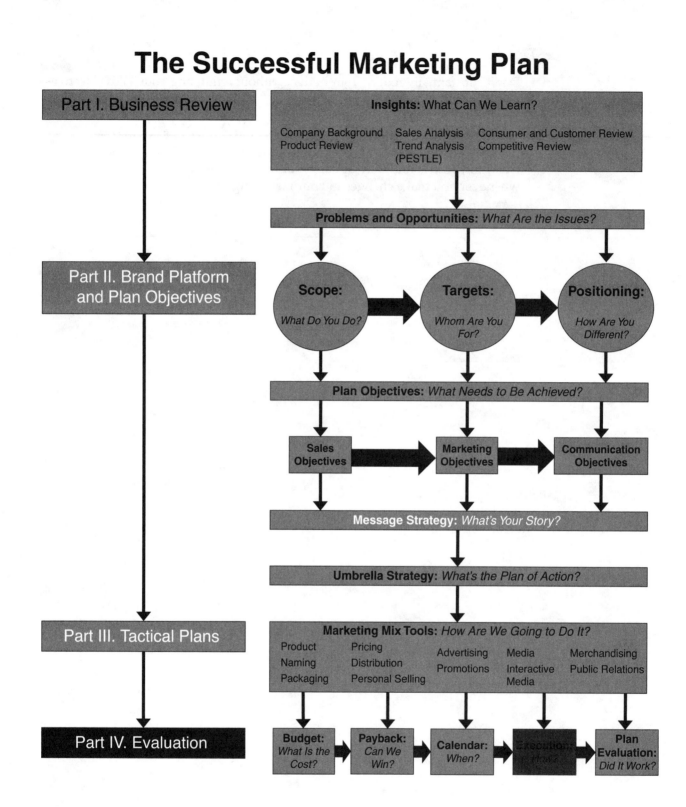

Part I. Business Review

Part II. Brand Platform and Plan Objectives

Part III. Tactical Plans

Part IV. Evaluation

Insights: What Can We Learn?

Company Background   Sales Analysis   Consumer and Customer Review
Product Review   Trend Analysis   Competitive Review
              (PESTLE)

Problems and Opportunities: *What Are the Issues?*

Scope: What Do You Do?

Targets: Whom Are You For?

Positioning: How Are You Different?

Plan Objectives: What Needs to Be Achieved?

Sales Objectives

Marketing Objectives

Communication Objectives

Message Strategy: *What's Your Story?*

Umbrella Strategy: *What's the Plan of Action?*

Marketing Mix Tools: *How Are We Going to Do It?*

Product   Pricing   Advertising   Media   Merchandising
Naming   Distribution   Promotions   Interactive   Public Relations
Packaging   Personal Selling   Media

Budget: What Is the Cost?

Payback: Can We Win?

Calendar: When?

Execution: How?

Plan Evaluation: Did It Work?

CHAPTER 23 Execution

Y*ou've completed your marketing plan. It's been reviewed and approved, and the budget is authorized. What may have seemed like a daunting task has been successfully completed. But the plan is only half of the equation; thorough execution is the other half. Remember:*

Disciplined marketing plan + thorough execution = successful marketing

FROM THIS CHAPTER YOU WILL LEARN

- What thorough execution encompasses and why it is important
- Key steps to successful execution

OVERVIEW

Webster's defines *execute* as "to carry out *fully*; to put *completely* into effect" (italics added).* By its very definition, *execution* implies comprehensiveness and thoroughness—attention to details. The genius of successful marketing plan execution is in those details.

A truly integrated marketing plan is greater than the sum of its parts, as the effect of each element is enhanced by the impact of the other elements. Salespeople have a greater chance of success calling on prospects who have already heard of their company through advertising because part of the selling has already begun— awareness has already started to build. It is attention to detail in every aspect of implementation that helps ensure that the synergistic effect of all the marketing plan activities will take place.

Thorough execution is critical to your success. A marketing plan, unless and until it is effectively executed, is nothing but a comprehensive list of good intentions. All of the work and resources that went into the business review, identification of problems and opportunities, and development of the plan itself are a substantial investment. The return on that investment and an accurate evaluation of the plan's activities for use in future planning can be realized only if you follow through with thorough execution of all the plan elements. A very good promotional idea may not give very good results not because the idea was bad but because the execution was poor. Unless you've given each marketing plan activity the best

---

* "Execute." *Webster's Third New International Dictionary, Unabridged,* Merriam-Webster, 2002, http://unabridged.merriam-webster.com (accessed May 1, 2011).

opportunity to work through careful execution, you won't be able to accurately evaluate it. If you can't evaluate your marketing activities, they are of little use in planning for the following year.

Most important of all, successful execution is the key to maximizing the dollars allocated to each of the marketing mix tools, with the ultimate goal of positively impacting sales and profits. For example, a well-targeted direct-mail campaign does the job of generating qualified leads. If these leads are not followed up on in a timely manner through personal selling, the dollars and effort of that campaign have been essentially wasted. Worse yet, prospect expectations have not been fulfilled, so a negative impression has been created.

Successful marketing plan execution generally requires the coordination of many people and resources. Participation and support will be required of many areas both within and outside the company. Ongoing follow-up with all participants is essential to ensure the following:

1. The people involved understand their role and the importance of their contribution to the overall marketing effort.
2. They have what they need to do their part in "making things happen."
3. They are actually doing what needs to be done.
4. They receive feedback on the results of their activities, as well as the overall marketing effort.

Without diligent follow-up and ongoing communication, execution will fall short and marketing objectives will be compromised. Moreover, these people will be far less enthusiastic the next time they are asked to participate. Like the effect on prospects, a negative impression may be created.

KEY STEPS TO SUCCESSFUL EXECUTION

There are three key steps in achieving the successful execution of a marketing plan:

Step 1. Review and understand all elements of the plan.
Step 2. Develop activity lists for the first six months.
Step 3. Communicate the plan.
- Gain the cooperation of key company staff.
- Gain the cooperation of company staff overall.
- Communicate the plan to the distribution channels.

STEP 1   ## *Review and Understand All Elements of the Plan*

No doubt some time will pass between submission of the marketing plan document for review and approval and the point at which you receive the go-ahead and budget authorization. No matter what this interval is, you should review the plan to be sure the needed components are in place.

1. Adequate Support Resources

Have adequate resources in place and committed to carrying out each plan activity. Allocation of supporting resources will have been addressed in the planning and budget approval process. In the planning process, you will have asked for—and hopefully received—input from appropriate personnel, both within and outside the company. Issues brought up by these key players—problems to be solved and opportunities to be taken advantage of—will have been addressed in the plan. Key participant involvement helps to make the plan their own and make them more committed and enthusiastic.

So as execution begins, the marketing plan activities are not a surprise; rather, they are confirmation of specific tactics designed to respond to the input received. This check is to ensure that those commitments have not been changed and that your need for them remains a high enough priority to accomplish the objectives within the timeframe called for by the plan.

For example, if the communications program will require establishing or updating a customer database, is your management information systems (MIS) department adequately staffed and scheduled to provide this service? If not, other resources will have to be used. If telemarketing is to be a major component, will assignments need to be changed, or should more staff be added?

2. Adequate Lead Time

Understand the lead time necessary for everyone who needs to participate in each executional element. Generally, more time is better. However, beware of the danger (rare though it is) of too much lead time for a project because it can allow other, more pressing assignments to interfere. Also, maintaining energy and enthusiasm for the work over an extended period of time can be difficult and may lead to inefficiencies and "restarts."

A good guideline is that you should always begin working *at least* three to six months in advance of the date on which a program or tactical project must be implemented. You will need a six-month lead time (or more) for major executional programs and communication campaigns. And the three- or six-month lead time needs to take into account the time necessary to presell and inform all those who need to participate. A promotion developed for consumers that will be executed by the trade target market or a dealer network needs to be developed in time to allow communication to the dealers, giving them time to plan and stock accordingly.

3. Adequate Human Resources

Understand completely and in detail what individual departments, vendors, and others need in order to execute the elements of the plan for which they are responsible and the time they will require. As you review each activity, if you can't answer the executional needs and time requirements with certainty, you must address them immediately. Even if you're confident about the processes and timetables, you will want to confirm these when you communicate with those involved.

STEP 2 ## *Develop Activity Lists for the First Six Months*

Begin with a summary list of all the major activities covered during the first six months of the marketing plan. You will already have prepared an annual marketing calendar showing these activities. A format like the following can be used to begin to provide more detail.

For each of the major activities, develop a detailed list of all the tasks that need to be completed to accomplish the given activity, along with due dates. Update this list on a monthly basis so that it always covers at least six months (or longer as projects dictate).

Always operate against specific due dates. Just as nothing gets under way until you actually start the activities, call the first meeting, or detail the parameters of each activity, nothing will be finished unless specific due dates are set, communicated, and agreed to by everyone involved. Without a specific date for a marketing activity, it can easily be postponed by any other task that the individual responsible for that activity has to do.

Setting specific due dates also provides momentum and a sense of urgency. Breaking down each major activity into its various segments and assigning due dates offers two important advantages. You not only help ensure that all the necessary details are covered but you also are breaking down into manageable pieces activities that, if taken as a whole, could seem overwhelming.

Segmenting in this way also forces you to think through the project in a step-by-step, detailed manner. Also, meeting a number of interim dates provides a sense of accomplishment for those involved.

Once these activity lists are completed, you have the structure and outline for the next steps: communication with all those involved.

STEP 3 ## Communicate the Plan

Just as you have consumer and end user target audiences with which you ultimately need to communicate, you also have a number of important internal and external target groups that you must communicate with in order to execute the marketing plan. Many of the same considerations—message content, tone, communication vehicle, and frequency—that you will give to developing communications for end users should be given to the communications with each of these groups. Your audiences for these communications fall into three general groups: key individuals within your organization (company), the company staff overall, and those within the distribution channels (noncompany).

Gain the Cooperation of Key Company Staff

To implement the marketing plan, you will need the cooperation of various departments throughout your company, including field sales, telemarketing, and MIS groups. Key personnel will include home office as well as field staff.

Ideally, you would have an initial personal meeting with key individuals, and subsequently with their staff members as needed, to review the activities with which you need their help and involvement and that they have the authority to accomplish. The activity lists described in the previous section give you the basis for these discussions. In each case it's important to present the key plan elements and then relate how the specific area is important and integral to the effective execution of these elements. For example, in the discussion with the MIS staff, details of the advertising are not critical, but how the advertising is expected to generate information for a prospect database is.

The goal is to have key staff members gain understanding of what needs to be done, why it needs to be done, when it needs to be done, and how each area's contribution is important to the overall marketing effort. These meetings also give you an opportunity to confirm what information each area will require and how much time is necessary to complete the tasks being discussed. It's essential that these communications be clear, specific, and concise and that all parties understand and agree to what is expected of them and when.

Gain the Cooperation of Company Staff Overall

Everyone within an organization, either directly or indirectly, impacts the company's marketing efforts because everyone contributes in some way to delivering the products or services being marketed. So the staff as a whole must understand what the overall marketing program is, what their role is in its execution, and why it is important. There are a variety of ways to communicate with staff, and the best choice will often depend on the size of your organization. Personal meetings with each department, group meetings, company newsletters, and bulletin boards are all methods that can be used effectively to gain interest and enthusiasm for the plan. The goal is to provide an overview of the marketing plan in easily understood terms and gain commitment from each staff member to do his or her part according to the timeline and guidelines developed.

Gain the Cooperation of the Distribution Channels

Noncompany staff, such as wholesalers, dealers, brokers, franchisees, and retail trade, is the other group that must be included in marketing plan communications. Without commitment from these channels to participate in the marketing program through carrying product, promoting produce in the store, and so on, effective marketing execution isn't possible.

These individuals, because they are not part of your company, need to be convinced that what you're asking them to do will enhance their business and will do so better than your competition—and certainly better than doing nothing at all. Communications with this group need to focus on the contribution your product or service will make to the profitability of their enterprise. Presentations at dealer and franchisee meetings, either regional or national, provide good opportunities to address these groups. Written and, possibly, phone follow-up will be required for those who do not attend such meetings and will serve as reminders to those who do. Dealer and trade newsletters provide other vehicles for these communications. Telemarketing, customer service phone support, and e-mail are other direct methods for communicating with these groups.

Clearly, commitment to carry and promote your product, participate in a given promotion, and so on, carries with it the obligation on your part to deliver product and promotional materials, as well as other services like field support, when promised and as needed.

ONGOING FOLLOW-UP

A disciplined system of regular, ongoing follow-up is necessary to ensure successful implementation of the marketing plan. Again, going back to the activity lists, you have determined specific due dates for all personnel involved in implementation. In addition, you need to determine interim dates at which you will follow up with each area to be sure progress is being made, obtain specific data on that progress, help to solve problems that have developed or take advantage of opportunities, and gain assurance that the projects are being given the priority needed. This needs to be done early and often enough in the timeline to allow for remedial action if needed. You can never assume that, if you hear nothing, everything is going as planned. Odds are, it isn't going at all.

In addition to following up, you must communicate results of the marketing efforts to the groups. This allows you to show your appreciation for their help and contribution and to build cooperation in the future.

Stay Committed to the Plan

Resist the temptation to make decisions and do things without regard to the plan. The plan must be looked on and embraced as a *working document*, guiding all of the marketing decisions you make during the period of the plan. If opportunities or ideas are brought up throughout the year (and they will be), they should be evaluated based on the plan that's being executed, which was designed to achieve very specific objectives.

A staff member brings up a media opportunity based on a "good deal" on the media cost. This "opportunity" must be evaluated against the target audience identified in the plan. Is it a valid plan supplement? Is it needed? Where will the money come from? If additional funds aren't available, what won't get done as a result of doing this? Go back to the plan.

The plan may already have tests built into it and, very possibly, dollars budgeted for contingencies or opportunities throughout the year, but even these dollars should be used only after consideration of the goals of the plan.

Focus is the key to keeping resources and attention committed to the task at hand—achieving the objectives detailed in the marketing plan. Review the plan and, particularly, the positioning frequently.

Maintain Top Management Support

If you have completed a thorough, comprehensive marketing plan, odds are you did so by providing strong, ongoing leadership and the driving energy to complete the task. And you had the support of your organization's leadership. Top executive involvement, support, and visibility are equally essential in the implementation of the plan. All those involved, both inside and outside the organization, need to know and understand that the marketing plan, and therefore its implementation, is a critical, integral part of the management of the organization. It is not something imposed on the organization but, rather, something developed out of the need to more effectively and efficiently operate and grow the business by those ultimately responsible for the success of the enterprise.

Top management's support and sponsorship need to be visible when the implementation is kicked off and throughout the year in the form of regular reports on status and evaluation of efforts. As discussed, implementation requires efforts and contributions from a number of different departments throughout a company. Management's involvement and active endorsement help ensure that the cooperation and support needed from the other areas will be provided in a timely and effective manner. Without this leadership support, successful execution will be very difficult, if not impossible.

DOS AND DON'TS

Do

- Be sure you have adequate, committed resources in place to carry out each plan activity.
- Be sure you understand the lead time necessary for everyone who needs to participate in each executional element.
- Be sure you understand completely and in detail what individual departments, vendors, and others need to do and what information and lead time they will require in order to execute the elements of the plan for which they are responsible.
- Develop a list of major activities for each six-month period of the plan, including the individuals responsible for each activity and the due date.
- Break down each major activity into the essential steps necessary to accomplish it. And identify the individuals responsible for the activities and the due dates.

- Communicate plan elements with key company personnel, detailing responsibilities and due dates.
- Gain commitment from company staff and noncompany distribution channels to execute the marketing plan.
- Consider message content, tone, communication vehicle, and frequency when developing communications about the marketing plan to internal and external participants.
- Follow up with status reports and the results of marketing plan activities with all of those responsible for execution.
- Review the marketing plan and the positioning frequently to stay focused on the objectives and means of accomplishing them.
- Enlist top management's endorsement of the marketing plan throughout its execution.
- Initiate every element of the plan. Nothing will happen until you make it happen.
- Always operate against specific due dates.

Don't

- Don't consider any executional detail too small. Make sure it's being taken care of.
- Don't accept that activities are going according to plan unless you have specific, concrete information to show that they are.
- Don't use the same communications regarding the marketing plan to audiences with different roles and different levels of marketing expertise.
- Don't communicate just once with those individuals enlisted to execute the marketing plan.
- Don't allow the calendar to slip away from you. Once major components of the plan are delayed, the entire system can unravel, which will negate the cumulative effect of the plan elements.
- Don't neglect internal support of external communication efforts. For example, preparations must be made for the sales and inquiry activity generated by advertising and other efforts.
- Don't ever *assume* that the plan is being implemented without personally checking on it.

The Successful Marketing Plan

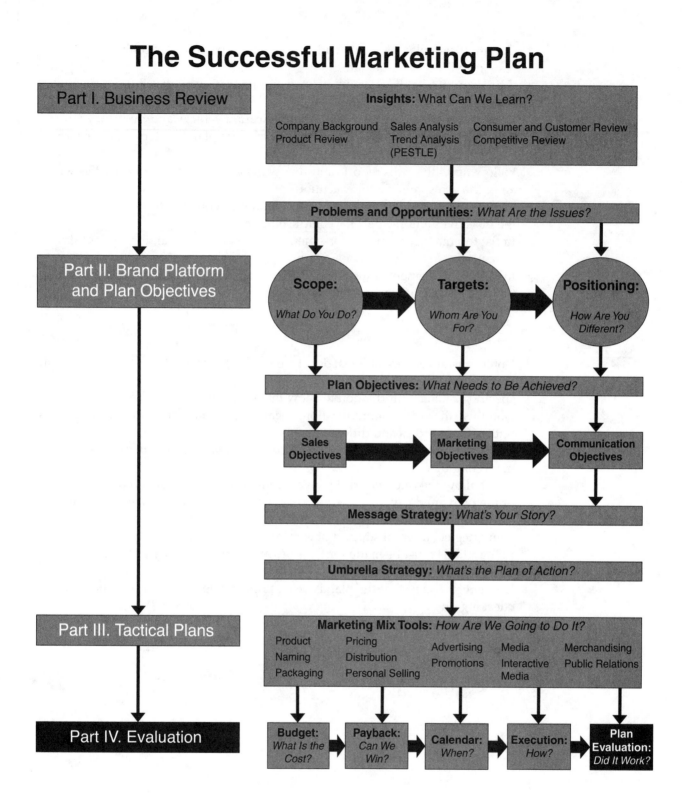

24 Plan Evaluation

After completing your marketing plan, you need to evaluate the results. To do so, you should establish an evaluation methodology with which to assess the success of the marketing plan itself and to ensure the ongoing evaluation of the marketing plan executions. In addition to providing a database from which to make strategic decisions for next year's plan, this information also provides invaluable feedback from which to make modifications during the execution of this year's plan.

FROM THIS CHAPTER YOU WILL LEARN

- How to evaluate the effectiveness of the marketing plan
- How to evaluate your marketing plan executions using two alternative methods: sales trend comparison and pre- and post-execution research

OVERVIEW

Upon completion of a year-long plan and specific marketing activities through the year, such as an individual advertising campaign, a promotion, a pricing change, or the use of a new media vehicle, there should be an evaluation of the results.

EVALUATION PERSPECTIVE 1. THE MARKETING PLAN AND ITS COMPONENTS

On an overall plan basis, you can determine the success of your plan by evaluating the following:

Sales and profit objectives
Marketing objectives
Marketing plan communication awareness and attitude goals

Sales and profit data should be readily available for evaluation. You should also have measurable target market behavior information to evaluate marketing objectives, such as customer retention, new customer trial, store visits, dollars per transaction, and so on. Survey research is required to evaluate target market awareness and attitude for the communication goals.

On a specific, *tactical tool* basis, you can evaluate the success of each tactical tool in fulfilling its function within the marketing mix. You should be able to accurately measure each tactical tool's performance because each tactical segment in your plan has an objective against which you can measure the tool's performance. An example of a measurable publicity objective would be "Achieve placement of one feature article in one of the two leading trade magazines."

In addition, although difficult, you should attempt to measure (most likely through interpolation) in a directional manner whether each tool has fulfilled its individual awareness and attitude communication goals. In order to make this tactical tool evaluation, it's important that you diligently collect the pertinent performance data for each tool. The tendency is to get caught up in the day-to-day fires of plan execution and ignore the plan evaluation. Subsequently, it will be difficult to plan for next year because you don't have the necessary data. It's therefore critical that you evaluate the effectiveness of each tool. While you can evaluate the overall plan's success to tell you "how well you did," the tool evaluation will help tell the "why" in terms of what generated the bulk of the success or caused the plan not to achieve the predetermined sales and profits.

EVALUATION PERSPECTIVE 2. SALES TREND COMPARISON

While the previous evaluation was *plan* based, this sales evaluation method compares current sales with the previous year's sales *prior to*, *during*, and *after* any given marketing execution. Sales are analyzed prior to the promotion period to determine if there was a downward, upward, or flat sales trend as compared to the previous year's sales. Sales are also compared to last year's both during and after the execution period.

In analyzing the preperiod, the execution period, and the postperiod separately, you will gain added insight into the effect of the individual test or marketing execution. Sales might have been trending down prior to the marketing execution. Even a small increase during the marketing execution period would mean that the marketing execution might have helped reverse a negative trend. Then, in analyzing sales after the marketing execution period, you can begin to determine if the marketing execution had any long-term effect on sales. If the marketing execution was designed to gain new users or trial of the product, the sales results in the months after the execution will help determine if repeat purchase or continuity of purchase was achieved.

There are two types of methods for comparing sales trends: with control markets and without control markets.

Sales Trend Analysis with Control Markets

This methodology utilizes control markets (markets with no marketing execution or markets receiving a mainline marketing execution) to compare against test markets receiving a new marketing execution or the marketing execution you want to analyze. Control and test markets should be similar in terms of sales volumes, sales trending, distribution levels, penetration and marketing coverage, size, demographic profiles, and other market and media characteristics. Also, there should be a minimum of two test and two control markets to guard against any anomalies.

In summary, a control market serves as a benchmark to determine whether the specific marketing execution was responsible for sales increases in the test market. If the analysis demonstrates that sales and profits in test markets that received advertising were substantially above control markets that received no advertising, then the decision should be made to consider expanding advertising to other markets.

Sales Trend Analysis without Control Markets

Whenever possible, we recommend using the sales trend analysis with control markets. However, for many businesses, control markets are not available because the business is located solely in one market or in a minimal number of markets, or there are no control markets comparable in their makeup to the test markets. In other situations, the marketer needs to analyze results of a marketing execution that was implemented across all markets. In these situations, a sales trend analysis without control markets is used.

Sales are analyzed before, during, and after the execution to determine if the period during the marketing execution received greater total sales and greater percentage sales increases or decreases over last year. Of course, without control markets, you can't be sure that the sales results are totally a function of the marketing execution. The results could be the effect of other market factors that caused marketwide sales increases or decreases not only for your company but for the competition as well. However, even without control markets, the analysis of sales trends provides general insight into the success or failure of individual marketing executions.

Sometimes test market performance is compared to national or total company sales. In this case, the national or company total is used as a benchmark. The method is not as accurate as a comparison of test versus control markets, but it does provide a basis for evaluation.

EVALUATION PERSPECTIVE 3. PRE- AND POST-EXECUTION RESEARCH

This evaluation method involves the use of primary research that is conducted both before and after the execution of the plan of activities. Most pre- and post-execution research involves awareness, attitude, and behavior tracking studies. These studies can measure the movement of awareness, attitude, and behavior both before and after the marketing plan was executed, and they can measure the movement of specific plan executions, such as promotions, campaigns, and merchandising programs.

While increased sales is a very valuable indicator of the success of a marketing execution, it is not the only one. Many times, though sales remain relatively flat, there is a significant movement in awareness and attitudes. These shifts signal the probability of future increases in sales. As has been proven time and time again, with increase in awareness there is a good probability that there will be an increased level of purchases.

Pre- and post-execution research can also serve as a diagnostic tool to help explain why sales went up or down. Research can identify changes in consumer awareness of your product, attitudes about your product, changing purchase behavior patterns, or competitive strengths and weaknesses as reasons for increases or decreases in sales. Thus, the research evaluation method has the ability to provide more in-depth information than the sales trend comparison method.

In summary, research allows the marketer to evaluate the success or failure of the overall marketing plan and communication programs. For example, research can determine whether you met your communication awareness objective of "increasing awareness from 50 to 55 percent."

EXHIBIT 24.1

Advertising Awareness and Attitudes Indexes

	NO ADVERTISING CONTROL MARKETS			ADVERTISING TEST MARKETS			
	Preperiod	Postperiod	Difference	Preperiod	Postperiod	Difference	Net Gain
Advertising awareness	(100)	(105)	+5	(100)	(152)	+52	+47
Better source of energy information	(100)	(82)	−18	(100)	(135)	+35	+53
More concerned about energy conservation	(100)	(84)	−16	(100)	(127)	+27	+43
More concerned with the environment	(100)	(100)	—	(100)	(115)	+15	+15

Research can help evaluate the success of the behavior objectives such as "increasing trial (percent of first-time purchasers) from 30 to 35 percent or increasing to some stated number the new customers obtained over the past year." Research can also help you measure whether you met the tactical objectives of specific executions. Above all, research is an evaluation tool that helps determine *why* your sales goals were or were not achieved.

The example in Exhibit 24.1 demonstrates the ability of pre- and post-execution research to evaluate the results of an advertising program. In this example, a public utility company was evaluating the effectiveness of its campaign to convince consumers that it was a good source of energy information and was concerned about energy conservation and environmental issues. The results clearly provided the utility company with insights into the effectiveness of the campaign.

EVALUATION METRICS EVERY MARKETER SHOULD CONSIDER

Too many measurements can result in a meaningless gluttony of information. Pick the metrics that are most important to your business and follow them over time, using the information they provide to help you evaluate your company's marketing. You should consider the key metrics listed below when making the final determination as to the key metrics you will follow that will help determine and communicate your company's success.

See also Worksheet 69 in Appendix C.

Share Numbers

- *Share of mind:* Company or product awareness as a percent of either the total market or a specific target segment.
- *Share of market:* Total company sales divided by the total market sales. This can be calculated using units, sales, retail shopping visits, or other pertinent measures to your company or category.
- *Share of wallet:* Similar to the share-of-market ratio. This figure is typically used in conjunction with the percent of total dollars spent on a particular product category for your company versus the total dollars spent on the total category or some other defined competitive set.
- *Share of closet:* A retail term used to evaluate the percent of your company's products in the consumer's closet or home versus the competitors' products. For example, a 30 percent share of closet for a shoe retailer would mean that 30 percent of some target segment (existing customers, young professionals, moms who value trend-right fashion, and so on) has items from your store versus items from your competitors' stores.

- *Brand Development Index (BDI):* The Brand Development Index measures a brand's performance in one market relative to the average performance across all markets. This is measured by examining the total population in a given market as a percent of the total population across all the brand's markets divided by the sales of your brand in that market as a percent of the total sales across all markets where the brand is present:

$$\text{BDI in Market A} = \frac{\text{population in Market A/population across all markets where brand is present}}{\text{sales in Market A/sales across all markets where brand is present}}$$

The Brand Development Index can also be used to quantify how well a brand is performing within a specific target market segment with its average performance across all target market consumers:

$$\text{Brand performanc within a specific target market} =$$
$$\frac{\text{brand sales to target market segment 1/total target market consumers in target market segment 1}}{\text{total brand sales across all targets/total consumers across all targets}}$$

- *Category Development Index (CDI):* The Category Development Index measures the industry category's performance in one market relative to the average performance across all markets. This is measured by examining the total population in a given market as a percent of the total population across all the category's markets divided by the sales of the category in that market as a percent of the total sales across all markets where the category is present.

$$\text{CDI in Market A} = \frac{\text{population in Market A/population across all markets in which the category is present}}{\text{sales in Market A/sales across all markets in which the category is present}}$$

The category development index can also be used to quantify how well the category is performing within a specific target market segment compared to its average performance across the total of all target segments.

$$\text{Category performance within a specific target market segment} =$$
$$\frac{\text{brand sales to target market segment 1/total target consumers in target market segment 1}}{\text{total brand sales across all targets/total potential consumers across all targets}}$$

- *Share of visits:* Visits from a customer segment to your store divided by the total visits to stores in your competitive set. These figures are obtained through primary research.
- *Average dollars spent per purchase:* The average dollar amount per purchase of your customers relative to the industry category average.
- *Market penetration of product category:* The percent of total consumers using the product category divided by all potential consumers of the product category. Put another way, this figure is the total number of users of the product in the marketplace divided by the total number of potential users, resulting in a measure of strength for the category.
- *Target market segment penetration:* Total size of target segment within the geographic trading areas of your company divided by the number of individuals from the segment who have been a customer in the past 12 months. Put another way, this figure is the total segment population divided by the number of customers from the segment, resulting in a measure of the target segment's strength relative to total purchases.
- *Purchase index:* The average consumption of the industry category in comparison to the average consumption of your users or customers. For example, if the

average frequency of purchases in the category were six per year and your customers were making only four purchases per year, the index would be 4 divided by 6, or 67 (0.67 × 100 = index of 67). This means your customers are 33 points below what would be the expected average number of purchases for the category. The same metric can be used for yearly dollar expenditures.

Measure of Awareness, Attitudes, and Perceptions

- *Unaided awareness:* The percent of any given target segment that is aware of your company or product based on unaided response: "Name the products that come to mind when you think about candy bars [or spray dried ingredients, or accounting firms, or some other product]." This figure is obtained from primary research.
- *First mention awareness:* The percent of respondents from a statistically representative sample that name your company first when asked an unaided awareness question. This figure is obtained from primary research.
- *Aided awareness:* The percent of people who recognize your company or product name when prompted with "Are you aware of [your company's name or product]?" This figure is obtained from primary research.
- *Knowledge ratio:* The percent of people who are aware of your company divided by the percent of people who are knowledgeable about a particular service or critical aspect of your company. Many times prospects and even customers are aware of your company but unaware of its specific products and services. This figure is obtained from primary research.
- *Awareness conversion rate:* The percent of individuals in a specific target segment that have unaided awareness and have purchased from your company in the last 12 months. This figure is obtained from primary research.
- *Key attribute perception shifts:* Measurements of top-box shifts over time. For example, on a scale of 1 to 5, with 5 being the highest, the top-box score would be the percent that rated your company or product a 5. On a scale of 10, you might look at the top-2 box or even the top-3 box relative to your competitors. Of critical importance would be the scores and movement around the attributes that link directly to your company or product positioning and brand promise. This figure is obtained from primary research.
- *Relevance:* The relevance that your company or products play in the target segment's life. If relevance is low, you need to find ways to improve it. Many options and promotional techniques exist for doing so. This figure is obtained from primary research.
- *Esteem:* The esteem in which your company or product is held relative to competitors in your category as a whole and across key attributes critical to your company's or product's positioning. This figure is obtained from primary research.
- *Differentiation:* Various mapping techniques (see Chapter 6, "Positioning") that provide a visual interpretation of your company's or product's differentiation relative to your competitive set. Most mapping techniques utilize some form of multivariate analysis that places your company in a section of the map that is determined by multiple variables that when combined shape a singular consumer focus relative to other places on the map. Additionally, perception shifts (discussed above) also provide measures of how you are differentiated versus your competition on key individual attributes. This figure is obtained from primary research.

Loyalty Measures

- *Retention ratio:* The percent of customers (often by customer segment) who were customers last year that purchased again this year. Said another way, this is a repeat purchase rate. Note, some industry categories have a long purchase cycle. In these cases, retention needs to be looked at over longer spans of time.
- *Sole purchase:* The customers who buy only your brand divided by the total customers. This information is commonly found from sources such as GfK MRI and Experian Simmons. This figure gives you a percent that are loyal to your brand. This measure can be compared to other competitors to gain insight into whether your customers are more or less loyal.
- *Satisfaction scores:* The percent of respondents who fall into the top box across key measures of satisfaction for your company or product. As with almost all of the primary research metrics, these measures are best examined over time and relative to competitive offerings. Similar to other measures of this kind, one way to provide a relative comparative score over time is to look at the percent of respondents that fall into the top box. So on a scale of 1 to 5 with 5 being the best, the top box would be the percent that chose 5. These figures are obtained from primary research.
- *Future purchase intent:* The percent of a given target segment that plan to purchase from your company or buy your product sometime into the future. This figure is typically gained from a 5- or 10-point score with the relevant score derived from a top box. If the purchase intent is a 1 on a scale of 1 to 5, with 5 being a certain purchase and 1 being no chance at all, the percentage of respondents who fall into the 5 box would be the future purchase intent score. These figures are obtained from primary research.
- *Definitely recommend to a friend:* The percentage of respondents in a survey who say they would recommend your product, company, or service to a friend.

HOW TO STRUCTURE A SALES EVALUATION PROCESS

The following method demonstrates how to measure the sales performance for your marketing activities. This method utilizes the *growth rate of improvement* (GRI) process, which is one specific type of sales trend comparison.

A retail example is used; however, a similar procedure could be established for any business type. The only changes that would need to be made would be in the evaluation categories. These would be made consistent with the business. A manufacturer would use product sales and units sold. A retailer could use such measurements as visits, transactions, dollars per transaction, units sold, and product sales. A service firm would use sales and people served. You should plan to use a similar method for your evaluation system.

See Worksheet 70 in Appendix C. However, wherever appropriate, we suggest that the pre- and post-execution research evaluation method also be utilized and that the research be executed by a professional research firm.

GROWTH RATE OF IMPROVEMENT (GRI) SALES TREND METHOD: EXECUTION AND EXAMPLE

The following are examples of retail evaluation objectives and strategies along with an execution format for the GRI sales trend evaluation process.

Example evaluation objective: Develop a data feedback methodology to monitor and determine the results of marketing test programs and executions.

Example evaluation strategies:

- Implement a disciplined data feedback system in order to quickly and easily evaluate sales activity for marketing planning and execution.
- Utilize the growth rate of improvement method.

Execution

Each test market is compared against a control market of similar type and the number of stores and per store sales averages. The test markets receive the test activity, and the control markets receive the regularly scheduled marketing activity. If you don't have control markets, you can compare the test market against your national system or all other markets.

Task 1. A *preperiod* is analyzed to determine sales trending prior to the test period.

Task 2. For the *test period*, the period during which the marketing program is executed, data are analyzed to determine sales trending.

Task 3. For the *postperiod*, the period immediately following a test period, data are analyzed to determine sales trending.

Task 4. Finally, a *growth rate of improvement* is determined by analyzing the difference between visits, transactions, and sales dollars per store in the preperiod, the test period, and the postperiod. The data enable the marketer to determine incremental visits, transactions, and sales during the test period for each market and to evaluate the rate of success.

Whenever feasible you should utilize the growth rate of improvement method to compare the preperiod to the test period, test period to the postperiod, and the preperiod to the postperiod. The preperiod is compared to the test period to determine if the test altered expected behavior. If the preperiod showed that sales were flat and the test period demonstrated a marked increase in sales, a determination would be made that the marketing program executed during the test period was effective. The test period is compared to the postperiod to determine if the marketing execution had a lasting effect and to gain knowledge on how much, if any, sales dropped off after the test period. Finally, a very important long-term analysis is the comparison of preperiod to postperiod. This comparison shows if the marketing execution had a positive effect on sales after the test as compared to sales trending before the marketing execution or test period.

Examples of Preperiod-to-Test-Period Comparisons

The examples in Exhibits 24.2 and 24.3 demonstrate a comparison of a preperiod to a test period. Exhibit 24.2 compares a test market to a control market, and Exhibit 24.3 compares a test market to the national system average.

See also Worksheet 70 in Appendix C.

MARKETING RESEARCH AND TESTING (R&T)

Evaluation also encompasses evaluating plans and tools *before* broadscale execution. This is what we define as testing. Because marketing is often as much art as it

EXHIBIT 24.2

Analysis of the Test versus the Control Market Dollar Sales
Test Period February 24 to March 30, Weekly per Store Average

	Last Year's Dollars, Thousands	This Year's Dollars, Thousands	Percent Change
Preperiod Jan. 20 to Feb. 23			
Test market: Detroit (2 stores)	$121.0	$185.1	+53%
Control market: Indianapolis (2 stores)	$118.0	$159.3	+35%
Test Period Feb. 24 to March 30			
Test market: Detroit (2 stores)	$ 29.0	$ 53.4	+84%
Control market: Indianapolis (2 stores)	$ 26.0	$ 25.7	−1%

	Preperiod Percent Change	Test Period Percent Change	Percent Point Gain or Loss
Growth Rate of Improvement (GRI)			
Test market: Detroit (2 stores)	+53%	+84%	+31%
Control market: Indianapolis (2 stores)	+35%	−1%	−36%
Net percent point difference	+18%	+85%	+67%

Incremental sales: GRI + 67% × test period sales $53,400 = net weekly gain $35,778

Note: The same method would be used for visits and/or transactions if the data are available.

is science, there is much chance for failure. For example, it has been estimated that up to 90 percent of new products fail. Accordingly, there will be no guarantee of success when you use new plans and plan elements, when you go against new target markets and use new strategy approaches, or when you implement new tactical tools. Attempting to try new marketing approaches on a broad scale will require a sizable outlay of dollars and have a significant impact on the effectiveness and success of your plan. Enhancing the success of these new marketing approaches requires marketing research and testing (R&T). Testing and research can help you stay ahead of the competition and avoid costly errors. What follows are just the

EXHIBIT 24.3

Analysis of the Test versus the National Market Dollar Sales
Test Period February 24 to March 30, Weekly per Store Average

	Last Year's Dollars, Thousands	This Year's Dollars, Thousands	Percent Change
Preperiod Jan. 20 to Feb. 23			
Test market: Detroit (2 stores)	$121.0	$185.1	+53%
National system average	$120.0	$144.0	+20%
Test Period Feb. 24 to March 30			
Test market: Detroit (2 stores)	$ 39.0	$ 53.4	+84%
National system average	$ 27.0	$ 31.6	+17%

	Preperiod Percent Change	Test Period Percent Change	Percent Point Gain or Loss
Growth Rate of Improvement (GRI)			
Test market: Detroit (2 stores)	+53%	+84%	+31%
National system average	+20%	+17%	−3%
Net percent point difference	+33%	+67%	+34%

Incremental sales: GRI + 34% × test period sales $53,400 = net weekly gain $18,156

Note: The same method would be used for visits and/or transactions if the data are available.

rudiments of this topic. Because research and testing are challenging and complex disciplines, we would recommend you seek professional assistance to help with their implementation.

Why the Need to Test

Every business situation can be thought of as a test. Many small entrepreneurs do not spend any money on a formal research and testing program. But they do "test" the market by posting a sign and setting up shop. Accordingly, the vast majority of them do not make it through their third year in business. However, with a research and testing program, one can significantly reduce the odds of failure. A testing program can be thought of as a form of risk management. You would not think about running your business without insurance. Why run your marketing plan without research and testing?

When to Test and When Not to Test

Not every marketing tool or tactical execution needs to be, or should be, tested. Testing every alternative would not be feasible from a cost or time standpoint. Thus, a prioritization approach should be considered. Some questions to consider when determining what to test include the following.

What Is the Risk of Not Having This Information?

This is probably the most critical question. If one is staking millions of dollars on a positioning strategy, then spending a few thousand dollars on research makes sense. However, taking the time and money to test a one-week, single-market media flight may not be worth the investment in research.

As an example, one of our clients, Mercury Marine, was introducing a revolutionary new propeller. They were to spend major dollars against this introduction. There was little consensus on the name for this propeller. Thus, they tested name alternatives against their consumer and dealer markets. In contrast, they also had a naming issue on another line of propellers. In this case, these propellers were a small part of a family of propellers geared to a small target niche market. It was decided to not spend the effort to test these names because the downside risk was minimal.

What Is the Cost of Obtaining Reliable Information?

The cost/benefit equation here would appear to be somewhat obvious. For example, in order to test the effectiveness of an advertising campaign, you need to conduct an in-market test, matching several markets with different advertising messages. It may cost almost as much to develop and test the campaign as it would to implement the campaign without testing, in which case the decision may be to not test.

What Are the Time Constraints?

If test results cannot be obtained in time to impact the decision-making process, then one must question the value of testing. However, the key here is to avoid this situation by planning for research and testing in the first year of your marketing plan, with a rollout to all markets in Years 2 and 3.

How Valid and Translatable Is the Testing Environment?

You must be able to take the research results and apply them to your marketing situation. You cannot measure the "effectiveness" of advertising in a "forced-exposure copy testing" environment. (Copy testing of advertising will be discussed later in this chapter.) Showing consumers a commercial once or twice in a research room and asking for their reactions will not help you assess the effectiveness of the advertising. Advertising does not work in that way. However, you can measure in this environment the "communication value" of the advertising. Did the commercial communicate the sponsor's name and intended message?

Types of Research and Testing Environments

For the purposes of this book, we can categorize marketing research and testing environments into four types: exploratory, experimental, the Internet, and in the market.

Exploratory

Marketers should always base their marketing objectives and strategies on what their consumers need. Marketing tools should relate to how the consumers think, what their attitudes are, and how they behave. In many instances, exploratory research can provide help in the development process of marketing tool alternatives and in preliminary evaluation of alternatives. Focus groups are probably the most prevalent form of exploratory research.

A focus group is a discussion among target group respondents. Typically, group sizes range from 8 to 10 participants, although groups of 4 to 6 participants are also common. The group discussion is led by a moderator who follows an outline of topics to cover. Focus groups are an excellent way to generate ideas and obtain feedback from target respondents on complex attitudinal issues such as positioning, product concepts, and advertising messages, and to increase understanding of the buying dynamics of a product or service category. When utilized early in the planning process, focus groups can help develop alternatives and provide initial qualitative feedback on alternatives. Focus groups are very qualitative in nature, although when the groups comprise sufficient numbers (6 or more preferably), marketers can gain an enlightened, but not a quantifiable, perspective on the target market.

Experimental

When focus groups are used extensively for exploring the dynamics of consumer attitudes and behavior, they are really a form of experimental research. Experimental research is any kind of research that is not an in-market testing situation under "real" conditions. Evaluating advertising copy via mall intercepts, testing pricing strategies via telephone interviews, and testing positioning concepts through a mail survey are all forms of experimental research.

With experimental research, you are generally forcing exposure of testing concepts onto your target market in an unnatural setting. This type of research is used for reasons of control, cost, and time constraints. In order to isolate and understand consumers' reactions and preferences regarding product, positioning, and marketing mix tools, the researcher needs to control the test environment. In this way, only one variable (for example, product feature, advertising message, brand name, or positioning alternative) is changed from one test exposure to the next. As a result, the researcher can determine that the differences in consumer preferences are due to the change in the one variable. If multiple variables were changed, then the researcher would not know to what to attribute the consumer's preference.

Marketers need feedback in a short amount of time (days to weeks) for decision-making purposes. Experimental research allows this to happen by controlling the exposure to different marketing alternatives. Compared to in-market testing, experimental research is also a more cost-effective form of gathering information.

The Internet

The Internet has affected global life in just about every aspect, and marketing research has certainly felt its impact. Over the past five years, online marketing research has grown faster than any other format of research, making research more affordable and accessible to generate both non-user and customer insights.

Online research has the advantage of speed and generally lower cost than traditional qualitative and quantitative methods such as focus groups and telephone surveys. Many companies, such as Survey Monkey and Zoomerang to name a couple, have formed online panels of respondents. Some of these companies have even produced questionnaire templates for common tools such as concept tests and attitude and usage studies that make it easy for companies to conduct research in-house. With the ability to show graphic images and stream audio or video, the testing possibilities are vast. And the global nature of the Internet now makes international research widely accessible whereas previously this was not economically feasible.

Internet research, however, is not without its detractors or cautious followers. There are questions of sample representativeness: online users tend to be younger, better educated, and of higher income. Also, response rates to online surveys are typically low, similar to mail surveys. As Internet access increases over time, some of these concerns may diminish.

In-Market

In-market testing is really a small-scale implementation of a specific marketing approach. The key to effective in-market tests is to match markets as much as possible, so that you are controlling for all variables except the one you are testing. The ability to accurately read test results relies heavily on the ability to match test markets as closely as possible.

Considerations for matching markets would include sales trends, competitive situation, penetration and distribution, media options, and geographic and demographic issues. In-market testing is used most notably for new product introductions, before rolling out the products nationally. Many companies with well-known brands will use in-market testing before rolling out package, product formulation, or positioning changes. In-market testing also can be used effectively for testing alternative media programs.

Examples of How to Develop Testing Programs

You can literally test anything related to your marketing plan. Also, there is no one absolute right way to test marketing alternatives. The following examples outline some parameters for research and testing of various marketing plan elements.

Positioning Testing

Positioning is the heart of the marketing plan. All marketing mix tools are developed to support the product's or service's positioning, which in turn is the link to the consumer's relationship with the product or service. Positioning concepts generally consist of complex attitude structures, which require a sensitive means of testing.

The objectives of testing positioning alternatives are to evaluate the connection between the target market and the product versus the competition. Important issues would include identifying the relevance of the positioning to the target, the importance of the positioning to the target, and the likelihood that the positioning would encourage trial. Positioning can be tested through many forms, including focus groups, mall intercepts, and mail surveys. Generally a "positioning concept board" is created. The concept board has a visual element and copy points to convey the benefits and positioning elements. Targeted consumers can be shown the concept board and then be asked to respond to a short survey covering attitudinal and intention types of questions.

One limitation to the concept board approach is that consumers tend to be very literal in research settings; they begin to be copywriters rather than focusing on the positioning "idea." An approach developed to counteract this tendency is the audio "concept board." Here, the positioning is stated on an audiotape that is played to respondents. Since they cannot read the concept, respondents are less likely to be quite so literal. They must take away the key positioning from what they heard. This method is very effective for positioning with a strong emotional appeal, as the tone of the audio can impart the desired emotion more easily than the writing on a concept board.

Product Testing

Probably the most testing dollars are associated with research for new product development. Product concepts are explored and formulated through numerous focus groups. Concepts are refined through more consumer testing using all of the methods previously discussed. There are also simulated test models that produce expected market shares when fed with market and benefit criteria. Much of the research on new product development is conducted to determine the ideal bundle of benefits, both rational and emotional, that a product should contain. The ultimate test of a new product is putting it into a real market situation.

Brand Name Testing

The target market will recognize your offering through the brand name of your product. But what is the best brand name? And how do you determine the best brand name? The process for name testing is to first develop alternative names for testing (see Chapter 12). As a rule, the number of names for consumer testing should not exceed seven. A number beyond seven creates respondent fatigue and results in a lack of name discrimination.

The objectives of naming research are to narrow the list of alternative names and to identify the strengths and weaknesses of each name alternative. There are factors other than consumer preferences to be considered in naming. Creative consideration is one example. If some names can be eliminated through naming research, then other factors can be considered in the final decision-making process. When evaluating name alternatives, three areas of questioning are utilized to achieve the research objectives: word association, ratings on product or service benefits, and preference scores.

Word Association

What connotations does the name elicit? Are they positive or negative? For example, when we were testing name alternatives for a merged pair of hospitals, as discussed in an earlier chapter, one of the test names generated for our client was Meriter. Through word associations, two common themes were Merit cigarettes and the word *merit* ("to be worthy"). The word association was tested outside the context of a hospital name. Thus, when the name was put in the context of a hospital, the cigarette association would be expected to disappear, while the merit—to be worthy—definition could be used in an advantageous way.

Ratings on Product or Service Benefits

Each name is rated against various product or service benefits to ascertain strengths and weaknesses. In the hospital example, the names were rated on leadership, caring, professional, state-of-the-art care, and quality.

Preference Scores

Respondents are asked for their name preferences, given a concept statement read to them. They are also asked for the reasons for their preferences.

All three types of measurement—word association, product or service benefit ratings, and preference scores—are analyzed to determine viable names. This type of testing can be conducted through telephone interviews or mall intercepts.

Promotion Testing

Promotion testing can be performed at the idea development stage or at the execution stage. The key objective in evaluating promotions is to determine the effectiveness of the promotion in generating incremental sales, new trial, or brand loyalty. At the idea generation stage, focus groups can be a useful tool for obtaining ideas and feedback. Mall intercepts can also be used to evaluate the stopping power and selling power of alternative promotions in an advertising context. At the execution stage, in-store exit surveys can be used to determine consumers' buying habits and profiles. For example, this type of survey can determine if the promotion was a specific reason that consumers shopped at a store. The profile of the customers can also be checked to determine first-time shoppers, improved purchase ratios, or higher average transaction amounts.

Advertising Message Communications Testing

Advertising is probably one of the most difficult marketing tools to measure. This is due, in part, to the long-term and cumulative effects of advertising and to the difficulty of isolating advertising effects. This is one of the most discussed and controversial research topics. The closest marketers can come to truly measuring the "effectiveness" of advertising is through in-market testing. However, controlling for all other variables is very difficult with in-market testing, and the necessary time and budget are seldom available for this type of measurement. On the other hand, assessing the communication value of advertising can be done more readily and efficiently.

Copy testing is a means of measuring the communication value of advertising. As a diagnostic tool rather than an evaluative tool, copy testing can be instrumental to the creative development process. There are two key objectives in a copy testing framework. One objective is to determine whether the advertising can cut through the clutter and make people stop and notice the ad. The second is to assess whether the ad communicates the intended message. There are several ways of copy testing ads, many through syndicated research sources that can provide norms to compare the test results with other products in the same category or format. The basic principle is common through most techniques. Respondents are shown the ad or commercial, often with other advertising clutter, and then asked questions pertaining to communication playback, negative and positive diagnostics, and feelings. Persuasion scores and purchase intentions can also be part of the questioning. Copy testing can be conducted on both broadcast and print forms of advertising.

Media Mix Testing

Which medium or media mix is the right one? How much media weight do I need? How many media dollars do I need to spend? Media testing can help answer these questions.

In testing media, there are two key variables to evaluate: media mix and media weight. Testing the impact of alternative media or weight levels is very difficult to accomplish in a forced-exposure experimental design. In-market tests are typically used for media mix and weight tests. Market tiers are derived that receive different weight levels of similar messages. Or the variable may be different types of media such as TV versus newspaper. There may be many combinations to consider, with markets and dollars available for testing being the limiting factor. The key is to control for all variables except for the media weight or mix. The typical measurement tool would be sales analysis. Survey research can also be utilized to determine awareness levels affected by the alternative media plans. Telephone research is generally utilized for this purpose.

DOS AND DON'TS

Do

- Evaluate using the overall plan objectives and tactical tool objectives of your marketing plan.
- Use what you learn from the evaluation process in the development of your plan for next year.
- Use primary research to help evaluate the "why" of the sales numbers in terms of awareness, attitude, and behavior.
- Assess the risk factor of *not* conducting research and testing on the various plan elements.
- Conduct research when the cost of implementing the marketing execution is high.
- As much as possible, control for all variables except the one test variable.
- Match the research technique with the type of information you want to obtain.

Don't

- Don't just evaluate only your total year's results. Whenever possible, evaluate each promotion, each campaign, and the effectiveness of each of your marketing tactical tools. Then, apply what you have learned.
- Don't wait until the plan is completed to begin to evaluate. Evaluate the specific plan executions as they are completed to determine their success.
- Don't implement a marketing execution without first determining an evaluation methodology.
- Don't expect the same results of your test market experience when you roll out the tested program to the other markets. Usually there is some falloff from the test market results because it's difficult to maintain the same attention to execution in all the markets as was achieved in the original test markets.
- Don't implement research if you intend to pursue the same path no matter what the research results say.
- Don't use research as the only tool for determining alternatives. Research is only one of many decision-making tools.
- Don't attempt a major new approach by trying it in all of your markets or across the country. In other words, don't make it a national test. It's expensive, and you may never have another chance because it may be a national failure.
- Don't implement the test yourself unless you are willing to pay the consequences. Use a professional to design and evaluate the results.

Idea Starters by Marketing Situation

On the following pages, the first of the 12 columns gives the idea starters, and then each of the 11 columns to the right corresponds to a different marketing situation you may encounter as you prepare and execute this marketing plan. The leftmost column contains idea starters grouped by marketing mix tool.

To use this idea grid, simply choose the marketing situation in which you find your product and the marketing mix tool with which you are currently working, and then select the best ideas for the specific situation.

For example, if you are looking for promotional event ideas for a store opening, check under the marketing situation column head New Product/Store Intro/Grand Opening in the Promotions/Events section of idea starters. Then follow the column down, and evaluate the suggestions that seem most appropriate.

Marketing Situations

Idea Starters for Each Marketing Mix Tool

Product/Service/Store	Flat/Continual Decline in Sales	Need to Increase Small User Base	Poor Repeat/Limited Loyalty	Need to Build Amount Purchased	New/Greater Competition	Low Awareness	Need to Improve/Change Image	New Product/Store Intro/Grand Opening	Seasonal Sales Problem/Opportunity	Need Support from Intermediate Markets/Channels	Regional/Local Market/Store Problem
Offer production more convenient, smaller/larger sizes	●	●	●	●				●			
Make store easier to shop	●			●							
Test new department/product extensions	●	●			●			●	●		●
Provide follow-up repair/maintenance program			●		●		●				
Reformulate/update product/retail concept	●	●	●		●			●			●
Add new products to line	●	●	●		●			●			●
New product for emerging market for specific need/use	●	●			●		●	●			
Test new shops/boutiques/services within store	●	●	●	●	●		●	●			●
Provide home delivery/shop-at-home service	●	●	●		●			●			
Provide product/service at home or on location	●	●	●		●		●	●			
Offer money-back guarantee	●	●	●	●	●			●			
Develop new products with existing products/materials or equipment/technology	●	●			●			●			
Develop new/more varied uses for product	●	●	●	●	●		●	●	●		
Develop private store brand/label and sell at value	●	●									
Develop a different product by price segment in same category	●	●		●	●						
Develop product for special uses/time of year (e.g., McDonald's Shamrock Shakes)	●	●			●				●		●
Develop special trial sizes	●	●	●		●			●			
Do primary research for the product/retail concept with potential target market/consumers/customers	●	●			●	●				●	●
Reposition product for alternative target markets	●	●	●			●	●				
Bundle products together	●			●							
Develop brand extensions/flankers	●●	●			●			●	●●	●	
Expand hours of store	●				●			●	●		
Offer longer/lifetime warranty	●	●	●		●		●				

Marketing Situations

Marketing Situations

Idea Starters for Each Marketing Mix Tool	Flat/Continual Decline in Sales	Need to Increase Small User Base	Poor Repeat/Limited Loyalty	Need to Build Amount Purchased	New/Greater Competition	Low Awareness	Need to Improve/Change Image	New Product/Store Intro/Grand Opening	Seasonal Sales Problem/Opportunity	Need Support from Intermediate Markets/Channels	Regional/Local Market/Store Problem
Naming											
Change name to reflect repositioning of store	•	•					•	•			
Brand for direct association with target market						•	•	•			
Brand for credibility		•	•				•				
Brand by price category (e.g., Budget Rent-a-Car)					•			•			
Brand for suggestion of quality or function						•	•	•			
Brand for communication and/or benefit						•	•	•			
Develop unique brands for each product line		•						•			
License use of brand for additional/supplementary products	•	•		•							
Provide different brand name in different markets											•
Develop alternative brands of product for various targets					•		•				
Put subliminal benefit in name (e.g., Acura Integra [integrity]; Legend [legendary])					•	•	•	•			
Packaging											
Update packaging/signage for changing target market		•			•		•				
Package multiple units of same item together			•	•	•						
Package different but compatible products together (e.g., shampoo with conditioner)		•		•	•						
Include handy feature on package (e.g., spout, carry handle)		•			•			•			
Include usage information inside or on package (e.g., recipe, additional uses)		•	•	•	•						
Include contest on package		•	•	•	•						
Redesign package or store to serve secondary benefit		•	•					•			
Develop package for disposability, and/or increased shelf life		•	•		•			•		•	

Marketing Situations

Marketing Situations

Idea Starters for Each Marketing Mix Tool	Flat/Continual Decline in Sales	Need to Increase Small User Base	Poor Repeat/Limited Loyalty	Need to Build Amount Purchased	New/Greater Competition	Low Awareness	Need to Improve/Change Image	New Product/Store Intro/Grand Opening	Seasonal Sales Problem/Opportunity	Need Support from Intermediate Markets/Channels	Regional/Local Market/Store Problem
Packaging, *continued*											
Develop permanent reader board inside and outside store that changes daily		•		•		•			•		
Package for visual sampling of product (see product through package window)		•			•		•	•			
Build in additional feature for after use (e.g., package container becomes drinking glass)		•	•		•		•			•	
Make package easy to stock for trade			•		•					•	
Make package and display piece one and the same/dependent on each other		•		•	•			•		•	
Research brand/package alternatives					•		•	•			
Provide on-pack toll-free number for assistance/tips			•		•						
Develop package that increases shelf life									•	•	
Develop package that takes less shelf space										•	
Introduce packages at various sizes/amounts for various targets/channels (e.g., individual, travel)	•	•		•	•			•		•	•
Develop environmentally friendly package (e.g., recyclable)		•	•		•	•	•				•
Pricing											
Set up customer panel that monitors competitive pricing											
Employ volume discount program				•	•					•	•
Vary price points by seasonality and market differences									•		•
Price to skim (introduce at high price, then reduce price to broaden consumer base)								•	•		
Price at lower level to steal share	•				•			•			•
Match price to intended perceived quality of product (e.g., high price to support premium image)			•				•	•			
Penetration pricing—introduce at low price and hold		•		•	•			•			•

Marketing Situations

Idea Starters for Each Marketing Mix Tool	Flat/Continual Decline in Sales	Need to Increase Small User Base	Poor Repeat/Limited Loyalty	Need to Build Amount Purchased	New/Greater Competition	Low Awareness	Need to Improve/Change Image	New Product/Store Intro/Grand Opening	Seasonal Sales Problem/Opportunity	Need Support from Intermediate Markets/Channels	Regional/Local Market/Store Problem
Pricing, continued											
Cream pricing—introduce at high price and hold				•			•	•			
Employ flexible pricing, negotiate with each customer from highest to lowest price				•	•						•
Price based on replacement cost, not what was paid for product		•			•					•	
Product line pricing (maintain similar price range for all products in line)								•		•	
Test higher/lower prices in various markets	•	•	•	•	•					•	•
Fit product to price ranges		•		•	•						
Price all merchandise at one price		•			•		•				•
Parity price but regularly feature lower-price specials for lower-price perception	•	•			•						
Provide renewal/repurchase discounts	•		•		•						•
Price by distribution channel	•			•	•					•	
Good, better, best pricing	•	•							•		•
Price some items as loss leaders			•		•						
Distribution/Store Penetration											
Fully distribute product; penetrate each market before rolling out to other markets		•			•	•		•		•	
Employ new channels (e.g., sell product in new/different retail outlets; retail through direct mail)		•			•					•	•
Use exclusive/selective distribution					•		•	•		•	•
Use extensive mass market distribution		•			•						•
Establish minimum distribution levels prior to use of other marketing activities (e.g., advertising)								•		•	•
Continually monitor distribution/out-of-stock versus competition to understand performance			•		•			•			•

Marketing Situations

Distribution/Store Penetration, *continued*

Idea Starters for Each Marketing Mix Tool	Flat/Continual Decline in Sales	Need to Increase Small User Base	Poor Repeat/Limited Loyalty	Need to Build Amount Purchased	New/Greater Competition	Low Awareness	Need to Improve/Change Image	New Product/Store Intro/Grand Opening	Seasonal Sales Problem/Opportunity	Need Support from Intermediate Markets/Channels	Regional/Local Market/Store Problem
Letter/printed piece/sample/premium to purchasing agent, trade, etc.			•	•						•	•
Concentrate store penetration in markets with high product usage and low media cost		•			•	•		•			•
Develop limited-service satellite outlets in outlying areas to feed main facility		•			•	•					•
Intensive distribution employing trade discounts		•	•		•						•
Send sample of product to home of buyer, purchasing agent, or spouse		•						•		•	•
Optimum distribution/inventory for new product introduction/grand opening		•						•		•	•
Offer merchandise on consignment, or guarantee return		•			•			•		•	•
Provide co-op advertising program		•			•	•		•	•	•	•
Offer exclusivity to outlets by market or within certain radius								•		•	•
Locate ministore within a larger store	•	•		•	•	•	•			•	•
Use electronic/vending machines	•	•		•	•	•				•	•
Just-in-time (JIT) delivery		•			•	•	•		•	•	•
Close unprofitable stores and relocate to better trading areas/locations/markets	•			•							•
Test larger superstores or ministores for greater selection and convenience, respectively	•	•			•						•
Personal Selling/Service											
Institute/strengthen sales commission programs	•	•	•	•					•	•	•
Institute highly visible peer-recognition program with reward	•	•		•						•	•
Research and then fulfill vocation and avocation needs of staff—graduated dollar incentive program; free vacation/prizes for winning sales contest	•			•						•	
Change method of selling product (e.g., direct versus manufacturer's representative)	•			•	•					•	•

540

Marketing Situations

Idea Starters for Each Marketing Mix Tool

	Flat/Continual Decline in Sales	Need to Increase Small User Base	Poor Repeat/Limited Loyalty	Need to Build Amount Purchased	New/Greater Competition	Low Awareness	Need to Improve/Change Image	New Product/Store Intro/Grand Opening	Seasonal Sales Problem/Opportunity	Need Support from Intermediate Markets/Channels	Regional/Local Market/Store Problem
Personal Selling/Service, *continued*											
Continuous sales training/seminars	•			•						•	•
Sponsor all-company events (convention, banquet, dinner, sales meeting, etc.)	•			•	•			•		•	•
Institute ongoing feedback program from field on promotion, selling, merchandising, product, inventory, etc.		•	•	•				•		•	•
Initiate ongoing internal competition among sales staff/districts/stores		•		•	•			•	•		•
Incentives/prizes for number of sales contacts and selling ratio	•	•	•		•						•
Develop lead-qualifying program to provide best prospects to sales staff	•				•			•		•	
Establish sales contests between regions and within regions	•				•			•			•
Adjust commission rate for current customers to emphasize retention			•								
Allow sales staff limited free product for sampling to gain new customer trial		•					•	•			
Establish service standards	•		•	•	•		•	•			•
Follow-up sales call after personal visit or direct-mail drop	•	•	•	•			•	•			•
Provide 24-hour toll-free expert trouble-shooting	•		•	•		•	•				•
New product seminars	•	•		•	•		•	•			•
Inventory control/services			•	•	•		•		•		
Promotions/Events											
Half-price sale (buy one, get a second at half price)	•			•	•			•	•		
Sampling—free product/gift/service; on pack/in mail	•	•				•	•	•		•	
Free goods with purchase	•	•		•	•			•	•		•
Media-carried coupon	•	•	•	•	•	•		•	•	•	•
Salesperson-carried coupon	•	•		•	•			•	•	•	•
Bounce-back coupon	•	•	•	•	•			•	•		
Multiple coupons for greater redemption	•	•	•	•	•			•	•	•	•

Marketing Situations

Idea Starters for Each Marketing Mix Tool	Flat/Continual Decline in Sales	Need to Increase Small User Base	Poor Repeat/Limited Loyalty	Need to Build Amount Purchased	New/Greater Competition	Low Awareness	Need to Improve/Change Image	New Product/Store Intro/Grand Opening	Seasonal Sales Problem/Opportunity	Need Support from Intermediate Markets/Channels	Regional/Local Market/Store Problem
Promotions/Events, *continued*											
Instant coupon redeemed when product purchased	•	•			•			•		•	•
Gambler's sale (everyone receives discount, but discount amount is left to chance)	•	•	•		•			•	•		•
Crossruff package couponing by similar demographic targets	•	•			•				•	•	•
Stage "Let's Make a Deal" auction on selected/sale merchandise	•		•	•					•		•
Tie-in offer with noncompetitor in store, on pack, in ad	•	•			•	•	•		•		•
Offer free/lower-cost financing	•	•		•	•						•
Trial sizes	•	•			•						•
Low price as loss leaders	•	•			•	•					•
Use trial-to-loyalty continuity program	•	•	•		•			•			•
Free product with series of purchases via punch/validation card	•		•	•				•			
Sweepstakes that require some show of product knowledge to enter						•	•	•		•	
Value packs	•	•		•	•						
Premiums	•	•	•	•	•						
In-store/department couponing	•	•	•		•			•		•	•
In-store demonstration with sampling	•	•	•	•	•			•		•	•
Free samples to the trade/buyers at office and home	•	•		•	•			•		•	•
Discounts for special groups (seniors, students, etc.)	•	•	•	•	•						
Sweepstakes—on/in pack, in store, in ad	•	•	•	•	•	•	•	•	•	•	•
Game with many/all instant winners and few big winners	•	•	•		•						
Continuous specials on specific days/hours	•	•	•	•	•				•		
Use a grand opening of one store to sell all market stores for month	•	•			•	•		•	•		•
Tie promotions to timely local, regional, and national events						•			•		•

Marketing Situations

Idea Starters for Each Marketing Mix Tool	Flat/Continual Decline in Sales	Need to Increase Small User Base	Poor Repeat/Limited Loyalty	Need to Build Amount Purchased	New/Greater Competition	Low Awareness	Need to Improve/Change Image	New Product/Store Intro/Grand Opening	Seasonal Sales Problem/Opportunity	Need Support from Intermediate Markets/Channels	Regional/Local Market/Store Problem
Promotions/Events, *continued*											
Free goods/discount for bringing/referring friend	X	X							X		
"2-for-1" special	X	X			X			X	X		X
Provide a free service to bring customers to outlet	X	X		X	X			X			X
In-pack/on-pack coupon	X	X	X	X	X			X			X
In-store/other retailer crossruff couponing	X			X	X			X			X
Graduated open or coupon sale (e.g., 10 percent off 1 item, 20 percent off 2 items, etc.)	X			X	X						
Premiums—free with purchase, self-liquidating; continuity (e.g., set of glasses)		X	X	X	X			X	X	X	X
Bonus pack (e.g., 20 percent extra product at no extra cost)	X	X	X	X	X						
Refunds—mail-in for cash/coupons; rebates	X	X	X	X						X	
Stamps										X	
Volume discounts—reduced price; free item with multiple purchases (punch card); free case with multiple purchases	X	X	X	X	X				X	X	
Make coupon as large as the page it is printed on						X		X			
Free appealing gift to first 50 to 500 customers	X	X	X		X			X			X
Establish customer club (e.g., free coffee breakfast club)			X				X				X
Coupon turnabout—promote acceptance of competitors' coupons	X	X			X						X
Preclearance/postclearance sales/specials	X	X	X						X		
Develop value-added specials by packaging items together at special price		X	X	X				X	X		
Contest		X				X	X	X			
In-store display allowance		X			X	X		X		X	X
Discount allowance for product feature in retailer ad		X			X	X				X	X

543

Promotions/Events, *continued*

Idea Starters for Each Marketing Mix Tool	Flat/Continual Decline in Sales	Need to Increase Small User Base	Poor Repeat/Limited Loyalty	Need to Build Amount Purchased	New/Greater Competition	Low Awareness	Need to Improve/Change Image	New Product/Store Intro/Grand Opening	Seasonal Sales Problem/Opportunity	Need Support from Intermediate Markets/Channels	Regional/Local Market/Store Problem
Free new product with purchase of an established product	●	●			●			●		●	
Premiums/prizes with contest for trade based on their knowledge of your product	●							●		●	
Have charity sell product/dollar savings certificate	●	●					●		●		●
Stage election/contest for naming the best local, regional, and national sports team		●				●	●		●		
Celebrate customer's birthday with free goods/services			●				●				
Sell gifts/dollar certificates (generates positive slippage)	●	●	●						●		
Gift with purchase of dollar certificates	●	●	●						●		
Dollars-off purchase with donation to charity (e.g., bring used coat for needy, receive dollar discount)	●	●					●		●		
Double coupon—instant and bounce-back coupons for immediate and subsequent purchase	●	●	●		●						
Crossruff coupon from high-volume to low-volume and complementary brands	●	●	●	●							
Retailers solicit co-op promotion support and tie-in with manufacturers and industry groups	●	●	●	●		●	●	●			●
Build a promotional event around a recognized celebrity or spokesperson		●			●	●	●	●	●	●	●
Develop a contest or award that shows real people using the product	●	●	●	●		●		●	●	●	●
Create a mascot, character, or vehicle (hot-air balloon, auto, etc.) that can tour parades, fairs, etc.						●		●	●	●	●
Create an event for employees that builds motivation and excitement for marketing initiatives							●		●		●
Off-hour/VIP customer sale	●		●					●	●		●
Have a grand open house to draw people and expose all areas of store	●	●		●					●		●

Marketing Situations

Idea Starters for Each Marketing Mix Tool	Flat/Continual Decline in Sales	Need to Increase Small User Base	Poor Repeat/Limited Loyalty	Need to Build Amount Purchased	New/Greater Competition	Low Awareness	Need to Improve/Change Image	New Product/Store Intro/Grand Opening	Seasonal Sales Problem/Opportunity	Need Support from Intermediate Markets/Channels	Regional/Local Market/Store Problem
Promotions/Events, *continued*											
Use store as deposit center for charity drive		•				•	•				
Use store as meeting place for groups/clubs			•				•				
Advertising Message											
Stress product's quality/inherent drama/uniqueness		•	•		•	•	•	•			
Stress brand name			•		•	•		•			•
Emphasize profitability of product to trade								•		•	
Feature consumer advertising to trade that will be supporting the product								•		•	
Use problem/solution approach when building market		•				•	•				
Use bandwagon (everyone-is-doing-it) approach		•	•			•	•	•			
Testimonial by authority/celebrity figure					•	•					
Comparative product/pricing	•	•			•	•					
Feature alternative product uses	•	•	•	•	•						
Use music for mood, entertainment, emotion, continuity, attention						•	•				
Use emotion to create difference for personalized commodity type of product like beer or wine				•		•	•				
Educational/editorial types of advertising (advertorial) to help build/preempt the market		•				•	•	•			•
Use company spokesperson					•	•	•	•			•
Use animation for greater interest/entertainment value					•		•				
For :30s use two integrated :15s/three :10s for different messages						•		•			
Provide key decision information to encourage purchase		•				•	•	•			
Borrowed interest/familiarity for imagery and/or memorability with established music, sound, phrase						•	•	•			

545

Idea Starters for Each Marketing Mix Tool	Flat/Continual Decline in Sales	Need to Increase Small User Base	Poor Repeat/Limited Loyalty	Need to Build Amount Purchased	New/Greater Competition	Low Awareness	Need to Improve/Change Image	New Product/Store Intro/Grand Opening	Seasonal Sales Problem/Opportunity	Need Support from Intermediate Markets/Channels	Regional/Local Market/Store Problem
Advertising Message, _continued_											
Make sure audio and video in TV sync together for most effective communication						•	•				
Make sure you have adequate name identification (early and late product identification) in broadcast commercials						•	•				
When logical and possible, "new," "grand opening," and "free" are powerful words to use in your advertising	•	•			•	•	•	•		•	•
Use teaser campaign to build interest prior to introduction	•	•	•			•	•	•			•
Use an involvement device (e.g., a puzzle)	•	•	•	•	•	•	•	•			•
Reduce message to a single word or picture	•	•	•	•	•	•	•	•			•
Copy test advertising before running						•		•			
Advertising Media											
Increase media weight	•	•			•	•	•	•			•
Use heavy TV	•	•				•	•	•			
Use direct mail in store's trading area	•	•				•		•			•
Use direct mail against competitor's customer trading area					•			•			•
Build and use direct mail customer list for all heavy users	•	•	•							•	•
Test direct mail to new target markets	•	•				•		•			
Use multiple, smaller ads in same issue of newspaper/magazine						•		•			
For target market impact, test medium never used before	•	•			•	•	•	•	•		•
Use cable TV for specially targeted groups by usage, demographics, and geography	•	•	•			•		•			•
Roadblock same time period/news on all TV stations								•			
Target outdoor/transit around store, in concentrated area, near company buying office, competition	•	•			•	•		•		•	•
If available and efficient, use :10s/:15s for additional frequency					•	•					•

Marketing Situations

Idea Starters for Each Marketing Mix Tool

Advertising Media, continued

Idea Starters for Each Marketing Mix Tool	Flat/Continual Decline in Sales	Need to Increase Small User Base	Poor Repeat/Limited Loyalty	Need to Build Amount Purchased	New/Greater Competition	Low Awareness	Need to Improve/Change Image	New Product/Store Intro/Grand Opening	Seasonal Sales Problem/Opportunity	Need Support from Intermediate Markets/Channels	Regional/Local Market/Store Problem
Provide radio station tie-in promotion in return for free spots	•					•		•			•
Sponsor high-rated/memorable television special once/twice a year if budget is limited						•	•	•			
Local/suburban newspapers to target selected areas		•			•	•	•	•			•
Stage periodic media blitz in TV/radio with spots every hour on all TV/top radio stations	•	•			•	•	•	•			•
Use :10/small-space ads as teasers with frequency for product intro, grand opening, promotion						•	•	•			
Follow up direct mail with telemarketing for increased response	•	•	•	•							•
Negotiate free radio bonus spots, remote broadcasts, etc., when purchasing radio spots from stations						•	•				•
Use heavy radio schedule for high frequency	•					•	•				•
Sponsor community events, local sports events (high school)			•			•	•				•
Place multiple spots within the same program for immediate message reinforcement						•		•			
Use broadcast medium/large print ads to attract new customers/build the market	•	•				•					
Use unique coupon insert in print medium (e.g., bag, cutout game, toy)	•	•						•			
Frequent trade mailings to office and home	•	•				•		•		•	•
Freestanding insert (FSI) in newspaper (good coupon carrier)					•			•		•	
Ethnic media to expand the user base	•	•				•	•	•			•
Tie in or sponsor programming/editorial that will enhance company's image as a leader/expert							•				

Marketing Situations

Idea Starters for Each Marketing Mix Tool	Flat/Continual Decline in Sales	Need to Increase Small User Base	Poor Repeat/Limited Loyalty	Need to Build Amount Purchased	New/Greater Competition	Low Awareness	Need to Improve/Change Image	New Product/Store Intro/Grand Opening	Seasonal Sales Problem/Opportunity	Need Support from Intermediate Markets/Channels	Regional/Local Market/Store Problem
Advertising Media, *continued*											
Develop trade-out agreement with broadcast station exchanging advertising for product/service	●					●		●			●
Use bag for home-delivered newspaper as medium		●			●	●		●	●		●
Use colored comics to reach whole family (adults, teens, kids) for cost of black-and-white		●				●					
Use direct mail/outdoor around new store in large multiple-store market						●		●			●
Manufacturers develop disciplined, aggressive media co-op program for dealers/retailers for added, efficient media weight						●		●		●	
Test alternative media mix and support levels		●				●					
Put a home page on the Internet	●	●	●		●	●	●	●	●		●
Create an interactive CD-ROM	●	●	●		●	●	●	●	●	●	●
Create editorial/programming and build into the message (e.g., health tips, auto safety tips)							●				
Bathroom stall messages (captive audience)					●	●					
Use in-store communication services (e.g., electronic reader boards, grocery carts)	●		●					●	●		●
Interactive Media											
Create an e-mail-based newsletter to which site visitors can subscribe		●	●			●					
Add links to your web page		●	●								
Add a press area to your website that contains press releases and contact information for media representatives				●		●					
Explore options for selling special items, such as overstocked or refurbished merchandise, only via the website	●			●					●		

548

Marketing Situations

Idea Starters for Each Marketing Mix Tool

Interactive Media, *continued*

Idea Starters for Each Marketing Mix Tool	Flat/Continual Decline in Sales	Need to Increase Small User Base	Poor Repeat/Limited Loyalty	Need to Build Amount Purchased	New/Greater Competition	Low Awareness	Need to Improve/Change Image	New Product/Store Intro/Grand Opening	Seasonal Sales Problem/Opportunity	Need Support from Intermediate Markets/Channels	Regional/Local Market/Store Problem
Identify a time each week or month to manually add/link your site to the most-used search engines		●	●								
Add customer testimonials to your website							●	●			
Add side-by-side quick-reference comparisons between products/services and those of competitors						●		●			
Build a micro website to focus on a specific target			●			●	●	●	●	●	
Implement a cell phone/PDA–friendly version of your site or its electronic newsletter			●		●						
Add an FAQ section to your website; provide a form that allows site visitors to submit questions			●				●				
Offer coupons via the Internet			●		●			●			
Provide product redemption				●			●				
Do research via the Internet			●	●			●				
Develop target involvement with product via the website	●			●				●			
Make sure web address is included in all advertising messages						●		●			
Purchase key search words on more heavily used sites						●		●			
Place banner ads on sites developed by the media being used						●		●			
Consider industry portals, Internet links, search engines, and online magazines when developing media relations plan		●				●				●	
Use the Internet to disseminate news releases and other materials to the press (Technology editors, in particular, prefer to receive information via the web. As an invaluable research tool, the Internet will increase efficiency and improve the quality of press materials, literature, and educational pieces.)		●									

Interactive Media, *continued*

Idea Starters for Each Marketing Mix Tool	Flat/Continual Decline in Sales	Need to Increase Small User Base	Poor Repeat/Limited Loyalty	Need to Build Amount Purchased	New/Greater Competition	Low Awareness	Need to Improve/Change Image	New Product/Store Intro/Grand Opening	Seasonal Sales Problem/Opportunity	Need Support from Intermediate Markets/Channels	Regional/Local Market/Store Problem
Boost the attendance of news conferences, roundtables, and annual meetings by webcasting the event		•	•							•	
Conduct a contest through social media	•	•	•			•	•	•	•		
Utilize hashtags (#) on Twitter to draw attention to events; share the hashtag with all event participants		•				•	•	•	•		
Create and participate in a discussion board pertaining to your area of expertise		•				•	•				
Create a Ning group of people most passionate about your brand				•		•	•	•			
Add social media icons and links to your company's website						•	•			•	
Add social media information in unexpected places: e-mail signatures, business cards, stationary, etc.						•	•				
Participate in Follow Friday on Twitter (recommending other users)		•		•		•	•		•		
Use social media as a polling forum to get feedback on your product			•	•			•	•		•	
Use social media as a customer service forum to answer questions and resolve issues (Best Buy is a great example.)			•	•			•	•		•	
Create a corporate blog, and post stories that are industry related (Be sure this isn't purely self-promotional.)	•	•				•	•			•	
Comment on other blog posts or news articles regarding your industry (You can also include your company's URL in this post, to draw more attention to your website.)		•				•	•			•	
Host a webinar surrounding your area of expertise, with your company as the main sponsor	•			•		•	•	•		•	
Mixing with public relations, use an online social media press release (for example, PitchEngine.com)	•	•		•		•	•	•		•	

Idea Starters for Each Marketing Mix Tool	Flat/Continual Decline in Sales	Need to Increase Small User Base	Poor Repeat/Limited Loyalty	Need to Build Amount Purchased	New/Greater Competition	Low Awareness	Need to Improve/Change Image	New Product/Store Intro/Grand Opening	Seasonal Sales Problem/Opportunity	Need Support from Intermediate Markets/Channels	Regional/Local Market/Store Problem
Interactive Media, *continued*											
Create how-to videos and post them to YouTube	●	●		●	●	●					●
Build buzz via social media for new stores/grand openings	●	●		●	●	●	●	●	●		●
Create an event on Facebook or LinkedIn, and invite all of your contacts; ask them to invite all their contacts as well		●				●	●	●			
Offer coupons or special promotions exclusively for social media fans/followers	●	●	●	●	●			●	●		●
Plan a giveaway for your company's first 1,000 followers					●			●	●		●
Use search engine optimization to make sure key words pertaining to your company appear often on its website		●		●		●	●				
Purchase Facebook advertisements to promote your page and get more likes		●		●		●	●				
Register your Twitter user name on Twitter directories such as WeFollow		●		●		●		●			
Use Foursquare to lure people into your business (Offer promotions for people who check in.)	●	●		●		●					
Merchandising											
Use crossruff display to sell other products/departments	●	●			●			●			●
Use buttons to suggestive sell				●			●				
Do tie-in display with noncompetitor		●		●				●			●
Announce timely specials in store via PA system				●							
Feature new/add-on products at checkout				●		●	●	●			
Use same window signs to sell inside as well as outside store				●			●	●			
Tie in all trade and in-store display materials to advertising						●	●			●	
Flyers/handouts in high-traffic areas, on neighborhood bulletin boards					●	●					

Marketing Situations

Idea Starters for Each Marketing Mix Tool

Merchandising, continued

Idea Starters for Each Marketing Mix Tool	Flat/Continual Decline in Sales	Need to Increase Small User Base	Poor Repeat/Limited Loyalty	Need to Build Amount Purchased	New/Greater Competition	Low Awareness	Need to Improve/Change Image	New Product/Store Intro/Grand Opening	Seasonal Sales Problem/Opportunity	Need Support from Intermediate Markets/Channels	Regional/Local Market/Store Problem
Communicate guarantee of product/lowest price in store to enhance sale	•	•	•	•	•		•	•			
Kids' play area in store		•	•	•							
Decorate store with unique mobiles/balloons				•		•	•	•			
Distribute coupons in store	•	•	•		•			•			•
Aisle, point-of-purchase displays to sell/sample product/distribute coupons		•		•				•			•
Use in-store advertising for point-of-sale awareness (e.g., grocery cart, video reader board)		•		•		•		•		•	•
Provide demonstrations/lessons on how to use product and expand its uses (e.g., use of fabrics for home decorating, not just for sewing clothes)	•	•	•	•							
Make display compatible with product and target market (e.g., in-store shoot-a-basket display for athletic shoes)			•		•		•	•	•		•
When purchasing radio, newspaper, and magazines, ask for free merchandising such as on-air contest and/or product merchandising to the intermediate/consumer markets						•		•		•	•
Bag stuffers with useful and changing message, including specials	•		•				•	•		•	•
Use TV monitor or large screen for in-store information, sales, entertainment			•	•			•				
Answer store phone with special message			•				•		•		
Customer newsletter with timely information, promotion announcements, crossruff/discount coupons			•	•	•	•	•				•
Shelf talkers whenever possible		•			•	•		•			•
Put product information on videocassette for review by purchasing agent at convenient time in home or office							•	•		•	
Use shopping bag as walking billboard/reminder			•			•			•		
Merchandise future sales	•		•			•					

552

Marketing Situations

Idea Starters for Each Marketing Mix Tool	Flat/Continual Decline in Sales	Need to Increase Small User Base	Poor Repeat/Limited Loyalty	Need to Build Amount Purchased	New/Greater Competition	Low Awareness	Need to Improve/Change Image	New Product/Store Intro/Grand Opening	Seasonal Sales Problem/Opportunity	Need Support from Intermediate Markets/Channels	Regional/Local Market/Store Problem
Merchandising, *continued*											
Place product information/coupons at point of purchase		•		•	•					•	•
Hold a product display contest for dealers/trade								•		•	•
Provide sales staff with ads/direct-mail reprints for in-person distribution						•	•				
Develop turnkey point-of-sale materials for retail outlets								•		•	
Develop video demonstration with TV/VCR/DVD incentive for retailers/dealers						•	•	•		•	
Provide removable signage for seasonal displays									•	•	•
Public Relations											
Tie in with radio/TV station and charity to sponsor event		•				•	•	•			•
Contribution to charity for every product sold		•	•	•			•		•		•
Tie in with charity, and secure free PSAs from broadcast stations		•				•	•	•			•
Request PSA support from media public affairs directors, salespersons, and station managers		•				•	•		•		
Sponsor community events (e.g., fairs, community interest programs)		•				•	•				•
Market-by-market visits by company representative with local news media people		•				•	•	•			•
Charity tie-ins on special days and gift-giving times of year						•	•				•
Provide game contest with prizes and coupons for spectator participation at sporting events, concerts, etc.		•				•	•		•		•
Sponsor celebrity market tour/in-store appearance		•				•	•	•			•
Feature representatives for various companies in retail outlet			•					•			•

Marketing Situations

Idea Starters for Each Marketing Mix Tool

Public Relations, *continued*

Idea Starter	Flat/Continual Decline in Sales	Need to Increase Small User Base	Poor Repeat/Limited Loyalty	Need to Build Amount Purchased	New/Greater Competition	Low Awareness	Need to Improve/Change Image	New Product/Store Intro/Grand Opening	Seasonal Sales Problem/Opportunity	Need Support from Intermediate Markets/Channels	Regional/Local Market/Store Problem
Provide news media with periodic stories on high-interest topics relative to product/store/company						●	●	●	●		●
Volunteer program for community activities (e.g., team physician for high school sports)							●				●
Tie publicity events to introduction/grand opening						●	●	●			●
Send/deliver news release to news/editorial staff with free product/premium and/or in unique manner						●	●	●			●
Establish company speakers' bureau to make presentations to key target groups	●	●				●	●				
Place a feature story that shows how product benefited a particular user		●	●		●	●				●	●
Place a feature story profiling a company executive/employee			●	●	●	●	●				●
Issue a news release announcing new product/new store/grand opening for the public and/or for charity						●		●		●	●
Publicize a newsworthy advertising campaign or promotion					●	●	●	●		●	●
Publicize a seasonal use for product	●			●	●	●			●	●	●
Offer to be a source of industry expertise for the media			●		●	●	●			●	●
Develop and publicize a seminar or educational event for specific target			●		●	●	●				●
Take an action that conveys image (e.g., donate product to charity, support employee volunteerism) and publicize it			●		●	●	●	●		●	●
Develop and place features with a local-interest angle					●	●	●	●			●
Submit an opinion piece on a local/regional issue						●	●			●	●
Editor briefing tours		●				●	●	●			●
Get industry expert advice on use of product and pass along to consumers		●	●		●	●	●				

Appendices B and C can be found online at
www.mhprofessional.com/successfulmarketingplan

Index

About the Authors

Roman G. Hiebing, Jr., is the retired president of The Hiebing Group, a full-service marketing and advertising agency serving clients such as McDonald's, Coors Beer, Culligan Water Filtration, Diaper Genie, and Mercury Marine.

Scott W. Cooper is principal of the marketing strategy firm Marketing Engine Group (www.marketingenginegroup.com). He formerly served as president of The Hiebing Group, senior vice president of marketing for Famous Footwear, and senior vice president of corporate brand marketing for Brown Shoe. Cooper lives in Madison, WI.

Steven J. Wehrenberg is CEO of Campbell Mithun, a full-service advertising and marketing communications firm (www.campbell-mithun.com), and also teaches a communications strategy course in the master's program at the University of Minnesota. He has served a range of clients, including Burger King, General Mills, H&R Block, and Verizon Wireless. Wehrenberg lives in Minneapolis, MN.